# COMPUTER TECHNICIAN'S HANDBOOK

## 3rd Edition

## Art Margolis

**TAB Books**
**Division of McGraw-Hill**
New York  San Francisco  Washington, D.C.  Auckland  Bogotá
Caracas  Lisbon  London  Madrid  Mexico City  Milan
Montreal  New Delhi  San Juan  Singapore
Sydney  Tokyo  Toronto

## Notices

| | |
|---|---|
| **IBM®** and **IBM PC®** | International Business Machines Inc. |
| **Zilog®** | Zilog Corp. |
| **Apple®** | Apple Corporation |
| **Atari®** | Atari, Inc. |
| **Commodore™** | Commodore Corporation |
| **Compaq®** | Compaq Computer Corporation |
| **Intel®** | Intel Corporation |
| **NEC®** and **Multisync®** | NEC Corporation |
| **Sony™** and **Multiscan™** | Sony Corporation of America |
| **RCA®** | Radio Corporation of America |
| **Texas Instruments™** | Texas Instruments Incorporated |
| **Motorola®** | Motorola Corporation |
| **Radio Shack®** and **Tandy®** | Tandy Corporation |

pbk   1617181920212223 KPKP 90210987
hc    91011121314151617 KPKP 902109876543

**Library of Congress Cataloging-in-Publication Data**

Margolis, Art.
    Computer technician's handbook / by Art Margolis.—3rd ed.
        p.  cm.
    ISBN 0-8306-9279-7   ISBN 0-8306-3279-4 (pbk.)
    1. Computers—Maintenance and repair.  I. Title.
TK7887.M36   1989
621.39′16—dc20                                    89-20147
                                                  CIP

Acquisitions Editor: Roland S. Phelps
Director of Production: Katherine G. Brown
Cover photograph courtesy of Motorola.
Back cover photograph of the author is courtesy of Michael Gorzeck.           3279

# Contents

# Acknowledgments

I'd like to thank my wife, Lea, for handling much of my paperwork and phone calls so I could do this third edition. I'd also like to thank my son-in-law, Michael Gorzeck, for the cover photo.

# Introduction

When I wrote the *Computer Technician's Handbook—2nd Edition* in the early '80s, microcomputer development was in an explosive phase. As the third edition goes to press, the microcomputer situation is even more explosive, and there is no letup in sight.

Technology leads the way. The focus in the previous edition was on 8-bit machines. Today, the 8-bit machines are just as popular, but in addition 16-bit and 32-bit computers are proliferating in the marketplace. Memories have expanded geometrically. While 64 k DRAM memory chips were the top of the line in the early '80s, 256 k and 1 megabyte chips are now routine. As technology leads the way, software is scrambling to keep up.

The more computers that are put into use, the more is the demand for technicians to aid during manufacturing, to set up and install computer systems, to maintain these systems, and to troubleshoot and repair them when they go down. In recent surveys, one of the most-needed workers is the computer technician. This need appears to be permanent and will only increase as time goes on.

In order to be able to do the job, you must be trained. In the future, working with micros will mean testing circuits the size of a virus. You will deal with events that take place in billionths of a second. Also, you will be dealing with locations in the machine that number in the millions, billions, trillions and even more. You'll be handling complicated codes within codes, within codes. As you work you must be precise and exact. One slight error could render a test worthless.

To be trained does not mean that you must be an engineer. You only need to be trained as a technician. As time goes by, you could reach an engineering level as you gain experience in the field.

In Part 1 of this book, you will be exposed to the basics in the field. Chapter 2 covers the mathematics you'll need right away. It is not really math but an understanding of the numbering systems that let you communicate with the computer. You already know one of the systems: decimal. The binary and hex that are also needed are just codes of the decimal.

Chapter 3 is a short course in digital electronics. Digital is different than analog electronics used in radio and TV. The transistors, resistors, capacitors, and other electronic components are no different in digital than in analog; they are just configured in different ways to operate on the digital signals.

Chapter 4 covers the usual pieces of test equipment needed to work on digital electronics. There are many more pieces available that you can make your life easier, but in this chapter you'll find the vital equipment that you need to get by.

Chapters 5, 6, 7, and 8 describe computer circuitry. Chapter 5 provides an overview of a computer, and the rest of the chapters begin the understandings of microprocessors, memories, inputs and outputs. Chapter 9 goes into how these circuits can be read by the way their voltages vary as they operate.

Part 2 discusses the way computers work from a technician's point of view. The accent is on the various microprocessors, which is the heart of any computer. In Chapter 10, there is a description of a typical 8-bit computer. Chapter 11 covers the instruction set of the computer and how to use it. Chapter 12 goes through a step-by-step short program that is run as instructions stimulate activity between the microprocessor and memory.

Chapter 13 begins the discussions of 16-bit processors. It uses as its example the 8086-8088 processors. Chapter 14 then describes another important processor, the 68000.

Chapters 14 and 15 describe some ways that computers input and output data and change data between analog and digital forms.

Chapters 17 and 18 delve into the 16-bit 80286 and 32-bit 80386 processors. These are the newer versions of the 8086-8088 family, and they are very popular.

Parts 1 and 2 deal mostly with the thoughts that go round in your head as you work on a computer. Part 3 is the ''hands on'' section. When a computer needs to be fixed, the first thing you do is diagnose the problem. In Chapter 19, the way to proceed during diagnosis is covered.

Once a defective chip is located, it must be replaced. When the previous edition was written, most chips were packaged in DIPs. Today, many chips have been packaged in SMDs. This chapter covers techniques to desolder and resolder both DIPs and SMDs. These techniques and soldering tools must be used if you want to succeed in a ticklish replacement.

Chapter 21 goes into details on testing chips and bus lines with test equipment. Chapter 22, in turn, provides the same type of test information for the I/O circuits.

Chapter 23 is the TV repair section of the book. Microcomputers use monochrome and color TV monitors to display their wares. A full 75 percent of computer troubles are caused by defects in the TV monitor or its video input circuits. TV monitors are simple devices in comparison to a home TV, and not too hard to fix. This chapter provides information that you'll find handy when the computer trouble is video related.

Chapter 24 discusses the computer and TV monitor power supplies. Power supply troubles in these units are very common, and fairly easy to diagnose and repair. This chapter shows you how to handle the supplies.

The Appendix to this book is a discussion on the way to go about buying replacement parts, test equipment, and service manuals. A few names and addresses of national electronic suppliers are listed. This discussion should answer a lot of questions that you might have when you need electronic supplies.

I wrote this book, as a technician, to be a guide and handbook for other technicians and all the computer users who desire to perform work on their computer hardware. It is also for those of you who would like to join our ranks and share in the status, security, and pleasure of spending our days with these devices that stimulate the imagination.

# PART 1
# TECHNIQUES AND CIRCUITRY

# 1

# The Computer Technician's Role

Becoming a computer technician is easier than becoming a TV serviceman. The microcomputer is not nearly as complicated as a modern color TV. The personal computer is also smaller in size, easier to take apart, and has circuit boards that are quite accessible. Servicing information and other aids are readily available. Manufacturers are helpful and will sell you diagnostic software that will often tell you which part has gone bad.

Employment as a computer technician is almost automatic, as long as you are qualified. On the other hand, if you have entrepreneurial leanings, there is always plenty of work you can drum up installing, maintaining, and repairing personal computers.

At the present time, the going rate for a computer technician's service charge, for an office or home call is $100. If the ailing computer is carried in to a service shop, the base charge is $50. These are national averages. Most of the money the computer user must put out is for the technician's labor and expertise. The cost of the parts usually do not come to more than 20% of the total repair bill.

In order to install, maintain or repair a personal computer, you as a technician, first of all, must know how the computer works. Servicing techniques is what this book is all about. Once you have mastered the theory of operation, it is then possible for you to intelligently observe problems, analyse the ailments, come to a conclusion what is wrong, and then make the installation, maintenance, or service moves to make things right.

## THE COMPUTER PEOPLE

There are four distinct categories of people, (Fig. 1-1) who work directly with personal computers. First, and most important, are the computer users, without the users' there would of course, be no need. They are the customers who buy the computers and put the other three categories, (the computer designers, the programmers, and the technicians) to work.

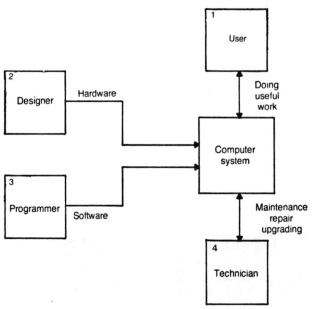

Fig. 1-1. The computer designer and software programmer create the computer systems that do jobs for users and are maintained and serviced by technicians.

The computer user, like the user of a good stereo music system, does not need to understand the workings of either the hardware or the programs on disks and cassettes in order to use his or her computer. An operating computer system is hardware with programs already installed. That is what computers do, they run programs. All the typical user needs to know is the ins and outs of how to operate the program.

It doesn't make any difference how educated or sophisticated the user might be. For example, the user might be an architect working with a CAD (computer-aided design) program. All he does, is turn on the computer, load the memory with the CAD program, and go to work. He conceives new designs for the building he is working on and all sorts of graphics are produced and printed out. The architect spends hours and days on the project looking at the display. The computer is his personal slave, yet the architect often doesn't know a resistor from an integrated chip, or machine language from BASIC.

Manufacturers put two of the categories of computer people together, the computer designers and the programmers, to produce the personal computer system for the user. The design engineer is the creator. Design people have the duty of dreaming up a configuration of print boards, chips, resistors, capacitors, keyboards, disk drives, TV displays, and other items that a computer system is made of. Once the designer forms a workable hardware system, he or she is through with that computer and goes on to another project.

While the designers produce the computer hardware, the programmers develop the software. The programmers study the way the computer is put together and pay particular attention to the chips the designer decided to install in the machine. Then they write programs that are carefully tailored to perform with the specific chip configuration of the computer. Each microprocessor unit has registers and gates that will operate only if the

4

program is written to conform precisely with the chip design. Besides the MPU there are other chips that need programming, such as the I/O types. The programmer, as he writes the software takes them into consideration too.

A computer user looks at the hardware in somewhat the same way a music lover looks at his record player. The computer user then views the software as the music lover sees his records. As the record player delivers music, the computer delivers some function such as word processing, number crunching or spreadsheeting.

The computer hardware does its job by moving and manipulating streams of binary bits electronically from place to place in the computer system. It is the job of the programmer to write the directions, in the program, that will cause the hardware to move the streams of data in a precise orderly fashion. In actuality, the binary bits, in the machine are formed as moving electrons and changing voltages. The programmer doesn't view them as such. The programmer sees the bits as binary or hexadecimal numbers. In fact, a large percentage of good programmers do not have any expertise in electronics. They can write the programs that make the chips do cartwheels, but they have little idea of how the electrons and voltages are working out on the inside of the

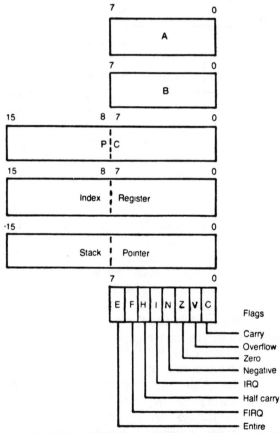

Fig. 1-2. The programmer looks at an MPU from a register and bit point of view. He uses block diagrams such as this one to aid him in writing machine language programs.

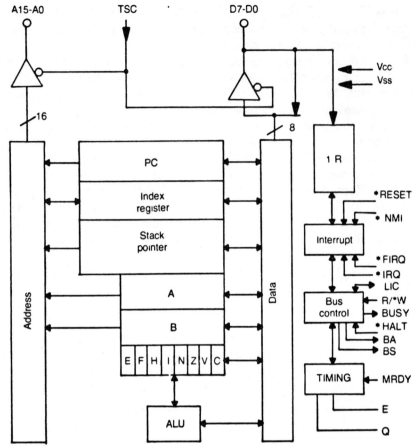

Fig. 1-3. The technician sees the MPU from a voltage and electron flow point of view. With this block diagram, he can check out the MPU with test equipment.

machine. Figures 1-2 and 1-3 illustrate the different ways the programmers and the designers see the insides of the computer.

Figure 1-2 is a block diagram of a typical 8-bit MPU from a software point of view. The programmer needs to know what registers are available and how many bits are contained in each register. With the aid of this block diagram, he can then write machine language programs. The diagram is not much help during troubleshooting.

Figure 1-3, on the other hand, is also the block diagram of an 8-bit processor, but from a hardware point of view. The same registers are shown but also shown is the way the registers are hooked up inside the MPU chip. In addition other registers and gates are drawn in and all the pin inputs and outputs are revealed. With this block diagram a technician can check out the voltages and pulses with appropriate test equipment.

This brings us to the fourth party involved with computers, you, the computer technician. While the designer is through with the computer once it goes into production, technicians are involved with it forever after. The technician could be assigned to the manufacturing assembly line to troubleshoot and watch quality control, or could be the one to deliver the computer and get a user started, or could be the one the user calls if the computer develops trouble. While the designer and programmer create the hardware and software that make up the computer system, it is the technician who takes over the creation and nurses it along for the rest of its life.

## HARDWARE AND SOFTWARE

The most valuable computer people are those who are expert in the use of both hardware and software. While a technician must be well versed in the computer hardware, it is also important to get a good grounding in software. In fact, the better you can handle BASIC and machine language, the more expert you will become in understanding the hardware. These two vital areas of expertise work hand-in-hand with each other. Being a decent programmer enables you to write diagnostic programs to root out subtle troubles.

The hardware is defined as the actual physical components the computer is made of; chips, resistors, capacitors, circuit boards and the rest. The software is the program that instructs the hardware during operation.

The workhorse of the hardware is the microprocessor, the MPU. It is a conglomeration of carefully-designed digital circuits that are photo-masked onto a tiny piece of semiconductor material such as silicon or gallium. The circuits are designed to respond in specific ways to certain digital signals. For instance, if you inject a square wave into one of the microscopic gate circuits, as shown in Fig. 1-4, and the gate is conducting, the square wave could stop the gate from conducting. The programmer would see this electronic turn off as a software binary bit 0 being changed to bit 1.

The circuit is carefully-designed hardware. The square wave, which you decided to inject into the hardware, is carefully designed software. The circuit could be called a

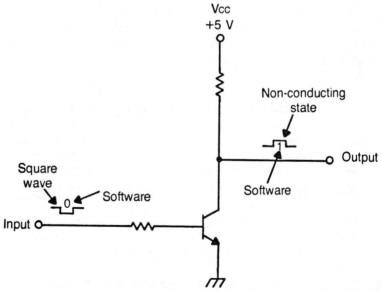

Fig. 1-4. A square wave can cause changes in the state of a circuit. The low level of the wave is electronic software code for the binary numeral 0. The high level of the wave represents a 1.

7

NOT gate. With the aid of the software, the gate, which was outputting a 0 by conducting, had its output state changed to a 1, as it was stopped from conducting. There will be more about NOT gates and other gates in Chapter 3.

The programmer writes a program line to change a logic state from 0 to 1. The computer responds to the program line, creates the square wave and inputs it to the conducting NOT gate. The NOT gate then stops conducting, which changes its output state from 0 to a 1. The programmer may neither know nor care that a software-generated square wave is actually forcing the job onto the hardware. All the programmer desires is a response to the coded program he or she wrote.

As a technician though, you are not only interested in the software instruction, but also with the square wave generating and the voltages and pulses on the gate circuit. You want to know the voltage level of the square wave and its frequency. You also want to know the circuit arrangement of the chip, what connections are going where, and all the other hardware facts needed to maintain and troubleshoot the equipment.

The amount of software expertise actually needed by a technician is really not that much. As mentioned before though, the more you do know about all aspects of the computer, the more of an expert you will become. However, all the software skills required are those that will enable you to compose little test programs or to utilize factory supplied test programs intelligently.

## THEORY OF OPERATION

In order to be able to fix and maintain a computer, you must know how it works. You do not need to understand the computer the way the design engineer does. The design engineer is charged with the responsibility of creating circuits, or changing circuits when they do not do the job they are supposed to. To learn his craft, the design engineer must spend many years in college and then more years on the drawing board.

As a technician, you don't have to create circuits. The circuits you work on already exist. Your responsibility is to know what is happening in the computer when you arrive to maintain or troubleshoot it. You are not the creator, you are the computer doctor. You need to comprehend the theory of operation so you are able to put together the pieces of a repair puzzle.

The theory of the computer's operation has to do with what goes on as the computer is loaded with a program and then runs the program. While there are many thousands of programs that could be used in a popular computer, they are all variations of the same electronic movements in the circuits. The programs simply drive square waves from chip to chip. While the programmer and the computer user are very concerned with the software activity and results, and couldn't care less about the actual electronic activity, the technician is mainly concerned with the square waves and voltages that move from circuit to circuit.

To understand the square wave movement, you must learn what circuits are in the computer, and how they go about processing the voltage highs and lows. Once you master how the circuits do their job, then you are in a position to accurately figure out how they fail and wear out.

Today's typical computer is, as electronic gear goes, relatively simple. For instance, it is not nearly as complex as a color TV. The computer is fairly easy to understand, from a technician's point of view, because most of the circuits have been shrunk to microscopic dimensions and buried in the integrated circuit chips. That way, if a trouble develops in a single circuit in a chip, all that is needed is to figure out which chip has the fault and change the whole chip, even though there might be 250,000 transistors on the chip.

This was not true years ago. Before the age of shrunken circuits, a computer literally took up the space in an entire floor of offices. For example, the original ENIAC in the late 40s had 18,000 vacuum tubes. If one circuit failed, that circuit had to be pinpointed, the circuit had to be analyzed, the defective component or connection found and fixed.

At that time, understanding the hardware theory of operation was a prodigious job. Technicians had to trace the flow of a square wave as they traveled from one end of the tube lineup to the other. The power supplies that fired up all the tubes were heavy-duty and large. The cooling system was massive. Punch card machines that fed programs on the cards into the computer, teletypewriters that input pulses as the keyboard and printed the computer output, and many other types of equipment were needed to operate the computer.

Maintenance and troubleshooting was conducted around the clock. Even so, the gigantic ENIAC was broken down more often than it was operating. The technicians were masters of ENIAC's theory of operation. They had to be or ENIAC wouldn't have operated at all.

Today's computers are four generations of circuits past the ancient ENIAC. All 18,000 vacuum tubes and more have been shrunk down into microscopic size on chips. It is no longer necessary for a technician to visualize the theory of operation of a square wave moving through thousands of tube circuits to thousands of tubes. All the technician has to imagine is the square moving from chip to chip. Even though there might be many thousands of circuits in a chip, the chip can be considered as a single component. It is replaced as a single component. We think of the chip as a "black box".

In electronics, a black box is thought of as a container that is permanently sealed shut. There is no practical way to see the insides or get a test probe directly onto an internal circuit. However, there are pins sticking out of the chip as seen in Fig. 1-5.

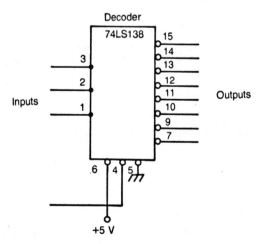

Fig. 1-5. The schematic of a chip shows the +5 V supply voltage, the ground connection, and the input and output pins. These pins are tested during troubleshooting.

These pins connect to the circuit inputs, the circuit outputs and the power supply inputs. The technician must know what signals are connected to the input pins, what happens to these signals in the black box and what signals exit the chip. In addition, the technician should know what type of power is needed by the chip. Once you understand these fundamentals, you can intelligently check out a chip. You can make input tests, output tests, and power supply tests. If you find one of the chip pins does not read the correct voltage, resistance, logic state or frequency, you have uncovered a clue to the trouble.

As a rule of thumb, if you find a pin with a wrong reading, if the pin is an output, odds are the chip is defective and needs replacement. Should the pin be an input, chances are good that the chip is ok and some circuit feeding the input pin has the defect. These conclusions are general. Sometimes the rule doesn't hold true so be prepared for the exceptions.

The theory of operation in the computer must encompass both digital and analog circuits. At certain stages of the signal path the circuits are processing digital square wave signals. At other stages the circuits are working on analog TV, audio, and joystick signals. Figure 1-6 shows typical digital and analog signals. As long as you know the way the computer you are working on operates, you can switch your techniques from digital to analog or analog to digital, and make the correct tests. For the most part, digital tests do not work in analog circuits and analog tests are meaningless in digital circuits.

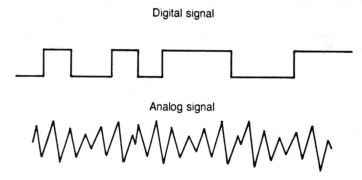

Digital signal

Analog signal

Fig. 1-6. The digital signal only has two possible states, high or low. The analog signal has an infinite number of states. Any spot on the constantly-changing analog signal is a state.

## INSTRUCTION SETS

As a technician you could encounter all sorts of computers in today's field. There are 8-bit computers such as the Apple IIs, TRS-80s, Commodore's VIC 20, 64, and 128, Atari 65XE and 130XE and others. These are representative of the first microcomputers to emerge on the scene. Incidentally, the 8-bit name refers to the number of lines in the computer's data bus.

Also in the field are 16-bit computers like Commodore's Amiga, the Macintoshes, the IBM PC series and the IBM clones. Then there are the recent 32-bit computers based around the 80386 MPU that Intel produces. There will be much more about all these computers further on in the book.

All of these computers run programs through the use of an instruction set. What in the world is an *instruction set*? It is the key to the computer operation. As a technician, you can use that key to test out various sections of the computer.

The MPU is the heart of the computer. Inside the MPU is a tiny permanent program called microcode. The microcode program can be made to run the MPU by injecting a machine instruction into the MPU. A set of machine instructions is called an instruction set.

A typical instruction set for a small computer like an 8-bit, might have about 75 machine instructions. The instructions order the microcode to make the MPU perform jobs like ADD, CLEAR, INCREMENT, SHIFT, and so on. There will be more detail on the machine instructions later in the book.

Each machine instruction is a group of square waves as seen in Fig. 1-7. When this voltage wave that varies between high and low voltages is injected into the input connections of the MPU, it turns on a section of the microcode, which in turn forces the registers in the MPU to respond by causing some of the registers to conduct and others to stop conducting. Each machine instruction produces its very own special response.

## Load Accumulator

| | |
|---|---|
| Mnemonic | LDA |
| Instruction Code | 86 (Hex) |
| Binary Equivalent | 1000 0110 |
| H-L Equivalent | HLLL LHHL |
| Voltage equivalent | +5000 0+5+50 |
| Square waves | |

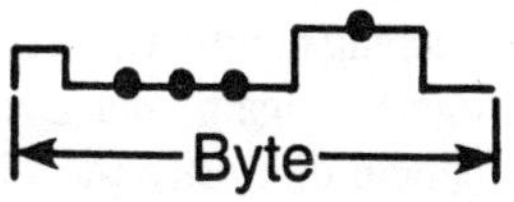

Fig. 1-7. A byte sized instruction is a group of 8-bits that vary from high to low and low to high. There are many ways to express the square wave configuration.

As a technician, you are vitally interested in noting the effect that the highs and lows in the instruction have on the registers in the MPU. One of the test techniques you will have in your arsenal is the injection of machine instructions. The instructions can affect all the circuits in the digital section of the computer. You an observe whether or not the instruction is producing the prescribed effect. If it is not, that could be an important servicing clue.

The instructions are nothing more than an assortment of high and low voltage levels in the square wave format. A high can be thought of as +5 V and a low as zero V. In the 8-bit machine instruction there is an assortment of eight highs and lows. In the 16-bit and 32- bit instructions there are instructions with 16 and 32 bits. Each high or low is considered one bit. A total of eight bits is known as a byte. 16 bits is two bytes and 32 bits comprise four bytes. In programming circles, two bytes are called a word. Four bytes are a double word.

The technician usually thinks of bits as either highs and lows or +5 V and zero V. The highs and lows are termed H and L. If you use test tables you'll find they contain H and L or +5 V and 0 V. To check test pins, you'll be using a logic probe or voltmeter. The logic probe reads out H and L. The voltmeter reads voltages.

The programmer, on the other hand, does not even think about voltage levels, H and L. To a programmer, and H is a 1 and an L is a 0. The 1s and 0s are the numbers in binary arithmetic that is natural and is used in the computer. The programmer could, if he wanted to, write his programs in binary arithmetic. This is true machine language. If you look at a program in binary form you'll see a long list of 1s and 0s.

These 1s and 0s the programmer uses are the same +5 V and zero V that you as a technician call highs and lows. The programmer is not very interested in voltages, but he is concerned with what the voltage levels represent in binary numbers. Binary arithmetic is covered in more detail in the next chapter.

Today, most programmers do not use 1s and 0s to write programs, although there are some experimentors and researchers who still stay with this pure form of machine language. On today's computers, programs are written in assembly or some other convenient language that uses hexadecimal, mnemonics or other special characters. This is also covered in more detail in Chapter 2.

As a technician, it will serve you well to be able to use the machine instructions of a computer you are working on. It would be of great value if in addition to being hardware knowledgeable you were also software oriented. From a strict hardware point of view, the instruction set is considered in terms of highs and lows as well as +5 V and 0 V. In the software view, the instruction set can be thought of as 1s and 0s, hexadecimal numbers and mnemonics. On certain jobs all you'll be doing is tracing voltages. At other times you could find yourself needing to use software numbers and letters.

## HANDLING EQUIPMENT

In the final analysis, the computer technician is a computer mechanic. An observer sees you taking the computer apart, conducting tests with meter and oscilloscope, touching points with a smoking soldering iron, changing parts, putting the computer back together again, and giving the machine checkout tests. Your expertise is judged by the manual dexterity the observer sees and by how rapidly the computer is transformed from a problem back to a working tool.

Most people have fairly good eye-hand coordination, are able to handle a screwdriver, and muddle through do-it-yourself projects with good success. With practice you can probably handle the physical moves required to take computers apart, take test readings, replace defective parts, and put it back together without forgetting any of the screws. It is vital that you have the proper tools and the correct techniques down pat to handle the tools. There are not that many items you'll need, in addition to ordinary electronic tools.

Most of us have at least average manual dexterity. The secret to getting the most out of the dexterity we have is to use the exact right tool to do a job. Even a simple job such as removing screws that hold a computer together, can go easily or with difficulty according to the screwdriver you use. For example, the screws might be slotted, phillips headed, torx types or others. The screws also come in many sizes. It is obvious that the driver you pick out of the tool box should be the correct type and size. If you try to remove a torx type with a thin slotted driver, you will have a hard time. When you use the correct driver and it is in good condition, the screws come out easily. This gets your repair job started on the right road. If you have to struggle to get the screws out you'll waste a lot of time, besides aggravating yourself.

This simple technique follows through on all the other aspects of a computer repair. You must use the right-sized soldering iron, your tools should always be clean and in good shape, there should be plenty of bright light, a magnifying glass or two, and a comfortable workbench with plenty of space. Then with a steady hand and some patience, every item on the circuit board, including the copper traces, can be replaced or repaired correctly.

Note I said, repaired correctly. That does not mean the defective part has to be repaired or replaced in such a magnificently perfect way that you can't tell the difference in your job from the way the factory originally produced it. From a practical standpoint, if you replace a part it is a good idea to use brightly-colored parts that are obvious replacements. This practice gives you or another technician who might work on the computer, a quick visual history of the breakdowns the machine had experienced up to that point in time.

Superior manual dexterity and expert techniques with computers gradually come about, as time goes by and you log completed job after completed job. As you learn the ins and outs of the computers you work on, not only do you become more and more familiar with the theory of operation, but your soldering and cutting techniques improve too. You will develop your own tricks to transport sensitive chips safely, to cut open and reattach the copper traces on the print board, to heatsink solder points correctly, to permanently repair open connections on small transformers instead of replacing them, and all other kinds of handy shortcuts and tricks of the trade.

You might start out with only average mechanical aptitude, but as time goes by, and as your experience grows, the observer who watches you will see a technician with expert manual dexterity and view a repair that progresses rapidly There will be more techniques on testing and replacing parts throughout the book.

## PUZZLE SOLVING TECHNIQUES

Most of the work a computer technician performs is solving puzzles. When a computer is placed in front of you to work on, it's because it has a problem. You must then marshall all your forces and solve the problem. Using this book as an aid, Fig. 1-8 will show you the problem solving path to take.

First of all, the computer is supposed to be able to run programs by processing highs and lows. You must understand the various numbering systems that describe the Hs and Ls. These numbering systems are found in Chapter 2.

Second, the voltages that make up the instructions and data in the programs are physically processed through electronic circuits. The circuits are composed of discrete and integrated transistors, capacitors, resistors, and so on. These circuits are shown and explained in Chapter 3. You must have a good grasp of how these circuits perform in order to fit their meanings into your puzzle-solving repertoire.

Third, the computer must be attached with test equipment that gives you an accurate reading of the various voltages, resistances, currents, frequencies, signals, etc. at the many test points (or as they are called, nodes) in the circuits. In addition other test

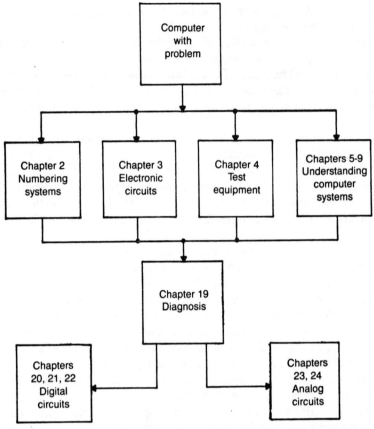

Fig. 1-8. A computer installation, maintenance or repair job requires the knowledge found in Chapters 2-9, diagnosis techniques are discussed in Chapter 19 and actual repair trouble techniques are covered in Chapters 20-24.

equipment to inject signals or test diagnostic programs is needed. Testing is discussed in Chapter 4.

Fourth, you must have a good idea of how the electronics is assembled to form the computer system. You should have a comprehensive block diagram of a typical computer in your mind's eye. This means you should have some briefing of the typical microprocessors out in the field, the memories the MPUs work with and other support chips and discrete components that you'll find in the computer. That way, as you look down on the print board you can imagine the way the chips are transporting the highs and lows from place to place. This information is given in Chapters 5-9.

With all of these forces in place, you can then begin to solve your puzzle by trying to obtain clues and then making a diagnosis of what's wrong. The diagnosis involves categorizing the trouble type in your mind, going to indicated trouble areas, physically probing the electronics and then trying to make sense out of the test results. You can make sense of your results as long as you understand what is happening. Diagnosing troubles is covered in Chapter 19.

You can then begin to apply the clues you come up with to the block diagram of the computer. Block diagrams and their uses are discussed in Chapter 5. At that point the technique narrows the indicated sources of the trouble to a specific area or areas of the computer. For example, suppose the problem you encounter is a computer that will run most of a program but not all of it. You run some diagnostic tests and find that some of the memory chips are responding correctly but a couple are not. This indicates that the source of the trouble could be in the circuits concerned with, and including, the incorrectly-responding memory chips. This points the finger at the blocks in the diagram that encompass these circuits. That narrows the search area to a great extent.

At that juncture, you abandon the block diagram overview and delve into the actual electronics. It is a good idea to have factory service notes and the computer schematic handy. While it is important to have an idea of the generic computer firmly implanted in your mind, it is improbable that you'll have the schematics of all computers memorized.

As time goes by, you will accumulate the schematics and other service notes that are important to install, maintain, and repair the computers you become involved with. A typical service manual will contain specific information and schematics like the illustrations and tables that will be found throughout this handbook.

With the factory manual available to clarify circuitry and parts, the rest of the repair consists of pinpointing the defective part or connection and replacing the part or repairing the connection. The discussions in Chapters 19-24 go into the actual troubleshooting and repair techniques. Once you have located the defect, you have solved the puzzle. As soon as you change or repair the part or connection that failed, the job is almost complete. All that is left to do is to check out the computer to make sure that nothing else is wrong.

# 2
# Mathematics for the Computer Technician

A few years ago an educator named Edwin M. Lieberthal came up with a system of counting on your fingers called Fingermath. While humans have been counting on their fingers for centuries, this system is so efficient, a practiced student can rival a calculator in speed and accuracy. Since we have ten digits on our hands, the system is based on the ability to count from one to ten. When we were created, our Maker designed us with a natural arrangement of working with a number system that consists of ten digits. This is called the decimal system (Fig. 2-1).

Humans, in turn, have created digital calculators and computers. However, the electronic counters do not naturally count from one to ten. They do not conveniently possess fingers. The electronic units can't do anything but turn on and turn off. Their digits are off and on, or zero and one. Zero is usually considered the *off* digit and one is the *on* digit. The computer is able to count from 0 to 1 and that's all.

As you can see, a conflict exists between human and computer numbering systems. While the human naturally works with decimals, a computer has to operate with the two-digit system known as binary. If a half-dozen oranges need to be counted, both the human and the computer can count them. Each uses a different system based on the different ways of numbering. This doesn't change the number of oranges; it remains the same. Only the two descriptions of the number are different.

In order for the human to enter the number of oranges into a computer, he punches the key labeled 6 (Fig. 2-2). When that happens an encoding circuit in the computer changes the number 6 to 0110. The 0110 is then sorted in the computer's memory.

If the computer is to display the number of oranges, the 0110 is sent to a display circuit. There the 0110 is decoded back to a 6 and shown on the screen. There are coding circuits that interface the gap between the human and the innards of the computer. The coding circuits simply change the decimal numbers you enter into the computer into binary, and then change the binary numbers back into decimal so you can use the output.

16

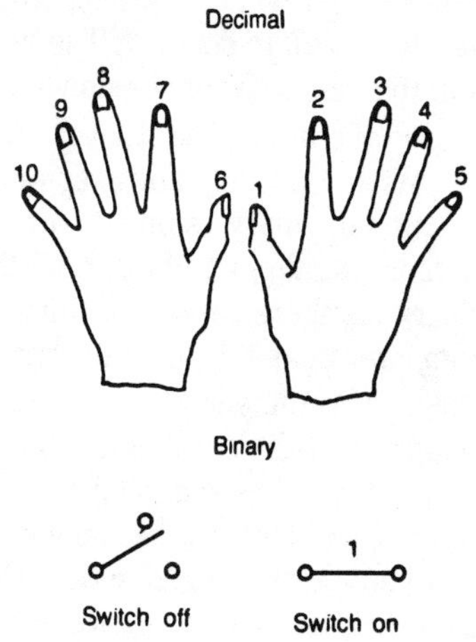

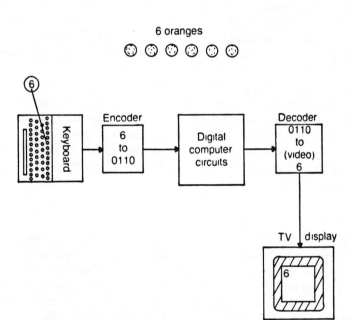

Fig. 2-1. The natural human numbering system is ten-fingered decimal. The computer numbering system is off/on switch binary.

Fig. 2-2. In order for the human to enter the number of oranges into the computer, he presses the key labeled 6.

Fortunately, computers move these numbers almost as fast as the speed of light so no real hardship exists in the circuits. The only hardship is that the technician must be very familiar with the mathematical process of coding the numbers from system to system. That is what the rest of this chapter is about.

## NUMBERING SYSTEMS USED WITH COMPUTERS

In order for a computer to be "user-friendly," the designers try to stay within the confines of the familiar decimal system. The computer professional can go through an

17

entire career without coming in contact with binary numbers. Most computer software is said to *default* to decimal. The word *default*, in the computer parlance, refers to the system that normally comes up when you first turn on the computer. This means decimal is usually the number system that comes up as you start using the computer.

While the computer user works with decimal numbers, deep down in the computer, streams of binary 1s and 0s are coursing through the circuits. An encoder changes the decimal numbers to binary as the operator enters them and a decoder changes the binary numbers back to decimal as the operator retrieves the processed numbers. The computer does this naturally and easily as a matter of course. The computer operator is oblivious of the encoding and decoding. All he or she is aware of is the decimal numbers going in and the decimal numbers coming out.

The most-used coding system in today's computer is called *hexadecimal*, or hex for short. Hex refers to the number six. Hexadecimal means decimal plus six. That means there are sixteen digits in the hex system. Since there are only ten numbers in decimal, the other six digits used are letters: capital A,B,C,D,E, and F.

The most-used coding system in years past was called *octal*. While octal is almost obsolete today as a code, the octal principle is used consistently in circuits, and we'll cover it. Octal refers to the number eight. In the octal numbering system, there are only eight numbers. They are 0,1,2,3,4,5,6, and 7. In octal, there are no numerals 8 and 9. When you count in octal, the number 10 comes after 7.

The reason these strange numbering systems are used is that they have a very important relationship with the binary digits. They are decimal representations of the binary system. It is quite difficult for a human to work with endless streams of 1s and 0s. It is much easier to manipulate our familiar numerals and letters.

The binary numbers, in addition to being coded with hex and octal, are also coded with systems called Binary Coded Decimal, ASCII, and other systems. Let's cover the actual systems.

## Hexadecimal

Hex has a very special relationship with the binary numbering system. Binary numbers are arranged in *bits*, *nybbles*, *bytes*, and *words*. A *bit* is a single binary digit, either a 1 or 0. A *nybble* is a row of four bits. The *byte* is composed of two nybbles, totaling eight bits. The *word* is a row of sixteen bits, which is four nybbles or two bytes. Knowing the relationships must become second nature to you. Stop and memorize them now, because they are the basis for the entire computer numbering system.

The hex system is designed so that one hex number equals one nybble or four bits. Let's examine the nybble. There are four bits and each bit can be either a 1 or a 0. What does that mean?

This means there are sixteen possible combinations of 1s and 0s in a nybble. These are the possible combinations:

| Binary | Hex | Binary | Hex | Binary | Hex |
|--------|-----|--------|-----|--------|-----|
| 0000 | 0 | 0001 | 1 | 0010 | 2 |
| 0011 | 3 | 0100 | 4 | 0101 | 5 |
| 0110 | 6 | 0111 | 7 | 1000 | 8 |

| Binary | Hex | Binary | Hex | Binary | Hex |
|--------|-----|--------|-----|--------|-----|
| 1001 | 9 | 1010 | A | 1011 | B |
| 1100 | C | 1101 | D | 1110 | E |
| 1111 | F | | | | |

The decimal numbers and letters next to the sixteen nybbles are the hex equivalents of the nybbles. It would be a good idea to memorize the sixteen possible nybbles and their hex equivalents, because the nybble is the most often used mathematical component in computers.

If you examine the list of nybbles, you'll realize that there are sixteen of them, in the same way there are ten integers in decimal. Note that the list begins with 0000, hex 0. The decimal integers also begin with 0. However, there is an important difference between 0 in hex-binary and 0 in decimal. When you count in hex-binary you start with 0. When you count in decimal you start with 1. For example, if you have a half-dozen oranges, in decimal you'd count 1, 2, 3, 4, 5, and 6. In hex, you'd count the oranges 0, 1, 2, 3, 4, and 5. In nybble form, the orange count would run 0000, 0001, 0010, 0011, 0100, and 0101.

This type of counting is indigenous to computers. Once in the computer even decimal counting begins with 0. Should you decide to number a set of 8 RAM chips, they'd be labeled 0, 1, 2, 3, 4, 5, 6, and 7. At this stage of the game, when it comes to computers, get used to this quirk in numbering. Eight items in a computer are 0-7. Sixteen components are counted 0 through 15, 256 bits are numbered 0-255, and so on.

Back to the nybble. A single nybble is rarely used alone. That's because computers are built to process instructions and data in multiples of 8 bits, or *bytes*. (Fig. 2-3). The byte is composed of two nybbles. When you look at a byte, visualize two nybbles. If you can automatically see a byte as 8 bits and at the same time recognize the two nybbles and know their hex equivalent, you will have mastered a valuable little technique that will

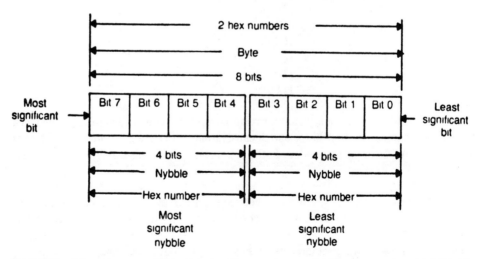

Fig. 2-3. Four bits make up a nybble which describes one hex number. Two hex numbers (eight bits) is a byte.

stand you in good stead in all areas of a technician's work. You'll be able to quickly read service notes intelligently.

Just as the nybble is able to form 16 different combinations of 1s and 0s, the byte is able to form 256 separate combinations. Actually, all the byte is doing is forming two nybbles of 16 combinations each. Since there can be 16 combinations of bits in the rightmost nybble for every one of the combinations in the leftmost nybble, there are 16 × 16 = 256 combinations of bits. Incidentally, the rightmost nybble has been given the name *Least Significant Nybble* and the leftmost nybble has the name *Most Significant Nybble*. Accordingly, the rightmost bit is called the least significant bit, and the leftmost bit is called the most significant bit.

## Octal

When you code a decimal number into hex, the decimal number is first changed into four binary numbers, and then the binary number is changed into its hex equivalent. For example, to change the decimal number 12, first change the 12 into 1100. Then turn the 1100 into the hex number C. It takes four binary digits to describe the decimal number. It also takes four binary digits to produce the single hex number. That is the decimal-binary-hex relationship.

The special decimal-binary-octal relationship is different. There are only eight numbers in the octal numbering system, in comparison to decimal, which has ten, and hex, which uses 16. Remember, there are no numbers 8 or 9 in octal. If you count to ten in octal it goes like this: 0,1,2,3,4,5,6,7, and then 10. Why use such a system?

In binary, if you count from 0 to 7, you only need to use three binary numbers, like this:

| Binary | Decimal |
|--------|---------|
| 000 | 0 |
| 001 | 1 |
| 010 | 2 |
| 011 | 3 |
| 100 | 4 |
| 101 | 5 |
| 110 | 6 |
| 111 | 7 |

Just as hex has a four binary number relationship to one decimal number, octal has a three binary number relationship to one decimal number. To code a decimal from 1 to 7 in octal, only three 1s or 0s are needed. In the electronic circuits this arrangement has a lot of convenient applications.

The octal system has little to do with the nybble-byte system. Octal is a separate system that has its own uses. However, between the hex and the octal numbering systems a relationship is established whereby decimals can be coded into three binary numbers or four binary numbers. This is useful and simplifies the manipulation of signals in circuits. The reasons will become clearer as you read about the circuits.

If you count from zero to fifteen in decimal, binary, hex, and octal, it goes like this:

| Decimal | Binary | Hex | Octal |
|---------|--------|-----|-------|
| 0 | 0000 | 0 | 0 |
| 1 | 0001 | 1 | 1 |
| 2 | 0010 | 2 | 2 |
| 3 | 0011 | 3 | 3 |
| 4 | 0100 | 4 | 4 |
| 5 | 0101 | 5 | 5 |
| 6 | 0110 | 6 | 6 |
| 7 | 0111 | 7 | 7 |
| 8 | 1000 | 8 | 10 |
| 9 | 1001 | 9 | 11 |
| 10 | 1010 | A | 12 |
| 11 | 1011 | B | 11 |
| 12 | 1100 | C | 14 |
| 13 | 1101 | D | 15 |
| 14 | 1110 | E | 16 |
| 15 | 1111 | F | 17 |

When you count sixteen numbers, computer-style in decimal, you begin with 0 and end with 15. The corresponding binary nybble starts with 0000 and ends in 1111. The hex representation goes from 0 to F. In octal 0 is the starting number, but the last number is 17, since 8 and 9 are left out of the octal.

It would be a good idea to memorize the first sixteen numbers of the decimal-binary-hex match up. The octal part only needs to be memorized from 0-7.

## HEX NUMBERS LARGER THAN F

The most important point to realize about octal and hex is their relationship to binary. Octal and hex are only handy ways to describe binary. They are shorthand for the cumbersome, hard-to-keep-track-of, binary rows of 1s and 0s. Octal and hex have no meaning in the circuits of the computer. The circuits can only process binary.

An octal number is shorthand for three binary numbers. The hex number is shorthand for four binary numbers. For the most part, we can bid adieu to octal right now. Octal is rarely (if ever) used in modern computers. Throughout the rest of the book, the binary system will use the hex system a its shorthand.

Hex numbers larger than F are shown in the Decimal-Binary-Hex Conversion (Table 2-1). Notice there are eight binary numbers and two hex numbers for every decimal number. The decimal list starts at zero and ends at 255, totaling 256 separate numbers. This is the entire table for the data bus in the common 8-bit computer. The reason a computer is called 8-bit is because its data bus has eight copper traces that can transport eight binary bits.

Also, each destination of the data bus terminates in a storage area called a register. Each storage area can store eight bits. The bits are either a 1 or a 0. If we place on the data bus a random arrangement of bits, it will be filled when eight bits are in place. Eight bits are called a byte. Each byte has two nybbles. There are four bits to a nybble. Since one nybble can be coded into one hex number, there are two hex numbers to a byte.

### Table 2-1. Byte Size Conversion Table.

| Decimal | Binary | | Hex | |
|---|---|---|---|---|
| 0 | 0000 | 0000 | 0 | 0 |
| 1 | 0000 | 0001 | 0 | 1 |
| 2 | 0000 | 0010 | 0 | 2 |
| 3 | 0000 | 0011 | 0 | 3 |
| 4 | 0000 | 0100 | 0 | 4 |
| 5 | 0000 | 0101 | 0 | 5 |
| 6 | 0000 | 0110 | 0 | 6 |
| 7 | 0000 | 0111 | 0 | 7 |
| 8 | 0000 | 1000 | 0 | 8 |
| 9 | 0000 | 1001 | 0 | 9 |
| 10 | 0000 | 1010 | 0 | A |
| 11 | 0000 | 1011 | 0 | B |
| 12 | 0000 | 1100 | 0 | C |
| 13 | 0000 | 1101 | 0 | D |
| 14 | 0000 | 1110 | 0 | E |
| 15 | 0000 | 1111 | 0 | F |
| 16 | 0001 | 0000 | 1 | 0 |
| 17 | 0001 | 0001 | 1 | 1 |
| 18 | 0001 | 0010 | 1 | 2 |
| 19 | 0001 | 0011 | 1 | 3 |
| 20 | 0001 | 0100 | 1 | 4 |
| 21 | 0001 | 0101 | 1 | 5 |
| 22 | 0001 | 0110 | 1 | 6 |
| 23 | 0001 | 0111 | 1 | 7 |
| 24 | 0001 | 1000 | 1 | 8 |
| 25 | 0001 | 1001 | 1 | 9 |
| 26 | 0001 | 1010 | 1 | A |
| 27 | 0001 | 1011 | 1 | B |
| 28 | 0001 | 1100 | 1 | C |
| 29 | 0001 | 1101 | 1 | D |
| 30 | 0001 | 1110 | 1 | E |
| 31 | 0001 | 1111 | 1 | F |
| 32 | 0010 | 0000 | 2 | 0 |
| 33 | 0010 | 0001 | 2 | 1 |
| 34 | 0010 | 0010 | 2 | 2 |
| 35 | 0010 | 0011 | 2 | 3 |
| 36 | 0010 | 0100 | 2 | 4 |
| 37 | 0010 | 0101 | 2 | 5 |
| 38 | 0010 | 0110 | 2 | 6 |
| 39 | 0010 | 0111 | 2 | 7 |
| 40 | 0010 | 1000 | 2 | 8 |
| 41 | 0010 | 1001 | 2 | 9 |
| 42 | 0010 | 1010 | 2 | A |
| 43 | 0010 | 1011 | 2 | B |
| 44 | 0010 | 1100 | 2 | C |
| 45 | 0010 | 1101 | 2 | D |
| 46 | 0010 | 1110 | 2 | E |
| 47 | 0010 | 1111 | 2 | F |
| 48 | 0011 | 0000 | 3 | 0 |
| 49 | 0011 | 0001 | 3 | 1 |
| 50 | 0011 | 0010 | 3 | 2 |
| 51 | 0011 | 0011 | 3 | 3 |
| 52 | 0011 | 0100 | 3 | 4 |
| 53 | 0011 | 0101 | 3 | 5 |

Table 2-1. Con't.

| Decimal | Binary | | Hex | |
|---|---|---|---|---|
| 54 | 0011 | 0110 | 3 | 6 |
| 55 | 0011 | 0111 | 3 | 7 |
| 56 | 0011 | 1000 | 3 | 8 |
| 57 | 0011 | 1001 | 3 | 9 |
| 58 | 0011 | 1010 | 3 | A |
| 59 | 0011 | 1011 | 3 | B |
| 60 | 0011 | 1100 | 3 | C |
| 61 | 0011 | 1101 | 3 | D |
| 62 | 0011 | 1110 | 3 | E |
| 63 | 0011 | 1111 | 3 | F |
| 64 | 0100 | 0000 | 4 | 0 |
| 65 | 0100 | 0001 | 4 | 1 |
| 66 | 0100 | 0010 | 4 | 2 |
| 67 | 0100 | 0011 | 4 | 3 |
| 68 | 0100 | 0100 | 4 | 4 |
| 69 | 0100 | 0101 | 4 | 5 |
| 70 | 0100 | 0110 | 4 | 6 |
| 71 | 0100 | 0111 | 4 | 7 |
| 72 | 0100 | 1000 | 4 | 8 |
| 73 | 0100 | 1001 | 4 | 9 |
| 74 | 0100 | 1010 | 4 | A |
| 75 | 0100 | 1011 | 4 | B |
| 76 | 0100 | 1100 | 4 | C |
| 77 | 0100 | 1101 | 4 | D |
| 78 | 0100 | 1110 | 4 | E |
| 79 | 0100 | 1111 | 4 | F |
| 80 | 0101 | 0000 | 5 | 0 |
| 81 | 0101 | 0001 | 5 | 1 |
| 82 | 0101 | 0010 | 5 | 2 |
| 83 | 0101 | 0011 | 5 | 3 |
| 84 | 0101 | 0100 | 5 | 4 |
| 85 | 0101 | 0101 | 5 | 5 |
| 86 | 0101 | 0110 | 5 | 6 |
| 87 | 0101 | 0111 | 5 | 7 |
| 88 | 0101 | 1000 | 5 | 8 |
| 89 | 0101 | 1001 | 5 | 9 |
| 90 | 0101 | 1010 | 5 | A |
| 91 | 0101 | 1011 | 5 | B |
| 92 | 0101 | 1100 | 5 | C |
| 93 | 0101 | 1101 | 5 | D |
| 94 | 0101 | 1110 | 5 | E |
| 95 | 0101 | 1111 | 5 | F |
| 96 | 0110 | 0000 | 6 | 0 |
| 97 | 0110 | 0001 | 6 | 1 |
| 98 | 0110 | 0010 | 6 | 2 |
| 99 | 0110 | 0011 | 6 | 3 |
| 100 | 0110 | 0100 | 6 | 4 |
| 101 | 0110 | 0101 | 6 | 5 |
| 102 | 0110 | 0110 | 6 | 6 |
| 103 | 0110 | 0111 | 6 | 7 |
| 104 | 0110 | 1000 | 6 | 8 |
| 105 | 0110 | 1001 | 6 | 9 |
| 106 | 0110 | 1010 | 6 | A |
| 107 | 0110 | 1011 | 6 | B |
| 108 | 0110 | 1100 | 6 | C |

Table 2-1. Con't.

| Decimal | Binary | | Hex | |
|---------|--------|------|-----|---|
| 109 | 0110 | 1101 | 6 | D |
| 110 | 0110 | 1110 | 6 | E |
| 111 | 0110 | 1111 | 6 | F |
| | | | | |
| 112 | 0111 | 0000 | 7 | 0 |
| 113 | 0111 | 0001 | 7 | 1 |
| 114 | 0111 | 0010 | 7 | 2 |
| 115 | 0111 | 0011 | 7 | 3 |
| 116 | 0111 | 0100 | 7 | 4 |
| 117 | 0111 | 0101 | 7 | 5 |
| 118 | 0111 | 0110 | 7 | 6 |
| 119 | 0111 | 0111 | 7 | 7 |
| 120 | 0111 | 1000 | 7 | 8 |
| 121 | 0111 | 1001 | 7 | 9 |
| 122 | 0111 | 1010 | 7 | A |
| 123 | 0111 | 1011 | 7 | B |
| 124 | 0111 | 1100 | 7 | C |
| 125 | 0111 | 1101 | 7 | D |
| 126 | 0111 | 1110 | 7 | E |
| 127 | 0111 | 1111 | 7 | F |
| | | | | |
| 128 | 1000 | 0000 | 8 | 0 |
| 129 | 1000 | 0001 | 8 | 1 |
| 130 | 1000 | 0010 | 8 | 2 |
| 131 | 1000 | 0011 | 8 | 3 |
| 132 | 1000 | 0100 | 8 | 4 |
| 133 | 1000 | 0101 | 8 | 5 |
| 134 | 1000 | 0110 | 8 | 6 |
| 135 | 1000 | 0111 | 8 | 7 |
| 136 | 1000 | 1000 | 8 | 8 |
| 137 | 1000 | 1001 | 8 | 9 |
| 138 | 1000 | 1010 | 8 | A |
| 139 | 1000 | 1011 | 8 | B |
| 140 | 1000 | 1100 | 8 | C |
| 141 | 1000 | 1101 | 8 | D |
| 142 | 1000 | 1110 | 8 | E |
| 143 | 1000 | 1111 | 8 | F |
| | | | | |
| 144 | 1001 | 0000 | 9 | 0 |
| 145 | 1001 | 0001 | 9 | 1 |
| 146 | 1001 | 0010 | 9 | 2 |
| 147 | 1001 | 0011 | 9 | 3 |
| 148 | 1001 | 0100 | 9 | 4 |
| 149 | 1001 | 0101 | 9 | 5 |
| 150 | 1001 | 0110 | 9 | 6 |
| 151 | 1001 | 0111 | 9 | 7 |
| 152 | 1001 | 1000 | 9 | 8 |
| 153 | 1001 | 1001 | 9 | 9 |
| 154 | 1001 | 1010 | 9 | A |
| 155 | 1001 | 1011 | 9 | B |
| 156 | 1001 | 1100 | 9 | C |
| 157 | 1001 | 1101 | 9 | D |
| 158 | 1001 | 1110 | 9 | E |
| 159 | 1001 | 1111 | 9 | F |
| | | | | |
| 160 | 1010 | 0000 | A | 0 |
| 161 | 1010 | 0001 | A | 1 |
| 162 | 1010 | 0010 | A | 2 |

| Decimal | Binary | | Hex | |
|---|---|---|---|---|
| 163 | 1010 | 0011 | A | 3 |
| 164 | 1010 | 0100 | A | 4 |
| 165 | 1010 | 0101 | A | 5 |
| 166 | 1010 | 0110 | A | 6 |
| 167 | 1010 | 0111 | A | 7 |
| 168 | 1010 | 1000 | A | 8 |
| 169 | 1010 | 1001 | A | 9 |
| 170 | 1010 | 1010 | A | A |
| 171 | 1010 | 1011 | A | B |
| 172 | 1010 | 1100 | A | C |
| 173 | 1010 | 1101 | A | D |
| 174 | 1010 | 1110 | A | E |
| 175 | 1010 | 1111 | A | F |
| 176 | 1011 | 0000 | B | 0 |
| 177 | 1011 | 0001 | B | 1 |
| 178 | 1011 | 0010 | B | 2 |
| 179 | 1011 | 0011 | B | 3 |
| 180 | 1011 | 0100 | B | 4 |
| 181 | 1011 | 0101 | B | 5 |
| 182 | 1011 | 0110 | B | 6 |
| 183 | 1011 | 0111 | B | 7 |
| 184 | 1011 | 1000 | B | 8 |
| 185 | 1011 | 1001 | B | 9 |
| 186 | 1011 | 1010 | B | A |
| 187 | 1011 | 1011 | B | B |
| 188 | 1011 | 1100 | B | C |
| 189 | 1011 | 1101 | B | D |
| 190 | 1011 | 1110 | B | E |
| 191 | 1011 | 1111 | B | F |
| 192 | 1100 | 0000 | C | 0 |
| 193 | 1100 | 0001 | C | 1 |
| 194 | 1100 | 0010 | C | 2 |
| 195 | 1100 | 0011 | C | 3 |
| 196 | 1100 | 0100 | C | 4 |
| 197 | 1100 | 0101 | C | 5 |
| 198 | 1100 | 0110 | C | 6 |
| 199 | 1100 | 0111 | C | 7 |
| 200 | 1100 | 1000 | C | 8 |
| 201 | 1100 | 1001 | C | 9 |
| 202 | 1100 | 1010 | C | A |
| 203 | 1100 | 1011 | C | B |
| 204 | 1100 | 1100 | C | C |
| 205 | 1100 | 1101 | C | D |
| 206 | 1100 | 1110 | C | E |
| 207 | 1100 | 1111 | C | F |
| 208 | 1101 | 0000 | D | 0 |
| 209 | 1101 | 0001 | D | 1 |
| 210 | 1101 | 0010 | D | 2 |
| 211 | 1101 | 0011 | D | 3 |
| 212 | 1101 | 0100 | D | 4 |
| 213 | 1101 | 0101 | D | 5 |
| 214 | 1101 | 0110 | D | 6 |
| 215 | 1101 | 0111 | D | 7 |
| 216 | 1101 | 1000 | D | 8 |
| 217 | 1101 | 1001 | D | 9 |
| 218 | 1101 | 1010 | D | A |

Table 2-1. Con't.

| Decimal | Binary | Hex |
|---|---|---|
| 219 | 1101 1011 | D B |
| 220 | 1101 1100 | D C |
| 221 | 1101 1101 | D D |
| 222 | 1101 1110 | D E |
| 223 | 1101 1111 | D F |
| | | |
| 224 | 1110 0000 | E 0 |
| 225 | 1110 0001 | E 1 |
| 226 | 1110 0010 | E 2 |
| 227 | 1110 0011 | E 3 |
| 228 | 1110 0100 | E 4 |
| 229 | 1110 0101 | E 5 |
| 230 | 1110 0110 | E 6 |
| 231 | 1110 0111 | E 7 |
| 232 | 1110 1000 | E 8 |
| 233 | 1110 1001 | E 9 |
| 234 | 1110 1010 | E A |
| 235 | 1110 1011 | E B |
| 236 | 1110 1100 | E C |
| 237 | 1110 1101 | E D |
| 238 | 1110 1110 | E E |
| 239 | 1110 1111 | E F |
| | | |
| 240 | 1111 0000 | F 0 |
| 241 | 1111 0001 | F 1 |
| 242 | 1111 0010 | F 2 |
| 243 | 1111 0011 | F 3 |
| 244 | 1111 0100 | F 4 |
| 245 | 1111 0101 | F 5 |
| 246 | 1111 0110 | F 6 |
| 247 | 1111 0111 | F 7 |
| 248 | 1111 1000 | F 8 |
| 249 | 1111 1001 | F 9 |
| 250 | 1111 1010 | F A |
| 251 | 1111 1011 | F B |
| 252 | 1111 1100 | F C |
| 253 | 1111 1101 | F D |
| 254 | 1111 1110 | F E |
| 255 | 1111 1111 | F F |

If you examine the Decimal-Binary-Hex Conversion Table in the binary section, you'll see a long list of eight bits that make up a byte. The list is a compilation of every single possible combination of 0s and 1s that can be formed in a byte size register. Starting with 00000000 and going to 11111111, there are 256 possibilities. While the registers are side by side without a break on the chip, there is a space between the two nybbles in Table 2-1 so they can be read in an easier fashion.

Corresponding with the binary bytes is a list of hexadecimal numbers, with a space between the two hex numbers for easier reading. To the left of the binary numbers are the decimal numbers. The 256 decimal numbers are matched up with their binary and hex equivalents. The first number is decimal 0.

Practically all numbering in computers starts with zero rather than one. For instance, the eight data bus copper traces on the print board are numbered D0, D1, D2,

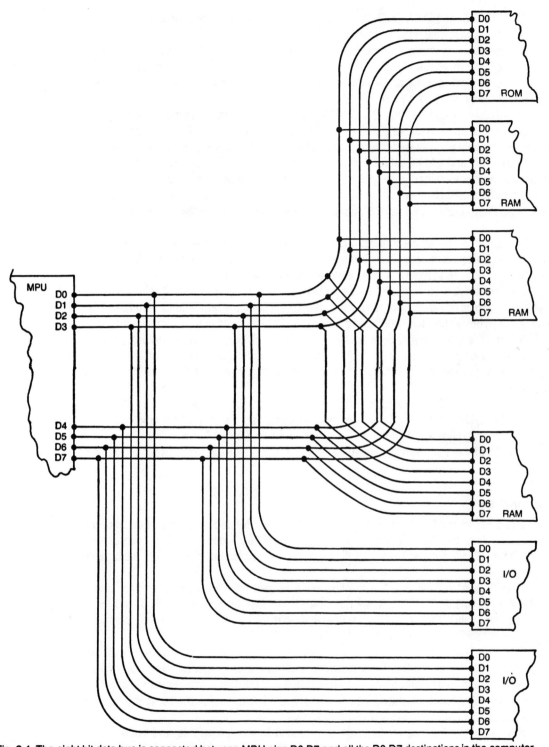

Fig. 2-4. The eight bit data bus is connected between MPU pins D0-D7 and all the D0-D7 destinations in the computer.

D3, D4, D5, D6, and D7 (Fig. 2-4). You must get used to this variation in our counting methods when you deal with computers.

All computer counting begins with zero because binary, the computer's natural numbering system, starts with 0. All the other number systems (decimal, octal, and hex) are forced to correspond with binary, since they are only substitutions for binary. Get used to counting starting with 0; it's the nature of the computer.

If you closely examine Table 2-1 you'll see some mathematical patterns emerge. It is useful to think through these patterns till they become established in your mind. The patterns will help you devise little test techniques during servicing and checkouts.

First of all, it would be useful if you could know by heart all 256 binary numbers in a byte and their hex codes. Obviously, to sit down and try to memorize all the bytes is a large, annoying job. However, you can already jot down a binary byte and its hex equivalent, if you have memorized the 16 binary numbers in a nybble and their 0 to F hex numbers.

The byte has no single number equivalent. It is, however, two nybbles, and each nybble has a single hex code. You already know all 16 of them. To code a byte of 8 bits all you have to do is to individually code each of its 4-bit nybbles.

There is a space in Table 2-1 every 16 bytes. This shows how easy it is to code the nybbles. Throughout the entire binary list, the 16 nybbles are repeated in patterns. The rightmost nybbles start with 0000 and proceed to 1111 over and over again. The leftmost nybbles start with 16 0000s, then continue with 16 each of every type, ending with 16 1111s. For coding, if you ignore the fact that a byte is eight bits but consider the byte as two nybbles, you can work with the 16 nybbles instead of having to deal with the 256 8-bit bytes.

This same nybble recognition technique works with 16-bit registers too. A 16-bit register holds four nybbles. There are 65,536 combinations in a 16-bit register. It is about as easy to code the 16-bit type as it is to code an 8-bit. All you have to do is consider the 16 bits as four individual nybbles. Then you can code each nybble with its single hex number.

## MS AND LS

The S in MS and LS stands for the word *significant*, defined as the digit contributing the most value. The M means Most and the L stands for Least. You'll encounter the terms Most Significant and Least Significant often during computer work. Let's examine them closer.

If we look at an 8-bit register, the bits are arranged from left to right and are numbered 7, 6, 5, 4, 3, 2, 1, and 0. As we discussed in the last section, bits 7, 6, 5, and 4 are the leftmost nybble. Bits 3, 2, 1, and 0 are rightmost nybble. Which nybble has the most significance?

The significance is illustrated easily (Fig. 2-5A). For instance, take two nybbles 1000 and 0001. Install 1000 in the left nybble and 0001 in the right nybble. This makes the register read 1000 0001. Since 1000 is 8 in hex and 0001 is 1, the register reads 8 1. 8 stands for eighty and 1 stands for 1. Obviously, the left nybble is the most significant, since eighty has more numerical weight than one.

Now we'll reverse the nybbles. 0001 is placed in the left nybble and 1000 in the right. What do we have? The hex now reads 1 8. The 1 stands for ten and the 8 stands

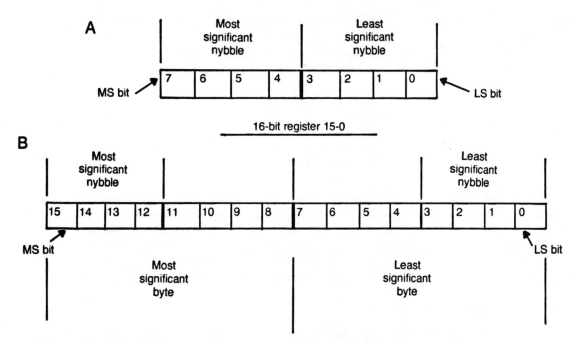

Fig. 2-5. A) Bits 7, 6, 5, and 4 are the leftmost MS nybble. Bits 3, 2, 1, and 0 are the rightmost LS nybble. B) Bits 15-8 are the leftmost MS byte. Bits 7-0 are the rightmost LS byte.

for eight. Now the 1 is the more significant digit. Again the left nybble is the more significant. It turns out that in a computer register, the leftmost nybble is always the Most Significant nybble and the rightmost is the Least Significant nybble. This holds true whether there are two nybbles in an 8-bit register, four nybbles in a 16-bit register, or eight nybbles in a 32-bit register. If there are more than two nybbles, the in-between nybbles would be called more significant or less significant according to their position in the register.

In a 16-bit register, the bits could be thought of as two bytes. In that case, the left-most byte would be the MS byte and the rightmost called the LS byte (Fig. 2-5B).

While the nybbles and bytes get a lot of reference to them as being the MSN, LSN, MSB, and LSB, the bits probably get the most of this attention. In a register the position of the bits produces a lot of mathematical manipulation. For example, let's look at the significance of the various bit positions in an 8-bit register. We'll start with a register that is completely clear of 1s. The register reads 0000 0000. The bits are numbered 7 to 0 from left to right.

If we set bit 0 with a 1, the total value of the register is 1. Next we reset bit 0 with a 0 and set bit 1 with a 1. This makes the total value of the register twice as much or 2. Bit 1 therefore is more significant than bit 0 since bit 0 being set only produces a value of 1. Bit 1 getting set in the same way produces a value of 2. There is no extra effort expended; the significant bit position is greater.

Now we will reset bit 1 to 0 and set bit 2 to 1. The register now reads 0000 0100. In hex, this is 0 4. This shows that bit position 2 is more significant than bit position 1. In fact the total value is again twice as much. When you reset bit 2 and then set bit three the register value again doubles, the register goes from 0000 0100 to 0000 10000, which is hex 0 8. Keeping up the leftwise shifting of the high pulse from a bit position to a more significant bit position causes the total value of the register to keep doubling.

| Register | Hex |
|----------|-----|
| 0001 0000 | 1 0 |
| 0010 0000 | 2 0 |
| 0100 0000 | 4 0 |
| 1000 0000 | 8 0 |

The bit positioning concept is an important one during troubleshooting, as you'll see later in the book. In the last few paragraphs, you've probably noticed a number of buzz words that you'll run across constantly in computer work. One word is *clear*. This means to remove any 1s in any bit position referred to, and replace the 1 with a 0. Another word is *set*. This is defined as the act of installing a 1 into a bit position. Then there is the term *reset*. This is often used instead of clear; in fact, clear and reset are used interchangeably.

## SIGNED NUMBERS

All the numbers in the conversion chart we have just examined (Table 2-1), are unsigned numbers—there are no + or − signs involved. Fortunately, most of the work a computer performs is with unsigned numbers and the chart can be used to convert decimal and hex numbers to a binary byte and vice versa. However, some work must be performed on numbers that need a + or − sign.

For example, let's take the listing of a computer program. The program is made up of one line after another of instructions and data. When the program is installed in the computer's memory and ordered to run, the computer automatically starts with the first line, fetches and executes it, goes to the next line, and so on.

As a program progresses, an instruction could tell the computer to stop the line-by-line sequence and branch to a line 50 numbers back. The computer obeys the branch instruction, subtracts 50 from the line numbers, and branches back. To do this, the signed number minus 50 must be used. An unsigned number 50 cannot be used. There are many maneuvers like this branch instruction that demand signed numbers. How are signs put on binary numbers?

In a byte-sized register, there are eight bits. The same registers must be used for signed as well as unsigned numbers. In the unsigned eight bits, all bits can be used to code a decimal or hex number. This permits coding all the decimal numbers from 0 to 255.

In the signed bits, one of the bits must be used to convey the + or − sign. It is common practice to use bit 7, the MSB. To represent a + sign, a 0 is placed in the MSB. To show a − sign, a 1 is installed in the MSB. The computer can handle the sign coding without any confusion (Fig. 2-6).

Let's see how this affects the conversion table (Table 2-2). Remember, in the MSB, 0 is + and 1 is −. Starting with 0000 0000 we have a decimal value of +0. Zero, by definition, is +. Continuing on, all the numbers up to 0111 1111 (which is +127) are

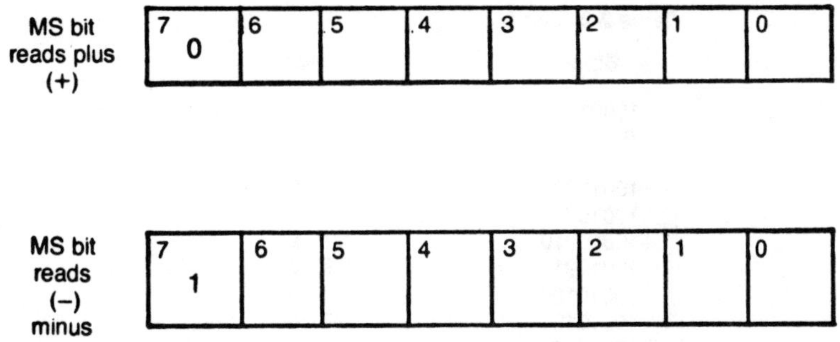

| MS bit reads plus (+) | 7 0 | 6 | 5 | 4 | 3 | 2 | 1 | 0 |
|---|---|---|---|---|---|---|---|---|

| MS bit reads (−) minus | 7 1 | 6 | 5 | 4 | 3 | 2 | 1 | 0 |
|---|---|---|---|---|---|---|---|---|

Fig. 2-6. In order to put a sign on a binary number, the MS bit is used. A 0 means the sign is + and 1 designates a − .

signed positively. With the MSB filled with the signs, there are only seven bits left for numbering. Seven bits can only have 128 possible combinations of 1s or 0s. This limits the + numbers to a range of 0 to 127.

The next binary number after 0111 1111 is 1000 0000. In unsigned decimal, this byte is valued at 128. However, we are now dealing with signed numbers. The entire table changes at this point. New arbitrary decimal numbers are assigned to the bytes starting with a 1. 1000 0000 is called −128. 1000 0001 is called −127. 1000 0010 is given the value −126. This is a complete departure from the values of the unsigned numbers. The numbers in order continue to decline till the binary 1111 1111 is reached. The signed value of 1111 1111 is −1. There is no −0.

**Table 2-2. Byte Size Conversion Table for Signed Numbers.**

| Decimal | Binary | Hex | |
|---|---|---|---|
| 0 | 00000000 | 0 | 0 |
| +1 | 00000001 | 0 | 1 |
| (Same as unsigned numbers in Table 2-1.) | | | |
| +126 | 01111110 | 7 | E |
| +127 | 01111111 | 7 | F |
| −128 | 10000000 | 8 | 0 |
| −127 | 10000001 | 8 | 1 |
| −126 | 10000010 | 8 | 2 |
| −125 | 10000011 | 8 | 3 |
| −124 | 10000100 | 8 | 4 |
| −123 | 10000101 | 8 | 5 |
| −122 | 10000110 | 8 | 6 |
| −121 | 10000111 | 8 | 7 |
| −120 | 10001000 | 8 | 8 |
| −119 | 10001001 | 9 | 9 |
| −118 | 10001010 | 8 | A |
| −117 | 10001011 | 8 | B |
| −116 | 10001100 | 8 | C |
| −115 | 10001101 | 8 | D |

Table 2-2. Con't.

| Decimal | Binary | Hex | |
|---|---|---|---|
| −114 | 10001110 | 8 | E |
| −113 | 10001111 | 8 | F |
| | | | |
| −112 | 10010000 | 9 | 0 |
| −111 | 10010001 | 9 | 1 |
| −110 | 10010010 | 9 | 2 |
| −109 | 10010011 | 9 | 3 |
| −108 | 10010100 | 9 | 4 |
| −107 | 10010101 | 9 | 5 |
| −106 | 10010110 | 9 | 6 |
| −105 | 10010111 | 9 | 7 |
| −104 | 10011000 | 9 | 8 |
| −103 | 10011001 | 9 | 9 |
| −102 | 10011010 | 9 | A |
| −101 | 10011011 | 9 | B |
| −100 | 10011100 | 9 | C |
| −99 | 10011101 | 9 | D |
| −98 | 10011110 | 9 | E |
| −97 | 10011111 | 9 | F |
| | | | |
| −96 | 10100000 | A | 0 |
| −95 | 10100001 | A | 1 |
| −94 | 10100010 | A | 2 |
| −93 | 10100011 | A | 3 |
| −92 | 10100100 | A | 4 |
| −91 | 10100101 | A | 5 |
| −90 | 10100110 | A | 6 |
| −89 | 10100111 | A | 7 |
| −88 | 10101000 | A | 8 |
| −87 | 10101001 | A | 9 |
| −86 | 10101010 | A | A |
| −85 | 10101011 | A | B |
| −84 | 10101100 | A | C |
| −83 | 10101101 | A | D |
| −82 | 10101110 | A | E |
| −81 | 10101111 | A | F |
| | | | |
| −80 | 10110000 | B | 0 |
| −79 | 10110001 | B | 1 |
| −78 | 10110010 | B | 2 |
| −77 | 10110011 | B | 3 |
| −76 | 10110100 | B | 4 |
| −75 | 10110101 | B | 5 |
| −74 | 10110110 | B | 6 |
| −73 | 10110111 | B | 7 |
| −72 | 10111000 | B | 8 |
| −71 | 10111001 | B | 9 |
| −70 | 10111010 | B | A |
| −69 | 10111011 | B | B |
| −68 | 10111100 | B | C |
| −67 | 10111101 | B | D |
| −66 | 10111110 | B | E |
| −65 | 10111111 | B | F |
| | | | |
| −64 | 11000000 | C | 0 |
| −63 | 11000001 | C | 1 |
| −62 | 11000010 | C | 2 |
| −61 | 11000011 | C | 3 |

| Decimal | Binary | Hex |
|---|---|---|
| −60 | 11000100 | C 4 |
| −59 | 11000101 | C 5 |
| −58 | 11000110 | C 6 |
| −57 | 11000111 | C 7 |
| −56 | 11001000 | C 8 |
| −55 | 11001001 | C 9 |
| −54 | 11001010 | C A |
| −53 | 11001011 | C B |
| −52 | 11001100 | C C |
| −51 | 11001101 | C D |
| −50 | 11001110 | C E |
| −49 | 11001111 | C F |
| −48 | 11010000 | D 0 |
| −47 | 11010001 | D 1 |
| −46 | 11010010 | D 2 |
| −45 | 11010011 | D 3 |
| −44 | 11010100 | D 4 |
| −43 | 11010101 | D 5 |
| −42 | 11010110 | D 6 |
| −41 | 11010111 | D 7 |
| −40 | 11011000 | D 8 |
| −39 | 11011001 | D 9 |
| −38 | 11011010 | D A |
| −37 | 11011011 | D B |
| −36 | 11011100 | D C |
| −35 | 11011101 | D D |
| −34 | 11011110 | D E |
| −33 | 11011111 | D F |
| −32 | 11100000 | E 0 |
| −31 | 11100001 | E 1 |
| −30 | 11100010 | E 2 |
| −29 | 11100011 | E 3 |
| −28 | 11100100 | E 4 |
| −27 | 11100101 | E 5 |
| −26 | 11100110 | E 6 |
| −25 | 11100111 | E 7 |
| −24 | 11101000 | E 8 |
| −23 | 11101001 | E 9 |
| −22 | 11101010 | E A |
| −21 | 11101011 | E B |
| −20 | 11101100 | E C |
| −19 | 11101101 | E D |
| −18 | 11101110 | E E |
| −17 | 11101111 | E F |
| −16 | 11110000 | F 0 |
| −15 | 11110001 | F 1 |
| −14 | 11110010 | F 2 |
| −13 | 11110011 | F 3 |
| −12 | 11110100 | F 4 |
| −11 | 11110101 | F 5 |
| −10 | 11110110 | F 6 |
| −9 | 11110111 | F 7 |
| −8 | 11111000 | F 8 |
| −7 | 11111001 | F 9 |
| −6 | 11111010 | F A |
| −5 | 11111011 | F B |

Table 2-2. Con't

| Decimal | Binary | Hex |
|---------|--------|-----|
| −4 | 11111100 | F C |
| −3 | 11111101 | F D |
| −2 | 11111110 | F E |
| −1 | 11111111 | F F |

As you can see, the conversion table for signed numbers is quite different than the one for unsigned numbers. While the unsigned number table proceeds smoothly in steadily-ascending decimal value from 0 to 255, the signed number table does not. The signed table proceeds from +0 to +127 in fine fashion, but then tops out at −128 and descends to a bottom of −1.

The limits of a byte-sized signed number ranges from +127 to −128, a total of 256 bit combinations. This is the same number of bit combinations in the same registers as the unsigned numbers. The binary bits do not change as you go from unsigned numbers to signed; only the arbitrary decimal coding is different. The computer goes about its electronics in exactly the same way.

A lot of the signed number activity deals with the BRANCH instruction from the CPU's instruction set. Branch instructions change the addresses of the instructions. With a byte-sized number, you are limited to changing the address by +127 or −128 places. Often, you'll want to change the address by more than that limited range. This can be done in a double byte-sized register, one with 16 bits. Having 16 bits increases the possible number of bit arrangements to 65,536 instead of the 256 possibilities in eight bits. The 16 bit signed numbers give you a range of +32,767 to −32,768 decimals to branch with.

## CONVERTING DECIMAL, BINARY AND HEX

The Conversion Table (Table 2-1) shows all the binary and hex equivalents for the decimal numbers 0 through 255. You will find the table very useful. At a glance, you can look down the number lists and quickly obtain the correct conversions you need for a single byte register. The table is limited to 256 entries.

After using the table awhile, you'll find that the conversion from binary to hex and back is rather easy. There is a relationship of one hex number for every four binary numbers. If you memorized the hex integers from 0 to F, you don't even need the table and are not limited to 256 entries. You can take a string of binary numbers, separate them into groups of four each, and quickly convert them to hex, or vice versa. For example, 0010/1100/1010/0101 is easily changed to 2 C A 5. 4 F 3 B becomes 0100/1111/0011/1011.

While the relationship between binary and hex is easily ascertained, the conversion to decimal is more difficult. The decimal is the natural human counting system, and the binary/hex is the computer way to count. The two do not mesh easily.

However, while human conversion of decimal numbers to binary/hex is slow the computer finds no difficulty performing the math. The computer makes the computation almost instantly. Most computers have a little program built in to convert hex to decimal and decimal to hex. Often, you will be able to type the decimal or hex number on the keyboard and the hex or decimal equivalent appears on the display. This is very convenient.

There are times that decimal must be converted to hex or hex to decimal by hand. If you have to change binary to decimal or decimal to binary, the best thing to do is turn the binary into hex first and then change the hex to decimal. This limits the conversion task to decimal and hex.

Let's use an example. In a typical 8-bit computer, there are usually 65,536 possible locations that the CPU is able to address. Every location has its very own numbered address. The numbers in decimal range from 0 to 65,535. During servicing, you find that you need to address a location. The address you have is in decimal and you want to address the location using hex. The address is 34,261. How can you convert 34,261 to its hex equivalent?

## Decimal to Hex

In order to convert the decimal number 34,261 to its hex equivalent, you must resort to some mathematical trickery that takes apart the five integers in 34,261 and reassembles them into four hex numbers. The procedure is quick but at first glance mysterious. First, let's try a simpler case of the same procedure that is more understandable, first (Fig. 2-7).

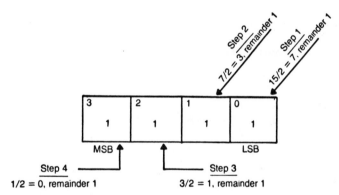

Fig. 2-7. Changing decimal to binary requires a repeated division of the decimal number by 2.

Let's convert the decimal number 15 to binary. We all know that decimal 15 is 1111 in binary. Another way to say that is 1111 is a nybble that can be installed in a register with four bits. The four bits are composed of an MSB, an LSB and two in between bits. The conversion from this view becomes, a disassembly of the decimal 15 into four bits, so they can be installed into the nybble register. How can this be done?

Since there are only two digits in binary in comparison to the 10 integers in decimal, changing decimal to a two-digit code requires a repeated division of the decimal by two. The remainders of the division become the binary equivalent. To begin with 15, is divided by 2.

15/2=7, with a remainder of 1. The remainder becomes the LSB and can be installed in that position in the nybble register. Next the answer to the division, 7, is divided by 2.

35

7/2 = 3, with a remainder of 1. This remainder becomes the next more significant bit and can be installed in that position in the nybble register. Next the answer to that division, 3, is divided by 2.

3/2 = 1, with a remainder of 1. This remainder becomes the next more significant bit and can be placed into the appropriate bit of the register. Last, the answer 1 is divided by 2.

1/2 = 0, with a remainder of 1. This one is the MSB and rounds out the binary conversion to 1111 from the decimal 15. It can be seen from this little exercise that a decimal can be taken apart and reassembled into binary with a repeated division by 2. What about changing the numbers into hex?

Once the decimal is converted into binary it is an easy matter to change the binary to hex. For instance, the binary 1111 is quickly changed to F, if you memorized the 16 binary/hex equivalents. However, by the same type of repeated division, you can change decimal to hex without going through a binary conversion stage. The only difference is that you must divide by 16 rather than by 2.

The relationship between decimal to hex is 10 to 16. While decimal only has 10 numerals, 0 to 9, hex has 16 numbers, 0 to F. Getting back to our original problem of converting decimal 34,261 to hex, it can be done in the following way. In Fig. 2-8, the first step is the division of 34,261 by 16. The answer is 2141. There is a remainder of 5.

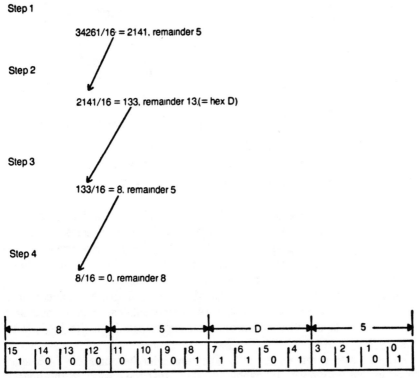

Fig. 2-8. Changing decimal to hex requires a repeated division of the decimal number by 16.

Like the previous binary conversion example, the first remainder becomes the LS hex number. Therefore, the 5 is jotted down as the last hex number. The next step is dividing the answer 2141 by 16.

2141/16 = 133, with a remainder of 13. The 13 in hex is coded as the letter D. The letter D then becomes the next more significant hex number. It is written in front of the 5.

The next division by 16 is into the previous answer 133. 133/16 = 8, and the remainder is 5. This becomes the next most significant hex number and is placed in front of the D.

The last step in the conversion is dividing the answer 8 by 16. 8/16 = 0, with a remainder of 8. This is the MS hex number. The conversion is complete. The decimal number 34,261 now is coded into hex 8 5 D 5.

This repeated division of a number is used when you must convert a decimal into binary, hex, or octal. While you need to divide by 2 for the binary answer and 16 for the hex number, you divide by 8 if you need an octal number. Fortunately, you will rarely need to use paper and pencil instead of the computer to do the conversion. For instance, to convert a number like decimal 34,261 to hex with one personal computer if you type in PRINT HEX$(34261), the computer responds almost instantly with 85D5.

However, there will be times when you'll need a decimal-hex conversion and a computer is not available or is broken down. Then it will be useful to be able to do the conversion by hand.

## Hex to Decimal

If the decimal repeated division conversion method is thought of as taking a decimal number apart, then the hex to decimal reverse procedure can be considered as putting the decimal back together.

Let's take an instance where a 16-bit register contains bits 0100 0011 1101 0101 (Fig. 2-9). In hex, that codes out to 4 3 D 5. The register could be a program counter and be pointing at memory location hex 4 3 D 5, which you need the decimal number for.

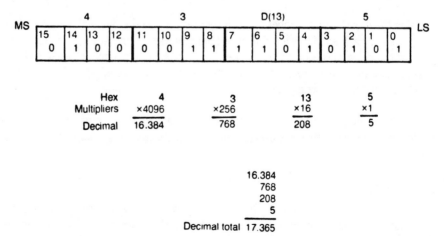

Fig. 2-9. In order to convert a hex number to decimal, each hex number must be multiplied by its nybble significance, and the nybble decimal totals added together.

There is no computer handy to do the conversion. You must construct the decimal number from the hex. How is it done?

There are four nybbles to deal with. The LS nybble contains the hex number 5. What is the relationship of the LS nybble to decimal?

The relationship is identical. For every hex number from 0 to F there is a corresponding decimal number from 0 to 15. Therefore the conversion of the LS nybble is exact. The hex 5 is converted to decimal 5. How about the next most significant nybble containing hex D?

This nybble, with the aid of the LS nybble, can contain the hex numbers 10 through FF. This corresponds with the decimal numbers 16 through 255. Table 2-1 shows this nybble stays at a single hex number for 16 counts. For instance, the hex number A remains in the nybble while the decimal count goes from 160 to 175. In order to obtain the decimal number that is stored in this more significant nybble, the hex number must be multiplied by 16. The hex number D then is multiplied by 16 (D(13) × 16) which equals 208.

In the next most significant nybble the hex number does not change for a decimal count of 256. In order to figure out what the decimal value of this nybble is, you must multiply the hex value by 256. This nybble is holding the hex number 3 (3 × 256 = 768).

The MS nybble in the 16-bit counter has the most significant value. In decimal the count must go 4096 times until hex number changes. This makes the decimal value of the MS nybble a result of the hex value times 4096. The nybble holds hex 4 (4 × 4096 = 16,384).

To obtain the total register value add up the decimal total in the four nybbles (Fig. 2-9):

| | |
|---|---:|
| MS nybble | 16384 |
| | 768 |
| | 208 |
| LS nybble | 5 |
| total | 17365 |

That is the way the hex number 4 3 D 5 is converted to the decimal number 17,365. The conversions back and forth are not too difficult by hand. However, it is much easier if you can do the conversions on the computer. To convert a hex number like 4 3 D 5 to a decimal number in some computers type in the code PRINT &H43D5. (The &H means hex.) Then, when the carriage return is pressed, the instantaneous reply of 17,365 appears.

If you constantly need to convert decimals to hex and vice versa, there are hand-held calculators available that will do the conversions as well as a computer can, which you might consider purchasing.

## ASCII and BCD

In the last few sections, we have discussed the way bits are installed in registers and the fact that each four bits represent a hex number. If there are eight bits in a row there are 256 possible arrangements. In hex, they are counted from 0 0 to F F. In decimal, the same bits are counted from 0 to 255. The eight bits do not change when hex is converted to decimal; only the description of the bits changes.

There are many other ways the bits in the byte can be coded. One other important way is a code called American Standard Code for Information Interchange, or ASCII for short.

Practically every computer you will ever come in contact with has a keyboard (similar to a typewriter's) for input and a screen display and printer for output. As you type on the keyboard, the keys you press are automatically displayed on the screen. If you want a hard (printed) copy of what you type the printer can be activated to print the letters and numbers. All this is accomplished with a code like ASCII.

ASCII can be described in decimal and hex just like any row of eight bits. However, the 256 possible bit arrangements are used to code all the keys on the keyboard. For example, the binary numbers from 0000 0000 to 0111 1111 are each assigned to represent a letter, number, or printer control figure. 0000 0000 is 0 0 in hex and 0 in decimal. 0111 1111 is 7 F in hex or 127 in decimal.

The capital letters A to Z are coded as 65 to 90 in decimal. The lower case letters a to z are coded from 97 to 122. Numerals 0 to 9 are coded from 48 to 57. As you can see the coding is strictly arbitrary, and the ASCII coding has no relationship to anything but the keyboard, display, and printer.

When you press a key on the keyboard, the key shorts out its own junction, which is different than any other key. That electrical impulse is sent to a device that generates the ASCII code for that key. For example, if you press the F key, the computer generates binary 0100 0110. The bits are stored in the computer memory, and sent to a chip called the Video Display Generator.

When the bits arrive at the VDG, they activate a display circuit. The circuit transmits the letter F to the display and F appears on the screen. Meanwhile, the F is also stored in bits on a memory register. To print the F, the computer sends the 0100 0110 to the printer. The printer is built to recognize those bits as F, and responds by printing F. The screen displays any of the ASCII codes it receives, and the printer prints any ASCII codes it receives, because they are designed to give that particular response.

Besides the letters and numbers, the symbols and other control keys can all generate an ASCII code. This includes quotation marks, exclamation marks, the space bar, and the carriage return. The important thing to remember is that ASCII is mostly used to install the keyboard characters into the computer, and to display or print the same characters as the need occurs. The jobs of running programs, instruction and data processing, and other binary manipulation are different. ASCII code is simply the binary DATA form that the keyboard characters take as they pass through the computer.

*BCD* stands for Binary Coded Decimal. This is a code like ASCII, except that it deals only with numbers and has no provision for letters or symbols, as ASCII does. In fact, BCD only has ten codes, not a possible 256 like ASCII.

ASCII uses eight bits to store a character. The byte sized code thus can describe 256 characters if all eight bits are used or 128 characters if only the seven least significant bits are put to work. In comparison, BCD uses only a nybble of four bits to code its numbers.

Four bits can code 16 numbers. Hex is four bits wide, and the four bits can code 0 through F. However, as the name binary coded decimal indicates, the binary of the BCD only codes decimal numbers. There are only ten decimals and only ten 4-bit binary codes are needed in BCD. the ten codes are identical to the first ten codes in hex. The BCD code consists of the following numbers:

| Binary Code | Decimal |
|:---:|:---:|
| 0000 | 0 |
| 0001 | 1 |
| 0010 | 2 |
| 0011 | 3 |
| 0100 | 4 |
| 0101 | 5 |
| 0110 | 6 |
| 0111 | 7 |
| 1000 | 8 |
| 1001 | 9 |

The nybble register that produced the code is able to make six more binary arrangements. It can set up the bits 1010, 1011, 1100, 1101, 1110, and 1111. These bit arrangements are not used in BCD. Those extra binary numbers not only are surplus, but their use is forbidden. If they accidentally do get used, they will ruin the calculation the computer is performing.

To avoid the complications that could occur, a special instruction is available in the Instruction Set to correct the calculation in case one of the results of an addition falls into the forbidden zone. (There is more about this in Chapter 11.)

BCD is handy since it codes decimal directly. There are many input devices that measure in decimal, like a voltmeter. If you are injecting the results of a voltage test directly with electrical impulses from the meter, it is handy to use BCD to code the decimal-counted pulses. Should you be sending a four bit code from a nybble register to an LED, it is convenient to conduct your data transfer using BCD. Most uses of BCD are performed by programmers. As a technician, you won't need it very much. However, knowing a little about it will keep you from being in the dark when the subject comes up. Also, you never know when a situation might arise that requires you to use or know about BCD.

Actual coding decimal to BCD is very easy. For example, suppose you want to code the decimal number 2356 to BCD and store it in the computer memory register. All you do is code the numbers 2 to 0010, 3 to 0011, 5 to 0101 and 6 to 0110. In an 8-bit computer, you'd install the numbers into two 8-bit registers like this.

00100011
01010110

If the number is to be placed in a 16-bit computer, only one register is needed.

0010001101010110

## ARITHMETIC

Decimal numbering uses 10 numerals, 0 through 9. Binary has only two digits, 0 and 1. Hexadecimal uses 16 characters, 0 through F. Last, octal has only 8 numbers, 0 through 7.

The mathemeticians describe these different numbering systems with the name *base*. All this means is decimal is called base 10, binary base 2, hexadecimal base 16, octal base 8. When you see a number and it has a tiny little number (either 10, 2, 16, or 8) attached as a tail, you can instantly tell whether it is decimal, binary, hexadecimal, or octal by its tail. For instance, the decimal number 2356 we coded into binary is described $2356_{10}$. The binary number 0010 is shown as $0010_2$. Hexadecimal 3F is $3F_{16}$, when the base is included in the description of number. Octal 25 is $25_8$.

You're used to the addition, subtraction, multiplication, and division of decimal numbers. However, the same mathematical manipulations of binary, hexadecimal, and octal are not second nature. In fact, the first few times you try to add base 2, 16, or 8 numbers together, you're likely to be perplexed.

Fortunately, you will rarely have to add or subtract hex or octal numbers. And if you do, the computer will be happy to do it for you. If the computer isn't available, you can always convert the hex or octal to decimal, do the addition, and then convert the answer back to hex or octal.

As a technician, you will occasionally need to add and subtract binary numbers. For instance, during signal tracing you might have to add a couple of registers together. The registers hold voltage levels. A voltage of +5 volts in a register could be a 1, while a zero voltage would be 0.

Suppose you have to add one 8-bit register containing 10101100 to a second register containing 00011001. There are only two possible numbers in binary, 0 and 1, in comparison to the ten numbers in decimal. Otherwise the addition is performed in exactly the same way as decimal.

| | Bits | 76543210 |
|---|---|---|
| Register one | | 10101100 |
| Register two | | 00011001 |
| Total | | 11000101 |

If you are adding the two bytes by hand, you start by adding the two LS bits together, just like decimal. Register one has a 0 in its LS while register two has a 1. $1+0=1$. All well and good. In the next bit to the left, each register has a 0. $0+0=0$. The next two leftmost bits are $1+0=1$. There are still no complications. However in bit positions 3, there are two 1s.

In binary, $1+1=10$. This is a departure from decimal. There are no other numbers between 1 and 10 and since the addition of $1+1$ cannot be 2, or 3 or any other decimal number, the next available characters are 10. (10 when converted to decimal is 2. The binary code for decimal 2 is 10.)

Therefore, when the 1s in bit positions 3 are added, they come to 10. Then, like decimal, the 0 is placed in the total and the 1 is carried.

In bit positions 4, the 1 carry is added to the 0 and 1. $0+1+1$ again equals 10. The 0 is put in the total and the 1 is carried. In bit positions 5, the 0 and 1 are added to the carry. $0+1+1=10$.

The new carry is added to bit positions 6. $0+0+1=1$, without any carry this time. Last, the MS bits are added. $1+0=1$.

That is how binary numbers are added together. The procedure is identical to the way you learned to add in grade school. The only difference is, the numbers 2 through 9 do not exist in the binary system. There are only two numbers, 1 and 0.

## Computer Subtraction

The digital circuits in the computer are designed for binary addition. They cannot do subtraction. If you tried to set up circuits to perform the subtraction, you'd find the design very difficult and expensive. Therefore, to perform subtraction, a tricky form of addition is used. That way the subtraction can be done in the registers that only conduct addition.

Most computers do their subtraction by a procedure called *addition of the 2's complement*. Like all simple math, the best way to do the job is by rote. The procedure is easy. Examine the definition. The complement of a binary number is its opposite. All 1s are changed to 0s, and all 0s are changed to 1s. That change makes the complement, what's called the *1's complement*. To get the 2's complement, simply add a 1 to the 1's complement. For example, take the binary byte 10011100.

| **Byte** | 10011100 |
| 1s | 01100011 |
| 2s | 01100100 |

Once you have the 2's complement, if you place it into a register and add it to another register, the answer is the same as if you had subtracted two binary numbers. That is how the computer does its subtraction in its circuits that can only perform addition.

There is another complication when you perform subtraction by addition of the 2's complement. This has to do with negative numbers. During subtraction the answer could turn out to be + or −. This brings up the subject of signed (+ or −) numbers again (Table 2-2). The 2's complement numbers are signed numbers, discussed earlier in this chapter. If you remember, the byte uses its MS bit to designate the sign of the number.

Between the eight bits, 256 possible arrangements can exist. The computer usually recognizes the arrangements of signed numbers as the following. The 128 bytes from 00000000 to 01111111 have decimal equivalents from 0 to +127. The 128 from 10000000 to 11111111 have decimal equivalents from −128 to −1. This is the range of numbers a byte can represent. Note that the first 128 bytes all have a 0 in the MS bit position, meaning +. The last 128 bytes all have a 1 in the MS position designating a −.

You will rarely need to use 2's complement addition during troubleshooting or maintenance, but you should know how the circuits are manipulating the voltage levels that are the 1s and 0s. Also, you are likely to run across the terminology elsewhere during your career, so you should be aware of it.

## Multiplication and Division by Computer

Binary multiplication and division are performed exactly like their decimal counterparts, except that the numbers 2 through 9 are not there. There are often no circuits in the computer to do this math work. In those cases the work is done with special multiplication and division software routines. The actual math is done in registers by shifting the value of the bits in the bytes from side to side. For example, it can be seen that if you have the number 1 in a byte, the 1 will reside in the LS bit, 00000001. To double the value, the bit is shifted once to the left, 00000010. To multiply again by two, the bit is shifted again, 00000100. This is how the multiplication can be conducted with the help of a program.

| Binary | Decimal |
| --- | --- |
| 00000000 | 0 |
| 00000001 | 1 |
| 00000010 | 2 |
| 00000100 | 4 |
| 00001000 | 8 |
| 00010000 | 16 |
| 00100000 | 32 |
| 01000000 | 64 |
| 10000000 | 128 |

The register does the multiplication after it receives instructions from a special program. In order to do the division, the bit positions are shifted to the right opposite in the direction the multiplication requires. A division program does that job. All of this is usually conducted automatically, but you must be aware of the procedures in case they stop operating automatically as they are designed to do.

# 3
# The Required Electronics

From the programmer's point of view, the computer is a device where a program can be entered and in some mysterious wonderful manner, the program goes to work and produces the desired results. The results get displayed on a screen, printed on paper, or stored on a cassette tape. The programmer might occasionally marvel at the speed and accuracy that the computer shows as it works, but rarely thinks about the electronic circuits that are faithfully doing the job.

The technician, on the other hand, is charged with the responsibility of installing the computer and then making sure that the computer is always operating. The electronics of the computer must be second nature to the technician. There is no way you can figure out what is wrong with electronic gear unless you know how it works. The more you understand the circuits, the more effective a technician you will be.

## DIGITAL AND ANALOG

As you stare down at a computer, you see a keyboard. When you strike a key, you short a row and column together. There can be 56 separate intersections where a short can take place under the keyboard. This is like 56 separate buttons, each one designating a character or symbol of the typing layout. When you push a button, the computer begins a complex coding process.

The coding, as mentioned earlier, is the manipulation of square waves. The square waves if viewed on an oscilloscope, go high or drop low (Fig. 3-1). The vertical height of the oscilloscope trace represents voltage. The horizontal base is the frequency of the wave, or to describe it another way, the timing of the wave. The square wave is digital. The circuits that process square waves are naturally called, digital circuits.

The reason a square wave is called digital is because it can be used to represent two digits (Fig. 3-2). The high voltage, which is typically +5 V, can be used as the digit 1.

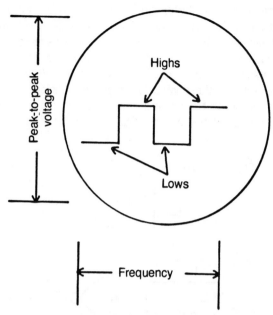

Fig. 3-1. A digital waveshape has two levels, high and low. The highs and low consume time. The time between highs and lows, the vertical lines, are practically instantaneous.

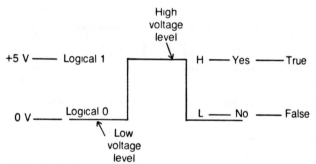

Fig. 3-2. The high voltage level represents the binary number 1. The low voltage level is used as the number 0.

The low voltage, which is usually 0 V, is utilized as the digit 0. The two states of the square wave are often referred to by technicians as H and L.

There are lots of different ways the two states of the square wave are shown. You might find them called Yes and No or True and False. Whatever they are called, however, in the digital circuit they are still the same square waves traveling through time and going from a high of +5 V to a low of 0 V.

The square waves are generated in the digital circuit areas and travel in those circuits from place to place as they are processed. All the processing consists of is changing the arrangements of the square waves. They are added to, stored, moved from place to place, and so forth. Then, after the manipulations are finished with, the square waves are output.

45

For the duration of time the square waves are processed in the computer, they encounter circuits that do nothing more than continously rearrange the states of the streams of highs and lows. Highs are changed to lows, lows are changed to highs (Fig. 3-3), the highs and lows are stored in the bit positions of the registers (Fig. 3-4), and the streams of logic states are transferred from place to place (Fig. 3-5).

The digital circuits do these jobs. When you test digital circuits, except for a few special instances, all you are testing for are the presence and absence of highs, lows, and the frequencies the two states are traveling at between digital circuits. There are no

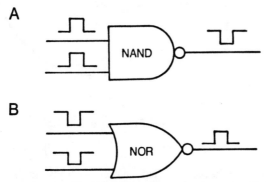

Fig. 3-3. Computer circuits rearrange the highs and lows according to design. A) A NAND circuit changes two highs into one low. B) A NOR circuit changes two lows into one high.

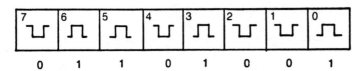

Fig. 3-4. Register circuits are able to store highs and lows during the processing.

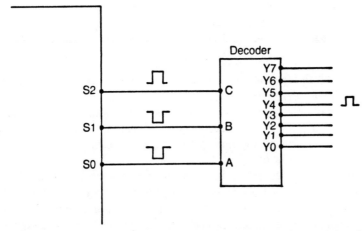

Fig. 3-5. These three highs and lows are transferred from circuit to circuit and decoded into one high.

46

other signals besides these square waves in the digital circuits. The tests are simple and straightforward. The circuits are easy to understand, but they may seem strange to the technician who has only been exposed to analog circuitry.

Once the digital signal has been processed, it is sent to analog circuits. Analog circuits are like those found in radios and TVs. While digital circuits only work on two logic levels, analog electronics have an infinite number of levels. The analog circuits, as a result, can perform jobs like amplification, detection, audio processing, video generating, color display, etc. (Fig. 3-6). The digital signal is output to circuits that are referred to as D/A, for *digital-to-analog* (Fig. 3-7).

Typically, the D/A circuits change outputs for audio circuits from 1s and 0s to sound. They turn outputs for cassette recorders from 1s to 0s into a recordable code, like sine waves; one frequency for a 1 and a second frequency for a 0. A complex D/A circuit generates a video signal with the logic states installed for the display. The inside world of the computer deals only with digital signal, but the outside, human-inhabited world can't work only with the two states. The human world connects to the computer by means of analog signals.

As a result, you will be working with both digital and analog signals and circuits. The testing of the computer requires digital techniques inside the computer itself. Once the signal is out of the computer and into the analog circuits, analog techniques are needed to examine the electronics. In the D/A circuits, digital circuit troubleshooting is used on the computer side while analog repairing is performed on the analog side. Just as the digital and analog circuits are not compatible, you cannot use digital techniques in the analog circuits or vice versa. Both methods are shown throughout the book.

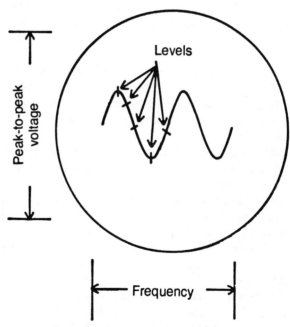

Fig. 3-6. The sine wave is an analog signal because it has a continuous infinite number of voltage levels. The digital square wave, in contrast, has only two levels, high and low.

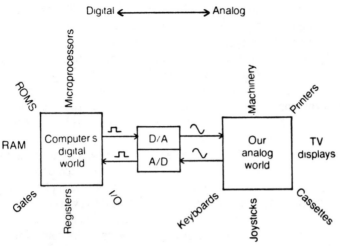

Fig. 3-7. Digital-to-analog circuits change highs and lows to signals like sine waves. The analog-to-digital converter changes sine wave signals to highs and lows.

## INTEGRATED AND DISCRETE

Years ago, all electronic circuits were made up of discrete components. The typical circuit, whether digital or analog, consisted of tubes, transistors, resistors, capacitors, and coils. Technicians typically traced trouble to a particular circuit by symptom analysis, signal tracing, and signal injection. Once a suspect circuit turned up, voltage and resistance readings were taken to pinpoint the actual discrete component that had failed. Usually there were a number of possible suspects. Each would then be tested individually by resistance or substitution. The defective discrete part would then be replaced and the equipment returned to operation.

About twenty years ago, small modules began to be made, mainly to aid technicians in that last step where the defective component was still not pinpointed, but was known to be one of a suspected group. The pinpointing was dispensed with. The entire module was replaced. This saved the pinpointing time which was more valuable than the cost of the inexpensive module.

These modules still contained discrete components but were often encased in plastic or tar and were considered a *black box*. A black box is a piece of electronic gear that cannot be accessed. It has wires sticking out, so you can test to see what signals or voltages are going in and out, but you cannot get to the components inside. A slick technician could shave open these early modules, locate the defective discrete component and replace it, completing a repair if necessary. Sometimes the module was not readily available, and technicians would repair the modules rather than go through the difficult job of obtaining a replacement module.

About 1970, these modules were built with integrated circuits instead of discrete components. There were a number of stages between the modules containing discrete components and the ICs. There was one stage where the module was built with subminiature capacitors, resistors and coils. They were made in what was called *cordwood*, as the illustration shows (Fig. 3-8). Then there were a number of hybrid modules that con-

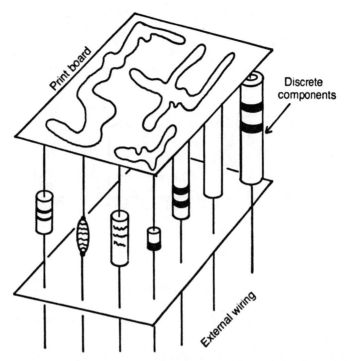

Fig. 3-8. The first modules were the cordwood stacked type. When encased in tar or plastic they were considered black boxes.

tained both integrated circuits and discrete components. All this is history, and if you are curious, there are books that trace this development.

We are mainly interested in the ICs called *monolithic*. These chips are the ones found in computers. They are encased in a package that is made of two kinds of materials. One is called *hermetic*, which is metal, ceramic, or glass. The second type is called *non-hermetic*, which is nothing more than plastic. The plastic is cheaper than the ceramic but is not as sturdy in hot, humid environments. You'll find both types in computers.

## CHIP PACKAGING

As a technician, you will spend a lot of your working hours dealing with the packages the silicon chips are encased in. In todays computers you are likely to encounter two different types of chip packaging. First of all there is the DIP. Its initials stand for Dual-In-line Package. As Fig. 3-9 shows, the package is rectangular in shape with two parallel rows of feet sticking out of the long sides of the rectangle. On one end is a keyway. It can be in the form of a notch, a paint dot or hole at one end of the package. The keyway is there to let you know where the first and last pin numbers are. Counting counterclockwise, the first pin from the notch is number 1. The pins are then counted until you reach the last number across from pin 1. Figure 3-9 shows a 14-pin DIP. Also shown are typical manufacturer markings on a chip. This one has the manufacturer's logo, a date code to give the chips' age, warranty information, and the part number of the chip.

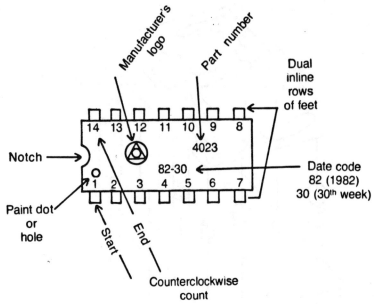

Fig. 3-9. Most of today's chips are called DIPs, because the legs are arranged in a Dual-Inline-Package.

When you look down at a print board and find a chip you are looking for, it could be positioned with its keyway in any convenient position. The keyway could be north, south, east or west. At first glance this could confuse the number count. Just remember to count DIP pins counterclockwise starting at the keyway. This rule only applies to DIPs, (unless otherwise noted in service notes). Other types of packages could require pin counting clockwise.

DIPs appear in data manuals and service notes in two different forms. They can be drawn in exactly the same shape as they appear on the print board. This means you can line up the data manual sketch with the actual package. This type of representation is called a pinout. Later on in this book you see pinouts showing pin numbers and the logic states that are typically found on each pin. These are convenient Test Point Charts that you can use to test the condition of chips with.

The chips are also drawn on schematics, as in Fig. 3-10. Here again the chip is drawn as a rectangle, but the positions of the pin numbers bear no correlation to the pinout. The pins show signal flow but are drawn for the convenience of the schematic layout. When you read the schematic, you must relate the pins on the schematic chip to the actual pinout. This is a required mental step when you attempt to compare the chip on the print board to the schematic. The pinout, on the other hand, compares directly and does not require the extra mental comparison step.

DIPs are very popular. When most people think of chips, they envision DIPs. However, DIPS represent the old-fashioned way to package integrated circuits. In today's microscopic electronic world, DIPs have disadvantages. First of all DIPs need both sides of the print board to be attached. They are plated through holes drilled in print boards to accomodate the DIPs. The little legs are poked through the holes and soldered in place on the bottom side of the board.

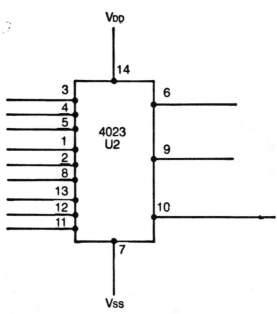

Fig. 3-10. The schematic drawing of a chip is usually a rectangle with the pin numbers arranged to show signal flow.

In addition, the circuits on chips are becoming denser and denser as time goes by. For example the 80386 processors have more than 250,000 transistors mounted. The pins on the 80386 number 132. If this chip was housed in a DIP there would be two rows of 66 pins on a side. The legs on a DIP, by convention, are spaced a tenth of an inch apart. If the 386 was installed in a DIP the chip would be six and a half inches long. Chips like this would really use up a lot of print board real estate. On both sides of the board too.

This brings us to the next type of package, the Surface-Mounted Device or SMD. From the above discussion it is indicated that the obvious advantages are probably the facts that SMDs only need to use one side of the print board and provide a smaller more convenient package than the DIP. This is indeed the case.

To begin with, SMDs, by convention have legs spaced closer than DIPs. While DIP legs are spaced one tenth of an inch apart, SMDs are spaced one twentieth of an inch apart. That feature alone could reduce the print board area the package takes up, by between 30 and 60 percent. In addition, the legs are not sticking out of only two sides. The legs are mounted on all four sides of the package. With these features two or three SMDs can be packed where one DIP had resided before.

Not only are the legs mounted on the four sides, but in larger chips such as the 132-pin 386 the pins are also mounted so they protrude out of the bottom of the chip.

Besides being able to package an IC in smaller quarters because the leg connections in SMDs are not restricted to just two sides of the package as in DIPs, the SMDs only use one side of the print board. The name Surface-Mounted Devices means the packages have legs that do not go through holes to the bottom of the print board. The legs are bent up in different ways so they simply sit on the board as in Fig. 3-11.

Surface—Mount IC Package.

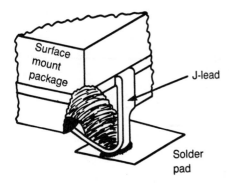

Fig. 3-11. An alternative leg shape on an SMD is the J-Lead. Note how the solder tends to accumulate in the crook of the leg providing a stronger solder joint.

This feature doubles the amount of available print board area. Since the SMDs only use one side of a print board, it is possible to have another complete set of circuits on the flip side of the board. This allows a designer to produce an SMD based printed circuit card that takes up the equivalent of two DIP based cards. This makes card-to-card wiring easier, and reduces wiring from other circuit sources to the card. In addition, the print board can be made thinner with less layers, is easier to produce and increases reliability.

Chip packages, by convention have been given a code letter. Just as a resistor is usually referred to as an R (R1, R2, R3, etc.), a capacitor as a C, the chip package has been called a U. For example the 99-chip packages on the system board of the IBM PC are designated U1 through U99.

The 99 packages are laid out on the system board in as coherent a pattern as possible as Fig. 3-12 shows. Incidentally, Fig. 3-12 is the chip location guide for the PC. It is very useful to locate chips during a repair.

Once you locate a chip you want to test, the package pinout shows the exact position of each pin on the package. The pin position on the package though is not present on the schematic. The pin location on the schematic has no physical relation to the pin location on the actual package. Only the pin numbers are the same but they are spread over the schematic symbol, a rectangle, in accordance to signal flow, as mentioned earlier.

The IC packages contain the bulk of the computer circuits. When you test a package, you are conducting tests on many thousands of circuits. However, all you do is make input-output tests. You can't gain access to most of the basic circuits. What you do is look for discrepancies. If a pin does not have the prescribed voltage, logic state or oscilloscope reading you have a clue to follow up.

When you do find a defunct chip it must be changed. That could be easy or difficult according to its package. If the package is plugged into a socket, replacing it can be a relatively easy task. Should the package be a DIP, careful, patient desoldering is in order. When the package is an SMD, tricky, calculated desoldering and resoldering is the order of the day. Chapters 20-22 go into considerable detail on the right ways to test and replace IC packages. Meanwhile, lets go into what types of transistors and circuits are cast in the silicon and find out how they work.

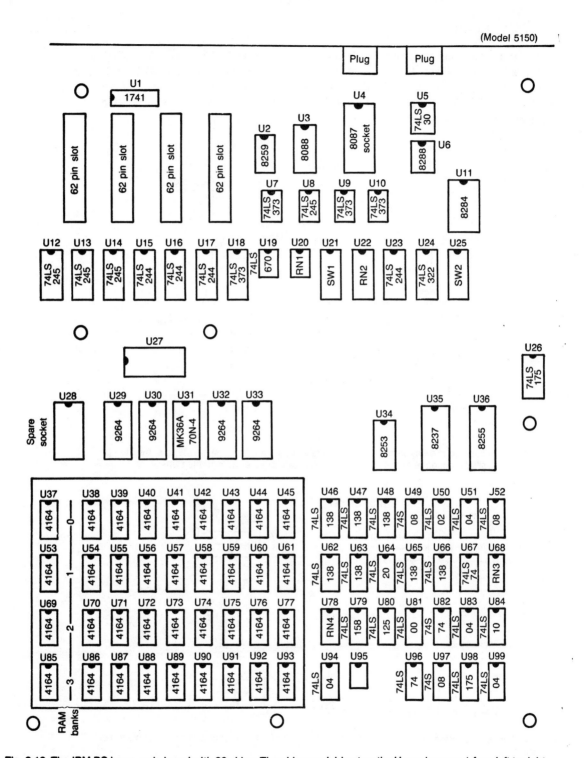

**Fig. 3-12.** The IBM PC has a main board with 99 chips. The chips are laid out so the U numbers read from left to right.

## TTL AND MOS

There are two important types of transistors that are installed on silicon chips to produce an intergrated circuit that is used in computers. One type is the bipolar transistor (Fig. 3-13). They are the pnp and the npn. The second type is the field effect transistor called the FET (Fig. 3-14). On TTL chips are found the pnp's and npn's. The MOS chips have FETs.

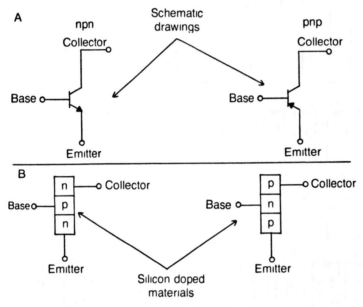

Fig. 3-13. The schematic drawing of bipolar transistors are drawn with arrow heads to show the npn and pnp. B) The silicon-doped N and P materials are stacked together to form the transistors.

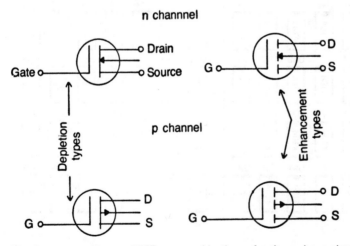

Fig. 3-14. The four common types of FETs are combinations of n channel or p channel, depletion or enhancement.

The typical chip has a silicon substrate that is smaller than a fingernail. The transistors are fabricated on the substrate. There can literally be hundreds of thousands of transistor circuits installed on one substrate. All of these microscopic circuits are hooked together internally. There is no way you can test an individual circuit with a test probe. The chips are true black boxes, and they must be tested as such.

The TTL's contain the bipolar transistors. The TTL stands for Transistor Transistor Logic. There are other kinds of bipolar transistor chips. They are called RTL (Fig. 3-15) and DTL (Fig. 3-16), for Resistor Transistor Logic and Diode Transistor Logic. The illustration shows the different types; however, you won't see much of RTL or DTL chips. The RTL was an inexpensive chip that was easily interfaced with discrete components, but it had poor noise immunity and low fanout ability.

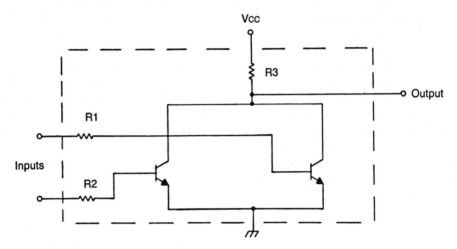

Fig. 3-15. The RTL circuit is named for the resistors in the input.

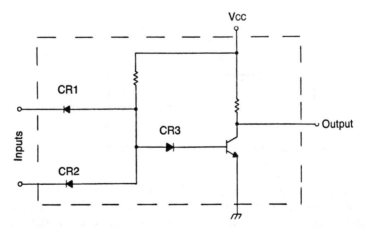

Fig. 3-16. The DTL circuit is named for the diodes in the input. This circuit is a NAND gate.

The characteristic called *fanout* is the measure of how well a chip is able to drive a number of parallel loads. The output of a chip is coupled to the next stage. When the fanout characteristic of the chip is excellent, the chip can drive a lot of parallel identical loads in its output. If the fanout is good, the chip can drive a few parallel loads. When the fanout is poor (as with the RTL), the chip can only drive a single load. The fanout of a chip is usually listed in the Absolute Maximum Ratings column of a chip's description. For instance, the 7473 TTL chip has a fanout of 10. That means it is strong enough to drive up to 10 identical parallel loads.

The RTL chip gets its name (Resistor Transistor Logic) from the placement of the resistors in the input base circuits of the npn transistors. In the same way, the DTL chip gets its name (Diode Transistor Logic) from the diodes in the input circuits. The diodes provide a clipping action that increases noise immunity and improves fanout.

The diodes also give the gate circuits on the chip excellent *fan-in* characteristics. This means the chip can receive a lot of parallel inputs. The fan-in characteristic is not always listed in the manufacturer's ratings, but it is sometimes a consideration.

RTLs and DTLs are rarely used in modern computers. When the need for bipolar transistor type chips arises, TTLs are usually used. TTLs are superior to RTLs and DTLs in most respects. They are faster. They act like DTLs since the transistors have built in diodes between their emitters and bases. In 1961, a special kind of transistor with two emitter diodes attached to a single base was invented by a man named Thompson. This is effectively a DTL as well as a TTL, combining the valuable characteristics of both types. All the inputs of the TTL can enter the gates through the multiple emitters and be diode-isolated, just as if the gate was DTL (Fig. 3-17).

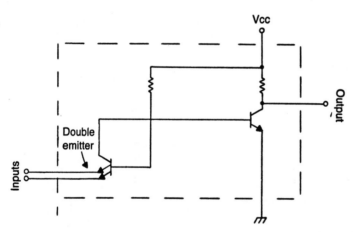

Fig. 3-17. The TTL with multiple emitters has eliminated the need for RTL or DTL circuits in today's computers.

There are a few hundred different types of TTLs. They have been given series numbers starting with 7400. They range in four digits from 7400 to 7499. Then they go into five digits from 74100 on up. The list shown here goes up to 74490 (Table 3-1).

The family of ordinary TTLs have cousins that are special TTLs. You'll recognize them by their LS middle initials. For instance, the 7400 has a counterpart cousin called 74LS00. The 74490 has a cousin called 74LS490 (Table 3-2).

56

**Table 3-1. Some of the TT1 Family of ICs.**

| | | | | | | | | | | | |
|---|---|---|---|---|---|---|---|---|---|---|---|
| 7400 | .19 | 7482 | .95 | 74170 | 1.65 | 7433 | .45 | 74136 | .50 | 74247 | 1.25 |
| 7401 | .19 | 7483 | .50 | 74172 | 5.95 | 7437 | .29 | 74141 | .65 | 74248 | 1.85 |
| 7402 | .19 | 7485 | .65 | 74173 | .75 | 7438 | .29 | 74142 | 2.95 | 74249 | 1.95 |
| 7403 | .19 | 7486 | .35 | 74174 | .89 | 7440 | .19 | 74143 | 2.95 | 74251 | .75 |
| 7404 | .19 | 7489 | 4.95 | 74175 | .89 | 7442 | .49 | 74145 | .60 | 74259 | 2.25 |
| 7405. | .25 | 7490 | .35 | 74176 | .89 | 7443 | .65 | 74147 | 1.75 | 74265 | 1.35 |
| 7406 | .29 | 7491 | .40 | 74177 | .75 | 7444 | .69 | 74148 | 1.20 | 74273 | 1.95 |
| 7407 | .29 | 7492 | .50 | 74178 | 1.15 | 7445 | .69 | 74150 | 1.35 | 74276 | 1.25 |
| 7408 | .24 | 7493 | .49 | 74179 | 1.75 | 7446 | .59 | 74151 | .65 | 74279 | .75 |
| 7409 | .19 | 7494 | .65 | 74180 | .75 | 7447 | .69 | 74152 | .65 | 74283 | 2.00 |
| 7410 | .19 | 7495 | .55 | 74181 | 2.25 | 7448 | .69 | 74153 | .55 | 74284 | 3.75 |
| 7411 | .25 | 7496 | .70 | 74182 | .75 | 7450 | .19 | 74154 | 1.40 | 74285 | 3.75 |
| 7412 | .30 | 7497 | 2.75 | 74184 | 2.00 | 7451 | .23 | 74155 | .75 | 74290 | .95 |
| 7413 | .35 | 74100 | 1.00 | 74185 | 2.00 | 7453 | .23 | 74156 | .65 | 74293 | .75 |
| 7414 | .55 | 74107 | .30 | 74186 | 18.50 | 7454 | .23 | 74157 | .55 | 74298 | .85 |
| 7416 | .25 | 74109 | .45 | 74190 | 1.15 | 7460 | .23 | 74159 | 1.65 | 74351 | 2.25 |
| 7417 | .25 | 74110 | .45 | 74191 | 1.15 | 7470 | .35 | 74160 | .85 | 74365 | .65 |
| 7420 | .19 | 74111 | .55 | 74192 | .79 | 7472 | .29 | 74161 | .70 | 74366 | .65 |
| 7421 | .35 | 74116 | 1.55 | 74193 | .79 | 7473 | .34 | 74162 | .85 | 74367 | .85 |
| 7422 | .29 | 74120 | 1.20 | 74194 | .85 | 7474 | .35 | 74163 | .85 | 74368 | .65 |
| 7423 | .29 | 74121 | .29 | 74195 | .85 | 7475 | .49 | 74164 | .85 | 74376 | 2.20 |
| 7425 | .29 | 74122 | .45 | 74196 | .79 | 7476 | .35 | 74165 | .85 | 74390 | 1.75 |
| 7426 | .29 | 74123 | .55 | 74197 | .75 | 7480 | .59 | 74166 | 1.00 | 74393 | 1.35 |
| 7427 | .29 | 74125 | .45 | 74198 | 1.35 | 7481 | 1.10 | 74167 | 2.95 | 74425 | 3.15 |
| 7428 | .45 | 74126 | .45 | 74199 | 1.35 | | | | | 74426 | .85 |
| 7430 | .19 | 74128 | .55 | 74221 | 1.35 | | | | | 74490 | 2.55 |
| 7432 | .29 | 74132 | .45 | 74246 | 1.35 | | | | | | |

**Table 3-2. Some of the LS TTL Family of ICs.**

| | | | | | | | | | | | |
|---|---|---|---|---|---|---|---|---|---|---|---|
| 74LS00 | .25 | 74LS113 | .45 | 74LS245 | 1.90 | 74LS42 | .55 | 74LS164 | .95 | 74LS366 | .95 |
| 74LS01 | .25 | 74LS114 | .50 | 74LS247 | .75 | 74LS47 | .75 | 74LS165 | .95 | 74LS367 | .70 |
| 74LS02 | .25 | 74LS122 | .45 | 74LS248 | 1.25 | 74LS48 | .75 | 74LS166 | 2.40 | 74LS368 | .70 |
| 74LS03 | .25 | 74LS123 | .95 | 74LS249 | .99 | 74LS49 | .75 | 74LS168 | 1.75 | 74LS373 | 1.75 |
| 74LS04 | .25 | 74LS124 | 2.99 | 74LS251 | 1.30 | 74LS51 | .25 | 74LS169 | 1.75 | 74LS374 | 1.75 |
| 74LS05 | .25 | 74LS125 | .95 | 74LS253 | .85 | 74LS54 | .35 | 74LS170 | 1.75 | 74LS377 | 1.45 |
| 74LS08 | .35 | 74LS126 | .85 | 74LS257 | .85 | 74LS55 | .35 | 74LS173 | .80 | 74LS378 | 1.18 |
| 74LS09 | .35 | 74LS132 | .75 | 74LS258 | .85 | 74LS63 | 1.25 | 74LS174 | .95 | 74LS379 | 1.35 |
| 74LS10 | .25 | 74LS136 | .55 | 74LS259 | 2.85 | 74LS73 | .40 | 74LS175 | .95 | 74LS385 | 1.90 |
| 74LS11 | .35 | 74LS137 | .99 | 74LS260 | .65 | 74LS74 | .45 | 74LS181 | 2.15 | 74LS386 | .65 |
| 74LS12 | .35 | 74LS138 | .75 | 74LS266 | .55 | 74LS75 | .50 | 74LS189 | 9.95 | 74LS390 | 1.90 |
| 74LS13 | .45 | 74LS139 | .75 | 74LS273 | 1.65 | 74LS76 | .40 | 74LS190 | 1.00 | 74LS393 | 1.90 |
| 74LS14 | 1.00 | 74LS145 | 1.20 | 74LS275 | 3.35 | 74LS78 | .50 | 74LS191 | 1.00 | 74LS395 | 1.65 |
| 74LS15 | .35 | 74LS147 | 2.49 | 74LS279 | .55 | 74LS83 | .75 | 74LS192 | .85 | 74LS399 | 1.70 |
| 74LS20 | .25 | 74LS148 | 1.35 | 74LS280 | 1.98 | 74LS85 | 1.15 | 74LS193 | .95 | 74LS424 | 2.95 |
| 74LS21 | .35 | 74LS151 | .75 | 74LS283 | 1.00 | 74LS86 | .40 | 74LS194 | 1.00 | 74LS447 | .37 |
| 74LS22 | .25 | 74LS153 | .75 | 74LS290 | 1.25 | 74LS90 | .65 | 74LS195 | .95 | 74LS490 | 1.95 |
| 74LS26 | .35 | 74LS154 | 2.35 | 74LS293 | 1.86 | 74LS91 | .89 | 74LS196 | .85 | 74LS624 | 3.99 |
| 74LS27 | .35 | 74LS155 | 1.15 | 74LS295 | 1.05 | 74LS92 | .70 | 74LS197 | .85 | 74LS668 | 1.69 |
| 74LS28 | .35 | 74LS156 | .95 | 74LS298 | 1.20 | 74LS93 | .65 | 74LS221 | 1.20 | 74LS669 | 1.89 |
| 74LS30 | .25 | 74LS157 | .75 | 74LS324 | 1.75 | 74LS95 | .85 | 74LS240 | 1.29 | 74LS670 | 2.20 |
| 74LS32 | .35 | 74LS158 | .75 | 74LS352 | 1.56 | 74LS96 | .95 | 74LS241 | 1.29 | 74LS674 | 9.65 |
| 74LS33 | .55 | 74LS160 | .90 | 74LS353 | 1.55 | 74LS107 | .40 | 74LS242 | 1.85 | 74LS682 | 3.20 |
| 74LS37 | .55 | 74LS161 | .95 | 74LS363 | 1.35 | 74LS109 | .40 | 74LS243 | 1.85 | 74LS683 | 2.30 |
| 74LS38 | .35 | 74LS162 | .95 | 74LS364 | 1.95 | 74LS112 | .45 | 74LS244 | 1.29 | 74LS684 | 2.40 |
| 74LS40 | .35 | 74LS163 | .95 | 74LS365 | .95 | | | | | 74LS685 | 2.40 |

The L initial stands for low power. The L-designated chips use 80 percent less power than their non-initialed cousins.

The S initial stands for Schottky diode. The Schottky barrier diode clamps the base circuits. This makes the gate quicker to turn off. This fast switching action makes the computer act faster—a very valuable asset.

Except for the LS characteristics, the 7400 series and 74LS00 series are identical TTL type chips. In lots of instances, they are completely interchangeable. It is good technique though, to change a defective chip with an exact replacement.

## THE THIRD LOGIC STATE

The illustrations of TTL, DTL, and RTL gates show NAND and NOR gates. These circuits will be discussed later in this chapter along with the other common gates. One ability that can be installed in any of those gates during manufacturing is called three-stating (Fig. 3-18). This name comes from the fact that gates usually output different logic states. You are familiar with the high and low states of the square waves that the gates process. Up until now, we have not mentioned the third state. When a chip can attain the third state, it is called a three-state chip. It can output a high, a low, or go into a three-state condition.

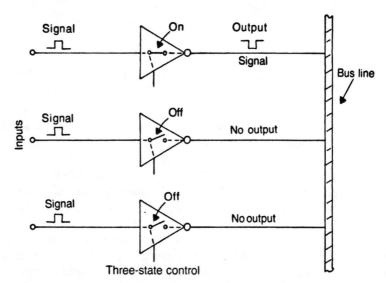

Fig. 3-18. The third logic state is when the circuit is shut off. This is useful when a number of circuits are all connected to the same line. In order to disconnect all the circuits except the one you want connected, you put them all except that one into a three-state condition.

What is the third state? Think of the square wave. It can do three things at the output of a chip. It can come out as a high, as a low, or fail to appear at all. The failure to show up at the output is the third state. The chip is turned off internally.

This state of non-state is not to be confused with a low. A low is a defined state. It is the bottom voltage of the square wave. If you take a VOM and measure the defined low, the dc voltage reads between 0 V and 0.8 V. In comparison, a high is defined at a voltage of 2.4 V to about 5 V. What about the three-state reading?

When the chip goes into a three-state condition, a circuit inside the chip disables the output. This makes the chip output go into a high impedance state. Technicians call the state *floating*. While the output is floating, the voltages and noise in the adjacent circuits develop some extraneous voltage levels at the chip output. If you test a chip output at three-state, you'll read about 1.5 V. That is the indication that the chip is floating. Any voltage between the defined 0.8 V upper limit of the low and the defined 2.4 V lower limit of high is a three-state condition (Fig. 3-19).

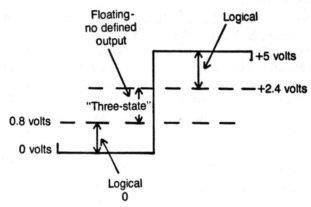

Fig. 3-19. The three-state condition will read between +0.9 V and +2.3 V on a VOM. The voltage is a result of a high impedance condition and the resultant buildup of static and noise.

What is the use of a three-state condition? As you will learn, there are many bus lines in a computer. One bus line can be connected to thousands of different circuits. Only the active circuit connection to the bus needs to be turned on while all the circuits that aren't being used are off. If all the circuits were on at the same time, the computer wouldn't operate. With the three-state ability, the one active circuit can be turned on while the rest of the circuits can be kept floating. The three-state ability is simply a way to turn a chip on or off at command.

The three-state control can be found on a chip with the aid of the schematic: TSC indicates the pin number. Internally, the circuit could be one like the illustration (Fig. 3-20). There are three npn's and a diode in the disable stage hooked in control of the data stage. They are Q2, Q3, Q5, and D1.

When the disable input is made to go low, Q2 will saturate. As a result, Q3 and Q5 will cut off. With Q3 and Q5 not conducting, the disable circuit is dead. The data stage is on and will process the square wave as it comes in. The chip thus runs well when the disable input is a low.

If a high is injected into the disable input, Q2 will be cut off. This makes Q3 and Q5 saturate. As they conduct heavily, they cause Q4 to lose its output current. The data stage output transistors then stop conduction. The chip starts floating. If you check the chip output, your VOM will read the noise level of about 1.5 V rather than a defined high or low.

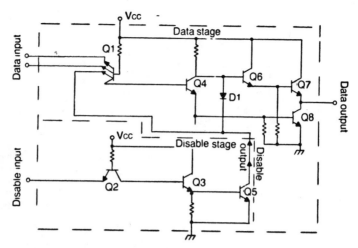

Fig. 3-20. The disable stage can cause an NAND circuit to three-state if it receives a low. The circuit will turn back on if the disable stage receives a high.

## MOS CHIPS

TTL chips were the chips that first became common in computers. About 1970, MOS chips arrived. MOS means *metal oxide silicon* and uses field effect transistors rather than bipolar. The MOS chips are packaged in a dual in-line format and look just like their TTL companions.

MOS chips appear as NMOS, PMOS, and CMOS. N stands for negative, P is for positive and C means complementary. N and P types are single-channel, while CMOS's are double-channel.

We'll discuss channels thoroughly in a minute. First, a little on transistor structure. Bipolar npn and pnp types are built as two back-to-back diodes. When an npn is powered, it is able to get electrons to flow from emitter to collector while holes travel from collector to emitter, all under the control of the current in the base. The pnp does the opposite. It sends electrons from collector to emitter and holes from emitter to collector. That is why they are called bipolar (Fig. 3-21).

In analog applications like amplication, a varying current between the base and the emitter is amplified in the emitter to collector current (Fig. 3-22). With digital applications of processing highs and lows, a high base current can cause the transistor to saturate (Fig. 3-23), while no base current makes the transistor cut off (Fig. 3-24). During saturation, if the collector is attached to +5 V through a load resistor, the resistor will drop the voltage on the collector to 0 V, a low. During cutoff the collector voltage will be pulled up to the supply of +5 V, a high.

Bipolar transistors are able to form lows and highs in that way, and do so on TTLs. MOS chips, however, do not use bipolar transistors; instead they use FETs. FETs are not like npn's or pnp's at all. First of all, MOS chips do not need a load resistor as such (Fig. 3-25). The circuit permits one FET to use a second FET as its load resistor. In the microscopic confines of the chip, the elimination of a load resistor for every transistor is a tremendous savings in space.

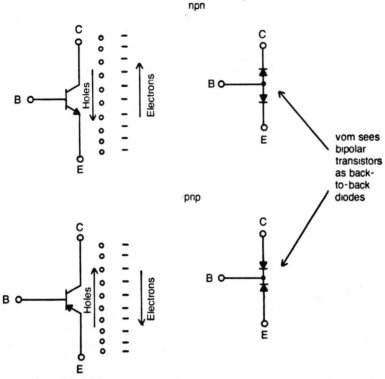

npn

pnp

vom sees
bipolar
transistors
as back-
to-back
diodes

Fig. 3-21. Bipolar transistors are so called because electrons and holes are both on the move in different directions during operation.

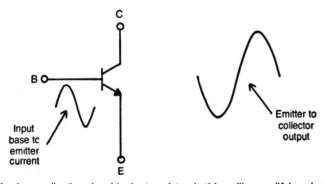

Input
base tc
emitter
current

Emitter to
collector
output

Fig. 3-22. Analog applications in a bipolar transistor do things like amplifying sine wave inputs.

## CHANNELS

A FET has a channel that operates like a vacuum tube channel. The channel is the section of the device that passes the electrons or holes (Fig. 3-26). In a bipolar transistor, the channel is directly through the two back-to-back diodes and their two junctions. In a vacuum tube, the channel is the vacuum space between the cathode and plate. The

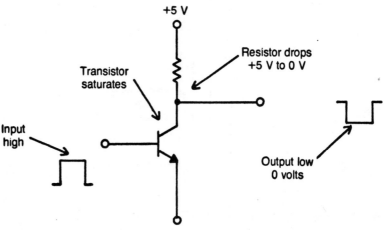

Fig. 3-23. Digital applications in a bipolar transistor do things like changing an input high to an output low as it saturates.

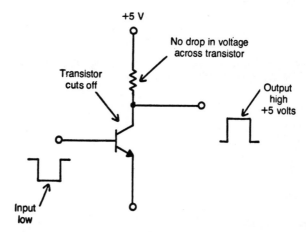

Fig. 3-24. In a digital application, an input low can be changed to an output high as the transistor cuts off.

control grid, screen grids, and suppressor grids are placed in the channel so they may influence the electrons as they pass. Early digital tube circuits let the cathode to plate current saturate, or be cut off, with the signal on the control grid. A positively-biased voltage made the tube saturate and a negative voltage cut the electron stream off.

The FET operates like the vacuum tube, except that it has a channel of semiconductor material. The NMOS has a channel of negative material, and the PMOS has a channel of positively-doped silicon.

If you attach a lead to one end of an n channel and call it *source*, and attach a second lead called *drain* at the other end, all you need to form an FET is a *gate* in the middle (Fig. 3-27). With a + voltage at the drain, the source grounded, and a bias voltage on the gate, electrons will flow from source to drain. Electrons can be controlled by a bias on the gate, either made to flow in a heavy stream with a positive bias, or cut off by a nega-

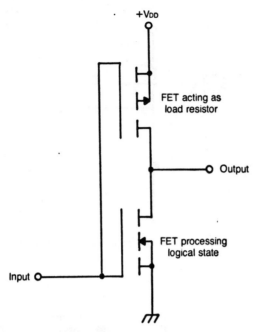

Fig. 3-25. The FETs are able to dispense with load resistors by using a second FET to do the job. This reduces the need for any space-wasting load resistors.

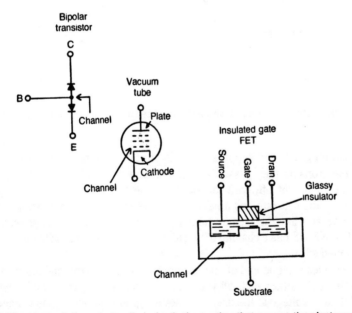

Fig. 3-26. The channel of an electronic device is the section that passes the electrons or holes. It can be the vacuum in a tube or the solid state pieces of N or P material in a transistor.

64

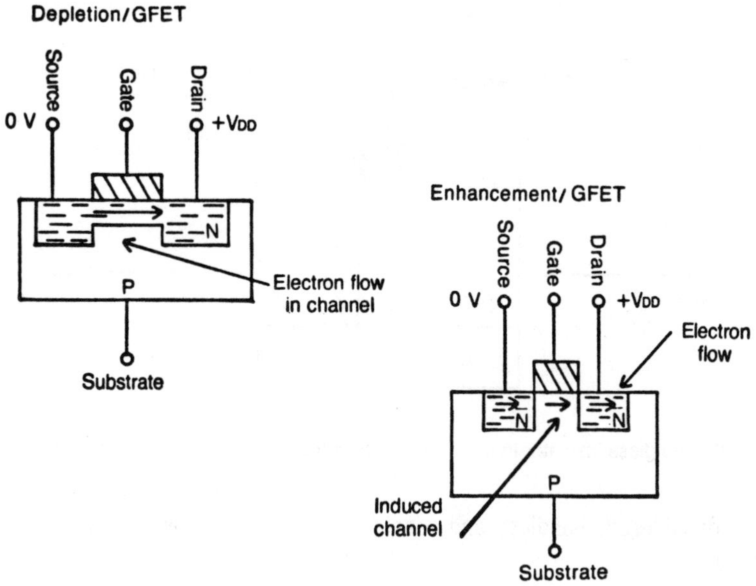

Fig. 3-27. The channels in different FETs can be one piece as in the depletion IGFET or three pieces in the enhancement IGFET.

tive bias, just like the vacuum tube. Also like the tube, the FET is a unipolar device. Only electrons or holes flow from source to drain. There is no simultaneous hole conduction from drain to source similar to the bipolar npn's and pnp's.

When there is conduction in a p channel FET, the conduction is the movement of holes. There is no electron conduction in p channel FETs. A negative voltage is attached to the drain and the source is grounded. Holes then travel from source to drain. A negative bias makes the holes conduct heavily, while a positive bias cuts them off. This circuit arrangement can be confusing since it is the exact opposite to the n channel layout. You should get the two types clear in your mind so there is no confusion during voltage testing.

MOS chips do not use ordinary FETs. They employ insulated gate FETs, called IGFETs, which have their gates insulated from the N or P channel material. The insulation is a piece of glassy silicon dioxide. The gate is nothing more than a lead connected to the glass insulator. In other FETs, the gate is a piece of N or P material that forms a pn junction with the channel. The junction is biased to prevent the dc level in the gate from getting into the channel.

The insulated gate, with its piece of glass installed between the gate lead and the channel, also stops dc but allows ac, or signal, to pass undisturbed. That way, the squares waves can cause the channel conduction to saturate or cut off according to whether the wave is in a high or low state.

The major problem with IGFETs is that the glass insulator is fragile. It is microscopic, and can easily rupture if subjected to static electricity, excess heat or humidity, or careless handling (Fig. 3-28). IGFETs are fairly safe while they are snugly soldered into their circuit. The troubles start when the circuit comes under test and IGFETs have

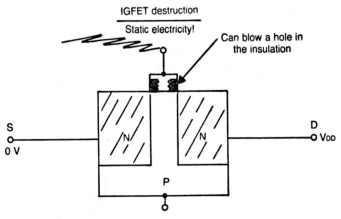

Fig. 3-28. The glass insulator in the IGFET gate is fragile and easily ruptured if not handled properly.

to be desoldered, handled, and resoldered. (Later on, we'll discuss how to do this safely.)

## NMOS

NMOS chips are often found in the large chips called *LSI* (for *large scale integration*.) These chips have, by definition, more than 100 gates on each chip. A chip with more than 1000 gates is called a *VLSI* (*very large scale integration*).

NMOS chips use a positive dc supply like +5 V. This is applied to the drains on the chip and attracts electrons from source to drain. The ground return is also connected to the FETs. The circuitry between the FETs is all configured individually according to the job on the chip each circuit is designed to do.

## PMOS

PMOS chips have p channels. Their supply voltage is always negative dc. PMOS chips can be easily identified for that reason. If you look at a chip on a schematic and you see it is receiving a minus dc voltage, you can be certain it is a PMOS. Both NMOS and CMOS chips have a plus voltage supply.

PMOS chips have hole conduction instead of electron conduction. During testing, the voltages are negative-going instead of positive-going. Otherwise, the chips operate in the same way. The glass-insulated gate in the PMOS is just as apt to rupture as the gates in the other IGFET chips.

## CMOS

The third member of this family is the CMOS chip. The complementary MOS is called that because it contains both p channel and n channel FETs. The CMOS chip is commonly used in SSI, small scale integration, with less than 10 to 100 gates to a chip. How can one substrate hold both p channel and n channel FETs?

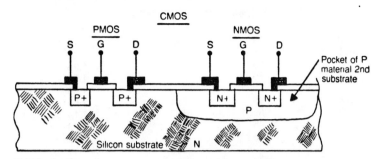

Fig. 3-29. The CMOS chip is designed to contain both NMOS and PMOS circuit areas.

Figure 3-29 shows a portion of a CMOS chip. The bottom or the substrate is a piece of silicon that is doped to be a piece of N material. The p channel FETs can be installed easily. On this piece, two small pockets of P material are diffused directly onto the n substrate. Then the source and drain are connected to the far ends of the p pieces. An insulated gate is attached to the close ends of the P material, and the PMOS FET is complete. The highs and lows that come into the gate determine if conduction takes place between the two pieces of P material or not.

To form the NMOS, a bed of P material is diffused into the n substrate. Then two small pieces of N material are diffused into the bed of P material. The source, gate, and drain connections are installed. The result is a chip with complementary FETs on the same large common substrate.

Typically, the supply voltage to a CMOS is a positive voltage like +5 V. Internal wiring takes care of getting the correct voltages on the source and drain. For example, the +5 V could be applied to the drains of the NMOS's and to the sources of the PMOS's. Then the sources of the NMOS FETs could be grounded and the drains of the PMOS FETs grounded. That effectively places +5 V on the n channel drains and −5 V on the p channel drains, which will work fine.

Just as the TTL chips were coded into the 7400 or 74LS00 series, some CMOS chips have been coded into a similar series. The code is C. If you see a chip numbered 74C00, it is like the TTL 7400 but it is an MOS type. The list shows the common ones and their approximate prices off the shelf (Table 3-3). In addition, MOS chips have a coding in the 4000 numbers. The list shows prices of the 4000 series.

## The Clock

Every computer has a clock circuit. The clock is based around an ordinary crystal-controlled oscillator circuit. Figure 3-30 shows the oscillator in a 16 K TRS-80 Color Computer with a D model print board.The crystal is set to resonate at precisely 14.31818 MHz. This is the *master frequency*.

This oscillator, like all crystal-controlled oscillators, produces a sine wave output. This circuit originates all the digital signals and produces an analog sine wave. However, the sine wave output is injected into a couple of pins on a large 40-pin n channel chip. In the chip, there are some circuits that act as a square wave generator. They take the sine wave and, without altering its frequency at all, block out the ups and downs. The master frequency is the source of all the frequencies in the computer.

## Table 3-3. Some of the CMCS Family of ICs.

| | | | |
|------|------|--------|-------|
| 4000 | .29 | 4528 | 1.19 |
| 4001 | .25 | 4531 | .95 |
| 4002 | .25 | 4532 | 1.95 |
| 4006 | .89 | 4538 | 1.95 |
| 4007 | .29 | 4539 | 1.95 |
| 4008 | .95 | 4541 | 2.64 |
| 4009 | .39 | 4543 | 1.19 |
| 4010 | .45 | 4553 | 5.79 |
| 4011 | .25 | 4555 | .95 |
| 4012 | .25 | 4556 | .95 |
| 4013 | .38 | 4581 | 1.95 |
| 4014 | .79 | 4582 | 1.95 |
| 4015 | .39 | 4584 | .75 |
| 4016 | .39 | 4585 | .75 |
| 4017 | .69 | 4702 | 12.95 |
| 4018 | .79 | 47C00 | .35 |
| 4019 | .39 | 74C02 | .35 |
| 4020 | .75 | 74C04 | .35 |
| 4021 | .79 | 74C08 | .35 |
| 4022 | .79 | 74C10 | .35 |
| 4023 | .29 | 74C14 | .59 |
| 4024 | .65 | 74C20 | .35 |
| 4025 | .29 | 74C30 | .35 |
| 4026 | 1.65 | 74C32 | .39 |
| 4027 | .45 | 74C42 | 1.29 |
| 4028 | .69 | 74C48 | 1.99 |
| 4029 | .79 | 74C73 | .65 |
| 4030 | .39 | 74C74 | .65 |
| 4034 | 1.95 | 74C76 | .80 |
| 4035 | .85 | 74C83 | 1.95 |
| 4040 | .75 | 74C85 | 1.95 |
| 4041 | .75 | 74C86 | .39 |
| 4042 | .69 | 74C89 | 4.50 |
| 4043 | .85 | 74C90 | 1.19 |
| 4044 | .79 | 74C93 | 1.75 |
| 4046 | .85 | 74C95 | .99 |
| 4047 | .95 | 74C107 | .89 |
| 4049 | .35 | 74C150 | 5.75 |
| 4050 | .35 | 74C151 | 2.25 |
| 4051 | .79 | 74C154 | 3.25 |
| 4053 | .79 | 74C157 | 1.75 |
| 4060 | .89 | 74C160 | 1.19 |
| 4066 | .39 | 74C161 | 1.19 |
| 4068 | .39 | 74C162 | 1.19 |
| 4069 | .29 | 74C163 | 1.19 |
| 4070 | .35 | 74C164 | 1.39 |
| 4071 | .29 | 74C165 | 2.00 |
| 4072 | .29 | 74C173 | .79 |
| 4073 | .29 | 74C174 | 1.19 |
| 4075 | .29 | 74C175 | 1.19 |
| 4076 | .79 | 73C192 | 1.49 |
| 4078 | .29 | 74C193 | 1.49 |
| 4081 | .29 | 74C195 | 1.39 |
| 4082 | .29 | 74C200 | 5.75 |
| 4085 | .95 | 74C221 | 1.75 |
| 4086 | .95 | 74C244 | 2.25 |
| 4093 | .49 | 74C373 | 2.45 |
| 4098 | 2.49 | 74C374 | 2.45 |
| 4099 | 1.95 | 74C901 | .39 |

| | | | |
|---|---|---|---|
| 14409 | 12.95 | 74C902 | .85 |
| 14410 | 12.95 | 74C903 | .85 |
| 14411 | 11.95 | 74C905 | 0.95 |
| 14412 | 12.95 | 74C906 | .95 |
| 14419 | 7.95 | 74C907 | 1.00 |
| 4502 | .95 | 74C908 | 2.00 |
| 4503 | .65 | 74C909 | 2.75 |
| 4508 | 1.95 | 74C910 | 9.95 |
| 4510 | .85 | 74C911 | 8.95 |
| 4511 | .85 | 74C912 | 8.95 |
| 4512 | .85 | 74C914 | 1.95 |
| 4514 | 1.25 | 74C915 | 1.19 |
| 4515 | 1.79 | 74C918 | 2.75 |
| 4516 | 1.55 | 74C920 | 17.95 |
| 4518 | .89 | 74C921 | 15.95 |
| 4519 | .39 | 74C922 | 4.49 |
| 4520 | .79 | 74C923 | 4.95 |
| 4522 | 1.25 | 74C925 | 5.95 |
| 4526 | 1.25 | 74C926 | 7.95 |
| 4527 | 1.95 | 74C928 | 7.95 |
| | | 74C929 | 19.95 |

In the service manual of most computers, a general timing diagram is provided showing all the pertinent frequencies. The timing diagram shows all the frequencies as perfect square waves. The horizontal lines are accurate. They represent time and they show a period of time that the wave stays at a high or at a low.

The vertical lines also represent time. However, the bottom of a vertical line and its top are both in the same time spot. That means no time has elapsed between the beginning of the vertical line to its end. This is clearly impossible. Some time has to take place. Therefore the vertical line in actuality is slanted. When the vertical line is rising, it slants to the right. When the line is falling it also slants to the right Fig. 3-31.

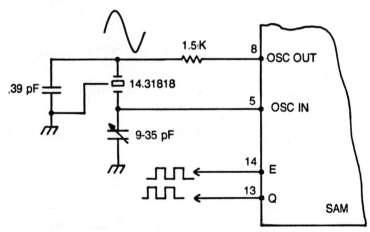

Fig. 3-30. The master oscillator in the typical computer produces a crystal controlled sine wave. Circuits then convert the sine wave into a square wave.

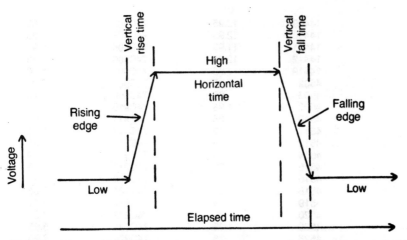

Fig. 3-31. The rising and falling edges of a square wave are really slanted and not straight up and down as timing diagrams seem to indicate.

These slant lines are important. They act as triggers to start off computer activity. The low-to-high is called the rising edge. The high-to-low is called the falling edge. In service notes, there are many references to rising and falling edges.

The timing diagram in Fig. 3-32 shows the master square wave going through 16 cycles. One cycle is shown as a square wave going through one low, one rising edge, one high, and one falling edge. The next cycle begins with the next low.

The first frequency derived from the master is produced in a circuit by dividing 14.31818 MHz by 2. This produces 7.15909 MHz. There are 8 cycles at this frequency in the same time as there were 16 cycles at 14.31818 MHz.

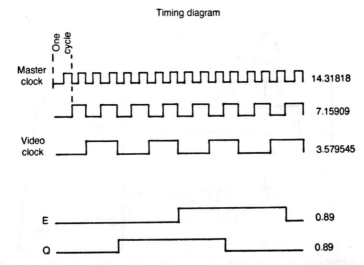

Fig. 3-32. All the frequencies used in the digital circuits are derived from the master clock.

70

The next frequency down is a familiar one to TV servicemen. It is obtained by dividing the master by 4, in a divider circuit on the large chip. 3.579545 MHz is the TV color oscillator frequency. It allows this computer to display colors. In this computer, this frequency is called the *video clock*. The 9-35 on the pF schematic drawing (Fig. 3-30) is a trimmer capacitor that can set this frequency exactly.

The two frequencies at the bottom of the chart are called E and Q. They are the square waves that run the data processing in the computer. In this computer, their frequency is 0.89 MHz, which is the crystal frequency divided by 16. 0.89 MHz could be roughly called 1 MHz. When a computer like this is described, it may be called a 1 MHz type. Other computers could be said to be a 4 MHz, 8 MHz, 10 MHz, 16 MHz, or what have you. The faster the operating frequency, the more quickly programs are run. The operating frequency is one of the indicators of computer power. The faster a computer can do its job of executing programs the more powerful it is.

Note the E and Q square waves are both 0.89 MHz. They are different, however, because they are out of phase with each other. The Q signal leads the E signal by 90 degrees. Note the rising edge of the Q signal occurs 90 degrees in advance of the rising edge of the E signal. This generation of two signals that are 90 degrees out of phase with each other takes place in a microscopic phase-splitting circuit, located near the circuits that are doing the frequency divisions to produce the chip frequency outputs.

The clock is the motor of the computer's electronics. It sends out square waves to all the circuit areas. The clock sends out the frequencies in a pure form, a regular even pattern of complete cycles, one after the other.

These complete cycles cause the main chip, the microprocessor, to run the program in the computer in a regular predictable fashion one program line after another. The process is discussed in detail in Chapter 6.

If the clock stops or runs at the wrong frequency, the computer stops operating properly . . . or simply stops operating altogether. Some of the important tests you'll be making are on the clock. The first easy test is to see if it is running. The second test is to find out if it is generating the correct frequency. These tests are covered in Chapters 4 and 19.

## LOGIC GATES

Most technicians who have worked on radios, TVs, stereos and the like, have been exposed to logic gates little, if at all. There are only a few types of gates yet; to the uninitiated, they appear mysterious and hard to understand. Actually, they are much easier to comprehend than some of the color TV and advanced stereo circuits. They are vital to computers, and the computer technician must be able to recognize, understand, and test them.

Besides being able to do arithmetic in the old-fashioned way, a computer also performs a form of math called logic. The computer can do three separate logical exercises (Fig. 3-33). They are called AND, OR and exclusive-OR (abbreviated XOR). It is not necessary to be a logic expert to work as a technician on the computers. Logic is reserved for advanced programming. However, you must recognize the AND gate, the OR gate, and the XOR gate. Also, you should know what logic state, high or low, comes

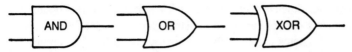

Fig. 3-33. The AND, OR, and XOR gate symbols are common on computer schematics.

out of a gate as a result of the highs and lows that are put into it. That way, you can test a gate's input and output and determine if the device is performing properly.

Modern logic gates are either a chip of their own or part of a chip. the little transistors and other miniscule components on the chip are not available to you. All you can test is their inputs and outputs, available at the pins of the packages. During testing you can almost ignore what is happening inside a gate. Consider a gate a discrete component. Just as discrete resistors, capacitors and transistors are tested at their leads, and their internals such as carbon, dielectrics, and back-to-back diodes are not really thought of, forget the circuits in the gate, and think of the gate as a component.

Besides AND, OR, and XOR gates, there are others. Actually, the rest of them are circuit variations of the basic three but they do separate logic jobs, so they must be considered as separate devices for testing purposes. These gates are called NOT, NAND, NOR, and XNOR (the abbreviation for exclusive-NOR). Let's go through all the gates one by one.

### Yes and Not

There is some dissension among engineers as to whether YES is really a gate, in the exact definition of the term. This is because a YES gate performs other work on the incoming square wave, besides manipulating the high or low that enters the gate. However, we technicians have no difficulty with the term. The YES gate, as far as we are concerned, is a bona fide gate.

On the schematic diagram, there are lots of triangles lying on their sides with two leads sticking out. One lead, the input, is fastened to the flat side. The other lead, the output, is attached to the pointy end. A logic state can be applied to the input and the following things will occur (Fig. 3-34).

This gate is named YES because it performs the logic function of passing the state without changing it. In other words, if a high is applied to the input, a high appears at the

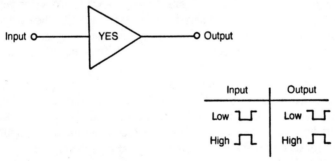

Fig. 3-34. The YES gate passes a single logic state without changing it. The gate will amplify and match the logic state into subsequent circuits.

72

output. In the same way, if a low is injected into the input, a low comes out of the output. The question arises, if the logic state doesn't change, why bother to pass the high or low through the gate?

That is where the other work on the signal comes in. The YES gate is also called a driver. From analog circuits, the word driver indicates that an amplifier is present. In digital circuits, this type of amplifier is also called a buffer.

Between the microprocessor and the rest of the computer circuits you'll find a lot of chips that are buffers. The microprocessor is an engineering miracle and produces all sorts of wonderful signals, but the signals are weak. They exit the pins with tiny currents.

The buffers are there as current amplifiers. The weak signals from the microprocessor are applied to the buffer inputs. The buffers amplify the amounts of current in the signal without changing the logic state. The amount of current that leaves a buffer is then able to work with the rest of the computer.

An example of a set of YES gates is found on a 74LS367 TTL chip (Fig. 3-35). It is described as a *three-state hex buffer. Three-state* means there is a three-state control whereby you can cause the chip to go into the third logic state of not passing the square waves. The word *hex* means there are six gates on the chip. The word *buffer* means the gate is a YES type.

74LS367

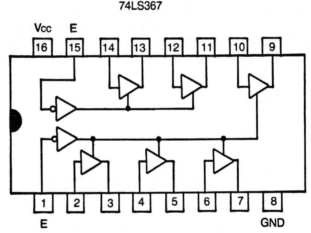

Fig. 3-35. The three-state hex buffer has six driver YES gates that are three-state controlled by two other buffers with inputs at pins 1 and 15.

The schematic drawing of the chip shows the in-line pins as they are actually laid out. The little YES triangles are simply indications of what gates are on the chip. The input and output connections to the pins are shown clearly. If you test the chip using this diagram, you have most of the chip information you need right there. Most of the rest of the manufacturer's information is more for designers than technicians.

The pin connection diagram shows a 16-pin DIP. Pins 16 and 8 are VCC and ground. The supply voltage calls for 5.25 V. This means if you read pin 16 while the computer is on, it should read about +5 V. Pin 8 should be at 0 V.

Pins 2, 4, 6, 14, 12, and 10 are inputs to the six gates. Pins 3, 5, 7, 13, 11, and 9 are corresponding outputs. When the chip is operating and is not in a three-state condition, whatever signal enters a gate must also exit the gate, without being changed. Therefore, if you are testing a buffer chip, the highs and lows on the input pins must also be present at their output pins. If a wrong reading is found, that could be a clue that one of the gates on the chip has failed.

Incidentally, there is a tiny gate delay between the time the signal enters a gate and when it exits. Typically it takes about 15 nanoseconds, which translates to 15 billionths of a second. The only way you could see if the gate delay is correct, is with an expensive dual trace oscilloscope. Gate delays are covered in more detail in the timing discussions of Chapter 9.

Note that there are two more YES gates on the chip. They have no exits! Their outputs attach to the sides of the other six gates. The gate at pin 1 connects to the four gates between pin 2 and 10. The pin 15 gate connects to the two gates between pins 11 and 14.

These gates that have their inputs attached to pins 1 and 15, are there to provide three-state control. Their outputs are connected to the disable stages of the six buffer gates. The two three-state control gates can hold the buffers on if they apply a high to the disable stages. If they send a low to the disable stages the buffers will three-state (turn off).

Let's examine the three-state control gates in a little more detail. Their outputs are attached to the three-state connection of the buffers. Their inputs are coming from pins 1 and 15 (Fig. 3-36). Note that the inputs connect to a little circle on the flat side of the gate. This circle is called a NOT circle. In computer logic, NOT is the opposite of YES.

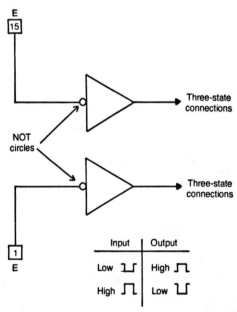

Fig. 3-36. The little NOT circles at the input of the buffers change them to NOT gates.

The NOT circle represents a complete circuit area just as the YES gate does. The NOT processes the square wave in the exact opposite manner that the YES does. The NOT circle also has a truth table. It looks like this:

| Input | Output |
|-------|--------|
| High  | Low    |
| Low   | High   |

Truth tables are mostly used in design work rather than technician work. We'll still call them truth tables, but we will do better to change the true and false to high and low or +5 V and 0 V, or 1 and 0, or set and clear, or set and reset. True and false can be confusing.

Technicians use truth tables as a guide to test the voltage inputs and outputs of a chip. You should really memorize the table for each logic gate. That way, when you take readings, you will recognize right away if the gate is doing its job correctly. The table for a YES gate is as follows:

| Input | Output |
|-------|--------|
| High  | High   |
| Low   | Low    |

It is rather simple. In the YES gate, whatever enters the input exits the output. Incidentally, aside from the 15 nanosecond delay, a gate like the YES gate is transparent. There is no storage capability in these gates. They are like a pane of glass. The signal, without more than the gate delay, passes right through.

Back on the chip shown in Fig. 3-35, there are two more gates that haven't been mentioned. They have inputs at pins 1 and 15.

The NOT circle at the input of the three-state gates inverts any square wave signal that is applied at pins 1 or 15. If a high is applied, the circle changes it to a low. When a low is applied, the NOT circuit changes it to a high. Since the circle is at the gate input, the inversion occurs before the signal enters the gate itself.

The chip then operates like this: Pin 1 is a three-state control that turns four of the buffers on and off. Pin 15 is also a three-state control that turns the remaining two buffers on and off. When pins 1 or 15 have a low applied, its buffers work. When a high is applied, the buffers three-state. The truth table for the chip then looks like this:

| Inputs | | Output |
|--------|--------|--------|
| Pins 1,15 | All others | |
| Low | Low | Low |
| Low | High | High |
| High | Low or High | Three-state |

The NOT circles on the 74LS367 chip are shown on the inputs of the three-state gates. Just as often, they are found on the output. For instance, a 7404 digital TTL chip is called a *Hex Inverter* (Fig.3-37). This means there are six gates on the chip and they are all inverters. An inverter is a YES gate with a NOT circle on its pointy output (Fig. 3-38). Figure 3-37 shows a 14-pin DIP. There are two supply voltage pins, 14 for the 5.25 $V_{dc}$ and 7 as the ground return. The other pins are all inputs and outputs for the six inverters. Note the NOT circles on the gate outputs. Whatever logic state enters the inputs gets inverted to the opposite state as it passes through the circles.

A NOT circle on the output of a buffer makes the buffer an *inverter*. Since there are six inverters on the 7404 it is called a *hex inverter*. The six inverters are separate circuits, except that they all share the same supply voltage of 5.25 $V_{dc}$ and ground return.

When a chip like this is suspected of a defect, it can be checked out inverter by inverter and conclusions can be drawn. A checkout would proceed like this:

First, the supply at pin 14 would be tested. It should read +5 V all the time the computer is on. If the +5 V is missing or incorrect, that is a clue that either the power supply is not providing enough voltage, or the chip has an internal short and is sinking too much current, dragging the voltage down. Either way you have a valid clue to follow up.

When the supply is ok, you go on to test the input and output of each inverter. according to the truth table, whatever state enters the inverter, the opposite state should

**7404**

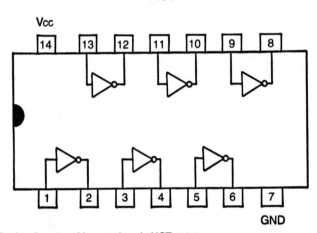

Fig. 3-37. The hex invertor chip contains six NOT gates.

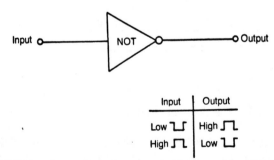

| Input | Output |
|-------|--------|
| Low ⊔̄ | High ⌐̄⌐ |
| High ⌐̄⌐ | Low ⊔̄ |

Fig. 3-38. The NOT gate changes input lows to output highs and input highs to output lows.

76

exit. For instance, if a high is at pin 13, an inverter input, then a low should be on pin 12, the inverter output.

In this case, if a high is also on pin 12, the inverter is not operating. It could be shorted internally, killing the inversion function, and letting the +5 V high bleed through. Should pin 12 be floating, the inverter could have opened up and not be YESing and NOTing. The output could go into a floating condition and read about +2 V.

While this procedure is fairly straightforward, there is one type of booby trap that you will encounter. During servicing, you will see a lot of unused gates on chips. This is because the chips, once they are on the shelf, are so cheap that it is much easier for manufacturers to use a chip from inventory rather than designing and developing a new chip. As a result, there are plenty of unused gates in computers. This 7404 could be one of these chips. The price list shows a 7404 can be purchased for 19 cents. In manufacturing quantities, the price is even lower. If one gate is utilized and the other five gates left unused, the user of the chip is still justified at that price.

Anyway, these unused gates can cause complications during servicing. They could give you false clues unless care is given to pin number detail. Since all the inverters on the chip use the same supply and ground lines, they must be wired up too, even though they are not being used. The manufacturer provides information with the chip. You must be aware of the extra wiring that goes with some chips. The 7404, for instance, comes with the following instructions in a Radio Shack catalog.

Two possible ways of handling unused inputs are: (1) Connect unused inputs to VCC. For all multi-emitter conventional TTL inputs, 1 to 10 K ohm current limiting series resistor is recommended, to protect against VCC transients that exceed 5.5 V.

(2) Connect the unused input to the output of an unused gate that is forced high.

The word NOT is used a lot in computers. It is a logic function. As you read schematics or look at drawings of chips, you'll see terminals with a straight line across the top of the name. Sometimes instead of a line there will be an asterisk in front of the name. Both the line and the asterisk mean the same thing, NOT. The asterisk is used since lots of computer printers have difficulty producing the line, but can print the asterisk easily. Whether the service notes show the line or the asterisk, they both indicate the same thing: the voltage that should be at that terminal, if you can interpret it.

The voltage at all the terminals of all the chips is in one of the three logical states: high, low, or floating. Floating occurs when the terminal is three-stating or has trouble. The NOT line or asterisk has no relationship with the three-state. The NOT line deals with highs and lows.

Suppose we take a terminal like *RESET. The terminal is designed to be held in a high state (+5 V) while the computer is operating normally. If it becomes necessary to reset the computer, the reset button is pressed, and a low (0 V) is generated and transferred to *RESET. The low changes the state and triggers the terminal into a reset routine. In other words, the asterisk means a low will turn on the reset.

On the other hand, the terminal could be named RESET, without the asterisk. When the asterisk is missing the terminal RESET is held low (0 V). When the reset button is pressed, a high (+5 V) is generated and sent to the terminal. The high changes the state and triggers the terminal into a reset routine. In the case without an asterisk, a high turns on the reset.

As a rule of thumb, when you are testing a terminal with a NOT sign like an asterisk or line, it is usually held high and should read a voltage high like +5 V. If the terminal does not have a NOT sign, then it is usually held low and should read a voltage low like 0 V.

There are some two-function terminals such as *READ/WRITE which could be in a high state or low state according to which function is going on. You can test them and puzzle out the correctness of the voltage with the aid of some theory of operation which you will learn in Chapter 6. For the most part, though, if a terminal has a NOT line, it is being held high. When the terminal lacks the NOT sign, it is being held low. Committing this fact to memory will enable you to check out many terminals very quickly.

## AND and NAND

Both AND and NAND gates are drawn on schematics as bullet looking objects, with two or more input leads on the flat side and a single output lead on the blunt rounded end. AND and NAND look exactly alike except that the NAND has a NOT circle attached between the rounded end and the output lead (Fig. 3-39). NAND is nothing more than AND plus the NOT circle, which makes NAND.

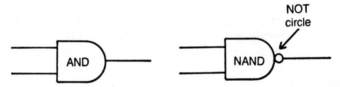

Fig. 3-39. The AND and NAND symbols look exactly alike except for the NOT circle on the end of the NAND.

Inside AND gates, just as in the rest of the microscopic gates, there are many transistors, resistors, diodes, and so on. Since we can't get to them, we treat them as all one component. We test them as a total. Then there are connections between gates that wire the smaller gates up as a larger gate. These configurations provide us with test points. In these cases, we can try to pinpoint the actual trouble. The key to what technique to use is determined by the availability of the test points. The schematic diagram usually reveals all the test points. It is necessary, though, to recognize what is happening.

The AND gate acts in a logical manner. A typical gate has two inputs and one output (Fig. 3-40). A logic state can be applied to each input. This means there are four possible combinations of highs or lows that can be applied. They are the following:

| Input A | Input B |
|---------|---------|
| Low | Low |
| Low | High |
| High | Low |
| High | High |

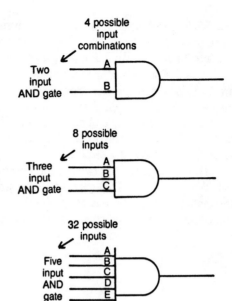

Fig. 3-40. When a gate has two inputs there are four possible combinations of highs and lows that can be input. If a gate has three inputs there are eight possible combinations. When there are five inputs, there are 32 possible combinations.

Other AND gates could have three inputs and one output. The addition of the third input permits eight possible combinations of highs and lows to be inputted into the AND gate. They are as follows:

| Input A | Input B | Input C |
|---------|---------|---------|
| Low | Low | Low |
| Low | Low | High |
| Low | High | Low |
| Low | High | High |
| High | Low | Low |
| High | Low | High |
| High | High | Low |
| High | High | High |

When an AND gate has four inputs there are 16 possible combinations that can be injected. With five inputs, 32 combinations can be put in, and so on.

While there are multiple inputs to an AND gate, there is only one output. AND is a function of the science of logic, just as addition is a function of mathematics. ANDing together a number of inputs results in the following truth table:

| Input A | Input B | Input C |
|---------|---------|---------|
| 0 | 0 | 0 |
| 0 | 1 | 0 |
| 1 | 0 | 0 |
| 1 | 1 | 1 |

While a technician finds it more convenient to use highs and lows in a truth table since the highs and lows are voltages, programmers find it more useful to code the voltage into 1s and 0s. We'll don the programmers' hat for the logic explanation.

Note the outputs of the four input possibilities; are all 0 except when all the inputs are 1. This is true whether there are two inputs or many. The AND gate outputs a 1 in only a single case, when all inputs are 1. When a programmer ANDs two bits together, he is applying AND logic in his program. This is an important ability the computer can perform. The programmer plans his ANDing with the aid of the truth table. He is not at all concerned about the electronics.

The computer ANDs two bits for a program instruction with an AND gate. The simplified version of the AND gate is a series circuit containing two or more switches. When the circuit is open, there is no conduction which can be represented as the output 0. If the circuit is closed and conduction is happening, the output is a logical 1 (Fig. 3-41).

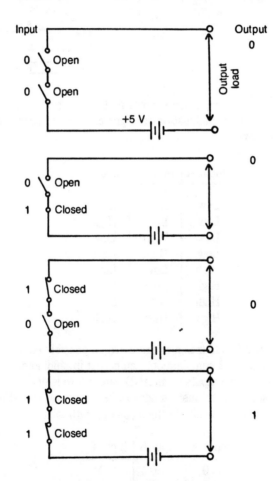

Fig. 3-41. In the four combinations of switch arrangements, conduction will take place only when both switches are closed.

There are four possible switch arrangements: both switches open, two cases of one switch open and one closed, and both switches closed. The only possibility of getting conduction and outputting a 1 is if both switches are closed. This is the way the AND function can actually be implemented.

On chips, the switches are inaccessible transistor circuits. The inputs and outputs are attached to the chip pins. A typical AND is the TTL 7408. It is called a *quad two-input AND gate*. This means there are four AND gates, and each gate has two inputs. The latest off-the-shelf price is 24 cents (Fig. 3-42).

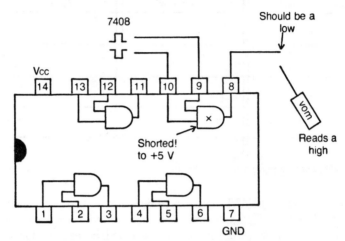

Fig. 3-42. If there is a high and low being input at pins 9 and 10, a good AND gate should output a low at pin 8. Should the VOM read a high, the gate is probably shorted to +5 V.

The 7408 is a 14-pin DIP. Pin 14 is Vcc and pin 7 is the ground connection. The other 12 pins are devoted to inputs and the outputs as Fig. 3-42 shows. When you test the chip, the voltages indicated by the truth table enables you to determine if the correct voltages are presented on the pins.

For instance, a high should be on pin 14 coming from supply. A low should be at pin 7 at ground level. If there is one high and one low on pins 9 and 10, two inputs, then there should be a low on pin 8 the output. If there is a high there instead, the gate could be shorted, letting the high bleed through from the input pin to the output.

It is possible that only the one gate is in use in the computer, and the other three gates are unused. If so, care must be taken not to become confused with the connections of the unused inputs and outputs. The 7408 unused inputs are handled in the same way as the 7404 hex inverter discussed earlier.

The NAND gate is a NOT AND gate. There is a little NOT circle sitting at the AND gate output. The AND output must pass through the circuit indicated by the circle. In the circle, all highs are changed to lows and all lows to highs (Fig. 3-43).

The truth table of the NAND gate is exactly like the AND gate, except that the outputs are reversed. A special truth table is shown with an interim step depicting first the ANDing of the inputs and then the NOTing of the AND results. The NAND gate has a high output in all input cases, except when all inputs are high. In that single instance, the NAND gate outputs a low.

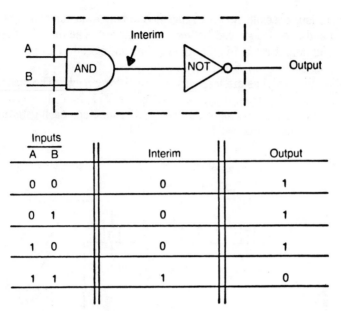

| Inputs | | Interim | Output |
|--------|---|---------|--------|
| A | B | | |
| 0 | 0 | 0 | 1 |
| 0 | 1 | 0 | 1 |
| 1 | 0 | 0 | 1 |
| 1 | 1 | 1 | 0 |

Fig. 3-43. The NAND gate is really a NOT AND gate.

A simplified version of a NAND gate can be built around two npn transistors in tandem (Fig. 3-44). There two inputs, on into each base. There is a single collector output from the top npn. A collector resistor goes to VCC and both bases are returned to ground through resistors. The NAND function operates in the following manner:

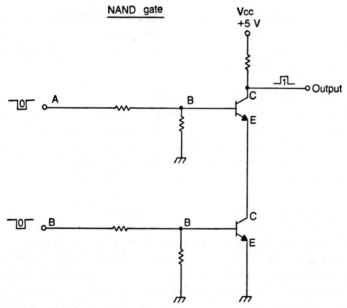

Fig. 3-44. A NAND gate can be constructed with two npn transistors connected in tandem.

If two lows are applied to the two npn bases, the npns will not conduct. They will be cut off. If there is no conduction, there is no current drawn through the collector resistor, and the collector output is pulled up to VCC which is a high. With two lows at the input producing a high at the output, the circuit acts like a NAND.

If one low and one high are input, conduction still can't take place, since the two npns are *in tandem* (that is, the collector of the bottom transistor is connected to the emitter of the top one). Therefore, if a low and a high, or a high and a low are applied, a high is still at the output. The circuit continues to act like a NAND.

When two highs are applied to the bases, the npns both turn on together. The simultaneous conduction draws current through the collector resistor and pulls down the collector voltage below the 0.8 V level, which makes the output a low. With the two inputs both highs and the resultant output a low, the gate shows itself to be an actual NAND.

If the inputs had been in the emitters instead of in the bases, the outputs would have been ANDed instead of NANDed. The NOT AND function is accomplished because base inputs are always the reverse polarity to collector outputs. Emitter inputs are always the same polarity as the collector output.

A typical NAND gate is a 7400 TTL. It is called a Quad Two-Input NAND Gate (Fig. 3-45). Pinwise, it is identical to the 7408. These chips are very versatile. By connecting the pins in different ways, the AND gate and NAND gate can both be transformed into many other types of gates. The illustrations show a number of chip wiring jobs that result in typical applications.

7400

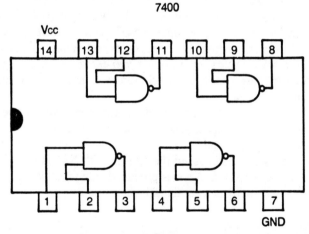

Fig. 3-45. The 7400 TTL is a typical group of NAND gates. By wiring them together, other gate types can be formed.

First of all, the NAND gate's most obvious application is as a *control gate*. The schematic in Fig. 3-46 shows one of the gates on the quad chip. Pins 1 and 2 are the inputs and pin 3 is the output. Pins 14 and 7 are VCC and ground. The VCC and ground pins are common to the entire chip.

The control gate is able to perform the following job. Suppose you want to be able to output a low, to turn on a three-state chip, when two highs are produced from two sepa-

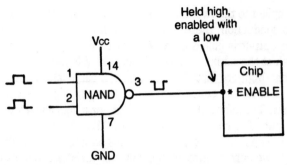

Fig. 3-46. When two highs are applied to a NAND gate it will output a low. The low can be used to enable a chip. The chip will stay off until the enabling low arrives.

rate sources. As long as one or both of the sources are producing a low, you want the three-state chip to stay off. The NAND gate controls the three-state off and on.

According to the truth table, the NAND gate will continually output a high, keeping the three-state chip off, except if both inputs are high. Then the NAND gate will go low and turn on the chip. The NAND gate is thus a control gate.

If you take the same chip and tie pins 1 and 2 together, the gate becomes a NOT gate (Fig. 3-47). If you input a low, it outputs a high. Should you input a high, it outputs a low.

Two of the NAND gates tied together can become an AND gate (Fig. 3-48). All you have to do is attach them in series and short the two input pins of the second gate together. That way, the second gate becomes a NOT gate. Whatever state exits, the first gate is changed. This changes the NAND gate output into an AND gate output.

Five of the little NAND gates can become a *four-input NAND gate* (Fig. 3-49). Two chips are needed, using four gates from one chip and one gate from the second chip. The four inputs are pins 1, 2, 4, and 5.

Inputs 1 and 2 are passed through and AND gate composed of two NAND gates. Inputs 4 and 5 are passed through a second makeup AND gate. This reduces the four inputs to two outputs at pins 8 and 11.

These two outputs are then passed through the fifth NAND gate. The results are that the four inputs and NANDed. A low is produced only when all four inputs are high; otherwise, the total gate outputs a continual high.

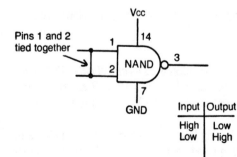

Fig. 3-47. A NAND gate can be changed to a NOT gate by tying the two input pins together.

| Input | Output |
|-------|--------|
| High  | Low    |
| Low   | High   |

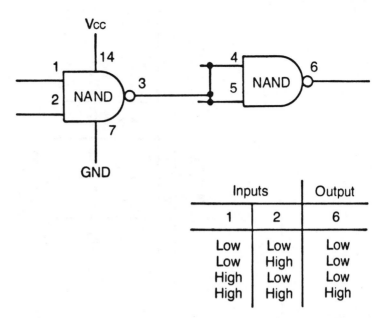

| Inputs | | Output |
|--------|--------|--------|
| 1 | 2 | 6 |
| Low | Low | Low |
| Low | High | Low |
| High | Low | Low |
| High | High | High |

Fig. 3-48. Two NAND gates can be wired at their pin connections and become an AND gate.

To check out the various configurations of gates that produce an overall gate, it is best to test each gate individually. Ignore the total gate during initial voltage readings. That way, as you check the inputs and resultant outputs, the voltages will be easier to comprehend and puzzle over. Also, one overall gate could have sections located on different chips requiring a lot of going back and forth between the schematic and hardware, causing much confusion.

It's easy, though, to memorize the few gate truth tables and test the individual gates quickly and accurately at the chip pins.

### OR and NOR

Another vital logic function the computer can do electronically is called OR. The NOR function is produced by adding a NOT circle to the OR gate (Fig. 3-50), just as NAND was accomplished by NOTing AND. OR is different than AND like series circuits are different than parallel circuits. If you think of ANDing two logic states electrically by inputting them via two series switches, then the ORing of two states is done by inputting them into two switches in parallel (Fig. 3-51).

While the AND circuit is energized (representing a high) only if both switches are closed, the OR circuit is energized if either or both switches are closed. The truth table for the OR circuit shows that the output is low only when both inputs are low. Otherwise, the OR circuit continually outputs a high. When an OR circuit is tested, a good one will follow the voltages shown in the truth table. Should a voltage not be true to its table, a defect is indicated.

The NOR gate is a NOT OR gate. The OR gate schematic symbol looks like an artillery shell. There is a curved bottom for the inputs and a pointy end where the output pin

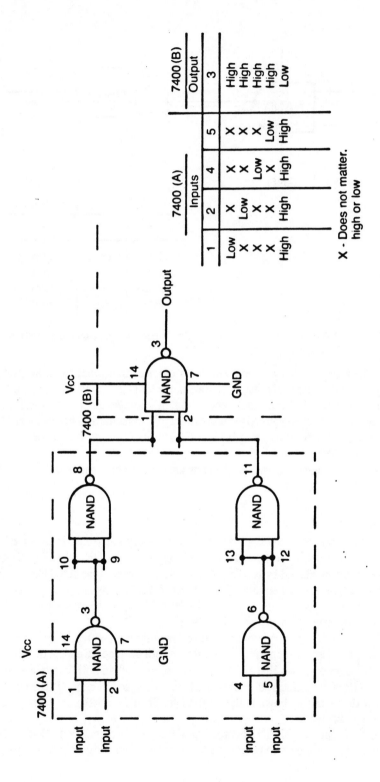

| 7400 (A) Inputs | | | | | 7400 (B) Output |
|---|---|---|---|---|---|
| 1 | 2 | 4 | 5 | | 3 |
| Low | X | X | X | | High |
| X | Low | X | X | | High |
| X | X | Low | X | | High |
| X | X | X | Low | | High |
| High | High | High | High | | Low |

X - Does not matter, high or low

**Fig. 3-49. Five two input NAND gates can be wired into a four input NAND gate.**

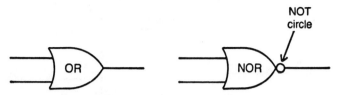

Fig. 3-50. The OR and NOR symbols are identical except for the little NOT circle on the end of the NOR.

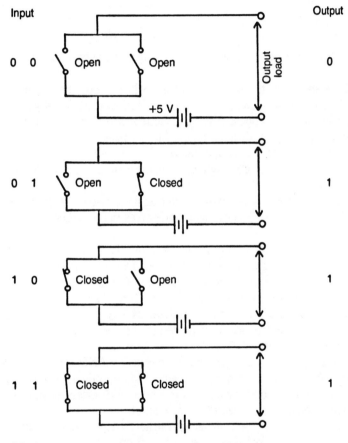

Fig. 3-51. The OR circuit will conduct except when both switches are open.

goes. When the symbol designates the NOT OR function, a NOT circle is installed on the pointy end between the lead and the body of the gate.

A simplified version of a NOR gate can be built around two diodes and a single npn transistor (Fig. 3-52). The two diodes are attached to the base of the npn. The collector is connected to VCC, and the emitter is attached to ground. This configuration keeps the transistor cut off. When there is no conduction, the collector stays high at the VCC level, around +5 V.

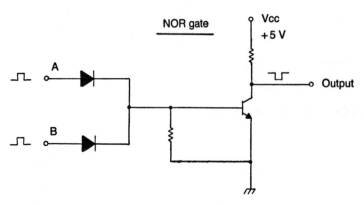

Fig. 3-52. A NOR gate can be built around two diodes and a single npn transistor.

If two lows are input, the npn stays cut off, which keeps the collector at VCC (the high state). Therefore, with two lows the output is high, like a NOR gate should act.

When a high and a low appear at the two diode inputs, it doesn't matter which input gets what; the transistor conducts. The conduction pulls current through the collector resistor dropping the collector voltage below 0.8 V (a low). This corresponds with the truth table for the NOR gate. One high and one low input producing a low is a NOR gate action.

Should two highs arrive at the diodes, the transistor also turns on, pulling the collector down to a low logic state. The configuration proves to be a NOR gate in the full sense of the word.

In the NAND sample circuit, the inputs were put through resistors. This makes the circuit an RTL (Resistor-Transistor-Logic) type. The NOR gate just discussed uses diode inputs, a DTL(Diode-Transistor-Logic) type. The diodes are useful because they reduce resistive input losses, permitting greater fanout and faster switching speeds. However, RTLs and DTLs are almost obsolete. Mostly you'll be working with TTLs (Transistor-Transistor-Logic), which work better and are easier to fabricate than their resistor and diode ancestors.

OR and NOR gates have applications somewhat like AND and NAND gates. There are times when AND gates are most convenient, and other times when OR gates will do the job better. You'll find both kinds in computers. For instance, suppose a terminal called *ENABLE must be activated every now and then.

Remember, when you see a terminal with an asterisk in its name, it means it is being held high while it is off and requires a low to turn it on.

(Get used to the word *enable*. It is commonly used when discussing computers. It is an action word that means to turn on. The opposite of enable is to *disable*.)

In order to activate *ENABLE on a chip, an OR gate could be used. The OR gate, according to what its truth table shows, outputs a high continually for all inputs except two lows. When two lows are sent in, the OR gate outputs a low (Fig. 3-53).

The output of the OR gate could be connected to the *ENABLE terminal. As long as one or both of the inputs are high, the OR gate holds *ENABLE high. When two lows are received by the gate, then it outputs a low and enables *ENABLE.

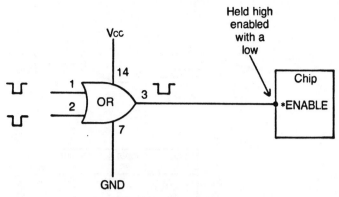

Fig. 3-53. Only when an OR gate receives two low inputs, will it output a low. This circuit can be used to control the *ENABLE pin.

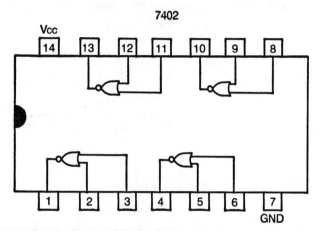

Fig. 3-54. The 7402 chip contains four NOR gates on a 14-pin DIP.

The 7402 TTL chip is a common quad two-input NOR gate. It is a DIP with 14 pins. Pins 14 and 7 are VCC and ground respectively. The other twelve pins are the inputs and outputs of the four NOR gates on the chip (Fig. 3-54).

Like the AND type gates, with some judicious wiring gates of this type can be made to perform all sorts of logic jobs. In different computers you'll see all sorts of configurations. For instance, this 7402, even though it contains four NOR gates, can be wired as an OR gate or and AND gate.

To produce an OR gate, two NOR gates are needed They are wired in series. The first NOR gate is allowed to do normal NOR work. That is, produce lows as long as there is a high in the inputs. If both inputs are low, though, then the output is high (Fig. 3-55).

The second NOR gate has its two inputs shorted together. This make the NOR gate into a NOT gate. Then, when the first gates output is passed through the formed NOT gate, the final output is that of an OR gate. That is, the final output is high as long as the beginning inputs have a high or two. When both initial inputs are low, a low appears in the final output.

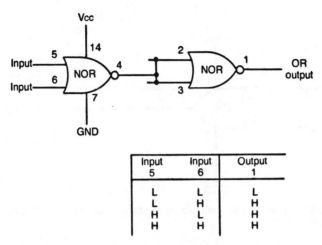

| Input 5 | Input 6 | Output 1 |
|:---:|:---:|:---:|
| L | L | L |
| L | H | H |
| H | L | H |
| H | H | H |

Fig. 3-55. An OR gate can be fabricated by wiring two NOR gates together.

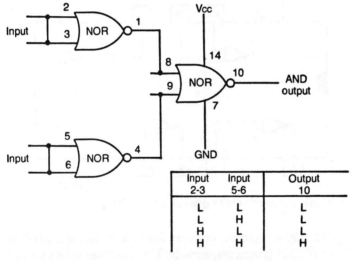

| Input 2-3 | Input 5-6 | Output 10 |
|:---:|:---:|:---:|
| L | L | L |
| L | H | L |
| H | L | L |
| H | H | H |

Fig. 3-56. An AND gate can be produced by wiring three NOR gates together.

In order to make the NOR chip into an AND chip, three of the gates are needed (Fig. 3-56). Two gates are made into NOT gates by shorting their input pins together. They then become the inputs to a third gate. The fact that the beginning inputs were reversed by the two now NOT gates makes the final NOR output AND.

Look at the truth table. When two lows are applied to the 7402, they are changed to highs and applied to the NOR gate. Two highs in the NOR gate produce a low output. Since the beginning inputs were both lows and the ending output is a low, the action is like an AND.

If one low and one high are applied to the beginning input, they are reversed and injected to the beginning NOR gate. One low and one high in a NOR gate produces a low. This again corresponds with the AND truth table.

Finally, if two highs are applied to the configuration, they are changed to lows in the two input gates and sent to the final NOR gate. There the two lows cause a high output. There might be three NOR gates in the circuit, but the beginning inputs and final outputs are right out of the AND truth table. You will encounter all sorts of tricky wiring jobs to accomplish specific purposes using whatever existing chips are handy.

Again, the trick during servicing is to start the checkout with each individual gate even though their total effect might be unusual. If you are testing a NOR gate, think of the NOR gate truth table, even though the gate might be one-third of an overall AND gate.

### Exclusive-OR and Exclusive-NOR

The third major logic gate type includes the XOR and XNOR, also called EOR and ENOR. They are similar to OR and NOR but not the same (Fig. 3-57). The word *exclusive* indicates the difference. XOR is different than the OR in the last category of outputs. XOR follows the logic definition of OR exactly, while OR itself does not.

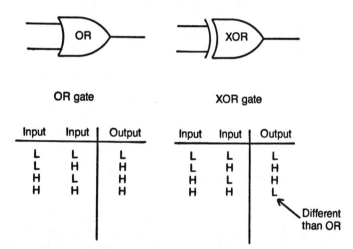

OR gate

| Input | Input | Output |
|-------|-------|--------|
| L | L | L |
| L | H | H |
| H | L | H |
| H | H | H |

XOR gate

| Input | Input | Output |
|-------|-------|--------|
| L | L | L |
| L | H | H |
| H | L | H |
| H | H | L |

Different than OR

Fig. 3-57. The XOR gate differs from the inclusive OR only when two highs are input.

To explain more clearly, let's view what the OR gate does again. The OR gate outputs a high if either one *or* the other of the inputs are high. In addition, the OR gate outputs a high if both inputs are high.

The XOR gate acts the same as the OR gate except when both inputs are high. If both inputs are low, the XOR gate outputs a low like the OR gate does. When either one or the other, but not both, of the inputs are high, the XOR gate outputs a high like the OR gate does. However, if both inputs are high, the XOR gate outputs a low! The OR gate, in contrast, outputs a high.

The XOR gate exclusively outputs a high only when one or the other of the inputs are high. It never outputs a high if both inputs are the same.

The XNOR gate is nothing more than an XOR with a NOT circle on its output point. The schematic diagrams of XOR and XNOR gates resemble OR gates, except for the curved input on the bottom. There are two bottom lines drawn with a space between them. One of the bottom lines is attached to the body of the drawing while the other curved line is attached to the input leads.

The 4070 CMOS chip is a quad two-input exclusive-OR gate (Fig. 3-58). It is a 14-pin DIP with VDD and VSS at pins 14 and 7, following the conventional layout we've seen in the 14-pin TTL chips in the previous discussions.

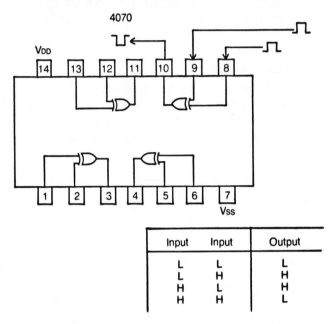

| Input | Input | Output |
|-------|-------|--------|
| L | L | L |
| L | H | H |
| H | L | H |
| H | H | L |

Fig. 3-58. The 4070 chip contains four XOR gates on a 14-pin DIP.

VCC, in TTLs, is defined as the collector dc supply voltage. In TTLs, this is invariably around +5 V and the supply is returned to ground. Therefore, you can test the TTLs with a VOM and feel confident that the highs and lows will be in the 0 V to +5 V range. MOS chips are not quite the same.

Instead of pin 7 being called ground, it is termed VSS. VSS is defined as source supply dc voltage. MOS chips use FETs and not bipolar transistors. FETs have sources, gates, and drains. VSS deals with the sources of FETs. VDD is defined as the drain supply dc on the MOS chips. It replaces VCC.

Another difference occurs during the testing of the MOS chips. It can get confusing with a VOM. While the voltages you read still relate to the supply voltage, the supply could be anywhere between $-0.5\ V_{dc}$ and $+18\ V_{dc}$. Interpreting the highs and lows, 1s and 0s, or sets and resets from a voltage that is not +5 V and 0 V can be misleading. Therefore, it is a good idea not to use the VOM if the VOM starts reading voltages not in 0 V to +5 V range. A logic probe that can read MOS chips is a more convenient instrument. The logic probe is covered in detail in Chapter 4.

With the XOR gate, it is also advisable to memorize the truth table. For technicians, the table is a service chart. When you take your input readings with the logic probe, the

92

output is predictable. If what should be at an output is not there, it indicates a possible defective gate on a chip. For instance, if there are two highs going into gate input pins 8 and 9 on the 4070, there should be an XOR made low at pin 10, the gate output.

The XNOR function is usually put together by attaching a number of other gates to form the complete XNOR gate. One such scheme uses five gates from a couple of 7400 TTLs (Fig. 3-59). The illustration shows all of one 7400 and one gate from the second 7400. There are two VCC and ground connections since there are two chips that have to be energized.

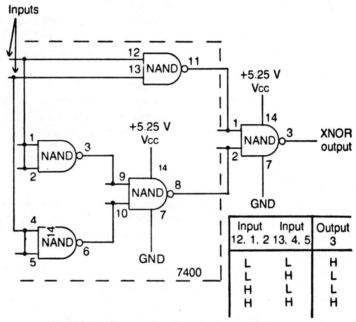

Fig. 3-59. When wiring five NAND gates together, the total is one XNOR gate.

The two inputs are connected to the NAND gate at pins 12 and 13, and are thus NANDed. The output is connected to the final stage NAND gate at pin 1.

The inputs are also injected into two more NAND gates. These gates have their input leads shorted together so they become NOT gates. The two gates' outputs are attached to another NAND gate. Its output also goes to the final NAND gate. The result is XNOR.

This total XNOR gate can easily be checked out. The first step is always to test for supply voltage. The VOM should read +5 V or the logic probe should show a high at all times. It does not change, no matter what the gates do properly. If a gate should short through to ground, then the +5 V might disappear.

This test is like any analog supply voltage reading, except it is more critical. The readings on both chips on pins 14 should be within 5 percent. If one is less, there could be a resistance short to ground sinking some of the current and lowering the voltage. Should a voltage be higher, an open gate could not be sinking enough current or the power supply could be sending out too high a voltage. After the supply is deemed ok and the ground connections intact, then you can leave this analog-type testing and begin logic troubleshooting.

There are two chips involved. The first chip uses all four gates. The second chip uses only one gate, which becomes the final output NAND. Suppose we inject two highs into the inputs. The two highs get NANDed as they enter pins 12 and 13, and exit pin 11. The two highs are NANDed to a single low. This low is sent over to the other chip and enters pin 1 there.

The other two highs enter the shorted input pins 1 and 2, and 4 and 5. The two highs are NOTed into two lows. They exit pins 3 and 6 and enter pins 9 and 10. They are then NANDed into a high and sent to the other chip to pin 2.

With a low on pin 1 and a high on pin 2, the NAND gate produces a high at pin 3, the final XNOR output. The net result of the total circuit should be the XNOR truth table reading, a high. If you apply the other three possible inputs, you'll they match up with the XNOR truth table too.

During an actual checkout, the fact that this total configuration is an XNOR gate will often never even be noticed. The five individual gates that are formed the total and the unused gates on the second chip are the main concern. If there is a short or an open, it will most likely be in only one gate out of the eight that are wired, unless the substrate is defective, which could involve an entire chip.

## STORAGE CHIPS

Gates are action devices. If you put logic states into them, the state immediately gets YESed, NOTed, ANDed, NANDed, ORed, NORed, XORed, or XNORed. There is no hesitation. The only way to stop the action for awhile is to three-state the gate and hold it in high impedance.

Besides the gates, there are storage devices that are not so hasty. They can hold a state snugly in their circuit for any length of time, as long as the electricity stays on.

Storing a logic state in a circuit is called *bit storage*. Bits can be stored in two different ways: static and dynamic. When TTL chips are used for bit storage, the procedure is accomplished with static storage. TTLs do not easily store bits in a dynamic fashion. If MOS chips are made to store bits, they can do it in a static manner, but they are also capable of dynamic storage. The ability to store bits in a computer is needed in many circuits. Among them are the microprocessors described in Chapter 6, the memory banks in Chapter 7, and various support chips with latches in Chapter 8.

The typical static storage circuit that has been around for many years is called a *flip-flop*. It was based around two triode tubes years ago, and graduated into using bipolar transistors and FETs as time went by. Today you'll find it using two logic gates as active devices. As an example, let's see how a logic state can be stored in two pnp transistor circuits.

The schematic in Fig. 3-60 shows two pnp's, Q1 and Q2, with their bases and collectors wired together in a criss-cross fashion through a couple of resistors. There are two base inputs and two collector outputs. Identical bias voltages are applied between the bases and emitters. $-V_{CC}$ is supplied to both collectors. The two pnp circuits are like a pair of Siamese twins, connected bases to collectors.

Even though they are identical, there is a minute amount of imbalance between the circuits. As a result, one pnp goes into saturation while the other cuts off. If Q1 cuts off

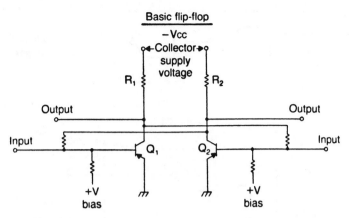

Fig. 3-60. The basic flip-flop circuit can be built around two pnp transistors.

and Q2 saturates, the total circuit holds that condition. It won't do anything else until it is disturbed.

With Q1 cut off and Q2 saturating, the circuit is said to be storing a high or 1. If the reverse has occurred, with Q1 saturating and Q2 cut off, the circuit is storing a low or 0. Either state is stored as long as the circuits are not disturbed.

To change the state, the circuit has to be disturbed. This is done by putting a high into the base of the cut-off pnp, or a low into the base of the saturating pnp. If either one of the changing pulses are applied, the circuits flip-flop and reverse states. The pnp that was cut off starts conducting, and the saturating pnp cuts off.

Instead of using two pnp's to construct the flip-flop you could just as easily use a couple of gates, like a pair of NANDs on a chip (Fig. 3-61). One of the inputs of a NAND could be connected to the other NAND's output and vice versa, producing the cross-coupling. The second input on each NAND is used as the actual input to receive the highs and lows. The NANDs or any other type of gate that is used could be either TTLs or MOSs to form static storage circuits.

A typical chip containing flip-flops is the 7474, a *dual-Dflip-flop* (Fig.3-62). As the name suggests, there are two complete flip-flop circuits of the D type on the 14-pin DIP. The chip is TTL and has VCC and ground at their usual pins, 14 and 7.

The D flip-flop is the type that changes states if a clock input is used. The state gets changed when the clock pulse rises to a high from a low. The rising edge triggers the change and causes the flip-flop.

The letter D stands for *data*. The data is input to the flip-flop as the clock ticks away. In this chip, the data is input at pins 2 and 12, to the two flip-flops. The two clock inputs are at pins 3 and 11. Every time a rising edge occurs, the data state is transferred to its Q output, either 5 or 9. The other outputs *Q, at pins 6 and 8, assume the opposite state to its Q.

The truth table shows what happens at the inputs and outputs of each flip-flop. The logic state shown at Input D is the state of the input immediately before the clock pulse. The logic state at Output Q and *Q is the state of the output immediately following the clock pulse. The clock pulse is not shown in the chart.

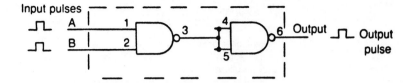

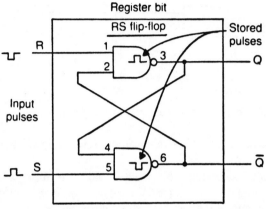

Fig. 3-61. Two NAND gates wired in series can be an AND gate. The same two NAND gates wired in a criss-cross fedback fashion is a flip-flop.

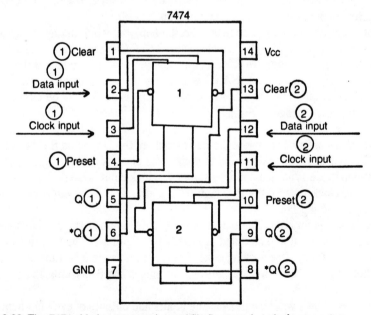

Fig. 3-62. The 7474 chip is a commonly used flip-flop type in today's computers.

| Input D | Output Q | Output *Q |
|---------|----------|-----------|
| Low | Low | High |
| High | High | Low |

The other pins on the chip, *PRESET* and *CLEAR*, are there to get the chip ready for action. The chip is liable to assume any logic state when it is first turned on. This, of course, is not good. The chip must be set to a desired state for duty. If you input a low to the pins labeled PRESET, the Q circuit in the flip-flop sets to a logical 1. If you input a low to the pins labeled CLEAR, the Q circuit clears to a logical 0. The PRESET and CLEAR pins are not affected by the clock pulse in any way.

## DYNAMIC STORAGE CELL

There will be more about the various static flip-flop circuits in Chapters 7, 8, and 9. Right now, let's examine a dynamic bit holder.

The schematic in Fig. 3-63 shows a dynamic storage cell on an MOS memory chip. There is a clock input and −VDD supply. The data is input at the first FET, Q1.

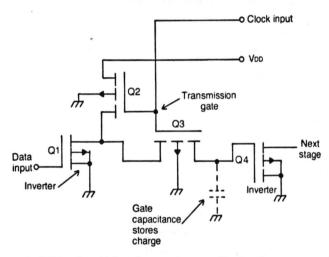

Fig. 3-63. In dynamic RAM cells a high or low can be stored in the charge or non-charge of a tiny capacitance in a FET gate.

If a low enters, as the clock goes low, Q2 and Q3 turn on. The output of Q1 is inverted to a high. The high is transferred through Q3 to another inverter Q4.

Meanwhile, between Q3 and Q4 there is a capacitance-to-ground gate. It charges up due to the very high input resistance of Q4. The charge can be used as one of the logic states.

If a high is applied to the input at Q1, at the first pulse of the clock, Q2 and Q3 turn off. The inversion of Q1 then outputs a low. The low is transferred through Q3 to Q4 and discharges the gate capacitor. The lack of a charge can be used as the other logic state.

This circuit then is able to store a high or a low in the gate capacitance. Q1 is a NOT gate. Q2 and Q3 are transmission FETs. The capacitance charges up or discharges during the clock phase. The charge or lack of charge is stored after the clock pulse passes because the input impedance of Q4 is very high. Q4 is the NOT gate for the next identical stage.

This storage of logic states in gate capacitance is different than storing a state in a flip-flop. Each has its advantages and disadvantages. Logic states storage is discussed in greater detail in Chapters 7, 8, and 9.

## VOLTAGE COMPARATORS

There is another circuit element found extensively in computers that is neither a gate nor a storage device. It is called a *comparator*, and it compares one form of voltage with another. It is used often in the input and output circuit areas to transfer and change analog to digital, digital to analog. The applications are shown throughout the book.

The circuit itself is easy to understand. A comparator can be built around a pair of pnp transistors. Figure 3-64 shows two pnp's with a common emitter resistor tied to ground. −VCC is applied to both Q1 and Q2 through a pair of collector resistors. There are two inputs and one output. The base inputs are a signal voltage into Q1 and a reference voltage into Q2. The output is in the collector of Q2.

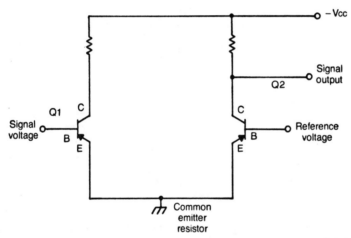

Fig. 3-64. The comparator circuit is used extensively in computers to help change digital to analog and analog to digital.

As you can see, the circuit is something like a flip-flop. When it is energized, one pnp saturates and the other one cuts off according to the circuit components. Once this happens, the stage stays that way and the output shows either a high or low according to which pnp is saturating and which is cut off. In other words, there are two stable states the circuit could possible assume.

With the aid of a signal voltage or the reference voltage, you can get either Q1 or Q2 to saturate or cut off and thus you can control which state the output should be in.

The comparator assumes the state of the voltage that is more negative. If the reference signal into the base of Q2 is more negative, Q2 saturates and Q1 cuts off. With Q2 saturating, the output is about the same as the reference voltage. When the signal voltage is more negative, Q1 saturates and Q2 cuts off. The output voltage is then equal to the supply voltage—VCC.

The simplified circuit we just examined will operate, but it is not too stable with only a resistor in the emitter. Actual comparator circuits put more pnps into emitter circuits along with a few diodes.

The 339 is a typical comparator chip (Fig. 3-65). It is a *quad comparator* on a 14-pin DIP. The supply voltage V + is on pin 3 and ground is at 12, unlike the other 14-pin chips we have looked at. The quad chip is considered *linear*, which indicates it is analog rather than digital. The fact is, in some applications it takes the role of an analog circuit, while at other times it is used to do digital work. Typical applications find it being used in all sorts of jobs. Besides being a basic comparator, it's an analog CMOS and TTL Driver, and AND or OR gate, and even a multivibrator (a form of flip-flop). It can and does do quite a bit.

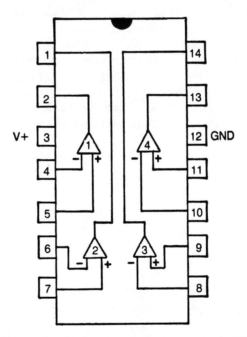

Fig. 3-65. The 339 chip contains four comparator circuits on a 14-pin DIP.

Figure 3-66 shows the two inputs + and −. The + indicates the signal voltage input and the − designates the reference voltage input. The two input voltages are compared in the stage to see which one is more negative. The one which is more negative then appears at the output as signal. The + and − signs on the inputs are often confusing. Keep them straight, since they have no meaning except to show which one is reference.

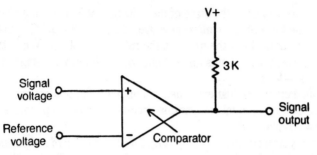

Fig. 3-66. The supply voltages on the comparator chips are quite different and usually higher than the regular logic chips.

The supply voltages are quite different than the supplies for TTL and MOS chips. The supply can be as much as 32 $V_{dc}$ or +/– 16 $V_{dc}$. This is because the applications often require a wide range of voltage comparisons.

Comparator circuits are used in the input and output interface circuits of computers. They can help in the conversion of a shaft position of a joystick, represented as a voltage level into the digital highs and lows the computer can use. They can help the highs and lows of a word processing output get to an external printer. They can aid in the changing of a special audio signal stored on a cassette tape to become the highs and lows of data the computer needs. They are very important chips. Some of the actual circuits using comparators are discussed in later chapters of the book.

Even though display circuits and power supply circuits are used in computers, they will not be discussed here. There is a full chapter each on the display and the power supply in Chapters 23 and 24.

# 4
# Test Equipment

In a computer, there are both analog and digital circuits. The way they operate and the jobs they do are very different. It is said that the two types of circuits live in different worlds. The analog circuits are in the human world. The digital world is the realm of the microprocessor and the circuits that the processor deals with.

However different the analog and digital circuits are from each other, they do have one thing in common. They die in the same way. They are all made of the same electronic materials, and when these materials fail, the failures are identical. Figures 4-1 and 3-28 will give you an idea of the way the electronic materials give up and bring the circuit function to a crashing halt.

The pieces of semiconductor materials that are doped to produce N material and P material and form junctions with each other and glassy insulators are all subject to breakage, electrical shorting, and change in their chemical makeup. The little resistances in resistors and dielectrics in capacitors can all burn through or break open. Transformer windings can disconnect or smoke their insulation off. Fuses can blow, plugs corrode, switches break, connections come apart, copper traces on print boards develop shorts between close spaces or can snap and come loose. These disasters happen often in electronics, no matter which type circuit is being used, analog or digital.

When these breakdowns happen, you as a technician will be responsible for first finding the component or connection that failed and then replacing or repairing the bad part. This chapter and Chapters 19 and 21-24 deals with finding the trouble. Chapter 20 describes the techniques required to replace or repair the bad part.

Sometimes, you are lucky and you can see, smell, hear or feel the defect right off. Then all you have to do is change the bad part or repair the connection. In those cases, you and your natural senses become the only pieces of test equipment needed.

Most times though, you are not so lucky. Then you must employ extensions of your natural senses to explore the troubled circuits and locate the defect.

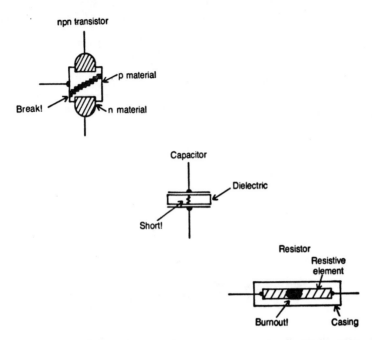

Fig. 4-1. The common reasons for electronic failure are breaks in semiconductor materials, shorting in dielectrics, and burns in resistive elements.

When you are performing an actual repair job the first step is the analyzing of the symptoms of trouble as described in Chapter 19. This diagnostic repair step indicates the circuits that most likely contain the defect. Once you decide on a circuit that should be tested you reach for your test equipment. The first pieces you reach for are the ones that will tell you the condition of the circuit.

These instruments are the low voltage continuity tester, the logic probe, and the VOM. The continuity tester will show up shorts and opens. This tester is used *only* when the computer is off and unplugged. The logic probe will reveal the highs, lows, and pulses at each and every pin in the digital circuits. The logic probe is used when the computer is energized, unlike the continuity tester. The VOM is an alternative to the logic probe and will also tell you the voltages in the analog circuit sections as well as the digital voltages. The logic probe only works in the digital circuits.

These three pieces of test equipment are used most of the time during a repair. A companion item to these three is not a piece of test equipment. It is the exact replacement of a suspect part. For instance if the microprocessor is suspect, if you unplug it and insert a good exact replacement, that is the best test of all. If the computer starts working again, the repair is complete. The processor was bad and you changed it. Should the replacement not fix the trouble, then you know the processor is not the culprit and is probably good.

Unfortunately, not all chips are socketed and a desoldering and resoldering job is so time consuming and fraught with danger, other procedures are best used to determine troubles. If you do suspect a socketed chip though, and have a good replacement, give it a try. You might get lucky.

When you can't get anyplace with continuity, logic, and voltage tests then you have to bring in the reserves. These additional test pieces are the following. There is a signal injection device called a logic pulser and another handy unit called a current tracer. Then there are various types of oscilloscopes and finally a frequency counter. These are the usual pieces of equipment to check out the computer. Additional pieces are needed to test the TV display monitor. These are covered in Chapter 23.

Diagnostic software can be considered in the test equipment category. There are often programs built right on the ROMs in the computer or on a disk supplied by the manufacturer. There are software companies that specialize in writing diagnostic programs. These programs usually exercise various circuits in the computer and if a circuit won't perform properly, a special trouble number will appear on the screen indicating the troubled circuit. There will be more about these diagnostics throughout the book. For right now let's examine the physical pieces of test equipment in more detail.

## VOLTMETER

The voltmeter is the most versatile and convenient piece of test equipment you'll need to check out the computer circuits. I said voltmeter, not VOM, because it is good practice to never, ever use the ohmmeter in the VOM to check resistance in the computer. The ordinary VOM ohmmeter section uses batteries. These batteries apply a voltage to the component under test.

For example, my old faithful Simpson 260 (1966 vintage) uses five 1.5 V batteries for the ohmmeter circuits (Fig. 4-2). One large cell provides 1.5 V for the R × 1 and R × 100 ranges. Four smaller cells are added together in series to furnish 7.5 V for the R × 10,000 range.

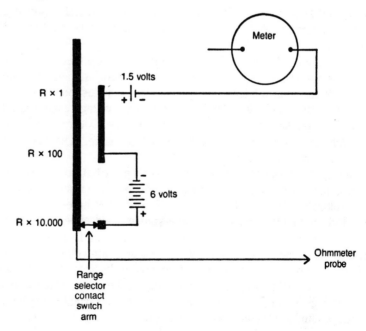

Fig. 4-2. Old-type ohmmeters use battery voltages that could damage newer integrated circuits.

If you test a sensitive transistor junction with these voltages, you are likely to destroy it. This induced extra trouble can lead to a lot of complications. Therefore, never use the VOM ohmmeter to check computer resistances. Often it is safe, but why take the chance? Use a special low voltage ohmmeter as described in the next section.

The voltmeter part of the VOM, however, is safe and convenient. The voltmeter is only a sensitive meter movement, and is moved by the voltage in the computer. The range scale processes the incoming voltage and deflects the needle safely for both meter and computer.

The voltmeter is even more convenient than the logic probe. The logic probe requires two connections to work. You must attach one connection to ground and the second connection to a place where there is a logical high, like +5 V. Only then will it operate. The logic probe test is made with a fat probe that you touch down on the test node.

The VOM, on the other hand, only requires one easy-to-locate ground connection. Then you can touch a test node with the second narrow test probe. In addition, the VOM can be used to check out all the circuits in the computer. Besides the digital circuits, you can test the power supply, both the digital and the analog sides of a digital-to-analog circuit, the video display area, and others. You can make all these tests without changing any connections and only turning the range switch.

The only VOM testing that requires digital interpretation is testing a node for its logic state. While you are checking analog circuits you are looking for actual voltages. In the display area, you might want to see if there is +56 V on a transistor collector. At the output of the power supply, there could be a +32 V point that requires a test. In digital circuits though, you will mostly be looking for the digital highs, lows, and three-statings (Fig. 4-3).

Typically, the VOM can be set to read 5 V to check the states. The negative probe is attached to 0 V, the computer is turned on, and the logic tests can begin. However, observe the following rules.

If the chip you are examining is a TTL, a high is any voltage that reads from +2.5 V to +5 V. A low is any voltage between 0 V and +0.8 V. Any voltage between +0.8 V and +2.5 V means the node is three-stating. That means the test point is in a high impedance state and is doing nothing but building up a static voltage charge due to circuit noise. The VOM is reading the meaningless static charge. You can double-check the three stating with the logic probe, discussed later in this chapter. The logic probe shows nothing during three-state condition.

When the chip is CMOS, the voltage levels are similar but not the same as TTL. The high state is any voltage of +4.2 V or higher. The low state is any voltage of +1.8 V or lower. The voltages between +1.8 V and +4.2 V are the three-state voltages.

On both TTL and CMOS chips, the three-stating could either be deliberate or a defect. Check to see if the chip is a three-state type when you find a three-state condition. If it is, then the condition could be normal. If you discover a three-state condition on a chip that is not able to usually three-state, then you might have uncovered a defect.

These tests are probably the ones you will perform the most. It won't take too long till the meter readings will register in your head as highs, lows, and three-state instead of the analog voltage numbers the needle is pointing to.

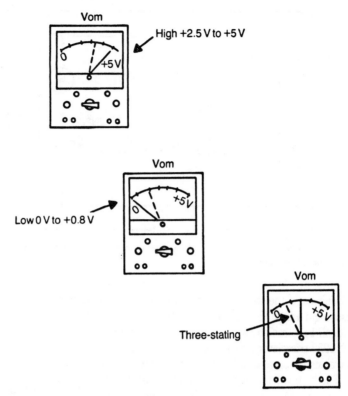

Fig. 4-3. The VOM is able to read highs, lows, and three stating.

## CONTINUITY TESTER

A resistance continuity tester does not read out a value of resistance. All it does is light up if a short circuit is across the input, or not light up if there is a high or infinite resistance across. It is actually a digital instrument. Its two states are named GO and NO GO.

As mentioned earlier, a tester like the VOM has batteries that drive voltages into components so it can read the amount of current that the component passes. This procedure, using normal battery voltages, could burst a MOS gate and cause additional troubles in a computer, and you are there to fix the device, not to cause more troubles.

The ordinary continuity tester also uses 1.5 V batteries. It could possibly blow a junction too. Therefore, you cannot safely use the ordinary tester. In order to render it safe it must be modified. The modification is easy, although getting the parts can be troublesome.

The tester must be made to put out a much lower test voltage than the battery voltage. This can be done with the commonly-used circuit in Fig. 4-4. The circuit can be built and installed into any inexpensive ordinary continuity tester. Just remove the old circuit. Of course, you could build you own enclosure, but it is more convenient to use one that already exists.

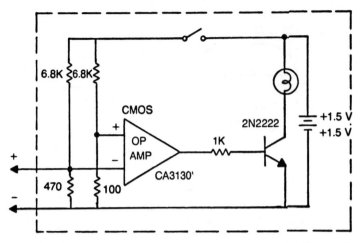

Fig. 4-4. A low-voltage continuity tester should be used in integrated circuits. One can be easily built with its common circuit arrangement.

The circuit uses the same batteries and bulb. The additional components are the npn transistor and a CMOS comparator such as a CA3130. The values of the two devices are not critical. Five resistors tie the devices together.

The 2N2222 transistor acts as a switch for the bulb. The CA3130 comparator output turns the transistor on and off. If the comparator is outputting a low, the npn will be biased off. The bulb will not light without conduction in the npn. When the comparator is putting out a high, the npn turns on, the bulb gets current, and it lights up.

The biasing resistors shown set the comparator so that the reference voltage is more negative than the + voltage. Under these conditions, the output of the comparator is a low. This keeps the bulb off.

Should the two input leads become shorted, the comparator changes states and its output goes high. This causes the npn to turn on, and the bulb lights. Therefore a state of NO GO occurs when the leads are open. A state of GO happens when the leads are shorted.

The beautiful part of this circuit is that only 0.2 V is output into the computer component under test. This is low enough that all transistor junctions can be safely tested. The 0.2 V is also well below the forward-biasing 0.6 V that a silicon junction requires to turn on. If some junctions were inadvertently turned on, the testing could get confusing. This tester is quite safe and you'll use it constantly during troubleshooting procedures.

## LOGIC PROBE

The logic probe was designed expressly to test digital circuits for logic states (Fig. 4-5). There is no interpretation of voltages necessary. When you touch down on a test node, the probe glows HIGH, LOW, or PULSE. There are two switches on some probes that require attention. One is a switch to select CMOS or TTL/LS. This selects the family of devices that are to be tested. The second switch selects MEM or PULSE. PULSE provides a means of detecting trains of pulses. MEM locates one-shot pulses and stores them.

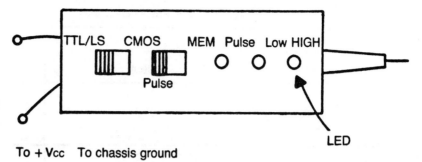

To +Vcc    To chassis ground

Fig. 4-5. The logic probe is the test instrument used most during the checkout of digital circuits.

The probe is not quite as easy to connect into the computer as the VOM or continuity tester. There are two leads to connect to power the probe, and then the stubby probe itself can be touched down on the test node.

My probe is a Micronta bought some time ago at Radio Shack. It can operate from any power supply from 5 to 15 V. There is a black lead that is connected to − , which is usually ground. Then the red lead is connected to the Vcc which powers the chips, usually +5 V. Be careful not to connect the red lead to a high voltage like +15 V. If you do, the readings will be incorrect. The probe will be looking for highs and lows that are proportional to +15 V instead of to +5 V.

When you are connecting the probe into the computer, you are really giving the probe a power supply. In some instances you won't want to use the computer's supply voltage, but instead give the probe its own separate power supply. In those instances, be sure to use a jumper wire between the external supply's common and the computer's common so a voltage level conflict does not occur.

The probe has three LEDs, HIGH, LOW and PULSE (Table 4-1), that can be lit or unlit. With three LEDs capable of two states each, the trio can attain eight possible conditions. One condition, the state of both HIGH and LOW lit, is impossible since a test point can't be both HIGH and LOW at the same instant. This leaves seven possible conditions the LEDs can show. Each condition indicates the state of the test node.

The first condition is when all three LEDs are not lit. This happens first of all if the probe is not attached properly or has come loose. This also happens if the test point is not getting any power, or during a three-state condition. There is a voltage there but it is undefined for the logic probe. The VOM will read it, but the logic probe is not turned on.

The second condition occurs when only the HIGH LED lights up. This is a clear indication that there is a HIGH on the test point. There is no square wave movement; only the high duration of the wave is holding steady on the node.

The third condition is the one where only the LOW LED is lit. There is a LOW on the test point. Like the HIGH reading, there is no pulsing going on; only the LOW duration of the wave is constantly at the test point.

The nest two conditions are combination PULSE and state indications. If the HIGH and PULSE LEDs are both lit, it means there is a wave train at the node, with the positive going durations between pulses. When the LOW and PULSE LEDs are both lit, it means there is a wave train at the node with negative going durations between pulses. The durations are on the bottom of the train between pulses.

**Table 4-1. Logic Probe Indications.**

| | LEDs | | | Signal | Explanation |
|---|---|---|---|---|---|
| | **High** | **Low** | **Pulse** | | |
| 0 | ○ | ○ | ○ | None | Probe not attached<br>Test point dead<br>Test point three-stating |
| 4 | ☀ | ○ | ○ | 5 V ⌐ ⌐ Л 0 V (Test point held high signal) | Test point held high |
| 2 | ○ | ☀ | ○ | 5 V 0 V (Test point held low signal) | Test point held low |
| 5 | ☀ | ○ | ☀ | High duration / Pulses | High with pulse |
| 3 | ○ | ☀ | ☀ | Low duration (pulses) | Low with pulse |
| 1 | ○ | ○ | ☀ | ЛЛЛЛЛ | Square wave more than 100 kHz |
| | ☀ | ☀ | ☀ | ЛЛЛ | Square wave less than 100 kHz |

Let's explain the words *duration* and *pulse* that were mentioned in the last paragraph. In a graph of a square wave the duration of a high takes exactly the same time as the duration of a low (Fig. 4-6). There are two duration times in one cycle, each duration taking 50 percent of the time in the cycle. To put it another way, each high and low does duration duty 50 percent of the time. The *duty cycle* of the high is the ratio of its duration with respect to the full cycle. Since the high is in place half of the time in a square wave, the duty cycle of the high is said to be 50 percent.

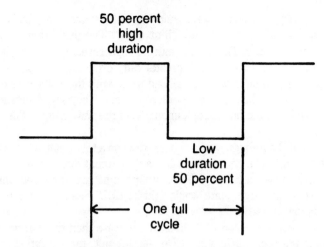

Fig. 4-6. In a square wave, the equal high and low periods of time are called durations.

In this case the same thing is true of the low. *Its* duty cycle is also 50 percent. This is the nature of a square wave. Since it is square, the highs and lows are both of the same duration. They share a cycle 50-50.

What if the high has a duty cycle of 75 percent and the low has a duty cycle of 25 percent? Then this wave is no longer square. When this happens, the high with its longer time stretch still retains the name duration, but the low with the shorter time elapsing is called a pulse (Fig. 4-7).

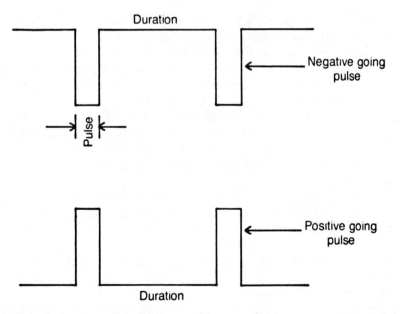

Fig. 4-7. When a high or low takes up less than 50 percent of a full cycle time period, it becomes a pulse.

That last test told you that the wave train was not a square wave but a pulsed wave. The duration time of each cycle was a high or a low. The pulse time of the cycle was opposite to the duration time. The high or low the LED revealed indicated the logic state of the duration time since it has a much greater duty cycle than the pulse time.

The last five logic probe indications all had to do with the voltage level of the wave train. The last two LED indications tell a different story. They give indications of square wave frequency, which is the horizontal dimension of the wave graph. The voltage is the vertical dimension.

To be specific, if the frequency of a square wave on a test point is less than 100 kHz, all three LEDs light up. The square wave has a 50 percent duty cycle for both the high and low durations, so both LEDs light. If it wasn't a square wave and one state had a larger duration, then that larger state would light its LED. Since they are both the same, they both light below 100 kHz.

When the frequency is above a 100 kHz square wave then the durations are too fast for the probe and they can't light the LEDs. As a result, the indication is a lit PULSE LED that tells you there is a square wave there but it's frequency is above 100 kHz. How much above? It won't tell you. that's the limitation of the probe. There is a lot more information about using the probe on actual troubles in Chapter 19 through 22.

## ORDINARY SERVICE OSCILLOSCOPE

The everyday, inexpensive service oscilloscope that is found on the benches of hobbyists and people who repair radios and TVs can perform a lot of computer tests. While most computers run high frequencies which are often beyond the ordinary oscilloscope's capabilities, there are still plenty of circuits in modern computers that provide interesting and valuable oscilloscope pictures.

The typical oscilloscope has a horizontal frequency range of about 100 kHz. The horizontal sweep on the oscilloscope is the frequency part of a graph. The vertical sweep on the oscilloscope is the voltage designation. When you take an oscilloscope picture at a test point, you are taking the varying voltage of a waveshape and applying it to the vertical sweep input (Fig. 4-8). The amount of voltage makes the vertical sweep rise and fall according to the instantaneous voltage at the moment.

Meanwhile, the horizontal sweep is drawing a horizontal line across and back on the oscilloscope face. If the repetition rate of the horizontal is the same as the repetition rate of the signal applied at the vertical, one complete cycle of the signal will appear on the oscilloscope face. When the repetition rate of the horizontal is half the vertical, two complete cycles will appear.

One easy test that an oscilloscope can do has to do with the clock. Since the clock frequency of most computers is a few MHz, one cycle of the clock cannot be seen. However, if the clock is, for example, 2 MHz, that is 20 times the top horizontal frequency of the oscilloscope. You would see 20 complete cycles if you took an oscilloscope picture at the clock. This is called an *envelope* (Fig. 4-9). If you can see an envelope, and you definitely recognize it, then you know the clock is running. This can be important servicing information during a repair job.

Besides the clock circuit, there are a number of other areas that can be tested with an inexpensive oscilloscope. For instance, the computer manufactures a composite

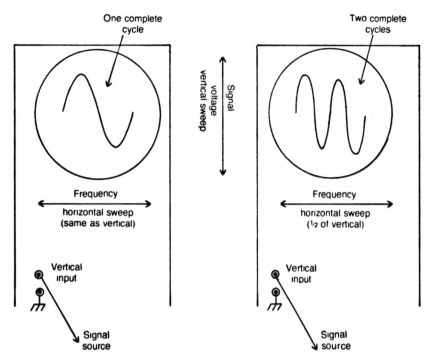

Fig. 4-8. The voltage signal under test becomes an oscilloscope picture as it causes the vertical sweep to rise and fall.

video signal plus CRT sweep and high voltages to display the computing activity. Once produced, it can be viewed on the oscilloscope. All the TV repair oscilloscope techniques can then be brought into play to solve troubles in these circuits.

The joystick circuits are analog-to-digital. The oscilloscope can be used to test the analog side of A/D circuits. There are many digital-to-analog circuits like audio output, and the oscilloscope can be used on the analog side of D/A circuits. There are a lot of copper trace bus lines that carry digital data from one side of the computer to the other in time to the beat of the clock. You can use the oscilloscope to see if the lines are active. The oscilloscope will also reveal if the states are changing in time with the clock.

The important thing is to know what you are looking for. This is explained throughout the book in the pertinent chapters.

The four pieces of test equipment just discussed are the ones used the most by technicians. Practically all computer troubles encountered in the field can be handled with these instruments. There are many more test devices available. If you own some of these other units and incorporate their use in your arsenal of test equipment, your speed and accuracy can only be enhanced. Let's see what some of them are.

## LOGIC PULSER

The small logic pulser is a form of signal injection device. It is usually in the form of a probe. It is attached into the circuit like the logic probe is; that is, there are two leads connected across the +5 V and 0 V supply.

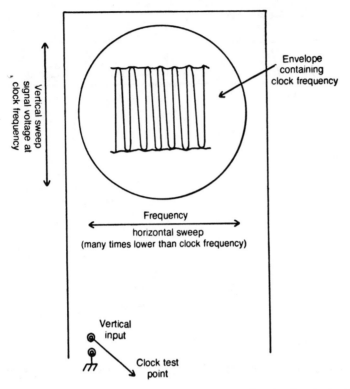

Fig. 4-9. An envelope appears as the oscilloscope picture when the signal under test has a much higher frequency than the oscilloscope internal horizontal frequency.

When the pulser is touched to a test point and *its* button is pressed, it sends a full cycle into the test point. The pulser tip is at a high at the start. Pressing the button causes it to go low and then high again.

With the injection of the single full cycle, a test of suspect circuits can be made. A node that is held high can be momentarily driven low. In some cases, this reveals if the digital circuit is operating. A test point that is held low can be pushed into a high state. Again, under certain circumstances the test provides important servicing news. A device like this is often found on the service bench in a manufacturing plant. It is used for specially-designed tests during design and manufacturing. If you get one and bring it into play, you can improve your troubleshooting abilities.

## CURRENT TRACER

The current tracer is a little probe-type device that picks out spots where ac current is flowing. There is a tiny pickup coil in its tip. When you touch a test point, the indicator light glows if a measurable ac (not dc) current is flowing. The tracer picks up the current flow as a wave train goes from high to low to high. It does not read a steady-state high or low.

There is a sensitivity control on the unit. The settings could be, for example, between 1 and 8. The current pickup at setting 1 is at 300 microamps which barely lights

112

the bulb, 1 milliamp which lights it to half-brightness, and 3 milliamps which fully lights it. This is the most sensitive setting. Be careful with the orientation of the tip. If the current path is 90 degrees out of phase with the pickup coil, the pickup won't work. Just rotate and change the position of the tracer tip to be sure the orientation is at maximum. If you use it a bit you'll quickly get the feel for the correct way to touch a test point.

The most convenient test is when a short develops in a circuit with a lot of parallel branches (Fig. 4-10). The continuity tester shows the short clearly but the trouble could be in any one of a dozen parallel branches. In order to isolate the branch which has the short, each branch must be disconnected one by one, so it can be tested for continuity. As each branch is lifted from the mutual circuit, it can then be tested individually. All the branches will then test good except the one with the trouble. This is a tedious chore, but without a current tracer it's the only way to do the job. The usual technique is to cut or desolder each branch in turn to free it from the group, which is always dangerous since you could induce more trouble with the knife and iron.

With the current tracer you check the current in each branch. How much current should be in a branch?

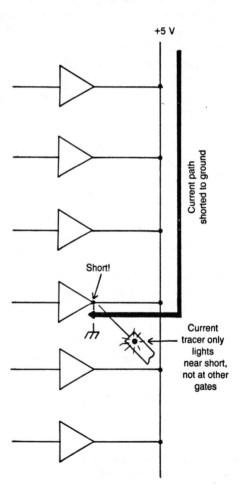

Fig. 4-10. A current tracer can often pick out a shorted parallel leg in a circuit of many parallel legs.

113

In a TTL with a normal high output, the current flow should measure about 40 microamps. A TTL with a low output should have a current of about 1.6 milliamps. In contrast, if the TTL is feeding a short circuit, the current could go up to 55 milliamps when the TTL tries to output a high. While the normal current of 40 microamps would not affect the light of the current tracer, the fault current of 55 milliamps would light the bulb brightly, indicating the short circuit.

To find the source of the short, the tracer is touched down at all the suspect parallel circuits one by one. The 55 milliamp fault current is only traveling on the wiring to the fault. The rest of the wiring will not light the bulb at all. The bad part can often be quickly pinpointed with the tracer.

## FREQUENCY COUNTER AND MULTITRACE OSCILLOSCOPE

These two instruments are expensive, and they rarely are used by the ordinary computer technician. In a design lab or a manufacturing quality control department, these instruments are necessary and valuable. For installation, maintenance, and troubleshooting they have very little use.

The frequency counter is occasionally needed when it is necessary to check the actual frequency of the clock, or the circuits driven by the clock. It is useful, when this job is required, to perform it with a pick-up loop rather than a direct probe connection. The direct connection could load the circuit down producing false frequencies, unless elaborate coupling methods are used. The pick-up loop avoids this type of complication.

The loop can be placed next to the crystal and obtain the frequency from the crystal frequency determining circuit. When the frequency is found to be way off, it is usually due to a defective crystal.

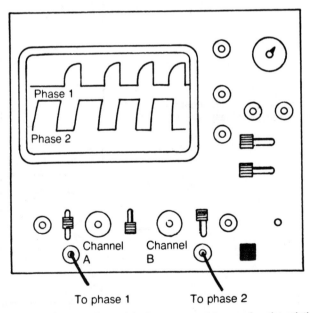

Fig. 4-11. A dual trace oscilloscope is useful when you want to examine the relationship of multiple timing signals at high frequencies.

The multitrace oscilloscope is needed during design work to match up the different chips that have to work together to do the computing (Fig. 4-11). For instance, the timing between the microprocessor and the memory is critical. The designers have to be sure that, when the microprocessor calls upon the memory to supply or store data, the memory responds with the best timing possible. These procedures are discussed in Chapter 9.

The multitrace oscilloscope is able to display a timing diagram. The clock signal is converted into a dual signal to drive the microprocessor. The two signal frequencies are identical, but they are 90 degrees out of phase with each other. The two phases are attached to the two traces of the oscilloscope, and then displayed on the oscilloscope face. Figure 4-11 shows a typical pattern of the two phases. Notice the peaks in the top trace coincide with the valleys of the bottom trace. They are 90 degrees apart in time.

There will be a lot more about these two clock frequencies in further chapters. However, displaying these phase traces is one of the main jobs of this expensive oscilloscope. While this job cannot be dispensed within design work and sophisticated assembly line troubleshooting, it is rarely done on equipment that is in common use and well-designed.

# 5
# Computer Block Diagram Overview

When you take the cover off an ailing computer and look down on it, in your mind's eye you should see a block diagram. The diagram should take form at first as a few blocks that encompass a lot of chips and discrete components in each block (Fig. 5-1). From the symptoms of trouble, you should be able to decide which general block is most likely to contain the trouble. For example, if the computer is acting completely dead, you pick out the power supply. If the computer doesn't remember all the data placed into it, the memory could be at fault. If the screen displays garbage instead of logic, the microprocessor might be messed up.

Once you have chosen a block that might be suspect, your mind should form a block diagram of that general block now under investigation. At this point, you might begin some test equipment measurements and continue zeroing in on the trouble.

The most general block diagram has four blocks. There is an input, the microprocessor, memory, and the output. The common inputs are the keyboard, cassette player, the floppy or hard disk system, joysticks, modems, and a mouse. The microprocessor (called the MPU) is usually an 8-bit, 16-bit, or even a 32-bit type. Memory is RAM, ROM, PROM, and EPROM. Outputs are the display, the printer, the cassette recorder, the disk drives, and modems. Cassette and disk are usually bunched together as I/O (input/output) devices, but from a technician's point of view it is best to consider the input and output as separate entities. The input and output circuits are not the same, even though both input and output functions work into the same devices.

## KEYBOARD

When you look at the keyboard, you'll usually see the QWERTY (first six letters, top left to right) layout. This is the same as any typewriter. In addition, there are some computer-specific keys like RETURN, CLEAR, and BREAK. The keys on the keyboard

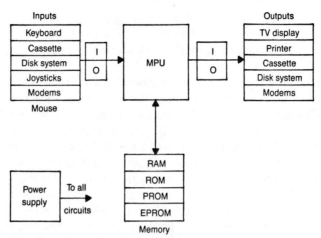

Fig. 5-1. The MPU is the heart of the computer. It reads from the inputs and writes to the outputs. It both reads from and writes to the memory.

are for the user's convenience only. The computer sees an entirely different layout: for example a grid made up of seven rows and eight columns (Fig. 5-2). There are 56 possible intersections on the grid. Every time one of the keys is pressed, one of the intersections is shorted together.

The eight columns are connected to eight pins on an output chip. The eight columns are scanned, pin by pin, by an output strobe pulse generated by the clock. The strobe

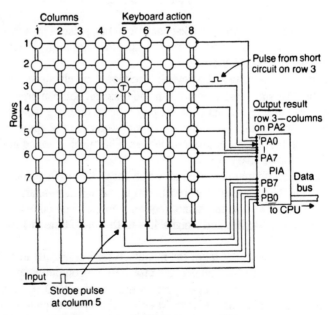

Fig. 5-2. The keyboard has 56 internal electrical intersections. One is shorted every time a key is struck. The electrical pulse due to the short enters the computer and generates a binary code to represent the character of the key.

117

pulse starts at column one and checks it for short circuits. If there is no short circuit at column one, the pulse checks column two. The pulse keeps testing each column in turn till it arrives at a column that has one of the rows shorted to it due to a human striking a key on the board.

The seven rows are connected to seven pins on an input chip. When a strobe pulse locates a row short it causes that row to input a pulse into the input chip pin that it's connected to. The correct row is thus registered at the input. At the same time, the strobe pulse has been keeping track of which column the row was shorted to by the user pressing the keys. With the knowledge of which one of the 56 intersections is shorted, row to column, the computer knows which key on the keyboard has been pressed.

In the memory, there is a little permanent program that codes the 56 intersections into 56 binary ASCII codes. The program acts instantly every time a key is pressed. The correct set of highs and lows are generated for the intersection that is shorted. For example, if the character T is struck on the keyboard, the pulses Low-High-Low-High Low-High-Low-Low are generated. This codes into the binary number 01010100.

A technician gets more out of the T being described as highs and lows. A programmer understands the 1s and 0s better. They are both only descriptions of the voltage levels generated by the permanent memory. As a technician, you must be prepared to constantly use both descriptions.

## CASSETTE PLAYER

A second form of input is the cassette player. (Remember the recording section of the cassette is an output, separate from the player.)

The most common type of cassette input is a software program that is stored on the cassette tape. The tape is inserted into the player and the player output is fed into the computer's tape input plug. We know the keyboard injects a pulse representing one of 56 possible shorts between the rows and columns of the keyboard grid. What type of signal does the cassette player send to the plug?

First of all, the cassette is an audio device. The tape can only store magnetic representations of audio. The signal then must be an audio signal. You can prove this to yourself by taking any tape with a program on it and play it on an ordinary tape player. You will hear audio. Specifically, you might hear it start off with a couple of beeps and then a rushing sound. The beeps are a form of program leader. The rushing sound is the program itself as it's heard on an ordinary speaker.

Before it was put onto tape, the program was a list of 1s and 0s made into a stream of highs and lows. The highs and lows were run through a digital-to-analog coding circuit to change the highs and lows into the audio frequency range. The code assigns a digital high to the audio tone of 2400 Hz, and a digital low to the audio tone of 1200 Hz (Fig. 5-3).

When you purchase a software tape, the manufacturer has already installed the program you bought into this code. As you play the tape into the computer, the signal enters an analog-to-digital decoding circuit. The circuit interprets the 2400 Hz signals as highs and the 1200 Hz signals as lows. If the letter M enters the cassette plug, it is in the form of 1200 Hz, 2400 Hz, 1200 Hz, 1200 Hz, 2400 Hz, 2400 Hz, 1200 Hz, 2400 Hz. This is coded in the A/D circuit to the binary number 01001101.

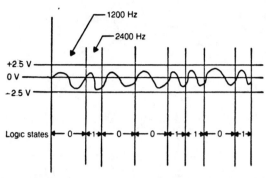

Fig. 5-3. In order for the cassette tape to be able to store data, the digital highs must be coded into a 2400 Hz audio tone and the lows into a 1200 Hz audio tone.

## DISK INPUT

Just as the music industry uses tape recordings and phonograph disks, the computer industry uses tape and disks. Computer disks, however, are far superior in performance to computer tapes. Taped software is only used with inexpensive computers where performance, speed, and reliability are not too critical. Tapes and cassette players are relatively cheap, while the disks and disk drives are much more expensive than tape equipment.

Disk drives, like cassette recorders, must record as well as play back the disk contents. The recording is an output function that will be discussed later in this chapter.

The computer disk is not like the phonograph record. The record has grooves cut in that a needle moves over producing the vibrations that are heard from the speakers. The computer disk is like the magnetic tape in that an oxide of iron is coated on the surface of the disk. The coating can be magnetized at any spot in the coating. The spots can be microscopic. When you magnetize a spot, it becomes a tiny magnet in the coating.

When a spot is magnetized, the little magnet that is formed lines up with all the other magnets that are made. The spots that are not magnetized are not lined up, but lie around in a haphazard way.

If a high is installed, the magnet could be lined up with the others in a north-south position. Should a low be installed the magnet is still lined up with the others, but in south-north position. The lineup could be the other way; it really doesn't matter. The important thing is the high bits are lined up one way, and the low bits are in the same line but with their north-south position reversed to the way the highs are positioned.

Each line is called a track. There could be thousands of bits in an inch of track. Systems easily record up to 15,000 bits per inch of track.

A small floppy disk (called that because it is flexible, in contrast to a hard disk that can't be bent) could have 40 concentric tracks. The tracks are numbered. The outermost track would be 0 and the innermost 39 (Fig. 5-4). The tracks are not one continuous track like a phonograph record. Each track is an individual closed circle.

In our sample disk, there could be ten sectors on each track. Each sector on each track has a numbered address. On the 40 tracks (each with ten sectors) there are 400 addresses numbered 0 to 39. Each sector can hold 256 bytes of data. Each of the eight data bits in each byte is represented by a tiny permanent magnet.

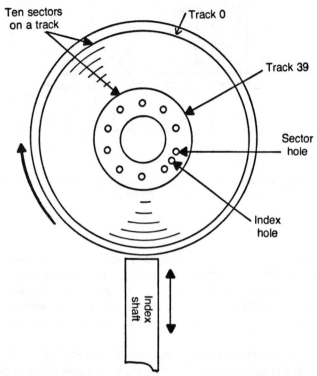

Fig. 5-4. A typical disk can have forty tracks, with ten sectors to a track. Each sector is able to contain 256 bytes of data.

Like a record player, the disk is made to rotate in the drive system. While a record player rotates at 33 revolutions per minute, an inexpensive disk drive has a rotation of 300 rpm. This is much faster than a record player, but 300 rpm represents a rather slow computer disk drive speed. In expensive disk systems, rotation speeds of 1500 rpm on disks with a few thousand tracks are not uncommon.

At a speed of 300 rpm, the disk rotates 20 or 30 microinches above a read/write magnetic head. The disk rotates continually. The head is on an index shaft. The shaft is arranged to move in a line from the outer edge of the disk to the center of the disk. That way, the head can be quickly placed over any one of the 40 tracks. Since the disk is rotating at 300 rpm, the ten sectors on each track are able to pass under the head five times a second. If you send an address to the disk drive, it will pick up any sector of data in less than a second. Each sector contains the equivalent of 256 keyboard characters, which can be sent from the disk to the computer very quickly.

## MOUSE

The mouse is an input only device. It can be used instead of some of the keys on the keyboard. It's a little vehicle that you can push around on your desk. It has wheels and a pushbutton. Some mice come with two pushbuttons. The mouse is used primarily to control the position of the cursor on the TV display. As you roll the mouse around, the cursor moves around the TV display. The mouse movement causes the same type of cursor movement that the arrow keys on the keyboard can produce.

The mouse is a "point and click" vehicle. As the mouse is moved around the wheels change positions and the voltages leaving the mouse and entering a pointing device port on the computer change. The changing voltages are usually injected into an RS232C port or another special assigned mouse port.

The mouse could operate in this way. Suppose you have a menu in place on the TV display. You desire to enter the category number 3 on the menu. You roll the mouse until the cursor covers the category number 3. This points the cursor. Then you press the button. Category number 3 then flicks into view and the menu disappears. You have thus dispensed with moving the cursor with arrowed keys and entered category number 3 without pressing the ENTER key.

The mouse is a mechanical device that can vary voltages that are coursing through its circuits. In the computer is some device driver software that receives the mouse voltage output and converts it into movement of the cursor on the TV display. The mouse is especially handy during the operation of complex graphics programs. It is also useful in other programs too.

## MICROPROCESSOR

The computer would not be a computer without a microprocessor, known as the MPU or CPU. This is the miracle chip that connects to and controls all the rest of the circuits. It is like the telephone company that connects to all the telephone users. The MPU is attached to all the input/output chips. It connects to all of the computer memory. It works directly with all the chips in the computer (Fig. 5-5).

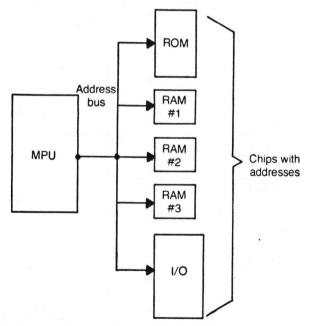

Fig. 5-5. The MPU is attached directly to all the chips with addresses, such as the memory and I/O.

121

The MPU assigns each input, memory cell, and output an address. This is like the telephone company assigns each user a telephone number. The telephone company publishes the Yellow Pages to let everyone know all the area codes and numbers. The MPU has a Memory Map that gives all the addresses of the I/O devices and memory chips (Table 5-1). When you are using the computer and you want to store data or obtain data, you dial up the I/O or memory cell where the data is stored or to be stored.

The MPU has a number of jobs that it is charged with performing. You tell the MPU what job you want to do. These orders have to be written in a language the MPU can understand. These orders are all contained in the software or the programming. The program, called an algorithm, is a copy of the orders written in the computer required form. The program is input by means of the keyboard, from a cassette tape, or a disk. The program is written in bytes. The MPU stores the program byte after byte, in empty byte-sized memory cells (Fig. 5-6). The MPU stores the program at an assigned memory map area; in this case, decimal 33,669 to 33,677. Each byte is stored by the MPU by first dialing up an address, then, once the address opens up, the MPU sends the address its byte. Each program byte is thus installed in its own memory cell group with its own private number.

**Table 5-1. Typical 64 K Memory Map in an 8-Bit Computer.**

| Decimal Address | Memory Map Hex Address | Resident of Address |
|---|---|---|
| 0 to 1023 | 0000 to 03FF | Housekeeper |
| 1024 to 1535 | 0400 to 05FF | Video RAM |
| 1536 to 16383 | 0600 to 3FFF | RAM |
| 16384 to 32767 | 4000 to 7FFF | Expansion RAM |
| 32768 to 40959 | 8000 to 9FFF | Expansion ROM |
| 40960 to 49151 | A000 to BFFF | Operating ROM |
| 49152 to 65279 | C000 to FEFF | Cartridge ROM |
| 65280 to 65535 | FF00 to FFFF | I/O devices |

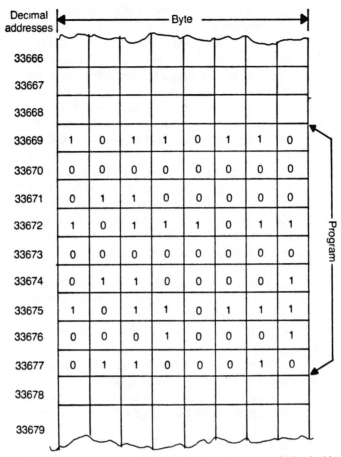

Fig. 5-6. This static RAM memory matrix stores this little program between decimal addresses 33,669 and 33,677.

Once the entire program is stored, the MPU is ready to run the program. The MPU dials up the address of the first byte of the program, 33,669. The address opens up and a copy of the data in the address is sent to the MPU. The MPU works on the data.

The MPU is able to perform a limited number of mathematical and logic jobs on the data. The work is covered in greater detail in the next three chapters. Once the work in the first byte is finished, the MPU goes to the next consecutive address of the memory, 33,670, for the next program byte. The MPU is built to go from byte to byte in order unless it's given specific instructions to do otherwise.

The MPU then proceeds to output address after consecutive address. The procedure is known as *fetch and execute*. The MPU keeps bringing byte-sized instructions and data from the memory to itself until the entire program has been run.

The above MPU description refers to a typical 8-bit computer. These were the ones that appeared on the market in the late '70s and held sway until a year or so after the IBM PC arrived on the scene in 1981. The PC is a form of 16-bit computer.

Examples of the popular 8-bit computers are the COMMODORE VIC-20, 64, and 128, the Tandy Color Computers 1, 2, and 3, the Atari's, the Apple Is and IIs and others. The Apple and COMMODORE machines were based on the 6502 family of microprocessors. The Color Computers use a 6800 family processor, the 6809. Other computers used the Z80 and 8085 processors. The 6800 was conceived and built by Motorola. Some ex-Motorola employees formed COMMODORE and came out with the 6502, which operates on similar principles. Intel produced the 8085 and Zilog made the Z80. In general, all the 8-bit processors operate as described in the beginning of this section. Their differences will become apparent as you proceed through the book.

When the IBM PC hit the market in the early '80s, it contained a so called 16-bit upgrade of the 8085, the 8088. Other computers came out from IBM and IBM clone manufacturers with a processor quite like the 8088, the 8086. At about the same time Motorola started marketing its 68000, a 16-bit processor. Zilog countered with its Z8000. Motorola was able to get its 68000 used by Apple in the Macintosh and by COMMODORE in its Amiga computer. The Z8000 did not penetrate the market to any great degree and is not found in very many machines in mass use.

The IBM PC astounded everyone and became an unprecedented success. Intel was supplying the 8088 and 8086 processors to IBM and its clones. Flushed with the success Intel began coming out with 16-bit upgrades. First there was the 80186. It was simply an improved 8086. Tandy used it in their 2000 Model.

Next came the 80286 16-bit processor from Intel. It had many features including a second operating mode. The good thing about the 80186 and 80286 is, they were compatible with the 8088-8086 processors. A standard was adopted, named after the PC-AT model. This is the most popular business standard today.

Then Intel came out with the 80386. This is not a 16-bit processor. It processes an astounding 32-bits. Here again, the 80386 is compatible with the 80286, the 80186 and the 8086-8088 processors.

The rest of the book goes into a lot more detail on all these processors that you are likely to encounter. The microprocessor is the most important chip in a computer. A machine is not a computer without a processor.

## BUS LINES

The MPU has three sets of lines between the memory-I/O circuits and itself. These lines of communication are copper traces on the print board. There are circuits like buffers, gates, and latches in with the sets of lines. These lines are called the data bus, address bus, and control lines (Fig. 5-7). The data bus transports the instructions and data in the memory locations back and forth between the MPU and the memory map. The address bus transmits the correct address to the residents in the memory map. The control lines make sure the data and addresses get to the right places at the right time in the right way.

The size of the data bus is the usual way a computer is classified (Fig. 5-8). If there are eight copper lines in a data bus, the computer is referred to as an 8-bit computer. When there are 16 lines in a data bus, the computer is a 16-bit computer. (16 bits which is two bytes, is often called a word. This is not a hard definition though; sometimes 32 bits is called a word also.)

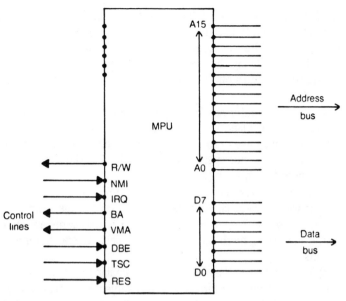

Fig. 5-7. The MPU communicates with the locations by means of the address bus, the data bus and its control lines.

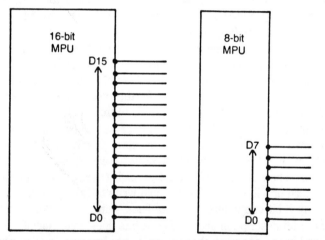

Fig. 5-8. The 16-bit computer has 16 data lines. The 8-bit computer only has eight data lines.

The 8-bit data bus has eight copper lines. These lines come out of the MPU pins and are labeled D7 through D0. They are attached to every address in the memory and the I/O system. Every address has eight bits connected together. The bits are labeled D7 through D0. When the MPU asks for data from the computer, it is connected to every byte on the memory map. However, none of the bytes are activated. Only the single byte designated by the address gets activated and only the contents of the addressed byte is transmitted to the MPU over the data bus. All the other bytes do nothing.

125

After the MPU completes its manipulation of the data, it can send new data back into memory over the data bus. It addresses a location on the map and that location opens its input. Only that single addressed location opens up. The data can then be output on the data bus, with the MPU being the transmitter and the location becoming the receiver. The data can travel both ways on the data bus, from the MPU to a location, and from a location to the MPU.

The typical 8-bit computer has 16 copper traces in its address bus. These 16 lines exit the MPU out of 16 pins labeled A15 through A0. From our earlier math discussions, we realize that 16 copper lines can carry 65,536 (64K) possible combinations of highs and lows. In binary the numbers are 0000000000000000 through 1111111111111111, each 0 being a low and each 1 a high.

This means the 16 lines can dial up a possible 65,536 individual locations on the memory map. If we use decimal addresses, they would range from 0 to 65,535. The same addresses in hex are 0000 to FFFF. The binary equivalents are shown above. Get used to all three addressing methods, since you are liable to encounter any or all of them in memory maps.

There are logic circuits in the address buses similar to those found in the data bus. The eight data lines and the 16 address lines are subject to shorts and opens. They are usually among the first circuits tested when trouble strikes.

The 16 address lines connect to all the memory-I/O locations as do the data lines. A simplified way of looking at the relationship between the two buses appears in Fig. 5-9.

In a static memory chip you can think of the individual bytes in the memory as one on top of another. If there are 64 bytes in the chip, then there are 64 bytes in the stack. All the D7 bytes are on top of each other, all the D6 bytes, and so on.

The 64 bytes from top to bottom are arranged in 64 rows. The D7 through D0 bits are arranged in columns. When you address a byte you send out its row number. For instance, suppose you want the contents of address 21. The MPU outputs address 21 on the address bus and row 21 gets activated. All the rest of the bytes stay off. The eight bits in row 21 are then sent out the data bus, D7 through D0.

The control lines make sure that the proper sequence of events take place. For example, the row 21 instruction is a *read* instruction. That is, the MPU wants to read the data out of a location. If the MPU wanted to *write* to that location it would have sent out a write instruction. There is a control line called read/write. It could send a high to get the location to be read or a low so the MPU could write to the location.

In the early 8-bit computers, the bus lines were straightforward and conformed closely to the brief description above. These bus lines were specific to the computer they were found in and not much thought needed to be given to them. If you wanted to check them out you had general rules of thumb for the simple address, data, and control lines. About the only complications revolved around the cartridge ports the machines might have built onto the print board. These ports permitted you to plug in a cartridge that could take over the machine and use the existing address, data, and control lines. Cartridges are not usually much more than a ROM chip or extra memory. Understanding the workings of these lines could be handled in a routine manner.

However, with the advent of the 16-bit processors, the print board came equipped with a number of slots, that cards full of circuits could be plugged into. For example, the first PC had five slots that would hold cards that performed all sorts of jobs. This was the

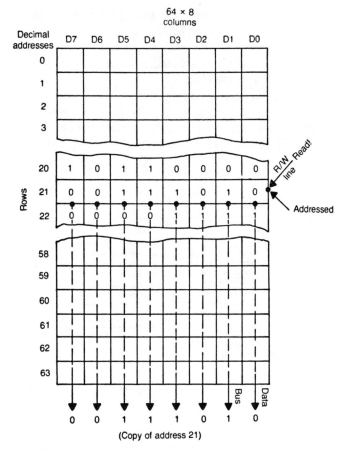

Fig. 5-9. In the static RAM chip, the bytes in the memory matrix are thought of as being stacked in one tall skinny column eight bits wide.

first standard. Next came a standard to handle the XT models of the PC. After that came the AT standard. Each standard has its differences. The AT became very popular. Recently IBM came out with a new, different standard for bus systems called Micro Channel Architecture, MCA. All of these bus systems work in different ways. Checking them out is a far cry from the original service moves needed to test the straightforward 8-bit bus systems. These bus lines get more detailed coverage in Chapters 10-18.

## RAM MEMORY

The sample memory map in Table 5-1 begins with RAM. The computer has 16 K, so the first 16,384 addresses are all RAM bytes. It is called a 16 K computer.

RAM is short for *Random Access Memory*. This means the memory is always accessible to the MPU for reading from or writing to. The only problem occurs if a RAM byte has data already in it and the MPU wants to write to it, the new data destroys the old data and takes up residence in the byte.

Actually, the term RAM and its random access terminology is a bit clumsy and is not used much today. While the abbreviation RAM is still retained, people define it as *read/ write memory*. This has more meaning especially when used in conjunction with the other type of memory called ROM. ROM stands for *Read Only Memory*, which means exactly what it says and is discussed next.

RAM is connected to the address and data buses. Also, there are some control lines that go through to the RAM chips (Fig. 5-10). The RAM receives addresses from the MPU and, if the address that arrives on the address bus is on one of the RAM chips, that address is opened up. If the address is not in RAM, the chips ignore it and keep all their addresses shut down.

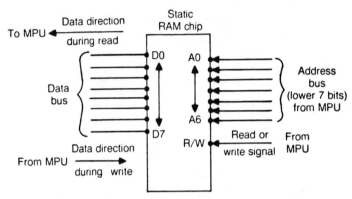

Fig. 5-10. The RAM chip uses the data bus to send data to the MPU or receive data from the MPU.

When a RAM address is opened, the RAM looks for a pulse from the read/write control line. If the pulse is a read, the RAM outputs the data contents of the address onto the data bus. The data then travels to the MPU as per its request.

Should the read/write pulse be a write, the RAM holds the address open and the MPU sends out some data on the data bus. The data travels the bus line to the address that is open and gets stored into the memory byte.

The RAM bytes are composed of eight bit holders. Each bit holder is a circuit that can store a high or a low. There are two types of RAM, static and dynamic. The static bit holders are flip-flop type of circuits. They can be TTL or CMOS. The dynamic bit holders are all CMOS.

Both types are known as *volatile*. This means they can only store bits if electricity is applied. When electricity goes off, even for a fraction of a second, all the data in the bit holder is completely wiped out. This is a major ongoing problem with computers. The only real solution is a backup source of electricity in case the power fails.

Using static RAM, as long as the power source is reliable, is a good way to store data in the computer. If a computer only needs a small amount of RAM, static flip-flops are the medium to use.

Dynamic RAM is also a reliable way to sort data, but it requires some additional circuits. If you remember, the dynamic bit holder keeps the stored 1 or 0 as a charge on a bit of distributed capacitance between a NOT gate and a few coupling FETs that go to the next bit holder. Well, this capacitance charge tends to leak off.

If the charge should leak off, the 1 or 0 that is stored there will be gone. A special circuit has to be installed that refreshes the charge every 20 milliseconds or so. The capacitance is recharged by simply reading the bit holder. Therefore, the MPU directs a constant reading of each bit in the dynamic RAM while the computer is operating. The circuit that does this is called a *refresh circuit*. It is easily implemented.

In the early 8-bit computers the number of bytes on a RAM chip were few in comparison to the gigantic number of bytes available today. The VIC-20 came with 5 K (K stands for 1024), of static RAM. Static RAM is also referred to as SRAM. The Tandy Color Computer at first had 4 K of Dynamic RAM. Dynamic RAM has the nickname, DRAM. The VIC-20's 5 K of SRAM was contained on ten chips. The CoCo's 4 K of DRAM was held on eight chips.

Then the state of the art in RAM began moving. Soon 16 K (16,384) of RAM could be installed on eight chips. Next 64 K (65,536) of RAM was placed on eight chips. After that technology allowed the installation of 256 K (262,144) on eight chips. Today there are eight chip sets that contain an astounding 1 Megabit (1,048,576 bytes) of RAM on an eight bit set. In todays computers it is not uncommon to have many millions of bytes of RAM installed. That's a far cry from the early 4 or 5 K that was available.

Note that there are typically eight chips in a byte sized RAM set. That's because these DRAM chips are each designed to hold one bit of each byte in an addressed memory location. One chip holds all the number 7 bits, a second chip holds all the number 6 bits, a third chip holds all the number 5 bits, and so on. There is much more detail on SRAMs and DRAMs coming up in Chapter 7 and the rest of the book.

## ROM MEMORY

As the name implies, *Read Only Memory* can't be written to; it can only be read from. The data bus is attached to the ROM chips just as it connects to the RAM, but the two-way feature of the data bus is not used (Fig. 5-11). The data from the ROM only travels one way, from the ROM chips to the MPU. The MPU could address a ROM loca-

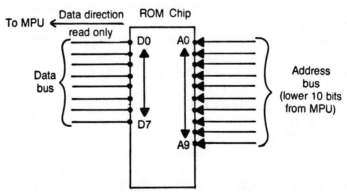

Fig. 5-11. The ROM chip only uses the data bus to send data to the MPU. It is not able to receive any data.

tion and try to write some data to the ROM, but the ROM is not capable of opening up a memory byte for the MPU to fill with data.

This is because the ROM bit holders are filled with permanent burned-in 1s and 0s, not flip-flops or charged capacitances. The ROM bit holders contain resistors, diodes or transistors (Fig. 5-12). If a 1 is installed, the component is intact and can operate. The conduction of the bit holder is designated a 1. When a 0 is to be installed in a bit holder, the component is destroyed and can't conduct. The nonconduction quality indicates a 0 resides there.

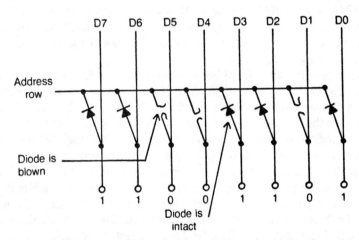

Fig. 5-12. The ROM chip has permanent data burnt into its circuits. For instance, intact diodes act electronically as highs while blown diodes act as lows.

While the RAM chips are available for the MPU to input programs and data and then draw from the stored material at will, the ROM chips are already occupied. The information that is in the factory-prepared ROM chips though, has to be nonvolatile because they run the computer. The ROM chips are the intelligence behind the MPU. The MPU can't do a thing without the ROM chips. The MPU must check with the ROM before it can make any move. The MPU doesn't do a logical thing unless it gets detailed instructions and data from ROM.

When you first turn on the computer one of the first things that happens is the MPU goes to the ROM address where its first instruction awaits. After the MPU fetches its first instruction, it executes it. The next thing the MPU does is go back to the ROM for its next instruction, and so on and so on.

The ROM, being the brains of the operation of the computer, contains what is called an *operating system*. The operating system is a detailed program burnt into ROM that gets all the computing done in its designed way. The operating system takes care of the programs as they are run. If any unexpected events take place, the ROM interrupts the program, takes emergency action, and returns the computer to normal operation.

Another thing ROM chips do is interpret special high-level languages into machine language. For example, there is a language you may be familiar with called BASIC. In computers, there is often a ROM that interprets BASIC as it comes in through the keyboard, cassette tape, or disk, and translates it into 1s and 0s. The BASIC program can then be installed in RAM and run.

The ROMs just discussed are usually plugged into the computer in a socket on the board. Other ROMs are available that you can buy in stores. They plug into the side or back of the computer in a special cartridge socket. That's what the game cartridges are. There are also applications cartridges for education, word processing, spreadsheet, and filing software. These ROMs usually contain complete operating systems as well as the programming needed for their special function.

Whether the ROMs are plugged into a board socket, soldered on the print board or inserted into a cartridge socket, they all do the same type of job; they control the action of the computer by telling the MPU what to do and how to do it every step of the way. Their rows of bytes are connected to the address bus, their columns D7 to D0 are connected to D7 through D0 of the data bus, and, if needed, the appropriate control lines are connected.

## OUTPUT CHIPS

The work of the computer is conducted in the digital circuit areas and is done by the manipulation of binary numbers. The digital areas are the MPU-RAM-ROM environs. The outside world gets its problems injected into the computer world with the keyboard, cassette player, disk drive and other devices. The input devices interface with the computer, which means having the analog inputs changed into digital in a group of I/O chips. It was mentioned in the keyboard and cassette discussions that some chips and their analog-to-digital circuits coupled the inputs into the computer. Once the work is completed, the computer is then ready to send the results back into the outside world. This is accomplished with the aid of the same group of I/O chips and their digital-to-analog circuits. Note the digital-to-analog output circuits do the opposite job of the analog-to-digital input circuits.

There are three main types of I/O chips. One is a chip that, besides handling both inputs and outputs, can interface both serial and parallel streams of data.

For instance, a cassette tape input sends a signal that enters the I/O chip one bit at a time, one bit after the next one (Fig. 5-13). Only one pin on the chip is needed to receive the input. The output is also one bit at a time. This is called a *serial* input-output. On the other hand, the keyboard has eight pins connected to the I/O chip. The keyboard output consists of eight simultaneous highs and lows. Since all eight pins receive a signal at the same time, it is called a *parallel* input. These chips are usually large ones, like a 40-pin DIP. Typical chips are the 6821, called a *Peripheral Interface Adapter* (PIA) and the 6522 called a *Versatile Interface Adapter* (VIA).

While the PIA and VIA I/O chips can do both serial and parallel work, they are usually thought of as parallel types. A second form of I/O chip exemplified by the UART and ACIA is a serial-only interface (Fig. 5-14). One end of it is serial and the other end is parallel. It does the job of changing serial to parallel or changing parallel to serial. It can't just interface a parallel to parallel or serial to serial; it must perform the conversion.

These chips are a little smaller than the PIA type. They are usually only 24-pin DIPs. They are very handy with an input/output device like a telephone modem.

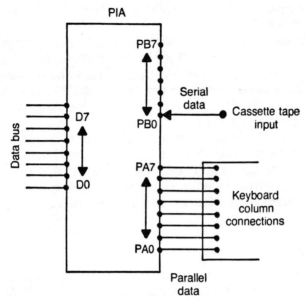

Fig. 5-13. Some I/O chips can perform parallel as well as serial transfers of data. This PIA is receiving cassette serial data and processing keyboard parallel data.

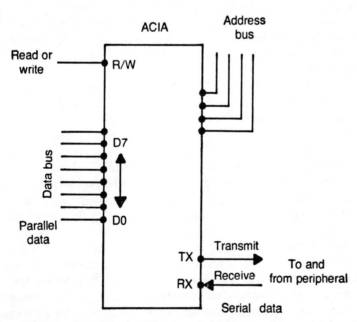

Fig. 5-14. Other I/O chips can change serial data to parallel data or parallel to serial data. The parallel connections are to the data bus while the serial is to a peripheral.

A telephone is by its very nature an I/O device. The modem is simply an external circuit that can change the analog signal that exits the telephone into a digital signal. The digital signal is composed of byte-sized pieces. The modem output is digital bytes but in a serial form, one bit after another. The UART or ACIA receives the serial signal into one pin and converts the serial signal into parallel eight bit units. Then the chip sends the signal out of eight pins simultaneously into the data bus of the computer.

The I/O chip can also perform the reverse action. When the computer talks to the telephone it has to have its byte-sized chunks changed into a serial form (Fig. 5-15). The computer puts a simultaneous eight bits into eight pins of the ACIA. It takes the bits, places them in a line, and sends them to the modem one at a time in true serial fashion. The modem then changes the digital bits into a coded tone that the telephone can transmit over its audio line.

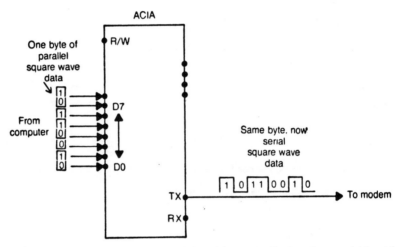

Fig. 5-15. When the computer is hooked to a modem, it is constantly changing a serial input from the modem to parallel and a parallel output from the data bus to serial.

## VIDEO OUTPUT

The third type of interface chip is a 40-pin wonder. Two examples are the 6847 Video Display Generator, known as the VDG, and the 6560 Video Interface Chip called the VIC. They take bytes from memory, change them into video signals and send them out into some video circuits so they will be displayed on the screen. The inputs into these chips are digital bytes. The outputs are video pictures.

These chips have three types of outputs. One is a mode called *alphanumerics*. All that means is the display will show letters and numbers. A second mode the chip can create is called *alpha semigraphics*. Besides displaying alphanumerics, the chip can generate a limited number of graphic characters too.

The third mode is pure graphics. With this mode you can draw actual pictures on the display. These modes are created by ROM circuits in the chip makeup. There will be more about these circuits in following chapters. Figure 5-16 is a diagram tying together all the chips just discussed.

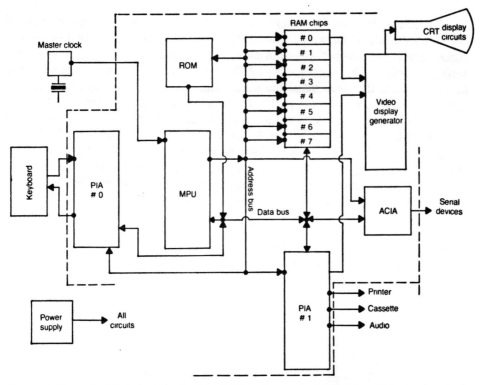

Fig. 5-16. The typical 8-bit computer has the ROM in charge, the MPU doing all the hard work, the RAM acting as storehouse, the PIAs and ACIA interfacing with the peripherals, the CLOCK as the pacemaker, and the power supply energizing all participants.

## OUTPUT TO A PRINTER

The computer is able to send signals to many, many kinds of output devices. Each device requires a special form of digital or analog signal. For example, a line printer needs a digital signal written in ASCII. ASCII is usually a seven bit signal with a 0 as its MSB, since the computer will be spewing out bytes. Some printers at certain times accept serial bytes and at other times parallel bytes. The computer must prepare the appropriate signal for the printer. If it is not exactly correct in format, the printer rejects it.

The reason the printer is able to receive digital signals is because it is really a computer itself. It has an MPU, some memory, plus all the other elements needed to perform its printing duties. The printer is not designed to do anything but its dedicated job: printing.

Let's discuss a sample dot-matrix printer. For example, this printer has both a serial and parallel interface connector. One or the other connector receives the digital signal from the main computer, and transfers the signal to the printer's MPU. The MPU sends the signal on to driver stages. From there, the ASCII signal, with each byte representing a letter or number, is translated into a series of dots. The dots then drive a little hammer that prints out the characters as the hammer strikes a typewriter ribbon onto the paper.

Printers have their own clocks and power supplies. A printer is a second computer dedicated to do nothing but printing for the main computer. The signal only travels from the main computer to the printer.

There are a couple of return signals from the printer, but they are only there to signal the computer the status of the printer. It tells the computer when it is ready, and if a complication arises, it tells the computer to hold everything until the complication is cleared up. The printing function is a case where two computers work with each other.

## CASSETTE RECORDER

The cassette input circuit assumes there is a signal on the tape that the computer could use. How does that signal get on the tape? It is placed there by the cassette output circuit, which is different than the input circuit.

The streams of highs and lows that are to be put on tape are in the RAM and ROM memory bytes. The ROM directs the MPU to take the bytes, put them into a prescribed format, and then output them to a PIA type chip. The output chip feeds the tape format into a digital-to-analog circuit. The D/A circuit codes the format into tones of 1200 Hz for the 0s and 2400 Hz for the 1s. The format starts off with a leader of alternating 1s and 0s followed by the blocks of data. A block of data, similar to the disk sectors, has 256 possible bytes in it, along with some control data that controls sync, tells the length of the block, and checks the accuracy of the block.

The streams of data leave the D/A circuit as audio tones and are recorded on the tape in a routine tape recording manner.

## VIDEO DISPLAY

There are all sorts of video display devices that can exhibit the computer's wares. First of all there is the home TV set. Next there is a large assortment of dedicated TV monitors both monochrome and polychrome. Lastly there are some flat screen devices. There is the LCD, liquid crystal display, the EL, electroluminescent display and the gas plasma.

The home TV can be used as a monitor as long as a special RF Modulator is used. Computers like the Tandy CoCo and the COMMODORE 64 and 128 are made with built in RF Modulators. This RF modulator is nothing more than an oscillator circuit that can output a channel 3 or 4 carrier frequency. A little switch provides either channel 3 or 4. These computers, in their video output circuits, construct an analog composite TV signal that is similar to the signals produced at a TV station. These signals are then mounted on an RF carrier signal that is the same frequency as channel 3 or 4. The signal is then wired to the home TV via a 72 ohm cable. The TV uses it just as it would use a signal from a TV station.

A dedicated computer monitor, on the other hand, does not have a TV channel selector, and tuner circuits between the antenna terminals and the innards of the TV. Therefore, the computer does not have to mount its video output onto a TV carrier wave to get it to the video circuits in the TV display. The dedicated TV display can receive the video output from the computer and inject the signal directly into its video circuits. In different computers there are many different types of video outputs. Some outputs are analog and some digital. Some are monochrome and others polychrome. Some signals are composite video and others are RGB or RGBI. The signals could have all sorts of voltage levels and frequencies. The input connections could have any number of pins in any kind of configuration. As you can imagine, you must be careful that when you hook up a monitor to a computer, that the two devices are compatible.

Most computer TV monitors have great resolution. If you compare the pictures on a monitor with a home TV you'll see the difference. The reasons for the better picture are discussed thoroughly in Chapter 23.

Figure 5-17 is the block diagram of a simple monochrome monitor that displays a conventional black and white, green and black or beige and black picture. There are three inputs, the video, a vertical sync signal at around 60 Hz and a horizontal sync signal at around 15,750 Hz.

The video first goes to a video amplifier where it is strengthened, and then goes on to the input of the CRT. In the CRT is an electron gun that fires a thin beam of electrons at a phosphor screen face. The electrons hit the phosphor and create light.

Around the neck of the CRT is a deflection yoke with two coils, one horizontal and the other vertical. These coils when energized create an electromagnetic field that the electron beam must pass through. As the electromagnetic field is varied by the sync signals the beam can be made to swerve in any desired direction.

The vertical sync signal is injected into a 60 Hz oscillator circuit. The sync signal locks the oscillator frequency to the same 60 Hz the computer is outputting. The synced 60 Hz signal is then amplified and fed to the vertical deflection coil.

The horizontal sync signal is injected into a 15,750 Hz oscillator circuit. The sync signal locks the oscillator frequency to the same 15,750 Hz the computer is outputting. The synchronized signal is then amplified and fed to the horizontal deflection coil.

The deflection coil proceeds to draw the beam across the TV screen at 15,750 Hz. At the same time the deflection coil pulls the beam down and up at 60 Hz rate. This makes the beam scan the TV screen and light up the screen one line at a time each line

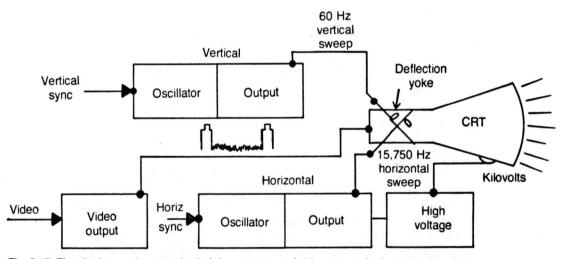

Fig. 5-17. The display can be comprised of the same type of video output, horizontal and vertical sweep, high voltage, and CRT found in TV sets.

beneath the preceding one. The scan rate is too fast for the human eye to follow and the screen appears to be a full screen of light.

Note the high voltage circuit. The voltage in a CRT could be anywhere between 10 and 30 Kilovolts (10,000 to 30,000 V). This high voltage is needed to attract the electron beam from the gun to the screen at sufficient velocity to light the phosphor.

In TV monitors, there could be many more circuits, producing much higher sweep frequencies. The higher frequencies are used to upgrade resolution. This is discussed further in Chapter 23.

## DISK OUTPUT

There are three general types of disk drives: floppy, hard, and Winchester. (Actually, a Winchester is a hard disk. It differs from many hard disks in that the disk is permanently sealed inside an airtight drive system. IBM names the Winchester after one of its proprietary projects, and not after somebody called Winchester.)

All three disks use similar systems with the bits of data stored in microscopic permanent magnets arranged in tracks around the disk. The tracks are broken up into sectors with each sector holding multiples of 256 bytes each.

The disks all rotate at high speeds a few microinches below a magnetic head that can move from the outer edge of the disk to the center upon command.

It was mentioned in the disk input section that the disks are read by moving the magnetic head across the disk as the disk rotates. The head is turned off and on according to the address of the sector that is applied by the computer's MPU. What about the write operation?

A disk system is a lot more complex than a cassette. The disk system usually has its own ROM. When the disk system is operating, it is in control of the computer. The disk is a source of memory that is used while a program is being run. While a cassette can be used in the same way, it is so much slower that, except in very special cases, it is not very useful. The cassette is fine to store a program and install the program at the beginning of a working day, but not a practical medium to be referred to constantly. A disk system, though, can produce data in a matter of milliseconds and is quite useful.

Data can be written onto a disk with the same rapidity that it can be read. When the data is written, there is one important interface process that must be performed, since the disk can only receive serial data. The data in the computer is traveling the eight lines of the data bus in parallel fashion. Therefore, the data must be passed through a parallel-to-serial interface chip before it can be written on a disk. Conversely, the data must be passed the other way (serial to parallel) when it is read from a disk. Often the same interface chip can be used for both read and write operations.

Data is packaged up in a special format for the disk operation. Every piece of the data including the packaging is still only highs and lows, but in a special disk operating system format. For example, a data bit whether it is a high or low is placed after a high that acts as a sync pulse. In a byte there are eight such sync pulses (Fig. 5-18).

The 256 data bytes in a sector are placed in a cocoon of bytes that take care of such functions as sync and addressing (Fig. 5-19). When a sector is filled with 256 bytes of data, it is also stuffed with a lot of control bytes. When the 256 data bytes are conditioned before being written to the disk, all these control bytes must be installed in with

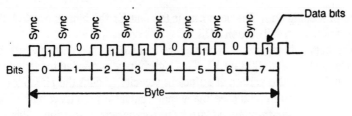

Fig. 5-18. A byte of data on a disk must be packaged up in a precise format.

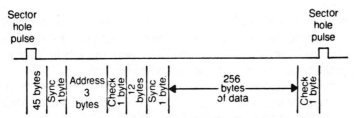

Fig. 5-19. The 256 bytes that are placed into a sector on a disk are also packaged with a large number of control bytes.

the data bytes. This conditioning takes place in the interface along with the parallel-to-serial processing.

The mechanical system that spins the disks and moves the arm that holds the magnetic recording head is nothing more than a glorified record player. The mechanical pieces wear out and break down like a record player does. However, the disk drive is a great deal more critical than the record player. To effect correct repairs, it is mandatory to scrupulously follow the detailed instructions in the factory service manual that goes with the unit.

Servicing the electronics is not as mechanically critical, but it is necessary to thoroughly understand what the circuits are doing. To service an actual disk system, the service manual is very handy.

# 6

# The Common Microprocessors

An MPU is likened to a heart. It is the major component of a computer, but it is not the brains. The brains are contained in the ROM chips. The MPU beats in time with its clock, which could be internal to the MPU or separate and attached to the MPU like a pacemaker. In step with the beat of the clock, the MPU pumps streams of data from place to place in the computer along arteries called the system bus. The MPU addresses specific locations on the memory map by means of highs and lows it sends out on the address lines of the system bus. Once a location is addressed and thus activated, the MPU is able to access the data contents of the location.

Accessing means either reading or writing to the addressed location. The MPU has a read/write control line. When it wants to receive the highs and lows that are stored in the location, it sends a read signal to the location. The data contents then leave the location and travel to the MPU over the data bus lines. Should the MPU want to write to the location it sends a write signal. The data then leaves the MPU and travels to the location where it is stored.

The MPU performs the work but it checks with the ROM every step of the way. The MPU is completely dependent on instructions from the ROM. If the MPU should somehow lose contact with the operating system program in the ROM and try to run itself, it would go wild, pulsing without sense much like a heart does when it starts to fibrillate.

There are only four common families of microprocessors. As mentioned earlier and shown in Table 6-1. The families are based from the Motorola 6800, the COMMODORE 6502, the Zilog Z80 and the Intel 8080. These were the first commercial processors that had wide acceptance.

**Table 6-1. The Four Common Microprocessor Families.**

| Motorola | | Commodore | |
|---|---|---|---|
| **6800** | | **6500** | |
| 6800 | 1.95 | 6502 | 2.25 |
| 6802 | 2.95 | 6502A | 2.69 |
| 6803 | 3.95 | 6502B | 4.25 |
| 6809 | 2.95 | 65C02* | 7.95 |
| 68B09 | 5.99 | 6520 | 1.65 |
| 6809E | 2.95 | 6522 | 2.95 |
| 68B09E | 5.49 | 6522A | 5.95 |
| 6810 | 1.95 | 6526 | 13.95 |
| 6820 | 2.95 | 6532 | 5.95 |
| 6821 | 1.25 | 6545A | 3.95 |
| 68B21 | 1.85 | 6551 | 2.95 |
| 6840 | 3.95 | 6551A | 6.95 |
| 6845 | 2.75 | | |
| 68B45 | 4.95 | *CMOS | |
| 6847 | 4.75 | | |
| 6850 | 1.95 | | |
| 68B50 | 1.75 | | |
| 6883 | 22.95 | | |
| 68000 | 9.95 | | |
| **Zilog** | | **Intel** | |
| **Z-80** | | **8000** | |
| Z80-CPU | 1.25 | 8031 | 3.95 |
| Z80A-CPU | 1.29 | 8035 | 1.49 |
| Z80B-CPU | 2.75 | 8039 | 1.95 |
| Z80A-CTC | 1.69 | 8052AH | |
| Z80B-CTC | 4.25 | BASIC | 34.95 |
| Z80A-DART | 5.95 | 8080 | 2.49 |
| Z80B-DART | 6.95 | 8085 | 1.95 |
| Z80A-DMA | 5.95 | 8085A-2 | 3.75 |
| Z80A-PIO | 1.89 | 8086 | 6.49 |
| Z80B-PIO | 4.25 | 8088 | 5.99 |
| Z80A-SIO/0 | 5.95 | 8088-1 | 12.95 |
| Z80B-SIO/0 | 12.95 | 8088-2 | 7.95 |
| Z80A-SIO/1 | 5.95 | 8155 | 2.49 |
| Z80A-SIO/2 | 5.95 | 8156 | 2.95 |
| Z80B-SIO/2 | 12.95 | 8155-2 | 3.95 |
| Z8671BASIC | 9.95 | 8741 | 9.95 |
| | | 8742 | 29.95 |
| | | 8748 | 7.95 |
| | | 8749 | 9.95 |
| | | 8755 | 14.95 |
| | | 80286 | 79.95 |
| | | 80286-8 | 249.95 |

## MICROPROCESSOR BACKGROUND

Integrated circuit chips were first produced in 1964. Texas Instruments and Fairchild pioneered the effort. The first Digital ICs were gates and registers as described in Chapter 3. Next some 1 K static memory chips were made. After that a UART was constructed. Then in late 1971 an MPU, the 4004 was made at Intel.

The Japanese were the first to order a machine with a processor. It was a desk calculator and it contained the 4-bit 4004. The calculator sold like hot cakes. Encouraged by the 4004's immediate success, Intel produced the 8008 in 1972. Processor development was then off and running. By 1974 Intel had produced the 8080, an 8-bit processor that worked well. Competition set in and Motorola produced the 6800 in 1975.

The 8080 and 6800 were smashing successes. More competition set in and a large number of processors were developed including the Z80 from Zilog. Some engineers originally with Motorola started COMMODORE and the 6502 appeared. The four main families of processors were then in place and the 8-bit processor caused the first mass market personal computers to be sold.

In September of 1977, Tandy unveiled the TRS-80 Model I containing the Z80. In the same year the Apple I with 6502 was on the market. COMMODORE's PET, also with a 6502 came out in 1979. The personal computer market then took off. A steady stream of computers came out with processors from the four families. The public and many business houses began snapping them up.

In 1981 IBM arrived on the personal computer scene with the first PC. It contained a 16-bit 8088. That was the beginning of IBM's domination of the market. Apple came out with the Macintosh that also had a 16-bit processor, the Motorola 68000. Zilog tried to penetrate the mass market with a 16-bit Z8000. The Z8000 did not catch on. The market was left to the 8088-8086 and the 68000.

In the late 70s, there was very little in the way of software available. As a result, most of the computer purchasers were experimenters, hobbyists, and other knowledgeable types. These people were able to utilize the 8-bit machines because they were able to write their own programs. The programs were mostly written in BASIC and machine language. Millions of COMMODORE, Tandy, Apple, Atari and some other 8-bit single board computers were sold.

These computers were sturdy and the knowledgeable enthusiasts who bought them and kept them going are still strong at it today. The Tandy CoCo and the COMMODORE VIC-20, 64, and 128 are all supported by monthly magazines. This hard core of computer enthusiasts number in the multimillions. Their contributions to the furtherance of education, business, and just plain fun is immeasurable. These -easy-to-handle machines are selling just as well today. Anyone who buys one of these machines becomes a member of an elite club and will improve his or her life in an important way.

Meanwhile back in 1981 IBM brought out the PC, a 16-bit machine with an 8088 processor. Actually the 8088 is a hybrid. It is not a complete 16-bit type since it only has eight data bus pins (Fig. 6-1). However, internally the 8088 has 16 data lines. It multiplexes the eight lines. It splits the 16-bit data signal into two 8-bit pieces to get the data in and out through the available eight pins.

The 8088 is actually a modified 8086 processor. The main difference between the two processors being, the 8086 has 16 data pins. The 8088 only has 8 data pins. The 16 data pins in the 8086 shares its pins with the 16 address outputs. The 8088 shares its 8 data pins with eight of the 16 address outputs. These arrangements can be seen in Figs. 6-1 and 6-2. The 8086 doesn't have to multiplex the 16-bits of data in two sections to get it in and out of the chip as the 8088 does.

Table 6-2 shows the evolutionary stages of the Intel 8080 family of MPUs. The 8-bit 8080 held sway until the late 70s. Then the 8086-8088 chips took over. They were Intel's

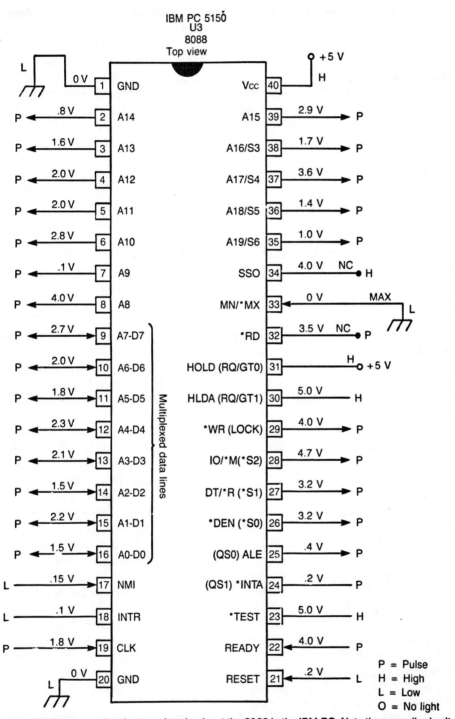

Fig. 6-1. This is a test point chart used to check out the 8088 in the IBM PC. Note the prescribed voltages and logic states of each pin. Also note that the 8088 only uses eight data bus lines, D7-D0, to operate its internal 16-bit data bus lines.

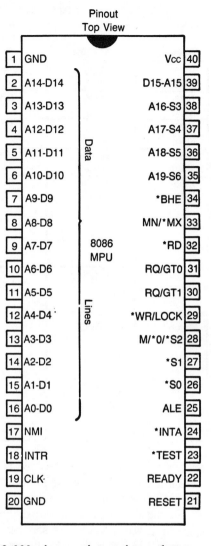

Pinout
Top View

| Pin | Signal | | Signal | Pin |
|---|---|---|---|---|
| 1 | GND | | Vcc | 40 |
| 2 | A14-D14 | | D15-A15 | 39 |
| 3 | A13-D13 | | A16-S3 | 38 |
| 4 | A12-D12 | | A17-S4 | 37 |
| 5 | A11-D11 | | A18-S5 | 36 |
| 6 | A10-D10 | | A19-S6 | 35 |
| 7 | A9-D9 | | *BHE | 34 |
| 8 | A8-D8 | | MN/*MX | 33 |
| 9 | A7-D7 | | *RD | 32 |
| 10 | A6-D6 | | RQ/GT0 | 31 |
| 11 | A5-D5 | | RQ/GT1 | 30 |
| 12 | A4-D4 | | *WR/LOCK | 29 |
| 13 | A3-D3 | | M/*0/*S2 | 28 |
| 14 | A2-D2 | | *S1 | 27 |
| 15 | A1-D1 | | *S0 | 26 |
| 16 | A0-D0 | | ALE | 25 |
| 17 | NMI | | *INTA | 24 |
| 18 | INTR | | *TEST | 23 |
| 19 | CLK | | READY | 22 |
| 20 | GND | | RESET | 21 |

8086 MPU — Data Lines

**Fig. 6-2.** The 8086 differs from the 8088 in that it uses 16 data bus lines, D15-D0, to operate its internal 16-bit data bus lines.

16-bit entry into the race. They contained about 29,000 microscopic transistors that performed the processing.

Lightning struck in 1981 when IBM came out with its PC that used the 8088. No one expected the instant success and large sales of the PC. The 8-bit machines up until that time were, for the most part, used to write BASIC programs and play games. Waiting in the wings were serious business users who were not interested in writing BASIC and playing games. They wanted a good computer that could run software and control their businesses. The IBM PC equipped with the VISICALC program could do just that. The acceptance was spectacular. The IBM machines and their clones were on their way. Good business software also proliferated notably Lotus 1-2-3 and Symphony.

The 8086-8088 processors have 40 pins. Intel then came out with a 68-pin pair of processors, the 80186 and the 80188, called the "computers on a chip". Each chip was

Table 6-2. The Evolutionary Stages of the 808 MPU Family.

| Dates | Processor | Data Bits | Address Bits | Physical Memory | Operating Modes |
|---|---|---|---|---|---|
| 1970-1979 | 8080 | 8 | 16 | 64 K Bytes | 8-Bit Operation |
| 1978-Today | 8086 | 8-16 | 20 | 1 Mega-Byte | 16-Bit Operation |
| 1979-Today | 8088 | 8-16 | 20 | 1 Mega-Byte | 16-Bit Operation |
| 1983-1985 | 80186-80188 | 8-16 | 20 | 1 Mega-Byte | 16-Bit Operation |
| 1983-Today | 80286 | 8-16 | 24 | 16 Mega-Bytes | Real Mode (16-Bit, Same as 8086) |
| | | | | (Virtual Memory 1 Giga-Byte) | Protected Mode 16-Bit |
| 1986-Today | 80386 | 8-16-32 | 32 | 4 Giga-Bytes (Billions) | Real Mode (16-Bit, Same As 8086) |
| March 17, 1989 | 80486 Introduced | | | (Virtual Memory 64 Tera-Bytes) (Trillions) | Protected Mode (16-Bit, Same as 80286) Protected Mode, 32-Bit |
| | | | | | Virtual 8086 Mode (Has Protection) |

actually only an upgrade of the 8086-8088 chips. It had the same instruction set plus 10 more instructions. Tandy used it in their Model 2000. This chip had a short existence during 1983 and 1984.

During this same time period, Intel introduced the 80286. This was not just an upgrade. It was a new processor that was upwardly compatible with the 8086-8088. It contained 130,000 transistors. It acts as if it is two separate processors. It operates in two different modes.

First of all there is the real-address mode. In real-address mode it acts exactly like an 8086 or an 8088. This allows it to run all the software that has been produced for those earlier processors. This provides the compatibility.

In addition, the 80286 has what is called a protected virtual-address mode. The protected mode is the native mode of the 80286. It is still only a 16-bit processor but it can do more than one job at a time, called multi-tasking, and it can address gigantic amounts of physical memory. This processor is the basis for the so called AT bus. Chapter 17 is devoted to the computers that use the 80286.

After the 80286, in 1987 came the 80386. This is the next step. The 80386 is a 32-bit processor. However, it is upwardly compatible to the 80286 and the 8086. It contains approximately 275,000 transistors. It has several different modes. One of the modes, the real-address mode is like the real-address mode of the 80286. It runs 8086 programs.

The 80386 also has a protected mode. This mode has two sections. First of all it makes the 80386 act like a 16-bit 80286. That way the 80386 can run the 80286 software. The second section of the protected mode is a 32-bit operation. It is unique to the 80386. It requires entirely new software of which there is very little around. As time goes by there will be more available 32-bit software. At this writing though, there is practically none.

Finally the 80386 has an 8086 Virtual mode. This is a mode like the real-address mode for the 8086 but is installed in the protected mode area. This permits the 80386 to run 8086 programs in the protected mode. This is a valuable feature to the programmer.

Table 6-2 gives a description of the compatibility relationship of the 8086-8088, 80286, and 80386. There will be more information on the 8086 in Chapters 13 and 14. Chapter 17 covers the 80286 and Chapter 18 the 80386. Meanwhile, let's examine what microprocessors are all about. We'll begin with typical 8-bit processors.

## INSIDE A PROCESSOR

Figure 6-3 is a block diagram of a typical 8-bit processor along the lines of a 6502. You can see the 16 address lines leaving the program counter on the left and the eight data lines connected to the instruction register and data bus buffer on the bottom. On the right is the large instruction decoder that has a number of control lines connected at its top and right side.

In the center is the accumulator, the index registers, the stack point register, a data latch, the program counter high, and the program counter low. Below the instruction decoder is the flag register. In the center of that internal register group is the Arithmetic Logic Unit, the ALU. Most of these registers are receiving single bit inputs from the instruction decoder. Note the important read/write line that goes to the data bus buffer, and to the outside of the processor.

These are the registers that perform the computing. In the center of things is the ALU. It does the main data manipulating in the processor. The rest of the registers are for support. Mostly they perform traffic duty on the data. Let's start the investigation of these internal registers with the ALU.

### Arithmetic Logic Unit

As the name implies, this register performs all the arithmetic and logic manipulation of the data. It performs its job by means of groups of registers, made up of flip-flops and a number of logic gates attached to the flip-flops. All the circuitry is, of course, smaller than the eye can see. There is no way to physically gain access to any of the circuits. When the ALU itself fails, the MPU has to be replaced.

The ALU can typically do only a few jobs. There are about 13 operations that boil down into ten jobs. To understand the jobs, think of the ALU in an 8-bit MPU as a group of 8-bit registers and some coupling logic gates. Into the electronics, there are two 8-bit data entrances and one data exit. The two inputs are sent to a pair of registers, where they are manipulated arithmetically or logically into one 8-bit result. Call one input A, and

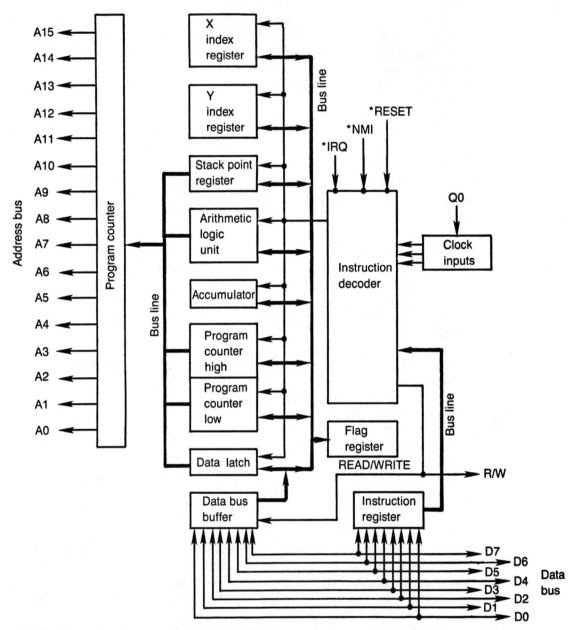

Fig. 6-3. The typical 8-bit MPU has 16 address lines, eight data lines and a number of various control lines. The workhorse of the MPU is the Arithmetic Logic Unit. The instructions enter the Instruction Register while the data passes in and out of the Data Bus Buffer.

the other input B as in Fig. 6-4. What are these miracle jobs that are causing such a change in the way the world is run?

In the 8-bit computer, the two input registers of the ALU can be thought of as eight flip-flops each, with coupling circuits between adjoining bit holders and coupling circuits between the two registers. Especially important are coupling circuits between corresponding bits of the two registers. For instance, there is a coupling circuit between bit D7 of register A and D7 of register B. These coupling circuits allow the individual bits in each of the registers to be arithmetically and logically manipulated with each other. This will be explained next.

The first obvious job the ALU can do as seen in Fig. 6-5, is add register A to register B. The number contained in an 8-bit register is, of course, in binary bits. The bits can be converted, with pencil and paper, into two hex integers or a decimal number, but in the register, the highs and lows can only be construed as binary 1s and 0s.

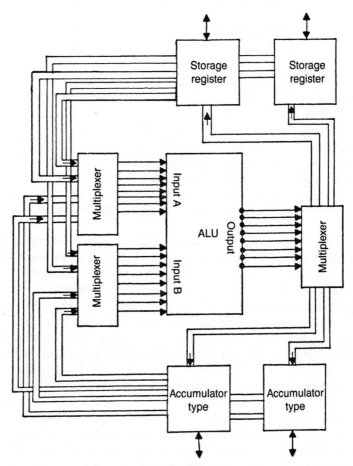

Fig. 6-4. The ALU is the centerpiece of a group of registers. These support registers send two 8-bit inputs to the ALU's input registers, A and B. The ALU then operates on the two inputs and produces one 8-bit output result.

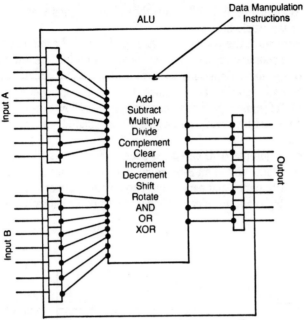

ALU

Data Manipulation
Instructions

Input A

Input B

Add
Subtract
Multiply
Divide
Complement
Clear
Increment
Decrement
Shift
Rotate
AND
OR
XOR

Output

Fig. 6-5. The core of the MPU is the ALU, arithmetic logic unit. It can perform about thirteen special jobs on computer data.

The contents of input A are added to the bits of input B bit by bit. D0 of A is added to D0 of B. D1 of A is added to D1 of B. Each bit of A is added to its matching bit in B. The addition is accomplished smoothly. If there are any arithmetical carries during the adding, they are performed in a normal arithmetic fashion. There is nothing strange about the addition, except that it is in binary and is done with blinding speed in electronic circuits.

The second job the ALU can do is subtract. While there are some computers that actually perform electronic subtraction, the extra circuits needed are wasteful. The computer can do the subtraction with 2's complement and not require any special circuits as Fig. 6-6 shows. The computer can do the 2's complement trick without a thought and at no hardship. The subtraction takes place in the two input registers as they add the contents of their registers together and then add an additional high pulse to the total.

The other two functions, multiplication and division, are also performed in the two registers by some tricky addition. For some of the less complex multiplying and dividing, the registers simply do continuous adding or subtracting. For example, if you want to multiply 4 x 3, the register adds 3 + 3 + 3 + 3.

If a lot of complex multiplying or dividing is required, then the user installs a small program that does the job. The software is called and does its multiplying or dividing job whenever it is necessary. The software still only uses the ability of the register to add to do all the math work. There is a lot of repetition, but the computer doesn't mind at all.

The next job the ALU can do is complement either or both A and B. This means the computer can change any or all of the bits to its complement. If there is a high being

148

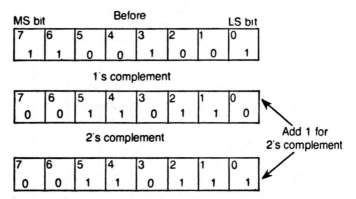

Fig. 6-6. The 1's complement of an 8-bit register is performed by changing all 0s to 1s and 1s to 0s. To obtain the 2's complement, simply add 1 to the 1's complement.

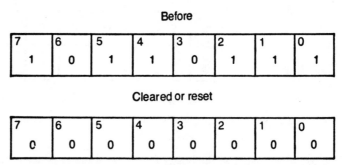

Fig. 6-7. When a register is cleared or reset, all 1s are changed to 0s.

stored in a bit, it can be changed to a low. Should a 0 be installed it can be changed to a 1 (Fig. 6-6).

An example of the complement tactic occurs during a 2's complement. The register being subtracted has all of its 1s changed to 0s and its 0s changed to 1s. That is called 1's complement. Then a 1 is added to the LSB and that result is called the 2's complement.

Next, the ALU can clear any or all of the bits of input registers (Fig. 6-7). To *clear* means to cause a bit to become a 0, no matter what binary number was in the bit. If there was a 1 and the bit gets cleared, the 1 is changed to a 0. Should a 0 be in the bit and it gets cleared, then the bit remains a 0.

The registers are able to do a job called *incrementing* and *decrementing*. This means the register can increase or decrease the binary number in the register. It can change the number by one or two or three or what have you.

The most common use requires a steady incrementing or decrementing by one. On occasion, there is a need to increment or decrement by two or three. Incrementing and decrementing is very useful during counting. For instance, a register could be used to keep track of a process. It keeps incrementing after every step, and a continuous count of how many steps were made is at hand (Fig. 6-8).

The incrementing and decrementing facility is valuable in the ALU but it has even greater use in some of the other registers in the MPU. Figure 6-8 shows incrementing the program counter.

Program counter incrementing by 1

First address

MSB ... LSB

| | 15 | 14 | 13 | 12 | 11 | 10 | 9 | 8 | 7 | 6 | 5 | 4 | 3 | 2 | 1 | 0 |
|---|---|---|---|---|---|---|---|---|---|---|---|---|---|---|---|---|
| | 0 | 0 | 0 | 0 | 0 | 0 | 0 | 0 | 0 | 0 | 0 | 0 | 0 | 0 | 0 | 0 |
| 2nd | 0 | 0 | 0 | 0 | 0 | 0 | 0 | 0 | 0 | 0 | 0 | 0 | 0 | 0 | 0 | 1 |
| 3rd | 0 | 0 | 0 | 0 | 0 | 0 | 0 | 0 | 0 | 0 | 0 | 0 | 0 | 0 | 1 | 0 |
| 4th | 0 | 0 | 0 | 0 | 0 | 0 | 0 | 0 | 0 | 0 | 0 | 0 | 0 | 0 | 1 | 1 |
| 5th | 0 | 0 | 0 | 0 | 0 | 0 | 0 | 0 | 0 | 0 | 0 | 0 | 0 | 1 | 0 | 0 |
| 6th | 0 | 0 | 0 | 0 | 0 | 0 | 0 | 0 | 0 | 0 | 0 | 0 | 0 | 1 | 0 | 1 |
| 7th | 0 | 0 | 0 | 0 | 0 | 0 | 0 | 0 | 0 | 0 | 0 | 0 | 0 | 1 | 1 | 0 |
| 8th | 0 | 0 | 0 | 0 | 0 | 0 | 0 | 0 | 0 | 0 | 0 | 0 | 0 | 1 | 1 | 1 |

Next addresses

Fig. 6-8. Registers can be incremented automatically and can keep track of steps in a process.

The ALU is also able to shift all the binary numbers, at once, either to the left or to the right (Fig. 6-9A). When all the numbers are shifted to the left their total value is doubled. If all the numbers are shifted to the right the total value of the register is divided by 2. This is a valuable ability in a math-logic device like an ALU.

When the numbers are shifted to the left, the MSB is pushed out of the register and the LSB is replaced with a 0. Should the numbers be shifted right, the LSB leaves the register, but the MSB is not affected. A programmer must take this effect into account when he writes his algorithm. As a technician, this fact is noteworthy but not of too much concern.

There is another ability the ALU registers do that is called *rotating*. This is like shifting, except you do not lose the end number that gets pushed out of the register. Instead, the end number is rotated out and installed into another register called the *condition code*.

For example, if a register executes a rotate right, the MSB becomes empty and the LSB is pushed out of the register. With the rotate ability, the LSB that was deposed is placed into the carry bit of the condition code register. The bit it replaced goes into the empty MSB position. In the same manner, during a rotate left, the MSB that is evicted is rotated into the carry bit and the carry bit's contents is rotated into the empty LSB (Fig. 6-9B).

Besides its knack for doing arithmetic, the ALU has additional computing power because it can also perform logic. Usually the ALU only needs to be able to AND, OR, and XOR. All the other logic functions can be derived from these basic three.

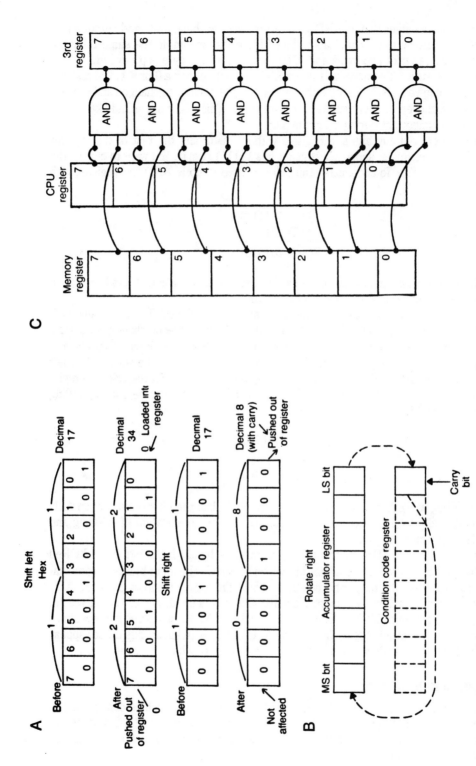

Fig. 6-9. A) Shift left doubles the value of the binary number. Shift right divides the binary in half. B) Rotate instructions use the C flag as a ninth bit for the accumulator register. C) ANDing and ORing registers is a logic technique that permits you to change individual register bits without disturbing the rest of the bits.

It was shown earlier that an AND gate can receive two binary bits and output a predictable bit according to its truth table. The ALU registers can do the same thing but more so. They can take two bytes and AND them, so a third byte is produced.

The AND truth table shows that if you AND a 0 with either a 0 or a 1, the result is always a 0. When you AND a 1 with either a 0 or a 1, the result is unchanged and remains a 0 or a 1, whichever number was ANDed with the 1. This might not sound like a great event, but it is important during programming.

You can zero out any bits in a register without disturbing the rest of the register (Fig. 6-9C). For example, suppose a register has 11111111 in it. You want to change the register to 10101010. To accomplish this, all you have to do is AND the register with 10101010.

$$11111111$$
$$\underline{AND\ 10101010}$$
$$Result\ 10101010$$

The actual ANDing took place bit by bit, but the final result was that bits 6, 4, 2, and 0 were masked out. This is an important computing technique.

In the same manner, the two ALU input registers can be ORed. The truth table indicates that if a bit holding a 0 is ORed with a 1 or 0 the result will be no change in the logic state of the bit. When a bit holding a 1 is ORed with a 1 or 0, the result will always be a 1.

Again this might not appear important, but bits of a register can be set to a 1 or left alone. This is a valuable ability. For example, suppose you want to set the LSB of a register with 10101010 to 1 and not disturb the rest of the bits. This can be done by ORing the register with 00000001.

$$10101010$$
$$\underline{OR\ 00000001}$$
$$Result\ 10101011$$

The ORing is another way the computer can manipulate the bit structure of an ALU register, as well as other sections of the computer. The combination of ANDing and ORing is very important.

The ALU can also XOR the two input registers, bit by bit. If the bits being XORed are both 0 or both 1 then the resultant bit will be 0. Should the input bits be a combination of 1 and 0, then the output bit will be 1. This third logical function gives the ALU additional flexibility. When even more maneuverability is needed, any of the bit results could be passed through NOT gates to produce NAND, NOR, or XNOR final results.

While at first glance these tricks that the ALU can do with binary bits do not appear earthshaking, in reality they are. They are the very core of what a computer is.

## ACCESSIBLE REGISTERS

The ALU is the very core of the MPU and will process any machine data applied to its input. Getting the data into the ALU from the computer memory and I/O devices and then back out into storage is what the rest of the MPU has to do. Let's examine the rest of the MPU register by register.

## Accumulator

In an 8-bit computer, the accumulator has eight bit holders in its register. In 16-bit or 32-bit computers, accumulators have 16-bit or 32-bit holders. An accumulator has been called a scratch pad because it is used as a temporary holding register for the input to the ALU and the output from the ALU. The MPU has a lot of instructions that concern themselves with the accumulator. The MPU could respond to an instruction such as "load the accumulator with the contents of hex address A0D3." The MPU would immediately address A0D3, the location would then open up, and a copy of its contents would travel the data bus to the MPU and be installed into a temporary holder, the accumulator. The accumulator is attached to the data pins D7-D0.

The accumulator is actually a group of registers and gates that surround the ALU (Fig. 6-10A). For example, an accumulator could be based around seven registers, consisting of three multiplexers, two storage and two actual accumulators. In the 8-bit computer, all these registers would be 8 bits and conduct their business with parallel inputs and outputs.

The three multiplexers are the closest to the ALU, and take up positions at the two inputs and the single output. They enter the bytes to be processed and remove the bytes that are completed.

The other four registers feed and remove the bytes to and from the multiplexers. Two are only storage, but two are actual accumulators. The storage registers can't do much except hold the logic states until the time arrives when the busy ALU can process them, or hold the highs and lows after the ALU did its work.

The accumulator is different. It is given the electronic circuitry that enables it to add. This extra feature makes it stand out in the ALU circuit section. When you work in this circuit area, it is all referred to as the accumulator. The accumulator is accessible for hardware testing at the data pins on the chip package. It is accessible for software work with a large number of instructions from the MPU Instruction Set.

## Instruction Register

The Instruction register is connected in parallel with the accumulator. As the MPU is addressing memory location after memory location during the running of a program, the bytes that travel the data bus enter the instruction register as in Fig. 6-3. The bytes could be binary instructions or binary data. The IR can decode the difference. If the byte received by the IR is a piece of data, the IR would let the data bus buffer store it. Should the byte be an instruction the IR decodes it.

The decoder in the IR is built to respond to the various arrangements of bits in an instruction byte. For example, the IR could receive an instruction listed in the Instruction Set as hex 86 from the data bus. The instruction stands for "load the accumulator with the bits in the next byte."

The byte the IR receives is 1000 0110, which in hex is 86. The IR responds to the bit arrangement. It instructs the accumulator to load up with the next byte, whenever it may be. The accumulator reacts by taking the next byte and storing it in its bit holders. The program continues (Fig. 6-10B).

The hex 86 or binary 1000 0110, whatever you want to call it, is a member of the Instruction Set the IR can respond to. The bytes are composed of eight bits. In eight

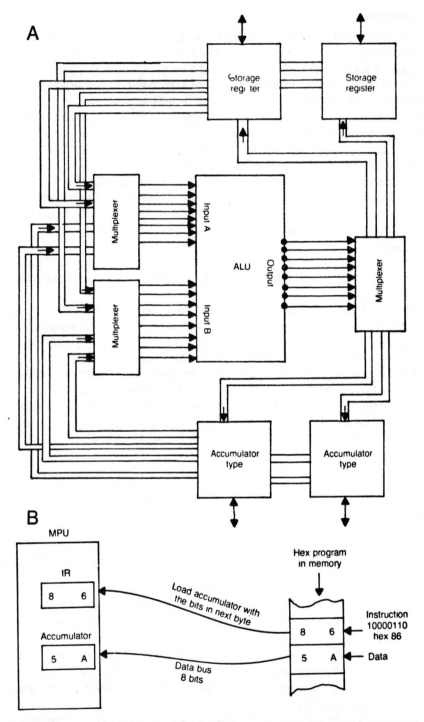

Fig. 6-10. A) The accumulator register is actually a group of registers that include the ALU. B) After the instruction register decodes the 8 6 instruction, it sends the next program byte 5 A to the accumulator.

bits, there are 256 individual arrangements of 1s and 0s. This means 256 individual instructions could be formed in the eight-bit set.

Typically, though, there are about 72 instructions created to do the computing job. There are a lot of the same jobs that are done on different registers. Each one gets its own codes. There are only about 24 general actual instructions if you don't count the instruction repetition for the different registers. About half of the 24 general instructions are to direct the ALU in the data manipulation we've already discussed.

The other 12 general instructions are in two groups. One group moves data. The movement is between the MPU and the memory-I/O circuits. The second small group has to do with addressing in general and another register called the program counter, which is discussed shortly. It would be useful to memorize the two dozen general jobs the Instruction Set performs (Table 6-3). Even though their usage might be fuzzy in your mind at this time, the jobs will become clearer as you go.

## Program Counter

The Program Counter in an 8-bit computer is a register with 16 bits, unlike the accumulator and IR that deals with the data bus lines and have eight bits (Fig. 6-11). The PC is connected to the 16 lines of the address bus A15 through A0. The address bus is a one-way bus, not two ways like the data bus. The addressing goes from the MPU out to the memory-I/O circuits. There is no return line from the memory back to the MPU.

It was mentioned earlier that the computer is built to access the memory map, starting at the first hex address 0000. Then it automatically continues to address each location in sequence. The program counter is the device that performs this automatic addressing chore. The program counter is driven by the clock. Every time the clock forms a full pulse, the program counter increments by one, unless instructed otherwise. There are six general instructions in the Set that can instruct it otherwise. These are covered later.

Since there are 16 bits in the PC, there are a possible 65,536 addresses the PC is able to dial up. The size of the memory map is determined by the number of bits in the PC.

Each additional bit in the PC doubles the number of locations the PC is able to address. If the PC has 17 bits, there are 131,072 possible bit arrangements. The MPU with a 17-bit PC is able to address all those locations. The number keeps doubling until

**Table 6-3. Generalized Instruction Set.**

| Addressing | Data Moving | Data Processing |
|------------|-------------|-----------------|
| Branch | Load | Increment |
| Jump | Store | Decrement |
| Call | Move | Shift |
| Return | I/O | Rotate |
| Skip | Exchange | Complement |
| Halt | | Clear |
| | | AND, OR, XOR |
| | | $+, -, \bullet, /$ |

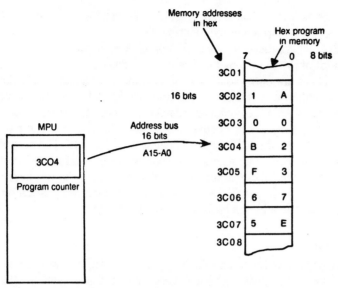

Fig. 6-11. The 16-bit program counter is connected to the 16-bit address bus. The program counter addresses 3 C 0 4.

gigantic amounts of memory can be addressed. Here are the numbers up to a 24-bit program counter.

| PC Bits | Possible Addresses |
|---|---|
| 18 | 262,144 |
| 19 | 524,288 |
| 20 | 1,048,576 |
| 21 | 2,097,152 |
| 22 | 4,194,304 |
| 23 | 8,388,608 |
| 24 | 16,777,216 |

These numbers are important. While the 8-bit computer has a 16-bit PC able to address 64 K, the 16-bit and 32-bit computers have larger PCs. For instance, an MPU could have a PC with 24 bits. A 32-bit computer could have 32 bits in its PC. That would enable it to address 4,294,967,296 individual locations; 4 G or 4 gigabytes.

The PC conducts its business, which is exclusively addressing, in the following manner. In a 16-bit PC, there are 65,536 locations the PC can address. The program that is to be run could be stored at the beginning of the addresses, starting at the binary number 0000 0000 0000 0000. Each 8-bit step of the program is placed in sequence into the memory. Each memory location has a 16-bit address (Fig. 6-12).

Incidentally, that last fact is one of the major difficulties that people have in understanding the way a computer operates. Let's pause here and review this.

These memory cells are a row of eight flip-flops that store eight bits. The bits enter and leave the cells through the 8-bit data bus.

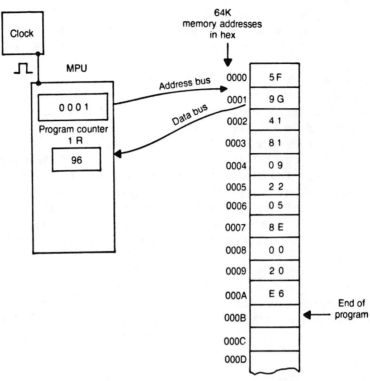

**Fig. 6-12. The program counter could start a program running with an output of the hex address 0000.**

Each cell has an address. Each address is 16 bits long. The cells have their data buses opened when they are addressed. Otherwise the data bus remains closed and the data is kept in storage.

Getting back to the program data that is placed in sequence in the memory, let's see what the PC does to an 11-step program installed in the first 11 addresses of the memory map.

The PC, when the computer is turned on, is initialized to its binary starting address 0000 0000 0000 0000, or hex 0000, like a car trip mile indicator is initialized to 0000 at the start of a journey. As soon as the program is begun, the PC sends out 16 low pulses over the address bus (Fig. 6-12).

There is only one location out of the 64 K that will respond to the 16 low pulse pattern on the address bus. That is the first location 0000 0000 0000 0000, hex 0000. We could call the location LLLLLLLLLLLLLLLL, if we wanted to, but we'll stay with the equivalent binary numbers.

The 16 low pulses activate the first address. The data lines open up and a copy of the program data that is in the location is placed on the data bus. The data bus is attached to the instruction register and the IR receives the program bits.

While the data is transmitting the program step, a pulse from the clock enters the PC and causes it to increment by one. As soon as the MPU executes the program step, the PC outputs 15 low pulses and one high onto the address bus. That turns off the first address and activates the second address 0000 0000 0000 0001, hex 0001.

The second address then outputs a copy of its contents onto the data bus. These eight data bits pulse their way to the IR and the rest of the MPU. At the same time, the clock increments the PC once again. As soon as the MPU completes that second step, the PC outputs the next address 0000 0000 0000 0010, hex 0002. This turns off the second address and activates the third address.

The PC continues its sequential addressing continually until it completes running the program. Then, when it reaches an empty location and there is no longer any program transmission to the MPU, the PC stops.

This is the PC's automatic mode. At the start, all the bits in the PC are initialized to 0s. Then as the program is run to the beat of the clock, the PC addresses location after location, in sequence. At each addressing the location opens up and outputs a copy of its contents. The data gets processed and the program gets run. All this is well and good if there is no need to suddenly stop the sequencing and branch off to an entirely different memory location that's not in the sequence. Then the entire automatic process must be switched to be a carefully-programmed new address that's out of numerical order.

The change is made with the aid of some other MPU registers. These other registers force the PC to stop outputting its sequential addresses. They cause a new calculated address to be placed on the address bus. The address bus doesn't care if the location is in sequence or not. It activates the address placed on its 16 lines.

It was mentioned earlier that there were six general instructions in the Set that deal with changes of address (Fig. 6-13). As the program is being run in a sequential manner,

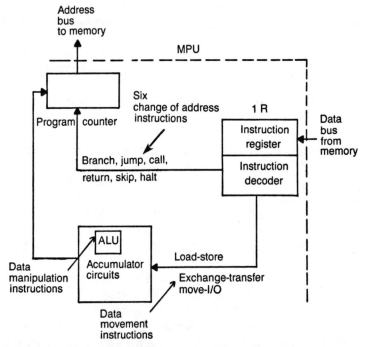

Fig. 6-13. The six change of address instructions are called Branch, Jump, Call, Return, Skip, and Halt. They go straight to the PC circuits from the IR.

158

if one of these instructions should be placed on the data bus and arrive at the IR, the following situation occurs.

Normally, when instructions arrive at the IR and they deal with the data processing and not addressing, the IR sends them to the accumulator registers. When some of the six addressing instructions arrive at the IR, they could be sent directly to the PC register circuits. The rest of the MPU is bypassed. The instruction can then do its addressing chore without wasting movement through circuits it is not going to affect.

The six general addressing instructions should be memorized. They are instructions called Branch, Jump, Call, Return, Skip, and Halt. They all affect the addresses the PC places in the address bus.

The Branch and Jump instructions are somewhat alike. (In some computers, they're exactly alike.) In general, the Branch instruction usually causes a number to be added or subtracted from the number that is on the PC. This changes the total address number and the PC places this new address on the bus. The change of location gets addressed. This change of address is normally caused by some flags that get set in another register nearby called the CCR. This will be discussed next.

The Jump instruction, rather than being caused by a thrown flag, is usually just the instruction with a new address trailing the instruction. When the IR receives the Jump instruction bits, it simply flashes the new address directly to the PC. The PC changes its number to the new address and the address bus takes it from there.

The Call and Return instructions have to do with using subroutines. A subroutine is a separate little program installed way off in the memory somewhere that can do a special job. For instance, suppose your ALU can't divide. To solve that shortcoming you write a little division program and install it in the backwoods of memory somewhere (Fig. 6-14).

When you write a program, every time you want to divide a number, you have some program lines that Call the subroutine, do the division and then return from the subroutine back to the main program. The Call instruction changes the PC to the subroutine address. The normal sequential incrementing of the PC continues, but now at the new address, and runs off the subroutine, dividing your number.

Once the subroutine finishes its division it comes to its last instruction: a Return instruction. This changes the PC address back into the main program location. The program then continues where it left off before it had to do the division.

The Skip instruction is something like a Jump, although it only skips a small number of addresses. Skip isn't used much anymore, but you might encounter it on occasion.

The Halt instruction is just that. It stops the program whatever the reason. Halt is often used as a form of stop in the middle of programs, unlike End that is mostly found at the very end of programs.

## Condition Code Register

In an 8-bit MPU, there is an 8-bit Condition Code Register. In a 16-bit computer, the CCR is 16 bits. The CCR is usually the same size as the data bus, although it does not have any direct connection to the data bus. It is connected through a two-way bus to the accumulator-ALU complex and a one-way bus to the PC (Fig. 6-15).

The CCR keeps up a steady two-way communication with the accumulator. The CCR samples the instructions that are being executed. Each of the CCR bits are individ-

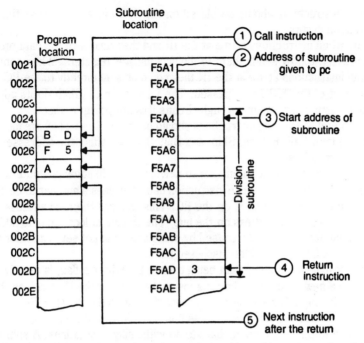

Fig. 6-14. The Call and Return instructions change the working address to a subroutine and then changes the address back to the main program.

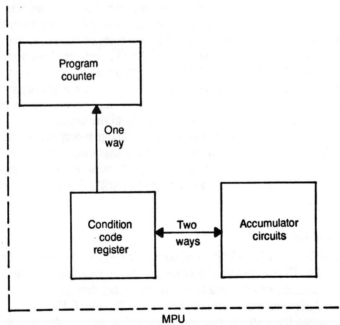

Fig. 6-15. The CCR is wired between the accumulator circuits and the program counter.

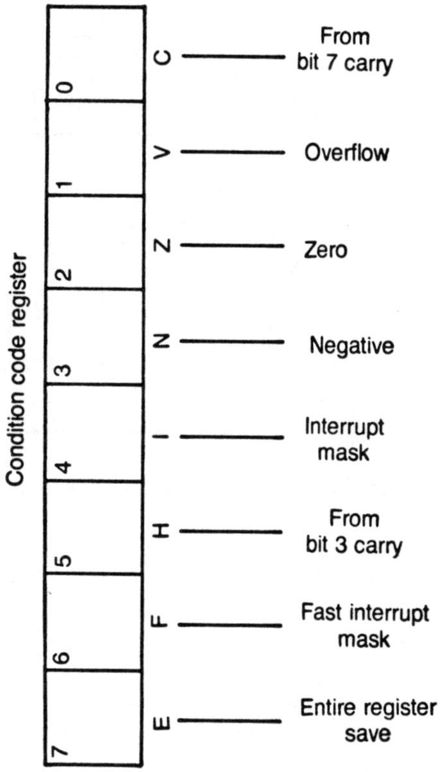

Fig. 6-16. The CCR contains individual bits called flags. The flag settings and resettings are a vital part of computing.

Condition code register

C ——— From bit 7 carry

V ——— Overflow

N ——— Zero

Z ——— Negative

— ——— Interrupt mask

H ——— From bit 3 carry

F ——— Fast interrupt mask

E ——— Entire register save

ual. They are called *flags*. Most of the instructions in the Set need the help of a flag or two (Fig. 6-16).

The flags can be set or cleared. When a flag gets set, it becomes a 1. If it is cleared or reset, it is 0. Each flag does its own type of job. Some of the jobs consist of changing the address number in the program counter.

For example, a common flag is the zero, named Z. It works in this way. Suppose the programmer is doing a countdown in the accumulator. He wants to bring the program to a halt when the number in the accumulator becomes 00000000.

The Z flag is built to get set whenever the accumulator reaches the value of 00000000 (Fig. 6-17). A program line is inserted into memory that halts the program when the Z flag is set. The Z flag is attached to the PC. As the end arrives, the accumulator becomes 00000000, the Z flag gets set to 1 and the PC is halted.

Another common flag is called N (negative). The N flag gets set whenever the accumulator becomes a negative number (Fig. 6-18). The accumulator is said to have a negative number when its MSB is a 1. Therefore, whenever the accumulator has a 1 in its MSB the N flag gets set. This signals the program counter and the ALU.They act to respond to the flag according to the dictates of the program.

The next common flag is the C (carry). This flag acts as an additional bit for the accumulator. In some computations the number being manipulated might be too large for the number of bits in the accumulator to hold it. The C flag will accept the extra bit as a

161

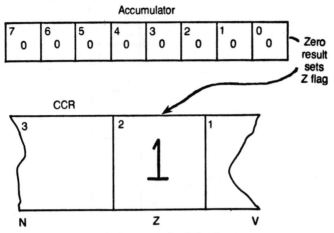

Fig. 6-17. When the accumulator turns into all 0s, the Z flag is set.

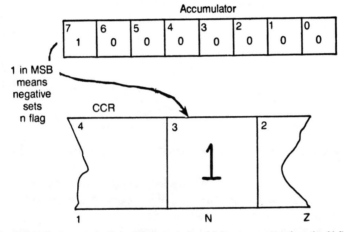

Fig. 6-18. If the MS bit in the accumulator becomes a 1, which means negative, the N flag is set.

carry (Fig. 6-19). The carry sets the flag. The flag is normally clear until it receives a carry.

Then there is the H flag (half-carry). It is often necessary to spot a carry during addition, from bit 3 to bit 4 in the accumulator (Fig. 6-20). The H flag gets set whenever there is a carry from bit 3 to bit 4. This is the dividing point between two hex or two BCD nybbles. Bits 7, 6, 5, and 4 represent the MS nybble in the accumulator. Bits 3, 2, 1, and 0 are the LS accumulator nybble. When a carry between the MSN and the LSN takes place it sets the H flag. The H flag normally remains clear until a half-carry happens.

Another flag is the V (overflow). It was mentioned that the MSB in the accumulator is often used to designate the sign of the number, either + or −. Sometimes during computation the MSB receives an overflow from bit 6 and the result is that the sign is

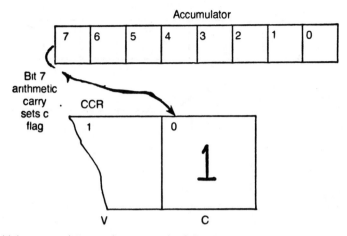

Fig. 6-19. Should the accumulator require a carry, the C flag is set.

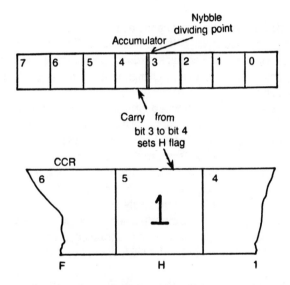

Fig. 6-20. When a carry takes place between bit 3 and bit 4 of the accumulator, the half carry flag H is set.

accidentally changed (Fig. 6-21). When this occurs, some corrective action must be taken by the programmer. The V flag gets set when this happens, and signals the fact that the sign was changed and could be trouble.

There are usually some flags that have an I (interrupt). The interrupt flags are what can be called *masks*. As interrupt is a method of stopping the running of a program.

If the interrupt flag is clear, then the interrupt can break into the program when it is necessary and cause the computer to go into the interrupt routine. However, when the interrupt flag is set, the interrupt is masked. If the interrupt occurs, the computer ignores it and continues running the program.

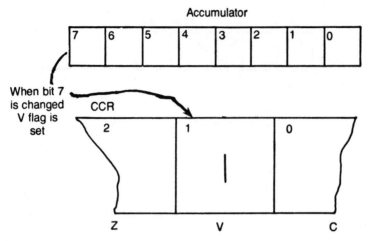

Fig. 6-21. When the MS bit of the accumulator becomes set due to an overflow from bit 6, the overflow flag V is set.

The Branch instructions in the Set depend heavily on the status of the CCR bits. For instance, the instruction could specify "if the Z flag is set branch forward to the following address. Or if the N flag is set branch backwards to the following address." The result of the flag and the instruction then causes a change in the address on the program counter and the Branch is made.

The CCR and its various bits are wired internally between the accumulator and the program counter. The instructions as they are executed set and reset the bits continually. The programmer has to be adept at knowing what instructions set and clear what flags. Then, when a flag is thrown, the programmer must know how the program is affected. Control over the flags is a vital part of his programming techniques. Most of the instructions affect one or more flags during the program run. The CCR register, if it was composed of lights, would be flashing continually.

As a technician, you need some comprehension of the part the CCR plays. It is activated by instruction register inputs and causes program counter change outputs. Since a lot of your tests are inputs and outputs, the CCR should be part of your repertoire.

## Index Register

The Index register is wired in parallel with the program counter. It is used as another method of changing the address from a sequential one to some other. When the Index register is in operation, it is in charge of addressing instead of the PC. It is a 16-bit addressing register just like the PC.

The Index register starts doing the addressing when an instruction arrives at the MPU specifying that the Index register should put addresses on the address bus. While the Index register is in action, the PC stands idle. Both of them are not permitted to operate at the same time; if they did, a conflict would occur.

The Index register is used by programmers. Indexing is an old addressing technique that is essential for certain types of programs. There will be more about the Index register and the techniques the programmer uses in the next chapter.

In the 8-bit computer, 16-bit Index registers are used. The 16-bit computer has the index type registers containing 32 bits. The bits are connected to the same address pins the program counter uses. The two types of address registers take turns using the pins. When you are reading logic states at the pins, you could be reading the Index register output or the program counter.

## Stack Pointer

There is another register, also in parallel with the program counter and the Index register. It also has 16 bits in an 8-bit computer and 32 bits in the 16-bit types. It is called the *stack pointer*.

This is a confusing name. What is the stack? Let's explore that first. First of all, the stack is a designated position in memory that can store a number of bytes of data. For example, if you were programming a computer with a 6800 MPU, you would assign seven byte locations as the stack. Why seven?

There are nine eight-bit programming register segments in the 6800. The programming registers are shown in Fig. 6-22. (Note the instruction register and the ALU are not shown. They are of great interest to the technician but not to the programmer, and this is a programmer's view of the MPU. The technician's view was shown in Fig. 6-3).

The registers here are shown with the emphasis on bits and not on circuit signal flow and voltages. There are eight bits each in the following nine register segments (Fig. 6-22).

Accumulator A
Accumulator B
Index High
Index Low

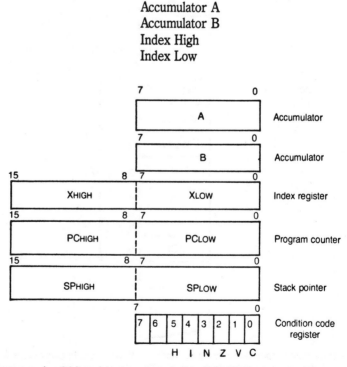

Fig. 6-22. There are nine 8-bit register segments in this 6800 MPU.

PC High
PC Low
Stack Pointer High
Stack Pointer Low
Condition Code Register

The stack is a storage place for the contents of the MPU registers. During a program run, an interrupt could happen or a jump to a subroutine might have to be made. Either way, the MPU is forced to stop operating and either service the interrupt or start running the subroutine program. In order to do so, the registers in the MPU must be used. However there are a lot of logic states already in the registers. What about them? Should they be destroyed because of the interruption? Of course not! These 1s and 0s are stored in the designated stack bytes.

There were seven bytes (0 to 6) reserved in RAM as stack storage for this 6800 MPU (Fig. 6-23). As the interrupt occurs, the MPU stacks up the register contents. It stores the PC Low and PC High in bytes 0 and 1. The Index Low and Index High are put in bytes 2 and 3. The Accumulator A and Accumulator B contents are placed in bytes 4 and 5. The contents of the CCR are installed in byte 6 of the stack memory area. What

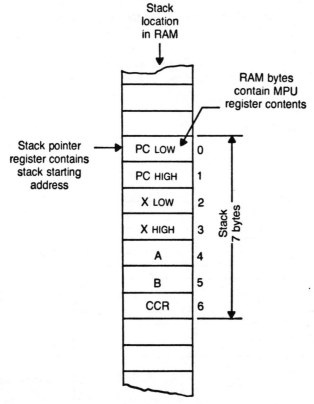

Fig. 6-23. The stack pointer register contains the address of the stack. In stack bytes of memory the MPU register contents can be stored during program interruptions.

about the contents of the Stack Pointer Low and High? There is no place in the stack for them.

That's because they are the Pointers. The Stack Pointer register in the MPU contains the starting address of the stack. If the stack was filled and the address was not readily available, after the interrupt or subroutine was serviced, how would the stack data be located? The stack pointer register does nothing but point to the starting address of the stack. That's its job.

During testing, the only time the stack pointer will be outputting an address on the bus is the quick instant that it points to the start address of the stack.

## TESTING THE MPU

The programmers' diagram (Fig. 6-22) with its emphasis on bit sizes of registers is of limited use to the technician. The block diagram (Fig. 6-3) has a lot more information and can indicate trouble areas of the MPU. The manufacturer's layout of the actual pins (Fig. 6-24) is quite valuable and will help out in many instances, but it might be misleading. Often, the original design arrangement the chip maker intended is radically changed by a clever design engineer during manufacturing resulting in a confusing operation the technician can have difficulty with.

The best piece of service information is the computer's schematic diagram (Fig. 6-25) and service notes. Then the only difficulty during testing is relating the schematic symbols to the actual hardware.

When there is *garbage* on the screen, the MPU is one of the suspects. Garbage includes all sorts of incorrect displays, from no video at all to a crazy patchwork of alphanumerics and graphics that looks like a cartoon character's swear words.

As you look down at the print board, the MPU is usually in a socket. 8-bit MPUs are in 40-pin DIPs, 16-bit MPUs could be in 64-pin DIPs, and a 32-bit MPU in a 132-pin package. Let's check out a 6502 8-bit MPU to see how it is done. There are 40 pins. The pins are numbered on the schematic in the old fashioned decimal manner from 1 through 40. The insides of the chip are numbered computer-style starting with 0. For instance the data lines are still D7 to D0.

As you look at the actual chip (Fig. 6-24), you'll notice a notch or painted dot on one end of the chip. To the left of the dot is pin 1. Then going in a counterclockwise manner, the count proceeds around the chip. On side goes from top to bottom, 1 to 20. The other side starting at the bottom goes from 21 to 40. Pins 1 and 40 are across from each other at the top near the dot, while 20 and 21 are adjacent at the bottom.

On the schematic you saw in Fig. 6-25, there was no such logical numbering. The numbers on the schematic 6502 are drawn so you can follow the signal flow, and are not necessarily in order. The confusion occurs when you read the schematic and find a pin number you want to test. Then you go to the DIP, test probe in hand, and look for that pin. It looks nothing like the schematic. You must relate the schematic information to the DIP and count pins with the paint dot or notch as a reference.

If you remember that the other end of the DIP has pins 20 and 21 you could count from that end too. Count from the end that the pin you are looking for is closest to. Always double-check your pin count before putting the probe onto an energized MPU.

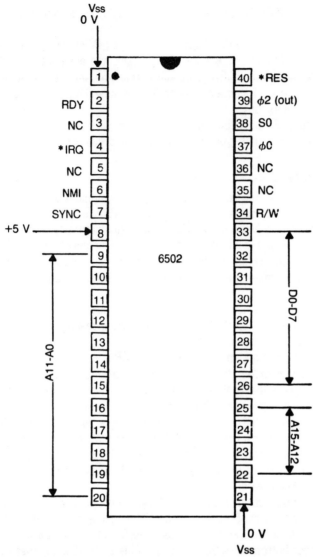

Fig. 6-24. Besides schematic drawings, hardware block diagrams, and software block diagrams, the actual physical pin layout of the MPU provides valuable technical information.

The first test is always power (Fig. 6-26). On the 6502, VCC is applied at pin 8. If you are testing with a VOM the meter should read +5 V. If you are using a logic probe, the HIGH LED light shines. If the +5 V or HIGH is not there, then the power supply is suspect. It may not be getting voltage to pin 8. There is always the possibility that a fault to ground in the chip has happened, and the +5 V is shorted to ground.

The 6502 is an MOS chip. The other end is the source connection. This is VSS on the schematic. There are two VSS connections, hooked together and grounded at pins 1 and 21. They should read 0 V on the VOM or the LOW LED should light on the logic

168

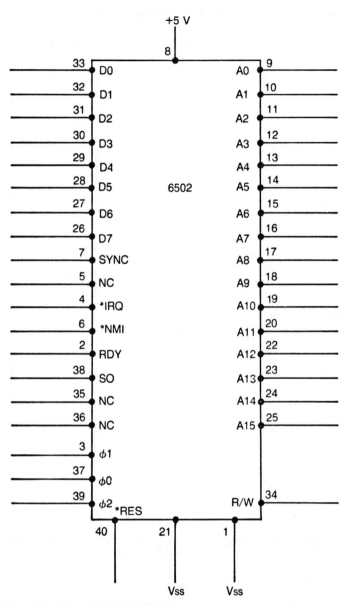

+5 V

8

| 33 | D0 | | A0 | 9 |
| 32 | D1 | | A1 | 10 |
| 31 | D2 | | A2 | 11 |
| 30 | D3 | | A3 | 12 |
| 29 | D4 | | A4 | 13 |
| 28 | D5 | 6502 | A5 | 14 |
| 27 | D6 | | A6 | 15 |
| 26 | D7 | | A7 | 16 |
| 7 | SYNC | | A8 | 17 |
| 5 | NC | | A9 | 18 |
| 4 | *IRQ | | A10 | 19 |
| 6 | *NMI | | A11 | 20 |
| 2 | RDY | | A12 | 22 |
| 38 | SO | | A13 | 23 |
| 35 | NC | | A14 | 24 |
| 36 | NC | | A15 | 25 |
| 3 | $\phi 1$ | | | |
| 37 | $\phi 0$ | | | |
| 39 | $\phi 2$ *RES | | R/W | 34 |

40    21    1

Vss    Vss

Fig. 6-25. A typical microprocessor is the 6502 shown here in a schematic diagram.

probe. If there is any voltage there, then the ground connection has come off and must be reconnected.

Next there are 24 pins that can be tested quickly. They are the eight data pins D7-D0 and the 16 address pins A15-A0. The data pins are 26 through 33. The logic probe shows them all with a lit PULSE LED. The VOM on this 6502 reads a three-state type voltage between 1.2 V and 2.5 V. During the test the data bus was on hold and in a

| Pin Number | | High (1) | Low (0) | Pulse |
|---|---|---|---|---|
| VSS | 1 | | ✓ | |
| RDY | 2 | ✓ | | |
| NC | 3 | | | ✓ |
| •IRQ | 4 | ✓ | | |
| NC | 5 | | | |
| NMI | 6 | ✓ | | |
| SYNC | 7 | | ✓ | ✓ |
| +5 V | 8 | ✓ | | |
| A0 | 9 | | | ✓ |
| A1 | 10 | | | ✓ |
| A2 | 11 | | | ✓ |
| A3 | 12 | | | ✓ |
| A4 | 13 | | | ✓ |
| A5 | 14 | | | ✓ |
| A6 | 15 | | | ✓ |
| A7 | 16 | | | ✓ |
| A8 | 17 | | | ✓ |
| A9 | 18 | | | ✓ |
| A10 | 19 | | | ✓ |
| A11 | 20 | | | ✓ |
| Vss | 21 | | ✓ | |
| A12 | 22 | | | ✓ |
| A13 | 23 | | | ✓ |
| A14 | 24 | | | ✓ |
| A15 | 25 | | | ✓ |
| D7 | 26 | | | ✓ |
| D6 | 27 | | | ✓ |
| D5 | 38 | | | ✓ |
| D4 | 29 | | | ✓ |
| D3 | 30 | | | ✓ |
| D2 | 31 | | | ✓ |
| D1 | 32 | | | ✓ |
| D0 | 33 | | | ✓ |
| R/W | 34 | | | ✓ |
| NC | 35 | | | |
| NC | 36 | | | |
| φ0 | 37 | | | ✓ |
| SO | 38 | ✓ | | |
| φ2 | 39 | | | ✓ |
| •RES | 40 | ✓ | | |

Fig. 6-26. A chart like this makes life easier for the technician during logic probe testing. If you draw one up the first time you test a new chip, you will gradually have a library of test charts for subsequent jobs.

three-state condition. That is what was read. On other MPUs there could be voltage variations, but the logic probe will show PULSE on the data pins if the clock is running.

The 16 address pins are 9 through 25, except for the VSS pin 21. They also show PULSE on all the pins, as the clock keeps sending out some pulses during the time the MPU is idling. After you test a few you'll get the feel of the two buses and know when the MPU is operating correctly with them. The pulses are referred to as *activity*. Another way the pulse is described is "the pins are changing." If they are not changing then the clock pulse is not present at the pin. That is a valid clue. The next trick is to figure out why.

If the clock is running and pulses are missing at any of the data or address pins, then the MPU is a good suspect. The clock is putting pulses into the MPU but they are not coming out. There could be a defect in some of the 50,000 odd FET circuits in the MPU. It could need replacement.

There are some other pins on the MPU DIP. They are control lines of various kinds. Usually there will be a few with no connection, labeled NC. It is rare that a manufacturer will utilize every pin assignment on a complex chip. Some computers use some of the control lines and others use different control lines.

They all use the output line read/write, labeled R/W. The R/W line is the traffic cop for the data bus. While the bus is two-way, it permits data to travel only one way at a time. The R/W line decides which direction the data is allowed to travel. In this 6502 MPU, the MPU is allowed to read from the memory when the R/W line is held high. The data travels from the memory I/O circuits to MPU.

The MPU is allowed to write to the memory when the R/W line is held low. In that case, the data travels the other way, from the MPU to the memory I/O circuits. When you test the R/W line while the MPU is idling, the logic probe shows a pulse. The voltage reads three-state. In this case, it read about 2 V. Some MPUs could have a normal standby high voltage, or low voltage; it varies with different computers.

As you glance from schematic to the chip and back, notice that some of the control lines have a line or asterisk by their label. As mentioned earlier, this means the pin is being held high and will read HIGH on the logic probe or near 5 V on the VOM. When a control lines does not have a line over its name or an asterisk in front of it, then the line is probably being held low.

When a line is held high, it needs a low to be activated. If a line is held low it needs a high to be enabled. If these lines read wrongly, chances are good you have a clue to trouble.

The *RES pin is a reset input pin. It is used to initialize the MPU registers when this machine is switched on. *IRQ and *NMI are also input lines. They are interrupts, and they make the MPU stop its program and service the interrupt before resuming the program.

The best test of an MPU is to try a new one, although this is often impossible. Then pin testing becomes a valuable technique. In order to test the pins intelligently, you should have an idea of how the MPU is operating and what the pins are doing. Then you can tell if the inputs are correct and if the proper outputs are occurring. Only then can you tell if the voltages and waveshapes are correct. When a wrong value is discovered, you can reason out how the MPU is in trouble to effect the required maintenance or repairs.

# 7
# **Memories**

Figure 7-1 is a retail price list of today's most common memory chips, static and dynamic, the SRAMs and the DRAMs. Besides the part numbers and the price, there are two other columns, size and speed. Let's examine these characteristics.

The *size* of the chips is actually the layout of the memory matrix. The first number describes the number of addresses that can hold data in the chip. In the static list the number of locations in the chips range from 256, 1024, 2048, 8192 to 32,768. These represent 1/4K, 1K, 2K, 8K, and 32K. There are some 16 K static RAM chips but they are not included on this particular list.

The second number in the size description is the number of bits that are found at each address on the chip. Note there are 4 bits, a nybble, on the 1/4K chip and 8 bits, a byte, on all the rest of the chips. If you want to store bytes in memory, two 4-bit chips will have to be wired together to do the job. The 8-bit chips, though, can be used singly to store bytes of data.

If you envision the matrix layouts, you can think of the 1024 × 4 chips as containing a tall pile of 1024 locations, each location 4 bits wide. The locations are numbered 0 to 1023. A 2048 × 8 matrix can be thought of as another pile of locations 8 bits wide. The locations are numbered 0 to 2047.

The dynamic RAM chip sizes range from 16,384 × 1, 32,768 × 1, 65,536 × 1, 262,144 × 1, to 1,048,576 × 1. These are 16K, 32K, 64K, 256 K, and finally 1MB (1 million bits). The most notable difference between the static and dynamic RAM layouts is the width of the locations. The static widths are mostly 4 or 8 bits while the dynamic widths are only one bit. Each address on a dynamic chip holds only one bit. In order to store a nybble you would need a set of four DRAMs. To make a byte sized location you will require a set of eight chips. Each chip in the set will hold one bit of the addressed byte. All the chips in the set must be wired together. When the processor needs a byte it must contact all eight chips at the same time and extract one bit from each chip.

## STATIC RAMS

| Part | Size | Speed | Price |
|---|---|---|---|
| 2102 | 1024 × 1 | 450ns | .99 |
| 2112 | 256 × 4 | 450ns | 2.99 |
| 2114 | 1024 × 4 | 450ns | .99 |
| 2114L-2 | 1024 × 4 | 200ns | 1.49 |
| TC5516 | 2048 × 8 | 250ns | 3.95 |
| TMM2016-200 | 2048 × 8 | 200ns | 3.25 |
| TMM2016-150 | 2048 × 8 | 150ns | 3.29 |
| TMM2016-100 | 2048 × 8 | 100ns | 4.29 |
| HM6116-4 | 2048 × 8 | 200ns | 4.95 |
| HM6116-3 | 2048 × 8 | 150ns | 5.95 |
| HM6116-2 | 2048 × 8 | 120ns | 6.45 |
| HM6116LP-4 | 2048 × 8 | 200ns | 5.95 |
| HM6116LP-3 | 2048 × 8 | 150ns | 6.45 |
| HM6116LP-2 | 2048 × 8 | 120ns | 6.95 |
| HM6264LP-15 | 8192 × 8 | 150ns | 9.95 |
| HM6264LP-12 | 8192 × 8 | 120ns | 10.95 |
| HM43256LP-15 | 32768 × 8 | 150ns | 12.95 |
| HM43256LP-12 | 32768 × 8 | 120ns | 14.95 |
| HM43256LP-10 | 32768 × 8 | 100ns | 19.95 |

## DYNAMIC RAMS

| Part | Size | Speed | Price |
|---|---|---|---|
| 4116-200 | 16384 × 1 | 200ns | .89 |
| 4116-150 | 16384 × 1 | 150ns | .99 |
| MK4332 | 32768 × 1 | 200ns | 6.95 |
| 4164-150 | 65536 × 1 | 150ns | 2.89 |
| 4164-120 | 65536 × 1 | 120ns | 3.19 |
| 4164-100 | 65536 × 1 | 100ns | 3.95 |
| TMS4164 | 65536 × 1 | 150ns | 2.89 |
| TMS4416 | 16384 × 4 | 150ns | 8.95 |
| 41128-150 | 131072 × 1 | 150ns | 5.95 |
| TMS4464-15 | 65536 × 4 | 150ns | 10.95 |
| TMS4464-12 | 65536 × 4 | 120ns | 11.95 |
| 41256-150 | 2612144 × 1 | 150ns | 12.45 |
| 41256-120 | 2612144 × 1 | 120ns | 12.95 |
| 41256-100 | 262144 × 1 | 100ns | 13.45 |
| 41256-80 | 262144 × 1 | 80ns | 13.95 |
| HM51258-100 | 262144 × 1 | 100ns | 13.95 |
| 1 MB-120 | 1048576 × 1 | 120ns | 34.95 |
| 1 MB-100 | 1048576 × 1 | 100ns | 37.95 |

Fig. 7-1. A memory chip is chosen by means of its size, speed, and price.

If the processor is an 8-bit type it will have eight lines in its data bus, D7-D0. All of the D7 bits will be on the D7 chip, all the D6 bits will be on the D6 chip and so on. There will be more about this further on in this chapter.

The other column on the price list is called *speed*. The speeds range from 450 ns for the 2112 and 2114 SRAMs to 80 ns for the 41256-80 DRAM. The speeds are measured in ns or nanoseconds. A nanosecond is a billionth of a second. Small 8-bit processors can be running at about 1 megahertz. This means it completes a typical cycle in 1000 ns. Should the processor be able to run at a faster 2 MHz it will have a cycle speed of only 500 ns. As the frequency is increased the cycle becomes less and less. With a new 16 MHz 80386 processor the cycle time would lower to a speedy 62.5 ns.

The speed time of RAM chips is the amount of time it takes a processor to obtain data from the addressed location. This is also referred to as access time. It can be seen that if the processor is running at 1 MHz and is taking 1000 ns to perform a cycle, if the accessed chip has a speed of 200 ns, the processor will have no problem accessing the chip. On the other hand if the processor is proceeding at a 16 MHz clip, the 200 ns access time is not enough for the cycle that is being completed in 62.5 ns. Much faster memory chips will have to be used in order for the processor to get the data it needs. There will be more about this problem in this chapter and Chapter 9.

RAM memory chips are installed in either DIPs or SMDs: There are advantages and disadvantages to both. Whatever the package though, the chips inside are the same. Figure 7-2 shows a common 64 K chip installed in a DIP and an SMD.

## MPU TO MEMORY AND BACK

A computer is basically an MPU and some memory. The MPU and the memory work together as a system. The main job that they do is ship streams of data back and

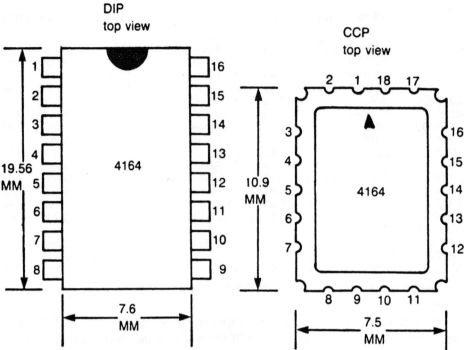

Fig. 7-2. On the left is a 4164 chip that is installed in a DIP. On the right is the same 4164 chip but it is installed on an SMD. The sketches are drawn relative to each other. Note the smaller size of the SMD package.

forth. The ROM part of memory contains the permanent program that operates the computer. It keeps the streams of data moving back and forth in a meaningful fashion.

The RAM part of memory starts out as empty storage bytes. If you want to do a job, you fill sections of RAM with a program. For example, if you want to make the computer into a word processor, you install the word processing program into RAM. The computer becomes a super typewriter. If you want the computer to do accounting work, you install a spreadsheet program into RAM. The computer puts on another hat and becomes an accountant's calculator and worksheet. If you want to play chess, install a chess game in RAM, and the computer becomes your opponent.

In addition to installing programs into RAM, you can also store your word processing text, the results of your accounting, and the score of chess games won and lost.

The procedure to send a copy of the ROM and the contents of RAM to the MPU is accomplished with a frequently-used instruction from the Set. The instruction is known as *Load* (Fig.7-3). In the program there will be many Load instructions. Three of the most common are *Load Accumulator, Load Index Register,* and *Load Stack Pointer.* If the instruction has an address with it, the MPU addresses the ROM or RAM location specified and loads the contents of that location into the specified MPU register.

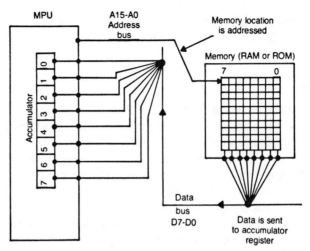

Fig. 7-3. The Load Accumulator instruction addresses a memory location and forwards the locations data contents to the MPU accumulator.

The Load instruction works on both ROM and RAM, because the data flows from the memory to empty waiting MPU registers. For data to flow in the other direction is not that easy because the ROMs are filled with permanent, burned-in data.

ROMs, remember, can be read but not written to. They are already full. Besides, ROMs are not flip-flop circuits, so they couldn't store data from the MPU even if they were empty.

In contrast, RAMs are easy to write to. The instruction used is *Store* (Fig. 7-4). The common instructions are *Store Accumulator, Store Index Register,* and *Store Stack Pointer.*

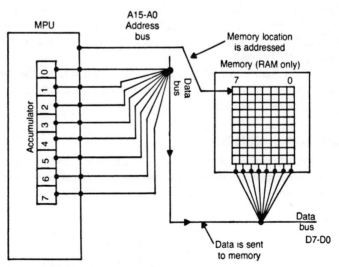

Fig. 7-4. The Store Accumulator instruction addresses a memory location and forwards the accumulator data contents to the addresses location.

If the MPU receives a Store instruction and it is properly addressed, it will send the contents of the indicated register out to the specified address and store the byte or bytes there.

## MPU MEMORY

There is a little bit of memory in the MPU. It is not much but it does come in handy in some programs. The memory storage places are the MPU registers themselves. That is, the accumulators, index registers, and stack pointers.

Our discussions so far have limited the number of these registers. In reality, common MPUs could have many accumulators, index registers, and stack pointers. In addition, these registers can be quite flexible and can easily be substituted for each other. Index registers and stack pointers are often interchanged and do each other's jobs. Lots of MPUs do not even designate the jobs; they simply have a number of registers called *General Purpose*. It is up to the programmer to arrange their operation as stack pointers or index registers.

Load and Store instructions are necessary to operate MPU registers. However, the inter-MPU register instructions are not called Load and Store; instead they are called Transfer or Exchange. Here's a typical list of these instructions:

Transfer from Accumulator A to Accumulator B
Transfer from Accumulator B to Accumulator A
Transfer from Accumulator A to Condition Code Register
Transfer from Condition Code Register to Accumulator A
Transfer from Index Register to Stack Pointer
Transfer from Stack Pointer to Index Register

There are many transfers and exchange possibilities especially in MPUs with a lot of general purpose registers. It is not necessary to memorize all the possibilities. There is only one general function here, transferring from one register to another in the MPU. If you are ever called upon to write a Transfer program line, just be sure you specify the correct origination and destination registers.

Load, Store, and Transfer are three main instructions that move the data being computed from place to place. Load and Store instructions are used in programs most often, while Transfer is not quite as popular.

## ACCESSING DATA IN MEMORY

There are a number of registers in the MPU which are made to operate as a program is run and instructions are fetched and executed. A typical program of high and low pulses could be coded and stored in memory bytes in the following manner:

| | | |
|---|---|---|
| 0 | 1000 | 0110 |
| 1 | 0001 | 1001 |
| 2 | 1000 | 1011 |
| 3 | 0010 | 0011 |

| 4 | 1000 | 1011 |
|---|------|------|
| 5 | 0011 | 0010 |
| 6 | 1000 | 1011 |
| 7 | 0001 | 0001 |
| 8 | 1001 | 0111 |
| 9 | 0000 | 1010 |

This is a little addition program which can be stored in ten bytes of memory. The addresses 0-9 are in decimal. The program contains instructions and data. Memory addresses 0, 2, 4, 6, and 8 are instructions. Addresses 1, 3, 5, and 7 are data. There is no easy way to tell which addresses have instructions and which ones are holding data. The computer, however, has no difficulty at all. It can tell electronically which are which by the highs and lows. The instructions are easily recognizable, and the Instruction Set number contains a code that tells the computer where (in memory) the data needed by the instruction is residing. For example, let's analyze this little program. First we'll convert it to hex, which is much easier to read.

| 0 | 8 | 6 | - INSTRUCTION LOAD |
|---|---|---|--------------------|
| 1 | 1 | 9 | - DATA |
| 2 | 8 | B | - INSTRUCTION (ADD) |
| 3 | 2 | 3 | - DATA |
| 4 | 8 | B | - INSTRUCTION (ADD) |
| 5 | 3 | 2 | - DATA |
| 6 | 8 | B | - INSTRUCTION (ADD) |
| 7 | 1 | 1 | - DATA |
| 8 | 9 | 7 | - INSTRUCTION (STORE) |
| 9 | 0 | A | - ADDRESS OF STORAGE LOCATION |

Address 0 holds highs and lows that can be described in hex as 8 6. In the Instruction Set list, 8 6 tells the instruction register to Load the accumulator with data. Where is the data? The instruction says the data is in the next address 1. The MPU goes to address 1, takes a copy of it contents, and loads the copy into the accumulator.

This type of data storage and data accessing is called the *Immediate Addressing Mode*. (Fig. 7-5). After the MPU loads the data in address 1, it continues to address 2. The contents of the address is the next instruction. It is hex 8 B.

8 B is an add instruction. It tells the MPU to add data to the numbers in the accumulator. It is also an Immediate Addressing Mode instruction. This means the data to be added to the accumulator will be found in the next memory byte, address 3.

After the data in address 3 is added, the MPU gets the next instruction out of address 4. This instruction is also 8 B and the instruction and the addressing mode are carried out. The contents of the next address, 5, is added to the accumulator's growing total.

After 5 has been accessed, the MPU addresses memory 6. This is an instruction and is again 8 B. The MPU goes to location 7, removes the data and adds it to the accu-

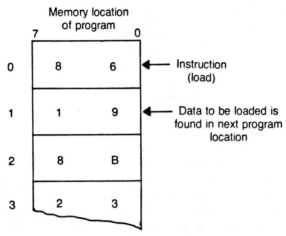

Memory location
of program

| 7 | | 0 | |
|---|---|---|---|
| 0 | 8 | 6 | ← Instruction (load) |
| 1 | 1 | 9 | ← Data to be loaded is found in next program location |
| 2 | 8 | B | |
| 3 | 2 | 3 | |

Fig. 7-5. When the data that the MPU needs to execute an instruction is found in the next program byte, the addressing mode to locate the data is called Immediate.

mulator for the grand total. The MPU then accesses location 8. There is an instruction there, 9 7.

Hex instruction 9 7 is a Store. Its Addressing Mode is not Immediate. In fact, it can't be Immediate, since there is no data to be accessed in memory. The data during a Store is sent to memory. The addressing mode in this case is called *Direct*.

While the Immediate Mode is used during a Load operation to show the data to be processed is in the next memory location, the direct mode is used during a Store operation to designate the address where the data is to be stored.

Therefore, at this spot in the program, the Direct Addressing Mode is used to tell you that the next location, 9, contains the address to store the data in the accumulator (Fig. 7-6). Locations 8 and 9 work together as a two-byte instruction. 8 holds the Store instruction itself in the Direct Addressing Mode. 9 holds a single byte address hex 0 A, where the accumulator's grand total is to be stored. The MPU executes the instruction and stores the data into hex memory location 0 A. Please note that the data in 9 is special—it is an address. The data in 1,3,5, and 7 were numbers in an addition problem and not addresses.

The main difference between the Immediate mode and the Direct modes is that the next byte of the Immediate mode is data to be worked on, while the next byte of the Direct mode is an address where data resides.

There is another addressing mode that works exactly like the Direct mode except for one thing. If you'll notice, the Direct mode address where data is to be found was contained in a single byte. This limits the range of the address to eight binary figures between 00000000 and 11111111. In hex, that only permits 256 addresses between 0 0 and F F.

256 bytes of memory is a very small range to be limited to. In an 8-bit computer 65,536, locations can be addressed. What is to be done about addresses above F F on up to F F F F? They also have to be addressed, and they can be, with another addressing mode called the *Extended Addressing Mode*.

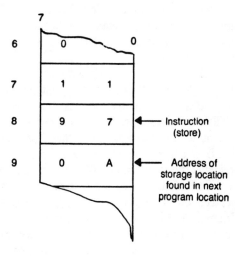

Fig. 7-6. When an address that the MPU needs to send data to is found in the next program byte, the addressing mode to locate the address is called Direct.

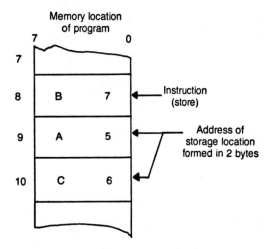

Fig. 7-7. When an address that the MPU needs to send data to is found in the next two program bytes, the addressing mode to locate the address is called Extended.

All that is needed is to change the Direct hex number from the Instruction Set to the Extended code number. Instead of the MPU looking for a single byte address, it will then look for an address contained in the next two-bytes. For example, let's change the program we have just exercised to fit the need. We will install the accumulator grand total into a two byte address, A 5 C 6. The data in memory locations 8 and 9 will be changed, and location 10 will now receive a program byte (Fig. 7-7).

$$
\begin{array}{rll}
8 & B & 7 \\
9 & A & 5 \\
10 & C & 6 \\
\end{array}
$$

Now, when the program is run, it executes the same way it did before until the contents of location 8 are fetched and executed.

From 8, the instruction B 7 is fetched. The instruction register decodes it as "store the contents of the accumulator in the address formed by the contents of the next two memory locations, 9 and 10." This is a Store Accumulator instruction in the Extended Addressing Mode.

The MPU executes by addressing A 5 C 6 in memory and transmitting the data in the single byte accumulator to the single byte of memory with the double byte address.

Accessing memory for data to be used in a program, is one of the most valuable skills a computer has. As you could see in the little addition program, the ability to move the numbers to be added together from memory to the accumulator was needed. The MPU had to able to locate them, bring them to the accumulator one by one, and then reinstall the total back into a memory location.

The MPU recognized that the numbers were installed in the byte after each add instruction. That's because the Load and Add instructions were given the code of the Immediate Addressing Mode. There are a lot of different ways to install and find data in memory for each instruction. The Immediate mode was chosen for the addition program since it appeared to be the most convenient.

The following is a typical Load Accumulator instruction code list. Note that each addressing mode has its own hex code. Each addressing mode is an instruction that is entirely separate from the others. When the program is written, the addressing mode for each byte must be decided on since it is just as important as the instruction itself.

| Addressing Mode | Instruction Code |
|---|---|
| Immediate | 8 6 |
| Direct | 9 6 |
| Extended | B 6 |
| Indexed | A 6 |

## INDEX REGISTER ADDRESSING

The code used for this example is something like one that the 6800 MPU Instruction Set contains. We've discussed the Immediate, Direct, and Extended means of locating data in memory. To repeat, the Immediate mode finds the data needed in the byte after the instruction. The Direct and Extended modes locate the data in memory with an address that is in the byte or bytes after the instruction.

There is another mode called Indexed, which uses the Index register. It is tricky, but very useful.

Some computers do not have Index registers. When they need indexing, they have to go about accessing memory in a roundabout manner with the other three addressing modes, which can waste a lot of time and effort.

Indexing is an old programming technique, which takes a programmer quite a while to perfect the skill. From a technician's viewpoint, indexing is not too important, but you should be familiar with its use.

The Index register in the 8-bit computer has 16 bits like the program counter. It is in parallel with the program counter, and can output an address to the memory map in the same way. However, the Index register can only output an address when the program counter is on hold between program steps.

This is how the memory accessing works. As a program is being run, an instruction like A 6 arrives at the instruction register (Fig. 7-8). The MPU is then alerted that the next byte trailing the instruction A 6 is a hex number to be added to the contents of the Index register. The hex number is called an *offset*.

The offset plus the Index registor form an address. At that address is some data that is to be loaded into the accumulator. The Index register places the address on the address bus and the location is opened up. The data is freed to the data bus and is loaded into the accumulator.

In various computers, there are many more addressing modes that make data accessing more and more valuable. There is the technique called Indirect. The data that is needed is in a location that can only be found in the following way.

Following the instruction byte is a trailer byte that is an address. This address in turn contains as its data a second address. At the second address is the data needed for the program. In other words, the Indirect Addressing Mode is a way of accessing data by means of obtaining the address of an address.

The list of addressing modes goes on and on. If you understand the Immediate, Direct, Extended and Indexed though, you will be able to intelligently check through a computer.

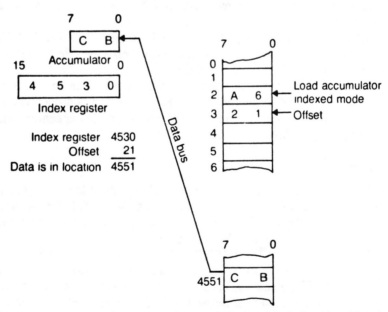

Fig. 7-8. When an address that the MPU needs to read data from is calculated by adding the contents of the index register to an offset found in the next program byte, the addressing mode is called Indexed.

181

## CHIPS IN THE MEMORY MAP

The memory map in Table 5-1 is for a typical 8-bit computer. The 16-bit program counter can address 65,536 individual byte sized locations. The address numbers are shown in decimal 0 to 65,535 and hex 0000 to FFFF. Of course, a location is a location and doesn't change whether it is addressed in decimal or hex. The actual addressing that is used depends on which one is the most convenient.

The two number systems get mixed up all the time. To avoid confusion, you must keep them straight. For example, in the addition program in the last section, we used decimal for the address locations of the program, but hex for the addresses that appeared in the program.

The 65,536 possible locations are, for the most part, filled with RAM and ROM chips. There are a few locations reserved for some I/O chips and devices and a few more locations left empty, in case some special need arises.

In this computer, the map (Table 5-1) is filled with eight RAM chips and three ROM chips. In the 16 K machine, the eight RAM chips are 16,384 × 1 each. The three ROM chips are 8 K each. The empty locations and the I/O together take up another 8 K.

In decimal, RAM occupies locations 0 to 16,383. The top of RAM is at location 16,383.

The first ROM address starts at 32,768. There is a large empty area between 16,383 and 32,768. The numbers are 16,384 to 32,767. These locations are empty and available for RAM, ROM, I/O, or other additions. The MPU would be able to address them without any further electronics.

Right now, there is a set of eight larger RAM chips in my bench drawer. These chips are to replace the 16 K DRAMS in my computer. The new set of chips would give me 32 K of RAM instead of the 16 K I've been putting up with.

If I install the new chips, the top of my RAM will become decimal 32,767. That's all the RAM my 8-bit MPU will address under normal circumstances. To go higher, special addressing techniques or chips must be used.

The first ROM is located at address 32,768 to 40,959. The second ROM is at 40,960 to 49,151. The third at 49,152 to 65,279. The last 8 K is divided between 256 locations for Input/Output and 7935 unused addresses. The I/O is conventionally stationed at the very top of the map, 65,280 to 65,535.

## STATIC RAM

The static chip is so named because it can hold a high or low as long as there is electricity applied. The storage does not require a constant clock that refreshes the bit holders continually, as dynamic RAM needs. The logic states are lost only if the programmer erases them or if the electricity goes off.

The 2102 is contained in a 16-pin DIP (Fig. 7-9). It needs a single +5 V supply connected to pin 10, VCC. VSS is at pin 9. The chip is a three-state type. At pin 13, there is a chip enable called *CE. (Remember, the asterisk means it is held high in the three-state condition.) When the chip is to be accessed the *CE pin is enabled with a low.

The 2102 is a special application static RAM chip. There is only one data IN and a separate data OUT at pins 11 and 12, because the internal organization of the bit holders is 1024 × 1. It's as if the 1024 bits are arranged one on top of another forming a tall,

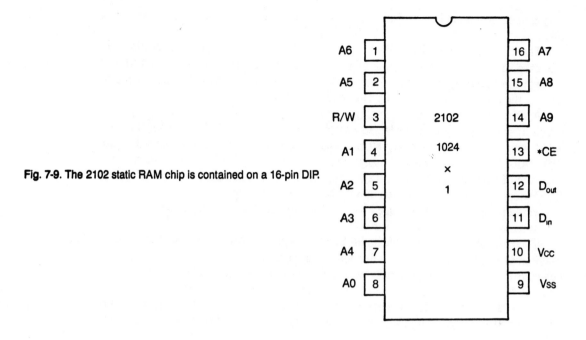

Fig. 7-9. The 2102 static RAM chip is contained on a 16-pin DIP.

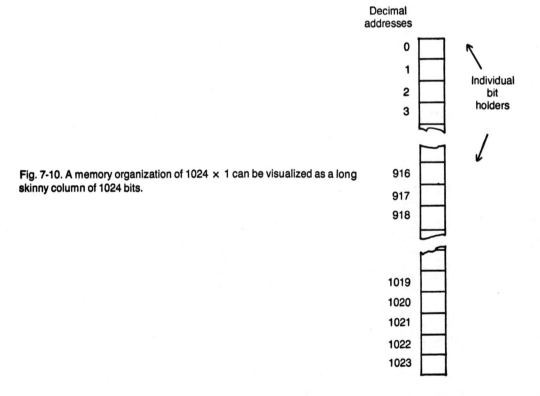

Decimal
addresses

Individual
bit
holders

Fig. 7-10. A memory organization of 1024 × 1 can be visualized as a long skinny column of 1024 bits.

very thin configuration one bit wide as in Fig. 7-10. Only one bit can be addressed at a time.

There are 10 address lines, A9-A0. Ten lines can address 1024 possible locations. In this case, a location consists of a single bit. The single bit can be read or written to through the single input and single output data lines. There is an R/W input at pin 3 to turn on the appropriate data line for the read or write operation.

Another static RAM in the catalog list is the 2114L. The L indicates low power, which means only +5 V is needed to energize the devices (Fig. 7-11). The 2114 is a RAM with 1024 bits available for storing logic states. It has 10 address lines like the 2102 (A9-A0), but four times as many bits. This is because it is organized in memory locations of four bits each (Fig. 7-12). Note the price list shows 1024 × 4. When the MPU accesses a location, it opens up four bits simultaneously.

Pins 11, 12, 13, and 4 are called I/Os, 1,2,3, and 4. One address allows four bits of data to be input or output at the same time.

The chip operates like the single bit 2102, except for a chip select pin *CS. This is really an eleventh address line. It is needed when there is more than one RAM chip to be selected The selected chip, normally lying in wait in a three-state condition, can be given a low at *CS. The addresses in the selected chip can then be accessed.

While the 2102 and the 2114 are valuable chips, they are not found in general purpose computers very often. They only store and output one or four bits at a time, and

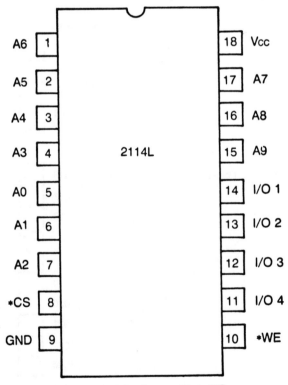

Fig. 7-11. The 2114L static RAM chip is contained on an 18-pin DIP.

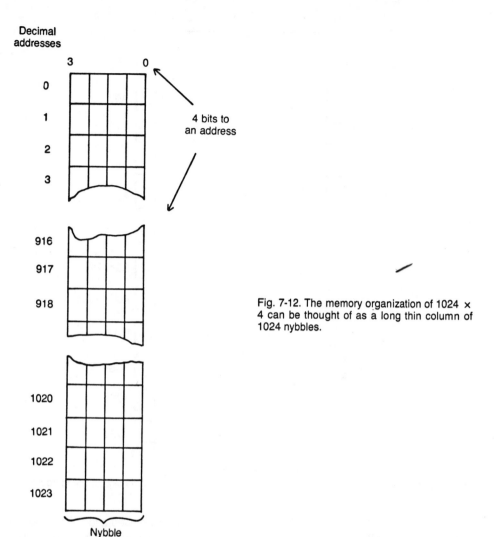

Fig. 7-12. The memory organization of 1024 × 4 can be thought of as a long thin column of 1024 nybbles.

the wiring becomes complex. The eight bits computer needs RAM that attaches easily to eight data lines. A 16-bit computer needs RAM chips that conveniently connect to 16 lines in a data bus.

## 8-BIT STATIC RAM

A RAM chip that has eight bits in a location is the MCM6810 (Fig. 7-13). It is an interesting chip, and is usually part of a set of chips. It has a 128 × 8 organization. There are seven address lines, A6-A0. They can address the 128 addresses perfectly. The complete byte at each address can open up and receive 8 bits or transmit 8 bits in parallel fashion. There is an R/W line to direct the data traffic. To read data from the 6810, the R/W line must be made high. To write into a byte, the R/W line must be forced low.

The 6810, like most full-byte RAMs, has a number of chip select lines. Typically, there could be eight 6810s in a RAM set. There are six CS lines in a 6810, CS5-CS0.

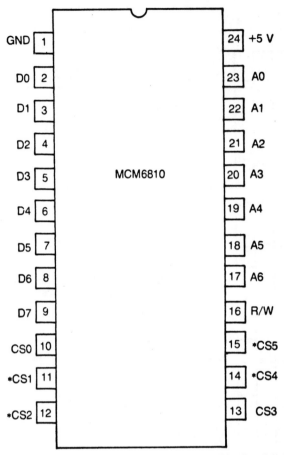

Fig. 7-13. The 128 × 8 RAM chip has eight data lines to accommodate the eight bit wide addresses.

If you'll note, CS1, CS2, CS4, and CS5 all have asterisks. CS0 and CS3 do not. In order to select a 6810 chip out of the possible eight, all six CS pins must have the correct logic state applied to it. 1, 2, 4, and 5 need lows. 0 and 3 need highs. Only when the correct combination of highs and lows are applied will the chip be enabled. Otherwise it remains on hold in a three-state condition.

## INSIDE THE MCM6810

The core of the 6810 is the memory matrix (Fig. 7-14). It can be thought of as a stack of 128 bytes piled one on top of another. They are addressed 0 to 127. The bits are called D7-D0. All 128 of the D7 bits are connected together, all of the D6 bits are connected, and so on.

The bits are connected to a three-state two-way buffer configuration. Each bit has its own buffering stage. The buffers are connected to the eight data pins 9 through 2. The pins, of course, are attached to the data bus, D7-D0.

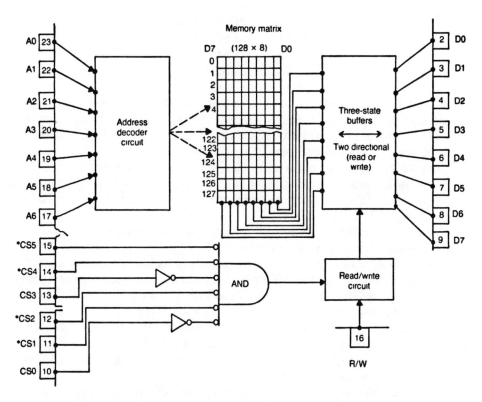

Fig. 7-14. A typical RAM circuit contains a memory matrix, an address input, a R/W input, and two directional three-state buffers.

There are seven address lines, A6-0, entering the chip at pins 17-23. These pins attach to an address decoder circuit on the chip. The decoder takes the incoming seven address bits and activates the chosen byte from the 128 on the chip.

The R/W high or low from the MPU enters at pin 16 and is routed to a read/write circuit. The circuit on the chip between the pins and the internal matrix and buffers, performs two duties. First, it sets up the matrix for either reading from or writing to, and second it turns on the correct buffers for the data flow.

The remaining pins on the chip are the chip selects. They are actually address pins and get connected to the address bus. The address pins named A6-A0 are attached to bus lines A6-A0. The chip select pins can be attached to any of the rest, A15-A7.

The A6-A0 lines are the addresses for the 128 byte holders in the matrix. The chip selects the chip to be accessed.

As mentioned, the pins with the asterisks are enabled by the application of a low. The pins without the asterisks are enabled with highs. A 6810 is turned on when the following signals are applied.

| Pin # | Name | Signal |
|-------|------|--------|
| 10 | CS0 | High |
| 11 | *CS1 | Low |

| 12 | *CS2 | Low |
| 13 | CS3 | High |
| 14 | *CS4 | Low |
| 15 | *CS5 | Low |

When this arrangement appears at these pins, the chip is addressed. The next step is attaching the pins to the address bus. The pins can be attached in any way to any of the A15-A7 address lines. If each chip arrangement is different, then each chip in a RAM set will be selected by a different address.

To add to the versatility of the addressing, you can keep the pins on all the time if you do not need all of them. That way they won't interfere in the addressing schemes. To keep a CS pin on all the time, it can be tied to any +5 V voltage point. Unused *CS pins can be connected to ground or 0 V.

The computer designer lays out the memory map. He connects the chip selects so their addresses are at convenient places on the map.

The chip select circuit for the 6810 is composed of a six input AND gate. Each of the inputs must pass through a little NOT circle to get into the AND gate. Two of the inputs are also through two NOT gates. The NOT gates are in the CS input lines of the AND gate. The rest of the input lines are straight wires without any gates.

The AND gate will output a high only if there are highs at all six inputs. Otherwise, the AND gate outputs a low. The three-state buffers and the matrix will only turn on when a high is applied to the control circuit. While the low is coming out of the AND gate the chip is in a three-state condition.

When four address bus lows are applied at the four *CS pins, they pass through the NOT circles, are reversed and enter the AND gate as highs. When two addressing highs are injected at the two CS pins, they are reversed to lows in the NOT gates and then reversed again in the NOT circles to highs.

Therefore, the six AND gate inputs are highs. The AND outputs a high and the chip is addressed. By switching around the connections to the address bus different addresses can be formed to enable the different chips in the RAM set.

This chip selection type of addressing is also used for other chips in the memory map such as ROM and I/O.

## THE ROM PACKAGE

The ROM chip looks like a RAM chip. Even the pin assignments are the same, except there isn't any R/W line. It's not needed, since the MPU can only read from ROM; it cannot successfully write to it.

The ROM in the illustration is an MCM6830 (Fig. 7-15). It has 24 pins. There are ten address pins A9-A0. This immediately tells the technician that there are 1024 byte locations in the memory matrix. It is described as an organization of 1024 × 8.

There are the usual eight data lines, D7-D0. Four chip selects, the +5 V, and ground make up the rest of the pins.

The address lines are connected to a ten-input, single-output address decoder to choose the byte that needs to be read. The data lines are connected to the outputs of a

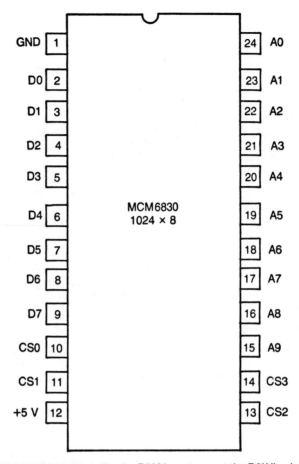

| | | | |
|---|---|---|---|
| GND | 1 | 24 | A0 |
| D0 | 2 | 23 | A1 |
| D1 | 3 | 22 | A2 |
| D2 | 4 | 21 | A3 |
| D3 | 5 | 20 | A4 |
| D4 | 6 | 19 | A5 |
| D5 | 7 | 18 | A6 |
| D6 | 8 | 17 | A7 |
| D7 | 9 | 16 | A8 |
| CS0 | 10 | 15 | A9 |
| CS1 | 11 | 14 | CS3 |
| +5 V | 12 | 13 | CS2 |

MCM6830
1024 × 8

Fig. 7-15. The MCM6830 ROM chip is like the RAM layout, except the R/W line is missing.

one way buffering system to output the byte in the matrix that was addressed (Fig. 7-16).

The buffers are three-state and are enabled by a high from an AND gate like the RAM package had. The AND gate has four chip inputs through four NOT circles. The inputs are from the four chip select pins.

When four lows are applied to the four chip select pins from the address bus, the ROM is addressed. The four lows find their way through the NOT circles and become highs. The four highs cause the AND gate to output a high. This enables the three-state buffers, and the chip can be read.

A typical ROM package contains neither flip-flop circuits like a static RAM, nor capacitance bit holders like dynamic RAM. ROMs contain components such as diodes or transistors at bit locations. The ROM has memory matrixes with rows and columns. The microscopic components can be typically wired at each intersection of row and column.

A typical ROM row holds eight bits. For example, Fig. 7-15 has a 1024 × 8 organization. Figure 7-17 shows ROMs numbered 4732 and 4764. The 4732 has a matrix of 4096 × 8 and the 4764 8196 × 8 organization. In Fig. 7-18 the 47128 has 16,384 × 8

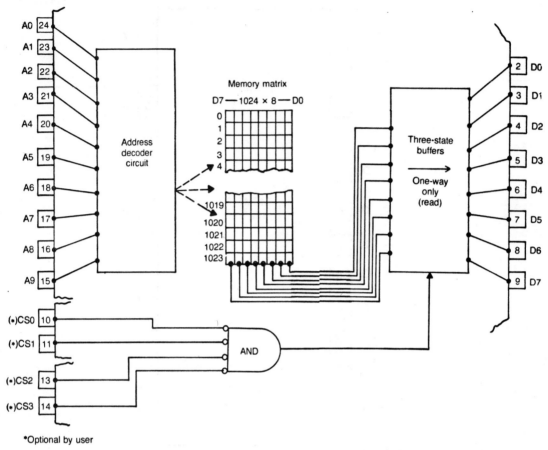

Fig. 7-16. A ROM circuit has a memory matrix, address input, and one-way three-state buffer outputs.

and the 47256 32,768 × 8. The 4732 is a 4 K ROM, the 4764 is an 8 K, the 47128 a 16 K and the 47256 has 32 K bytes in its matrix.

The first two numbers, 47, denotes the fact that these chips are ROMs. The 47 number shows that the ROMs were originated at Texas Instruments. The MCM lettering of the MCM6830 in Fig. 7-15 is the Motorola designation. IBM uses the numbers 92 for their ROMs in their PC. The second two or three numbers gives the thousands of bits, not bytes. For instance, the 47256 has 256 bits in the matrix. Since there are eight bits to a byte, this makes 32 K bytes.

## ROM PROGRAMS

Before it receives its programming, if you would read a typical ROM location, the bit holders could output HHHHHHHH. Such a ROM starts out as a chip with all Hs in its bit holders. When a row is addressed, it is energized. If there are diodes or transistors in the row, they are all intact. Each diode or transistor will conduct from the row line to

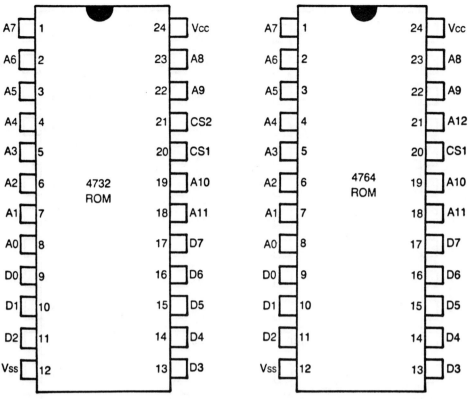

Fig. 7-17. The common 4732 and 4764 are found in 24-pin DIPs. Both have eight data pins. The 4732 has two chip selects and 12 address register selects. The 4764 only has one chip select because it needs an extra pin for its 13 address register selects.

each of the eight columns. The conduction results in highs emerging from all eight bits. (According to its design, a ROM could have all Hs or perhaps all Ls before it is programmed.

The columns are connected to the data bus lines, D7-D0 and the eight highs emerge and go to the processor as HHHHHHHH. Obviously a chip full of highs or lows is not very useful. Therefore it needs programming. Some ROMs have operating systems installed. Others contain tables and language interpretation programs. Still others can hold character patterns. Whatever the useful contents might be, it must be installed.

The first step in the installation process is to write the program. It must be written in pure machine language, that is, in Hs and Ls. Machine language is normally a list of bytes. Each byte contains an assortment of highs and lows. Once the program is written it is then burned into the ROM chip bit holders. Since the ROM in this example started life with a matrix full of Hs, all that is needed is to burn in the Ls at the appropriate bit positions.

Since the Hs are read from the ROM as a result of a diode or transistor conducting, to install an L into a bit holder, the component must be put into a condition whereby it cannot conduct.

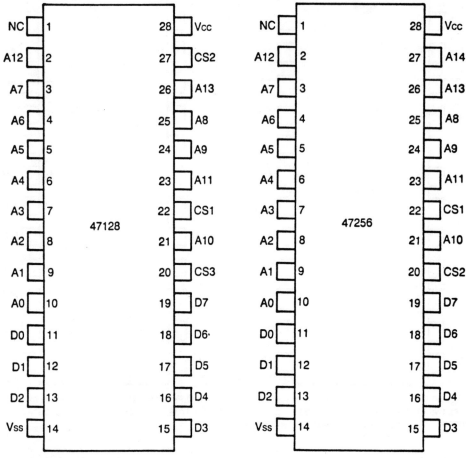

| | 47128 | | | 47256 | |
|---|---|---|---|---|---|
| NC | 1 | 28 Vcc | NC | 1 | 28 Vcc |
| A12 | 2 | 27 CS2 | A12 | 2 | 27 A14 |
| A7 | 3 | 26 A13 | A7 | 3 | 26 A13 |
| A6 | 4 | 25 A8 | A6 | 4 | 25 A8 |
| A5 | 5 | 24 A9 | A5 | 5 | 24 A9 |
| A4 | 6 | 23 A11 | A4 | 6 | 23 A11 |
| A3 | 7 | 22 CS1 | A3 | 7 | 22 CS1 |
| A2 | 8 | 21 A10 | A2 | 8 | 21 A10 |
| A1 | 9 | 20 CS3 | A1 | 9 | 20 CS2 |
| A0 | 10 | 19 D7 | A0 | 10 | 19 D7 |
| D0 | 11 | 18 D6· | D0 | 11 | 18 D6 |
| D1 | 12 | 17 D5 | D1 | 12 | 17 D5 |
| D2 | 13 | 16 D4 | D2 | 13 | 16 D4 |
| Vss | 14 | 15 D3 | Vss | 14 | 15 D3 |

Fig. 7-18. The larger 47128 and 47256 ROMs come in 28-pin DIPs. There are still only eight data pins. The 47128 has three chip selects and 14 address register selects. The 47256 only has two chip selects to allow an extra pin for the 15th address register select bit.

The procedure consists of applying a special destruction voltage to all the bit holders that are to read Ls. The voltage then goes ahead and blows the diode or transistor apart. That way they can no longer conduct. After the destructive force has been applied, the machine language is permanently installed into the matrix. When the processor then reads an address it will receive the byte of data that has been burnt into the location.

This procedure is used when individual custom ROMs are fabricated. It is too slow for mass production. For large production runs, the program is installed in a master printed circuit pattern. The photo masking pattern has the junctions drawn between the rows and columns. If the bit junction is supposed to provide an H, a diode or transistor that works is drawn there. Should the bit holder be supposed to provide an L, the junction is left empty. Once the pattern contains the program, it is reduced photographically and used to mass produce the desired ROM.

## EPROMS

The ordinary ROM described above, once programmed is permanent. In some applications, it is desirable to erase the program and install a new program. This can't be done with the permanent type ROMs but it can be done with Erasable ROMs like the one in Fig. 7-19.

The EPROM is a ROM that can be programmed, erased and reprogrammed again and again. The EPROM uses special metal-oxide-silicon-field-effect-transistors, MOS-FETs, at the bit holder junctions. It so happens that if you apply about 20 to 25 V between the source and drain electrodes, a phenomenon called avalanche injection takes place and causes the gate electrode to lose its ability to conduct. The FET then takes up residence in the bit holder as an open circuit, just as if it had been blown. Since no conduction takes place the bit holder acts as if it was an L.

Except for the FETs that received the 20-25 V shots, all the rest of the FETs still are able to conduct. This makes the conducting FETs the Hs. That is how the Hs and Ls of the program are installed in the EPROM matrix.

Once the program has served its usefulness, it is time to erase it. This is accomplished with ultraviolet light. There is a little quartz window on the top of the package. Ultraviolet light is shined through the window onto the exposed FETs for about a half hour. The avalanche injection effect gradually subsides and the FETs that were not conducting, begin conducting again. This programming and erasure procedure can be done over and over again. In the computer, the EPROM performs exactly like an ordinary ROM.

The only precaution that is needed is, once the program is installed, the window must be covered with some sort of opaque covering. Normal room lighting contains some ultraviolet light. If the little window is not covered, the room lights could, over time, erase the program. If the window is carefully kept covered, the EPROM will hold the program intact indefinitely.

EPROMs are programmed with little computer devices called IC programmers. Figure 7-20 illustrates a typical programmer. Note it has a socket to place the EPROM chip into, a keyboard and a control panel. This programmer can handle DIPs up to 28 pins.

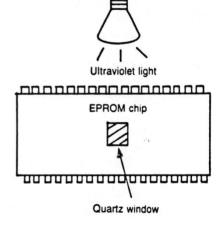

Fig. 7-19. The EPROMs can be erased by opening up its quartz window and shining an ultraviolet light onto the matrix.

Ultraviolet light

EPROM chip

Quartz window

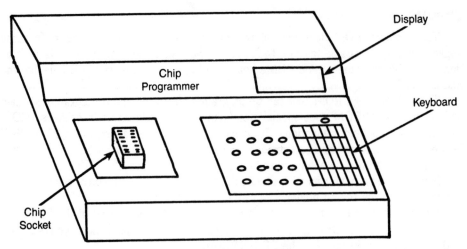

Fig. 7-20. An EPROM chip can be programmed with a device such as this. It has a chip socket, a keyboard and control panel.

The matrix can vary between 16 K and 512 K. For more information contact one of the mail order parts houses listed in the back of the book.

## DYNAMIC RAM

Except for special applications, static RAM is not installed in general purpose computers very often. Static RAM is feasible in applications where small amounts of RAM are used. If there is a need for large amounts (4K or more) it is more practical to use dynamic RAM. Dynamic RAM takes up less circuit board area, uses less power, and, most importantly, costs much less than static RAM. It is important to understand the theory of static RAM so it can be compared with the dynamic circuit activity.

As mentioned earlier, a static bit holder is a flip-flop that can store a high or low and hold it as long as the chip is energized. On the other hand, a dynamic bit holder is a NOT gate with some coupling FETS that are connected to the next holder. While the logic state in the flip-flop is contained in transistors that are either saturated or cut off, the high or low in the NOT gate-coupling circuit is contained as a charge or a non-charge in a grid of tiny amounts of capacitance developed between the FET gates and ground.

Once a logic state is installed, static RAM holds the state without any assistance. Dynamic RAM, though, is not that stable. The charge in the capacitors will leak off in a few milliseconds unless it can be recharged. This means the dynamic logic state must be refreshed every few milliseconds.

This sounds like a prodigious task, but it is not too hard to handle. All the dynamic bits need to retain their charge is to be addressed every few milliseconds while the computer is on. In order to keep the dynamic RAM intact, special circuitry is installed in the computer. The Z-80 MPU has a special refresh counter that constantly addresses the memory bits. Other MPUs like the 6800 or 6502 employ additional chips to do the refreshing job.

Refreshing takes place as a counting circuit starts at the bottom row of memory and addresses to the top row. The signal is a strobe and is called *RAS-only*. This means *Row*

*Address Strobe-only.* The RAS-only is a separate signal devised only for the refreshing job. It plays no other part in the computer. There is another strobe signal called *RAS but it has to do with the actual addressing and is not the same as RAS-only which is only giving all the capacitances in each row a boost.

A common dynamic RAM chip is the 4116 (Fig. 7-21). It is organized in a 16,384 × 1 format. This layout is not like the static RAM arrangement. If you recall, the 2102 static RAM was also organized in a one bit setup; 1024 × 1. It could be thought of as a tall skinny arrangement with one bit on top of another. Each bit has its own individual address. There are ten address lines, A9-A0, to address the 1024 addresses.

Dynamic RAM is different. The 4116 has its 16,384 bits laid out in a matrix 128 bits high and 128 bits wide (Fig. 7-22). Each bit is individual. Each bit has its own address. Each address requires 14 bits to address one out of 16,384 separate bits.

The matrix thus has 128 rows and 128 columns. The 16 address bits then can be utilized in the following way. The two most significant bits are used as the chip select. The next seven most significant bits are used to address the 128 rows. The seven least significant bits address the 128 columns.

Each bit can be addressed by first addressing a row and then addressing a column. The intersection where the row and column meet becomes the bit chosen.

The 4116 chip comes in sets of eight. They are all identical. They are all wired up together in parallel. They all have the same chip select address and are all addressed simultaneously. They all have the same bit organization. If the first bit is addressed, all the first bits in each of the eight chips are addressed at the same time. If the third bit is addressed, then all the third bits are addressed together. Each databyte is spread throughout the eight chips, one bit in each corresponding location. In order to read one byte, the MPU must access eight chips.

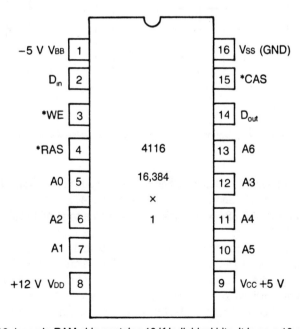

Fig. 7-21. The 4116 dynamic RAM chip contains 16 K individual bits. It is on a 16-pin DIP.

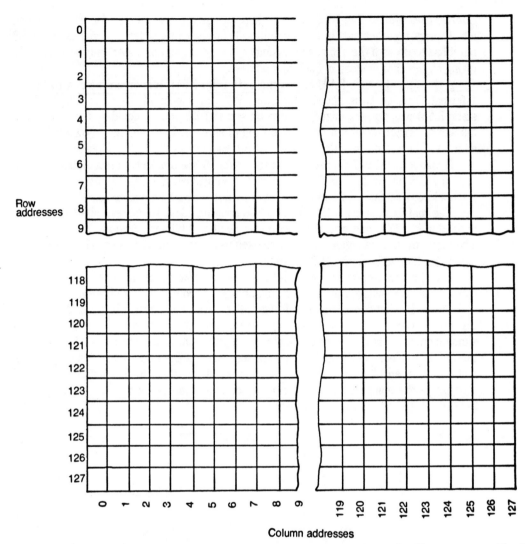

Row addresses

Column addresses

Fig. 7-22. The 16,834 × 1 organization of the 4116 16 K dynamic RAM chip is contained in a memory matrix of 128 × 128 individual bits.

Each chip is attached to a separate line of the data bus (Fig. 7-23). Chip 7 connects to D7, chip 6 connects to D6 and so on. Let's examine a 4116 chip.

The array of eight 16,384 × 1 chips add up to to a total of 131,072 individual bits. This bit total is 16,384 total bytes, or 16 K bytes. The eight chips are numbered 0-7. Let's pull chip number 3, the fourth one in the array, and examine it pin by pin.

The top view shows a 16-pin DIP (Fig. 7-21). There are both TTL circuits and MOS circuits on the chip. The TTLs are in the input-outputs of the chip, while the MOSFETs are in the memory matrix to hold the capacitance logic state charges. The TTLs are powered with +5 V at VCC pin 9 and VBB with −5 V at pin 1. The FETs are powered

196

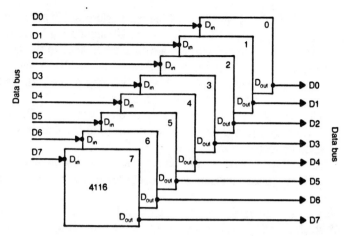

Fig. 7-23. In order to read a byte, all eight chips must be addressed simultaneously. Each byte is spread out over the eight chips, one bit to a chip.

with +12 V at VDD pin 8 and VSS at ground pin 16. There are three input voltages, +12 V, +5 V, and −5 V, that run the chip.

There are seven address lines, A6-A0 (Fig. 7-20). These seven lines are in parallel with all the address lines of the rest of the chips in the 16 K byte array. However, there are 14 address bits that are needed to fully address the memory matrix. There are seven bits needed to address the 128 rows and seven bits needed to address the 128 columns. This is accomplished by the multiplexing scheme.

On pin 4 there is a signal being input called *RAS (Fig. 7-21). On pin 15 there is another input signal called *CAS. These are *Row Address Strobe* and *Column Address Strobe*. The row address bits approach the memory array on address bus lines A6-A0. The column address bits arrive on lines A13-A7 (Fig. 7-24).

Multiplex chips stand between the address lines and the memory array. They receive the 14 address bits and separate them into two sets of bits. Then they feed the

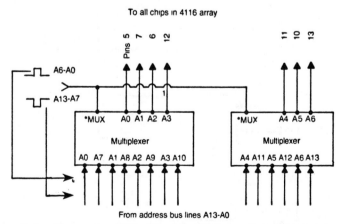

Fig. 7-24. The multiplex chips receive 14 bits from the address bus. During *RAS they send the seven bits A6-A0 to the 4116 RAM array. During *CAS they send the seven bits A13-A7 to the array.

two bit sets alternately to the array. The multiplexer performs this alternate feeding in sync with *RAS and *CAS. During *RAS it feeds A6-A0, and during *CAS it feeds A13-A7. That way, all 14 bits are injected into the seven address lines to the array.

The array accepts A6-A0 during *RAS and A13-A7 during *CAS, all into its seven address lines, which are numbered A6-A0. This multiplexing of the address lines saves seven pins. The chip can be kept small in a 16-pin package.

There are only two data pins needed on a chip, one Data In, pin 2, and the other Data Out, pin 14. On chip 3, the Data In pin is connected to the data bus line D3. The Data Out pin is also connected to D3.

The pin called *WE is the write enable pin. It is like a read/write line. When the pin is held low, the MPU is signaling it wants to write into the memory. If the pin is high, the MPU wants a read.

The memory array is controlled by the three signals *RAS, *CRS and *WE (Fig. 7-25). The *RAS strobes in the seven lowest bits into the array (Fig. 7-26). Row address latch in each chip accepts the row address and feeds it into its address decoder. The decoder chooses the same row in each chip. The *CAS strobes in the next seven bits into the array. A column address latch in each chip accepts the column address and feeds it into a column decoder. The decoder chooses the column addresses. The corresponding bits in each chip are chosen at the same time.

Meanwhile, the *WE signal sets up either a read or a write for the eight bits chosen. The contents of the eight bits are either made to leave the eight chips, or the eight bits are loaded with data.

Dynamic memories are quite different from static types. In comparison to static memories, the dynamics are many times more difficult to design. This is because of the multiple timing considerations between the multiplexing, row selection, column selection, and input/output of data. There will be discussions of the timing in Chapter 9.

To a technician, the timing designs are not too much of a problem. The computers are already in existence when we arrive on the scene. Designers, though, can have fits when they are making dynamic memories with MPUs.

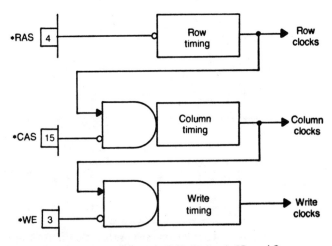

Fig. 7-25. The timing signals are applied to each 4116 at pins 4, 15, and 3.

198

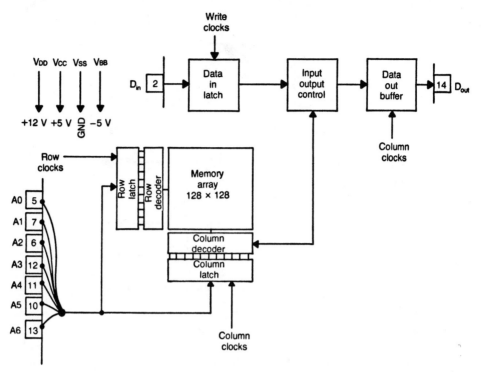

Fig. 7-26. Data being read can exit the 4116 at pin 14. Data being written can enter at pin 2.

## RAM CHIP UPGRADES

The 16 K 4116 RAM chip is not dead but it is over the hill. It is still used in certain applications but it has been supplanted by denser chips. There are, right now, three steps of upgrades. First of all there is the popular 64 K 4164. It has been around for quite awhile. One of the first things 16 K computer users did was upgrade their machines from 16 K to 64 K as soon as the chips were available. The 16 K chips each held 16,384 capacitance circuits to store bits. The upgrade raised the total to 65,536. This is a fourfold increase. The upgrade was relatively easy since the 4164 chips came on the same 16-pin chip the 4116 used. The pins are almost the same pin for pin.

The 4164 is constructed like the 4116 at about the same cost. The bit density is increased by doubling the bit matrix sizes. The 128 × 128 4116 matrix is increased to 256 × 256 in the 4164. Note that doubling the numbers of rows and columns, quadruples the number of bits in the matrix. 128 × 128 = 16,384. 256 × 256 = 65,536.

There are a few different pin assignments in the 4164 in comparison to the 4116. Note in Fig. 7-21 the 4116 has four power supply inputs at pins 1,8,9, and 16, the corner pins. These supply pins are reduced to two in the 4164. Pin 8 remains VDD and pin 16 remains VSS. Internally the chip has some new supply wiring to fulfill the needs that pins 1 and 9 were supplying.

In the 4164, shown in Fig. 7-27, pin 1 is removed from the circuit and becomes NC for no connection. It is being saved for further upgrades, as you'll learn in the next section. Pin 9 in the 4164 becomes a new address pin, A7. For addressing 16 K all that is

199

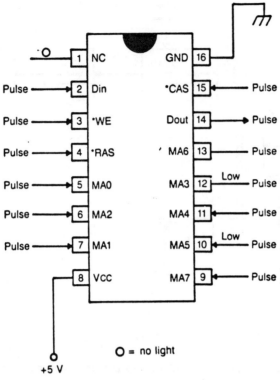

Fig. 7-27. This is the top view of a 4164 chip showing typical voltage states, which pins are receiving inputs and which pins are yielding outputs.

needed is address pins A6-A0. For addressing 64 K one more multiplexed address pin is required. Thus pin 9 is given the job of being A7. Other than the pin 1 and pin 9 changes, the 4116 and the 4164 are externally identical. In most cases, but not all the 4164 can be plugged in for the 4116 with just a few minor wiring changes.

The next step up in density is the 41256, shown in Fig. 7-28. Whereas the 4164 has 65,536 bit holders, the 41256 has 262,144 bit holders, a fourfold density increase over the 4164. The density is again achieved by doubling the numbers of rows and columns. The 41256 has a matrix that contains 512 rows by 512 columns. $512 \times 512 = 262,144$.

The 41256 is upwardly compatible with the 4164 in the same limited way the 4164 is upwardly compatible with the 4116. Figure 7-29 shows the pin by pin layout of the 4164 and 41256. Figure 7-21 shows the pinout of the 4116. Figure 7-28 displays the matrix arrangements for all three chips and the newer one megabit chips that we will get to shortly. The 4116, 4164, and 41256 chips have a lot in common. They are each organized by 1 bit. That is, $16,384 \times 1$, $65,536 \times 1$ and $262,144 \times 1$. Each uses a $+5$ V power supply, each has one data input pin and one data output pin at pins 2 and 14. They all have a *RAS input pin 4, a *CAS input pin 15, and a *WE input pin 3. The only striking difference from chip to chip are the address lines. The 4116 only needs A6-A0 to input 14 multiplexed address bits, seven at a time. The 4164 requires A7-A0 to input 16 multiplexed address bits, eight at a time. The 41256 has to have A8-A0 to input 18 multi-

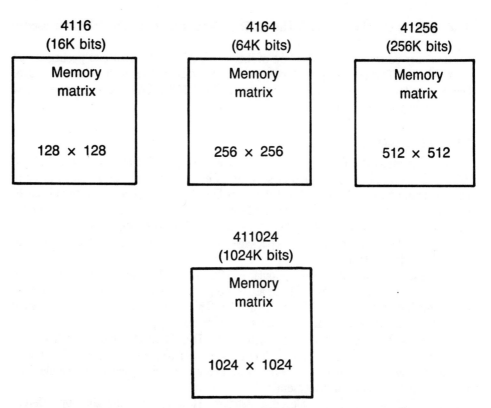

Fig. 7-28. The 4164 chip has a matrix density of 256 × 256 bits in comparison to the 128 × 128 of the 4116 chip. The 41256 chip has an even more dense matrix, 512 × 512 bits. The 411024 chip's density is 1024 × 1024.

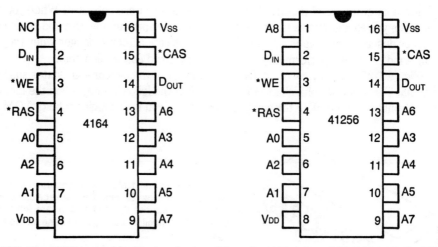

Fig. 7-29. The 41256 is considered upward compatible to the 4164 and 4116. Note the only pin difference between the 4164 and the 41256 needs one more address bit.

plexed address bits nine at a time. The 41256 uses the pin 1 connection that is unused in the 4164, as address bit A8.

It is very convenient that all three of these DRAMs can be built into packages that are so similar. The next step up though, could not follow along in the same package. There were too many additional pins required. The 1 MB DRAMs has an entirely new package designed for them.

## THE 1MB DRAM

The one megabit DRAM arrived on the scene in 1986. It has a matrix of 1024 × 1024. 1024 × 1024 = 1,048, 576 bits. A set of eight provides over a million bytes of dynamic memory. In order to address this large DRAM set, a processor with at least 20 address bits must be used. This more or less eliminates the use of chips with an 8-bit processor. The 16-bit and 32-bit processors though, work well with these chips.

The 1 MB chips need 20 pins in a package. Ten pins, A9-A0 are needed for the multiplexed 20 address bits.

One package that has become popular is a 26-pin sized surface mount device. The unusual feature of the package is, there are three pins on each side of the dual in-line pin arrangement that are removed from the middle. This provides space that can be used beneath the chip for decoupling capacitors or board traces.

Figure 7-30 shows a Texas Instrument 1 MB DRAM surface mount package. On one side there is space for 13 pins but the three center pins are not there. This leaves five pins at one end, five pins at the other end, and a three pin space in the middle. The other side has the same arrangement.

This SMD package is considered a standard. However, as time goes by different packages could be built to hold the chip. There will be more detail on the assortment of possible package types that chips might appear in.

## TESTING MEMORIES

Memory chips are of the MOS variety and as a result are sensitive. When you test memories you should wear a wrist strap and take other precautions to avoid static electricity as described in Chapters 20 and 21. Memories are in mortal danger when they are being handled. A test performed in a careless way could easily kill a chip.

Figure 7-27 is a top view of a 4164 chip with typical voltages or logic states shown at each pin. This is a test point chart. You can use it in the following way when the memory needs troubleshooting. With the computer energized you take a logic probe or VOM and

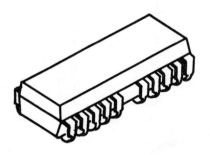

Fig. 7-30. A typical 1 MB DRAM comes in this SMD package. It requires 20 pins. The package can accommodate 26 pins but the center pins are left out so decoupling capacitors can be used beneath the package.

take a reading at each pin. If there is no trouble anywhere around the chip, all the pre-scribed readings should be found at each pin.

If one or more of the readings do not match up, that is a clue. Note the arrows at each pin. They show you whether the pin is an input or output. If a wrong reading is found at an input, for example a pulse is missing at an address pin, chances are, the trouble is not due to the chip under test. The signal is not arriving from the address bus. The address bus and specifically the circuit feeding that pin is under suspicion.

On the other hand if you find an output pin is incorrect, such as the $D_{out}$ at pin 14, the chip itself falls under suspicion. There could be no $D_{out}$ because the signal is being killed somewhere inside the chip.

Because you cannot gain physical access to the silicon circuits inside the chip, the information on the test point pins are the way to manually service the chip. It helps if you can visualize what is happening inside the chip. Figure 7-31 is a block diagram of the inside of the 4164 chip.

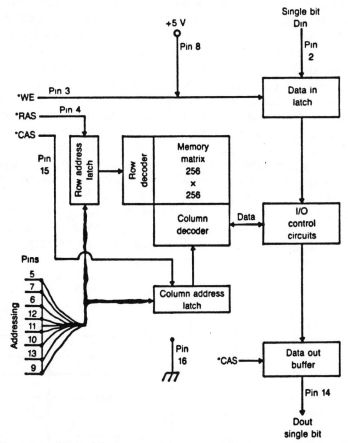

Fig. 7-31. In the 4164 chip the eight row and eight column address bits take turns entering through the eight address pins. *RAS strobes the row address into its latch and *CAS strobes the column address into its latch. The memory matrix outputs a bit when a read operation takes place. The matrix takes in a bit during a write.

As mentioned, the 4164s usually operate in a set of eight. There might be a ninth chip in the set, but it will usually be the controller of the set and not one of the memory participants. The eight chips that form the byte-sized registers are all working together to produce a 64 K × 8 total memory.

In the 64 K set the addresses range from 0 to 65,535 in decimal. In hex they are counted as 0000 to FFFF. In binary they are LLLLLLLLLLLLLLLL to HHHHHHHHHHHHHHHH. In Fig. 7-31 the bit matrix is in the center. Figure 7-32 is a closeup of the bit matrix arrangements in the 4116, the 4164 and the 41256. Note the sense amplifiers separating two sections of the matrix. The sense amplifiers aid in the capacitor refreshing business. The 4164 chips also have their bit matrixes divided in two. Each section has a 128 × 256 bit layout. Between the two sections are 256 sense amplifiers that aid in the refreshing. Incidentally, the refreshing of the 4164 chips need not be completed in 2 milliseconds as the 4116 chips require. Improved designs permit the refreshing to take place in 4 ms or even longer times.

The 41256 chips have their matrixes divided into four sections. Each of the four sections resembles a 4164. It is as if the 41256 chip is four 4164s squeezed into one 16-pin package. Following the same design stategy but taking the design one step further, the 1 MB chip squeezes the bits together even more. The 1 MB chip takes four of the 41256 chip arrangements, shrinks them as much as possible, and installs the four 41256 type layouts onto one 20-pin chip.

Whatever the number of bits on a chip, when a RAM or ROM fails, it either shorts or opens somewhere in the many circuits. Most of the time, what exactly happens is inconsequential. The main thing is, it died, and it is causing a performance problem. The trick is to locate the bad chip and change it to restore operation. If you are lucky and the short produces some smoke from the chip or if the chip if charred or visually broken, the bad chip is easily pinpointed. Most of the time though, the bad chip looks as good as the good chips. One fortunate feature is usually present. Typically only one chip at a time is defective, although multiple chip failure is always a possibility.

When a memory chip dies, one of the symptoms is the inability to run a part of a program. For instance, an address or two on a chip might have shorted out. When the program tries to access that address, the program, at that juncture fails. Other times the program runs but doesn't produce accurate results.

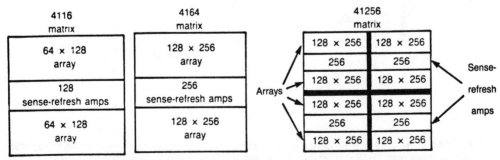

Fig. 7-32. The matrix layouts in the dynamic chips require amplifiers for refreshing as well as the bit holders. Note the 41256 layout is the same as four 4164 layouts.

Once the memory banks are suspected, the memory can be tested with a diagnostic program. There are many such programs for practically every popular computer. In fact, many of the computers come with an automatic diagnostic program that is run everytime the computer is turned on.

The test program often will pick out a bad memory chip and print some sort of identification number for the bad chip on the screen. The diagnostics could operate in the following way.

The MPU writes to all the RAM locations. Next the MPU reads all the locations to see if the data had arrived safely and was correctly installed. If the data is intact the memory location is deemed okay. Should a location not have received its assigned data, that indicates a defective location. A chip needs replacement.

The actual techniques of the test process is covered in more detail in Chapters 19-22.

# 8
# I/O Chips

The core of the digital computer is the MPU and memory chips. When you turn on your computer, the MPU contacts the operating system in ROM. A ROM program starts running. The program typically starts filling sections of RAM with operating instructions, initializes all the chips that will be involved in the data processing, and tests the chips to make sure there aren't any software or hardware faults. Once the ROM and MPU set up, the computer is ready to compute.

The data that needs processing is outside the computer. There are programs on disks or cassette tape. The keyboard stands ready to receive instructions and data from your fingertips. Joysticks, trackballs, and mice stand waiting to get moving. Light pens, kaola pads, modems, and other input devices are on call to input their forms of data.

Some of the data that needs to get into the computer and be processed is analog in nature. Other forms of data are digital. The analog data must be converted to digital before it can be used. The digital data can be used directly. Examples of analog data are cassette tape signals, audio, and video. Digital data is exemplified by keyboard strikes and cartridge inputs.

Once the data has been processed it is then ready to be output. Disks and cassette tape stand ready to receive an output. Mechanical contrivances are waiting for instructions on how to move. Modems are looking for data to send out over the telephone wires. TV displays need information to show text or graphics. Audio systems await sound information to make noises.

Therefore, besides the MPU and memory, a computer must also possess an input and an output system, commonly known as I/O. The I/O system consists of two distinct categories. One is the hardware. There are some wonderfully clever chips that input data to the computer from input devices both analog and digital. There are also equally smart chips that are able to output data to the peripheral devices. Most of these chips do a dual job consisting of both input and output.

The second item that is needed is software to run the chips that are doing I/O duty. There are usually several layers of I/O software that cushion the input and output chips from the external I/O devices. In addition there is more software installed between the I/O chips and the computer's insides. The software can be called BIOS, which stands for *basic input-output system*. Between the actual I/O chips and the BIOS the communication between the computer and its peripherals takes place smoothly.

In this chapter some typical I/O chips are discussed. One type of chip handles inputs such as the keyboard, joysticks and so forth. It also handles outputs to places like the RS-232 ports, modems and the like. Another type of chip that will be examined is the video output, which sends pictures to the TV display system. There will be more detail on the keyboard type I/O chip in Chapters 15, 16, and 22. Chapter 23 has more information on the video output type chip. The discussion starts with the PIA or peripheral interface adapter.

## PERIPHERAL INTERFACE ADAPTER

A common I/O chip that was designed by Motorola to operate in the 6800 family is the MC6821. It is found operating with the 6800 8-bit computers. It is also found performing I/O jobs in 16 -bit computers based around the 68000.

There are similar I/O chips that act in practically the same way. For example the Complex Interface Adapter, the 6526. It is a COMMODORE chip and is designed to operate with the family of MPU 6502 chips.

The 6821 PIA is a 40-pin chip made in an NMOS format. It comes in a DIP. It should receive careful handling, although it is not as touchy as a DRAM.

Today it costs between $3 and $4. Years ago, equivalent circuits cost thousands of dollars.

The PIA is connected directly to the data bus D7-D0 at pins 26-33 (Fig. 8-1). The MPU can write data to the PIA or read data from the PIA as if it were a memory location.

The chip itself can be addressed with three bits. There are three chip selects at pins 22, 23, and 24. They are CS0, *CS2, and CS1. To select the chip, the address bus must send a high to pin 22, a low to pin 23 and a high to pin 24.

Inside the chip, there are four addressable register systems. When the MPU sends out the chip select address, it uses the 14 MS bits. The remaining two LS bits are used to address the internal four locations.

Pins 35 and 36 are the two address lines used for the internal locations. Two address lines can choose from four locations.

The pins are named RS0 and RS1, standing for register selects 0 and 1. Between the three chip selects and the two register selects, one of the four locations in the PIA can be accessed.

The PIA is in a high impedance state until it is addressed. At that time, when the data is moved in or out of the PIA to the data bus, an Enable signal is applied at pin 25. The enable signal is the complete $\phi2$ signal from the MPU. Just as the $\phi2$ signal connects memory with the data bus, the $\phi2$ enables the PIA. The PIA reacts with the data bus during $\phi2$.

At pin 21, there is an R/W line. This signal is generated by the MPU and it controls the direction of the streams of data move on the data bus. When the R/W line is low, the

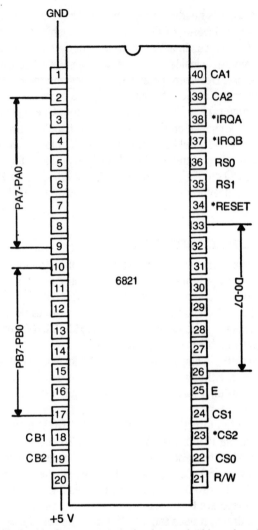

Fig. 8-1. The PIA is a 40-pin chip that connects to the data and address bus. It also has I/O ports to communicate with external circuits and devices.

input buffers are turned on and the data is sent from the MPU to the PIA address. If the R/W line is made high it sets up the PIA for outputting data from a PIA address to the MPU.

The MPU's addressing and data transfer chores to the four locations in the PIA are quite like the interfacing the MPU conducts with RAM. The other end of the PIA is where the differences show up. The PIA has two 8-bit input-output registers.

On this PIA, the I/O registers are pins 2-9 for PA0-PA7 and pins 10-17 for PB0-PB7. These two ports can input and output highs and lows to all the peripherals except the display. The highs and lows must be changed to analog signals or different level digital signals before the peripherals can use them. However, these ports are places where the new data enters the MPU-memory circuits or the finished data exits.

## Inside the PIA

Inside the PIA are four addressable circuits. There are two circuits on a side and two sides. The two sides are identical twins from a technician's point of view. We'll discuss the A side; except for its addresses, the B side is the same (Fig. 8-2).

On the A side, there is a circuit for the I/O function. Its output is PA7-PA0 at pins 9-2. This output is called the *Peripheral Data Register A*. It is connected internally bit by bit to a *Data Direction Register A*. The two registers work together and they are considered one location on the chip. Both are assigned one address.

The data direction register has one function: It decides whether a bit in the PDRA is to be an input bit or an output bit. When the computer is first turned on, the DDR is the register that receives the data from the MPU. If the DDR receives a 1 in one of its bits, the corresponding bit in the PDR is made an output. Should the DDR receive a 0, the bit in the PDR is defined as an input (Fig. 8-3). The MPU thus sets up the various bits in the PDR as inputs or outputs according to the 1s and 0s the MPU sends to the bit positions in the DDR.

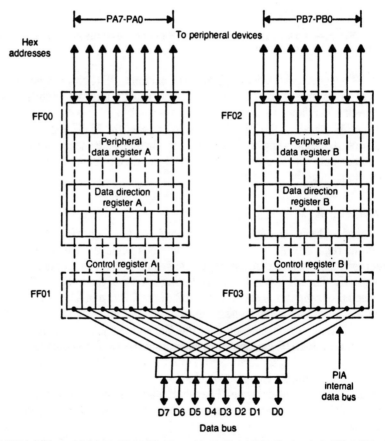

Fig. 8-2. A PIA has four addresses. There are two addresses each for the two twin sides. The data bus connects to both sides.

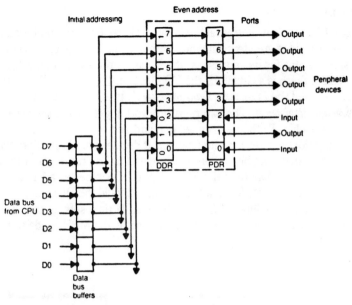

Fig. 8-3. The DDR bits set up the PDR bits. A 1 in a DDR makes the corresponding PDR bit act as an output. A 0 makes the bit into an input.

The PDR doesn't receive any assigned bit positions. PDR bits can be either state. The DDR receives an assigned bit position. The DDR's internal circuits control the direction the data can flow in the PDR.

Once the MPU assigns the DDR with its I/O duties, the MPU sends a signal to the PIA to turn off the addressing to the DDR. Any further addressing to the PDR-DDR circuit shall then only access the PDR. The DDR will then remain out of action until the MPU wants to change the I/O status of the PDR.

## Control Register A

The second address on each PIA side belongs to the Control Register, CR. The eight bits in the register are connected to the data bus when the CR is addressed.

It was mentioned before that the MPU can switch addressing contact between the PDR and its DDR. The MPU can do this by writing to bit 2 of the CR (Fig. 8-4). It works like this. When the computer is started up, bit 2 of the CR is a 0. The MPU then writes to the DDR and gives the bit positions their input and output assignments. Once that is done, the MPU writes to bit position 2 of the CR and installs a 1. This switches the addressing at the PDR-DDR location from contacting the DDR to contacting the PDR.

Besides bit 2 in the CR, there are seven other bits. They perform PIA control functions too. The seven bits get two control jobs done.

CA1 at pin 40 is an input-only line. The input, a square wave, can come from various devices or circuits. A circuit receives the wave and determines if the edge on the wave is rising or falling.

According to what use the CA1 line is assigned to , bit 1 of the CR register is made a 0 or 1. Bit 0 and bit 1 operate together. They control bit 7. Figure 8-5 shows the way bit

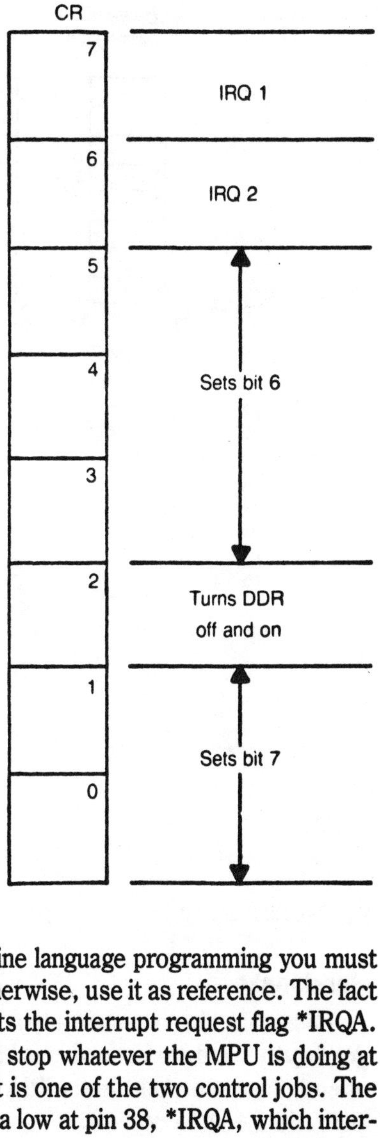

CR

7

IRQ 1

6

IRQ 2

5

4

Sets bit 6

3

2

Turns DDR
off and on

1

Sets bit 7

0

Fig. 8-4. Bit 2 of the CR determine if the DDR or the PDR is being addressed. A 1 in bit 2 of the CR puts the DDR on hold and the PDR is addressed.

7 is controlled. If you are going to do a lot of machine language programming you must learn all the little complicated steps of the chart. Otherwise, use it as reference. The fact that bits 0 and 1 control bit 7 is important. Bit 7 sets the interrupt request flag *IRQA. When the flag is set, *IRQA is ready to go low and stop whatever the MPU is doing at the end of its cycle, and service the interrupt. That is one of the two control jobs. The CA1 input at pin 40 with bits 0, 1, and 7, can cause a low at pin 38, *IRQA, which interrupts the MPU.

The second job the CR register can do is similar to the way bits 0 and 1 control bit 7. This job has bits 3, 4, and 5 controlling bit 6. Bit 6 in turn determines the role line CA2 performs (Fig. 8-6).

CA2 at pin 39 can play one of two parts. It can be an input or an output line. If it is an input line, then it is an interrupt like CA1. When CA2 is an interrupt, it works with *IRQA as its connection to the MPU like CA1 did.

Bit 5 determines if CA2 is an interrupt or not. When bit 5 is 0, CA2 is an interrupt. When bit 5 is set to 1, CA2 becomes an output and does not act as an interrupt.

As an output, line CA2 has bit 5 set as 1 and bit 6 becomes a 0 (Fig.8-7). This idles the *IRQA line, which is held high.

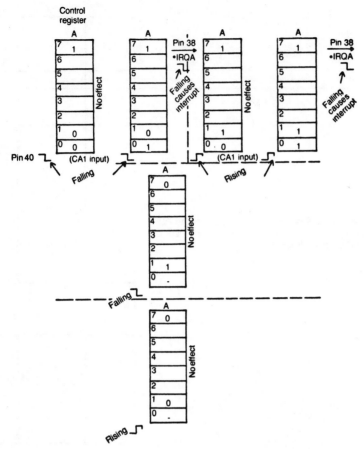

Fig. 8-5. Bit 0 and bit 1 of the CR operate together and control the state of bit 7.

## Handshake

When CA2 becomes an output-only line, it goes to work with CA1. The two of them get together and perform what is known as a *handshake*. The handshake is a term used often in computer talk. In the PIA lines, CA1 an input only and CA2 in its output only state, do the job (Fig. 8-8).

The handshake mode is set up when bits 5, 4, and 3 have bits 1 0 0 installed. The handshake takes place between a peripheral and the PIA. The peripheral is attached to PA7-PA0. The CA1 and CA2 lines are also attached to the peripheral. The CA1 is an input from the external device, and the CA2 is an output to it.

The handshake begins when the peripheral sends a signal to the PIA through CA1. The signal configures bits 0 and 1 of the CR (Fig. 8-4, Fig. 8-5). This in turn sets bit 7, the IRQA1 flag. This interrupt goes to the MPU and in effect says, "This is the peripheral calling. I have some data for you."

When the IRQA1 flag gets set, the CA2 output line to the peripheral, which was held low, goes high. This in effect is a message from the MPU saying, "I am ready, send the data."

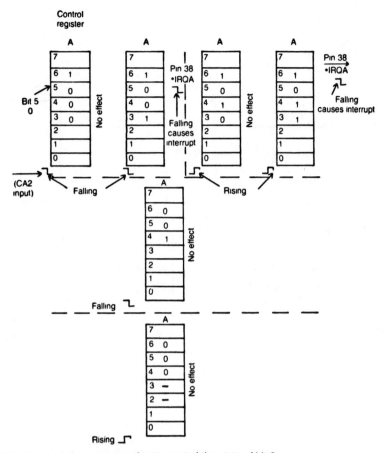

Fig. 8-6. Bits 3, 4, and 5 operate together to control the state of bit 6.

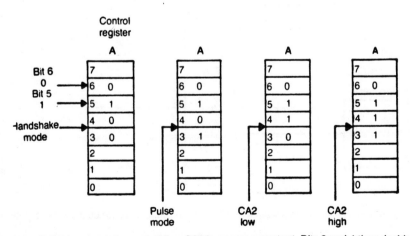

Fig. 8-7. When bit 5 is set to 1 the control line CA2 becomes an output. Bits 3 and 4 then decide what output mode to adopt.

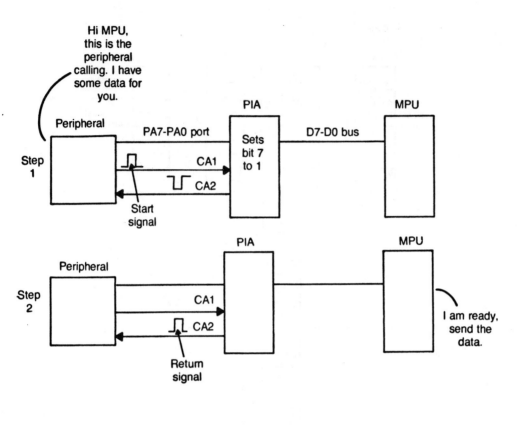

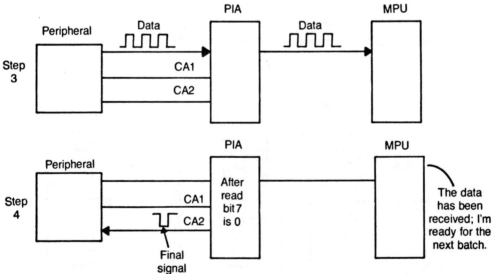

Fig. 8-8. Control lines CA1 as an input line and CA2 as an output line, conduct the handshake.

The peripheral sends the data which arrives at the port PA7-PA0. The MPU reads the data by accessing PDRA. At the end of the read operation, IRQA1 flag gets reset to 0. This in turn makes CA2 revert back to a low. This is the electronic signal from the MPU to the peripheral, "The data has been received, I'm ready for the next batch."

The handshake is simply messages back and forth between devices, in the form of highs and lows, that signals when to transmit data and then acknowledge receipt of the data.

The bit positions 5, 4, and 3 are configured as 1 0 0 for the handshake. There are three other modes possible, 1 0 1, 1 1 0, and 1 1 1. All of these modes are used by machine language programmers. They all keep the CA2 line in an output state. They are used when a full handshake is not needed. As a technician, it is important that you have an idea of what is going on, but it is rare that you will be called upon to use these procedures in your work. If you are placed in a job that requires you to write machine language programs, then you can master these software procedures. The register illustrations (Figs. 8-5, 8-6, and 8-7) will prove helpful.

## PIA Input and Output Tests

Chances are good that the PIAs or VIAs (Versatile Interface Adapters) or other such I/O 40-pin chips will be found plugged into a socket. If so, and if you have a replacement chip, testing it by direct replacement is your best bet. If it is not socketed, then it is a good idea to check it pin by pin with the logic probe or VOM rather than undertaking a desoldering operation. Also, if you do not have a replacement and the chip is a suspect, logic state and voltage tests must be used (Table 8-1).

First, test the inputs and see if all voltages and signals are entering the pins. Then test the outputs to see if the signals made it through the chip intact. Any deviation from the norm is a clue, and could lead you to the source of trouble.

The first inputs are the supply voltage. Pin 20 should have +5 V, and pin 1 ground or 0 V. This chip responds best to the logic probe, so pin 20 should have a high and pin 1 a low. With the energized chip, both the high and low should light the LEDs brightly.

The next inputs are the control lines. These are *RESET at pin 34, Enable at pin 25, and R/W at pin 21. The asterisk in front of reset means the pin is held high and will be activated with a low. If the line reads a high during the test, then reset is ok.

If you want to try the reset, you will reset all the registers in the PIA. When you press the reset button, all the interrupts will be disabled. The PA7-PA0 and PB7-PB0 ports will all become inputs. CA2 and CB2 will also become inputs.

If you probe pin 25, Enable, the LED named PULSE should light up. The $\phi 2$ pulse is entering the chip at the pin. It is the only timing for the chip and should always be present. If it is not there, that's a sign of trouble. It could have been lost at a short or open between the generator circuit and pin 25.

The third control line is R/W. When the line is R/W, the pin is held high and there should be a pulse on the line. The R/W line is an MPU output and a PIA input. If either the high or the pulse is missing, that is a valid clue, and the circuits back to the MPU origin can be checked for trouble.

Once the control inputs are tested and exonerated, the address lines are next. There are five input address lines, CS0, *CS2, CS1, RS0, and RS1. This means only five

Table 8-1. PIA Service Checkout Chart.

| KEYBOARD PIA SERVICE CHECKOUT CHART | | | |
|---|---|---|---|
| **Pin Number** | **High (1)** | **Low (0)** | **Pulse** |
| Ground 1 | | | |
| PA0 2 | ✔ | | |
| PA1 3 | ✔ | | |
| PA2 4 | ✔ | | |
| PA3 5 | ✔ | | |
| PA4 6 | ✔ | | |
| PA5 7 | ✔ | | |
| PA6 8 | ✔ | | |
| PA7 9 | ✔ | | |
| PB0 10 | ✔ | ✔ | |
| PB1 11 | ✔ | ✔ | |
| PB2 12 | ✔ | ✔ | |
| PB3 13 | ✔ | ✔ | |
| PB4 14 | ✔ | ✔ | |
| PB5 15 | ✔ | ✔ | |
| PB6 16 | ✔ | ✔ | |
| PB7 17 | ✔ | | ✔ |
| CB1 18 | ✔ | ✔ | ✔ |
| CB2 19 | | ✔ | |
| Vcc 20 | ✔ | | |
| R/W 21 | ✔ | | |
| CS0 22 | ✔ | | ✔ |
| *CS2 23 | ✔ | | ✔ |
| CS1 24 | ✔ | | |
| ENABLE 25 | | | ✔ |
| D7 26 | | | ✔ |
| D6 27 | | | ✔ |
| D5 28 | | | ✔ |
| D4 29 | | | ✔ |
| D3 30 | | | ✔ |
| D2 31 | | | ✔ |
| D1 32 | | | ✔ |
| D0 33 | | | ✔ |
| *RESET 34 | ✔ | | |
| RS1 35 | | | ✔ |
| RS2 36 | | | ✔ |
| *IRQB 37 | ✔ | | ✔ |
| *IRQA 38 | ✔ | | ✔ |
| CA2 39 | | ✔ | |
| CA1 40 | ✔ | | ✔ |

of the 16 address bus lines are connected to the chip. The chip selects CS0, *CS2, and CS1 are attached to any of the 14 higher order address lines, A15-A2. The designer assigned the combinations according to the address he wanted to give the chip.

The register selects RS0 and RS1 are connected to the lowest order lines A1 and A0. When you probe the five address pin connections, you will be reading whatever is on the address bus at that time. If there are other chips—like a decoder, for instance—between the address bus and the PIA, then the probe will show the decoder output. The schematic of the unit will tell what circuits are in the addressing scheme and you can judge the results of your address probing accordingly.

The next input tests to be made are the internal data bus connections, D7-D0, at pins 26-33. The data bus should show activity. The logic probe glows PULSE on all pins. If it is active, it is probably intact. Should you find one of the pins is not active, but the rest are, that is a good indication that somewhere in the strange acting line there could be a short or open.

The data pins were called an input even though the pins can be sending data in either direction. However, the data bus is inside the computer environs and connects at the internal side of the PIA. Pins on the other side of the PIA that attach to the external D/A, A/D circuits, and devices are considered the outputs, even though they ship data both ways. During checkout the internal connections are best thought of as inputs to the PIA, and the external connections the PIA outputs.

The external connections are the twin PDR registers, PA7-PA0 and PB7-PB0, and the twin control lines, CA1-CA2 and CB1-CB2. They work with the last two internal connections, *IRQA and *IRQB.

*IRQA and *IRQB at pins 37 and 38 are usually tied together and find their way to the interrupt pin on the MPU. They are held high (as the asterisk indicates) until an interrupt occurs. Then they go low which sets off a chain of events in the MPU interrupt priority circuits. When you are probing the *IRQ pins they should read a high. If they do not, trouble is nearby, possibly a defective PIA chip.

The external connections CA1 and CB1 are coming from the peripheral devices. They connect to their respective CRs and bits 0 and 1. These bits in turn set the interrupt flag bit 7. The interrupt flag works *IRQA and *IRQB that interrupts the MPU when the peripheral sends some data.

CA1 and CB1, at pins 40 and 18, will probe out as a high or low, with or without a pulse, according to what device is sending a signal to them. If the signal is pulsed, then the probe will light the PULSE LED. If the signal is just a high, then there won't be any pulse probed.

The external connections CA2 and CB2 at pins 39 and 19 can be programmed as inputs from a peripheral device, like CA1 and CB1, or as outputs to the device. When one is an output it can do the handshaking trick like the following.

During $\phi2$ the CA2 line starts off as a low. As the $\phi2$ cycle goes high CA1 causes the MPU interrupt by setting bit 7 of the CR. When bit 7 is set to CA2 line goes high. This tells the peripheral that the MPU is ready for the data (Fig. 8-9).

The peripheral sends the data to the PIA. The falling edge of $\phi2$ occurs and the data gets taken. This also clears bits 6 and 7. This makes CA2 go low. This tells the peripheral that the MPU has read the data and is ready for more.

The three other output CA2 modes are shown in the illustration (Fig. 8-7). When CR bits 5, 4, and 3 are 1 0 1, the CA2 line goes low from a high when it wants to convey a data received message from the MPU to the peripheral.

When the bits are 1 1 0 the CA2 line is set low. If 1 1 1 is the setting, the CA2 line is made into a high.

For testing, you could encounter any of these reading on the CA2 line. There is no hard and fast rule on what will be found there. You must read the schematic, and from your understanding of the circuit puzzle out if the reading is indicating a problem or not.

The remaining 16 pins 2-17 of the PIA are the two byte sized data ports. They are the link to the outside world from the innards of the computer. The data to and from the

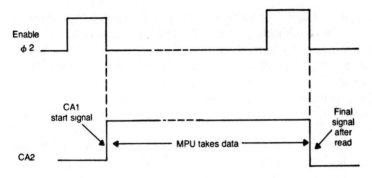

Fig. 8-9. The handshake timing is driven in step with the φ2 Enable clock signal.

computer is connected at D7-D0. The data is then attached inside the computer to the two Peripheral Data Registers A and B. A switching circuit lets the one data bus register maintain contact with both PDRs.

Remember that the PDRs share their address with a pair of corresponding Data Direction Registers. The DDRs configure the PDRs. The DDRs can be programmed to have either a 1 or 0 in each bit position. When a DDR has a 1 in a bit position, the corresponding PDR bit is made to do the job of an output. A 0 in a DDR bit makes the PDR bit into an input.

The programming of the DDR does not install any 1s or 0s into the PDR. It only configures the circuits of the PDR to be an output or an input.

The PDR operates like this. Suppose you configure bits 7, 5, 3, and 1 of the PDR as outputs by installing 1s in bits 7, 5, 3, and 1 of the DDR. Also, you place 0s in bits 6, 4, 2, and 0 of the DDR, making bits 6, 4, 2, and 0 of the PDR into inputs.

When you want to read the PDR, you have the MPU send a load instruction to its address. The contents of bits 6, 4, 2, and 0 will be transferred to the data bus and then to the MPU register designated in the instruction.

If you want to write to the PDR, have the MPU send a store instruction to its address. The byte that is to be transferred is placed on the data bus, enters the PIA, and is switched to bits 7, 5, 3, and 1 of the PDR. These bits can then output the byte to a peripheral circuit.

There are ways that the PDR can be forced to input from a bit that is configured as an output, but these are programming problems and not in the technician's province.

Most of the information on how the PIA operates is needed by the machine language programmer as well as by the technician. A lot of overlapping takes place between the programmer and the technician. The programmer who understands the hardware is a better programmer. The technician who understands machine language is a better technician.

When you probe the PIA's Peripheral Data Register pins, you are liable to read highs or lows with or without pulses. There could even be a three-state effect since the output buffers are three-state types. If you have a Service Chart like the one shown in Table 8-1, you can take reading of these 16 data lines and compare them with the desired states. A deviation indicates a problem.

A good test of the 16 pins is to treat them as two memory registers. Write to the output pins and see if they are able to perform their output job. For instance, if the output pin is sending audio to a TV set, try to get the audio bits to sound off. If they do, the PDR bits that are sending sound are ok.

## Diagnostic Programs

Like the memory registers, there are diagnostic programs to test all the I/O circuits. There is a program to test the audio circuits, one to check the joysticks, the keyboard, the printer, and so on. Run one by one, these tests check the bits in the PIA output data lines at the same time. If the peripheral devices are working, then it follows that the bits that are interfaced with them are ok too. When one of the peripheral circuits is down, then the bits become one of the suspects. The connections near the pins tend to short on occasion.

## VIDEO DISPLAY GENERATOR

When computers were young and large, the outputs were sent to teletypewriters and printing machines. All program composition was done with pencil and paper. The

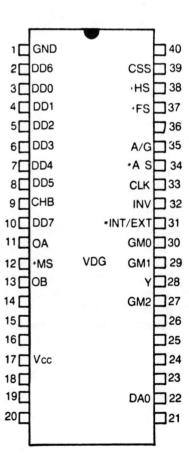

Fig. 8-10. The VDG chip is full of ROM circuits that generate alphanumerics and graphic characters to be displayed on the screen.

219

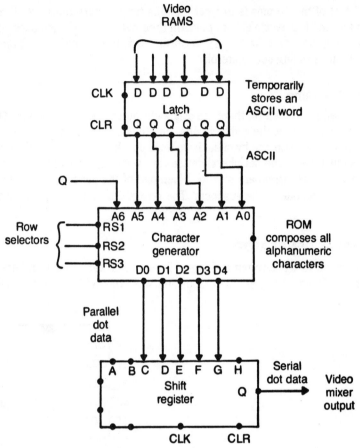

Fig. 8-11. A video interface can be fabricated with a character generator that has a latch input and a shift generator output.

programs were then installed on punch cards and read into the computer on a punch card reader. Video displays were hardly utilized at all.

In recent years the video display has changed all that. They are now an indispensable, integral part of the computer system. They became feasible when some clever designers developed the video interface chips (Fig. 8-10). They are output chips sending the digital data from memory locations to the video display, which is a special type of television receiver.

The video display chip had its beginnings in a ROM chip that is called a Character Generator. If you put the character generator together with a flip-flop latch on one side and a shift register on the other side, you have a video interface system (Fig. 8-11). The circuit operates in the following manner.

## Video RAM

In the typical microcomputer, a portion of RAM is set aside to hold the characters that appear on the TV display. This section is called video RAM. For instance, 512 bytes can be reserved.

When there are 512 bytes the video display block on the screen is laid out into 512 little blocks (Fig. 8-12). There are 32 blocks for a horizontal line and 16 blocks vertically. Each block is able to display one alphanumeric character.

As the keyboard is pressed during computing, the character is coded into ASCII and stored into video RAM in the sequence that the typing takes place. Each character becomes seven ASCII bits and is stored in the video RAM byte.

Meanwhile, the display is lit up. The light is actually 192 electron beam scan lines that are occurring 60 times a second, On a line there are 256 dots of light (Fig. 8-13). A properly-synced signal can turn any of the dots off and on according to plan.

The character generator is a ROM coding device. The character generator can receive an input of ASCII bits and output seven rows of five dots each. One of the little character blocks on the TV face displays a character that is seven rows high and five dots wide (Fig. 8-14). If the display receives information on which dots should be on and which ones off, it will show a character in its block.

The circuit operates by coinciding with the CRT scanning. As the scan begins in the top left block, the first video RAM location, that coincides with that block, outputs its

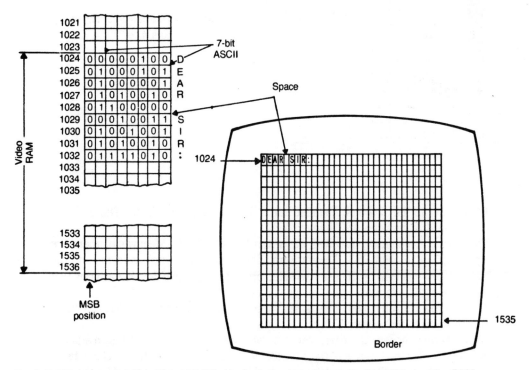

Fig. 8-12. The screen is laid out into 512 little blocks that act as windows for the 512 byte video RAM.

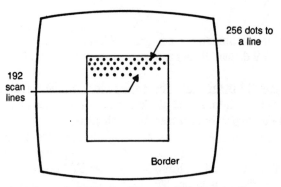

Fig. 8-13. The display is composed of 192 scan lines with 256 dots on a line.

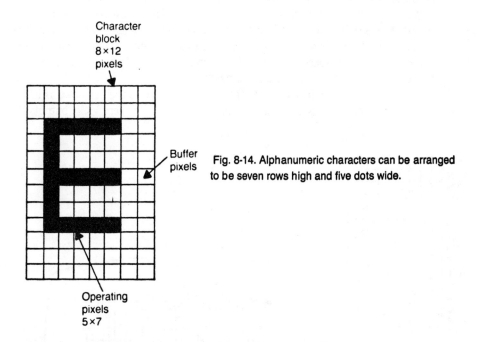

Fig. 8-14. Alphanumeric characters can be arranged to be seven rows high and five dots wide.

ASCII character to the data bus. Installed in the data bus is a video latch. The latch is a hex D flip-flop. It stores the ASCII seven bits.

The character generator receives the seven bits at A6-A0. Meanwhile, there are three pins RS1, RS2, and RS3. They are row selectors. There are seven rows in the display block that can light up. These row selectors choose the five dots in each row that should light according to what character should be displayed.

The first row chosen is 000. This is the top row number. Row two is 001, row three is 010, and so on to row seven, 110.

With 000 row chosen, the character generator outputs the five dot information to the shift register for the top row of the first character. Then the next ASCII character is output to the generator. The generator outputs the top row dot information for the second little block in the display. As the top scan line continues, the ASCII characters are applied to the generator and have their top rows illuminated properly.

At the end of the first scan line, there is a complete row of dots some lit and others off. The cathode ray then scans line after line until the entire display block and all 512 characters are on the screen. Then it repeats the scanning over and over. The display is a window into the contents of the video RAM.

Between the character generator and the video output circuits there is a shift register. The shift register is a parallel-to-serial converter. The five dots for each row of each character exit the generator at D4-D0. The five dots are injected into the shift register. They exit the generator in parallel fashion. The shift register then outputs them one at a time (serially) to the video mixer and output circuits. From there they are sent to the CRT gun to modulate the cathode ray and be seen.

Early character generators were individual chips that were connected with other individual chips and produced a video interface. In recent years the latches, character generation, and shift registers along with a number of other circuits have all been successfully contained on large DIPs. They operate in essentially the same way, but they are easier to service because of the multiple containment.

## Testing a Video Generator

To check out large chips, input and output tests are used. On the input side, from the computer, digital tests are required. On the output side, to the display, analog tests are required.

A typical 40-pin video interface chip schematic drawing shows most of the pins are inputs (Fig. 8-15). There are only a few outputs. First of all, there are the ASCII bit inputs that come from the video RAM. They enter the D7-D0 data bus pins.

The next inputs are there to select the mode that the chip is going to output. In most computers, there are a number of graphic modes besides alphanumerics which let the computer draw charts, graphs, and pictures. These modes are ROM-controlled like the keyboard characters. Between the alphanumerics, the graphics, and alphasemigraphics the chip can generate a dozen or more different display modes. The pins that select the particular ROM inside the chip and control it are GM2-GM0, *INT/EXT and A/G.

This particular chip (shown earlier in Fig. 8-10) is a 6847 and is a member of the 6800 family. It sells for $11.25 and contains circuits that years ago would have cost about $1000 in discrete form. The chip is a 40-pin DIP and is powered with +5 V at pin 17; ground is at pin 1. The supply voltage is usually the first area to check when the 6847 is under suspicion.

After you determine that the supply is ok, the next tests should be made at the outputs. There are only five output pins.

The signals put out by these pins produce a complete color TV display. They are individual signals that are applied to a color video mixer chip. The video mixer chip is an analog circuit exactly like the ones found in color TV receiver. These circuits are discussed in Chapter 23.

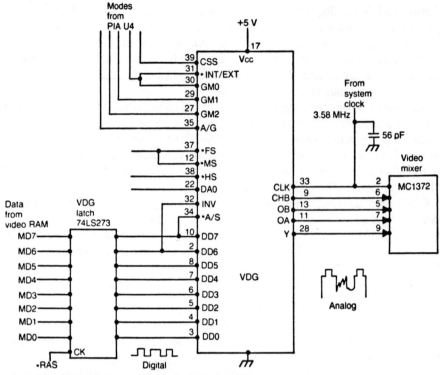

Fig. 8-15. The VDG chip has a few outputs but a lot of inputs.

Coming out of pin 28 is the Y signal (Fig. 8-16.) Y is the designation for the composite black and white video signal. It contains the horizontal and vertical sync pulses and the blanking level. the signal is given four levels of brightness.

The digital coding to turn the dots off and on is contained in the Y signal. The dots are the only actual video that is displayed. Alphanumerics and graphics are formed by the dot off and on patterns.

The best way to test for the presence of the Y signal is with an ordinary service oscilloscope with a high impedance probe. The signal is the same composite monochrome Y signal found in any TV. The oscilloscope displays the signal. It will be very weak on the oscilloscope but it will be viewable.

When the Y signal is present, that means the chip was able to put together the horizontal sync, coming in at pin 38, *HS, and vertical sync, entering the chip at pin 37, *FS. There could still be problems in the internal ROM mode circuits, which do not show up in the oscilloscope picture.

The other output pins, OA OB, and CHB, have no definitive tests. In the computer tested, OA and OB probe LOW (Table 8-2). CHB does not affect the probe at all. The CLK pin is the input from the clock. 14.31818 MHz is divided by four, and this result is the frequency on pin 33, CLK. This is the color video reference signal needed to produce the color picture.

224

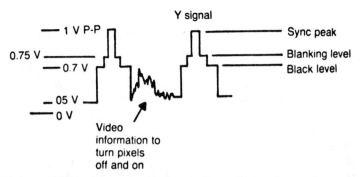

Fig. 8-16. The Y signal exits pin 28 and is one of the first signals to look for during video failure.

Inside the chip, there are ROM circuits that can generate a lot of different display modes. This one has four alpha semigraphic modes and eight full graphics modes. There are also a few more modes hidden in the chip that the manufacturer's notes do not even mention. These can be accessed by the machine language programmer, but are not usually bothered with. These are all developed in addition to the usual alphanumerics. Any one of these modes can be activated and will appear on the TV face.

The modes are set by the control lines. At the pins at the top left of the schematic are control lines that come from a PIA (Fig. 8-15). Then there are two other mode controllers in the center batch of lines. At the bottom left are D7-D0 from the data bus. These are the bits from video memory that will turn the dots off and on after the ROM character-graphic generators finish with them.

Table 8-2. VDG Service Checkout Chart.

| VDG | | | | | |
|---|---|---|---|---|---|
| | | | | SERVICE CHECKOUT CHART | |
| Pin Numbers | | Logic Probe | Pin Numbers | | Logic Probe |
| 1 | GND | Low | 39 | CSS | Low |
| 2 | DD6 | Pulse | 38 | *HS | Low-Pulse |
| 3 | DD0 | Low-Pulse | 37 | *FS | Hi-Low-Pulse |
| 4 | DD1 | Low-Pulse | 35 | A/G | Low |
| 5 | DD2 | Low-Pulse | 34 | *A/S | Low-Pulse |
| 6 | DD3 | Low-Pulse | 33 | CLK | Nothing |
| 7 | DD4 | Low-Pulse | 32 | INV | Pulse |
| 8 | DD5 | Low-Pulse | 31 | *INT/EXT | Low |
| 9 | CHB | Nothing | 30 | GM0 | Low |
| 10 | DD7 | Low-Pulse | 29 | GM1 | Low |
| 11 | 0A | Low | 28 | Y | Oscilloscope ⎍⎍ (Very Weak) |
| 12 | *MS | Hi-Low-Pulse | 27 | GM2 | Low |
| 13 | 0B | Low | | | |
| 17 | Vcc | High | 22 | DA0 | Hi-Low-Pulse |

## Pin-By-Pin Checkout

When you probe these pins the following results can be expected when the inputs are ok. Any deviation indicates possible trouble (Table 8-2).

Pin 39, CSS, should be low. CSS controls the color of the border around the display block. CSS is said to *default* to a low. This means that if no other signal is applied, the pin will automatically be given a low. When CSS is held low, the normal border color will be displayed and the mode has a choice of four given colors. If CSS is programmed high, then a different border color is shown and a choice of four other colors are given. Unless it is set differently, the pin should read low.

Pins 30 and 31 are tied together in this chip. *INT/EXT is a graphic mode called "semigraphic −6": It is tied to GM0, which is one of the selectors of the eight full graphic modes. The two pins probe low. GM1 and GM2 at pins 29 and 27 also read low.

Pin 35, A*/G, selects between semigraphics and full graphics. It is normally held low. Pin 34, A*/S, selects between alphanumerics and semigraphics. It reads low-pulse. The pulse is there because pin 34 is shorted to one of the data lines.

Another mode control has a limited function. On a black and green screen, it chooses between black characters on a green background or green characters on a black background. It is at pin 32, called INV (for inversion). It is held low which keeps a black character. There is also a pulse since it is tied to a data line too.

At pin 22 is DA0. It probes high, low, and pulse, all at the same time. It is a color sync signal and works with the CLK 3.58 MHz color oscillator signal coming in at 33.

## Display Block

Pins 37, *FS, and 38, *HS, are the signals that produce the Display Block that is shown inside the border on the TV raster. These are two interrupt type signals. *FS stands for *Field Sync* and *HS stands for *Horizontal Sync*. Field sync is just another way to say vertical sync.

The video raster fills the entire screen with light. The light is composed of about 256 scanning lines, starting at the upper left and like writing is scanned to the bottom right. The computer display block is developed in the raster. The block uses 192 of the 256 raster lines. This produces a border at the top and bottom of the screen when the 192 lines are centered.

The block does not use the entire scan from side to side. Each block scan line goes through 32 little blocks. The blocks each have 8 picture dots. This makes 256 dots on a scan line. A raster scan line has many more than 256 available dot spots. If the 256 block scan lines are centered in the raster, there a border is formed on the right and the left of the block scanning area.

The dots are called *dot clocks* or *pixels*. The term *pixel* is coined from a contraction of the words picture element. The dot clock expression comes from the fact that a multiple of the clock frequency forms the dots. In this case, the dots are formed as one half of the 3.58 MHz color reference frequency, originated by dividing the master clock frequency.

The *FS signal is a 60 Hz frequency that is sent to the display along with the video to sync the raster into running along with the computer's field sync. The *FS signal is made to coincide with the trailing edge of the TV raster's vertical sync pulse as it goes from high to low. That way, the raster and the display block run in step.

## Raster

The *FS signal is tied to pin 12, *MS, a three-state line. The low forces the chips inputs into a high impedance state. This stops all signal output during the vertical retrace of the TV raster.

As *FS pulses from low back to high, the three-stating stops and the chip starts, sending signal again. The signal is in perfect sync vertically with the raster beginning scan lines. When you probe the *FS-*MS pins, there should be a high, low, and pulse reading all at the same time. The 60 Hz signals are picked up by the probe. The probe reads the low that causes the three-stating and syncing. It also reads the high component and reveals the activity of 60 Hz.

The *HS pin is receiving the horizontal sync for the display block. The horizontal sync pulse is also added to the video output of the chip and is sent to the horizontal oscillator that is forming the raster. The high to low pulse at *HS is made to coincide with the leading edge of the horizontal pulse that is driving the raster across the screen.

The raster starts scanning of the 256 line field with dark lines, as it scans the top border. The dot clock information does not start till the border has been scanned. The dot clocks are centered in the raster scanning lines. As each scanning line that has pixel information in it is scanned, it starts off dark till the centered pixels arrive at the cathode gun. The pixels then modulate the cathode ray. Each pixel either cuts off the ray or lets it through to light the phosphor screen. At the end of the pixels, the ray is cut off for the rest of the scan forming the right border. Then it retraces and begins the next scan line beneath the previous line. It continues line after line until the entire display block of 192 lines are shown. The raster continues until the 256 lines have been scanned. Then it retraces from the bottom of the screen back to the top.

When you probe the *HS line, there is a low and a pulse present. This is the response the logic probe gives to an active *HS pulse.

## Data on the Screen

The remaining pins on the chip are D7-D0. They receive the data from the data bus to be placed into the composite video signal. The data enters the chip and is directed to the ROM stage that controls the mode that has been selected. The ROM accepts the data and changes it into highs and lows that form the characters or graphics in color on the TV screen. The digital information from the ROM is inserted into the video signal. The highs and lows turn the pixels off or on according to the ROM plan.

# 9
# Reading Timing Diagrams

The timing for any computer starts with the beating of its clock. The sine wave frequency is then sent to the confines of a square wave generator. The output of the generator then becomes the driving force throughout the computer. All of the system timing is derived from the original basic frequency the crystal in the clock oscillates at. Some computers have two crystal oscillator circuits that produce two different frequencies as a convenience. The clocks can produce all sorts of frequencies according to the computer's needs.

If the computer is an 8-bit type such as the ones using the 6800, 6502, Z80, or 8080, the processor frequency could be anywhere between one to four megahertz. A 16-bit computer using an 8086 or 68000 could run the processor at four, six, or eight megahertz. As the processors become larger, their frequencies could be ten megahertz or more. The 32-bit 80386 uses frequencies that range from 16 MHz to 25 MHz. All of the clocks operate in a similar manner; the higher frequencies do the same things as the lower frequencies, they just do them faster.

All of the processors have their own family of support chips. They all work into memories, I/O, video output display generators, audio output chips, and other specially designed circuits. Proper timing is a must in order for the streams of data traveling in the address, data, and control buses to do so at precisely the right times and go to the right places. The timing jobs are essential and tricky. For the most part, timings are measured in nanoseconds or billionths of a second. There is little room for timing errors.

Designers must spend a lot of effort, figuring out how to time the MPU with the rest of the chips. The technician, on the other hand, comes in contact with computers that have the timing parameters all worked out. The technician must understand the timings in case they need to be tested during troubleshooting. Some subtle troubles require the use of an expensive multitrace oscilloscope to check the highs and lows for their timings.

## CLOCK FREQUENCY

Let's examine a clock frequency for an 8-bit MPU. The 16-bit and 32-bit frequencies operate in a similar way, just faster. The 8-bit clocks typically run around 1 MHz. A crystal in the clock oscillator circuit, for this frequency is cut to run precisely at 14.31818 MHz. Divided by four, the frequency becomes 3.579545 MHz. If you are a TV technician, you will recognize that as the color reference frequency. The 8-bit computers usually provide color so it can be displayed on any home TV receiver. This exact frequency is vital if the computer is to show a color display.

Not quite as exact is the frequency the processor itself is supposed to run at. A 1 MHz frequency to run the processor is allowed to be off a bit. Therefore, the master frequency of 14.31818 MHz can be divided by 16. This produces a processor driving frequency of 0.89 MHz. This is close enough to 1.0 MHz that the processor runs without any difficulty. Take note that this approximate 1 MHz signal is beating at approximately a million times a second, making one full processor cycle one microsecond long. One microsecond is 1000 nanoseconds. Figure 9-1 shows a typical square wave cycle when the processor frequency is 1 MHz.

In the Z80 and 8080, the 1 MHz can be used directly to drive the processors. In the 6800 and 6502, the 1 MHz frequency is put through a phase splitter circuit that outputs two 1 MHz signals. They are the same frequency but out of phase with each other. They could be called (phase) 1 and 2. They each do different jobs as shown in Fig. 9-2.

## BUS CONTROL

The two individual 1 MHz square waves, which are symmetrical and out of phase with each other, control the traffic on the address bus and the data bus. $\phi1$ is assigned to the address bus. $\phi2$ keeps the data bus straight. $\phi2$ has an assistant on the data bus because it goes in two directions. The assistant is the R/W line.

$\phi1$ is able to take control of the address bus by running the program counter. $\phi1$ is injected into the PC's circuits, and they are wired to respond.

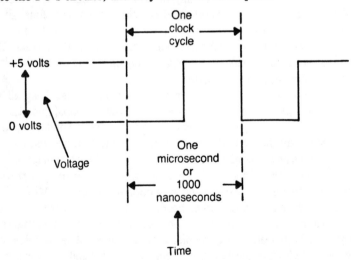

Fig. 9-1. A one megahertz clock cycle is timed as happening in one microsecond.

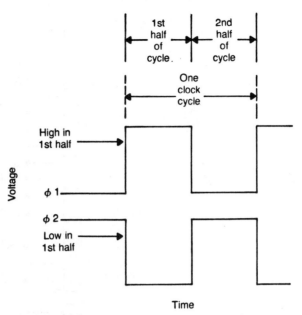

1st
half
of
cycle.

2nd
half
of
cycle

One
clock
cycle

High in
1st half

$\phi$ 1

$\phi$ 2

Low in
1st half

Voltage

Time

Fig. 9-2. In the 6502 and 6800 MPUs, the master frequency is made into two square waves that are identical but out of phase with each other.

As the $\phi$1 cycle begins it goes high. The rising edge triggers the PC to place its contents on the address bus (Fig. 9-3A). This initiates the addressing. At the start of a program run, address 0000000000000000 is placed on the bus. That address is activated. The $\phi$1 cycle continues.

The time required to execute a full $\phi$1 cycle is about 1000 nanoseconds. The high takes up about 500 nanoseconds. Then the falling edge arrives. The falling edge triggers the PC too. It forces the PC to increment by one (Fig. 9-3B). This places the next address 0000000000000001 on the PC. The low of the cycle then runs for about 500 nanoseconds.

Actually, the timings are not exactly 500 and 500 for the high and low. There is about a 25 nanosecond time lapse for the rising edge and another 25 nanosecond period for the falling edge. From an overall approach though the 500-500 thinking will be close enough. If actual timings are needed for some reason, take them off the manufacturers spec sheets.

$\phi$2 runs behind $\phi$1. About the same time that $\phi$1 is experiencing its falling edge and incrementing the PC, $\phi$2's rising edge takes place.

$\phi$1 has activated the address. The $\phi$2 rising edge then attaches the data bus to the address (Fig. 9-4A). A read or write could take place at that time.

If the read/write line is an R/*W, then a high will be on the R/*W line for a read and a low for a write. Standby R/*W voltage is usually a high.

If the $\phi$2 rising edge occurs and the R/*W is high then the location that was addressed outputs the data in the location to the data bus. The high persists for 500 ns and then the falling edge occurs.

231

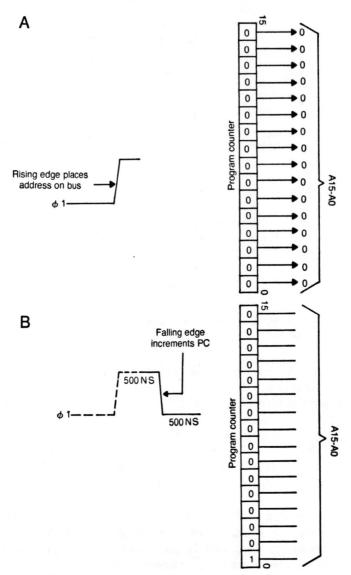

A

Rising edge places
address on bus →

φ1

Program counter

A15-A0

B

Falling edge
increments PC

500 NS

φ1

500 NS

Program counter

A15-A0

Fig. 9-3. The φ1 signal is assigned the jobs of placing addresses from the program counter on the address bus and then incrementing the PC.

The falling edge latches the data into the instruction register of the MPU (Fig. 9-4B). The MPU takes it from there. It decodes the instruction or piece of data, and directs it to the accumulator, index register, PC or what have you.

Then the next cycle begins, and the next location is addressed.

φ1 is internal to the MPU. It drives the PC to place the desired locations on the address bus and then increments the PC. It doesn't do much else. φ2, on the other hand, acts outside the MPU. In addition to placing data on the data bus and latching it into the data destination, it performs other timing jobs.

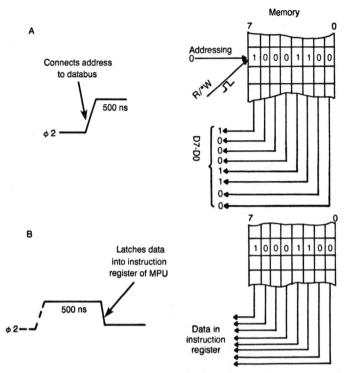

Fig. 9-4. The φ2 signal is assigned the jobs of connecting a location to the data bus and then latching or gating the data into its destination, φ2 is aided in its task by the R/W control line.

## MEMORY ACCESS TIME

When the program counter places an address on the 16-bit address bus, a number of things must happen. A few of the MS bits are removed and decoded first. They are the chip selects. They pick out the chips that are to be accessed.

The rest of the bits are applied to the address lines of the memory chips. In a dynamic memory array, seven bits are sent to the row address decoder. Next seven bits are sent to the column address decoder. Then the memory bit selected in each chip of the array is readied for the data bus line. This all takes time. From the time the 16 bits are placed on the address bus till the address is located and the data is in a stable position to be output, a lot of nanoseconds go by. This all must go on within one cycle for either a read or write operation. Let's examine a read.

### Read Operation

The first time period that elapses is the rise time of φ1 (Fig. 9-5). This places the address on the PC. A typical amount of time is 25 ns. The next time period occurs when the address goes out over the address bus and reaches the location. This time is about 300 ns.

The next period is the time when the location is read, or in other words the memory is accessed and the data put on the data bus. This is the longest delay and takes about 575 ns.

233

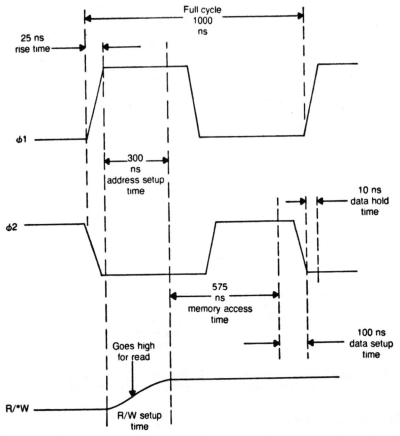

Fig. 9-5. The memory access time for this 1000 ns cycle is about 575 ns.

So far, 900 ns out of the 1000 ns cycle are used up. That leaves 100 ns for the data to be latched into the instruction register in the MPU before the next cycle starts—just enough time.

The 100 ns is the *data setup time*. This is an important parameter. Immediately after the data setup time, $\phi 2$ falls and the cycle ends. However, the data must remain stable for a short time after it is latched into the MPU. In this case, the data is held stable for another 10 nanoseconds after $\phi 2$ falls. This is called *data hold time*. The data setup time stability before the $\phi 2$ fall and the data hold time after the $\phi 2$ fall are critical for the data to be read correctly.

In catalogs, the memory chips all have a timings like 80 ns, 100 ns, 120 ns, 200 ns, and 250 ns listed. The memory access time of this MPU example was that long period of 575 ns. All chips up to and including the 450 ns type would have plenty of time left over if they were working with this MPU. The memory access time of an MPU must be greater than the amount of time it takes the memory chip to be read.

In computers that use faster clocks, faster memory chips must be used. The cycle time reduces from the leisurely 1000 ns to much less. This reduces the memory access times, making faster memory chips necessary.

## Write Operation

During a write operation, the sequence of events is similar but not the same. The read operation has the MPU opening up a memory address, the data in the memory placed on the data bus, and the MPU takes the bits into its instruction register.

In contrast, the write operation has the MPU placing bits on the data bus. Then the MPU opens up the memory address where it wants to store the data. After that, the MPU causes the RAM to accept the data (Fig. 9-6).

The first time period that elapses, like the read operation, has the rising edge of $\phi 1$, forcing the PC to place an address on the address bus. The address rides out on the bus and becomes stable. It takes about 300 nanoseconds for the address to settle into place. Manufacturers call this the *Address Setup Time*. Don't confuse this with Data Setup Time. The address time indicates a period of addressing in both the read and write operation.

At the same time the address is setting up, the R/*W is made low by the MPU. Making the R/*W line low indicates to the memory devices that the MPU is writing to

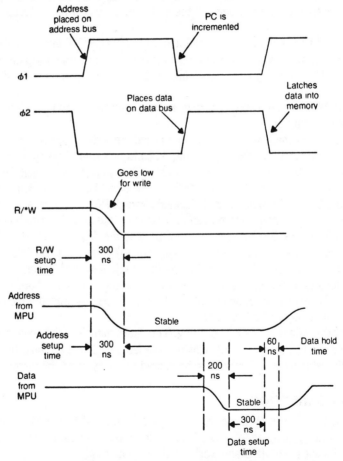

Fig. 9-6. The R/*W line goes low for the write operation. The address setup takes place at the same time.

them. The R/*W line also takes 300 ns to get stable. However, it is getting low at the same time as the address is settling on the address lines so no time is used up.

Meanwhile $\phi 1$ continues. The falling edge of $\phi 1$ increments the PC. Down at $\phi 2$ as $\phi 1$ is falling, $\phi 2$ is rising. The rising edge of $\phi 2$ places the data from the MPU onto the data bus. This takes place 500 ns into the cycle. It takes the data 200 ns to get on the data bus and become stable. This leaves the remaining 300 ns in the 1000 ns cycle for the data to be available to the falling edge of $\phi 2$. This is plenty of setup time for the data.

The falling edge of $\phi 2$ latches the data from the bus into the memory location. The data then remains stable on the data bus for 60 ns. This hold time is usually satisfactory.

To summarize the read and write timings, the complex-looking waveshapes must be closely examined. This is easier than it first appears. There are a number of very similar patterns that accentuates the differences.

First of all, in both the read and write drawings, the $\phi 1$ and $\phi 2$ waveshapes are identical. They do not vary. The $\phi 1$ handles the addressing and $\phi 2$ the data movement.

The addressing waveform is also exactly the same whether the data is going one way or the other. The Address Setup Time is 300 ns during every addressing operation. The memory accessing does not begin till the address takes 300 ns to occupy the address bus.

The R/*W line is different for read and write. The R/*W line is made high by the rising edge of $\phi 1$ when a read operation is to take place. The waveform on the read chart shows the R/*W line going from low to high and then staying high for the duration of the read cycle.

The R/*W line on the write chart goes from high to low and then stays low for the duration of the write cycle.

The data movement is where the complications arise. During a read, the data is coming out of memory. Nothing comes out till halfway through the cycle, the rising edge of $\phi 2$. Then the data emerges and gets stable. The stability must last for its specified Data Setup Time of 100 ns. Then the falling edge of $\phi 2$ latches the data into the MPU.

The data line on the write chart is labeled *From MPU*. The data is coming out of the MPU and going to memory. Here again, no data is placed on the data bus till the rising edge of $\phi 2$. The data then moves out and traverses the data bus. It takes 200 ns to get stable and sets up for 300 ns. The $\phi 2$'s falling edge then strobes the data into the memory location. The 60 ns hold time maintains the stable data installation.

The memory locations are accessed by the address bus for both read and write operations. The access must be completed before the data is moved. Once the access is stable then the data can be transmitted.

Moving the data requires strict timing. The data timing is mainly concerned with stability around the falling edge of $\phi 2$, which is the latcher. The data must be stable before and after the latching in order for it to be seated properly after the move.

## MEMORY CONNECTION

The MPU is driven by the clock cycles. $\phi 1$ is internal to the MPU and keeps the program counter placing addresses on the address bus and incrementing address after address. $\phi 2$ leaves the MPU and works with the data bus.

$\phi2$ is low at the beginning of a cycle. While it is low, the address bus and the R/W line take 300 ns and become active. As soon as they are both stable, the MPU's memory access time begins.

The access time is the amount of time the MPU has to either place data on the data bus or have the addressed location place data on the bus. Once the data is on the bus, access time is over and the setup time begins.

The $\phi2$ rising edge occurs in the middle of the access time. $\phi2$ actually gets the data out on the bus. Then $\phi2$ stays high for the rest of the cycle.

After access time, the data gets stable during setup time. Once the data is stable, the cycle comes to an end as the falling edge of $\phi2$ latches the data into the MPU during a read or into the memory during a write. After the latching, a small amount of hold time keeps the data stable on the data bus so the latching doesn't fail.

ROM and RAM chips are listed in catalogs with a nanosecond timing. This is the access time of the chip. A 150 ns listing means the chip is fast. A 450 ns listing denotes a slower speed access time. A 1000 ns chip speed is very slow and could be a problem unless special circuits are installed to match the MPU accessing speed.

The 6502 MPU has a memory access time of about 575 ns. It can access the 150 ns chip with plenty of nanoseconds left over. The 450 ns chip can also be accessed by the 6502 comfortably. The 1000 ns chip though is a problem. The chip takes it good old time and won't permit being accessed in less than the 1000 ns. The 6502 is all finished accessing after 575 ns. The 6502 can't work with a 1000 ns chip unless special circuits are installed.

## ACCESSING ROMs

ROM chips are usually expensive to replace. It's not because the bare chip itself is expensive; the cost comes from the programs that are burnt into the address in the chip. ROM chips contain permanent programs.

The ROM hardware connection to the MPU is not overly complex. The ROM doesn't have any write operation. The MPU can only read its burnt in programs. If the MPU tries to write to the ROM, the ROM cannot respond.

As a result, there are less signals traveling the lines between the MPU and the ROMs. Figure 9-7 shows a 450 ns ROM chip. There is one chip select line, and an R/W line. Then there is an 11-bit address connection and the usual eight-bit data connections. The 11 bits in the internal address lines means there are 2048 byte sized memory locations the MPU can read from.

There is only one chip select, because this chip is usually selected by a direct connection from a separate decoder chip. The other five address bits are attached to the decoder. When they are all selected, the decoder enables the ROM.

The R/W line also enables the chip if a read signal is applied. If a write signal is on the line, the chip stays in a three-state condition. The chip will not turn on unless both the chip select and the read signal are applied together.

## ROM TIMING

The ROM times itself with the MPU in the following way. As the MPU reacts to the clock and begins its cycle, the address and the read function line turn on. It takes them

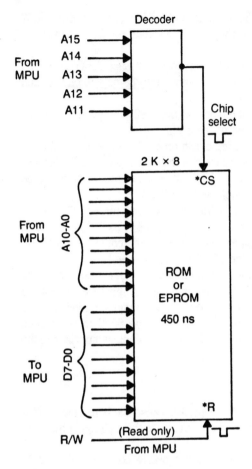

From MPU
- A15
- A14
- A13
- A12
- A11

Decoder

Chip select

2 K × 8

*CS

From MPU — A10-A0

ROM or EPROM

450 ns

To MPU — D7-D0

*R

R/W — (Read only) From MPU

Fig. 9-7. The eleven lines A10-A0 are able to address 2048 internal byte locations.

300 ns to do so. Meanwhile, at the ROM, the chip select and the read function are enabled. At this point, the ROM starts allowing the MPU to access it, and the 450 ns timing begins (Fig. 9-8).

The $\phi 2$ rising edge arrives, and the data from the location addressed is placed on the data bus. The data has sufficient time to set up on the bus. The $\phi 2$ falling edge closes out the cycle by latching the data into the instruction register. The data remains on the bus for a short hold time, and the read is complete.

## STATIC RAM

Static RAM is used in computers in areas that require small amounts of memory. For example, the video RAM could be static while the rest of the computer memory is dynamic. Another case could be a small computer that only needs 4 K or less. Static RAM is very stable and feasible in these applications. However, static RAM takes up a lot of circuit board room and is expensive in comparison to dynamic RAM. When a lot of RAM is required, dynamic RAM is chosen over static RAM. The technician must be familiar with both types.

238

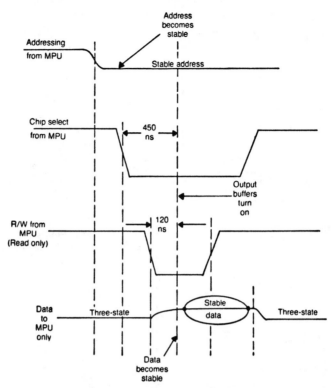

Fig. 9-8. The internal addressing, the chip select, and the R/W line when activated turn on the ROM output buffers. Stable data then exits the ROM chip onto the data bus.

The 2114 is a common static RAM chip. It is organized in a 1 K × 4 bit layout (Fig. 9-9). It is built on an 18-pin DIP, and it operates like the ROM except that it can be written to as well as read from. There is one chip select that is enabled by an external decoder chip. Address lines A15-A10 are connected to the decoder. When they apply the chip address to the decoder, a low turns on the Enable circuit.

There are ten internal addresses, lines A9-A0. They can choose individual nybble locations from the 1024. There is a read/write type line called *WE, for write enable. When *WE is high, the chip is in a read state. When *WE goes low, it is in a write state.

Four data lines attach to four lines of the data bus. Two 2144s attach to the eight data bus lines to form a byte. The 2144's data bus lines are called I/04-I/01. They can, of course, handle data in or data out.

### Read Operation

The timing for a read operation is begun in the MPU. The $\phi 1$ rising edge causes the program counter to output the RAM address. There is a small amount of delay, about 30 nanoseconds, for the address to reach the decoder and the RAM address pins. Once there, voltage impulses turn on the enable pin and find the dialed address. As soon as the addressing becomes stable, the RAM accessing begins (Fig. 9-10).

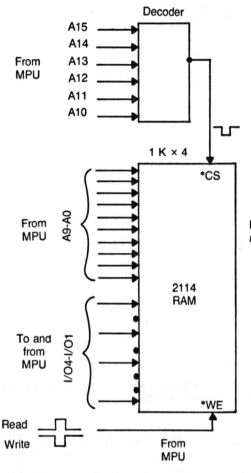

Fig. 9-9. The 2114 chip only needs ten address lines A9-A0 for internal byte locating.

The output buffers turn on. The data in the addressed location enters the buffers as they activate. It takes the buffers about 20 ns to turn on once the chip select is enabled. The data becomes stable as it passes through the buffers. The data is considered stable and valid for 120 ns, while the chip select is on.

Once enough stable data has passed through the buffers, the read cycle draws to a close. The rising edge of $\phi2$ places the data bits into the data bus. The output buffers turn off. About the same time, the falling edge of $\phi1$ increments the program counter changing the address bits.

As the address bits change and the output buffers turn off, the data is held stable for 50 to 100 ns to satisfy data hold time requirements. $\phi2$ at the MPU then falls, and latches the data into its instruction register.

## Write Operation

After $\phi1$ rises and causes the addressing of the RAM chip, the accessing of the RAM by the MPU begins (Fig. 9-11). The addressing produces a low from the decoder

240

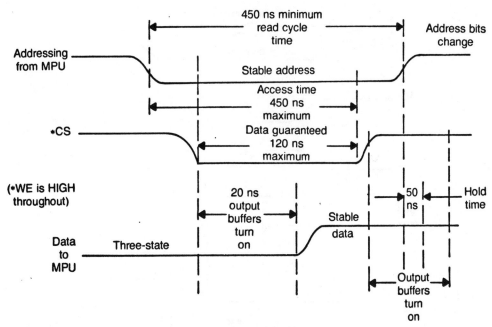

Read timing at the 2114 RAM

Addressing from MPU

450 ns minimum read cycle time

Address bits change

Stable address

Access time 450 ns maximum

*CS

Data guaranteed 120 ns maximum

(*WE is HIGH throughout)

20 ns output buffers turn on

50 ns

Hold time

Data to MPU

Three-state

Stable data

Output buffers turn on

**Fig. 9-10. The 2114 RAM output buffers turn on about 20 ns after the chip select is enabled.**

to the chip select pin *CS. The MPU sends a low to the *WE pin for the write operation. Both the *CS and *WE inputs have about a 200 ns low duration.

The first thing that must happen is that the output buffers must be turned off. This is done in the first 100 ns of the *WE low duration. The next event is to turn the input buffers on and get the data from the MPU to the RAM I/O pins. There is plenty of time since the MPU has an access time well over 500 ns.

The stable data must overlap the *WE low by 200 ns. This 200 ns includes the data setup time and the data hold time. After the overlap, $\phi1$ falls and changes the address bits. $\phi2$ rises and has the data on the data bus from the MPU. Then $\phi2$ falls and injects the data into the RAM input buffers and to the memory nybble area the four bits are assigned to.

That is the way the static RAM is mated timewise to the MPU. The circuits are all dc, and there are no complicated extra clock signals needed to constantly refresh the memory bits as the dynamic memories require.

## DYNAMIC RAM

Dynamic RAM's physical makeup has many advantages over static RAM. A static RAM bit is a flip-flop composed of a group of logic gates in a feedback design. Each gate has a number of transistors and resistors. In comparison, a dynamic RAM bit is only one transistor. In addition, there are a couple of FETs that couple one bit to the next. The number of components in a dynamic bit is a fraction of the number in a static bit. As a

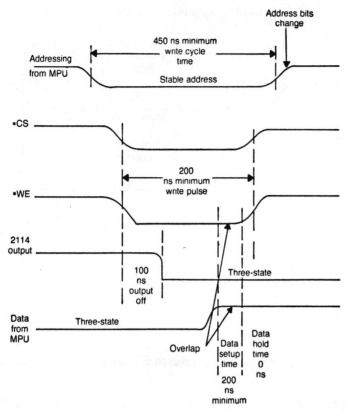

Fig. 9-11. At the beginning of the write cycle, the 2114 RAM output buffers must be turned off and the input buffers turned on.

result, the per-bit cost of dynamic memory is a fraction of the cost of static memory. Any microcomputer that needs a lot of memory will use dynamic chips. This includes all the general purpose personal computers.

There is one drawback of dynamic memory: it needs refreshing. Remember, the logic states in 4116 chips are contained in a grid of gate capacitances. If a capacitance is charged, the state is a high. When there is no charge, a low is being stored. The charge will leak off in a few milliseconds unless it is refreshed. To refresh a bit all you have to do is address it. The accessing of the bit brings the capacitor charge up to full. Any electron leak loss of the charge is restored.

The 4116 dynamic RAM chip described earlier has a matrix of 128 rows with 128 columns across. Actually, the matrix is composed of two 64 × 128 arrays that are connected together by 128 sense amplifiers, but this is all internal and can't be tested. The best way for you to view the matrix is the 128 × 128 layout (Figs. 7-22 and 7-26).

The 4116-equipped dynamic RAM typically comes with eight chips wired together. The address wiring is the same for all eight chips. When you address one chip, you automatically address all eight at the same time in the same way.

The eight-bit data bus is the only wiring connected to the eight chips that is not the same on all eight chips. Each chip is wired to its own data bus bit (Fig. 7-23). When a

242

byte is transferred from the bus to the eight chips, each bit takes up residence in the same number bit in one of the chips. If a byte is sent, there is one bit of the byte from the same bit location in each of the chips.

Bits are addressed with the aid of signals called *RAS and *CAS, the *row address strobe* and the *column address strobe*. The row address itself is contained in the seven least bits of the total 16 bit address.

The refreshing can be conducted by addressing all 128 rows in the eight bits. When a row is addressed, it refreshes every bit in the row. When a row is refreshed, it refreshes that same number row in all eight chips at the same time.

To refresh the matrix, a complete read operation is not needed. Transferring data can be eliminated from the routine. All that is needed is to address the 128 common rows and applying an *RAS signal to strobe the address into the row address latches in the chips.

If the MPU is a 6502, then the refreshing can be done during the cycle after $\phi1$ has completed its normal addressing. At that time $\phi1$ is low and $\phi2$ is busy with its job. If the refresh addressing is sent out over the address bus at this time, it won't disturb any other signals.

During $\phi1$ low, the refresh address is sent out and the *RAS strobe occurs. Each row can be addressed in 16 microseconds, which is fast enough to maintain the charges on the capacitors.

The 6502 needs additional circuits to conduct the refreshing. The circuits are counting circuits that are clocked. One such circuit is part of a chip called a *dynamic memory controller*. It starts counting at the first row address and increments automatically until it counts to the last row. Then it starts over. This is a special little program counter used expressly for refreshing.

The Z-80 chip contains its very own refresh counter. It has its own *RFSH line, at pin 28, that connects to the RAM circuit (Fig. 9-12).

The refresh signal is not involved in the fetch and execute operation of the MPU-memory. It does not enter into the data transferring in any way. The MPU starts a cycle as the program counter places all 16 bits on the address line at one time, in response to the rising edge of the clock signal.

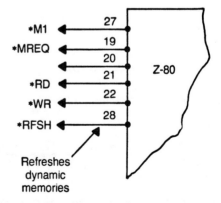

Fig. 9-12. The Z-80 MPU is designed with a special circuit called *RFSH. It sends out a constant refresh signal for dynamic RAM.

243

## 4116 DYNAMIC MEMORY CHIPS

The two MS bits are used to select an array of eight 4116 chips. The typical chip has a 250 ns access time, but faster access times are available, down to 150 ns. On one chip the organization is 16,384 × 1. Eight chips provide 16 K bytes of memory. The two MS bits can choose from one of four arrays. Four arrays provide 64 K bytes.

The other 14 bits are divided into the seven lowest bits A6-A0 and the next higher bits A13-A7. These bits will address the 128 rows and the 128 columns. The two sets of seven bits are sent to a multiplexer (Fig. 7-24). They are latched into the multiplexer and are output upon command. The multiplexer selects for output A6-A0 when it receives a control signal high. A13-A7 outputs upon a control low. The signal can be labeled *MUX. The multiplexer signals is external circuitry as is refresh.

*MUX is timed to be high when *RAS executes its falling edge, and be low when *CAS goes through its falling edge (Fig. 9-13). That way, the A6-A0 bits are on the 4116's row address latch during *RAS, and A13-A7 bits are on the column address latch during *CAS. As their respective falling edges arrive one after another, the bits will select the desired row and column. The accessing times out in the following way.

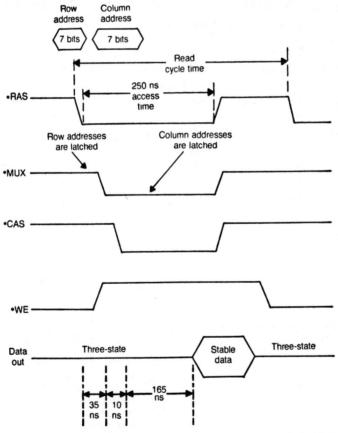

Fig. 9-13. For the read cycle the stable data can leave the 4116 array when *RAS, *CAS and *MUX all arise.

244

The read cycle begins when the row address bits, A6-A0, leave the multiplexer and arrive at the seven address pins of each 4116 in the eight-chip array. Then the *RAS signal arrives and latches the row address into the chip.

Once the row addresses are latched, *MUX, which was in a high state, falls. The *MUX after the fall needs 10 ns to stabilize. The column address bits are placed on the same chip address pins the row addresses had just passed through. Then *CAS arrives and falls. The falling edge latches the column addresses into the chip array.

While *CAS is low, the three-state chip data output circuits are removed from their high impedance state and made active. The output stays active until *CAS goes high again. This means the data must have left the circuit and be out on the data bus before *CAS goes high.

The time is a 250 ns chip, from the falling edge of *RAS to the falling of *CAS cannot be more than 85 ns according to the spec sheet. In this example, the timing is 45 ns, which is satisfactory. Any timing under 85 ns that the MPU provides will work well.

The rest of the total access time is the period that ends with the data becoming available from the memory. The row addresses must go into the row decoders from the latch and then access the selected row. The column addresses must enter the column decoders and select the desired column. The bits that are intersected by the row and column selections are then drained of their charges. The charge is then compared with a reference charge to determine if it is a high or low. The results are then sent to the data-out buffer. Meanwhile *RAS and *CAS are held low to replenish the drained charges. All this takes time.

The data must be available no later than 165 ns after the *CAS falls. The data must be past the three-state buffers before they go into a high impedance state once again as *CAS rises.

The 85 ns maximum for the *RAS-*CAS activity, plus the 165 ns data availability time, adds up to the 250 ns access time requirement of these 4116s. The cycle time determined by the MPU is always greater by a comfortable margin than the access time of the memory. For this 250 ns chip a cycle would be about 400 ns or more.

The other chip control line, *WE, controls the read/write operation. The MPU originates the line. It is designed to be active during the time that *CAS is low. Therefore, the falling edge of *CAS allows *WE to become active in the chip. *WE only has to be active 75 ns to do its job. *WE is an individual control line and does not have any effect on the various other signals that are coursing through the chips.

## I/O Timing

From the point of view of the MPU, chips like the PIA and VIA that interface the digital circuits to the analog circuits look like static RAM. The MPU has to address, transfer data, and control only the internal address and data bus side of the fence. The data transfer to the external circuits is accomplished by the PIA or VIA, and not the MPU.

Let's examine the timing on the 6522 VIA, versatile interface chip. There are two main operations like the memory chips, read and write (Fig. 9-14).

The read and write operations both take place during the $\phi 2$ clock. One complete cycle takes place during a full clock cycle. If the computer is a 1 MHz type, that means the cycle is 1000 nanoseconds.

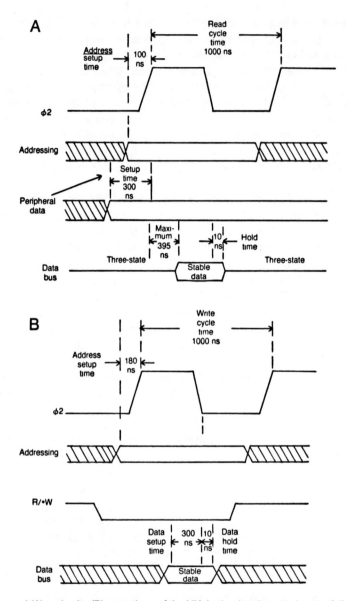

Fig. 9-14. The read (A) and write (B) operations of the VIA both take place during the fall of φ2.

The address set up time is 180 ns and starts at the end of the low section of the φ2 cycle. The chip selects, register selects, and R/*W line all get settled during the set up time. There is no time needed for address hold. This addressing time is the same for both a read or write to the VIA.

For a read operation, the data from the peripheral must be received by the VIA and readied. This is called *peripheral data setup time*. The external device must output to the VIA's registers. The MPU is addressing the registers. Both the address set up time and the data from the peripheral must be in place before the $\phi2$ rising edge arrives. The peripheral data time starts before the address setup time.

The peripheral data time begins 300 ns before $\phi2$, the address setup time begins 180 ns before $\phi2$. Both setup times end as the $\phi2$ signal completes its rising edge.

Once the peripheral data is settled, $\phi2$ moves on. The timing from the$\phi2$ rising edge to the point where the data enters the data bus is 395 ns. Then the falling edge of $\phi2$ arrives and latches the data into the MPU. Another 10 ns hold time is needed for the data bus to hold the data after the MPU receives it.

The write operation for the VIA has the identical addressing timing. The timing is the same on the R/W* line too, except R/*W has a falling edge for the write while it has a rising edge for the read.

The data bus receives the write data from the MPU during the rising edge of $\phi2$. The data becomes valid after a data bus setup time of 300 ns. The falling edge of $\phi2$ then arrives and strobes the data into the VIA address. Then the data bus must hold the data another 10 ns to ensure stability.

To summarize, the MPU develops address, data, and control signals that let it connect to ROMs, RAMs and peripheral interface chips. The timing of the MPU signals must match up with the chips the MPU has to work with. The MPU, according to its basic frequency, develops a cycle. The chips must be able to be accessed during the cycle. The chips must be able to be read and, with the exception of ROM, be written to.

During designing, understanding these timings is a must. For the technicians who work with the designers, it is an important part of their job to determine if designed times are accurate. For the maintenance and service technician, timing rarely will play any part in his job unless a strange replacement must be used.

To test timing patterns, an expensive high frequency multitrace oscilloscope must be used to display the various patterns.

# PART 2
# ANALYSIS OF TYPICAL COMPUTERS

# 10

# General Description of an 8-Bit Computer

If you ever put together an electronic kit, you have acted the part of a computer. Your brain was the operating system, as if it was a ROM. The step-by-step instruction sheet was the program. The sheet of paper held the program like a RAM. The numbers of the steps were the addresses. Your body acted out the part of the MPU. Your eyes were the address and data bus and your fingers the output. The kit was the peripheral device that received manipulation according to the step-by-step instructions.

The construction probably proceeded like this: at the start your brain told you to read step number 1. The step was located on the paper and read. The instruction told you to lay out the parts of the kit in careful fashion on the work bench.

Your brain then told your hands to perform the job according to the instructions. As soon as you finished laying out the parts according to step number 1, you automatically incremented and read step number 2. It instructed you to install a capacitor on the circuit board. Your brain then told your hands to install the capacitor. The kit gradually became a piece of electronic gear as you the computer, ran the step-by-step program. When you finished, the program was filed away. You were then free to do another task, step-by-step.

Admittedly, the human computer is infinitely more complex than the most expensive super computer ever made, but there is a similarity. In a crude, elementary way, the computer is fashioned after some of the characteristics and habit patterns that human beings perform naturally all of the time.

The millions of "imitation humans" filling our world now come in three general types. They are 8-bit, 16-bit and 32-bit machines. The next step is indicated to be 64-bit and who knows what will appear after that. Of course, there are all sorts of other individual types of computers but the above types represent the majority of machines.

The bit type, as mentioned earlier, refers to the MPU's internal data bus and the bit size, one byte, of each individual address in memory. In 8-bit machines all data is arranged in 8-bit pieces, 16-bit machines place data in 16-bit units, and 32-bit computers have data in 32-bit arrangements. Some data can be handled in units that are smaller than the designated size. When that happens, 0s could be installed in the bit holders that are left empty. Other data can be arranged in units that are larger than the designated size. In those cases extra locations are used to hold the extra bits or bytes. As many memory bytes as necessary are used until the data is safely stored in the addresses.

8-bit computers usually have 16 address lines. 16-bit computers can have one of a number of different address bus lines. For example, the 8088-8086 has 20 address lines. The 68000 puts out 24 address lines. The 80386 addresses with 32 bits. This chapter is about the 8-bit computers that have 16 address lines and can address 64 K memory locations. The 16-bit computers are described in Chapters 13, 14, and 17. Chapter 18 goes into the 80386 processor. Let's continue with the 8-bit computer and how it evolved.

## WHAT DOES A COMPUTER DO?

Computers perform literally millions of jobs. Yet all these duties are only variations of three fundamental types of performances. First of all, the computer is a great calculator. It can do all the jobs a calculator can and more.

Second, the computer is able to aid you in writing programs. Years ago, programs were written with paper and pencil. There were special program paper forms printed up that a programmer used as he created the step by step software (Fig. 10-1).

Once the program was completed, a punch card operator converted the lines of code into a deck of cards with a punch card machine (Fig. 10-2). In order to run the program, the cards were placed into a card reader which felt the position of the holes in the card

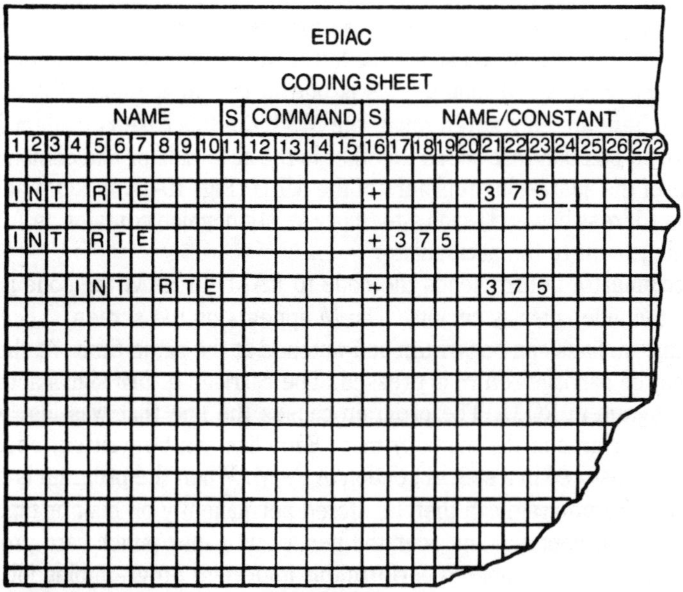

| EDIAC | | | | | | |
|---|---|---|---|---|---|---|
| CODING SHEET | | | | | | |
| NAME | S | COMMAND | S | NAME/CONSTANT | | |
| 1 2 3 4 5 6 7 8 9 10 | 11 | 12 13 14 15 | 16 | 17 18 19 20 21 22 23 24 25 26 27 2 | | |
| I N T   R T E | | | + | 3 7 5 | | |
| I N T   R T E | | | + 3 7 5 | | | |
| I N T   R T E | | | + | 3 7 5 | | |

Fig. 10-1. This old-time program form is hardly used anymore. Computer programming is now done with a keyboard and a video display.

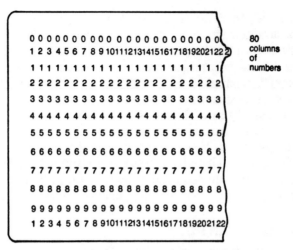

0 0 0 0 0 0 0 0 0 0 0 0 0 0 0 0 0 0 0 0 0 0
1 2 3 4 5 6 7 8 9 10 11 12 13 14 15 16 17 18 19 20 21 22

1 1 1 1 1 1 1 1 1 1 1 1 1 1 1 1 1 1 1 1 1 1

2 2 2 2 2 2 2 2 2 2 2 2 2 2 2 2 2 2 2 2 2 2

3 3 3 3 3 3 3 3 3 3 3 3 3 3 3 3 3 3 3 3 3 3

4 4 4 4 4 4 4 4 4 4 4 4 4 4 4 4 4 4 4 4 4 4

5 5 5 5 5 5 5 5 5 5 5 5 5 5 5 5 5 5 5 5 5 5

6 6 6 6 6 6 6 6 6 6 6 6 6 6 6 6 6 6 6 6 6 6

7 7 7 7 7 7 7 7 7 7 7 7 7 7 7 7 7 7 7 7 7 7

8 8 8 8 8 8 8 8 8 8 8 8 8 8 8 8 8 8 8 8 8 8

9 9 9 9 9 9 9 9 9 9 9 9 9 9 9 9 9 9 9 9 9 9
1 2 3 4 5 6 7 8 9 10 11 12 13 14 15 16 17 18 19 20 21 22

80
columns
of
numbers

Fig. 10-2. Once a program was written on paper, a keypunch operator converted it to a deck of cards like this one.

and converted the holes into highs and lows. The digital states were stored in the computer memory.

Today's machines are equipped with keyboards which are connected, rows and columns, to an I/O chip like a PIA. The columns are strobed from the PIA and the rows are output to the PIA. When an intersection is shorted, the row bit position is sent out the data bus to the MPU. In addition, the column strobe bit position is also sent to the MPU.

On a 56-key board, there are seven rows and eight columns. Each key can produce an individual combination of highs and lows for the 16 bits produced by striking a key (Fig. 10-3). For example, if you strike the letter M, the strobe bit position is 00000100. The row bit position is 00100000. This is one of the 56 possible PIA outputs to the MPU. Since there are only seven rows, the MS bit in this case is made a 0.

The two bit positions are added together in the accumulator and combined with a set value in one of the addressing registers of the MPU (Fig. 10-4). A ROM address is sent out over the address bus and reads a memory location which contains an ASCII code for M. The code is sent to the accumulator.

The accumulator in turn sends the code to RAM. In RAM the code is both stored and sent to the video display circuits. The M appears on the screen.

The program lines can be written and watched at the same time. At the end of each program line the carriage return is pressed. The carriage return signal activates a small operating program in ROM. The program causes the line that was just written to be stored in a buffer area in the memory map. Each line can be written, observed on the screen, and then stored in a special section of RAM. When the program is complete it is also in RAM. The program can then be stored permanently on disk or tape.

This is a great improvement over the pencil and paper/punch card procedure. The older computers were not able to perform this important programming job.

The third duty the computer is charged with is running programs. The older computers were also good at this job. In today's computers, programs can be placed into

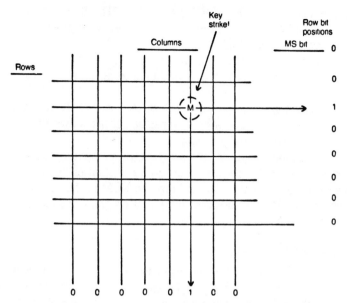

Fig. 10-3. Each of the intersections can be shorted and will generate an ASCII code to form a character.

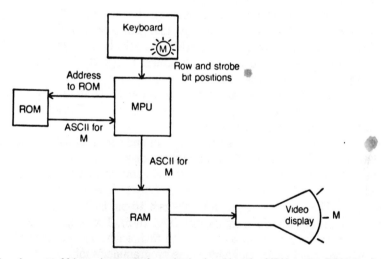

Fig. 10-4. The character M in code travels from the keyboard to the MPU, to the ROM, back to the MPU, to RAM, is then decoded, and appears on the screen.

action a few ways. First of all, you can type a program into the computer by hand. This is fine for tiny programs, but can be a chore as the program size increases.

The second way to get a program into the computer is by having a program on disk or tape. That way, the highs and lows enter the computer through disk or tape I/O interfaces. The process is like the keyboard's method of installing a byte.

The third method is by means of ROM cartridges. The ROM cartridge has a complete program installed on it. They often contain games, word processors, and spreadsheets. The programs are burnt into the chip.

There is a cartridge holder in the computer that can handle these items. The cartridge plugs into the cartridge holder. It is designed to work only on the computer it is made for.

When it is plugged in, the cartridge disables the internal ROM that had been the brains of the computer. It becomes a brain transplant. It takes over the operation of the MPU as well as being a dedicated program.

Whatever the method of installing the program, the computer is able to run the program. The programs in RAM are run under the jurisdiction of the internal ROM. The programs in a cartridge ROM are controlled by the ROM in the cartridge. Either way, the MPU is directed by ROM to begin with the first program line and automatically run through the program line after line.

## MICROPROCESSOR

The MPU is very exclusive. Besides its clock crystal, it will not connect with any other circuits other than the residents of the memory map. This means the MPU will only work with ROM, RAM, and peripheral interface chips like PIAs and ACIAs. All of these chips have addresses.

The MPU doesn't work directly with video display generator chips which don't have any addresses, even though they are connected to the data bus. The VDG receives data from the video RAM that is holding the data that is displayed on the screen.

ROM has a program installed that the MPU checks before executing an instruction. The ROM program is installed by the manufacturer to operate the computer properly. It is in control.

RAM is the immediate storage area where the MPU stores the program that is being used. A portion of RAM is set aside to be video RAM. The screen will display the bytes that are stored in the video RAM.

PIA chips concern themselves with the input and output of data to and from peripherals like the keyboard, joysticks, cassettes, and disks.

The 6800 is an example of a relatively simple, commonly-used MPU. The programmer looks at it with an eye for the registers he can utilize and particularly the bit size of the registers. The technician sees the 6800 as a 40-pin DIP with lines coming out and connecting to the chips in the memory map (Fig. 10-5). The programmer has practically no interest in the electrical connections. The technician, on the other hand, becomes increasingly proficient as he understands the programmer's job.

The pinouts show 16 address pins, 9-25, with the exception of pin 21 which is ground. The address lines, A15-A0, are output only.

The signal that appears at the address pins originates in the program counter, index register, and the stack pointer. The two accumulators can also contribute data to these registers, so they are also involved in the addressing.

These three registers are in parallel and connect inside the MPU to an internal address bus (Fig. 10-6). In turn, this 16 bit attaches to three-state bus drivers that can be turned off and on, which connects or disconnects the pins from the external address bus.

254

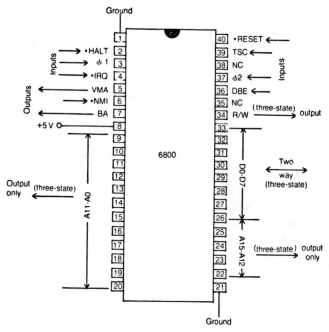

Ground

•HALT 2        40 •RESET

φ1 3        39 TSC

•IRQ 4        38 NC

VMA 5        37 φ2

•NMI 6        36 DBE

BA 7        35 NC

+5 V 8        34 R/W (three-state) output

Fig. 10-5. The technician sees the 6800 MPU chip as a 40-pin DIP with lines connecting to the locations on the memory map.

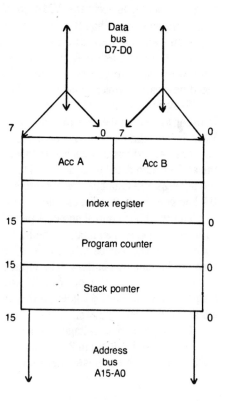

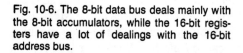

Fig. 10-6. The 8-bit data bus deals mainly with the 8-bit accumulators, while the 16-bit registers have a lot of dealings with the 16-bit address bus.

255

At pin 39, TSC, there is a three-state control. When it goes high it turns off the 16 address pins, the eight data pins, and the read/write line (which we will get to shortly). The TSC line, when high, also forces two other lines low and holds the $\phi 1$ and $\phi 2$ high and low. (These lines will also be covered shortly.) When TSC is held low, it has no effect.

D7-D0 are at pins 26-33. These eight data lines are two-way. They can transfer data back and forth to the members of the memory map. The outputs of the eight lines are passed through their own three-state bus drivers. The three-state buffers can turn off in one direction while leaving the other direction on.

Pin 34 is the R/*W line. It connects to all the memory map residents and lets them know it is reading from them when it is high and writing to them when low. It goes into a three-state when TSC goes high.

When the computer is idling, the R/*W line goes high and is in a read state, because the read/write line is attached to +5 V through a pullup resistor. This is a protective measure which makes sure the line goes into a high state when there is no activity. During a test, it will probably show a high.

The R/*W line is an important bus control line. There are three other bus control lines. The first one we'll discuss is called *Valid Memory Address*, or VMA, at pin 5.

VMA is needed to protect the memory map from being written to accidentally. If the writing takes place at the wrong time, data can be destroyed. The VMA is not needed by the ROM since the data in the ROM is permanent.

VMA isn't always used but it is held high as long as the address coming out of the program counter is accurate. VMA goes low when TSC three-states the address lines. VMA also goes low while the MPU is operating and the program counter is changing its states and working towards a valid address but hasn't arrived at it yet.

The I/O chips like PIA are especially vulnerable to an accidental read. If they are read when they are setting up flags for an interrupt to conduct a handshake, the flags could be cleared, which could cause the program being run to crash.

To avoid this, the VMA lines are ANDed with a chip select address line (Fig. 10-7). In order for the chip select to address a chip, both it and the VMA line must be high. If VMA is low, the chip will not be selected by the AND gate output.

The second bus control line is called *Bus Available*, BA, at pin 7. It is an indicator of the address and data bus condition. During operation it is usually held low, indicating that the address and data bus are operating properly under the auspices of the MPU. If the BA line goes high, it indicates the buses are available in a standby three-state condition.

The third bus control line is at pin 36. It's called *Data Bus Enable*, or DBE. As the name indicates, it is an input to the MPU that enables the data bus when it is high. During enabling, data can be placed on the bus for a write operation. If it receives a low it will turn off the data bus buffers. The input comes from $\phi 2$.

$\phi 1$ and $\phi 2$ from the clock circuits are input at pins 3 and 37. At this stage, they are in a square wave format. $\phi 1$ goes to the program counter timing circuits, and $\phi 2$ does its job at the data bus circuits.

The +5 V supply voltage is applied at pin 8, and pins 1 and 21 are grounded.

*HALT, an input at pin 2, is a sort of master bus controller. While it is held high, the MPU works with the buses and their individual control lines in a normal fashion. The

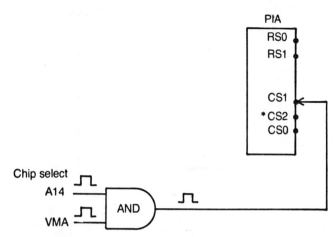

Fig. 10-7. The PIAs are protected from crashing by the VMA line. A PIA chip select is ANDed with VMA. That way, the chip can't be selected unless VMA is high.

*HALT line is normally high because it is tied to the supply line +5 V. You can force a halt by grounding pin 2. When pin 2 goes low, the following happens:

First the MPU finishes the instruction it was working on when the halt occurred. Then the read/write line, the address bus, and the data bus all go into a three-state condition.

When they do, BA goes high indicating that the buses are three-stating. In addition, VMA goes low which tells all the devices on the address bus that the current address, whatever it is, is not valid.

The halt line is handy when you want to put the MPU into a three-state condition during test procedures.

## CALLS FOR HELP

In order for the computer to be automatic, every possible contingency must be handled. This means the designer should be able to anticipate complications and arrange for the computer to solve problems as they occur.

The problem-solving is based around programs that are burnt into the ROM chip during production of the computer. For different computers doing different jobs, these emergency programs vary. Whatever they are, when these programs are needed the MPU must call them from the ROM and put them into operation. The 6800 has three pins that are capable of receiving these signals to call for the emergency sequences. They are *RESET at pin 40, *IRQ at pin 4, and *NMI at pin 6. They work like this.

*RESET. There is a reset button on computers that connect into circuitry consisting of some discrete resistors, capacitors and diodes (Fig. 10-8). When the button is pressed, a pulse is sent to the reset pins of the chips that have such pins. The 6800 has one, and so does each PIA the 6800 is working with. The reset button only needs to be pressed after the computer has lost power and needs to be started up again.

The 0.1 second input pulse from the reset circuit enters pin 40 of the MPU, and sets in motion an initialization sequence. During the outage, the various registers in the MPU

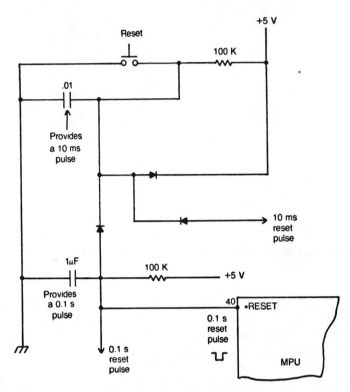

Fig. 10-8. The reset button, when pressed, sends out pulses to the MPU and the PIAs.

and PIA could have become inaccurate. The program counter could have any address on it. The accumulator, index register, stack pointer, and flags could be in disarray. In the PIA, the PDRs, DDRs, and CRs could be set wrong. They all have to be initialized to their start states. There is a special initialization program stored in ROM that initializes all the pertinent registers. The reset pulse into pin 40 begins the sequence of events that will run the program.

After the power returns and reset is pressed, the pulse must be held low on pin 40 for at least eight clock cycles (Fig. 10-9). Then the reset pulse can go high once again. The rising edge of *RESET signals the MPU to begin the restart sequence. The *RESET low automatically caused the address 1111111111111110 to appear on the address bus. This is ROM hex location FFFE. Notice that FFFE is the next to the last address on the map.

The address FFFE on the address bus places the contents of FFFE, which is one byte, into the most significant byte of the program counter. Then address FFFF appears on the address bus and its contents are placed in the least significant byte of the program counter.

FFFE and FFFF are both addresses on the ROM. The contents were installed in the factory. The contents of these two bytes form another address in ROM.

Since this address is now on the program counter, the address is put out on the address bus during $\phi1$. At that address is the first byte of the initialization program. The

258

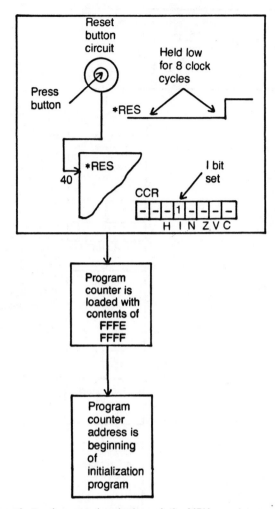

Fig. 10-9. After the reset button is pressed and released, the MPU goes into a restart sequence.

program is then run. The pertinent registers are all initialized and the computer is ready to go.

**\*NMI.** At pin 6, there is an input called *Nonmaskable Interrupt.* A nonmaskable interrupt is used for emergencies like loss of power. As the power loss occurs, some systems are able to save data by switching to a backup battery. The nonmaskable interrupt cannot be stopped once it occurs. A pulse is sent to pin 6, and the interrupt sequence goes through the routine.

When the pulse enters pin 6, the MPU completes the current instruction before it recognizes the interrupt (Fig. 10-10). Then the MPU begins the routine by storing the stack. In memory, there is a stack of registers that are reserved for this purpose. The 16-bit stack pointer contains the address of the first memory register of the stack.

The MPU then stores the contents of the Index register, the program counter, the two accumulators, and the condition code register in the stack, so they are available once

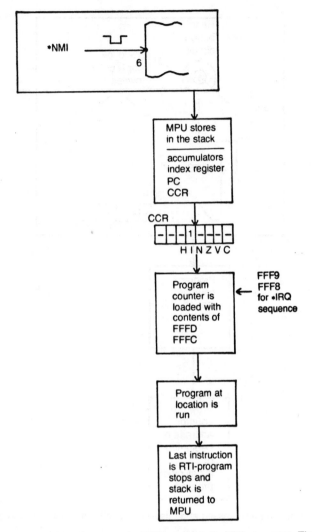

Fig. 10-10. During an emergency interrupt, the MPU goes into its NMI sequence. The same sequence with a different vector address is used for the IRQ interrupt.

the interrupt has been serviced. Next, the I bit in the condition code register is set to 1 so that no more interrupts can occur.

The contents of the ROM addresses FFFD and FFFC are then loaded into the program counter. This is the address of the ROM program that will service the nonmaskable interrupt. The program gets run and solves the problem that caused the interrupt. The MPU unloads the stack into the appropriate registers and gets back to its normal business.

*IRQ. Pin 4 is called the *Interrupt Request Line*. When pin 4 is pulled low, it goes into its interrupt sequence. *IRQ is maskable and is used a lot, unlike *NMI which is needed mostly for emergencies.

For example, *IRQ is connected to the two interrupts that are coming out of the PIA. That way, the PIA can pull *IRQ low and get the immediate attention of the MPU when it has data to send or wants data.

The maskable part means the interrupt can be disabled if the programmer desires. That way it won't work, which sometimes is the way a program must be run. In comparison, the nonmaskable interrupt cannot be disabled. Except for this, the *IRQ runs like the *NMI shown in Fig. 10-10.

When pin 4 is pulled low, the MPU immediately stores the contents of the Index register, the program counter, the accumulators, and the condition code register in the stack for use after the interrupt is serviced. Then a 1 is placed in the I bit of the condition code register. No other interrupts can happen at pin 4 as long as the Interrupt bit is set with a 1.

The *IRQ interrupt also has a vectoring or guiding address stored in the ROM chip that mates with the 6800. Specifically, the 16-bit address is stored in two bytes at minus 6 and minus 7 of the highest ROM address. The highest address is FFFF. *IRQ's vector is at FFF9 and FFF8.

The address at FFF9 and FFF8 is placed on the program counter, and goes out on the address bus during $\phi 1$. Then the contents of the address are placed on the data bus during $\phi 2$.

The data byte is the first instruction of the *IRQ interrupt service routine. The clock keeps cycling and the entire service program is run.

The last instruction in the program is called *Return from Interrupt*. This allows the MPU to unload the stack into the program counter, Index register, accumulators, and condition code registers. Then the MPU continues with the program it was running before the interrupt.

To summarize, the 40 lines out of the MPU are either inputs or outputs. The technician should know which are which so intelligent tests can be made at the pins.

## Inputs

The MPU inputs are as follows:

1. +5 V is applied at pin 5, and ground is attached to pins 1 and 21.
2. *HALT is held high at pin 2. You can stop the MPU by grounding * HALT.
3. *RESET is held high at pin 40. You can get the restart sequence going by pressing the reset button, which causes a low at pin 40.
4. TSC is held low at pin 39. If a high is applied, the address bus and read/write line are three-stated.
5. DBE turns the data bus drivers off and on at pin 36. It is driven by $\phi 2$ and is high during a write.
6. The clock inputs are $\phi 1$ at pin 3 and $\phi 2$ at pin 37.
7. The two interrupts are inputs. *IRQ enters as a low at pin 4, and *NMI as a low at pin 6. When an interrupt is not present, the pins are held high.

## Outputs

The MPU outputs are as follows:

1. When VMA at pin 5 is high, it tells the devices it connects to that the address on the bus is valid. If VMA outputs a low, the address is not guaranteed.
2. R/*W from pin 34 signals the chips it connects to that a read operation is in progress when it is high. If R/*W is low, it is conducting a write. During stand-by, it is held in a high read position.

R/*W is one of the three types of three-state lines in the MPU. During a three-state MPU condition, the R/*W line goes into the high impedance condition, neither high nor low. The other two three-state lines are the address and data bus connections.

3. The 16 address lines at pins 9-20 and 22-25 are all output lines and can address every location on the memory map. While in a three-state condition, the lines are in a high impedance state.
4. The eight data lines at pins 26-33 are both output and input lines. They both send data and receive data. They also possess the three-state ability.

## MEMORY MAP RESIDENTS

The MPU conducts its business with the residents of the memory map. The business is the transferring of data bits back and forth. The ROM contains permanent data the MPU constantly reads to keep the activity under control. The RAM is the data bit storage files the MPU is constantly reading and writing to. The I/O chips are the doorways to the external device circuits the MPU also must read and write to.

Each of these chips contains byte-sized registers. Each chip has an address called the chip select. Also, each byte on the chips has an address. The chip selects are found on the most significant bits of the address. The bytes on each chip are addressed with the least significant bits (Fig. 10-11).

The 6800 can address 64 K with 16 bits. A typical arrangement can locate the RAM chips anywhere on the memory map. 4 K of static RAM can be formed with four 1 K chips. Each chip is organized as 1024 × 8, and needs 10 address lines to select one out of the 1024 bytes on each chip.

The same ten address lines can be used for all four chips. Each chip has the same internal structure. There are 1024 byte-sized registers numbered 0-1023 in decimal. It takes ten bits to address 1024 individual locations. Each of the four chips can have their A9-A0 address lines connected to A9-A0 of the address bus. This means that all four chips are addressed simultaneously at A9-A0. How can one out of the four chips be chosen? That is the job of the chip selects, and will be discussed next.

## ADDRESSING LAYOUT

To control the 6800 and the 4 K RAM we could use two 2 K ROMs. The ROMs could be installed on the map starting at 32,768 decimal (Table 10-1). In the 2 K ROM, there are 2048 byte sized registers, numbered 0-2047. It takes eleven bits to address

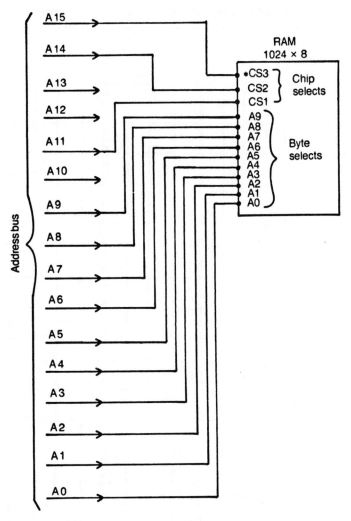

Fig. 10-11. The chip selects are usually connected to the address bus high order bits. The byte selects inside the chip are usually connected to the low order bits.

2048 locations. The ROM thus has its A10-A0 lines connected to the A10-A0 address bus.

For I/O duty we could install two PIAs (Fig. 10-12). One PIA can be attached in memory starting at decimal 16,416 and the second one at 16,448. In the PIAs, there are only four registers that are addressed. The PDRs and DDRs share the same address. It only takes two bits to address four locations. There are two register selects that connect to the register addressing circuits. The two selects, RS0 and RS1, can be connected to address bus lines A1 and A0. The two address bits will choose the addressed register.

Connecting the MPU's least significant address bits to address lines and register selects is straightforward. All the connections on RAM are the same. The connections on ROM are identical. The two PIAs, RS0s, and RS1s are the same. The chip selects,

**Table 10-1. Chip Select Chart to Calculate Memory Map Addresses.**

| Chip | Starting Decimal Address | 15 | 14 | 13 | 12 | 11 | 10 | 9 | 8 | 7 | 6 | 5 | 4 | 3 | 2 | 1 | 0 | Starting Hex Address |
|---|---|---|---|---|---|---|---|---|---|---|---|---|---|---|---|---|---|---|
| ROM #1 | 32,768 | 1 | | | | 0 | | | | | | | | | | | | 8000 |
| | | CS1 | | | | •CS3 | | | | | | | | | | | | |
| ROM #2 | 34,816 | 1 | | | | 1 | | | | | | | | | | | | 8800 |
| | | CS1 | | | | CS2 | | | | | | | | | | | | |
| PIA #1 | 16,416 | 0 | 1 | | | | | | | | | 1 | | | | — | — | 4020 |
| | | •CS2 | CS1 | | | | | | | | | CS0 | | | | RS1 | RS0 | |
| PIA #2 | 16,448 | 0 | 1 | | | | | | | | 1 | | | | | | | 4040 |
| | | •CS2 | CS1 | | | | | | | | CS0 | | | | | RS1 | RS0 | |
| RAM #1 | 0 | 0 | 0 | | | 0 | 0 | | | | | | | | | | | 0000 |
| | | •CS5 | •CS4 | | | •CS3 | •CS2 | | | | | | | | | | | |
| RAM #2 | 1024 | 0 | 0 | | | 0 | 1 | | | | | | | | | | | 0400 |
| | | •CS5 | •CS4 | | | •CS3 | CS1 | | | | | | | | | | | |
| RAM #3 | 2048 | 0 | 0 | | | 1 | 0 | | | | | | | | | | | 0800 |
| | | •CS5 | •CS4 | | | | •CS3 | | | | | | | | | | | |
| RAM #4 | 3072 | 0 | 0 | | | 1 | 1 | | | | | | | | | | | 0C00 |
| | | •CS5 | •CS4 | | | | CS0 | | | | | | | | | | | |

264

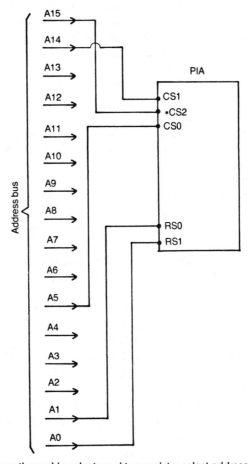

Fig. 10-12. The PIAs have three chip selects and two register select address.

though, are all different. No two chip select sets are wired the same. That's because they all have to connect to different addresses.

Remember the block diagram of a ROM we saw in Fig. 7-16? The ROM has ten lower address lines, A9-A0. These are straightforward. Then there are four chip selects. The four selects are connected to the input of an AND gate. The output of the gate enables the three-state buffer of the ROM. All four AND inputs must be high in order for the output to be high and turn on the ROM chip. If one chip select input is low, the ROM won't be addressed by the chip selects.

## CONNECTING THE ROMs

Getting back to the two ROMs in our 6800 system, there are four chip selects, CS0, CS1, CS2, and *CS3. The selects are wired so the ROM is addressed when highs are on CS0 CS1, and CS2, and a low is on *CS3. The low is easily turned into a high inside the chip by passing it through a NOT gate.

When the H-H-H-L is applied to the ROM, the chip is addressed. Both ROMs in the map are identical, but they are to have different addresses. The addresses are worked out by connecting the chip selects to the higher address bits in such a manner that the highs and lows of the desired address form the H-H-H-L to enable the chip.

For bit manipulations, it is best to use hex rather than decimal. The first ROM at 32,768 can be addressed first. The hex address is 8000. In binary the address is 1000 0000 0000 0000.

When this address comes over the address bus, line A15 will have 1 and all the rest of the lines will be 0s. If A15 is connected to a positive chip select like CS1, the hex address 8000 is almost addressed. (*Almost* always, because the rest of the chip selects are still open. They must be enabled.)

This is accomplished by the following connections (Fig. 10-13). CS0 and CS2 are tied to +5 V. This gives them a constant high. *CS3 is tied to 0 V. This makes it always low. If this ROM stationed at hex 8000 was the only chip in the computer, its addressing would be complete. However there are other chips to worry about. We will hold off tieing the extra chip selects to +5 V and 0 V till the rest of the chips are settled into the map.

The next ROM is at hex 8800. This is 1000 1000 0000 0000 in binary. There are highs needed from address lines A15 and also from A11. The rest of the address bits are all lows.

The wiring consists of attaching two positive chip selects to the address lines that will carry highs when this chip will be addressed. Therefore, A15 and A11 are connected to CS1 and CS2. If this ROM was the only chip, the remaining selects could be connected to +5 V and 0 V and it would be addressed at this point. However, there are two ROMs in place now. #1 is at address 8000 and #2 is at 8800 (Fig. 10-14). Look at Table 10-1. When you address 8000 only that address will be activated. The single high at A15 can't turn on the ROM at 8800 due to the high needed at A11.

When you address the ROM at 8800, the ROM at 8000 will also turn on. All it needs is a high at A15, which the 8800 address will supply. Don't be concerned—that's where the negative select, *CS3 enters the picture.

*CS3 from ROM #1 is connected to A11. That way, when 8800 is addressed, a high is applied to A11. ROM #2 will turn on because its positive select CS2 is connected to

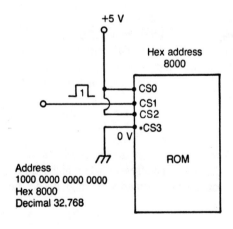

Fig. 10-13. This single ROM can be addressed by attaching CS1 to A15, CS0 and CS2 to +5 V, and *CS3 to ground.

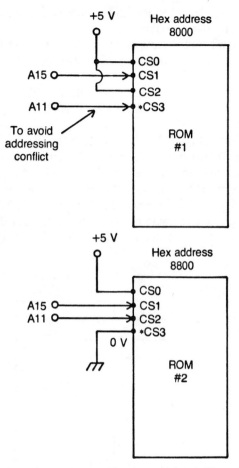

Fig. 10-14. Two ROMs can be addressed by attaching A15 and A11 to CS1 and *CS3 on ROM #1, and CS1 and CS2 on ROM #2.

A11. ROM #1 has *CS3 connected to A11. There will be no response at *CS3 to a positive pulse. Only 8000 will activate ROM #1.

Left over in the addressing scheme are CS0 and CS2 from ROM #1, and CS0 and *CS3 from ROM #2. The extra positive selects are connected to +5 V and the negative to 0 V. That way, when the chip is selected all the CSs will enable the internal AND gate and activate the chip.

The ROM chips are selected by the correct bits on the higher address lines. The internal registers are addressed by the correct bits on the lower address lines. The higher lines connect to the chip selects while the lower lines connect to the address pins.

## CONNECTING THE PIAs

Once the ROM chips have their addresses wired in, the PIAs can receive their connections. The ROMs were wired first because they have the largest address numbers. It is best to start the layout with the biggest numbers because all of the bits are involved.

That way, when negative selects are needed to avoid turning on more than one address at a time, the problem reveals itself quickly.

The PIAs are to be wired at starting decimal addresses 16,416 and 16,448 which are hex 4020 and 4040 (Fig. 10-15). The binary addresses are

$$0100\ 0000\ 0010\ 0000$$
$$0100\ 0000\ 0100\ 0000$$

The 16 bits match up with A15-A0 of the address bus. Both A14s of the address bus are connected to the CS1 pins of PIA's #1 and #2. This produces the hex character 4 as the MS hex address number. A5 is connected to CS0 of #1 and A6 is wired to CS0 of #2. This produces a hex number 2 for the first PIA and hex 4 for the second. Since A5 and A6 represent the third hex digit, the two addresses 4020 and 4040 are thus installed.

To avoid any conflict in addressing between the ROMs and the PIAs, the negative selects *CS2, on both chips are connected to A15. That way when the ROM is

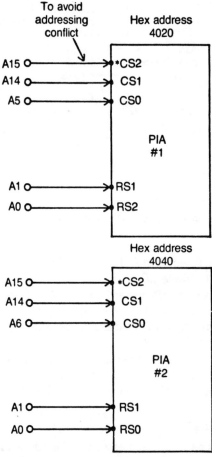

Fig. 10-15. To avoid any conflict in addressing between the PIAs and the ROMs, A15 is connected to *CS2 of the PIAs.

addressed and a high is on A15, the PIA can't accidentally turn on too. There are no extra chip selects left over that have to be enabled by connecting to +5 V or 0 V.

## CONNECTING THE RAMs

The remaining chip selects to be wired are the RAMs. The four 1 K × 8 chips have four negative selects and two positive selects each. They are CS0, CS1, *CS2, *CS3, *CS4 and *CS5 (Fig. 10-16). The RAMs in this case are started at hex address 0000.

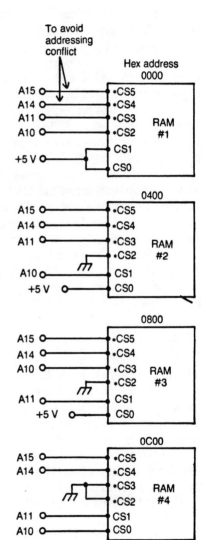

Fig. 10-16. The RAMs are equipped with six chip select pins to give the addressing flexibility.

They contain 1024 bytes each. The second chip starts at hex 0400, the third at hex 0800, and the final one at hex 0C00. The equivalent binary starting addresses are:

0000 0000 0000 0000
0000 0100 0000 0000
0000 1000 0000 0000
0000 1100 0000 0000

To connect the correct select addresses, the first chip requires all negative chip selects. At first glance it would seem that since all the bit positions are lows, the negative chip selects could be connected in any position. However, the chip must be protected from accidentally being turned on. Therefore, the negative selects are installed in bit positions 15, 14, 11, and 10, because these address lines are used for selecting other chips and there should be protection.

With those bits connected, when the program counter starts off at location 0, the RAM #1 chip is selected. To connect chip #2, the hex number 0400 must be dialed instead of 0000. Since 0400 is addressed by placing a 1 in A10, the connections remain the same except that the negative connection at A10 is changed to a positive select pin.

RAM #3 has a starting address of hex 0800. To attach the correct address, A10 is then connected to negative and A11 is wired to a positive select. RAM #4 has an address of 0C00. This address is achieved by connecting both address lines A10 and A11 to positive selects. With careful attention to these wiring details, only one RAM can possibly be addressed at a time.

The four RAMs end up with some extra chip select pins. #1 has CS0 and CS1 empty, #2 has left with *CS2 and CS0, #3 has *CS2 and CS0 unwired, and #4 leaves *CS3 and *CS2 open. The unused positive selects must be wired to +5 V and the negatives to 0 V.

## DATA BUS

The data bus has only eight types of destinations. They are simple to understand; they don't present a puzzle like the address bus. The eight bus connections from the data pins D7-D0 on the MPU connect to all the data pins D7-D0 of all the ROMs, PIAs, and RAMs (Fig. 10-17). There is usually no variation or complication. D7-D0 travels the circuit board from one end to another and all the connections on all the chips are the same.

The R/*W line from the MPU gets connected to the RAMs and the PIAs (Fig. 10-18). The line is normally held high which is the read state. That way, the RAMs and PIAs are always ready to be read.

The R/*W line is not connected to the ROMs. The Read Only Memories are never written to, and the standby high state of the line has the data bus sending data from the ROM to the MPU and not the other way.

To ensure the standby read condition, the line is connected to a +5 V source, because the R/*W line along with the data bus and address bus are three-state circuits. If the +5 V was not connected, the line could three-state and extraneous data could accidentally be written into a member of the memory map.

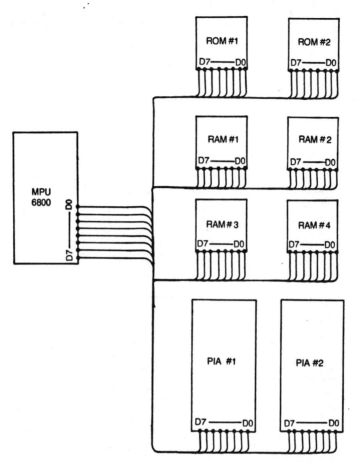

**Fig. 10-17.** The data bus is connected to all the residents of the memory map at pins D7-D0.

When the Valid Memory Address signal, VMA, is used, it is a backup to the read/write line. It further ensures that a location does not accidentally get written to. The main chips the VMA signal protects are the I/O chips. For instance, this configuration we've been discussing has two PIAs as I/O.

VMA is high when the addresses on the bus are valid. If an invalid address should be output by the MPU, VMA goes low. This state change is used to protect the PIA's addressing. If the PIA is accidentally read or written to, its internal flag settings could be erased.

Instead of connecting their CS1s to A14, they are attached to the output of an AND gate. Then the two inputs of the gate are connected to A14 and the VMA line. That way, when the PIA is addressed and A14 is high, the VMA line must be high too, in order for the gate to output a high and the address to be validated. If the VMA line is low, the PIA is being accidentally addressed and it will not respond.

Since the PIAs are both input and output devices, they not only receive data from the MPU, but they also send data to the MPU. One of the signals that participate in the PIA sending data are the *IRQ PIA outputs. They are *RQA and *IRQB. Typically, they

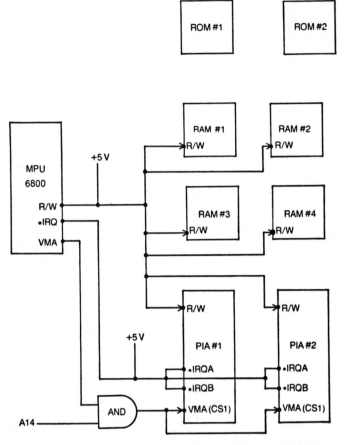

Fig. 10-18. The R/W, VMA, and IRQ lines are connected to the PIAs and RAM chips but not to ROM.

are tied together and are connected to *IRQ of the MPU. *IRQ is normally held high. When the PIA wants to send data to the MPU from an external device, it outputs a low over *IRQ and the MPU goes into the receiving sequence described earlier.

Those are the connections between the MPU on one side and the memory map residents on the other side. There are some other lines attached to the map chips that are common to the MPU but are not coming from the MPU.

First of all, there is a common +5 V source and ground. Next there is the reset circuit that connects to the PIA as well as the MPU (Fig. 10-19).

Then there is the $\phi2$ clock signal mentioned earlier. It connects to the RAMs and to the Enable pin of the PIAs. It syncs the RAMs and PIAs with the rhythm of the clock.

This $\phi2$ clock signal is produced differently than the $\phi2$ signal applied to the MPU. The MPU is an NMOS chip and has a non-TTL-compatible signal. The RAMs and the PIA require a TTL-compatible signal. This TTL $\phi2$ signal is generated by hardware in addition to the signal produced for the MPU data work. The two $\phi2$s coincide with each other but are separate signals, each with its own job to do.

272

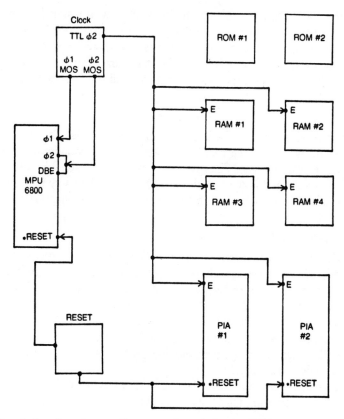

Fig. 10-19. The clock and reset connections are not needed at the ROMs.

The computer part of the total computing system is not that extensive. It is made up of the MPU, the residents of the memory map, and connecting wires. All the computing is done by transferring digital states between the MPU and the memory locations. The next two chapters show how a small machine language program is processed in these circuits.

## OTHER 8-BIT PROCESSORS

The 6800 type of processor, just discussed and also used as an example in Chapters 11 and 12, is very popular. It found its way into many machines. It was used in industry as controllers, in game devices like Pac-Man, and in many microcomputers. The 6809 is still found today in Tandy's CoCo.

The 6502 processor family operates quite like the 6800. COMMODORE uses a lot of different 6502 types. You'll find the 6502 family members in the VIC-20, C64, and C128. Apple uses 6502 types in their Apple I and II series.

The 8080 family of processors started with Intel. The 8085 became very popular. Then two of Intel's microprocessor designers left Intel and formed a company called Zilog. Zilog then introduced the Z80 which was similar to the 8085 in the same way the

6502 is like the 6800. From the technician's point of view, if you understand the workings of the 6800, you can apply the same thinking patterns to the 6502. In the same way, if you comprehend the operation of the Z80, you can easily switch your thinking to handle the 8085. Since we have discussed the 6800, let us now examine the workings of the Z80. Between the two processors you'll have most 8-bit processors under control.

## THE Z80

The Z80 had quite a run in the late 70s and the early 80s. Tandy used it in their Model I and is still using it in their Model 4, which is today's evolutionary upgrade of the I. The Z80 was used in the small Sinclair models that never made it in the marketplace. The Z80 today is still used in many devices, and has found its way into the COMMODORE 128 as a coprocessor, working alongside an 8502 (6502 upgrade).

## Z80 BLOCK DIAGRAM

The Z80 has many more registers than the 6800. There are eighteen 8-bit and four 16-bit registers. They are all accessible by the machine language programmer. With the proliferation of registers, the Z80 is said to be "register oriented." This means that since there are so many registers, they can be used to manipulate and store data, that is being worked on, rather than having to ship data back and forth to RAM. This speeds up the operation and reduces the number of shipping instructions that have to be written for the program. This is an advantage over the 6800, which is not particularly register oriented, as it has fewer registers.

The address bus is one-way out and is the exit for the bits generated in the four 16-bit registers. That is, the program counter PC, the two index registers, X and Y, and the stack pointer SP.

The 18 other 8-bit registers connect to the 8-bit internal data bus. These registers are grouped as two accumulators, two flag registers, 12 general purpose registers, an interrupt register, and a special DRAM refresh register.

The internal data bus in turn connects to the ALU, the instruction register and the data input-output circuits. In the instruction register are the instruction decoder and processor control circuits. The decoder-control areas receive and output 13 control signals through the register pins. The Z80 is able to run when a clock signal that is generated externally is fed in through a pin.

### The Register Jobs

The accumulators, Flag registers, and general purpose registers are separated into two groups. One is called the Main registers and the other the Alternate registers. They are arranged for the programmer in two groups each with one accumulator, one Flag register, and six general purpose registers.

The accumulators act in their usual scratch pad fashion and the flags set up special conditions as they should. The general purpose registers though are versatile. They can perform as if they were RAM or they can become a group of extra accumulators.

The program counter has no surprises. It outputs a 16-bit address, and then increments if the next byte in a program is to be addressed in sequence. If a program line specifies a jump operation, the program counter is not incremented but has its contents replaced with the new jump address.

The X and Y Index registers are two independent 16-bit registers that hold the special address data needed for index modes. The stack pointer is still another 16-bit register that holds the start address of the stack. The Z80 stack area in RAM is of the last-in-first-out variety. That way, if there is anything in the RAM stack addresses, the stack pointer register will hold the address of the last byte that was stored in the stack.

The Z80 has two registers that the 6800 and 6502 processors do not have. One is the 8-bit interrupt vector. This register holds the address of a memory page where an interrupt-service routine is stored. During some types of interrupts, this vector will be placed on the address bus to call that desired page.

The Z80 has a special 8-bit DRAM refresh register. This is a seven-bit address that is designed to refresh the RAM rows after every instruction is completed. This register can be used or not, according to the application the Z80 is performing.

Besides the above programmable registers, there are the other performing registers that just do jobs that are needed. The ALU handles all the arithmetic and logic calculations that go on in the Z80. Specifically, the Z80 ALU performs the following operations on data. It ADDs, SUBTRACTs, ANDs, ORs, Exclusive ORs, SHIFTs left and right, INCREMENTs, DECREMENTs, COMPAREs, SETs a bit, RESETs a bit and TESTs a bit. These are all machine language programming concerns and only of passing interest to a technician. However, being aware of what the ALU in the Z80 can do could help out during some technical job.

In the instruction register circuits are some more registers that can't be programmed. The instruction register is loaded from the system data bus, D7-D0. After it has a register loaded, the IR then uses control registers to get the defined instruction performed. These control registers generate all the control signals that send the instruction results to the other designated registers in the processor.

## Z80 in Action

The Z80 has been around since the beginnings of microcomputers. A lot of software has been written for it. For instance there are thousands of programs written in CP/M. To take advantage of the CP/M wealth, the COMMODORE 128 has a Z80 installed on the print board. The Z80 acts as a coprocessor along with an 8502 from the 6502 family. The support chips match the Z80 into the 8502 processor's environment. This circuit is a good example of what is done with Z80s in today's computer environment.

The 16 address pins, 1-5 and 30-40, are connected directly to the system address bus. There is no conflict there. The eight data bus pins, D7-D0, are connected to a special Z80 data bus. There is a conflict in the data lines. The Z80 data bus connects to the support chips, a 74LS373, a latch, and a 74LS244, a buffer. These chips in turn connect to the system data bus and match the Z80 data bus into the 8502 system data bus. The buffer acts as an interface during a write, while the latch acts as an interface during a read.

Besides the 16 address lines and the 8 data lines, the Z80 has 16 other pins. There are three control pins, 18, 19, and 28 that are not connected. Pin 18 is a signal from the Z80 called *HALT. When *HALT is operating it goes low. Since it is not needed in this application it is held high. If you read it with a logic probe it will read HIGH. It goes low when the Z80 is awaiting a non-maskable interrupt, which won't happen in this circuit. Pin 19 is also a signal from the Z80 called *MREQ, memory request. This signal is also active low. It is supposed to indicate that there is a valid address on the address bus. *MREQ is a tri-state signal when not active. There will be no logic probe reading present on the pin. Pin 28 is the *RFSH, refresh signal for the DRAMs. In this computer the DRAM refresh is conducted by the video interface chip elsewhere on the board. Since *RFSH is not needed, it is held high and kept inactive.

There are often many unused pins on a chip. A technician must be aware of what is happening with the unused pins as well as the active pins. For instance if one of these pins were not inactive it could interfere with the operation. If you probe a pin and find a wrong reading, that is a clue.

There are ten more control pins. The first four are to handle system control. Pin 27, *MI, is an output that signals when the Z80 is idling or in the midst of a fetch. While idling it is held high. During an operation it signals a low. Pin 20, *IORQ, shows that the lower half of the address bus is valid when low.

Pins 21 and 22 are the read and write outputs, *RD and *WR. During a Z80 read, *RD goes low. If the Z80 is writing to the memory map, then *WR goes low. Otherwise *RD is tri-stating and *WR is held high with a connection through a 3300 ohm resistor to +5 V. In the 6800 processor there is one read/write line, R/*W. The Z80 uses two pins for its reading and writing.

The next four control lines are all inputs from the rest of the computer. They signal the Z80 that certain conditions are occurring. Pin 24 is called *WAIT. It is an input active low. When it goes low it tells the Z80 to wait because the memory or I/O device that is addressed, is not ready to transfer data. However, in this example circuit, there is no need to signal a wait state. Therefore, the pin is held high and inactive by tieing it to +5 V. As long as it is high it can't accidentally put the Z80 into a wait state. Pin 17, the non-maskable interrupt, *NMI, is also not needed in this circuit so it gets the same treatment. It is inactive high and gets tied to +5 V. Pin 16, *INT is the interrupt that is allowed to work. It is held high and inactive until an interrupt when an I/O device sends a low and overrides the high it is held at. Pin 26 is the *RESET line. It is held high until the reset is triggered. Then it causes the Z80 to go into its reset sequence.

The last two control lines are 25 and 23, *BUSREQ and *BUSAK. They are the bus request and bus acknowledge lines. They indicate that the Z80 is idling, and has relinquished control of the computer to another device, in this case the other processor, the 8502. These pins go low and become active when the Z80 is on standby. The bus request receives a low from another device and causes the address bus, the data bus and the control lines to tri-state. The bus acknowledge then sends out a signal and tells the other device that the Z80 has indeed tri-stated. The other device then can take over the bus lines and not worry about interference from the Z80.

Pin 6 is the input from an external clock circuit. The Z80 does not use a two phase clock like the 6800 or 6502. It performs with a single phase clock. This is discussed in more detail later in this chapter.

## Z80 Instruction Set

The Z80 has an instruction set containing 158 different instructions. If you want to write programs in machine language, you should use an assembler, or, as it is sometimes called, a monitor. This is a program that you install into the Z80 computer. It allows you to write ML programs with the aid of mnemonics. Mnemonics are code for the binary bits in each instruction. A detailed description of all 158 instructions will accompany the monitor. A monitor is quite like a program that lets you write BASIC programs. The different statements and functions in BASIC are code for sets of binary bits in the machine's instructions. There will be a lot more about mnemonics as we get into discussions on the 16- and 32-bit processors.

In all programs, the most used instructions deal with the processor moving data from place to place, either to and from the memory map or within its own internal registers. Probably 70 to 80 percent of the instructions you'll find in a program are of the read/write and exchange variety that transfers data from place to place.

The next group of instructions have to do with using the ALU. These instructions run data through the ALU, which results in arithmetic or logic being executed. The results of the data processing are then placed into the accumulator and the flags relating to the ALU operations are cleared or set accordingly.

One group of instructions shifts or rotates data in the accumulator, in other Z80 registers, or in memory. These instructions also have the ability to do binary coded decimal manipulations.

Another group of instructions stops the program counter from automatic incrementing and places special addresses in the program counter. These are the JUMP, CALL, and RETURN instructions. The I/O group is next. The Z80 is able to address 256 input and 256 output ports. The I/O instructions transfer data back and forth between the processor and memory, and between the memory and I/O devices.

There are some instructions that are able to halt the Z80 in its tracks, and manipulate interrupts. One instruction NOP, makes the Z80 do nothing, no operation, during the time the NOP is processed. There are some bit handling instructions. They are able to set, reset, and test bits in some Z80 registers or memory. The results of the bit manipulation are then recorded in the Flag register.

Lastly, the Z80 is able to transfer any size block of memory to any group of next-door memory locations. Another instruction lets the Z80 search through a block of memory for a desired byte that might be needed.

## The Z80 Timing

Back in Chapter 9, the 6800 dual phase clock was used as an example to describe processor timing. The Z80 is not a dual phase processor. It uses a single-phase clock. This single-phase wave enters the Z80 at pin 6, running at the frequency of the computer. Typically this is a low frequency, 1 MHz for instance. Each square wave, consisting of a low, rising to a high, then falling to the low level, is called a clock period. The clock energy makes the program counter output an address and causes the Z80 to move data. The clock energy inside the Z80 has its signal split into separate energy bundles, and is fed separately to the address circuits and the "fetch and execute" circuits.

A clock period is not a cycle. There are a lot of clock periods in a cycle. The single phase wave train consists of one identical clock period after another. In the Z80 the wave train is called phase ($\phi$). On the first rising edge of $\phi$, the address circuits receive an input and the program counter in the Z80 places its contents onto the system address bus. A register in the memory map is addressed by the counter's bits.

Stored in memory is a program that is to be run. The address put out on the bus contacts the first byte of the program. Typically, the storage arrangement consists of first an instruction byte, and then one or more data bytes. The instruction tells the processor what it should do with the following data bytes.

$\phi$ will run the program to match the memory instruction-data arrangement. The instruction fetch is called a machine cycle. Memory reads or writes are also called machine cycles. Typically these three machine cycles each take place in three to six clock periods.

The $\phi$ wave train is shown performing one instruction cycle. The first four clocks, a machine cycle conducts the instruction op code fetch. The next three clocks, another machine cycle performs a memory read. The next three clocks, another machine cycle performs a memory write.

The wave train is built to run steady and apply the clocks to their appropriate circuits in the processor. The op code fetch clocks go to the circuits that will be working on the op codes as they arrive. The op code fetch is always a read operation because it is obtaining an instruction from memory. The memory read clocks are applied to the read circuits and the write clocks to the write circuits. All three machine cycles occur every time.

In order to trigger the activity in a read or write circuit there are read and write lines in the program. Their logic states tell the processor which direction the data should be conducted over the data bus.

## Op Code Fetch

The Z80 carefully counts the incoming clock periods. The first four clocks are then input to the op code's circuitry. The first rising edge of the first clock triggers the program counter to address the first register in memory that is holding the program bytes.

The falling edge of the same clock triggers off a signal called *MREQ, memory request. A low leaves the *MREQ pin and enables the memory chips. The same falling edge also triggers an individual signal called *RD, which is the read line.

A copy of the contents of the addressed memory byte, an op code, is placed on the data bus as a result of these signals activating and opening up the memory location. The data becomes stable on the bus during the second clock period. As the rising edge of the third period arrives, the processor is able to absorb the contents of the data bus. The same rising edge also extinguishes the *MREQ and *RD signals.

The first four clock periods are there expressly to fetch op codes. They do the job easily by triggering circuits on and off as the edges of the periods rise and fall. Once the op code reaches the processor, the circuits are set up to follow the instruction on processing the data that will follow.

278

## Data Movement

Once the first op code fetch machine cycle is completed and an instruction is fetched, the next machine cycle, consisting of three clock periods, arrives. Actually the cycle could be four or five clocks long but we'll use three for our example.

These three clocks are readers. They cause a fetch operation very similar to the op code fetch except they are fetching data and not an instruction. The timing diagram shows the similarities and the differences. Upon the rise of the first clocks, in both the op code and data fetches, the address of the register holding the instruction or the data is placed on the address bus. As the first clocks fall, the signal *MREQ is made to output a low. At the same time *RD is also made to output an enabling low. The op code or the data moves out onto the data bus in the same way.

The main difference between the op code fetch and the data read happens when the bits are strobed into the processor from the data bus. If you look at the timing charts, the memory output bits, whether they are an op code or data byte, are represented by a straight line and then a little energy container. The containers have highs and lows. This represents the highs and lows of the op code or data that are in the bus lines D7-D0.

Under the op code clocks, the contents of the data bus, the instruction bits are strobed into the Z80 during the rise of the third clock. Under the memory read clocks the data bits are strobed into the Z80 during the fall of the third clock.

Immediately following the data read machine cycle are the clocks that can drive the data write machine cycle. Like the data read operation the data write operation typically uses three clocks, but often it uses more than three. The write operation is the act of sending data from the processor to memory, unlike the read that sends data from the memory to the processor. The clock periods though are quite alike. Only the circuits the clock drives are different.

Upon the rise of the write's first clock, the 16 address bits are placed onto the address bus exactly like the op code fetch and the data read did. As the first clock has its falling edge, a low is output from *MREQ, *RD remains high and inactive, since this is a write operation and *RD is not needed.

With the address bus and the *MREQ turned on, the memory location opens up and is ready to receive data from the Z80. The Z80 lets data bleed out onto the data bus. The data then becomes stable on the bus. During the fall of the second write clock a low from the *WR write pin is output. This low strobes the data in the bus into the memory chips and specifically into the addressed location that had just been opened up by the address bits.

That is the way the clock periods are used in single-phase clocks to fetch instructions, read data from memory, and write data to memory. The clock crystal starts vibrating at its resonant frequency as voltage is impressed onto its crystalline structure when you turn on a computer. This vibration is an analog sine-wave voltage that is then converted to a digital square-wave voltage and adjusted in circuits to become lows such as zero volts and highs like +5 V. A prescribed number of clocks becomes the op code fetch ;machine cycle, the data read cycle, and the write cycle.

## Z80 Computer

A typical Z80 computer is similar to the 6800 computer in a general way. The Z80 is the center piece and it needs the same type of power supply, clock circuits and reset mechanism. The Z80 addressing system is quite like the 6800, and the memory arrangement is also the same. There is ROM, RAM, and the I/O interfaces.

The major differences between the 6800 and Z80 computer is due to the fact that the 6800 is a dual phase and the Z80 is single phase. This makes some of the control lines act in different ways. The most obvious difference is the way the two processors conduct reading and writing. The 6800 uses one line called R/*W. When it is high the 6800 reads. As it goes low the 6800 writes.

The Z80 uses two lines, *RD and *WR. These lines are inactive high or tri-stating, and become active when low. Only one can go low at a time. When you are working with the different 8-bit computers, take note of the differences in the processors.

# 11
# Using The Instruction Set

ROMs and RAMs store computer programs in the form of highs and lows. A program is a list of eight-bit lines that has been written by a programmer. Each program line is either an instruction or a piece of data. The electronic activity between the MPU and the memory map is known as the fetch-interpret-execute cycle (Fig. 11-1). As the clock pulses, it keeps the cycles moving step after step.

The MPU has a multitude of gates and registers that are built to respond to certain arrangements of the eight bits. Eight bits can have 256 individual arrangements. The MPU circuits react differently to each individual bit possibility. The result is that the 8-bit computer is capable of following 256 instructions, if the circuits are designed into the MPU.

When a memory location is addressed and its eight-bit contents are fetched, the byte is latched into the instruction register of the MPU. The register decodes the byte. First, it decides if the byte is an instruction or a piece of data. If it is an instruction, it sends the order to the register where it is to be executed. When the byte is data, it stores the bits in a register like the accumulator, so an instruction can work on it.

There are only three major categories of instructions. One has to do with transferring data from place to place. The second is the arithmetic and logical manipulation of the data. The third kind of instruction has nothing to do with the data; instead, it deals with the manipulation of addresses.

## ADDRESSING MODES

In the 6800, there are 72 individual instructions. However, the instruction set shows 197 hex codes in the list. The hex, of course, is only a code for the actual highs and lows that pass through the wiring, gates, and registers. How can there be 197 codes if there are only 72 instructions? The answer: each instruction can have more than one addressing mode.

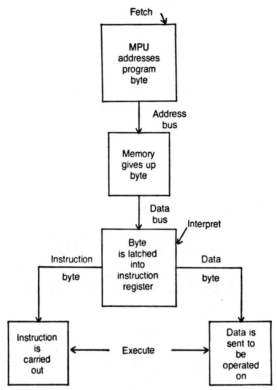

Fetch

MPU
addresses
program
byte

Address
bus

Memory
gives up
byte

Data
bus

Interpret

Byte
is latched
into
instruction
register

Instruction

byte

Data

byte

Instruction
is
carried
out

Execute

Data is
sent to
be
operated
on

Fig. 11-1. The electronic activity between the MPU and memory map is known as the Fetch-Interpret-Execute cycle.

Addressing modes, which were introduced in Chapter 7, and are illustrated in Fig. 11-2, show the different methods the MPU can use to find data. If the data to be processed is found in the next program byte after the instruction, the mode is Immediate.

When the data needed is a in a memory location that can be addressed with one byte (any location between 0 and 255), an address is found in the byte after the instruction. This is called the Direct mode.

If the data needed is in a memory location that requires two bytes (all locations above 255), an address is found in the two bytes after the instruction. This is called the Extended mode.

Should the instruction be in the Indexed mode, the Index register is involved. In the byte after the instruction is a number called on offset. This offset is added to whatever is in the Index register. The total of the offset and the Index register forms an address. This address is where the data needed will be found.

To obtain the data, the MPU puts the index register contents out on the address bus. The location is accessed and the data it contains is brought back to the MPU.

For instance, let's examine one of the most used instructions that needs at one time or another all four addressing modes to operate. The instruction is called *Load Accumulator* (Fig. 11-2). This instruction causes a copy of the contents of the memory location addressed to be installed in the accumulator register.

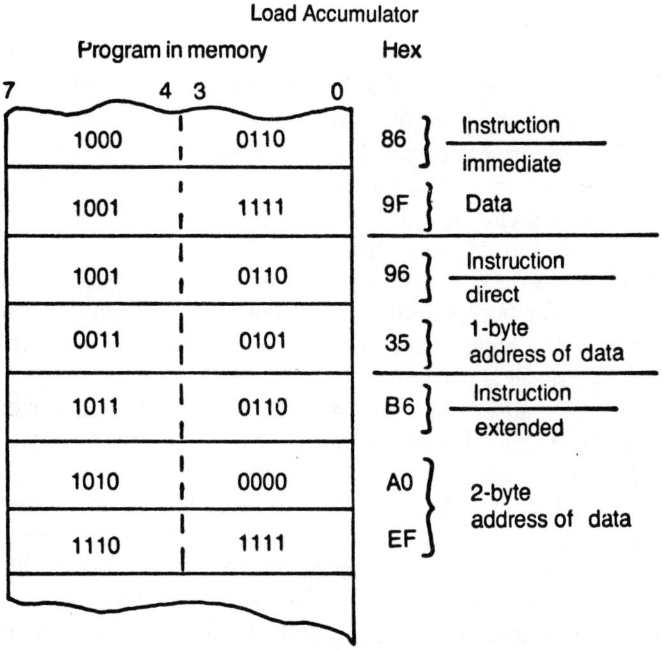

Fig. 11-2. Immediate, direct and extended addressing modes for the Load Accumulator.

There are four hex codes to perform the load operation. The first one is hex 86. When the instruction register receives the bits that code into 86, it recognizes the Immediate mode. The MPU then looks for the data to put into the accumulator in the next memory location after the instruction. The data is fetched and placed into the accumulator for processing.

The next load code is 96. When the instruction register receives the 96, it is built to know that the data to be loaded is in a memory location that is specified by a one byte address. The address is in the next byte after the 96. The MPU receives that address and sends it out over the address bus. The contents of that address is then installed into the accumulator.

The third load code is B6. When the IR receives the B6, it recognizes the Extended mode. It knows that the data to be loaded is in the location specified by the next two bytes in the program. The MPU then receives the two bytes and forms the 16-bit address. The single data byte in that address is then loaded into the accumulator.

The fourth load mode is A6. The A6 tells the IR that the data needed will be found by the trickery of the Index mode. The IR takes the byte after the A6 and adds it to the contents of the Index register. The address formed then goes out on the address bus. The contents of the location addressed is loaded in the accumulator.

There are a lot of variations of addressing modes. The modes are only different ways to find data that is stashed in various places in the computer. They add a lot of versatility to the programming. The more useful ways that the MPU has to address locations that hold data, the more powerful it is said to be.

## FLAGS

The condition code register in the MPU was mentioned earlier. It is an 8-bit register and each bit contains what is called a *flag*. Flag bits can be either set or clear. Each flag signals a particular condition in the data processing. An instruction can throw one or more flags. The flags in turn can cause changes in different registers.

In the 6800, there are six flags in the eight bits. They are located in the lowest bits. The extra two bits can contain more flags in other processors. The six flags are initialed H, I, N, Z, and C. Each has its own duties.

In bit 0, the CCR has the C (carry) flag. A lot of the 72 instructions affect the C flag. A typical use of the C flag occurs during an add instruction. When two binary numbers are added together in the accumulator, sometimes their total exceeds the eight bits of the accumulator. The result is nine bits.

When the arithmetic answer must be nine bits long, the accumulator needs a carry. The C bit is set in these cases. In fact, whatever the reason, when a carry from the most significant bit of the accumulator happens, the C bit in the CCR is set.

Bit 1 of the CCR has the V flag. The V represents an overflow. Overflow is not a carry. The overflow has to do with the state of the MS bit in the accumulator. If you recall, the MS bit during the two's complement addition (that is, the substitute for computer subtraction) keeps its sign in the MS bit. A 0 means + and a 1 is −. This restricts the range of two's complement numbers to seven bits. The highest number is +127 and the lowest is −128.

If the activity in the accumulator overflows the seven bits and changes the sign bit, the V flag is set. Otherwise, the V bit is clear.

In bit 2 of the CCR, the Z (zero) flag is located. Whenever all the bits of a computed result ends in 0s throughout the accumulator, the Z flag is set. Otherwise the Z flag is clear.

Bit 3 of the CCR has the N (negative) flag. This negative refers to the MS bit of the accumulator. During two's complement activity, the MS bit could get set and designate a minus number. The N flag will be set when this happens. However, when the MS bit of the accumulator gets set, the N flag gets set. Otherwise, it is cleared.

In bit 4, there is a mechanism called the I (interrupt mask) bit. If you recall, the IRQ interrupt is maskable. This bit is the mask. When the I bit is clear, the interrupt is able to get through to the MPU and get service. If the I bit is set, the interrupt is masked off and the MPU pays no attention to the interrupt requests.

The IRQ Interrupt is not to be confused with the more powerful NMI nonmaskable interrupt. When it interrupts the MPU, it's due to an emergency and it gets through any masking attempt.

The last flag in the 6800 is bit 5. Bits 6 and 7 are set with 1s. Sophisticated hardware-software people are able to utilize these bits but they can largely be ignored. Bit 5 is the H flag.

The H flag is used conventionally during binary-coded-decimal operations, BCD. This is the coding of numbers 0-9 in binary. The hex numbers A-F are not used and the corresponding binary numbers are forbidden. If there is a carry from bit 3 of the accumulator to bit 4, the result could be one of the forbidden binary numbers. There is an instruction called *Decimal Adjust the A Accumulator*. If his instruction is used immediately after a BCD operation, it adjusts all forbidden numbers to valid ones.

The H (half carry) bit is set if there is a carry from bit 3 to bit 4. This is an alert that a half carry, from the LS nybble to the MS nybble, has taken place.

The flags are automatic devices and they detect a lot of special conditions that happen in the computer. They are very important to any program.

A programmer writing a machine language program must take into consideration every flag that might get thrown on every instruction and after every data process.

There are some instructions that cause the computer to make decisions. These are the Branch group. For example, take the instruction that says, "Branch if the Z flag is set." The setting or clearing of the flag decides if the branch is to be made. If the Z flag is set, the branch is made. When the Z flag is clear, the branch is not made. All the flags perform similar jobs according to their functions. More discussion on this follows.

## INSTRUCTION SET

There are three general forms of instructions in the 72 separate instructions. The first type has to do with the movement of data. The second type involves the processing of data. The third type of instruction deals with changing addresses. Also covered are several instructions that do not fit into any of the general categories and interrupt instruction codes.

### Data Movement

These instructions are the most often used, especially the Load and Store instructions, which are used in about 70 percent of the total program lines. The Load instruction is a read instruction. The Store instruction is a write. There are three Load instructions that will work in the 6800 circuits. There are also three Store instructions.

When you enter a machine language program into the computer, the hex instruction code for each binary instruction number is the one you type into the computer. The keyboard input to the PIA changes the hex characters you strike into bytes. The keyboard bytes are then encoded into a ROM address by the MPU registers. The binary instruction number that represents the hex is at the ROM address. The binary bits are the ones that are stored in the memory.

The addresses and data that accompany the instruction code are also typed in hex. After instruction code numbers, the address where the data to be processed is stored, or the data itself is found.

The three Load instructions always have a hex number following them. The hex is either an address or a piece of data. The casual observer sees no difference between the instruction code number and the address or data number. That is why programmers place comments after program lines.

The first Load instruction is *Load Accumulator*. There are eight hex numbers to load the accumulator, because there are two accumulators in the 6800 and four addressing modes for each accumulator.

The instruction causes the MPU to load the contents of a memory location into one of the accumulators. The memory location is determined by the addressing mode. If the mode is Immediate, then the location is the one immediately after the instruction. If the mode is Direct or Extended, the location is the one shown by the address following the instruction. When the mode is Indexed, the address is the location derived by adding the offset, contained in the byte after the instruction, to the contents of the index register.

The condition code register can have two of its flags altered by the Load instruction: N and Z. If the execution of the instruction causes a negative or zero effect, the flags will be set. The V flag stays clear during a Load operation.

The next Load instruction is called *Load Stack Pointer*. There is only one stack pointer register in the 6800. There are the usual four addressing modes though. This gives a total of four separate instructions.

The stack point register has 16 bits. The program is processing bytes. When the stack pointer is loaded from the bytes being processed, two bytes are needed. The first byte along gets loaded into the most significant bits. The second byte is loaded into the least significant bits. The bytes are automatically found in the memory according to what addressing mode is used.

The N or Z flags can be set if bit 15 of the pointer gets set or is cleared. The V flag stays clear during the operation so not to interfere with anything.

The third Load instruction is called *Load Index Register*. The index register is loaded from memory in exactly the same way the stack pointer is loaded. The placement of bytes and the flag alterations are identical. The only difference is the hex instruction code.

There are three Store instructions that work in the 6800. They resemble the Load instructions, except that they send data in the other direction. When a Store instruction is received by the MPU it addresses a location and sends it data from the register defined by the instruction.

The first Store instruction is called *Store Accumulator*. There are two accumulators and three addressing modes for each accumulator. This gives a total of six Stored Accumulator instructions.

There are only six instead of eight like the Load instructions because there is no Immediate mode for the Store instruction. There is no way the data to be stored can follow the instruction in the program, as the mode requires. The data to be stored is already in an MPU register. The Immediate mode is useless in this instance.

When the MPU receives a Store Accumulator A instruction, hex 97, there is a memory address in hex immediately following the Instruction Code. The MPU activates the address and writes the contents of the A accumulator into the address.

The address is either in RAM or I/O. It is not in ROM because you can't store in ROM. The Load instructions, on the other hand, can be followed by a ROM address because you can load from ROM.

The storing in memory from the accumulator can use the Direct, Extended, and Indexed addressing modes. The byte following the instruction byte contains the addressing means.

Like the Load instructions, the Store Accumulator affects the N and Z flags. If the accumulator has a 1 in bit 7 the N flag is set. Should the accumulator be cleared, the Z flag is set. Also like the Load, the V flag remains clear.

The next store instruction is *Store Stack Pointer*. There are three instruction codes; one each for the Direct, Extended, and Indexed addressing modes. The instruction stores the contents of the stack pointer into memory.

Since the stack pointer is composed of two bytes, it must be stored in two bytes of memory. The most significant byte is stored in the address that is in the byte following the instruction. The least significant byte is stored in the next byte after the one in the program.

The store causes the Z flag to be set if the stack pointer is all 0s. The N flag becomes set if bit 15 of the stack pointer is set. The V flag is cleared and is not affected otherwise by the instruction.

The third store is *Store Index Register*. The instruction has three instruction codes; one each for the Direct, Extended, and Indexed addressing modes. The instructions store the contents of the Index register into memory. Like the stack pointer instructions, the 16-bit Index register is automatically stored in two consecutive bytes. The first storage location byte is the one specified in the program. It receives the MS byte from the Index register. The second storage byte receives the LS byte from the Index register.

The same flags (N, A, and V) are involved, like the stack pointer.

**PUSH and Pull.** There are two more instructions that transfer data back and forth between the accumulator and the stack location in memory, when the accumulator is needed for some operations but the current contents of the accumulator must be saved. One of the instructions stores the accumulator contents into the address specified in the stack pointer. It is called *Push Data onto Stack*.

There are two instruction codes; one for the A accumulator and the other for the B accumulator. When the instruction is executed, the stack pointer decrements its contents by 1. The decrementing is performed so the pointer address is to an empty byte holder and not to the byte that is storing the accumulator data.

The other instruction is *Pull Data from Stack*. There are two instruction codes; one for the A accumulator and the other for the B. This instruction is used to return the former contents of the accumulator back to an accumulator after stacking them. The instruction causes the stack pointer to increment by 1 first. This makes the address in the stack pointer the original one, that the contents of the accumulator had been sent to. The instruction then makes the MPU return the stacked data back to an accumulator. The data can return to either the A or B accumulator. The data is not necessarily forced to return to its original accumulator.

During these two instructions, the flags play no part and are not affected in anyway.

**Microprocessor Transfers.** The other kind of data transfers take place in the MPU. The registers in the MPU are able to transfer data from one to the other in a number of ways. There are no special addressing modes required. Each instruction has a single instruction code.

The two accumulators have two instructions that force them to transfer their contents from one to the other. One instruction is called *Transfer from Accumulator A to Accumulator B*. The second instruction is *Transfer from Accumulator B to Accumulator A*.

When the transfers take place, the originating accumulator retains a copy of the data it transferred. Any data that was in the destination accumulator is destroyed as the entering data takes its place.

The N and Z flags are affected by the accumulator transfers. The V flag is cleared.

Another pair of similar instructions are able to send data from the index register to the stack pointer and vice versa. They are called *Transfer from Index Register to Stack Pointer* and *Transfer from Stack Pointer to Index Register*. None of the flags are altered during these operations.

When the stack pointer sends a copy of its contents to the Index register, the stack pointer doesn't change its value. The stack data that appears in the Index register is, however, not the same as the value that was transferred. The value was incremented by 1 during the transfer.

Conversely, when the Index register sends a copy of its contents to the stack pointer, the value of the data is decremented by 1. These slight alterations by 1 are needed by the programmer to save steps.

The last two inter-MPU data transfers are between the accumulator A and the flag bit holder, the condition code register (Fig. 11-3). One instruction is called *Transfer from Accumulator A to Condition Code Register*. The other instruction is *Transfer from Condition Code Register to Accumulator A*. They are tricky, and flags are affected as the transfers take place. There are no corresponding instructions involving the B accumulator. The A accumulator handles are eventualities.

When the transfer is from the accumulator to the CCR, the accumulator transfers only the data from bits 0-5. Bits 6 and 7 are not transferred. Bits 6 and 7of the CCR have

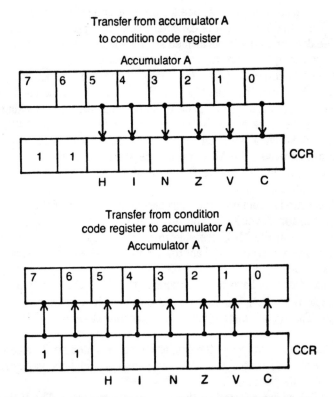

Fig. 11-3. The Transfer instruction between Accumulator A and the CCR is not the same both ways. Accumulator to CCR only transfers five of the eight bits.

permanent 1s installed. If these 1s are removed, programming complications could occur.

When the accumulator bits are transferred to 0-5 of the CCR, the flags will be set or cleared according to the bits that are sent. This is a useful way for the programmer to set or clear flags as needed.

The converse instruction transfers a copy of the contents of the CCR to the accumulator. In this direction, the CCR transfers all eight bits, 0-7, to the accumulator. The two MS bits are both 1s. Transferring a copy of them to the accumulator does not upset anything. They remain 1s in the CCR as they should. Transferring to the accumulator does not affect any of the flags in any way.

These data-moving instructions are very useful during advanced maintenance and troubleshooting. Most diagnostic programs use the transfer program heavily. Data can be sent and retrieved from every section of the computer. When one section doesn't perform in the manner it was designed to, this constitutes a valid clue that requires further investigation.


## Data Processing

While moving data is the first major category of instructions the MPU responds to, processing data is the second. There are three general ways data is processed. It all happens in the MPU. First, the registers are manipulated while the data bits are in them. Second, the MPU performs arithmetic with the data. Third, the MPU applies logic to the data. We'll look at the instructions that manipulate the registers first.

There is a group of six instructions that increment and decrement registers. There are three increment instructions and three decrements. The first one is simply called *Increment*. Increment has four instruction codes. It is able to affect both accumulators A and B, and it can also increment a memory location.

The first two instructions increment the accumulators by 1. All that means is when the instruction occurs the indicated accumulator gets 1 added to its value. The N and Z flags will be affected if the accumulator, due to the increment code, affects bit 8 or goes to all 0s. The V flag is also affected with Increment since the accumulator could have a signed number. If the sign in bit 7 is accidentally changed due to an overflow from bit 6, the V flag is thrown.

There are separate instruction codes for incrementing the A and B accumulators. There are also two separate codes for incrementing a memory location. One code number is used to increment a location that is found by addressing it in the Extended mode. The other code number increments the location that is addressed in the Indexed mode.

There are two instructions that increment the stack pointer and the Index register. Incrementing the stack pointer does not affect the flags at all. Incrementing the Index register sets the Z flag if all 16 bits are cleared; otherwise, the flags stay cleared.

The *Decrement* instruction performs almost the same activity as Increment, except it decreases the indicated register by 1 instead of increasing it. Decrement can subtract 1 from either accumulator or a memory location. There are four instruction codes, one for the A accumulator, one for the B accumulator, one for the Extended addressing of a memory location, and one for Indexed addressing of a location.

**Table 11-1. 6800 Machine Instruction Set.**

**1** LOAD ACCUMULATOR A
86
96
B6
A6

ADDRESSING MODE
IMMEDIATE
DIRECT
EXTENDED
INDEXED

LOAD ACCUMULATOR B
C6
D6
F6
E6

IMMEDIATE
DIRECT
EXTENDED
INDEXED

Flags affected. N, Z. Flag cleared, V.

**2** LOAD STACK POINTER
8E
9E
BE
AE

IMMEDIATE
DIRECT
EXTENDED
INDEXED
Flags affected. N, Z. Flag cleared. V.

**3** LOAD INDEX REGISTER
CE
DE
FE
EE

IMMEDIATE
DIRECT
EXTENDED
INDEXED

Flags affected. N, Z Flag cleared. V.

**4** STORE ACCUMULATOR A
97
B7
A7

DIRECT
EXTENDED
INDEXED

STORE ACCUMULATOR B
D7
F7
E7

DIRECT
EXTENDED
INDEXED

Flags affected. N, Z. Flag cleared. V.

**5** STORE STACK POINTER
9FBF
AF

DIRECT
EXTENDED
INDEXED
Flags affected. N, Z. Flag cleared, V.

**6** STORE INDEX REGISTER
DF
FF
EF

DIRECT
EXTENDED
INDEXED

Flags affected, N, Z. Flag cleared, V.

**7** PUSH DATA onto STACK
36 (Push accumulator A onto stack)
37 (Push accumulator B onto stack)
No flags are affected by these instructions.

**8** PULL DATA from STACK
32 (load the A accumulator from stack)
33 (load the B accumulator from stack)
No flags are affected by these instructions.

**9** TRANSFER from AC-CUMULATOR A to AC-CUMULATOR B
16
TRANSFER from AC-CUMULATOR B to AC-CUMULATOR A
17
Flags affected. N, Z. Flag cleared. V.

**10** TRANSFER from INDEX RE-GISTER to STACK POINTER
35
TRANSFER from STACK POINTER to INDEX REGISTER
30
No flags are affected by these instructions.

**11** TRANSFER from AC-CUMULATOR A to CONDITION CODE REGISTER
06
TRANSFER from CONDITION CODE REGISTER to AC-CUMULATOR A
07
Flags are affected when accumulator A transfers contents into CCR. Whatever was in the accumulator register bits 0-5 will be in bits 0-5 of the CCR.

**12** INCREMENT
4C    ACCUMULATOR A
5C    ACCUMULATOR B
7C    EXTENDED ADDRESS
6C    INDEXED ADDRESS
Flags affected are N, Z, V.
INCREMENT STACK POINTER
31
No flags affected.
INCREMENT INDEX RE-GISTER
08
The Z flag is set if all 16 bits are cleared

**13** Decrement
4A    ACCUMULATOR A
5A    ACCUMULATOR B
7A    EXTENDED ADDRESS
6A    INDEXED ADDRESS
Flags affected are N, Z, v.
DECREMENT STACK

**Table 11-1. Continued.**

POINTER
34
No flags are affected.
DECREMENT INDEX RE-
GISTER
09
The Z flag can be affected.
**14** CLEAR
4F ACCUMULATOR A
5F ACCUMULATOR B
7F EXTENDED ADDRESS
6F INDEXED ADDRESS
the Z flag is set The N, V, and C
flags are cleared.
CLEAR 2'S COMPLEMENT
OVERFLOW BIT
0A
The V flag is cleared.
CLEAR CARRY
0C
The C flag is cleared
CLEAR INTERRUPT MASK
0E
The I flag is cleared
**15** SET 2'S COMPLEMENT
OVERFLOW BIT
0B
The V flag is set to 1
SET INTERRUPT MASK
0F
The I flag is set to 1
SET CARRY
0D
The C flag is set to 1
**16** TEST N or Z
4d ACCUMULATOR A
5D ACCUMULATOR B
7D EXTENDED ADDRESS
6D INDEXED ADDRESS
Flags affected. N, Z. The V flag is
cleared
**17** LOGICAL SHIFT RIGHT
44 ACCUMULATOR A
54 ACCUMULATOR B
74 EXTENDED ADDRESS
64 INDEXED ADDRESS
Flags that can be affected. Z, V.
C The N flag is cleared
ROTATE LEFT
49 ACCUMULATOR A
59 ACCUMULATOR B
79 EXTENDED ADDRESS
69 INDEXED ADDRESS
Flags that can be affected. N, Z,
C. V
ROTATE RIGHT
46 ACCUMULATOR A
56 ACCUMULATOR B
76 EXTENDED ADDRESS
66 INDEXED ADDRESS
Flags that can be affected. N, Z,
C. V
ARITHMETIC SHIFT RIGHT
47 ACCUMULATOR A
57 ACCUMULATOR B
77 EXTENDED ADDRESS
67 INDEXED ADDRESS
Flags that can be affected, N, Z,
V. C.
ARITHMETIC SHIFT LEFT
48 ACCUMULATOR A
58 ACCUMULATOR B
78 EXTENDED ADDRESS
68 INDEXED ADDRESS
Flags that can be affected, N, Z,
V. C.
**18** COMPLEMENT
43 ACCUMULATOR A
53 ACCUMULATOR B

73 EXTENDED ADDRESS
63 INDEXED ADDRESS
Flags that can be affected. N, Z,
C is set to 1. V is cleared.
NEGATE
40 ACCUMULATOR A
50 ACCUMULATOR B
70 EXTENDED ADDRESS
60 INDEXED ADDRESS
Flags that can be affected. N, Z,
V. C.
**19** ADD ACCUMULATOR A to AC-
CUMULATOR B
1b
Flags that can be affected. N, Z,
V. C. H.
SUBTRACT ACCUMULATORS
10
Flags that can be affected. N, Z,
V. C
ADD WITH CARRY IN AC-
CUMULATOR A
89 IMMEDIATE
99 DIRECT
B9 EXTENDED
A9 INDEXED
Flags affected are. N, Z, V, C. H.
ADD WITH CARRY in AC-
CUMULATOR B
C9 IMMEDIATE
D9 DIRECT
F9 EXTENDED
E9 INDEXED
Flags affected are. N, Z, V, C.
ADD WITHOUT CARRY IN AC-
CUMULATOR A
8B IMMEDIATE
9B DIRECT
BB EXTENDED
AB INDEXED
Flags affected are. N, Z, V, C. H.
ADD WITHOUT CARRY in AC-
CUMULATOR B
CB IMMEDIATE
DB DIRECT
FB EXTENDED
EB INDEXED
Flags affected are. N, Z, V, C. H.
SUBSTRACT WITH CARRY in
ACCUMULATOR A
82 IMMEDIATE
92 DIRECT
B2 EXTENDED
A2 INDEXED
Flags that can be affected are, N,
Z. V. C.
SUBTRACT WITH CARRY in
ACCUMULATOR B
C2 IMMEDIATE
D2 DIRECT
F2 EXTENDED
E2 INDEXED
Flags that can be affected are, N,
Z. V. C.
SUBTRACT (memory byte from
ACCUMULATOR A)
80 IMMEDIATE
90 DIRECT
B0 EXTENDED
A0 INDEXED
Flags that can be affected. N, Z,
V. C.
SUBTRACT (memory byte from
ACCUMULATOR B)
C0 IMMEDIATE
D0 DIRECT
F0 EXTENDED
E0 INDEXED
Flags that can be affected, N, Z,

**Table 11-1. Continued.**

V. C
DECIMAL ADJUST the A AC-
CUMULATOR
Flags that can be affected are. N.
Z. C.
**20** LOGICAL AND AC-
CUMULATOR A
    84 IMMEIDATE
    94 DIRECT
    B4 EXTENDED
A4 INDEXED
Flags that can be affected. N. Z
The V flag is cleared
LOGICAL AND AC-
CUMULATOR B
    C4 IMMEDIATE
    D4 DIRECT
    F4 EXTENDED
    E4 INDEXED
Flags that can be affected. N. Z.
The V flag is cleared
INCLUSIVE OR (Logical OR)
ACCUMULATOR A
    8A IMMEDIATE
    9A DIRECT
BA EXTENDED
    AA INDEXED
Flags that can be affected. N. Z.
The V flag is cleared
INCLUSIVE OR (LOGICAL OR)
ACCUMULATOR B
    CA IMMEDIATE
    DA
DIRECT
FA EXTENDED
    EA INDEXED
Flags that can be affected. N. Z
The V flag is cleared
EXCLUSIVE OR AC-
CUMULATOR A
    88 IMMEDIATE
    98 DIRECT
    B8 EXTENDED
    A8 INDEXED
Flags that can be affected. N. Z
The V flag is cleared
EXCLUSIVE OR AC-
CUMULATOR B
    C8 IMMEDIATE
    D8 DIRECT
    F8 Extended
    E8 INDEX
Flags that can be affected. N. Z
The V flag is cleared.
**21** BRANCH ALWAYS
    20 Unconditional
BRANCH to SUBROUTINE
    8D UNCONDITIONAL
RETURN from SUBROUTINE
    39
**22** BRANCH if CARRY SET
    25 CONDITION. C is set
      to 1.
BRANCH if CARRY CLEAR
    24 CONDITION. C is
      cleared to 0.
BRANCH if OVERFLOW SET
    29 CONDITION. V is set
      to 1.
BRANCH if OVERFLOW
CLEAR
    28 CONDITION. V is
      cleared to 0.
BRANCH if ZERO SET
    27 CONDITION. Z is set
      to 1.
BRANCH if ZERO CLEAR
    26 CONDITION. Z is
      cleared to 0.

BRANCH if NEGATIVE SET
    2B CONDITION. N is set
      to 1
BRANCH if NEGATIVE CLEAR
    2A CONDITION. N is
      cleared to 0.
BRANCH if HIGHER
    22 CONDITION. C or Z is
      cleared to 0.
BRANCH if LOWER or SAME
    23 CONDITION. C or Z is
      set to 1
BRANCH if LESS THAN ZERO
    2D CONDITION. N is set
      to 1 and V is cleared to
      0. or N is cleared to 0
      and V is set to 1
BRANCH if LESS THAN or
EQUAL TO ZERO
    2F CONDITION. Z is set
      to 1. N is set to 1 and V
      is cleared to 0. or. Z is
      set to 1. N is cleared to
      0 and V is set to 1
BRANCH if GREATER THAN
ZERO
    2E CONDITION. Z is cleared
      to 0. N is set to 1 and V is
      set to 1 Or Z is cleared to
      0. N is cleared to 0 and V is
      cleared to 0
BRANCH if GREATER THAN or
EQUAL TO ZERO
    2C CONDITION. N and V
      are set to 1. or. N and V
      are cleared to 0
**23** JUMP
7E EXTENDED ADDRESS
6E INDEXED ADDRESS
JUMP to SUBROUTINE
DB EXTENDED ADDRESS
AD INDEXED ADDRESS
    RETURN from SUBROUTINE
    39
**24** NO OPERATION
    01
    COMPARE ACCUMULATORS
    11
    Flags that could be affected. N.
    Z. V. C
    COMPARE ACCUMULATOR A
81 IMMEDIATE
91 DIRECT
B1 EXTENDED
A1 INDEXED
    Flags that could be affected. N.
    Z. V. C
    COMPARE ACCUMULATOR B
C1 IMMEDIATE
D1 DIRECT
F1 EXTENDED
E1 INDEXED
    Flags that could be affected. N.
    Z. V. C.
    COMPARE INDEX REGISTER
8C IMMEDIATE
9C DIRECT
BC EXTENDED
AC INDEXED
    Flags that could be affected. N.
    Z. V.
**25** RETURN from INTERRUPT
    3B
    SOFTWARE INTERRUPT
    3F
    The I flag is set to 1.
    WAIT for INTERRUPT
    3F
    The I flag can be affected.

The N and Z flags can both be affected. The V flag can also be set if there is a 2's complement computation and an overflow occurs. The overflow can only happen in one situation.

If the register contains a hex 80, which is binary 1000 0000, and the Decrement is executed, the register changes to 0111 1111, hex 7F. Bit 7 changes from 1 to 0. The V flag is set.

There are two other Decrement instructions for the Stack Pointer and the Index Register. The instruction code for the stack pointer decrements the 16 bit register and does not affect the flags. The instruction code for the Index register decrements the bit total by 1 and will set the Z flag if the register is completely cleared.

Another useful register manipulation instruction is named *Clear*. When this instruction is executed, the target register has all its bits, no matter what they are, changed to 0s. The instruction can be performed in either accumulator or a memory location. There are four instruction codes to execute Clear.

Each accumulator is affected by a separate code number. Then there is a code to address a location by the Extended mode and one for the Indexed mode.

Whenever a Clear is made, the Z flag is set. In addition the N, V, and C flags are cleared.

In addition to the straight Clear instruction there is a separate instruction called *Clear 2's Complement Overflow Bit*. That bit is the V flag in the CCR. When the instruction is executed it clears the V flag. Next is an instruction called *Clear Carry*. This clears the C bit to a 0. Following that is an instruction called *Clear Interrupt Mask*. This clears the I bit to a 0.

The flags themselves have three other instructions that cause them to be set. There is one called *Set 2's Complement Overflow Bit*. When executed, it set the V bit. Then there is *Set Interrupt Mask*. Its instruction code sets the I bit. Thirdly, there is *Set Carry*. It sets the C bit. This ability to clear and set bits and registers helps both the programmer during software debugging and the technician during hardware testing.

The preceding single bit set and clear instructions give you the ability to control the contents of the I, V, and C bits in the CCR. There is one more instruction that gives you the power to set the N and Z bits. It is called *Test (Z or N)*. With this instruction, the N and Z bits can be set according to the contents of either accumulator or a memory location. The C and V bits are cleared during the operation.

**Shift Registers.** The next few instructions take advantage of the ability of a register to shift the bits from side to side (Fig. 11-4). The bit shifting is the basis of the shift registers used extensively in all computers.

First of all, there is the instruction *Logical Shift Right*. This instruction can operate on the two accumulators and the memory locations. When executed, it forces the target register to shift all the bits 0-7, one place to the right.

When the shift takes place, all bits are moved without complication except for bits 7 and 0. Bit 7 is loaded with a 0. Bit 0 is pushed out of the register. It is not lost, but is loaded into the C bit of the Flag register.

There are four instruction codes for the Logical Shift Right. There is one each for the accumulators, a code for Extended addressing, and one for Indexed addressing. The accumulators are shifted with their codes and the addressed memory locations with their codes.

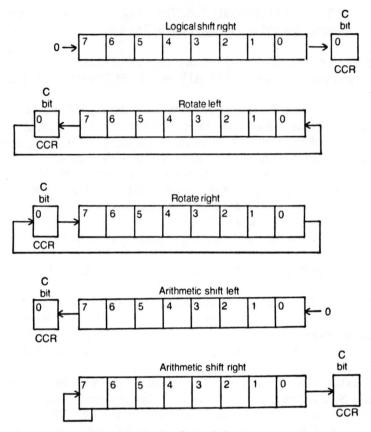

Fig. 11-4. The 6800 shift register instruction has five variations.

During a shift right, the flags could be affected. The Z flag could be set if the shift produces all 0s in the target register. The V flag will be set if the shift somehow produces a C flag of 0 and an N flag of 1, or a C of 1 and an N that is 0. Otherwise V stays 0. The C flag becomes whatever bit 0 was and the N stays clear under most circumstances, since bit 7 has a 0.

In other MPU's, there is a logical shift left instruction besides the shift right. There is no logical shift left op code in the 6800. There are two other shift instructions called *Rotate Left* and *Rotate Right*. They are almost like shift, except that they do not destroy whatever was in the C flag.

*Rotate Left* shifts all the bits one place to the left. Then the logic state that was in the C bit is loaded into bit 0 that was emptied by the shift. The state that was a bit 7 and pushed out of the register gets placed into the now-empty C bit. The C bit becomes in effect a ninth bit, so the eight register bits can be rotated without destroying any of the eight.

*Rotate Right* shifts all the bits one place to the right. Bit 0 is pushed out of the register and bit 7 is vacated. Bit 0 is loaded into the C flag and whatever was in the C flag is

294

loaded into the bit 7. The rotation is complete. The C flag acts like a ninth bit with one side connected to bit 0 and the other side hooked to bit 7.

Both Rotate Left and Rotate Right have four Instruction codes. There are two codes for rotating each accumulator and two for rotating a memory location. The memory registers are found with an Extended address or an Indexed address.

The N, Z, and V flags are affected exactly like the shift instruction affects them. The C flag assumes the state of bit 7 after a Rotate Left or bit 0 after a Rotate Right.

The Logical shift Right discussed above has two related shift instructions. *Arithmetic Shift Right* and *Arithmetic Shift Left*. The Arithmetic Right and Logical Right shifts are identical except for one bit replacement. Logical Right loads the vacated bit 7 with a 0. Arithmetic Right does not vacate bit 7 as it shifts all the bits to the right. The state that was in bit 7 is reproduced in bit 6, but the state also remains intact in bit 7.

This is because the Arithmetic Right could be working with a signed number. By keeping bit 7 the same as before the shift, the sign of the number remains the same. The Logical Right instruction is not concerned with signed numbers, so its execution merely loads a 0 into bit 7. Aside from this one quirk, the two instructions act in an identical manner.

Arithmetic Shift Left has no Logical counterpart instruction for the 6800. The instruction works on both accumulators and memory locations. There are four instruction codes, one for each accumulator and two addressing modes, Extended and Indexed.

The instruction shifts all the bits in a targeted register one place to the left. Bit 7 is loaded into the C flag and a 0 is loaded into the vacated bit 0. If the result is a register full of 0s, the Z flag becomes set. Should bit 7 become a 1, the N flag is set. When N becomes 1 and C receives a 0 from bit 7, the V flag is set. Should N become 0 and the C flag receive a 1, this sets the V flag too.

These shifts and rotates are straightforward except for the complications of the flag settings. Programmers have to be on their toes to keep these constant automatic flag settings and clearings in order. The flags are vital to the automatic running of a program.

**Arithmetic.** The second major section of data processing is arithmetic. This means addition, subtraction, multiplication, and division. There are a number of arithmetic instructions. They all move the binary bits around the registers affected to produce addition and subtraction. There are no multiplication or division instructions. These operations have to be performed by special little subroutine programs, which could be installed as part of a major program. They could also be contained in a ROM. When a multiplication or division operation is needed in a program, the instructions cause the program to Jump to the Subroutine, pass the data, have it multiplied or divided, and then return the results to the main program.

Adding and subtracting can be accomplished by the Instruction Set. The following are the instructions that will do the job. First of all, there is an instruction called *Complement*. It operates with four instruction codes.

Complement takes each bit in either accumulator or a memory location, and changes it. All 1s are changed to 0s and all 0s are made into 1s. The result is called the 1's complement. The 1's complement is useful during additions and subtractions.

The four codes address the two accumulators and memory locations in the Extended and Indexed modes. The operation can affect flags. If the results in the target register are all 0s, the Z flag is set. Should the result be a 1 in bit 7, the N flag is set. V is cleared, and C is set to 1.

A companion instruction to Complement is called *Negate*. It has the same type of instruction codes to address the two accumulators or a memory location by Extended or Indexed modes.

When Negate is executed, it simply replaces the bits in the target register with its 2's complement. The 1's complement is replacing the 1s with 0s and the 0s with 1s. The 2's complement is arrived at by adding 1 to the 1's complement. Negate can be thought of as two instructions tied together. First, there is the Complement, second is the Increment. The result in the register is a 2's complement of the original value.

The instruction is called Negate because the value creates the opportunity for an implied subtraction. The 6800 is built so that adding the 2's complement to a binary number results in an implied subtraction.

The 2's complement method of subtraction is a tricky way to obtain a subtraction by using addition. The procedure works whether the sign of the number is + or −. On more complex computers the subtraction scheme could use 1's complement, but then the answer must be corrected, which requires additional circuitry. For simple microprocessors, the 2's complement is usually employed and works well with the Carry and Overflow flags.

The *Negate Instruction Codes* operate in the same way as the Complement codes. There are two codes to change the accumulator's values to 2's complement through an Extended addressing mode, and one in the Indexed mode. The N flag is set if the result is a negative number due to bit 7 becoming a 1. The Z flag is set if the result is all 0s.

The V flag is set if the value in the target register becomes hex 80, which is binary 1000 0000. For example, if the addition 01000000+01000000=10000000 occurs, an accidental Carry from bit 6 to 7 happens. 01000000 is 64 in decimal. The addition in decimal should be 64+64=128. However 10000000 equals −128. The V flag is set and the incorrect minus sign is detected. The sign can be changed to +. The accidental 2's complement overflow is handled with the help of the V flag.

The C flag is used with the Negate instruction when a ninth bit is needed for the math work. For example, 128+129=257. In binary this is 10000000+10000001=1 (in the C bit) 00000001. If a carry or a borrow is needed, the C flag will be set. The only time the C flag will not be set in ninth bit cases is when the result is 00000000.

These concerns are mostly for the machine language programmer, but the technician should be aware of them.

The 6800 has a group of codes that add and subtract. The subtraction in the circuits is actually being performed with 2's complement, but the instruction performs subtraction and the user does not have to concern himself with the mechanics of the operation. As far as the programmer goes, he sees a subtraction take place. This is unlike the codes like Negate which require some attention to the 2's complement situation.

The first two pure math codes are *Add Accumulators* and *Subtract Accumulators*. The Add instruction is called *Add Accumulator B to Accumulator A*. The code forces the B accumulator to add a copy of its binary contents to the A accumulator. The sum goes into the A accumulator and the contents of the B accumulator remain the same. The flags H, N, Z, V, and C can each be affected if the A accumulator is changed in a way to affect a flag.

The converse instruction is called *Subtract Accumulators*. This code causes a copy of the contents of the B accumulator to be subtracted from the A accumulator and the results placed in the A accumulator. The B accumulator contents remain intact. The C, N, Z, and V flags can all be affected by the operation.

The last two codes dealt with operations that took place only in the MPU. The memory locations were not concerned in any way. Flags could be thrown but these complications were still inside the MPU. There are four other similar operations that bring the memory locations into play.

The first one is called *Add with Carry*. This code adds the contents of the ninth bit, the C bit, with one of the accumulators and a memory location. The results are installed into the accumulator that takes place in the addition. The H,N, Z, V, and C flags can all be affected.

In the previous codes that operated only inside the MPU, addressing modes were not considered, since memory was not concerned. In this operation the memory does play a part, so addressing modes are considered. There are eight instruction codes to handle the Add with Carry operation. There are two possible accumulators that can be used and four addressing modes needed to find the data in the memory. Each accumulator can receive data found by the Immediate, Direct, Extended, or Indexed modes.

The second such instruction is called *Add without Carry*. As the name describes, the addition takes place without the contents of the C bit. The addition consists of adding the contents of a memory location to either the A or B accumulators, whichever is designated. The sum remains in the accumulator that takes part in the operation.

Even though the C bit is not involved in the addition, it can be affected by the operation if a carry is needed. Also, the H, N, Z,and V flags are involved.

The data in memory is found by means of the same four addressing modes: Immediate, Direct, Extended,and Indexed.

The third instruction of this group is *Subtract with Carry*. The codes cause the contents of the C bit to be subtracted from one of the accumulators. Next, the code subtracts the contents of an addressed location to be subtracted from the results. The final result of the two subtractions is placed in the involved accumulator. There are the same eight codes because there are two accumulators and four addressing modes that can be used. The N, Z, V, and C flags can be affected.

The subtract without carry instruction is simply called *Subtract*. There are eight codes to be used according to which of the two accumulators and which of the four addressing modes are used. The N, Z, V, and C bits are all involved.

The instruction subtracts the contents of an addressed location from either the A or B accumulator. The results of the subtraction are then placed into the accumulator that the operation was performed with.

The last arithmetic code is called *Decimal Adjust the A Accumulator*. This instruction is only used when the binary bits are code for Binary Coded Decimal. If you recall, the BCD numbers range from 0-9. The hex codes A-F are forbidden in a BCD computation. When the math operations we described are performed, the computer assumes they are hex. Mistakes can occur if results come out with forbidden numbers.

As a result, the need for an operation code that will alter possible forbidden bit arrangements to workable numbers arose. The decimal adjust instruction is designed to correct invalid nybbles.

The decimal adjust instruction code is included in 6800 programs. It is installed after the three add instructions just discussed. The decimal adjust instruction checks the addition that takes place. If one or more of the nybbles is a forbidden code, the instruction adds six to the invalid nybble which raises it out of the forbidden zone into the valid BCD range.

**Logic.** The last three processing instructions deal with performing logic on the data. There are usually only three logic functions an MPU performs directly: AND, OR, and XOR. If any other logic jobs must be done, a combination of the basic three instructions is used.

When any of the three logic instructions are employed, the ANDing, ORing, and XORing takes place between a selected memory register and one of the accumulators. For example, each bit of the memory location can be ANDed with each bit of the selected accumulator. The results of the bit-by-bit ANDing is left in the accumulator that is used.

For all three operations, the V flag is cleared since any overflow into bit 7 that might take place is meaningless. The N and Z flags can either be set or cleared. In some programs, the N and Z flag activity might be needed.

There are eight instruction codes for each logic operation. The locating of the data in memory requires one of the four addressing modes: Immediate, Direct, Extended, or Indexed. Once the data is located and sent to the MPU, a copy of the data remains in the location for further reference.

When you logically AND a bit with a 0, the result is always a 0 whether the target bit is a 1 or 0. If you logically AND a bit with a 1, the value of the target bit remains unchanged. These results are very useful to clear certain bit positions that are obstructing the results of a program. To get rid of the unwanted bits, a byte containing 0s in those bit positions is ANDed with the problem byte to *mask off* the problem bits.

When you logically OR a bit with a 1, the result is always a 1. If you OR a bit with a 0, the resultant bit is unchanged from the original. ORing is useful whenever you want to set a bit or bits in a byte. The bit that requires setting to 1 is ORed with a byte that has a 1 in the desired bit position. All the bits that are to remain the same have 0s in those bit positions.

XOR is not as useful as AND and OR, but it is available and programmers use it to test for changes in bit status and to calculate code corrections.

These are sophisticated machine language uses. The XOR operation produces a 1 output only when both input bits are 0 and 1 or not equal. When both input bits are the same, either 1s or 0s, the output is 0.

## Changing Addresses

As a 6800 computer runs a program, it is built to have the program counter automatically incremented by 1 as the $\phi 1$ clock has a falling edge. The program counter continues counting sequentially as the clock cycles. It causes the memory area where the program is stored to be accessed location by location.

As the program moves data from place to place, and processes the data in the MPU, situations arise whereby the sequential addressing will not do the job. Instead of accessing the next memory address in line, the MPU must change the address put out on the address bus to some other section of memory. There are a number of instructions that are placed in the program expressly to cause the change of address. They are known as Branches, Jumps, Returns, and Interrupts. When the MPU receives one of these change of address instruction codes, it sends the change directly over to the addressing mechanism. The program counter stops its sequential addressing. A new location somewhere else in memory is addressed.

The major change of address instruction in the 6800 is called *Branch*. There are 16 branch instructions in the 6800. There are two categories in the branch family of instructions. One is called *unconditional* and the other *conditional*.

There are two unconditional instruction codes, *Branch Always* and *Branch to Subroutine*. As unconditional codes, whenever one of them arrives at the MPU the branch is on. The program counter puts out the address the branch orders and the location is accessed without further ado.

At the end of every Branch to Subroutine excursion, there must be a final instruction code that returns the run back to the addresses of the main program. This subroutine ending code is called Return from Subroutine. It instructs the MPU that the subroutine is finished. The MPU then puts out an address on the address bus. This new address is the original address plus 2. The main program again starts running from there.

On the other hand, the Conditional Branch codes must check the status of the bits in the condition code register before the branch is allowed to occur. The CCR has had its bits set and cleared by all the instructions before the branch. The last code before a branch instruction also might have made some changes in the CCR bits.

The Conditional Branch code checks the status of the bits immediately before it executes. The status of the bit determines whether the program counter should simply address the next memory location or get changed to a new branch address. This IF-OR situation is the condition.

After the Branch code is a byte. If the condition of the branch is met, this byte plus 2 is added to the contents of the program counter. The addition forms the new address. When the condition for the branch is not met, the byte is not added to the program counter contents. The plus 2, added to skip over that byte, is not needed. The CCR is checked during the conditional branch but it is not altered by the test.

Adding the next byte plus 2 to the program counter in response to a Branch code is called the *Relative Addressing Mode* (Fig. 11-5). It is another way to locate data in the memory that's used only with branch instructions. The branch instruction method is the Relative Addressing mode.

The 6800 uses one byte of data after the branch instruction, which limits the branching to 256 locations. Also, the branching can be forward from the program location or backward. Bit 7 is used to determine if the branch is forward or backward. A 0 indicates forward. A 1 means the branch is backward. The limit forward is the signed binary number 01111111. This is +127 decimal locations forward. The backward limit is 10000000. This is decimal −128 in 2's complement code. The 10000000 added to the program counter reduces the program counter by 128 locations.

The branching limit of −128 to +127 around the program's location is all the 6800 can branch. Other MPUs have long branches that use two address bytes after the branch instruction. This gives a branch range of −32,769 to +32,767, which is the entire memory map.

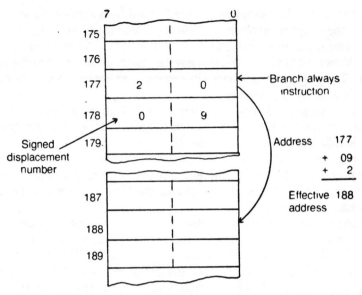

Fig. 11-5. The relative addressing mode makes the program sequence branch to a far-away address.

The conditional branches are dependent on the N, Z, C, and V flags in the CCR. For example, there are two branch codes that are governed by the C flag. One is *Branch if the Carry is Set*. Another is *Branch if the Carry is Clear*. Another pair are *Branch if the V Flag is Set* and *Branch if the V Flag is Clear*. Still another pair is *Branch if Z is Set* and *Branch if Z is Clear*.

The *Branch Always code* has no conditions. When it arrives at the MPU the branch is executed. The *Branch to Subroutine* is also unconditional. In programs, there can be lots of subroutines, some in RAM and others in ROM. These little subprograms save a lot of memory. For example, suppose you are doing a math program that needs a logarithm on several occasions. A small log program can be installed in memory and branched to for every log that is needed.

The next address-changing instruction is called *Jump*. Jump is something like Branch Always. If you recall, Branch Always did not use flag bits to tell it when a branch was needed. It always branched either forward or backwards. It was restricted to a range of −128 to +127 locations on either side of the main program's current location. The byte that followed the instruction code was an offset that was added or subtracted from the current location on the program counter to form the branch location (Fig. 11-5).

The Jump code is not restricted to a range of one byte; instead, it handles two bytes. Also, the Jump byte is not added to the program counter to form a new address. The bytes after the Jump are the new address. They are installed in the program counter. The new location goes right out over the address bus. The program continues running at the new address.

The Jump instruction has two codes to accommodate two addressing modes, Extended and Indexed. The Extended code is followed by four hex numbers that form an address with a range of 64 K. The Jump code can address the entire memory map.

The Indexed code is followed by a single byte offset. The offset is added to the contents of the Index register to form a new address. This address also can be anywhere in the map, according to the basic address contained in the Index register.

A variation of the Jump is called *Jump to Subroutine*. When the Branch to Subroutine is used, an offset is combined with the current address in the program counter to form the branch address. Jump to Subroutine does not use an offset. The hex number following the Instruction Code is the address. It replaces the current address from the MPU.

Jump to Subroutine also has two codes, one for Extended addressing and the other for Indexed. There are four hex numbers after the Extended code that are installed in the program counter to form the subroutines address. There are two hex numbers after the Indexed code to be added to the Index register to form the subroutine address.

Like Branch to Subroutine, Jump to Subroutine instructions need a final code at the end of the subroutine to return the program run back to the original addresses. The same Return from Subroutine code is used.

When the MPU receives the Return from Subroutine code, it changes the program counter back to the original address plus 3 if it is an Extended location. The Extended location was found with two bytes after the Jump code and requires the plus 3. If the subroutine was found by Indexed addressing only, plus 2 needs be added to the original location for the next starting address. There is only one offset byte after the Indexed code.

## Miscellaneous Instruction Codes

In the 6800, there are seven other instruction codes that do not fit easily under the categories of data movement, data processing, or address-changing. Three is one instruction called *No Operation*. This instruction code does nothing. When the MPU receives this code from the program in memory, it simply goes on to the next instruction. The instruction gives the computer a two-cycle breather. It is used when a pause in the program is needed.

Next, there are three instructions called *Compare*. One is *Compare Accumulators*. The instruction is used to set or clear the N, Z, V, and C flags in the CCR. The operation consists of subtracting the contents of the B accumulator from the A accumulator.

The bits in the two accumulators are not changed by the operation. The N, Z, V, and C bits are changed if the subtraction causes them to react in their normal fashion. The programmer needs this code to be in control of the action of the flags.

Another instruction code is simply called *Compare*. This comparing brings into play a memory location besides one or the other of the accumulators. The instruction subtracts a memory location from a selected accumulator. After the operation, nothing is changed but affected flags. The memory location and the selected accumulator are both left as they were.

The instruction is often used before a branch instruction to control the action of the branch. This instruction can control the N, Z, V, and C flags and thus decide if a branch should take place.

The desired memory location can be found by Immediate, Direct, Extended, or Indexed addressing modes. Since there are two accumulators and four addressing modes, eight instruction codes are assigned to perform the Compare instruction.

The third comparing is done with an instruction called *Compare Index Register*. The comparing is done by subtracting two consecutive memory locations from the Index register. The register is 16 bits wide, so two bytes are needed for the subtraction. The first byte is subtracted from the MS byte of the register and the second memory byte from the LS index byte.

There are four instruction codes assigned to the instruction. The codes are for the Immediate, Direct, Extended, and Indexed addressing modes. The subtracting takes place inside the MPU. The Index register is not involved in the subtraction, except for the fact that a copy of the Index register's contents is used for the subtraction. The Indexed addressing mode can, therefore, be used to locate the memory registers for the operations.

The three flags that can be affected by this operation are N, Z, and V. The C flag is not involved in this comparing. The N flag can be set by obtaining a result of 1 if the subtraction from bit 15 of the Index register by bit 7 of the first memory location is 1. The N flag is otherwise cleared.

The Z flag becomes set if the results of the operation are 16 clear bits. If one or more of the results are 1, the Z flag is cleared. The V flag will be set if the result of the operation causes an overflow into bit 15.

## Interrupt Instruction Codes

The 6800 has three instruction codes that deal with interrupts. One is a return and the other two are actual interrupts. The first one is called *Return from Interrupt*. It is needed in situations like the following.

When a peripheral interface like a PIA receives data from a peripheral, it will interrupt the MPU during a program to send it the data. As soon as the MPU gets a valid interrupt, it will stack the contents of the accumulators, Index register, program counter, and flags in the memory stack locations.

The MPU then concentrates on the peripheral data with the aid of its interrupt program. At the end of the interrupt program a Return from Interrupt instruction code is included.

This final code instructs the MPU that it has completed servicing the interrupt. It further instructs the MPU to go into the stack; retrieve all the former contents of its registers; reinstall these contents back into the accumulators, Index register, program counter, and flag bits; and continue on where it left off when the interrupt arrived.

The *Instruction Code Software Interrupt* is an actual interrupt. It is written into the program when it is required to run some special program during a main program run. When the code is encountered during a program, the following procedure takes place in the 6800.

First, the contents of the accumulators, Index register, program counter, and flag bits are stored in the memory reserved for the stack. Next, the I flag is set. This will stop any other such interrupts from interfering while this software interrupt is being serviced.

Then, in an automatic fashion, the contents of locations FFFA and FFFB are loaded into the program counter. These locations are usually in ROM and are there expressly to aid in this interrupt.

The contents of those locations are an address. That address is the start location of the program that will service the software interrupt. The program runs as the MPU begins with that address and then continues addressing consecutively.

At the end of the program is the *Return from Interrupt* instruction code. The final instruction tells the MPU to restore all its registers and continue on the main program, as it was doing before the software interrupt.

The last interrupt code is called *Wait for Interrupt*. This code is used when you want the MPU to stop and wait for some special event to happen. Upon receipt of the instruction code, the MPU gets everything ready for some form of interrupt. It could be an *IRQ or and *NMI. Either one performs the following.

The accumulators, Index register, program counter, and flags are stored in the stack. The I flag is not changed. It will be set if an *IRQ or *NMI arrives. It will be clear if they are to be accepted by the MPU.

Once the interrupt the MPU is waiting for arrives, it is serviced and ended with the usual Return from Interrupt previously discussed.

The 6800 programmer must know all these instruction codes as second nature. The technician will be aided by knowing these codes too. The programmer needs these codes to get the computer to perform the jobs it is built to do. The technician needs these codes in order to test the various sections and activities of the computer.

For the technician, the codes are forms of signal injection tests. All diagnostic programs use these codes extensively.

Some computers are built with automatic testing procedures that run every time the computer is powered up. If a problem is discovered during power up, the computer is shut down until the trouble is cleared.

While this chapter concentrated on the instruction codes for the 6800 MPU, you'll find that once you get these codes under your hat, it will be relatively easy to assimilate the instruction codes for the 6502, Z-80, and other 8-bit families.

This chapter also prepares you for the instruction sets for the 16-bit and 32-bit MPUs that are covered in chapters 14, 17, and 18.

# 12

# A Program Run

The last chapter discussed the 72 instructions the 6800 MPU responds to. As each byte of highs and lows enters the instruction register, it is decoded and causes an electronic reaction: computing.

Each instruction can cause data to be moved or processed, or consecutive addressing to be replaced with a different addressing method, or a few other things. However, individual instructions really do not do very much. Computing takes place when a lot of instruction codes and data are lined up in careful order to form a program. The program is stored in memory and then it's run. That is what computing is all about.

The programmer writes the programs and the user has the programs perform the jobs. Neither is concerned with the electronic activity that is taking place. You, as the technician, however, are very concerned with the mechanics of the program operation. In this chapter, we will run a small program and examine the details of the MPU, bus lines, and memory as the instructions and data are computed.

## AN ASSEMBLER

The chart in the last chapter showed a list of the 6800 instruction codes, called the Instruction Set. The numbers are the hex code itself. Programmers call it the *op* (operation) *code*. The two hex numbers represent two binary nybbles or one byte. The hex code and the binary are also known as the *object code*. It is important to understand the terms without confusion.

Table 12-1 contains an alphabetical list of another type of code using lettering. The letters are chosen to resemble the name of the instruction it represents. For example, the letters JMP represent a Jump instruction. ASR indicates the Arithmetic Shift Right instruction. These letters are called *mnemonics*. They are also known as *source code*.

Mnemonics letters are meaningless to the computer. The computer only responds to binary, or hex that gets converted to binary. Mnemonics, however, are much easier

Table 12-1. A 6800 Assembly Language Mnemonics.

| Mnemonic | Meaning |
| --- | --- |
| ABA | Add accumulators, A to B |
| ADCA/ADCB | Add with carry |
| ADDA/ADDB | Add without carry |
| ANDA/ANDB | Logical and |
| ASL | Arithmetic shift left |
| ASR | Arithmetic shift right |
|  | BRANCH IF |
| BCC | Carry clear |
| BCS | Carry set |
| BEQ | = to 0 |
| BGE | > or= to 0 |
| BGT | > than 0 |
| BHI | Higher |
| BLE | < or= to 0 |
| BLS | Lower or same |
| BLT | Less than 0 |
| BMI | Minus |
| BNE | Not = 0 |
| BPL | Plus |
| BRA | Always |
| BSR | To subroutine |
| BVC | Overflow clear |
| BVS | Overflow set |
| BIT | Bit test |
| CLR | Clear |
| CMPA/CMPB | Compare |
| CBA | Compare accumulators |
| CLC | Clear carry |
| CLI | Clear interrupt |
| CLV | Clear 2's comp, overflow bit |
| COM | Complement |
| CPX | Compare index register |
| DAA | Decimal adjust a accumulator |
| DEC | Decrement |
| DEX | Decrement index register |
| DES | Decrement stack pointer |
| EOR | Exclusive OR |
| INC | Increment |
| INS | Increment stack pointer |
| INX | Increment index register |
| JMP | Jump |
| JSR | Jump to subroutine |
| LDAA/LDAB | Load accumulator |
| LDS | Load stack pointer |
| LDX | Load index register |
| LSR | Logical shift right |
| NEG | Negate |
| NOP | No operation |
| ORAA/ORAB | Inclusive OR |
| PSHA/PSHB | Push data onto stack |
| PULA/PULB | Pull data from stack |

Table 12-1. Continued.

| Mnemonic | Meaning |
|----------|---------|
| ROL | Rotate left |
| ROR | Rotate right |
| RTI | Return from interrupt |
| RTS | Return from subroutine |
| SBC | Substract with carry |
| SBA | Subtract accumulators |
| SEC | Set carry |
| SEI | Set interrupt |
| SEV | Set 2's comp. overflow bit |
| STAA/STAB | Store accumulator |
| STS | Store stack pointer |
| STX | Store index register |
| SUBA/SUBB | Subtract |
| SWI | Software interrupt |
| TST | Test (Z or N) |
| TAB | Transfer accumulator A to B |
| TAP | Transfer accumulator A to CCR |
| TBA | Transfer accumulator B to A |
| TPA | Transfer CCR to A accumulator |
| TSX | Transfer stack pointer to index register |
| TXS | Transfer index register to stack pointer |
| WAI | Wait for interrupt |

#, means "immediate" addressing mode
$, means "HEX"

for the programmer to work with than either hex or binary. A program of mnemonics is written quicker and makes more sense to a human than a string of hex or binary numbers.

As a result, it is customary for machine language programmers to write their programs with mnemonics rather than hex. Once the program is written, it is then converted into hex so the computer can use it. The conversion can be done either by hand or by computer.

Hand assembly, which is rarely done anymore, is simply writing the mnemonic program on a sheet of paper and then looking up each hex op code for the mnemonics. Once all the op codes are written in, they can be poked into the computer. This is the hard way, and it can be a difficult, error-prone job. It is rarely done by the programmer. For the technician who composes small test programs, it can be a useful method.

The programmer usually employs an *assembler*. This is nothing more than a special program that is written to change mnemonics to binary. When the assembly program is installed in a computer memory, you can type the program into the computer in mnemonics. Then when the program is run, the binary output of the program is stored in memory. You can put the binary on disk or tape, or run it.

Mnemonics are limited. They only represent the name of the instruction. For example, the mnemonic AND is short for Logical AND. There are eight instruction codes for AND (Fig. 12-1). Each op code not only contains the name of the instruction, but it also indicates which accumulator is being used and what addressing mode is going to find the

| AND (op code) Instruction Code In Hex | | Addressing Modes | | Cycles |
|---|---|---|---|---|
| 8 | 4 | Immediate | A | 2 |
| 9 | 4 | Direct | A | 3 |
| B | 4 | Extended | A | 4 |
| A | 4 | Indexed | A | 5 |
| C | 4 | Immediate | B | 2 |
| D | 4 | Direct | B | 3 |
| F | 4 | Extended | B | 4 |
| E | 4 | Indexed | B | 5 |

Fig. 12-1. The mnemonic letters do not contain the amount of information the hex set number does. The addressing mode is not in the mnemonic. For instance, it takes eight hex codes to cover all AND cases in the 6800.

data location. When a mnemonic is written it also must contain this information. Therefore, the AND mnemonic comes in eight versions.

The hex code 84 is written in this way: AND A #$BF (Fig. 12-2). All the information those symbols stand for is installed in the hex 84. When the assembler receives the line of symbols, it recognizes them and converts them to the binary 10000100 (hex 84).

The assembler recognizes AND A as meaning "AND accumulator A with a memory location." The # sign means the addressing mode is Immediate. Therefore, the assembler knows that the memory location holding the data is the one after the instruction code (Fig. 12-3).

$BF is in the location. The $ sign simply means hex. This is to show the assembler that the BF is not decimal. (The BF is obviously not decimal but other hex numbers have exact decimal counterparts.) The meanings of all those symbols are tied up in the hex code. In addition, the number of cycles the instruction takes to execute is included. While this is important information for the programmer, the technician rarely needs the cycle numbers.

The next hex code 94 can be written as AND A $BF. The AND A means AND the A accumulator with a memory location. The location is hex BF. The code shows the

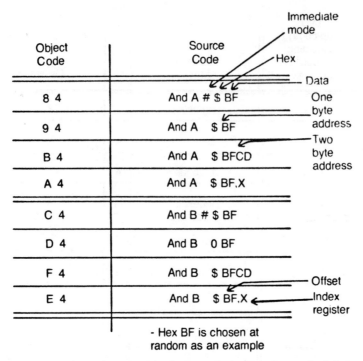

Fig. 12-2. The # sign indicates to the assembler the Immediate addressing mode. A $ sign means the number is in hex.

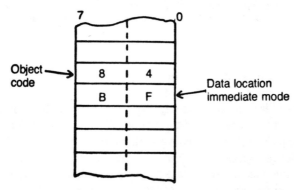

Fig. 12-3. When the assembler receives AND A #$BF, it converts the source code to 84 BF object code.

addressing is Direct because the address is only one byte long. The BF can be changed to any one-byte location. The rest of the mnemonic doesn't change (Fig. 12-4).

When the assembler receives AND A $BFCD it recognizes the Extended mode. It produces B4. The hex code B4 is similar to 94, except the mode is Extended because a two byte address is used (Fig. 12-5). When the assembler receives a Direct mode, it expects one byte. If the mnemonic it gets is Extended it expects a two byte address.

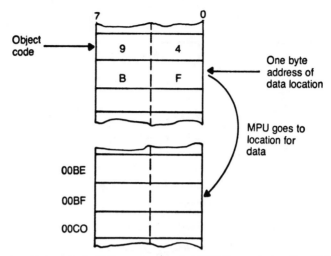

Fig. 12-4. When the object code 94 BF is received by the MPU, it goes to location 00BF for data.

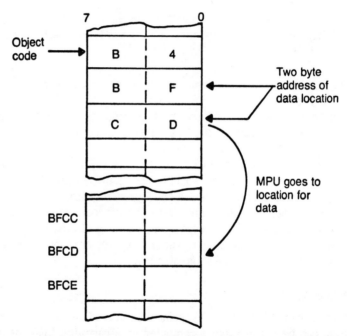

Fig. 12-5. When the object code B4 BF CD is received by the MPU, it goes to location BFCD for data.

Whatever the mode, the assembler knows the contents of the address will be a one byte piece of data. The data is to be ANDed with the contents of the A accumulator.

    The mnemonic AND A $BF,X is the symbolization for the Indexed mode (Fig. 12-6). It means AND the contents of a memory location with the A accumulator. The location is found by adding hex BF to the contents of the X register, which is the Index

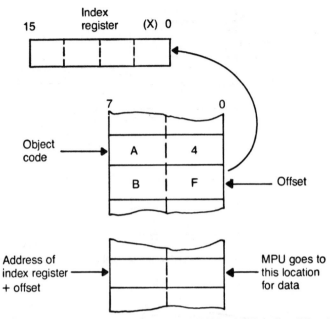

Fig. 12-6. When the object code A4 BF is received by the MPU, it adds the offset BF to the index register and goes to the resultant address formed in the index register.

register. The assembler changes the assembly code into the binary representation of hex A4. The binary is sent to the MPU for execution.

The assembler program is considered machine language because the mnemonics are simply another representation of the binary-hex instruction codes. The mnemonic goes one-on-one with the bytes of highs and lows.

Other so-called higher-level languages like BASIC and COBOL do not go one-on-one with the binary codes. In fact, you would be hard put to uncover the relationships. High-level language words each represent a small program rather than a single binary code. When you run a high level word, a number of binary codes produce the computing instead of one code like assembly language does. Because of this, high-level language programs are easier to write. Assembly language programs are more difficult, but they run much faster and you can accomplish greater feats.

## A SIMPLE PROGRAM

A program can be installed in RAM by typing it in, or reading it from cassette tape or disk. A program can be plugged into a computer on a cartridge ROM or into a DIP socket. Once the program is in memory, it is in bytes of highs and lows. When a program is run, the program counter starts things off on the rising edge of $\phi1$. That electronic trigger places the contents of the program counter onto the address bus. The address is the first location of the program.

The program is continued by the falling edge of $\phi1$. That trigger increments the program counter by 1. At the next addressing cycle, the second address is put on the bus. This automatic addressing of the program continues until the entire program is run, unless it is desirable to stop the action for some reason. We are going to run off a small program that is stored in seven consecutive addresses in RAM. The addresses are the following in decimal, hex, and binary.

| Decimal | Hex | Binary |
|---------|------|-------------------|
| 0 | 0000 | 0000000000000000 |
| 1 | 0001 | 0000000000000001 |
| 2 | 0002 | 0000000000000010 |
| 3 | 0003 | 0000000000000011 |
| 4 | 0004 | 0000000000000100 |
| 5 | 0005 | 0000000000000101 |
| 6 | 0006 | 0000000000000110 |

Most of the time, addresses in the memory map are listed in decimal and hex. The binary is rarely shown. Nevertheless, it is always present, and it is the number representation of the high and low voltages that actually emerge from the pins attached to the program counter. The programmer doesn't give the binary a thought. The technician works with it constantly as he tests the address pins with a voltmeter or logic probe.

In these seven addresses, there are three instruction codes and four bytes of data. The program is going to read one location by the Immediate addressing mode. It will then find a second location by the Direct mode and read its contents. Last, it will find a third location by the Extended mode and write to it, storing a byte of data. We will observe the activity and see how the MPU registers and the memory locations handle the highs and lows that will travel back and forth. The seven contents of the program locations and their mnemonics are listed in the following way. Notice there are only three lines of hex numbers with their corresponding assembly language. There are seven hex numbers though, one for each program location. The reason the numbers are listed this way is because one line of assembly language can be stored in two or more locations (Fig. 12-7).

| Hex Numbers | Mnemonics |
|-------------|-------------|
| 86 31 | LDA A # $31 |
| D6 45 | LDA B  $45 |
| B7 80 05 | STA A $8005 |

The first hex number in each line is the instruction. The second and third numbers are the data or an address of the data, according to the dictates of the addressing mode. In this program, the first line is in the Immediate mode so the second number is data. The second line is the Direct mode, so the following hex number is an address of data. The last line is the Extended mode, so the two hex bytes are an address where data is to be stored. The electronics of the program run can now commence.

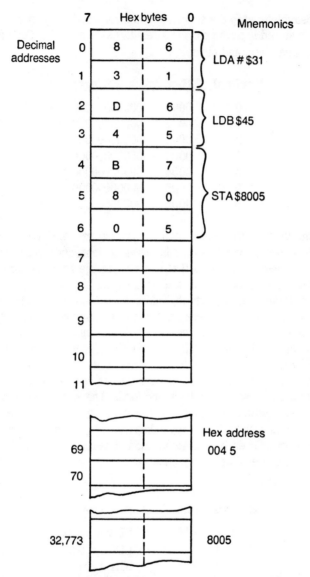

Fig. 12-7. The small program is written in mnemonics by the program installed into the memory by the assembler program, and then run by the MPU and ROM.

The seven bytes in the program are stored in decimal addresses 0-6 in the following way:

| Address | Contents | Hex Code |
|---------|----------|----------|
| 0 | 10000110 | 86 |
| 1 | 00110001 | 31 |
| 2 | 11010110 | D6 |
| 3 | 01000101 | 45 |

| 4 | 10110111 | B7 |
| 5 | 10000000 | 80 |
| 6 | 00000101 | 05 |

The 1s and 0s are, of course, high and low voltages stored in RAM circuits. If the RAM is static, the logic states are stored in flip-flops. When the RAM is dynamic, they are stored in capacitor charges. Either way, they do their job because they are voltage levels.

### First Cycle

The program starts as the $\phi1$ rising edge places the first 16-bit address on the address bus. It is 0000000000000000, the start address of the program counter. The $\phi1$ falling edge then increments the program counter in anticipation of the next addressing chore.

The first address is activated, and 10000110 (86) is in the location. $\phi2$'s rising edge comes along, and the eight bits are placed on the data bus. Incidentally, these two actions of placing the address on the address bus and then placing the contents of the address on the data bus, can be the most puzzling part of computers. Once you can clearly view this little procedure, a lot of confusion is eliminated.

$\phi2$'s falling edge then appears and latches the data bus contents into the MPU's instruction register. The IR then decodes the bits. They are interpreted as "load the A accumulator with the contents of the next byte."

The MPU then has its accumulator A loading circuits unlocked by the combination of bits in the instruction byte. The R/*W line is made high which is the read mode. That is the end of the first cycle.

### Second Cycle

Then $\phi1$'s rising edge places the next location, 0000000000000001, on the address bus. The second location is actuated. $\phi1$'s falling edge increments the program counter in preparation for the subsequent step.

$\phi2$'s rising edge puts 00110001 (31) on the data bus. This is a copy of the contents of the second location. $\phi2$'s falling edge then latches the data into the awaiting A accumulator. The R/*W line is still high. That ends the second cycle.

The instruction has two cycles. The clock is able to address two memory locations, receive an instruction and install a byte of data into the accumulator during the two cycles.

### Third Cycle

The third cycle puts 0000000000000010 on the address bus. This activates the third location and turns off the second location. The program counter then increments in preparation for the fourth location which will be accessed next.

The third location contains 11100110 (D6). This is an instruction that states, "Load the B accumulator with the contents of a memory location. The address of the location is the next byte in the program.'' The byte is placed on the data bus and is latched into the IR in the MPU.

The bits are decoded and their combination starts up the circuits that load the B accumulators. The R/*W line is held high since the load instruction is a read type. That concludes the third full cycle. The B accumulator is waiting for the byte of data somewhere in the memory.

## Fourth Cycle

The next cycle has the $\phi1$ rising edge place 0000000000000011 on the address bus. The falling edge increments the program counter. The contents of the location are placed on the data bus upon the rising edge of $\phi2$. The instruction was in the Direct addressing mode. The data is therefore not sent to the accumulator. It is not straight data, but an address form of data.

The eight-bit address is placed into an address bus register in the MPU. The address is 01000101 (45). It is latched into the register during the fall of $\phi2$. The R/*W line is held high for the read type instruction. That finishes the cycle.

## Fifth Cycle

The next cycle starts with $\phi1$ rising and placing the contents of the internal address bus register into the lower eight bits of the address bus. The higher eight bits are all 0s. The address 0000000001000101 is activated. The falling edge of $\phi1$ does not increment the program counter; in fact, the falling edge does nothing much at this time.

The rising edge of 2, though, places the contents of the location hex 0045 onto the data bus. The falling edge of $\phi2$ latches the data from hex 0045 into the B accumulator. All this time, the R/*W line has been held high since data has been moving only from the memory to the MPU during read operations. This is the end of that cycle.

Up to this point, the A accumulator has been loaded with data that was installed in the program and was found with the Immediate addressing mode. In addition, the B accumulator has been loaded with data from a location that is not in the program proper. This distant location hex 0045 was found with the direct addressing mode. If you are wondering how the data from hex 0045 got there, it had to be installed before the program was run. In the next instruction execution, we will access a location even further away than 0045.

## Sixth Cycle

The next cycle begins, as usual, with the rise of $\phi1$. This places 0000000000000100 on the address bus. The program counter is then incremented. The location is opened up and as the rise of $\phi2$ arrives the contents are put out on the data bus. The fall of $\phi2$ latches the contents into the IR. The instruction 10110111 (B7) is decoded. It instructs the MPU, ''Store the contents of the A accumulator in one memory location. The location's address is in the next two bytes in the program.''

The R/*W line is going to be changed to a low for the write operation. However, the actual write does not take place for a few cycles yet. The R/*W line stays high until then because address data traffic will be coming from the memory to the MPU until the actual writing of the accumulator data to the memory.

The execution of this instruction takes five cycles. The first cycle ends with the decoding of the instruction byte. The next cycle begins with the rise of $\phi2$ putting the contents of the program counter on the address bus. It is 0000000000000101. The PC is then incremented.

The contents of the address is 1000000 (80). It is placed onto the data bus and then latched into the eight highest bits of an internal address register. With the R/*W line remaining high that ends that cycle.

The next address, 0000000000000110, is put out on the bus and the PC incremented. This is the last address of the program but not the last step. This address contains the lower eight bits of the address where the accumulator data is to be stored. As the cycle progresses, the eight bits 00000101 (05) are put out on the data bus. Next, they are latched into the lower byte of the internal address register. With the R/*W still holding high, this cycle comes to an end.

The fourth cycle of this series begins with the $\phi1$ rise placing the 16-bit address 1000000000000101 (hex 8005) from the internal address register to the address bus. This activates the location in memory.

Meanwhile, the cycle continues. The A accumulator circuit is turned on and prepares to send its contents out over the data bus. This finishes that cycle. The R/*W line is still high but getting ready to change.

The fifth cycle then begins. The address hex 8005 is activated. The R/*W line is finally brought low. $\phi2$ puts the contents of the A accumulator, 00110001 (31), onto the data bus. The fall of $\phi2$ then writes the data into the accessed memory location. The program is over.

Admittedly, this program does not do very much. It was able to load the A accumulator with a byte from the program. It was able to load the B accumulator with a byte from memory location hex 0045, which was not in the program. The byte had been stored in the location before the program was run. Last, the program stored the contents of the A accumulator in a memory location distant from the main program (hex 8005). None of this may seem consequential, but it is. This is what computing is all about.

This is the way programs run from the technician's point of view. There are many more instructions than Load and Store, but they all operate in a similar manner. Each one does a little bit, and together they are a colossus.

# 13

# General Description of 16-Bit Processors

Computers are generally classified as 8-bit, 16-bit or 32-bit by the number of wires in their data bus. The data bus winds its way from the MPU to all the locations on the memory map. The data bus is the route the instructions and data in the programs take to and from the MPU. The 16-bit computer is able to transport two bytes, called a *word*, between the MPU and memory. (Fig. 13-1)

In contrast, an 8-bit computer is only able to transfer one byte at a time.

## 16-BIT MEMORY

In a 16-bit computer, compared to an 8-bit, memory locations have twice as many bit positions. There are many memory schemes that can be used to fill the memory locations, but they are usually dynamic types. For example, a set of 64 K bit chips can be used (Fig. 13-2). The chips are organized as 64 K × 1 each. If you use 16 such chips with a 16 line data bus, the MPU can address one location, one bit position on each chip, at one time.

In the 8-bit computer, the same type of dynamic memory can be used. Only in the eight line data bus are eight bit positions on eight memory chips addressed at one time. The 16-bit MPU, therefore, addresses twice as many bits at the same time as the 8-bit MPU. This automatically doubles the rate of operations possible in the 16-bit type.

## ADDRESSING

There a lot of 16-bit MPUs on the market, which transport 16 bits at a time over a 16-bit data bus. However, the address bus size of many of them do not follow the same pattern. The 8-bit computer typically has eight data lines in the data bus and 16 address lines in the address bus. It should follow, then, that a 16-bit computer should have twice

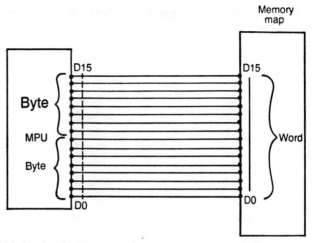

Fig. 13-1. The 16-bit data bus is able to transfer a word at a time. A word is composed of two bytes.

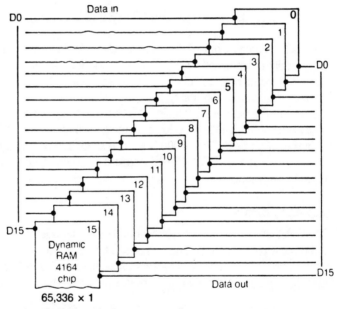

Fig. 13-2. One 16-bit design scheme could have sixteen 4164 dynamic memory chips attached to the data bus.

as many address lines as the 8-bit. This means a 16-bit MPU should have 32 address lines.

32 address lines gives the MPU an almost inconceivable ability to directly address a memory map. Let's examine the address line numbers.

In an 8-bit computer there are 16 address lines. This enables the MPU to directly access 64 K individual locations. There are addressing schemes that use a special addressing chip to place additional address lines into a computer. If the lines are increased from 16 the number of addresses the MPU can contact doubles with each additional line.

| Address Lines | 8-Bit Locations |
|:---:|:---:|
| 16 | 64 K |
| 17 | 128 K |
| 18 | 256 K |
| 19 | 512 K |
| 20 | 1024 K |
| 21 | 2058 K |
| 22 | 4096 K |
| 23 | 8192 K |
| 24 | 16 MBYTES |
| . | |
| . | |
| . | |
| 32 | 4 GIGABYTES (BILLIONS) |

The 16 address lines coming out of the 8-bit MPU can be increased in number with the addition of specially-constructed chips. The address lines in the 16-bit MPU can come out of a 32-bit program counter and are able to address 4 billion locations directly. This is indeed a powerful increase in ability.

In this chapter, and the next we'll examine the two most popular 16-bit processors, the 8088-8086 and the 68000. The 8088-8086 became very popular as the IBM PC took over leadership in the 16-bit field. The 68000 is a close second in popularity when Apple used it for the Macintosh and COMMODORE chose it for their Amiga. Let's examine the 8088-8086 processors first.

## THE 8088 AND 8086 CHIPS

In the IBM PC/XT and all its clones, you will find either an 8088 or 8086 type chip. The chips, for the most part are made and numbered by Intel, but you could find them with other brand names and numbers. The two chips have some differences in their internal circuitry and their pin assignments, however they use the exact same Instruction Set.

Figure 13-3 shows the two chips. They are both 40-pin DIPs like the 8-bit processors. If you look closely at the two pinouts, the 8086 has 16 data pins. They are pins 2-16 and 39. These 16 pins are used by both the address bus and the data bus. On the other hand, the 8088 only uses eight data pins, 9-16. This makes the 8088 appear at first glance, to be an 8-bit processor while the 8086 looks like a 16-bit processor. The 8088 is just as much a 16-bit processor as the 8086. The 8088 has a slight handicap. It must make two passes to access a 16-bit data register in memory, eight bits at a time. The 8086 can access 16-bits with a single pass.

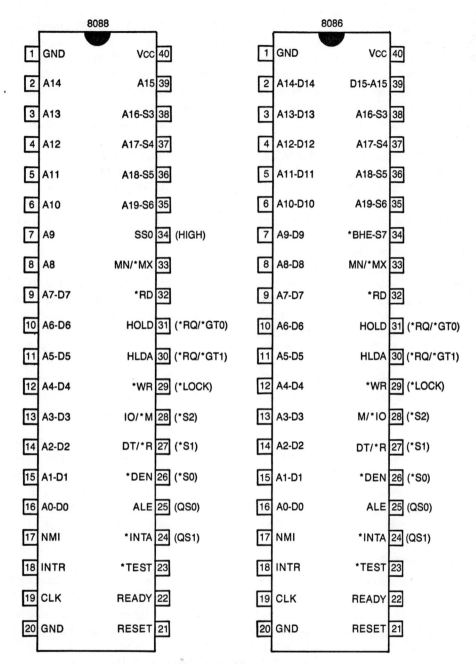

Note pins 33 on both chips, MN/*MX, minimum
and maximum mode controls. In minimum mode
the pin functions inside chip area are active.
In maximum mode the functions in parentheses
outside chip area take over their pins.

Fig. 13-3. The 8088 and 8086 chips are able to be installed in 40-pin DIPs since they output the
address and data bits out of the same pins in a multiplex fashion.

Aside from the difference in the layout of the data pins, the 8088 and 8086 are similar in most other ways. They both output the same address, data, and control signals to transfer data back and forth between themselves and the residents of the memory map.

They both have 20 address lines, A0-A19. This allows the 8088-8086 to directly address 1,048,576 memory map bytes. This is called 1 MB. These are 8-bit registers in the 1 MB map. The map can also be considered in terms of 2 byte registers, called words. The 8088-8086 therefore is said to be able to directly address 524,288 memory map words.

The 8088-8086 is equipped with fourteen 16-bit registers, shown in Fig. 13-4. Note there are no registers larger than 16-bits. This makes the register set resemble an 8-bit processor. In many respects there are 8-bit processors that can perform as well as the 8088-8086. However, the 8088-8086 has 20 address lines and can address 1 MB while an 8-bit processor only has 16 address lines and can only address 64 K. This is one of the advantages the 8088-8086 has, among other things, over an 8-bit processor and is considered a 16-bit processor.

In order to fully utilize the 1 MB address space the 8088-8086 is given an Instruction Set with 135 instructions. These instructions are designed to perform operations on data of many sizes. It can work on single bit data, 8-bit bytes, 16-bit words and 32-bit double words. Most of the instructions though, operate only on 8-bit and 16-bit data. The single bit and 32-bit operations are available but few in number.

The 8088-8086 is said to be "register oriented." This means the processor and its instructions tend to use the internal registers to manipulate data as much as possible rather than transferring data back and forth to memory. This saves all sorts of time. To implement this specialized activity, eight of the fourteen internal 16-bit registers are general purpose. The processor can use them in many ways including making them act as RAM.

The 8088-8086 clock speed can be made to run between 4 MHz and 8 MHz. The 8-bit processors ran around 1 or 2 MHz. The 8088-8086 is considerably faster. For example, in a processor running at 5 MHz, a short instruction such as register to register transfer would take 400 nanoseconds to execute. A long instruction like a signed 16-bit by 16-bit division takes 42 microseconds to run off. In a processor with 1 MHz speed, these instructions would take many times longer to complete an instruction cycle.

## The Fourteen Registers

There are three sections to the fourteen registers. There are the accumulator data handling group, the pointers and indexes, and the segment registers. Figure 13-4 shows the programmer's diagram. The accumulator group, the pointers and indexes make up the group of general purpose registers. The four accumulator types are divided even further. Each 16-bit register comprises two useful 8-bit registers, with high and low bytes.

The eight 8-bit or four 16-bit accumulator type registers, however you want to describe them, are primarily data handlers. The other four general purpose registers, the pointers and the indexers, are primarily addressers.

The data handlers are named accumulator, base, count, and data. Each 16-bit register has two 8-bit sections called high and low. They are somewhat interchangeable

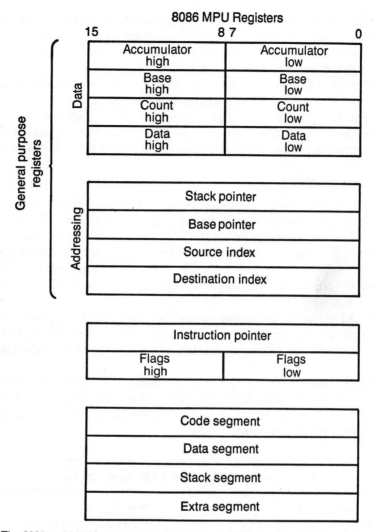

Fig. 13-4. The 8088 and 8068 both use fourteen 16-bit registers to conduct their business.

according to the instruction being executed. Some instructions specify a particular register, while other instructions are able to be more flexible.

The four other general purpose registers also can be used for specific purposes. The stack pointer can be used to provide the 16 most significant bits of the address of the stack. The four least significant bits for the stack address is provided by the stack segment register, which we will get to shortly. The base pointer, source index, and destination index can be used to provide 16 bits of 20-bit addresses when the 8088-8086 addresses the 1 MB memory map. Sometimes just the base pointer is used. Other times the source index or destination index could be added to the base pointer to produce a final address. Still other times the base pointer and indexes could be used with the data segment register to generate an address. The 8088-8086 addressing ability is quite versatile. Don't forget these eight 16-bit registers, besides doing assigned duties are also general purpose. They are all capable of performing general operations between all eight registers. Data can be transferred, added, subtracted, shifted, rotated, incremented, decremented, etc., between them.

The four segment registers, code, data, stack, and extra are not really thought of as general purpose, although there are some instructions that can change the contents of the registers. These registers are there primarily to aid in the addressing of the 1 MB address space. These registers are used to store 16-bit segment addresses. Let's examine the way the 8088-8086 is able to get 20 address bits out of the 16-bit registers.

### Generating a 20-Bit Address

Figure 13-5 shows a segment register 16 bits wide in the center of the illustration. It could be any of the four segment registers, code, data, stack or extra. The segment register has its 16 bits in address positions 19-4. Address positions 3-0 are appended zeros. If you add an address to the segment that is offset from the segment address position by four bits, you will have a 20-bit address. The offset could come from any of the other registers in the processor. With the proper selection of bits all 1,048,576 bytes in the map can be addressed.

Table 13-1 shows the addressing modes than can be used in the 8088-8086. The modes are immediate, register, base index, index, base, indirect, direct, and relative. The mode is attained by adding together the indicated registers and obtaining a 20-bit result.

Actual addressing is performed by machine language programmers. Combining all these values to produce these 20-bit addresses can get very complex. The technician will usually not have to do very much in this area but you never know what you might have to do when working on these machines.

**Table 13-1. Data Can Be Located in the 8088-8086**
**Memory by Use of These Eight Addressing Modes.**

| Addressing Mode | Data Location |
|---|---|
| Immediate | In the instruction itself |
| Register | In designated register |
| Register Indirect | In memory addressed by offset in register |
| Direct | In memory addressed by offset in instruction |
| Index | In memory addressed by adding index register to displacement in instruction |
| Base | In memory addressed by adding base register to displacement in instruction |
| Base-index | In memory addressed by adding base register plus index register plus displacement |
| Relative | In memory addressed by adding displacement to a segment register |

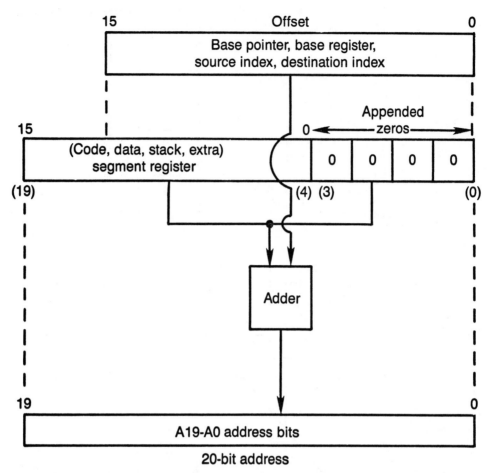

Fig. 13-5. A 20-bit address can be derived from 16-bit registers. For instance, place a segment register into bit positions 19-4. Then append four zeros to bit positions 3-0. Finally add an offset to the created 20-bit register.

One of the features of this ability to add 16-bit registers together to produce 20-bit addresses is the allocation of separate memory areas for the program code, the needed data, and the stack. In the 8-bit computer all of the code, data, and stack registers had to be in the same 64 K section of RAM. With separate 16-bit segment registers, a separate 64 K RAM area can be allocated for code, data, and stack. In addition there is the extra segment register that can be used if needed. Figure 13-6 shows the way the segment registers can allocate separate map areas for these purposes. An adept programmer makes good use of the qualities that are not found on the 8-bit computer.

## The Addressing Modes

Referring back to Table 13-1 the different addressing modes are shown. In immediate addressing the instruction itself contains an 8-bit or 16-bit piece of data that needs work. According to the instruction being executed, the byte or word of data could be

323

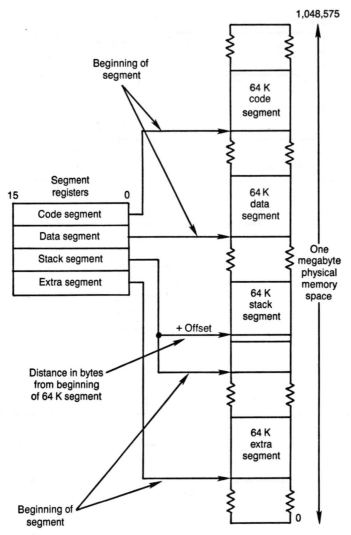

Fig. 13-6. Each of the 16-bit segment registers can set up its own 64 K memory area in the 1 megabyte physical memory space.

stored into a processor register or a memory location. The data also could be sent to the ALU and be added, subtracted, ANDed or ORed. The immediate designation means that the data does not have to be read separately from memory. It is read at the same time that the instruction is. Immediate is the only mode that does not use segment addresses, pointers, indexes, and so forth.

When the Register addressing mode is employed, the instruction op code contains the name of the processor register whose contents need work. The processor then quickly accesses the register and performs the dictates of the instruction on the contents. The instruction could simply be, move the specified register contents to another register. The processor will then execute the instruction.

The reason for all these addressing modes is to give the processor many different ways it can access storage areas and obtain operands to work on. The Immediate mode is the simplest. The processor doesn't have to address anything. The operand is contained in the instruction line with the op code. The Register mode is also simple. The operand to be worked on is already in an 8088-8086 register. The op code specifies the register and the processor goes to work on it. These two modes are the only simple ones. The rest of them get tricky.

The first tricky one is called Indirect Register addressing. The trick is to generate a 20-bit address. In this address is an operand the processor needs for the program being run. The typical way the address is generated is to take the contents of the data segment register and add it to the contents of one of the following registers, the base, base pointer, source index or destination index. The results of this addition is the 20-bit address where the needed operand resides. The operand is then brought to the processor and used in the program.

The contents of the base, BP, SI, and DI registers are called EA, effective address. Effective addresses when added to segment registers produce actual 20-bit addresses to be accessed.

A variation on the Indirect addressing is Direct addressing. Here again a 20-bit address must be generated with the aid of a segment register. However, the bits needed to supplement the segment register are not in another processor register. These address bits are contained in the instruction along with the op code. This arrangement is something like Immediate addressing. The difference is, in Immediate addressing, the actual operand is in with the op code. With Direct addressing, the address bits to be added to the segment register are in with the op code.

Once these bits are added with the segment register, a 20-bit address is generated and the location accessed. The operand in the location is read and the processor uses it in the program.

The next type of addressing mode is the Index .This brings into play another kind of address bits. In the preceding modes, address bits were found in the segment registers, in the base, base pointer, and Index registers. They were also found in with the op codes. There are also other address bits that are found in with the op codes. These bits are called a displacement. They can be added to the other involved registers to form other addressing modes.

A good example is the Index addressing mode. When a displacement arrives with an op code, it can be added to one of the Index registers. Together they form an EA. The effective address is then added to a segment register to form the 20-bit address. The address is then accessed and the desired operand is retrieved. Note that if there is no displacement, the mode is an Indirect Register type. The two modes are almost identical, except for the displacement.

The modes become more complex. The next one is Base addressing. This is somewhat like Indirect Register addressing but one step further. In Indirect, the contents of the Base, Base Pointer or Index registers are EAs. They are added to a segment register to form the 20-bit address. If you add a displacement to the EAs in Indirect, you will have performed Base addressing. The 20-bit address formed with the Indirect EA, displacement, and segment register, contains the needed operand.

Taking the addition one step further and Base Index addressing occurs. To obtain a Base Index EA, you must add together the contents of the base register, to an Index register, plus an optional displacement. Once you have the Base Index EA, the EA is then added to the contents of a segment register. The result is the 20-bit address where the needed operand is stored. It can then be obtained and used by the processor.

The last mode is called Relative addressing. It is a simple one but very important. It permits programmers to enjoy position-independent programs. All that is needed is to add a displacement to a segment register to form the 20-bit address. This is the mode that works to aid the processor to perform Jumps and Calls.

The many different ways the 8088-8086 is able to obtain operands is one of the great strengths the processor is endowed with. The operands are stashed all over. They are found contained in program lines along with the op code in the internal processor registers, in RAM and ROM. When the operands are accompanying the op code and when they are in processor registers the Immediate and Register addressing modes fetch them without further ado.

When the operands are stashed around in the 1 MB memory map, then the other addressing modes must be used to gather them up. The other modes, Indirect, Direct, Index, Base Address, Base index, and Relative are all various schemes to generate the 20-bit address to access the location containing the desired operand.

The schemes consist of adding together combinations of segments, pointers, displacements and indexes. To find instructions in memory the instruction pointer is added to the code segment register contents. To locate stack bytes the stack pointer is added to the stack segment register. To obtain databytes in memory the base register is added to the base pointer, an index, and a displacement when required. The result is added to the data segment contents. The extra segment register can also be used in the same way. Adding a base register to an index plus a displacement to the extra segment register will also locate data.

Getting the various addressing modes under your hat is not easy. However, if you want to be able to write machine language programs for the 8088-8086, the addressing techniques must be learned. It is important for the technician to know about them. The more you understand the workings of the processor in a computer you are working on, the easier it will be to do your job.

## The 8088-8086 Instruction Set

In the addressing mode section we discussed the way operands are located and brought to the processor to be worked on. Mention was made that operands might be installed along with op codes, that addresses are installed with op codes, and that displacements also can accompany op codes. It is now time to look closer at the way op codes travel along with these other bit set types. Figure 13-7 illustrates different sized instructions. The sizes vary from one to six bytes long.

The number of bytes in an instruction is dependent on what entities are contained in the instruction. The bytes can consist of the op code, the addressing mode, displacement bits, address bits and data.

The 8088-8086 had been given 8-bit op codes. The first byte in the total instruction length is the op code. The op code defines the operation that is to be performed. For

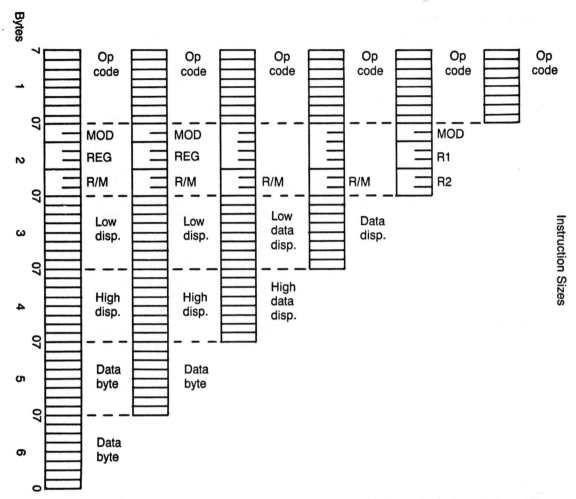

**Bytes**

**Instruction Sizes**

Fig. 13-7. The instructions come in sizes from one to six bytes. The op code of the instruction is always in first position.

example, MOVE, ADD, JUMP, etc. The second byte (when there is a second byte), specifies the addressing mode in the two MOD bits and the three R/M bits.

When the addressing mode specifies that a displacement is to be in the instruction length, one or two bytes are assigned to hold the displacement. In the three byte instruction the third byte will hold the displacement bits. In the four, five or six byte instructions, two bytes can be assigned to hold the displacement. The displacement is then used by the processor as needed to generate the 20-bit address that contains data for the program.

The op code and addressing mode could specify one or two bytes of immediate data. When that happens the data will be found after or instead of the displacement byte or bytes. Figure 13-7 shows the example arrangements of op codes, addressing modes, displacements, and data in one to six byte instruction lengths.

327

## Storing the Instructions

A program consists of a long list of these one to six byte instruction lengths. They are stored byte after byte in memory. The processor accesses the bytes one after another, unless it makes a jump or some other addressing change.

Memory for the 8088-8086 is organized in 16-bit words. There are 16 data lines, D15-D0. However, either a byte or a word can be addressed and accessed. The programmer must know the organization if he is addressing bytes so he can keep the data lines straight. What this means is, where are the D15-D8 bytes and where are the D7-D0 bytes stored?

In the 8088-8086 computer, the even byte numbers, starting with zero, hold the low data bits, D7-D0. The odd byte numbers, starting with location 1, hold all the high data bits, D15-D8. When the program is addressed byte by byte the data bus acts like an 8-bit computer, except that when an even numbered byte location is accessed, the even byte uses data bus lines D7-D0 to transfer its bit contents. When an odd numbered byte location is accessed, the odd byte uses data bus lines D15-D8 to transfer its contents.

When the processor is acting as a 16-bit computer, and is accessing 16 bits at a time, the addressing situation changes. The processor accesses two bytes at a time. One even numbered byte and one odd numbered byte, in that order, are both accessed at the same time. The 16 bits are then transferred simultaneously over all of the data bus lines, D15-D0. Figure 13-8 shows the map format for 8-bit and 16-bit accesses. The 8-bit access works as if the computer is an 8-bit type. For the 16- bit access, the computer changes hats and assumes the identity of a 16-bit computer.

| 8-Bit memory address | Byte format |
|---|---|
| 0000 | D7-D0 |
| 0001 | D15-D8 |
| 0002 | D7-D0 |
| 0003 | D15-D8 |
| 0004 | D7-D0 |
| 0005 | D15-D8 |

Fig. 13-8. The even byte addresses starting with zero hold the lower bits of a word, D7-D0, while the odd addresses contain the higher bits, D15-D8.

| 16-Bit memory address | Word format |
|---|---|
| 0000 | D7-D0, D15-D8 |
| 0002 | D7-D0, D15-D8 |
| 0004 | D7-D0, D15-D8 |

## The 135 Instructions

Intel breaks down the 135 instructions into seven categories. The categories are called, Data Transfer, Arithmetic, Logic, Control Transfer, String Manipulation, Interrupt, and Processor Control.

The instructions make use of all the registers in the 8088-8086. Earlier we discussed the general purpose and segment registers, there was no mention of the 16-bit Status Flag register. No discussion of the Instruction Set would be complete without the Flag register. As programs are run and instructions are processed, the Flag register is deeply involved. As an instruction is executed, chances are good that one or more of the flags in the register will have its state changed.

There are nine bits of the 16-bit Flag register that are in action in the 8086 I am using right now. As time goes by and newer versions of the 8086 are produced, more bits in the register could be assigned jobs. Meanwhile there are the following nine single bit registers installed in the 16-bit space.

Figure 13-9 illustrates the 16-bit Status Flag register. The nine flags in use are:

| | | |
|---|---|---|
| Bit 0 | C | the Carry Flag |
| 2 | P | the Parity Flag |
| 4 | A | the Auxiliary Carry Flag |
| 6 | Z | the Zero Flag |
| 7 | S | the Sign Flag |
| 8 | T | the Trap Flag |
| 9 | I | the Interrupt Enable Flag |
| 10 | D | the Direction Flag |
| 11 | Q | the Overflow Flag |

Bits 1,3,5,12,13,14, and 15 are unused. They represent excess capacity that will eventually be filled.

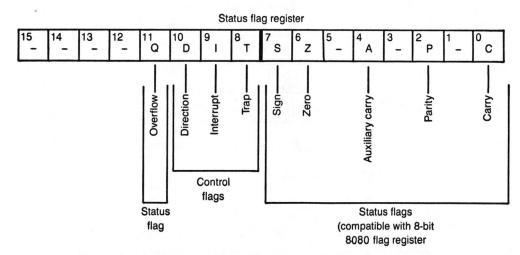

Fig. 13-9. The 16-bit Status Flag register holds six status flag bits and three control flag bits.

If you'll notice the names of some of the flags are similar to the names of the flags in the 8-bit 6800 processor discussed earlier. They perform similar jobs in the 8088-8086. They are especially active as Arithmetic and Logic instructions are executed. There will be more information on the flags and their activity as we go through the instructions and see what they do and what registers they use.

### Data Transfer

Intel further breaks down the data transfer category into six subcategories. Their mnemonics used to write machine language programs are MOV(move), PUSH(push), POP(pop), XCHG(exchange), IN(input from) and OUT(output to).

There are seven kinds of MOV instructions. These type of instructions in 8-bit processors were called Load and Store. In the 8088-8086 they are all lumped together as MOV. There are some load and store instructions that supplement the MOV instructions. They will be covered later in this section. According to the bit structure of the instruction bytes, the direction of the data movement is specified. In Fig. 13-10 the

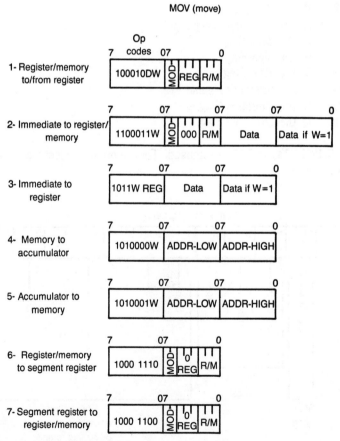

Fig. 13-10. The seven MOV instructions are constructed as two, three, and four bytes structures.

seven bit structures are shown. As you can see, the moves can go either way. For instance, the fourth instruction specifies a data movement from memory to accumulator. The fifth instruction, using the same pathway but in the other direction, specifies accumulator to memory. According to the instruction either an 8-bit or 16-bit piece of data can be moved.

The PUSH and POP instructions, in Fig. 13-11 deal exclusively with 16-bit data that is pushed onto the stack or popped off of the stack. The stack is simply a set of assigned registers in RAM that store contents of the 8088-8086 registers during the time the processor is busy servicing interrupts.

The XCHG instructions shown in Fig. 13-12 handles either 8-bit or 16-bit data. The instruction causes data in two registers to be swapped with each other. The registers affected can be either in memory or in the processor. The exchange instruction causes swaps between two processor registers or between a processor register and a memory location. It does not swap data between two memory locations.

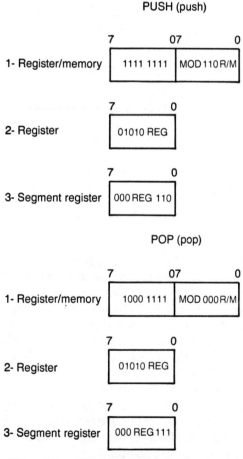

Fig. 13-11. The three PUSH and three POP instructions deal with pushing register contents onto the stack or popping them off.

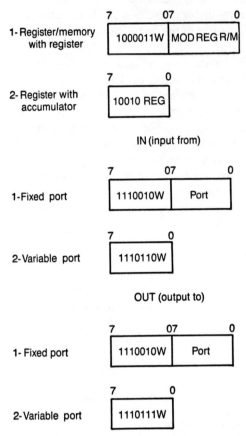

XCHG (exchange)

| | 7 | 07 | 0 |
|---|---|---|---|
| 1- Register/memory with register | 1000011W | MOD REG R/M | |

| | 7 | 0 |
|---|---|---|
| 2- Register with accumulator | 10010 REG | |

IN (input from)

| | 7 | 07 | 0 |
|---|---|---|---|
| 1-Fixed port | 1110010W | Port | |

| | 7 | 0 |
|---|---|---|
| 2-Variable port | 1110110W | |

OUT (output to)

| | 7 | 07 | 0 |
|---|---|---|---|
| 1- Fixed port | 1110010W | Port | |

| | 7 | 0 |
|---|---|---|
| 2-Variable port | 1110111W | |

Fig. 13-12. The six XCHG instructions are able to swap register contents in the computer or with peripherals.

The IN (input) instruction and the OUT (output) instructions, also in Fig. 13-12, deal with transferring data to and from the accumulator register and peripheral devices. As their name suggests, they are I/O instructions that transfer data.

There are eight instructions in Fig. 13-13 that are not in any of the above groups. XLAT is said to translate a byte to the low bits of the accumulator register. This description relates to transferring the contents of a register in a lookup table to the low bytes in the accumulator. This is a valuable programming technique. Next, there are four load instructions and one store. These instructions are additional to all the MOV instructions. There is LEA. This means load the effective address into the specified register. After that there is LDS and LES. They instruct the loading of the data segment and extra segment registers with 16-bit data from memory. There is LAHF which means load the high bits of the accumulator with a byte from the Flag register and SAHF, which means store the accumulator high bits into the Flag register.

The last two data transfer instructions are PUSHF and POPF. The push and pop instruction again deal with the stack in RAM. The F at the end of the mnemonic indicates

332

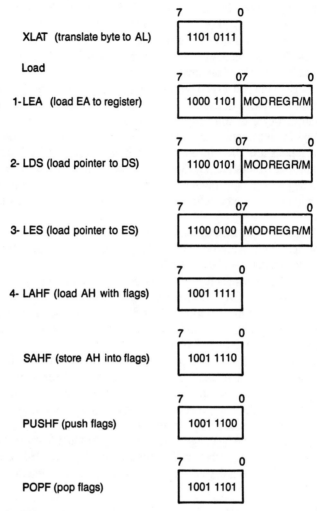

XLAT  (translate byte to AL)

```
7           0
1101 0111
```

Load

1-LEA  (load EA to register)

```
7        07          0
1000 1101 MOD REG R/M
```

2- LDS (load pointer to DS)

```
7        07          0
1100 0101 MODREGR/M
```

3- LES (load pointer to ES)

```
7        07          0
1100 0100 MODREGR/M
```

4- LAHF (load AH with flags)

```
7           0
1001 1111
```

SAHF (store AH into flags)

```
7           0
1001 1110
```

PUSHF (push flags)

```
7           0
1001 1100
```

POPF (pop flags)

```
7           0
1001 1101
```

Fig. 13-13. These eight instructions move data but are not in any of the previous categories. They are one and two byte types.

the operation is concerned with the Flag register. The instructions mean push and pop the 16-bits of the Flag register onto and off of the stack.

## Performing Arithmetic

The preceding data transfer instructions dealt with the task of moving 8-bit or 16-bit data from place to place in the digital circuits. The arithmetic instructions, move data around somewhat, but the main job these instructions perform is simply elementary school type 'rithmetic, one of the three R's.

The 8088-8086 is endowed with instructions that permit it to perform addition, subtraction, multiplication and division. This is a long step from the 8-bit processors that can only add and performs subtraction, multiplication, and division by roundabout means.

There are ten instructions for addition, seen in Fig. 13-14. Three of the instructions are ADD (add a byte or word), three as ADC (add a byte or word with carry) and two INC (increment byte or word by 1). All the add instructions do the job on signed or unsigned numbers. Instruction AAA adds and adjusts ASCII back to the correct binary numbers. DAA adds and adjusts decimal numbers.

There are instructions concerned with subtract in Fig. 13-15 and Fig. 13-16. Five of them are direct counterparts of the add instructions. They are SUB (subtract byte or word ), SBB (subtract byte or word with borrow), DEC (decrement byte or word by 1), ASS (ASCII adjust for subtraction) and DAS (decimal adjust for subtraction). The other subtraction instructions are NEG (change the sign of a byte or word ) and CMP (compare a byte or word, subtracts memory location contents from a processor register contents and sets a flag accordingly, does not change value of involved memory location or register). The addition and subtraction instructions do their job on 8-bit, 16-bit, and larger numbers.

There are three multiply instructions shown in Fig. 13-17, MUL performs straight multiplication on unsigned bytes or words. IMUL multiplys integers that are signed. AAM multiplys and adjusts the ASCII number.

There are three divide instructions, counterparts of the multiply types. DIV divides two unsigned numbers and IDIV divides two signed numbers. AAD does the job on ASCII. The multiply instructions multiply either 8-bit or 16-bit numbers with the results being either 16 bits or 32 bits. The divide instructions divide 16-bit or 32-bit numbers and the results are either 16 bits or 8 bits.

All of the arithmetic instructions affect the individual bits in the Flag Register. Figure 13-9 shows the bit positions and functions of the nine flags. As the instructions are executed, flags get set and reset according to the instruction. Some of the flags such as carry, zero, interrupt enable, and overflow act somewhat like the flags in the 8-bit processors. Other bits, the direction flag, single step and parity are new in the 8088-8086. If you are going to do machine language programming you must learn the job each does from the table. They are an important part of programming. The 8088-8086 makes a lot of decisions according to which flags are set and which ones are cleared.

## The Logicals

Besides being able to do arithmetic, the Arithmetic Logic Unit in the 8088-8086 is able to perform tricks of logic. The logicals, as Intel calls them, consist of the usual ANDing, ORing, NOTing, XORing, and an instruction called TEST. Besides those the shifting and rotating that an accumulator register is able to do, round out the rest of the logicals.

Figure 13-18 lists the AND, OR, NOT, and XOR logic instructions. All the instructions are able to perform logic on bytes or words. All the logic instructions are quite the same as the AND, OR, and XOR, shift and rotate instructions in an 8-bit processor except that 16-bit pieces of data can also receive treatment. There is only one NOT instruction and three each for logic operations, AND, OR and XOR (exclusive or). There are three shift operations and four rotates as listed in Fig. 13-19.

The TESTing operation is also like an 8-bit processor's TEST but using 16-bit data. The instruction is used to determine what will happen to the flags when two 16-bit regis-

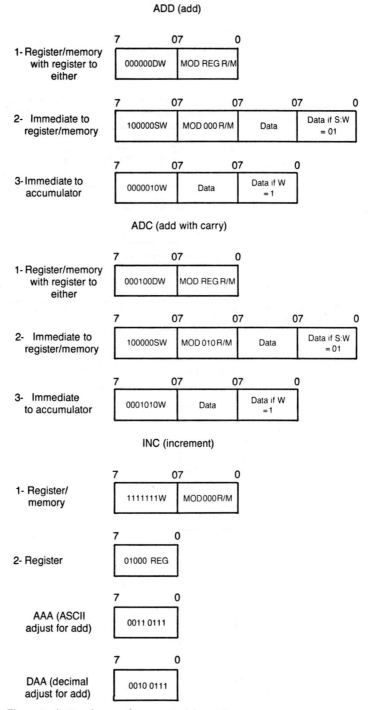

Fig. 13-14. These ten instructions perform most of the adding.

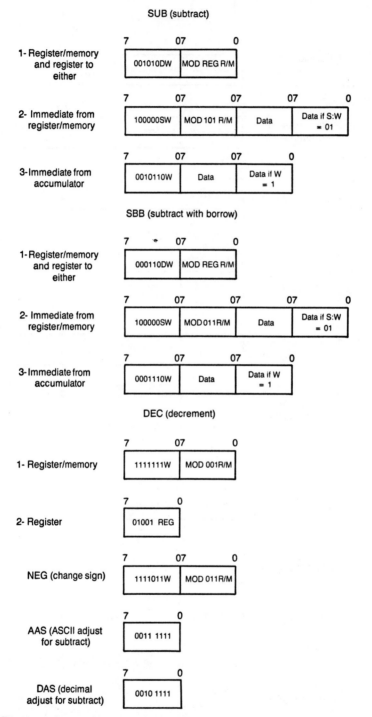

Fig. 13-15. There are eleven subtract type instructions.

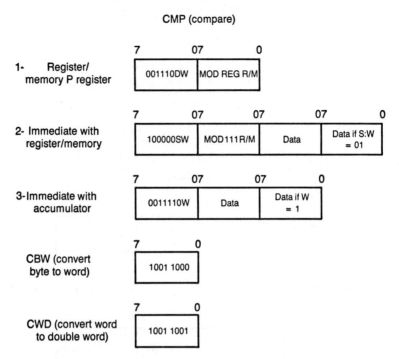

CMP (compare)

1- Register/ memory P register

| 7 | 07 | 0 |
|---|----|---|
| 001110DW | MOD REG R/M | |

2- Immediate with register/memory

| 7 | 07 | 07 | 07 | 0 |
|---|----|----|----|---|
| 100000SW | MOD 111 R/M | Data | Data if S:W = 01 | |

3- Immediate with accumulator

| 7 | 07 | 07 | 0 |
|---|----|----|---|
| 0011110W | Data | Data if W = 1 | |

CBW (convert byte to word)

| 7 | 0 |
|---|---|
| 1001 1000 | |

CWD (convert word to double word)

| 7 | 0 |
|---|---|
| 1001 1001 | |

Fig. 13-16. The CMP instructions compare registers. This is a form of subtraction without changing any of the register contents. The results will only set a flag if required.

ters are ANDed together. The flags will change when TEST is executed but the two registers being ANDed do not have their contents altered. All the TEST instruction does is set or reset flags. The programmer finds this instruction valuable during his efforts to keep control of the many flag changes that go on as arithmetic and logic instructions are executed.

## Control Transfer

The control transfer instructions could also be called change of address instructions. They deal with addressing. The program counter circuits are built to start their addressing at address zero and automatically increment by one at each succeeding address move. A control transfer instruction, stops the automatic incrementing and causes an entirely different memory location to be addressed, not in the arithmetical order.

There are three kinds of control transfer instructions. First there are 16 conditional JUMP type instructions. These instructions are shown in Fig. 13-20. They take a reading of the Flag register, and according to the state of the flags, can either ignore the flags or cause a change of address to take place. Then at the change of address site in memory, the processor continues on with its automatic incremental addressing. All these conditional jumps are made in relation to whatever the contents of the instruction pointer is at that instant. The jump is restricted to a range of −128 to +127 bytes.

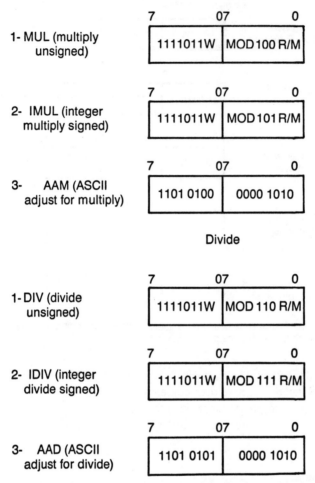

Fig. 13-17. This processor is able to perform multiplication and division, features an 8-bit processor cannot do directly.

A JUMP instruction will contain a displacement or might address registers for their contents to be placed into the code segment register or the instruction pointer. The use of these new address bits forms a new address where the processor jumps to.

An example of the JUMP type instruction is JO (jump on overflow). The overflow flag is bit 11 in the Flag register. As JO is run it notes the state of bit 11. If bit 11 is set to a 1, the instruction will make the processor JUMP to the new address that is specified. Should bit 11 be cleared to 0, the processor will simply increment the addressing register and ignore the JO instruction. Programmers say that this ability gives the processor decision making qualities. It can decide to jump or not according to its Flag register.

These listed JUMP instructions in Fig. 13-20 are said to be Conditional. That is, they will make the jump or not according to the condition of the Flag register. There is

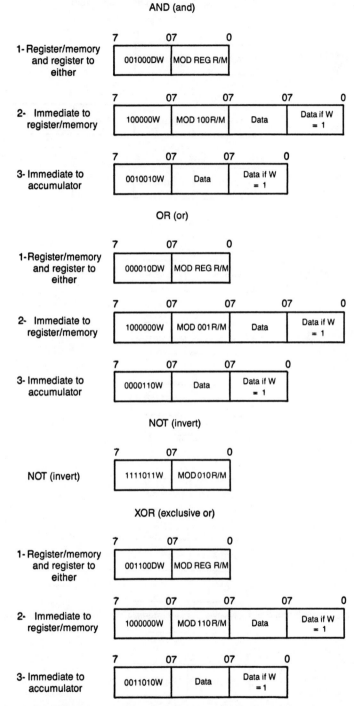

Fig. 13-18. The AND, OR, NOT, and XOR logic is conducted with these instructions.

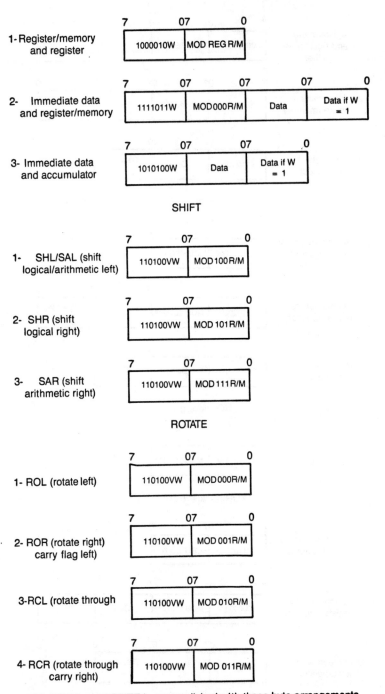

Fig. 13-19. TEST, SHIFT, and ROTATE is accomplished with these byte arrangements.

| | 7      0 | 7      0 |
|---|---|---|
| 1-JE/JZ (jump on equal/zero) | 0111 0100 | Displacement |
| 2-JL/JNGE (jump on less/not greater or equal) | 0111 1100 | " |
| 3-JLE/JNG (jump on less or equal/not greater) | 0111 1110 | " |
| 4-JB/JNAE (jump on below/not above or equal) | 0111 0010 | " |
| 5-JBE/JNE (jump on below or equal/not above) | 0111 0110 | " |
| 6-JP/JPE (jump on parity/parity even) | 0111 1010 | " |
| 7-JO (jump on overflow) | 0111 0000 | " |
| 8-JS (jump on sign) | 0111 1000 | " |
| 9-JNE/JNZ (jump on not equal/not zero) | 0111 0101 | " |
| 10-JNL/JGE (jump on not less/greater or equal) | 0111 1101 | " |
| 11-JNLE/JG (jump on not less or equal/greater) | 0111 1111 | " |
| 12-JNB/JAE (jump on not below/above or equal) | 0111 0011 | " |
| 13-JNBE/JA (jump on not below or equal above) | 0111 0111 | " |
| 14-JNP/JPO (jump on not par/par odd) | 0111 1011 | " |
| 15-JNO (jump on not overflow) | 0111 0001 | " |
| 16-JNS (jump on not sign) | 0111 1001 | " |
| 1-LOOP (loop CX times, count not zero) | 0111 0010 | " |
| 2-LOOPE/LOOPZ (loop while zero(equal) ) | 0111 0001 | " |
| 3-LOOPNE/LOOPNZ (loop while not zero(equal) ) | 0111 0000 | " |
| JCXZ (jump on CX zero) | 0111 0011 | " |

Fig. 13-20. These instructions will cause a change of address or put a program into a loop if the proper conditions occur as the program is run. They are unconditional.

one more JUMP group of instructions that are unconditional. They are found in Fig. 13-21. When their specific bits arrive at the processor, the processor will execute a jump no matter what the state of the Flag register bits. There are two more unconditional transfer instructions that also change addresses no matter the state of flag bits in Fig. 13-22.

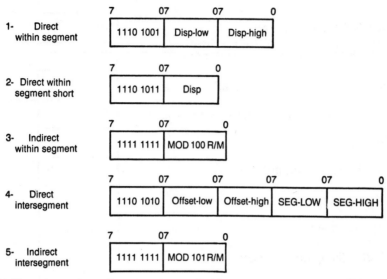

JMP (unconditional jumps)

| | | 7    07 | 07    0 |
|---|---|---|---|
| 1- | Direct within segment | 1110 1001 | Disp-low | Disp-high |

| | | 7    07    0 |
|---|---|---|
| 2- | Direct within segment short | 1110 1011 | Disp |

| | | 7    07    0 |
|---|---|---|
| 3- | Indirect within segment | 1111 1111 | MOD 100 R/M |

| | | 7    07    07    07    07    0 |
|---|---|---|
| 4- | Direct intersegment | 1110 1010 | Offset-low | Offset-high | SEG-LOW | SEG-HIGH |

| | | 7    07    0 |
|---|---|---|
| 5- | Indirect intersegment | 1111 1111 | MOD 101 R/M |

Fig. 13-21. These instructions will cause a change of address no matter what the conditions are. They are unconditional.

They are CALL and RETURN. These instructions are valuable to cause a jump to a subroutine stashed away in memory someplace and then after the subroutine is run the processor can return to the main program. For example, suppose you needed to compute the log of numbers in a program time and time again. All that is needed is to install a log conversion subroutine program somewhere memory. When the subroutine is needed to compute a log, it is CALLed. After the log is computed, a RETURN instruction is executed, the processor returns to the instruction just after the CALL instruction.

The last group of control transfer instructions are called Iteration Controls. Iteration refers to repeating a program area over and over again. Accordingly the iteration instructions are in the LOOP family. A LOOP keeps running the same instructions over and over. There are three loop instructions and another special JUMP in the Iteration group. The three LOOP instructions are found in in Fig. 13-20. They work hand-in-hand with the Count register. They all make the Count register decrement by 1. The plain LOOP instruction, as long as the Count register is not zero makes the processor loop back to an instruction within the range of −128 to +127 bytes. This makes the Count register decrement by 1 after every loop and keep count of the process.

The LOOPE/LOOPZ will execute its loop after it checks both the zero flag bit and the Count register. The loop will be executed only when they are zero. The other loop instruction, LOOPNE/LOOPNZ acts in the opposite way. It will cause a loop to be executed when the Count register and Z flag are not equal to zero. These instructions let the processor get into loops and then to get out of loops when the Count register reaches zero or when other zero-non-zero conditions occur.

The last jump instruction JCXZ in Fig. 13-20 also deals with the Count register. It causes the processor to execute a jump to a new address when the Count register is

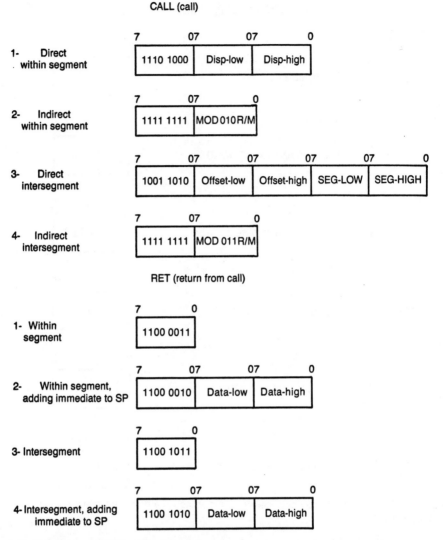

Fig. 13-22. The CALL and RET instructions are like the unconditional jumps. The CALL causes a jump to a subroutine somewhere in memory. The RET returns the addressing back to the main program where the CALL had caused the jump.

equal to zero. It is different than the other JUMP instructions. The other jumps are made with reference to the flags. JCXZ depends on the Count register.

## String Manipulation

A string to a programmer is usually a sequence of characters. Strings are written from left to right and are connected. The analogy to a computer string is a string of beads. The beads are usually characters. The group of characters ABCDEF is a string. Numbers can be in strings but when they are they're considered to be characters.

343

# String Manipulation

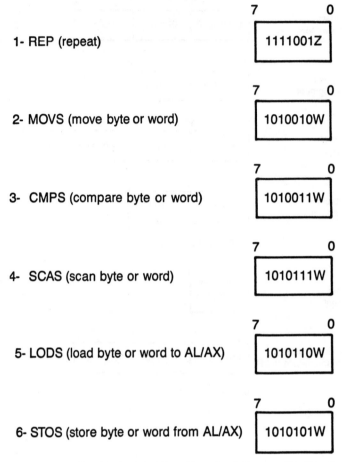

1- REP (repeat)

```
7        0
1111001Z
```

2- MOVS (move byte or word)

```
7        0
1010010W
```

3- CMPS (compare byte or word)

```
7        0
1010011W
```

4- SCAS (scan byte or word)

```
7        0
1010111W
```

5- LODS (load byte or word to AL/AX)

```
7        0
1010110W
```

6- STOS (store byte or word from AL/AX)

```
7        0
1010101W
```

Fig. 13-23. These string instructions operate on the strings in a program while the other instructions deal with ordinary data.

The 8088-8086 only has six string op codes (Fig. 13-23). There are only a few jobs that are needed on strings. One job required is called concatenation. This is the process of adding one string section to another to form a total string. Another required job is called pattern matching. This is the process of comparing and scanning strings with each other to find substrings in the total string that have specific relationships with each other.

A third job is to change strings around after pattern matching to get desired strings. These jobs are essential when handling characters and numbers in many applications.

The string instructions in the 8088-8086 provide the abilities of moving, comparing, and scanning strings of binary bits. Other instructions can load and store strings to and from the accumulator register. The string instructions simply handle binary bits. The instructions will do the jobs whether the bits represent the six bit per character BCD set, the seven bit per character ASCII set, the eight bit per character EBCDIC set, or any alphanumeric or numerical arrangement of binary bits.

The instruction group includes MOVS (move string). All the string instructions use the source index and data segment registers for addresses. They can also use a combination of the source index, data segment, and the destination index and extra segment registers. The MOVS instruction uses these registers to move strings from one section of memory to another.

The MOVS instruction is only able to move one 8-bit or one 16-bit of data at a time. After one move the source index and destination index will be incremented or decremented by 1 or 2 according to the nature of the MOVS op code that is used.

If a number of bytes or words are to be used, another string instruction, REP (repeat) is employed. The repeat op code is placed in memory in the address preceding the MOVS instruction. When REP is utilized, the MOVS instruction will keep repeating itself for the number of times that is specified in the Count register. This repeat instruction saves the programmer from having to write a MOVS instruction over and over again.

The CMPS (compare string) instruction will compare two strings byte by byte or word for word. The source index and destination index registers are automatically incremented or decremented during this operation. The repeat instruction can be placed in front of the compare in the same way REP is used for the MOVS instruction. When REP is used the compare instruction will keep repeating itself as long as the strings match perfectly bit for bit. The processor will stop the operation as soon as the strings do not match. The operation will also stop when the counter register decrements down to zero.

The SCAS (scan string) works like the compare except when the repeat instruction is used the processor will keep comparing until a byte or word match is found. When the repeat instruction is used, the processor will stop comparing when the counter register decrements to zero, just like the CMPS instruction.

The last two instructions LODS (load accumulator with string) and STOS (store string from accumulator) are straightforward. The load instruction places a string into the accumulator. The store instruction sends a string in the accumulator to a memory location. The repeat instruction is rarely used with the load and store.

## The Interrupts

There are three different types of interrupts in the 8088-8086. No matter which interrupt is activated the processor starts off with the same procedure. It pushes the contents of the Instruction Pointer, the code segment register and the flags onto the stack. The processor then goes to the first 1 K of memory where new Instruction Pointers and new code segment register contents are stored. The processor will then choose contents according to what interrupt occurred. These new contents are placed into the Instruction Pointer and code segment register. They form an address where the interrupt service routine is stored.

The INT (interrupt) instructions shown in Fig. 13-24, are used to get the interrupt service programs stored in memory to start running. There are 256 possible interrupt programs stored in memory. These subroutines are used to help peripheral devices communicate with the processor. The INT instruction is two bytes long. The first byte is

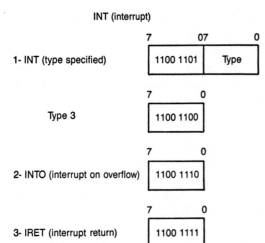

INT (interrupt)

| 7 | 07 | 0 |
|---|---|---|
1- INT (type specified)

| 1100 1101 | Type |
|---|---|

7       0

Type 3

| 1100 1100 |
|---|

Fig. 13-24. The three INT instructions all interrupt the processor and have register contents stored in the stack.

7       0

2- INTO (interrupt on overflow)

| 1100 1110 |
|---|

7       0

3- IRET (interrupt return)

| 1100 1111 |
|---|

the interrupt op code. The second byte, according to its bit structure, specifies which of the 256 subroutines should be run to service the interrupt.

In the first 1 K of memory, hex addresses 000-3FF, is an interrupt vector table that contains the vectors to be placed into the Instruction Pointer and code segment register. With the correct vectors installed in the IP and CS the processor is then able to address the service subroutine and get it running, once the original contents of the IP, the CS and flags have been pushed onto the stack.

Once the interrupt service subroutine has been run, the processor is ready to return to the main program it had been running before the interrupt from the peripheral had arrived. Accordingly there is an instruction to get the processor back to the main program. It is called IRET (interrupt return).

This instruction is always placed at the end of all interrupt service routines. It is a one byte instruction. As the last instruction in an interrupt service routine, the first thing it does is pop the original contents of the Flag register, the Instruction Pointer and the code segment register, off the stack and back into their original registers in the processor. Then the IRET instruction returns the processor to the next instruction in the main program, after the one that was last executed when the interrupt occurred.

The other interrupt is called INTO (interrupt on overflow). This is a one byte instruction that allows the processor to interrupt itself. The interrupt will be executed if an overflow occurs. It has a four byte interrupt vector starting at hex address 010. This interrupt is a time saver. The same procedure could also be accomplished by a jump instruction with a lot of bytes. One byte runs faster than five or six.

## Processor Control

The last category of instructions deal with controlling the processor. Most of these are single byte instructions that set and clear some of the flag register bits. There is a CLC (clear carry), STC (set carry), CLI (clear interrupt), and others that are in Fig. 13-25.

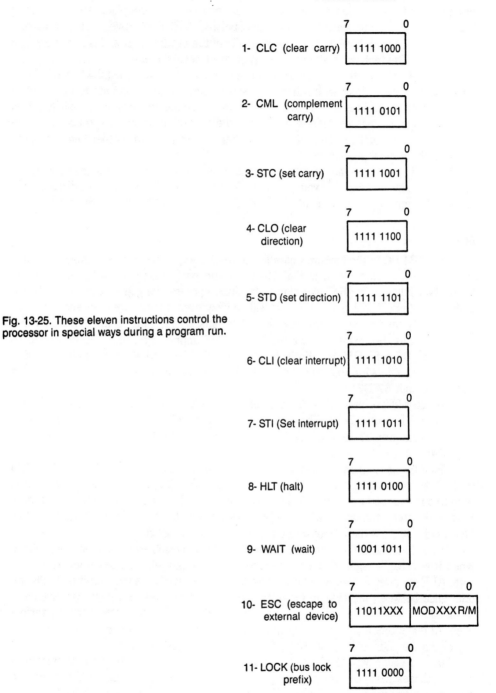

1- CLC (clear carry)

7        0
1111 1000

2- CML (complement carry)

7        0
1111 0101

3- STC (set carry)

7        0
1111 1001

4- CLO (clear direction)

7        0
1111 1100

5- STD (set direction)

7        0
1111 1101

**Fig. 13-25. These eleven instructions control the processor in special ways during a program run.**

6- CLI (clear interrupt)

7        0
1111 1010

7- STI (Set interrupt)

7        0
1111 1011

8- HLT (halt)

7        0
1111 0100

9- WAIT (wait)

7        0
1001 1011

10- ESC (escape to external device)

7    07    0
11011XXX | MODXXXR/M

11- LOCK (bus lock prefix)

7        0
1111 0000

347

The last four instructions are used for external synchronization. If it is desirable to bring HLT (halt) to operations until an interrupt or reset can take place, that instruction is used. Should it be necessary to WAIT until pin 23, *TEST, is active, then that instruction is used. These instructions are in the realm of the programmer and is rarely used by technicians. The technician should know they exist nevertheless.

The ESC (escape to external device) is an instruction that is useful when the 8088-8086 must operate along with other processors. The LOCK (bus lock prefix) is used when a special register is chosen to be used rather than the normal one. If an instruction normally uses the data segment register, but the programmer decides to use the extra segment register instead, the LOCK instruction is used along with other instructions to override the normal procedure.

If you find machine language instructions fascinating and want to learn more there are many books available that you can study. The preceding Instruction Set discussion is needed to acquaint you as a technician with the way the 8088-8086 operates.

## 8088 Pinout

The IBM PC is the base machine for all the PC-type machines that follow. I'll use the 8088 in the original PC, in Fig. 13-26, as the pinout example. All the 8088s and 8086s that followed in IBM and clone machines operate along the same lines. If you understand the original pinout the rest will be easy even if there are differences.

As mentioned earlier, there are eight data pins D7-D0 that do multiplex duty and transfer 16 bits, but eight bits at a time. The 8086 improves on this by transferring 16 bits through 16 pins, D15-D0. Both the 8088 and 8086 use some of the address pins to also handle the data ins and outs. The 8088 shares pins with A0-A7. The pins are called A0-D0 through A7-D7.

The 20 address pins A19-A0 are numbered 35-39 and 2-16. The data pins D7-D0 share pins 9-16 with A7-A0. These pins transfer both address bits and data pins but at different moments. The address and data pins handle 8-bit bytes, 16-bit words and 32-bit long words.

The 8088 has separate read and write output pins. Pin 32 is called *RD and pin *29 is *WR. Both pins are dormant when they are held high. They become active when it is time to direct a read or a write. When *RD goes low, the processor reads the contents of an addressed memory location. *WR stays high at that time. When *WR goes low *RD holds high and the processor can write data to a location.

At pin 25 is ALE, the address latch enable. ALE is disabled low and starts enabling when it is brought high. The address pins do not output address bits until ALE goes high. ALE operates in coordination with pin 28, IO/*M. IO/*M is the circuit that tells the difference between the system memory and I/O devices. When a memory location is being addressed, IO/*M goes low. The address bits travel to memory without interference. At that moment, I/O devices cannot be addressed. If IO/*M goes high, then memory cannot be addressed. Only I/O circuits will accept address bits.

Pin 33 is called MN/*MX for minimum/maximum mode. Note the various pin initials in parentheses alongside the regular pin initials. These letters in parentheses are the maximum mode indicators. The regular initials show the 8088's minimum mode.

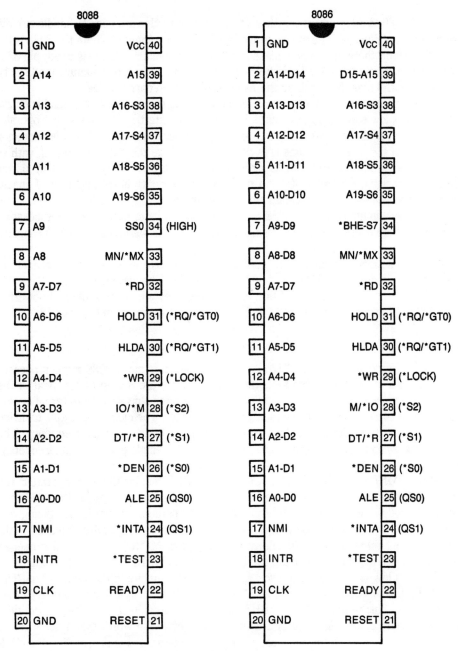

Note pins 33 on both chips, MN/*MX, minimum and maximum mode controls. In minimum mode the pin functions inside chip area are active. In maximum mode the functions in parentheses outside chip area take over their pins.

Fig. 13-26. It is a good idea to understand the function of every pin, what typical voltages and logic states are present, and whether a pin is an input or output. During testing the knowledge will help you pick out wrong values.

For the 8088-8086 processor, these two different modes are used to handle two different types of designs. The minimum mode is used in a computer where the 8088 is the only processor, there are no coprocessors. When the minimum mode is used, pin 33 is wired permanently to +5 V. This holds the pin high and in the minimum mode. The involved control pins then assume the name that is not in parentheses.

On t¹ ɔ other hand, the 8088 could have pin 33 tied to zero volts or ground and have a permanent low state. The pin names in parentheses are then the ones that operate. When this happens the 8088 is able to coexist with other processors. The most common application of the maximum mode is in the IBM PC where the 8088 is wired up with an 8087 coprocessor. The 8087 works along with the 8088 and speeds things up during number crunching. The minimum and maximum modes each have a number of special circuits in the 8088 that they use on an exclusive basis.

In the maximum mode the 8088 could work with a large number of coprocessors. Typical uses are coprocessors that have specialties such as mathematics and I/O applications.

These two different modes the 8088-8086 can operate in were the forerunners of the different modes in the 80286 and 80386 processors. The various modes in these 16-bit and 32-bit processors is one of the main reasons they are so versatile and powerful. The 80286 is discussed in Chapter 17. The 80386 gets coverage in Chapter 18.

## 8086 Chip Timing

Figure 13-27 shows a block diagram of a small minimum mode 8086 single processor computer. All of the operations the processor conducts are driven by the beat of the clock. This small computer uses an 8284 clock generator chip with an external crystal cut to run at 14.31818 MHz, a commonly used frequency. The clock chip is able to divide up the crystal frequency and output an approximate 5 MHz operating frequency. The timing diagram in Fig. 13-28 shows the clock output as a single phase driving frequency. One bus cycle of the processor consists of four clock cycles.

Pin 33, MN/*MX, of the 8086 is connected to +5 V making the 8086 operate in the minimum mode on a permanent basis. With the minimum mode in place, the 8086 then needs the following connections to conduct a read operation shown in the timing diagram, Fig. 13-28. First of all there are the address and data pins, A19-A16 and A15-A0, D15-D0. Next there is ALE, the address enable latch, M/*IO and *RD. Also needed and shown with the A19-A16 bits in the timing diagram is *BHE the bus high enable.

The first low of the processor cycle applies the A19-A0 bits to the address bus. The signal *BHE is ANDed with A0. A0 and *BHE are able to form four different AND output patterns. This permits A0 and *BHE to choose from among the following entities. There is available, the high byte of a word, the low byte of a word, the entire word or none of the word at an addressed location. Whatever the access choice of bits, the clock applies the correct address bit to the A19-A0 address output circuits.

The falling edge of the first clock period also triggers a high from ALE. This fulfills the next step in getting the processor to access a memory location. Also at the same instant, the M/*IO is made high if the read is going to be made from a memory location. Should the read be one from a peripheral, the M/*IO pin is forced low.

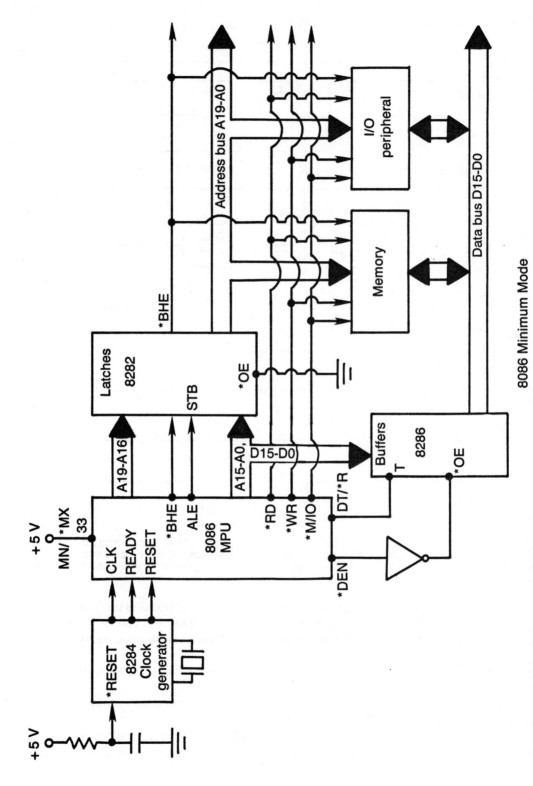

Fig. 13-27. A typical 8086 based computer system can be wired up in this manner.

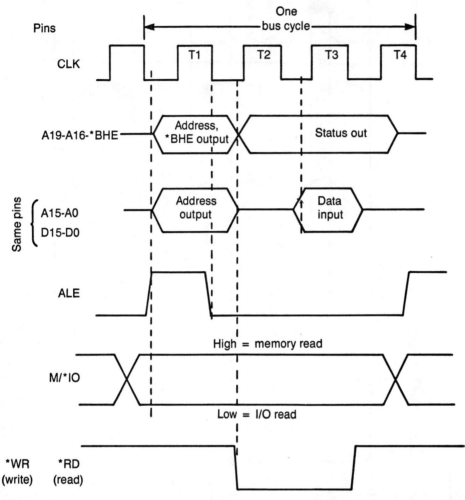

Fig. 13-28. A single phase CLK signal drives the 8086. The first low of CLK triggers the addressing bits and *BHE. The falling edge of the first clock period also triggers a high from ALE. If the read is from memory then M/*IO is high, if it is from a peripheral it goes low. *RD is triggered at the second clock low.

Once all these accessing prerequisites have occurred, the processor makes the *RD pin output a low during the second low of the processor cycle. The *WR pin, at that time, is held high and thus inactive during the read cycle. When all these clock events have taken place, then and only then, the addressed location is ready to let a copy of its contents out on the system data bus. The data does not leave the location until *RD goes low.

Once the data is out on the data bus, the processor, during the third clock cycle low, strobes the data into the awaiting data pins, D15-D0.

The write operation is just about the same as the read except for the logic states on *RD and *WR. The read operation takes place when *RD goes low and *WR is held high. The write operation takes place with all the same signals except the *RD goes high and the *WR pin outputs a low.

Figure 13-29 illustrates an 8088 performing in a maximum mode. Note the MN/*MX pin 33 is tied to ground. The maximum differs in that pins 24-31, the memory and peripheral signals are shut down. Another chip, an 8288 bus controller is added to the circuitry and connected to pins 26, 27, and 28, S0, S1, and S2 that become status outputs when the processor goes into a maximum mode.

The bus controller chip in turn decodes the status outputs and generates the required signals to control the memory and I/O addresses. These new signals are called, *MRDC, memory read control, *MWTC, memory write control, IORC, input output read control and IOWC, input output write control.

In the two block diagrams, the address bus and data bus lines appropriately go to the memory data holders and the peripherals that also deal in data. In the address lines are inserted a pair of chips. This design is an application developed at Intel. These chips in the address lines are latches. They are needed in the address lines because of ALE. ALE works with A0 to direct the address bits, as mentioned earlier.

Note in the timing diagram that ALE is only high for a short period of time. In this 5 MHz system, ALE is active only about 100 ns. Many memory and peripheral devices need more time than that to be addressed. A peripheral could need 400 or 500 ns to be addressed. That's where the latches come into play. When an address in this circuit is generated, it is latched. This keeps the address at memory or a peripheral long enough to be addressed and be able to transfer data back and forth. The address will then hold until the next address and ALE comes out of the 8088.

The 8088-8086 processors are very popular. There are millions upon millions of them around the world residing in personal computers from IBM and clone manufacturers. They will remain in style for a long time to come. Manufacturers are still churning out the machines based around these processors despite all the new processors that are also appearing on the scene. The 8088-8086 has become the standard for most IBM compatible computers. As a technician you will be encountering them often.

Another 16-bit processor family that is also important and sets a standard in the Apple world, is the Motorola 68000. It is the processor of choice that Apple placed in the original Macintosh. Commodore installed it in their Amiga. In the next chapter we will discuss the original 68000 in some detail.

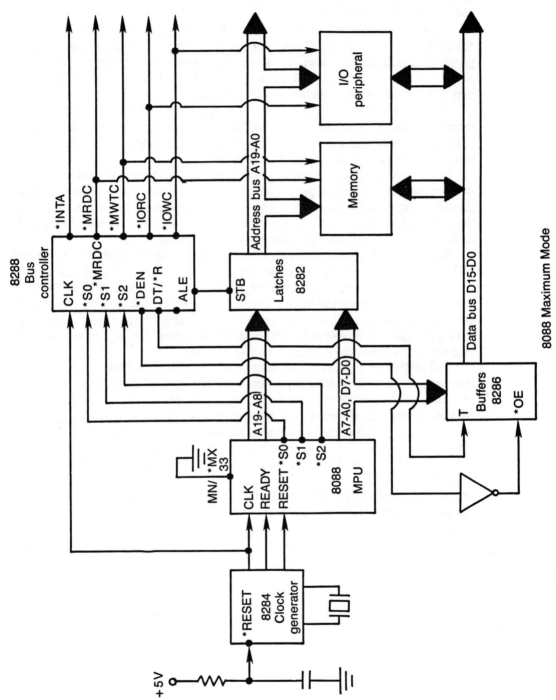

Fig. 13-29. This is a typical 8088 computer system operating in a maximum mode. Note pin 33 the MN/ *MX is tied to ground.

8088 Maximum Mode

# 14

# The 68000 Processor

The 68000 is packaged in a larger DIP then the 8086 and 8088. Figure 14-1 shows the 68000 has 64 pins in comparison to the 40 pins on the 8088-8086 packages. One of the reasons for the increase in pins on the 68000 package is an increase in the number of address pins. Inside the 68000, the addressing registers use 24 bits to conduct the addressing. With 24 address bits in use, the 68000 is able to directly address 16 megabytes. In contrast the 8088 only has 20 address bits and is restricted to addressing 1 megabyte. The four additional address bits in the 68000 permits a 16 fold increase in addressing ability. The 68000's addressing is also conducted without any segmenting. The 8088, as you'll recall, needed segment manipulating in order to get the 20 correct bits out on the address bus.

Actually, the 68000 chip has addressing registers with 32 bits. However, only A23-A0 is used. The other eight address bits, A31-A24, are used in other members of the 68000 family of processors, for instance the 68020. If these additional address bits are used, the package must be larger and provide more pins for addressing. When all 32 address bits are used, the processor is able to address 4 gigabytes (billions) of direct memory. This large capability is impressive as far as direct memory addressing goes.

Figure 14-1 is the pinout of the 64 pin 68000 in this discussion. As the pins are examined one by one, VCC is found at both pins 14 and 49. Ground connects to both pins 16 and 53. The 16 data pins, D15-D0, are arranged clockwise, starting with pin 5, going to pin 1, crossing the top of the package and continuing through pins 64 to 54. The address pins are arranged counterclockwise at pins 29-48 and 50-52. Note the address pins are labeled A1-A23. A0 is conspicuously missing. A0 is encoded internally and is controlled with two external pins. These A0 involved pins will be covered shortly.

The 16 data pins are the link to eight 32-bit data registers on the chip. These 32-bit registers, shown in Fig. 14-2, can be accessed in a few different ways. Since they are 32-

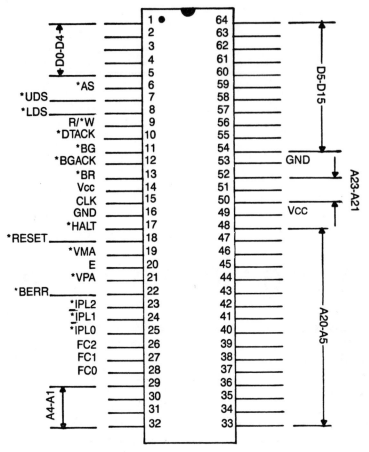

Fig. 14-1. The 68000 MPU has its circuits contained in a 64-pin DIP.

bits wide the 68000 can use them to handle 8-bit bytes, 16-bit words or 32-bit long words. Their register addresses are D7-D0.

The 68000 has seven address-type registers. These are also 32 bits and can be used in a general purpose fashion. They are not quite as versatile as the data registers. They can only be accessed by 16-bit words and 32-bit long words. They do not respond as single byte registers. Their register addresses are A0-A6.

The A7 register address is the stack pointer. There are two stack pointers, but they share the same address since they do not both operate at the same time. The 68000 operates in one of two states, a user state and a supervisor state. The two stack pointers are a user pointer and a supervisor pointer.

The program counter is also a 32-bit register as mentioned earlier. However, in the 68000, the highest eight bits are not connected to external pins. They have been designed into the configuration for the future. When they are put into use, the 68000 will be able to address 4 billion byte-sized locations. This chip is able to address 16,777,216 byte-sized locations with the 24 lower address bits.

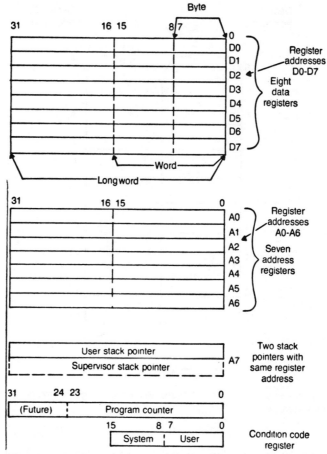

Fig. 14-2. The 68000 has 32-bit data registers, address registers, stack pointers, and program counter. The CCR has 16 bits.

It was mentioned that only 23 of the 24 address bits, A1-A23, exited through pins to the address bus. A0 is not pinned directly. This complication is there so the address can choose either a byte transfer or a word transfer from the 16-bit memory locations. Figure 14-3 shows the memory locations are arranged in 16-bit sizes. However, each 16-bit location has a high byte and a low byte. The bytes are the numbers on the memory map not the 16-bit locations. All the high bytes are the even numbers. All the lower bytes are the odd numbers on the map.

The 16-bit location can be accessed in three ways. The high byte, bits 15-8, can be retrieved by itself. The low byte, bits 7-0, can be retrieved by itself. The complete word, bits 15-0, can be accessed in its entirety.

On the chip pinout, A0 is missing. In its place, there are two pins, *UDS pin 7 and *LDS pin 8. They are called *Upper Data Strobe* and *Lower Data Strobe*. They produce outputs when A0 is gated internally with the instruction size as the program is run. They can produce three forms of data transfers between the MPU and memory.

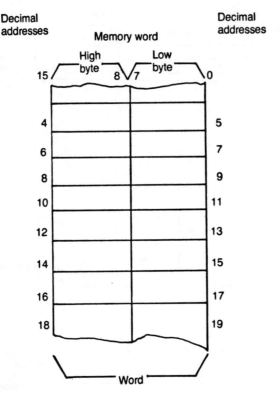

Decimal addresses

Decimal addresses

Memory word

High byte · 8 · 7 · Low byte

15 / 8 \/ 7 \ 0

4                5
6                7
8                9
10               11
12               13
14               15
16               17
18               19

Word

Fig. 14-3. The memory words each have two addresses. The high byte is always an even address and the low byte an odd address.

When the 68000 accesses bytes and there are two bytes to a 16-bit location, the 68000 is addressing 16 megabytes of individual locations. If the 68000 is addressing words, and there is only one word to a 16-bit location, the addressing is thought of as eight *megawords*. Eight megawords of locations have the same number of bits as 16 megabytes.

The actual accessing is accomplished with the aid of the two control lines *UDS and *LDS. When *UDS goes low, the bits that travel in the data bus lines D15-D8 are transferred. If *LDS goes low, the data bus lines D7-D0 carry the low order bits between the MPU and memory. Should both *UDS and *LDS go low, then the entire word length of 16 bits traverses the full data bus.

There is a routine R/*W line coming out of pin 9. It operates by sending a high during a read and a low during a write to the memory or I/O device the MPU has addressed. The device then knows whether to place copy on the data bus or gate copy from the data bus.

Next to the R/*W pin is an input line *DTACK at pin 10. It operates with the R/*W line. Once the bus line has data in transit, it sends a low to pin 10 of the MPU. When the low is received at *DTACK, which is a data acknowledgment, the MPU reacts. It latches the data during a read and shuts down the bus. If the operation is a write, the external

358

chip is sending a message that the data is received. The MPU knows it is to shut down the bus.

The 68000 always waits for the *DTACK input signal before it completes the operation. This feature matches the timing of the MPU operation with the timing of the external device. This feature allows the 68000 to speed up access with fast chips and slow access down with slower chips, an amazing ability.

The combination of the data strobe lines, the *R/*W line and the *DTACK connection from the external chip forms what is known as *asynchronous control*. This type of control is not in sync with the clock. The transferring of data is accomplished independently. The clock is running and the operation takes place during cycles, but the number of cycles the MPU takes to complete the operation is dependent on the speed of the external chip.

The other type of control is *synchronous*. Asynchronous control is usually needed when the MPU is interfaced with chips that are not in the 68000 family. Those chips that are members of the family can be synced in with the clock cycles. The 68000 is designed to operate with the same chips the 6800 used. Synchronous control connections are like the 6800 control lines.

Two identical control lines are E, enable, and *VMA, valid memory address. There is a third sync signal called *VPA at pin 21. The E pin 20, outputs a $\phi2$ type signal to the chips the MPU is in contact with. The E signal syncs all chips into the same sync frequency. It is derived from the CLK input at pin 15. E is $1/10$ the frequency of the CLK signal.

*VPA is a signal from the external chips that tells the MPU that a chip in sync is being addressed. It is the counterpart of the *DTACK. *DTACK notifies the MPU that an asynchronous chip is transferring data. *VPA tells the MPU that a synchronous chip is transferring data. When the MPU receives a *VPA low, it responds with a *VMA signal.

The rest of the pins on the chip perform their own jobs. *AS on pin 6 is an address strobe. It announces to all the chips that a valid address is on the address bus. FC2, FC1, and FC0 on pins 26, 27, and 28 work together to set up the operating state of the MPU. The three functions can arrange eight different functions.

*IPL2, *IPL1, and *IPL0 at pins 23, 24, and 25 are interrupt lines. *BG, *BGACK, and *BR at pins 11, 12, and 13 are used by other microprocessors to gain control over the bus lines. *BERR, *HALT and *RESET are other controls and state indicators. *HALT and *RESET can be useful to the technician if you want to reset or halt the operation of the MPU.

During voltage or logic probe testing of the pins, a good idea of the operation can be obtained. The pins with asterisks are usually held high and the pins without are held low. The asterisk pins are enabled with a low and the others are enabled with a high. The bus lines should all show activity. VCC and ground, of course, must have the correct supply voltages in order to operate.

## PIAs AND 16-BIT OPERATION

The same PIAs that are used with the 6800 can be connected directly to the 68000 data bus. It is a synchronous chip and connects to the address bus and control lines. The

PIA also connects to the outside world peripherals without any undue complications. The PIA's circuits to the outside world are discussed later.

The 6821 PIAs that the 68000 uses are the same ones that the 6800 use. The 6800 has an eight-line data bus and the 68000 has a 16-line data bus. How is the difference in bus line numbers handled by the PIAs?

Two PIAs are used for the 68000 where one was used for the 6800. Two PIAs wired in parallel are connected to the data bus. Eight data pins on one PIA are attached to data lines D15-D8 and eight data pins on the other PIA are attached to bus lines D7-D0 (Fig. 14-4).

The 68000 is designed to transfer 16 bits at a time and the two parallel PIAs are able to each transfer eight of the 16.

The PIAs are typically interfaced to the 68000 in the following way. They are installed in the memory map near the top between hex FEF800 and FEFFFF. Each PIA needs four addresses.

| Registers | PIA #1 | PIA#2 |
|-----------|--------|-------|
| PDRA/DDRAs | FEFF00 | FEFF01 |
| CRAs | FEFF02 | FEFF03 |
| PDRB/DDRBs | FEFF04 | FEFF05 |
| CRBs | FEFF06 | FEFF07 |

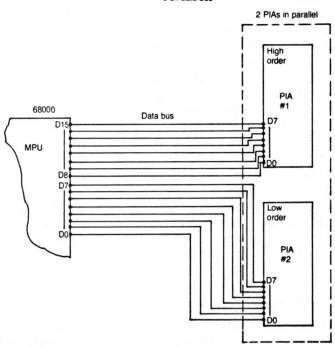

Fig. 14-4. The 68000 is able to interface directly with a lot of the 8-bit chips that were originally designed for the 68000. This is a 68000-PIA hookup.

Note that each 24 address bits are described with six hex characters. Each address is able to output eight bits of data. It takes two addresses of data to fill the 16-bit data bus.

When the MPU accesses locations FEFF00 and FEFF01, it can transfer data over the 16-bit data bus to and from both Peripheral Data Registers A in the two PIAs. If the MPU accesses locations FEFF04 and FEFF05, it can transfer data between itself and the PDRB registers in the two PIAs. As far as the MPU is concerned, the two PIAs look like one large PIA with a 16-bit data bus and 16-bit internal registers.

To dial up the PIAs, 23 bits are used: A23-A1 (Fig. 14-5). The PIAs are wired in parallel. Bits A1 and A2 of the address are connected to the internal register pins of the PIAs. A1 and A2 are connected to both RS0s and RS1s of the PIAs. When one of the four registers in a PIA is selected, the same register in the parallel PIA is also selected at the same time.

In this addressing scheme, the chip selects (*CS2, CS1, and CS0) on each PIA are also connected together. A3, A4, and A5 address lines select the PIAs when they are high. They enter a decoder that enables *CS2 when A3, A4, and A5 are high. The CS1s receive a low from the address bus. The CS0s are wired to VMA.

The R/*W lines decide if the PIAs are to be read from or written to. E syncs the PIAs in step with the clock. *RESET is there in case the PIA must be started over after a problem.

The 68000 must learn if the peripheral has been satisfactorily addressed by having *VPA turned on. *VPA needs a low to turn on. *VPA has two inputs, one from the address strobe, *AS, and the other from a multiple NAND gate.

*AS goes low at the beginning of the cycle. This low into one of the *VPA gates inputs is the enabling pulse. The low enters a NOT circle and becomes a high.

The other *VPA gate input comes from a multiple NAND gate that has 13 address bits as its inputs. When all thirteen address bits enter with the correct combination of highs and lows, the gate will be enabled. When that gate and *AS enter the *VPA gate, the MPU is notified that the PIAs have been addressed.

## THE 68000 INSTRUCTION SET

The 8-bit computer uses instructions that are one byte wide. The 16-bit computer uses instructions that are two bytes wide. The hex code for a byte is two hex characters. The instruction set for the 8-bit computer is a collection of two hex characters. Since there are 256 possible combinations of two hex characters, 00 to FF, the 8-bit instruction set is able to have 256 individual instructions. The 16-bit instruction set's hex code requires four hex characters. There are more than 64,000 possible combinations of four hex characters, 0000 to FFFF. The 16-bit instruction set is able to have 64 K individual instructions (Fig 14-6).

## REGISTER AND MEMORY ARRANGEMENT

The 68000 faces a memory arranged in 8-bit bytes. The basic address layout is byte-sized, not 16- or 32-bit size. If the memory bank is 64 K, that means there are 64 K bytes being addressed. 32 K bytes are at even addresses and 32 K bytes at odd addresses.

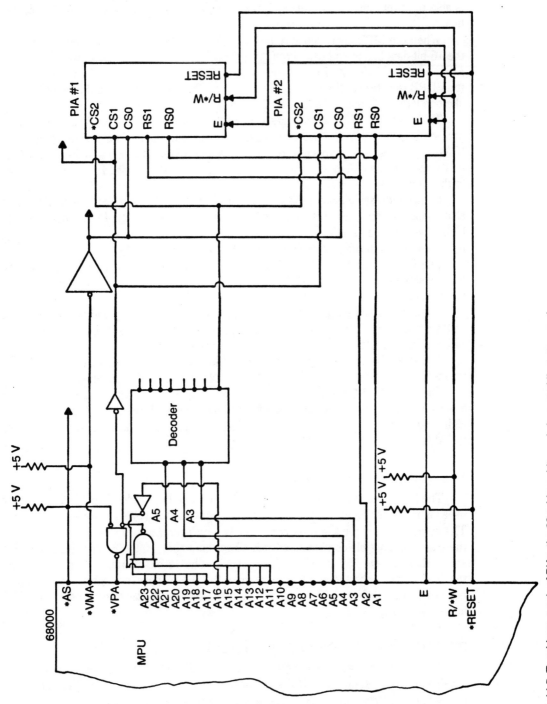

**Fig. 14-5. To address a pair of PIAs, the 23 address bits and six control lines are used.**

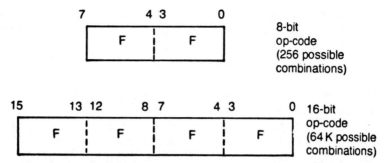

Fig. 14-6. The two hex number op-code has 256 possible combinations. Four hex numbers can be arranged in 64 K different ways.

One even address and one odd address comprise a memory station. At each station, there are 16 bits. Bits 15-8 are always the even address and 7-0 is the odd address at each memory station. The 16-bit data bus connects to each station, which consists of one even address and one odd address, bits 15-0. This memory setup lets the MPU address a single byte, eight bits, a double byte (word), 16 bits (a quadruple byte or long word), or 32 bits. In addition, the MPU is capable of working on individual bits, when the need arises.

In the MPU, there are 19 registers to work with the memory. The registers are like the accumulators, Index registers, stack pointers, program counter, and condition code registers in the 8-bit computer. However, they have considerably more versatility and general purpose qualities.

There are eight 32-bit data registers. The data registers are used as accumulators, although they are so versatile they can be used for most register purposes. The registers are designed to handle data of any size. They can use individual bit, bytes, words, and long words. They are 32 bits wide. Bits 7-0 can be accessed as bytes, bits 15-0 as words, and all 32 bits can be accessed for a long word transfer or manipulation. The eight data registers have register addresses. These addresses are not included in the memory map. They are MPU internal addresses, D0 through D7.

In the MPU, there is a Condition Code register. All the data registers affect the condition code bits. This is mentioned because other registers in the MPU do not affect the CCR bits, an important 68000 feature.

The data registers are all identical. Each one is able to handle bytes in bits 7-0. Two bytes or a word is worked on in bits 15-0. Long words are manipulated in the full 32-bit register.

There are seven 32-bit address registers. They are a lot like the data registers except for a few details. First of all, an address register cannot access bytes directly. It can deal with words and long words easily enough, but individual bytes cannot be accessed. In Fig. 14-2, you saw the data registers with dotted lines at the byte and word separations. The address registers are only separated at the word marker between bits 16 and 15.

The address register does not affect the flags in the CCR as the data registers do. This is a carefully thought-out feature that makes life easier for the programmer. For the technician, it is only a feature to be aware of during maintenance or repair.

In the eight-bit processor, most of the registers affect the flags. They are changing states constantly during a program run. A large percentage of the flags that change are not needed in the program run. In fact, the flag changing is often a nuisance and extra instructions must be used to nullify their effects.

Flags are very important to the data processing. Flags can be a nuisance during addressing. The 68000 is designed therefore to throw flags during data register processing and to have the flags left alone when the address registers are in action.

The seven address registers are given the MPU addresses A0 through A6. The registers are able to handle 16 and 32-bit wide pieces of data.

The stack pointer, which is a form of address register, has the address A7. A7 is really the address for two stack pointers. The two pointers are never used in the same operating state, so they can both share the same address. The two states are called the *user* and the *supervisor*. The user state is the normal way the computer operates. The supervisor state is a special state needed in certain instances.

The program counter in the 68000 is 32 bits wide. It can address up to 4 billion individual byte addresses directly. However, the 32-bit address is not needed at this time in the 68000. It is used in the 68020.

There are only 23 bits used directly; the 24th bit is controlled by *UDS and *LDS circuits. The total of 24 bits allows addressing up to 16 million bytes. The bytes are divided in two, with 8 million even and 8 million odd bytes. Each even and odd byte adds up to a 16-bit word. The program counter can address 8 million 16-bit words. Each word address usually starts off with an even number. The program counter can address 4 million long word addresses. Each long word starts off with an even number but skips every other number.

The 68000 is built to operate quickly on word and long word addresses that start with even numbers. In those instances where the 68000 must start with an odd address, the operation runs more slowly because two operations must be made to access the address. Every effort is usually made to start word and long word accesses with even addresses. When single bytes are accessed, the addressing can be odd or even.

The Condition Code register (also called the Status register) is a 16-bit register (Fig. 14-7). It is the only 16-bit register in the group. The 16 bits are divided between two groups of eight. The upper bits are reserved for the system's work and lower bits are for the user.

The lower bits contain five flags that can be set or cleared by the actions of the data registers. Four of the registers are the same as the 6800. Bit 0 is C for carry, bit 1 is V for overflow, bit 2 is Z for zero, and bit 3 is N for negative. In addition, bit 4 is X for extend.

The X bit is a helpmate to C. In the 68000 the C bit performs two jobs. It is used both as an arithmetic carry and for program control. During the execution of some branch instructions, the bit is tested. According to its state and the dictates of the instruction, the program may or may not branch.

The X bit takes over the arithmetic carry operation. The C bit is used as a test for the branch operations. This gives the programmer some simplification and more control.

The system byte has several bits. Bits 8, 9, and 10 are an interrupt mask. Bit 13 shows the operating state of the MPU. If the bit is 1, the MPU is in the supervisor state. When the bit is 0, the user state is in effect.

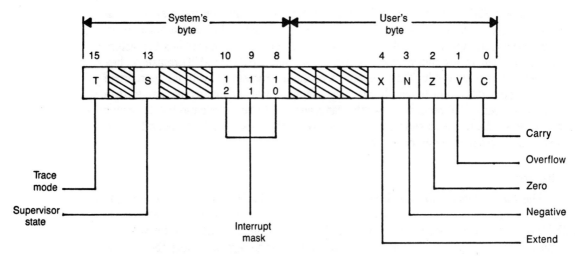

Fig. 14-7. The 16-bit CCR register is divided into a user's byte and a system byte.

Bit 15 is of great use to the sophisticated technician. When bit 15 is set, the computer is in a trace mode. The 68000 has built-in tracing circuits.

You can install a user written trace service routine. When it is necessary to debug a problem, the trace mode can be set with bit 15. The 68000 then runs through a program one step at a time. As each step is run, the 68000 is in the supervisor state. With bit 15 set and the 68000 in the supervisor state, the program counter develops a specific vector address. The vector sends the 68000 to a special trace service program. The service program can be used to trace the contents of the memory map, registers, flag settings, and so forth. This trace mode is valuable to the programmer for debugging software and to the technician when you check out hardware.

## ADDRESSING MODES

In the vast memory map of the 68000, there can be storage areas of data, or *operands* in many places. The operands can be in the form of bytes, words, and long words, in odd or even addresses. It could be in a table of numbers or stored as individual operands. In order to locate operands, it is useful to have many ways to address them. The 68000 has 14 addressing modes that fall under only six categories.

This discussion will cover the six general addressing modes; the six are called Inherent, Register, Immediate, Absolute, Indirect, and Relative. They are similar to the addressing modes of the 6800, with the addition of the Indirect mode.

You'll notice that in the discussion of the op codes and operands in the 6800, we used hex numbers in the instruction set rather than mnemonics. Mnemonics are needed when assembly language is used to describe the hex code numbers. Assembly language is the realm of the programmer. Technicians usually do not need assembly language to work on the hardware; you'll probably prefer using the hex codes. In fact, binary is ideal for tests, but most microcomputers cannot accept binary directly. Therefore, you'll end up coding your tiny binary test programs into hex, and installing the hex into the machines.

With only 256 possible byte-sized op codes, byte-sized data bus and memory locations, and only a few MPU registers, hex can be used without undue hardship. However, in 16-bit computers with a possible 64,000 word-sized op codes of four hex characters each, 16-bit data buses and memory locations, and multiple 32-bit MPU registers, hex numbers are very unwieldy. The mnemonics of the instruction set with its appropriate addressing mode is easier to use. In this discussion, we will use mnemonics rather than the hex numbers. The resulting assembly language has to be installed in the computer with an assembler. The assembler will take care of the massive job of generating the hex/binary version of the op code the computer uses.

## Inherent

The *Inherent addressing* mode is an automatic one. The location of the operand is implied in the mnemonic. For example, there is an op code called jump. the mnemonic is JMP. When executed, the jump instruction always loads the program counter with the jump address. The program counter is always implied as the register where the address is destined to be loaded. The program counter is called the *destination* register of the jump load instruction. The program counter, although never mentioned by name, is inherent in the instruction JMP (Table 14-1).

## Register

The next addressing mode is like Inherent, except the name of the destination is mentioned. It is called *Register addressing*. In the MPU, the registers all have their own MPU addresses. These addresses are not located on the memory map, only inside the MPU.

There is a general instruction in the 68000 called *MOVE*. It is a powerful instruction that is described in detail later in this chapter. One of the MOVE instructions can move data from one MPU register to another. For instance, the assembly language instruction MOVE D7, D6 will move the contents of data register D7 to register D6 (Fig. 14-8).

Table 14-1. Implied Addressing Mode.

| Mnemonic | Some Implied Instructions | Implied Register |
|---|---|---|
| BRA | Branch always | Program counter |
| JMP | Jump | Program counter |
| JSR | Jump to subroutine | Program counter stack pointer |
| MOVE CCR | Move condition codes | Condition code register |
| RTE | Return from exception | Program counter stack pointer condition code register |

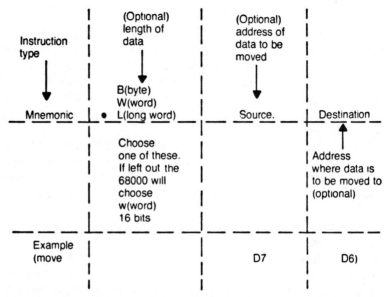

Fig. 14-8. One line of the 16-bit assembly language format can accommodate both the source and destination address codes.

This is a Register addressing mode. The register D7 is called the *source* address. It is specified with 16 bits. The register D6 is the destination address. It is also specified with its own 16 bits. The instruction moves the data contents from source to destination.

The instruction MOVE is also specified with 16 bits. The 16 bits in the instruction contains both the exact nature of the operation and the type of addressing mode.

## Absolute

The next mode is called *Absolute addressing*. This can be compared to the Direct and Extended modes used in the 6800. The operand address is specified directly and absolutely found after the instruction. For example, the mnemonic MOVE can be followed with the source and destination addresses, $FF23,D4. This says to move the contents of hex FF23 to data register D4.

## Immediate

The next addressing mode is almost exactly the same as the 6800 Immediate addressing mode. It is also called *Immediate*. It works like this. Suppose an instruction line to be executed is MOVE #9,D1. The MPU interprets the symbol # as the Immediate mode of addressing. This means the number immediately following the symbol is the operand. The location of the operand is the memory location in the program immediately following the location of the binary bits that specify the # symbol. The MPU, according to the instruction, moves the 9 from the program location to data register D1.

## Indirect

The next category is *Indirect*. In this case, the addressing after the mnemonic is not the address of the operand. It is the address of an address where the operand is found.

With this addressing mode, the indirect address is enclosed in parenthesis. The address in the parenthesis is the address of the address of the operand. An example is an instruction like MOVE (A3),D4. The contents of register A3 is 200. The contents of address 200 in the memory map is 32F. Here is what happens when the instruction MOVE (A3),D4 is executed (Fig. 14-9).

The MPU goes to its address register A3 as a source address. The MPU sees the parenthesis and knows that the contents of A3 is not the operand, but is instead the address of the operand. It finds the address 200 there. The MPU then knows that the 200 is its source address. It goes to 200 and finds the number 32F there. That is the operand.

Once the source address is located indirectly, the MPU moves the contents 32F into the destination address, data register D4.

This Indirect addressing mode has a number of variations. While they are essential to the programmer, as a technician, you can get by with only a brief overview of the variations. If you ever get into a particular situation where you must use this addressing mode, you can learn the variation in detail at that time.

*Indirect addressing with predecrement* or *postincrement* is one pair of variations. Predecrement means that the address register is decremented before its contents are used as the effective address. Postincrement means that the address register is incremented after the contents are used as the address.

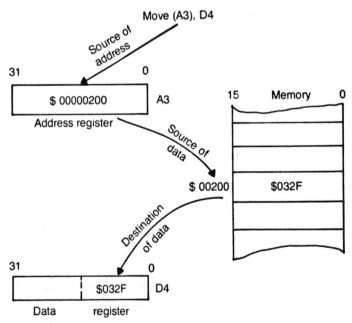

Fig. 14-9. The parentheses around A3 tells the assembler that this source address contains an address of the data that is needed.

For instance, to keep predecrementing address register A3, the assembly code – (A3) is used. To keep postincrementing the address register A3, the code (A3) + is used. Preincrementing and postdecrementing is especially valuable when the program has to loop through a program section that is numbered in sequence. It automatically performs the MOVE operation on all the addresses in order. It works on bytes, words, and long words.

There are a number of other variations the Indirect address mode uses. Most of them become very complex, and are not needed by the technician except in isolated cases. If you are curious, you can study 68000 assembly language for more details.

## Relative

The last general category of addressing is *Relative addressing* modes. Like the 6800, the Relative addressing mode refers to the program counter. There are two variations of the technique. One simply adds an offset to the value of the program counter. The second adds an offset plus another value found in one of the address or data registers.

The addressing mode changes the address in the program counter to one above or below the address of the current instruction being run. The main difference between the Relative mode and the others is that there is no destination operand in the instruction. The source address is specified, but the destination location for the data in the source location is not given.

There is no destination for the data. The source operand is the beginning of a program to be run. The offset from the program counter is the address of a piece of position-independent code relative to the main program being run. Position-independent code can be a subroutine in RAM or a program in ROM. The nice part of position-independent code is the location of the code can be anywhere that is convenient on the memory map. It can be used with any combination of other programs. This might not appear significant to the new technician, but a programmer finds the position-independent capability of Relative addressing very convenient.

## INSTRUCTION MNEMONICS

The 16-bit instruction set programs are best written in assembly language. Since the instructions are defined in 16 bits and 16 bits have 64 K possible combinations, there can really be more than 64,000 individual hex op codes. Each code specifies an operation, the size of the data to be handled, plus the addressing mode to locate the operands in storage.

The layout of the assembly language in bits is in full 16-bit words. The instruction format starts off with the mnemonic and the size of the data to be handled. Not all the instructions handle data, but those that do receive a B, W, or L for byte, word, or long word after the mnemonic. This part of the instruction line is contained in the first 16 bits of the line. A period (.) is placed between the mnemonic and the data length initial. If no length is specified, the 68000 assumes a 16-bit word is in the works.

The next set of 16 bits provide the data source. If the data source is in the Immediate addressing mode, the bits are the data itself. Otherwise, the bits are the source address of the data. The remaining sets of 16 bits on the line are the destination addresses of the data. There is a comma (,) between the source and destination addresses of the data.

The op code and modes are specified in one word. The operands, Immediate mode, source address, and destination address are either one or two words each. An assembly language line can occupy one to ten words in memory. A one-word line could be one of the Inherent addressing mode instructions. A five-word line could have two word source and destination addresses.

When you write an instruction, you must first find the mnemonic to do the job. Next, figure out the data size. These are contained in the first part of the line. Decide on one of the 14 addressing modes that will locate the operands. Then work out the address of the operand to be moved. Lastly, decide where the results of the operation should be located. A second addressing mode is decided on in many operations. When data is moved, however, any mode can be used. These decisions are contained in the last part of the line.

The op codes in the 68000 are defined in 16 bits. This is deliberate. One of the benefits is that instructions can always be started on even-byte addresses. The 68000 works fastest with 16-bit quantities. The 16-bit even-odd unit is the basic unit of the computer. The fact that it can operate on 8-bit units is only a special feature.

The 68000 has 56 mnemonics (Table 14-2). This is less than the 6800, which uses 72. However, the mnemonics are only code for part of the general instruction. The 16 bits that specify the operation also contain information on data size, addressing mode, and other tidbits. There are three data sizes and 14 possible addressing modes. Each mnemonic is multiplied by the factors that apply to them. One instruction mnemonic can produce one of many binary bit possibilities.

## Data Movement Instructions

The most amazing mnemonic is MOVE, with its variations (Table 14-2, Mnemonic # 1). The 68000 has streamlined its data movement mnemonics into MOVE. There are no LOAD, STORE, stack pointer PUSH and PULL, or I/O instructions. They are all variations of MOVE. In addition, moving data in the 68000 is much freer of restrictions than in older MPUs. Binary data can be moved from almost any place in the environs of the digital circuits to anywhere else in the digital circuits.

MOVE comes in three general versions. One is *MOVE* itself, which replaces the LOAD and STORE instructions used in 8-bit computers. Second is *MOVEM*. MOVEM is a change of mnemonic for the stack pointer instructions of PUSH, PULL, and POP used on smaller MPUs. *MOVEP* is a mnemonic reserved for use on peripheral I/O type chips in the memory map.

The straight MOVE mnemonic has tremendous power when coupled with the many addressing modes. It can copy bytes, words, or long words between most any registers in the MPU or memory map. The data contents of registers can be copied not only between MPU registers and memory, but also from a memory location directly to another memory location. There are ten addressing modes that locate the source address and seven modes that find the destination address.

MOVEM is used to save MPU registers when a subroutine must be called or an interrupt must be serviced by the MPU. During the change from sequential addressing

**Table 14-2. 68000 Assembly Language Mnemonics.**

| | Mnemonic | Meaning |
|---|---|---|
| #1 | MOVE<br>MOVEM<br>MOVEP | Move<br>Move multiple registers<br>Move peripheral data |
| #2 | EXG<br>SWAP | Exchange registers<br>Swap data register values |
| #3 | LEA<br>PEA | Load effective address<br>Push effective address |
| #4 | ADD<br>ABCE<br>SUB<br>SBCD, NBCP<br>MULS<br>MULU<br>DIVS<br>DIVU<br>CMP<br>CLR<br>NEG<br>TST, TAS<br>EXT | Add<br>Add decimal with extend<br>Subtract<br>Subtract decimal with extend<br>Signed multiply<br>Unsigned multiply<br>Signed divide<br>Unsigned divide<br>Compare<br>Clear operand<br>Negate<br>Test, test and set operand<br>Sign extend |
| #5 | AND<br>OR<br>EXCLUSIVE OR<br>NOT | Logical AND<br>Logical OR<br>Exclusive OR<br>One's complement |
| #6 | ASR<br>ASL<br>LSR<br>LSL<br>ROR<br>ROL<br>ROXR<br>ROXL | Arithmetic shift right<br>Arithmetic shift left<br>Logical shift right<br>Logical shift left<br>Rotate right without extend<br>Rotate left without extend<br>Rotate right with extend<br>Rotate left with extend |
| #7 | BTST<br>BSET<br>BCLR<br>BCHG | Bit test<br>Bit test and set<br>Bit test and clear<br>Bit test and change |
| #8 | Unconditional<br>BRA<br>BSR<br>JMP<br>JSR<br>Conditional<br>ALL BRANCH<br>Conditionals, 14<br>  Conditions | <br>Branch always<br>Branch to subroutine<br>Jump<br>Jump to subroutine<br>Scc set conditionally<br>Bcc branch conditionally<br>DBcc decrement & branch<br> |
| #9 | RTR<br>RTS | Return & restore condition code<br>Return from subroutine |

Table 14-2. Continued.

| #10 | TRAP<br>TRAPV | Trap<br>Trap on overflow |
|---|---|---|
| #11 | Privileged<br>STOP<br>RESET<br>RTE | Stop<br>Reset external devices<br>Return from exception |
| #12 | LINK<br>UNLK | Link stack<br>Unlink |
| | CHK | Check register against bounds |
| | NOP | No operation |

to the subroutine or interrupt, the MPU register contents have to be saved. The MOVEM instruction transfers any or all of the 16 address and data registers to a stack place in memory. The register contents can be saved there safely until the MPU is ready to resume the main program after the subroutine or interrupt is over.

MOVEP is needed in a new way. There are no similar instructions in the 8-bit computer. The MOVEP instruction is needed to make the 16-bit computer compatible in certain ways with the earlier 8-bit types.

Since the 8-bit MPU has had such a wide and popular acceptance, there are many 8-bit peripherals that have been developed, perfected, and are readily available. The designers of the 68000 figured that, if these 8-bit devices could be easily used by the 68000, many uses for the 68000 would be immediately available. The Move Peripheral or MOVEP instruction was created to allow the 8-bit periphreals to be used by the 68000.

It was shown earlier how two 8-bit PIAs were connected in parallel to the 16-bit data bus, one PIA to lines D15-D8 and the other one to D7-D0. In the memory map where the PIAs are addressed, all D15-D8 bits are at an even address and D7-D0 bits are an odd address.

Suppose you want to use one of the PIAs, the one connected to data bus lines D15-D8. In order to load memory in preparation of the use, the data in the 32-bit registers in the MPU must be all placed into even addresses. Otherwise, the data bus will not be able to transfer data from memory to the peripheral over the correct data lines.

The MOVEP instruction lets you take the data in an MPU 32-bit register, break it up into four-byte pieces and transfer it to four even addresses in memory. The even addresses are connected to data lines D15-D8 which are also connected to the desired PIA of the parallel pair.

Besides the MOVE type instructions there are a pair of mnemonics that swap data inside the MPU from one register to another (Table 14-2, Mnemonic #2). The exchanges can be made between any of the address and data registers. One of the instructions is called *EXG*, which exchanges entire registers. The second is called *SWAP*, which is able to swap only the high order or low order 16 bits.

## Effective Addresses

Another pair of instructions, *LEA* and *PEA*, deal with *effective addresses* (Table 14-2, Mnemonic #3). The effective address is the final computed address where the MPU finds or stores the actual data or operand it uses. The effective address can be simple or difficult to find. When the Immediate addressing mode is used, the EA is simple. The operand is found in the memory location immediately following the location in the program the instruction came from.

The EA is hard to figure out when the Indirect addressing mode is used. The EA is found by first going to an address specified by the program line. The contents of that address is itself an address. The MPU then goes to that second address. That is the residence of the operand. That address is the effective address.

LEA loads the effective address into an address register rather than the contents of the effective address. PEA pushes the effective address onto the stack rather than the contents of the address. These two instructions are valuable to programmers while they're writing machine language programs. They are interesting to technicians.

The various data movement instructions are used about 70 percent of the time a program is being run. The other types of instructions have to split up the remaining program time.

## Computation Instructions

While moving data around from place to place in the digital world of the computer takes up most of the program line, the actual computing is accomplished with the arithmetic and logic instructions.

The 68000 is able to do the arithmetic operations listed on Table 14-2, Mnemonic # 4. It can add (ADD), subtract (SUB), multiply (MULS, MULU), divide (DIVS, DIVU), and compare (CMP) a pair of operands. It can also clear (CLR), negate (NEG), test (TST), and sign extend (EXT). The instructions are quite like the 6800 comparable instructions and the accompanying table shows the differences.

The logic instructions are AND, OR, Exclusive OR, and NOT. They are written with source and destination addresses that are logically combined. If you want to logically affect a register with a constant, you can use ANDI, ORI, and XORI (Table 14-2, Mnemonic #5). This is the Immediate mode. The constant can be installed in the program line as the source operand. An important use of the I mode is to set or clear individual flag bits in the Condition Code register.

The 68000 has instructions for arithmetic shift right (ASR), arithmetic shift left (ASL), logic shift right (LSR), and logic shift left (LSL) (Table 14-2, Mnemonic #6). The ASR mnemonic causes the least significant bit to be placed in the X and C flag positions. The MS bit remains intact and a copy of the MOS bit is installed next to the MS bit.

The other three shift operations install the bit that is pushed out of the shifted register into the X or C flag position. The empty bit in the register, due to the shift, is filled with a 0.

The rotate instructions are rotate right (ROR) and rotate left (ROL). Rotation shifts the bits around so the end bit that loses its place in the register is installed in the other end. In addition, the bit is copied into the C flag. If you want a copy of that rotating bit in the X flag too, *ROXR* or *ROXL* is used instead of ROR or ROL.

In the 68000, the programmer has strong bit-testing capabilities. Specifically, it does this for him. First, the test instruction can target a bit in a memory location or MPU register. Next, it is able to place a copy of the target bit into the Z flag. Finally, the instruction can make a decision on the test result and perform an operation.

For example, a single bit is often the off-on switch of a machine. With control of the bit, the MPU can tell if the machine is off or on and take appropriate action. The programmer writes the appropriate action into the program. The decision to take the action is determined by the bit tests.

The mnemonics for the tests are bit test (BTST), bit set (BSET), bit test and clear (BCLR), and bit test and change (BCHG) (Table 14-2, Mnemonic #7). With these tests, individual bits can be tested to see if they are high or low. Then, according to their logical state, they can be set, cleared, or both (toggled). This provides control over the devices or programs the bit will affect.

## Address Manipulation

The data movement instructions get the data into the right registers at the right time so it can be processed. The computation instructions process the data. The program runs smoothly, since the MPU is built to automatically start at the first address in the program and run the program lines in sequence. However, the sequential processing of address locations is not enough to accomplish satisfactory results. The time comes in programs when the next address in the row will not do the job. The MPU must branch or jump to some other location in the memory map for the next instruction (Table 14-2, Mnemonic #8).

Branch and jump instructions look the same at first glance. They are not. One important difference is the type of code that each will produce. When a branch instruction is written, position-independent code is produced. Jump instructions result in transferring program control to absolute addresses. A second difference between them is the word *if*. Branch instructions will perform if one of the flags is set or cleared in a specified way. Branch instructions will not perform if the designated flag is not affected. This makes branch instructions conditional. Except for Branch Always and Branch to Subroutine, they will only work if certain flag conditions are met. Jump instructions are unconditional. They always perform as written. They can use any of the addressing modes to locate the destination address in the program line.

Both types of instructions fit into the same instruction category: program address manipulators. All they do is change the program run from executing automatically address by sequential address to some other specified arrangement.

Branch instructions do this by adding an offset to the program counter. The offset is a signed 8- or 16-bit number that is in the program followed by the branch instruction. When the MPU receives the instruction, it checks the flags to see if the flag condition is met. If the flag condition is not met, the MPU ignores the offset and proceeds to the next instruction. However, when the flag condition is met, the MPU adds the offset to the program counter. The resultant PC value becomes the next location to be addressed. The automatic sequential addressing is altered.

Since the offset is signed, it is either a + number or a − number. A + offset makes the branch advance in a forward way. A − number causes a backward branch. If the offset is an 8-bit number, the offset is restricted to the 256 combinations of the byte. The sign bit causes the 256 possibilities to be from $-128$ to $+127$. The branch can be up to 128 addresses backward or 127 addresses forward.

When the offset is a 16-bit signed number, the range of addresses the branch can locate is $-32,768$ to $+32,767$.

The offset added to the program counter is said to produce an address *relative to* the value in the program counter. The effective address can be made anywhere in the memory map according to the PC value. The offset is absolute but not the effective address. This is position-independent code that is so convenient for the programmer.

The jump instruction has absolute addresses and is unconditional. The address for the jump is contained in the instruction line. When the MPU receives the jump instruction, it changes the program counter to the address following the instruction. The new absolute address goes out on the address bus and the normal sequential addressing is jumped to the new memory location.

The branch–jump address manipulation instructions are shown in two tables. One table shows the unconditional instructions and the other the flag conditional instructions. There are only four unconditional instructions. Branch Always and Jump are both unconditional. They differ only in the way they affect the program counter. Branch uses an offset added to the PC and jump changes the PC entirely. This limits the branch instruction to $-32,768$ and $+32,767$. Jump has no numerical limit and can address the entire memory map.

Branch to Subroutine and Jump to Subroutine are also both unconditional. The branch instruction has the same limiting offset, while the jump instruction is not so encumbered.

The change of address to a subroutine needs another instruction once the subroutine is run. This is a Return instruction, which changes the address back to the main program. There are two Return instructions, RTS and RTR (Table 14-2, Mnemonic #9). They are *Return from Subroutine* and *Return and Restore condition*.

When you branch or jump to a subroutine, the call saves the return address on the stack. When the subroutine has been completed, RTS could be the last instruction in the routine. This instruction restores the stacked value back into the program counter. The program counter places the value onto the address bus and the MPU starts processing the main program again.

Often it is necessary to save the value of the flags in the MPU too. In those cases, RTR will be the last subroutine instruction. It will restore all the flag states that were stored in the stack, at the beginning of the subroutine, back into the Condition Code register.

## OTHER 68000 INSTRUCTIONS

The 68000 has two general modes. One is called the User mode and the other is the Supervisor. All the instructions discussed so far operate in the User mode. The 68000 spends most of its time in the User mode. The User mode is considered the lower level of operation and the Supervisor the higher level. Bit 13 of the Condition Code register controls which mode the 68000 will operate in.

The Supervisor mode is a protection level. It sets up electronic walls around the operating system and its resources so defects in a user program can't cause troubles.

Switching from mode to mode is handled in the following way.

If the computer is in the Supervisor mode and needs to run a User program, the operating system changes the state of bit 13 in the CCR. The system goes into the User mode and begins program execution.

The program runs and stays out of the Supervisor level unless a TRAP instruction occurs (Table 14-2, Mnemonic #10). There are 16 TRAP instructions, and all are triggered if a troublesome User program happening occurs. Some of these happenings are an attempt to divide by zero, an attempt to execute an illegal instruction or a bad address. The MPU is forced to save the contents of the PC and CCR on the Supervisor stack.

The MPU then goes to a vector table where it gets an address that is loaded into the program counter. The address is the start of a special routine to service the TRAP. Each type of TRAP has its own service routine that corrects the problem and returns the program counter back to the original program.

The 68000 has a few privileged instructions which can be used only when the 68000 is in the Supervisor mode—most of them would cause trouble in the User mode (Table 14-2, Mnemonic #11). The first such instruction is STOP. The instruction stops execution but also loads the CCR with a 16-bit value. The change in the CCR bits would throw off the program operation in the User mode.

Another privileged instruction is RESET. This instruction resets the entire computing environment except for the MPU itself. This must be done in the Supervisor mode.

RTE is a privilege instruction, *Return from Exception*. What constitutes an exception? Any eventuality that stops the MPU from running its normal instructions. For example, traps are exceptions. Interrupts are exceptions. At the end of the exception the RTE takes the values of the program counter and Condition Code register from the stack and restores them to their registers in the MPU.

*MOVE USP* means access the user stack pointer. During activity in the Supervisor mode the supervisor stack pointer that shares register address A7 is used. There are periods when the User Stack Pointer register must be initialized for activity. MOVE USP will access the user stack pointer.

The instructions MOVE AND, OR, and XOR, when used to move a 16-bit value to the CCR or combine a value with the CCR, become privilege instructions. This is because the high order bits in the CCR, the S/U bit 13, the Trace mode bit 15, and the three interrupt bits 8, 9, and 10, all must be under the control of the operating system and not the user program.

You'll find it helpful to understand how the application of instruction bits into the data pin of the MPU forces the MPU to perform tasks such as data movement, data processing, and addressing changes. During sophisticated maintenance and servicing, you'll be called upon to test voltages, logic states, and oscilloscope patterns, and you must be able to detect incorrect readings. You can't do that unless you know what the correct readings were in the first place.

Quite often, you are required to write little test programs to see if the MPU and memory map is responding to various instructions. These programs are usually written in machine or assembly language. This requires some expertise in working with the Instruction Set of the computer. Three will be more about these techniques in Chapters 19-23.

# 15
# Digital to Analog and Back

We live in an analog world. The steering wheel of your car rotates smoothly through 360 degrees. The temperature in your neighborhood changes from hot to cold and back on a sliding scale. Voltages start at zero EMF and increase in a linear manner. Currents begin at zero when electrons are at rest and increase as the electron flow becomes heavier and heavier.

Inside the computer, however, a digital world exists. The MPU operates with the residents of the memory map in terms of highs and lows. The starts and fits of highs and lows are measured in a high voltage like +5 V and a low voltage of 0 V. There are only three states of existence in the digital world: high, low, and no state. There are no in-betweens.

When you work in the analog world, you must think and test in terms of voltage, current, and analog waveforms. When you test in the digital world, the square wave, with its highs, lows, and absence, is your indicator.

The world inside the computer and the outside world we live in are connected through electronic circuits. They convert digital to analog when digital bits leave the ports of the I/O circuits, or convert analog to digital when the voltages need to enter the confines of the computer. Let's examine this further.

## EQUIVALENT VALUES

In order to convert D/A or A/D, some relationship must be established between the two different types of values. One of the common conversions in computers is relating digital bits to a varying voltage. If we take a voltage that is varying smoothly between 0 and 7 V, an oscilloscope picture will show a sine wave with a peak to peak reading of 7 V. How can this be changed to digital bits?

The first question: how many spots on the sine wave do we want to represent in a bit pattern? A bit pattern can be coded into a single voltage. We decide to produce bit patterns for each voltage, 0, 1, 2, 3, 4, 5, 6, and 7 V. This means if we store eight bit patterns in memory, they could represent the eight voltages the sine wave is traversing as it varies between 0 and 7 V. The bit patterns could be stored in sequential locations in RAM. The RAM would then output them one at a time or in serial fashion. A digital-to-analog circuit would then convert each bit pattern to its coded voltage level. The voltage levels could then be merged together in a filtering network. This would be a varying voltage and displayed on the oscilloscope face.

If the output chip was a PIA three port pins would be needed to carry the eight bit patterns (Fig. 15-1). The relationship between the analog voltages and the digital voltages follows.

| Analog Voltages | Digital Voltages | | |
|:---:|:---:|:---:|:---:|
| Volts | Bit 1 | Bit 2 | Bit 3 |
| 0 | LOW | LOW | LOW |
| 1 | LOW | LOW | HIGH |
| 2 | LOW | HIGH | LOW |
| 3 | LOW | HIGH | HIGH |
| 4 | HIGH | LOW | LOW |
| 5 | HIGH | LOW | HIGH |
| 6 | HIGH | HIGH | LOW |
| 7 | HIGH | HIGH | HIGH |

The three ports will output the bit patterns in the serial order the oscilloscope needs to display the 0 to 7 V pattern (Fig. 15-2). The bit patterns are combined and filtered in a voltage divider network in the D/A circuit. The serial output of the D/A circuit is the desired shape when seen on the oscilloscope. A similar, more complex actual circuit is discussed later in this chapter.

The circuit just shown will convert bit patterns to a specific voltage. What about converting a voltage to a bit or bits? It is a little trickier.

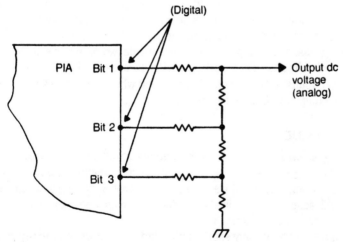

Fig. 15-1. Three digital bits can produce eight analog voltage levels.

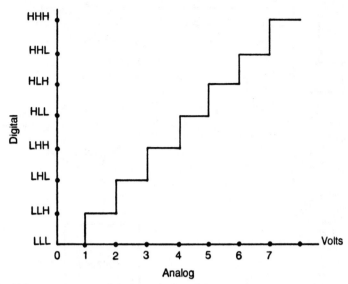

Fig. 15-2. The D/A waveshape produced by plotting digital logic states versus voltage resembles a stairstep.

You need a counter chip, a D/A circuit like the one just discussed, and a comparator chip covered earlier in the book (Fig. 15-3). The comparator chip has two inputs designated + *and* −. The − input is connected to the analog voltage input. The + input comes from the D/A circuit. The comparator chip will output a low as long as the comparator circuit does not respond. The comparator circuit will not fire unless the two inputs are correct. When the comparator conducts, its output goes high.

The counter circuit, driven by a clock, keeps counting. Its three outputs into the D/A converter keep changing states from LLL to HHH. The D/A outputs single analog voltage results into + of the comparator. The voltage levels could be 0 to 7. This changing voltage is coupled into + of the comparator.

Meanwhile, down at the − input, the analog voltage is present. When the analog voltage at − matches the changing analog voltage at +, the comparator output goes positive. At that time, the counter chip holds the correct bit pattern for the voltage.

A coupling circuit from the output of the comparator is connected back to the counter. When the comparator goes positive, the circuit enables the counter to output the digital combination of bits to an I/O input to the computer. The analog voltage has been converted to three bits that is the code of the voltage.

## STAIRSTEP VOLTAGE CIRCUITS

The stairstep voltage waveform can be seen with the ordinary service oscilloscope in digital-analog circuits (Fig. 15-2). *Stairstep* is the name of the waveshape formed by voltage over a cycle or so of circuit activity. It's usually generated by the computer for its D/A converters.

The stairstep shape shows each level of voltage as it relates to its corresponding bit pattern. As the clock pulses the counter circuit, the count goes on. In the previous cir-

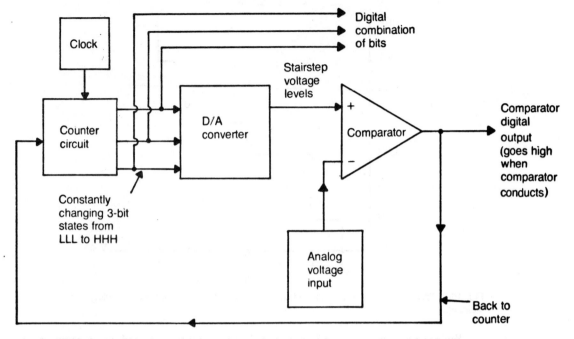

Fig. 15-3. By comparing a stairstep voltage with an analog voltage, a comparator will go high when they match up. A feedback line causes the counter to output the analog to digital conversion.

cuit there were three output pins from the counter chip. Each output pin came from a single flip-flop. The flip-flops respond to the clock. They count in binary from 000 to 111, over and over again. The three output pins send the count to the D/A converter.

The converter has eight possible voltage output levels due to a set of resistors acting as a voltage divider. The resistor network is able to take the high and low voltages produced by the binary counting and blend them into one voltage output. The network varies the voltage from a low of near 0 V to a high of 7 V. The voltage output corresponds to the bit patterns in the count. The stairstep is the oscilloscope picture of the output analog voltages.

## D/A OUTPUT

A typical use of the D/A output circuit is to transfer audio generated in the digital circuits to an analog audio output circuit. The sound can then be heard from a speaker.

The TRS-80 Color Computer provides a good example. One of its PIAs has a D/A circuit connected to six port pins, PA2-PA7 (Fig. 15-4). Six bits encompass 64-bit positions. This means the six bit sound is able to produce 64 different voltage level steps. The six bits are connected to six buffers on a chip.

The buffers output their voltages to a voltage divider network with a filter capacitor. According to the six bit pattern, one voltage is generated, a slightly different voltage for each of the 64 combinations of the Hs and Ls. The single voltage is then sent to the audio output circuits and eventually to the speaker. Each different six bit pattern produces a different tone. If a lot of bit patterns are emitted serially, a number of tones are produced

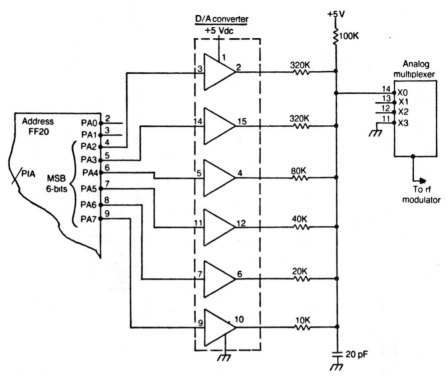

Fig. 15-4. This 6-bit D/A circuit is used for sound effects.

one after the other. Simple tunes can be stored in memory and played through the circuits.

## D/A INPUTS

The same D/A circuit can be used to convert the analog positions of a joystick into the digital environment (Fig. 15-5). The six pins for this operation, PA2-PA7, output the results of an internal counter. The counter starts at LLLLLL and counts to HHHHHH. It keeps counting over and over again.

This constant count is converted in the buffer-filtered voltage divider to a single output voltage for each of the 64 separate counts. The serial output voltages are sent to — of a comparator chip.

The joystick itself is composed of a pair of potentiometers. They are connected to +5 V, and they output a portion of the +5 V. The amount of voltage is determined by the position of the stick. When the voltage level of the joystick corresponds with the quickly-changing voltage level of the internal counter and D/A output, the comparator goes positive.

This H from the comparator is coupled back to the joystick comparison input at another PIA pin, PA7. The H enables the counter. It outputs the six bits it had when fired upon by the H from the comparator. The six bits is the digital pattern that corresponds with the analog voltage. The six bits thus adjusts the display according to the physical position of the joystick.

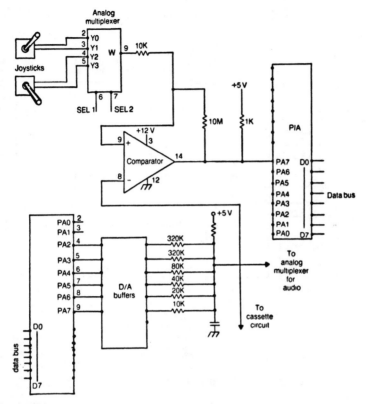

Fig. 15-5. The 6-bit D/A circuit, when connected to a comparator circuit, becomes part of a joystick A/D circuit.

## CASSETTE D/A INTERFACE

The cassette recorder is an analog device. It is able to record audio frequencies on magnetic tape. Once the audio frequency is on the tape, the player is able to output a magnetic copy of the tape audio contents. A computer finds the cassette recorder very useful.

In order for the computer to record its intelligence onto magnetic tape, it must change the binary 1s and 0s into audio frequencies. A standard has been arranged to code the logic states into audio. Typical use has been to code a 1 into one cycle of 2400 Hz, and a 0 into one cycle of 1200 Hz. The program tape is a carefully arranged line of 2400 and 1200 Hz audio tones. The audio tones are produced in a D/A converter and output to the cassette recorder. The cassette player is then able to output the tones into a computer where an A/D arrangement converts the tones back into binary states.

The output circuit starts with a D/A circuit like the one used for the audio and joystick interfaces. When a program is to be sent to tape from inside the computer, the internal software codes the 1s and 0s in RAM into a form that will produce the 2400 and 1200 Hz outputs. For example, a 1 is changed to 10. The 0 is converted to 1100. These codes for the original states are then output to the D/A converter through the PIA ports.

After buffering and passage through the filtered voltage divider, the 10 produces one cycle of 2400 Hz. After its journey through the D/A circuit, the 1100 becomes a 1200 Hz cycle. The output of the D/A circuit is a continuous parade of carefully arranged audio tones. The tones are attenuated and cleaned up by a few resistors and capacitors. Then they proceed directly to the input of the cassette recorder where they are placed on tape.

When the cassette player sends the program back into the computer, an A/D circuit arrangement is used. This circuit needs a comparator, but does not use a D/A circuit in order to get the comparator to output highs and lows. A typical circuit follows is shown Fig. 15-6.

The input tones are first filtered to get any RF picked up by the cable out of the line. The filter is a .02 μF capacitor to ground. In parallel with capacitor is a 220 ohm resistor that matches the cassette output to the input circuit.

The heart of the circuit is a diode and a comparator. The + input of the comparator is biased at 1 V with a tap between 56 K and a 15 K resistor. They are dividing +5 V to ground. The − input is also biased at 1 V by a tap between another 56 K and three other resistors, 6.8 K, 8.2 K and the 220 ohm mentioned before. The four resistors are also dividing +5 V to ground.

The comparator is an open collector and connected to +5 V through a 1 K pullup resistor. The output is connected directly to a single PIA pin. This is the digital connection to the PIA from the comparator. The output of the comparator will be serial highs and lows. The input of the comparator is the audio cycles. The comparator is actually the A/D converter.

The comparator is aided by the diode attached in the input line. As the cycles occur, the following happens. When the cycle is negative, the diode turns on. The current drain lowers the 1 V bias to about a half volt. With the other input still at 1 V, the comparator output is switched to a high.

When the input line goes positive, the diode turns off peaking the pulse larger than 1 V. This switches the comparator to a low.

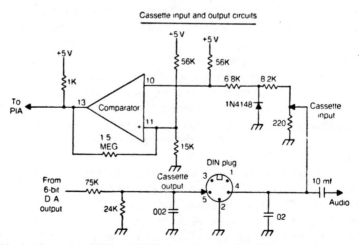

Fig. 15-6. This circuit converts 2400 and 1200 Hz audio tones into highs and lows.

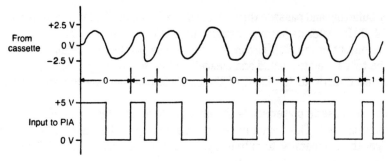

Fig. 15-7. The wide cycles contain two highs and two lows, HHLL. The narrow cycles contain one high and one low, HL. The HHLL is code for 0. The HL is code for a 1.

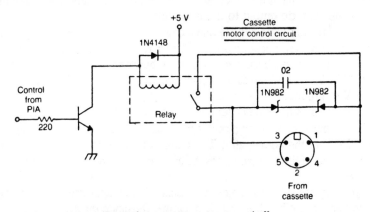

Fig. 15-8. One PIA control line will turn the cassette motor on and off.

If you examine the cassette format waveshapes, the cassette output cycles are varying between ±2.5 V (Fig. 15-7). The negative analog voltages produce digital highs and the positive cycle swings produce digital lows. One low and one high is a digital cycle which is the code for a digital state. The faster cycles are 1s and the slower cycles are 0s. The highs and lows are input at the PIA pin. They are then decoded and sent to RAM.

The cassette interface must have an off/on switch. This is handled by one of the control lines from the PIA; specifically, bit 3 of the Control register. This is the CA2 output. CA2 goes high if the IRQA1 flag in bit 7 of the register gets set to a 1. The MPU has control over this action, so a program line or a direct instruction can set IRQA1 bit 7.

When CA2 is high, the off/on circuit to the cassette is on. If CA2 is low, then the cassette is off. This is because CA2 is connected directly from PIA pin 39 to an npn switching transistor. The high turns the npn on and a low cuts it off (Fig. 15-8).

When the npn is on, the relay coil in the collector circuit is activated and the relay contact is closed. The diode across the relay coil is there to smooth out any voltage surges that might occur in the transistor as the switch is closed. The other two diodes shunt the relay contacts for the same reason. The parallel capacitor across the twin diodes filters out any RF that has developed during switching.

The motor is connected across the diode and runs when the transistor is conducting. The off/on switch itself is not a true D/A circuit. It is shown since it is part of the overall cassette activity.

# 16
# Digital to Digital Interfacing

Quite often the computer does not have to interface with the analog world. It might only have to connect to a printer, disk operating system, or another computer. In these cases, it is not necessary to change the digital bits to analog values. All that is needed is to interface the digital bits to the other digital device. While the methodology is simpler, there are problems the interface must be able to overcome.

One of the problems is that the external device could be operating at a different speed than the computer. Another concern has to do with voltage levels. The receiving device could require a voltage at a different level than the transmitting device (the computer) is putting out.

Other differences that complicate the transfer of data are current outputs instead of voltages, different word lengths, special control signals, and different data formats. The interface must be able to match the transmitter to the receiver or else the transfer will not take place properly.

## RS-232C INTERFACE

The RS-232C connection circuit is a good example of how two digital devices are hooked together. The RS-232 general interface uses one line to transmit serial data and another line to receive. There can be a number of other lines that all perform control work. The control signals are specifically designed to operate with specific data.

*RS-232C* is a four pin connection circuit. Counting clockwise from the keyway, pin 1 is called CD (Fig. 16-1). It is an input line and brings the status of the external device into the computer. The status is either high or low and means different things for different circuits.

Pin 2 is also an input; it's called *RS232IN*. It operates with CD to bring signals into the computer. Pin 3 is ground and is used as a zero voltage reference point.

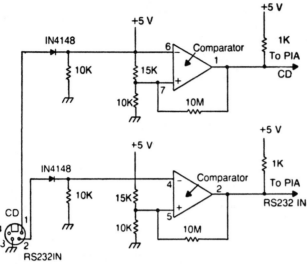

Fig. 16-1. The input to this typical RS-232 circuit enters pins 1 and 2. Pin 1 receives a control signal and pin 2 receives serial data.

Pin 4 is *RS232 OUT* (Fig. 16-2). The computer serial signal leaves through this exit. For instance, if a printer is being fed ASCII, it leaves the computer here.

### Inputs

A typical RS-232C configuration is shown in Fig. 16-1. The circuit is able to receive digital signals from an external device through pin 2, RS-232 IN. The status of the external device enters through pin 1, CD.

The RS-232C signal that enters pins 2 and 1 have highs with a voltage of +3 V or more, and lows with a voltage of −3 V or less. The voltages between +3 and −3 are meaningless. They will not be received.

At the PIA pins called RS232 IN and CD, a high is any voltage at or above +2.6. A low is defined as voltages below +0.8. The circuit between pins 2 and 1 of the input plug and PIA pins RS232 IN and CD must rearrange the input voltage highs and lows to PIA compatible highs and lows. Two identical circuits convert the two inputs.

The two inputs first encounter two diodes. The inputs connect to the anodes of the diodes. The cathodes of the diodes connect to the − input pins of comparators. The diodes prevent any negative signals from being applied to the comparators. However, when a positive signal is input the diodes conduct.

The comparators are referenced at the + input by a connection between two resistors, 15 K and 10 K, tied from +5 V to ground. The reference voltage is 2 V. Therefore, the comparator will turn on only if a voltage greater than +2.6 V enters the − input. If +3 V enters, the comparator turns on and outputs a high to the serial input at the PIA. If − V enters, the comparator is off and a low is applied to the PIA. Thus the input +3 V highs and the −3 V lows are converted to +2.6 V highs and 0.8 V lows.

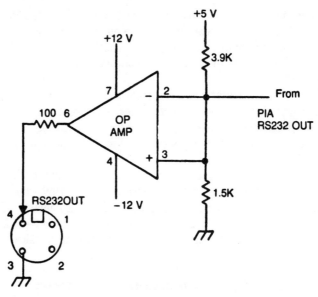

Fig. 16-2. The computer can output serial data through pin 4 to a peripheral like a printer.

The comparator outputs are open collector, and a pullup resistor is needed to the +5 V supply. The bypass 10 M resistor is there to prevent the comparators from going into oscillation.

### Outputs

At pin 4 of the plug, the computer is able to output binary bits (Fig. 16-2). At the plug, the highs are +3 V and the lows are −3 V. When the highs and lows leave the PIA pin in serial fashion, they are at +2.6 V and +0.8 V levels. The circuit in between converts the voltage levels to the correct I/O values.

The PIA serial output is sent to an *op amp*. The op amp has its + input connected between two resistors, 3.9 K and 1.5 K, that drop +5 V to ground. This references the op amp at +1.4 V.

The op amp has two power supply voltages, +12 V and −12 V. As the highs and lows of +2.6 V and +0.8 V enter the − input of the op amp, the output voltage is forced to swing towards +12 V when +2.6 V enters and towards − 12 V when the +0.8 enters. The resultant output voltage becomes, more than +3 V as a high and less than −3 V as a low. This is coupled to the external device through a 100 ohm resistor and pin 4 of the plug, which meets the requirements of the RS-232C general standard.

### CARTRIDGE I/O

All computers have an MPU and a memory map full of storage places and I/O ports. An important I/O circuit is the cartridge connector. It permits the same computer to be a lot of different computers. The cartridge connector can allow the same computer to be a dedicated word processor, a spreadsheet, a filing cabinet, an assembler, or an arcade game. By changing the cartridge, the computer's ROM brain is transplanted.

Besides containing ROMs, a cartridge can hold an I/O chip like a PIA and become a multiple I/O port. In addition, the cartridge can be equipped with RAM and increase the storage capacity of the computer; it can even have another MPU. The cartridge connector is an interface that enables the computer to do many, many jobs. Let's examine the connection in detail.

The TRS-80 Color Computer has a 40-pin cartridge connector (Table 16-1). The 40 pins are connected to signals all over the computer. The first thing that usually happens when a cartridge is inserted into the connector is that pins 7 and 8 of the connector are shorted together. Most of the cartridges designed for this computer have pins 7 and 8 tied together.

In the computer, pin 7 is connected to the clock signal Qin on the MPU. Pin 8 is connected to CB1 or a PIA. The Q signal generates an interrupt from the PIA as CB1 causes the flag in bit 7 of the Control register to be set. This causes *FIRQ on the PIA to go low. When *FIRQ goes low, the MPU is interrupted and forces the MPU to get a vector address from the top of memory. The vector is then installed in the program

**Table 16-1. ROM Cartridge Connector Signals.**

| Pin Numbers | Signal Name | Job Description | Origination Circuit |
|---|---|---|---|
| 19 ↓ 39 | A0 A15 | Address Bus | MPU |
| 10 ↓ 17 | D0 D7 | Data Bus | MPU |
| 6 7 | E Q | CLOCK | SAM |
| 32 | *CTS | ROM or I/O Select | Decoder Chip |
| 36 | *SCS | ROM or I/O Select | Decoder Chip |
| 40 | *SLENB | Disable Select | External |
| 3 4 5 | *HALT *NMI *RESET | Halts CPU NMI Interrupt Main Reset | External External |
| 8 | *CART | Cartridge Interrupt | External |
| 18 | R/*W | Read/Write | MPU |
| 35 | SND | Sound Input | External |
| 33,34 1 2 9 | Ground −12 V +12 V +5 V | Signal Ground −12 Volts, 100 mA +12 Volts, 300 mA +9 Volts, 300 mA | Power Supply |

counter. The vector is the start address of the cartridge. The MPU then begins addressing the cartridge in sequence. The cartridge at that point is in control of the computer.

A typical ROM cartridge contains 8 K of addresses. The actual address range of this cartridge is from hex C000 to DFFF. The ROM in the cartridge can contain an operating system as well as the program for a dedicated use. The computer becomes whatever the programs in the cartridge dictates.

A general-purpose cartridge with a peripheral interface chip on it has only a few addresses on it. The number of address lines need only be enough to address the chip and internal registers. The numbers of lines to external devices depend on the chip. Some chips have 16 external lines and others have 24.

The cartridge connector on this TRS-80 Color Computer has lines for all 16 address lines. That doesn't mean they all have to be used. The 16 address lines can handle a cartridge with up to 64 K addresses. This can take up the entire memory map of the 8-bit computer.

Pin 18 is connected to the R/*W line of the MPU. This line is needed if the cartridge has chips that require reading and writing. The MPU will read the cartridge when the line is high and write to the cartridge if the line is low. When the cartridge is a ROM, the write signal is not needed. (The ROM, remember, is a read only chip.) If the cartridge is a peripheral I/O chip or RAM then the write signal is required.

Pin 32, *CTS, is the cartridge select signal. It comes from the address bus through some circuitry. Whenever an address between hex C000 and DFFF (the cartridge-assigned addresses) is dialed up, *CTS goes active, which enables the cartridge.

There are a number of other pin connections to the cartridge interface that are useful and make the interface very flexible. First of all, there is a second I/O select called *SCS, spare select signal. It also comes from the addressing circuits. It indicates that the entire cartridge is not being addressed. Only the addresses between FF40 and FF5F are being used. Second, a signal called *SLENB attaches from the cartridge to the addressing circuit. When it goes low, it turns off the address decoder that is doing all the chip selecting. This gives the cartridge the power to turn off all the chips that are selected by this decoder.

Pin 5 of the cartridge is *RESET. When reset is needed in the computer the cartridge is reset at the same time. Pin 3 is *HALT. This gives the cartridge the power to halt the MPU. Pin 4 is *NMI. This lets the cartridge interrupt the MPU with a non-maskable interrupt in case of dire emergency like impending power failure. Lastly, there is a sound input at pin 35. It allows the cartridge to input audio generated on the cartridge directly into the computer's audio decoding circuits.

When the cartridge is plugged into the 40-pin connector the MPU sees it as part of the memory map. The MPU will address it and transfer data just like any ROM, RAM, or I/O on the map. It will perform step by step in the following way.

When eight bits in an address on the cartridge is to be read, a "load the accumulator from the address hex xxxx on the cartridge" instruction is executed. The *CTS signal goes active and the address bus contains the cartridge address bits that defines hex xxxx.

The R/*W line goes high for the read operation. The combination of the *CTS, the R/*W line and the constant pulsing of the E and Q clock signals readies the cartridg′

addresses for the read operation. The cartridge address places the eight bits of data onto the data bus. The falling edge of the clock pulse strobes the data into the MPU.

For a write operation the following steps occur. First a "store accumulator in the address hex xxxx on the cartridge" is executed.

*CTS goes active and the address hex xxxx is placed on the address bus. The R/*W line goes low. The MPU places the eight bits to be written on the data bus. The cartridge receives the *CTS and R/*W signals and prepares the address to receive the bits. The pulsing of the clock strobes the bits from the data bus into the cartridge address.

The cartridge connector can be very useful to the experienced computer technician. Practically all the signals used by the computer have lines into the connector. This gives you a convenient test entrance to the computer. The lines can be tested individually and collectively by various test probes and diagnostic programs.

## EXPANSION SLOTS

In the inexpensive 8-bit computers like the COMMODORE 64 and CoCo, a cartridge connector such as the one just covered is present. Besides plugging a ROM cartridge into these connectors, these large plugs provided a way to tap into the computer's insides and expand the usefulness. However, there is only one such large connector on these single print boards.

On the slightly more expensive Apple *IIe* machine the connector idea was taken a step further. Apple figured that a number of slots would be better than one. They installed seven such connectors on the print board as seen in Fig. 16-3. This changed the single board to a motherboard. Seven more circuits on printed board cards could be installed. Apple then came out with a line of cards that plugged into the seven slots.

Smaller manufacturers recognized opportunity and began creating all sorts of circuit cards that plugged into the Apple slots. This greatly expanded the usability of the Apple. Even though the Apple was using an 8-bit 6502 processor, these seven slots made the Apple *IIe* series of computers very popular.

Then IBM came out with their Personal Computer. It had five slots, Fig. 16-4. The PC is a bare bones computer that depends on the slots for all sorts of its features. For instance, in order to run most of the peripherals, you must use a card to provide the interface. There is one card that permits you to run a monochrome monitor (Fig. 16-5) and another card to operate a color monitor, (Fig. 16-6).

Figure 16-7 is the layout of an 8-bit expansion slot in an IBM or IBM PC compatible. The same sort of slot is found in the PC/XT. Standardization in these compatible machines is the name of the game. The cards are mass produced and there is a large demand for cards that use the standard. The PC/XT standard has an 8-bit data bus that the 8088-8086 processors can use.

When the PC/AT came out it had an 80286 processor. A 16-bit card standard was used. Smaller manufacturers immediately jumped on the bandwagon and mass produced 16-bit cards that mate with 16-bit data buses. The AT bus cards have become very popular. The fact that precise standards were set made the IBM PC/AT very popular in the business and school environment. A very large following is in existance and a lot of dollars are spent on the AT bus. It appeared that standardization was going to reign and simplify the computer field for all concerned.

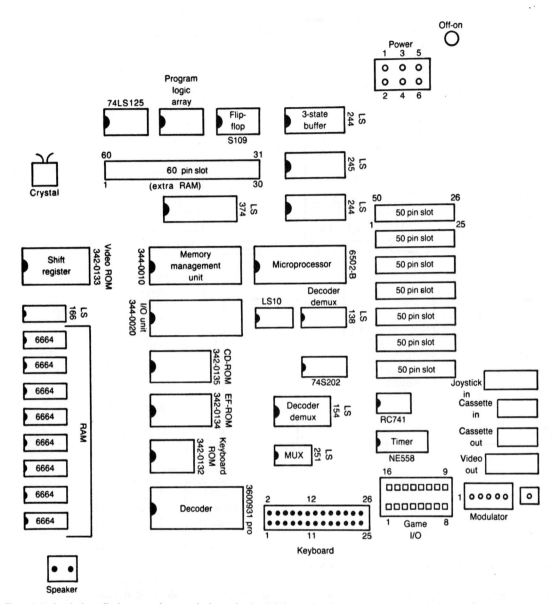

Fig. 16-3. Apple installed seven slots on their motherboard that printed circuit cards can be plugged into.

In 1987 IBM came out with its new line of computers, the PS/2 series. Standing atop the PS/2 line of computers are 32-bit machines that use the Intel 80386 processor. Compaq also came out with a 80386 machine. To everyones surprise, IBM deviated sharply from their AT standard bus systems and surfaced with a new bus called the Micro Channel Architecture, MCA to work with the 80386. The new slots were smaller and required a smaller sized card. The signals were changed around and appeared on different pins. Compaq though, did not follow IBM's lead. They stayed with the standard AT type bus.

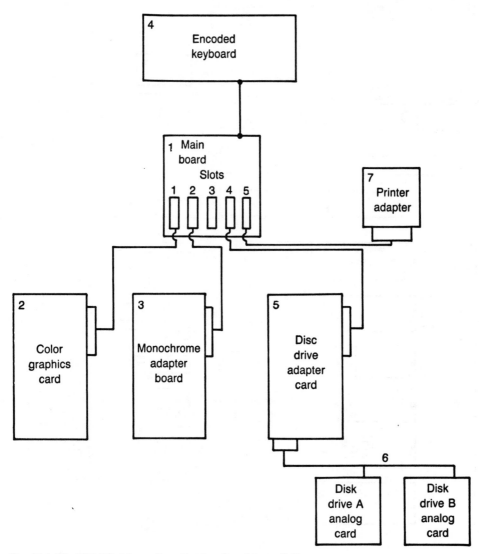

Fig. 16-4. The IBM PC style configuration has five slots available.

Meanwhile, a consortium of other manufacturers led by COMPAQ decided to stay with the popular AT bus too. Tandy and Dell decided to play both ends. They came out with both AT and MCA machines. As of right now standardization is muddled, and both the new MCA and the AT buses are being marketed. As a technician you must be aware of the different bus lines. Using the schematic of the machine you might be working on, you can handle the differences in size, pins, and signals.

## THE PC, THE AT AND THE MCA BUS SYSTEMS

The different bus systems are extensions of the internal bus lines in the processor being used. The original PC bus is an extension of the 8088 bus used in the PC. The

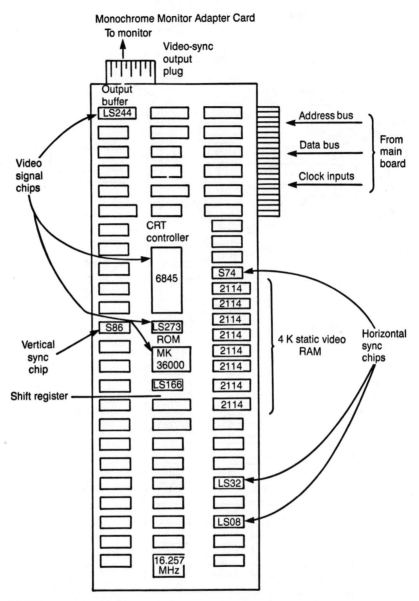

**Fig. 16-5.** This monochrome adapter card contains the video generator and output to drive a monitor.

8088 has eight data pins and the 8088 slot has eight data pins and is called an 8-bit slot. The AT bus originates in the 16-bit 80286 and accordingly has what is called 16-bit slots.

Along came the 32-bit 80386 processor. Compaq expanded the AT bus to 32-bits to accomodate the internal bus lines of the 80386. This made the expanded AT bus upwardly compatible with the 16-bit AT bus. IBM didn't follow suit. They came out with the new incompatible MCA bus. The MCA bus also originates in the 80386 but IBM

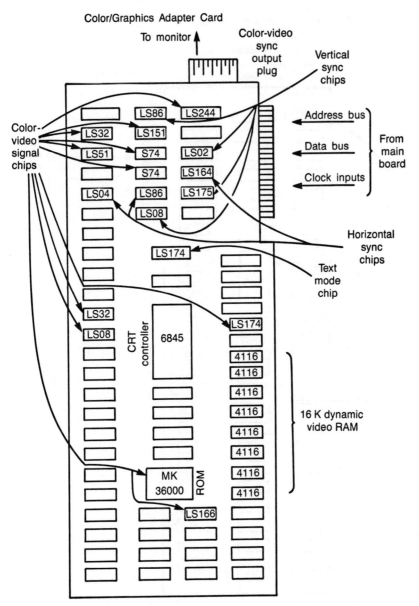

Fig. 16-6. The color adapter card contains the color video generator and output to drive a color monitor.

gave the slot a smaller size, different pin numbers, and changed the timing, signals, and voltages around. Figure 16-8 shows the difference in sizes between the AT and MCA cards that plug into the expansion slots.

The AT expanded bus slot has 24 address lines and 16 data lines. The MCA has 32 address lines and 32 data lines. The AT though uses 32-bit address and data lines connected internally to memory. That way they are able to use the same type of fast mem-

394

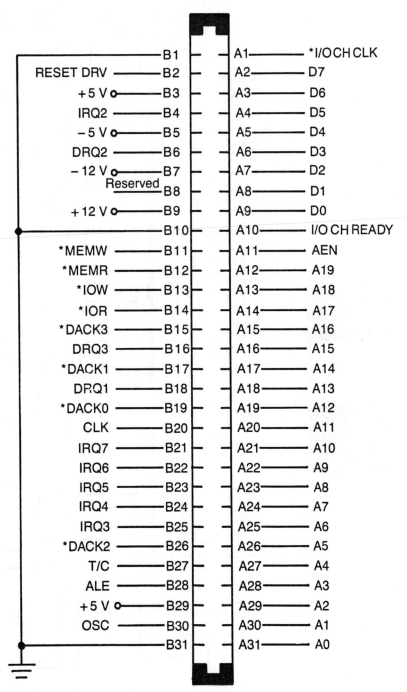

Fig. 16-7. The PC style slot connects to all of these circuit lines in the computer.

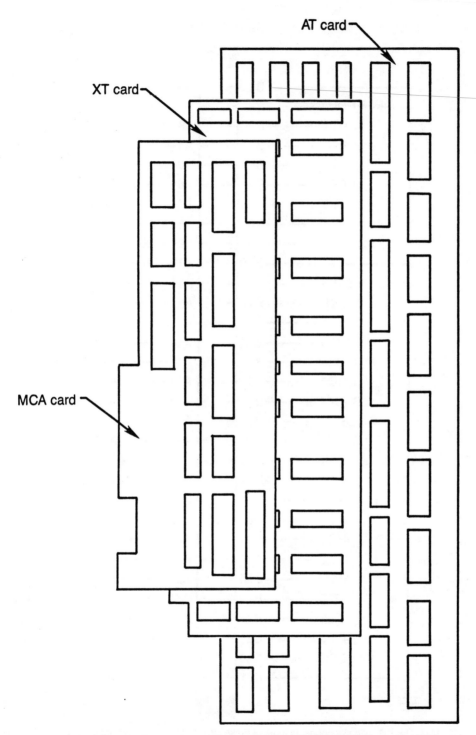

Fig. 16-8. Note the differences in size between typical AT, XT, and MCA cards. The newer MCA cards are appreciably smaller; which restricts the number of components it can hold.

**Table 16-2. Each Board in a Configuration Produces Its Own Symptoms of Trouble. By Analyzing the Symptom, the Defective Board Can Be Indicated. A Swap of the Board with a Known Good One Can Produce an Instant Repair.**

| Typical IBM PC Style Boards | Troubles Board Can Cause |
| --- | --- |
| Main Board | Dead Computer<br>Garbage |
| Color/Graphics Card | No Color or Poor Color<br>No Video<br>Garbage<br>Loss of Graphics<br>Cursor Missing<br>No Horizontal Sync<br>No Vertical Sync |
| Monochrome Adapter Card | No Video<br>Garbage<br>Loss of Graphics<br>Cursor Missing<br>No Horizontal Sync<br>No Vertical Sync |
| Keyboard Circuit Board | Wrong Character<br>Garbage |
| Disk Drive Adapter Card | Both Drives have Trouble<br>Reading or Writing |
| Disk Drive Analog Circuit Board | One Drive will not Read<br>or Write |

ory chips as the MCA does. The 80386 runs at fast speeds, for instance, 16, 20 or 25 MHz. When the expanded AT bus system is compared performancewise to the MCA, it turns out they are both about the same. At this time there does not appear to be any advantage to using one over the other. However, it is hinted that IBM has some features that it will unveil that will prove the MCA to be superior. Time will tell.

There are many programming and user pros and cons between the two 32-bit systems. One complication that could concern a technician working on the machine has to do with inserting and removing cards. On the AT bus when you want to insert and test a card, you simply insert the card and turn on the machine. Not so with the MCA bus.

After you install an MCA card you must then install a reference disk and put a configuration program into the machine that will set up the card for use. Then when you are finished with the card, you must configure the computer to forget the card. This process can get very complicated if there is a hardware defect in the card or machine that gets involved with the bus.

In the AT you can simply pull the card. If the trouble disappears, you had a bad card. Should the trouble stay the defect is in the computer. You can't do that with an MCA system defect. You must take into consideration configuring the machine both before and after you pull the card for the trouble isolation test.

Standardization is a trying problem for computer users, programmers, and manufacturers. It is less of a problem to technicians. As long as you comprehend the different standards that are out there with the aid of the manufacturers service information, one computer is pretty much the same as another.

# 17
# General Description
# of the 80286

The Intel family of processors, is used in about 40% of all the microcomputers in the world. Besides the fact that they are viable machines, giant computer maker IBM decided to use them in their microcomputers. IBM then set the standard for the PC line of computers. The PCs and their clones all sell and work well. The magic words are IBM-compatible.

In Chapter 13 the 8088-8086 processors were covered. In this chapter the 80286 is discussed. What happened to the 80186? Let's examine this interim processor that appeared between the 8088-8086 and the 80286 before we cover the 80286. These circuits are similar to those found in the 80286.

## A Look at the 80186

The 80186 does not look like an 8086. The 8086 chip is contained in a 40-pin DIP. The 80186 package, in contrast, has 68 pins. The chip is packaged as a square device in a surface mount socket as shown in Fig. 17-1. The 80186 chip contains a complete 8086 processor. The 8086 on the 80186 chip is complete and uses the same instruction set. The 80186 is a superset of the 8088-8086 instruction set. The 80186 has ten more instruction types. These additional instructions are used to handle the additional circuits the 80186 chip has on board.

The 80186 is upwardly compatible to the 8086 and the 8088. Whatever software can be run on the 8088-8086 can also be run on the 80186 without any changes necessary. If the 80186 is so similar to the 8086, what is the reason for the additional 28 pins?

The 80186 chip has a number of circuits that were not on the 8086. These circuits were in additional chips that were installed along with the 8086 in the PCs and clones. The 80186 is therefore a collection of 15 to 20 individual chips. The 8086 processor is only one of the group of chips.

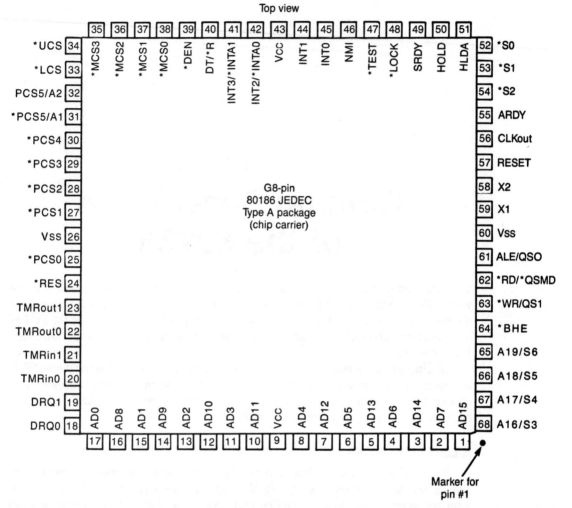

Fig. 17-1. The 80186 does not look like an 8086. It is packaged as a 68-pin square surface mount device. The package is called a Chip Carrier. Note that the pins are arranged around all four sides of the package, not on only two sides like the DIP.

The 80186 block diagram in Fig. 17-2 displays the different integrated circuits the chip contains. Besides the 8086 circuits, there is a clock generator, a programmable interrupt controller, programmable timers, a bus interface unit, chip select unit, and a programmable DMA unit.

The clock generator needs an external crystal to run. The clock comes in two versions, 8 and 6 MHz. When the 80186 is ordered the purchaser has the option to buy either one. The 6 MHz version is considered cost effective.

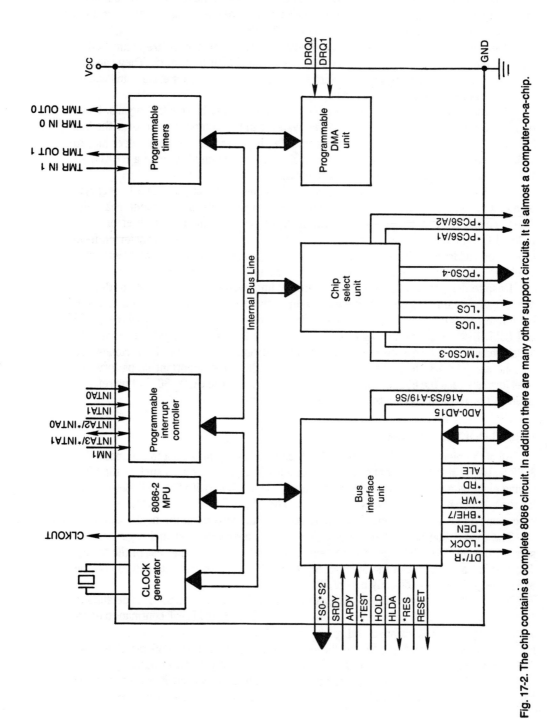

Fig. 17-2. The chip contains a complete 8086 circuit. In addition there are many other support circuits. It is almost a computer-on-a-chip.

401

The 8086 MPU section is souped up in comparison to the conventional 8086. It has twice the throughput as the regular 8086. The 8086 unit is aided by a programmable interrupt controller. Some of the additional instructions are used to get these circuits in use. There are five types of interrupts that can be utilized.

There are three 16-bit programmable timers. Two of the timers are connected to external pins. They can be used to count events in the computer system. They can also be used to generate waveforms. The third timer is not connected externally and can be used internally for coding and time delay operations.

The Bus Interface unit is a bus controller. It generates the bus control signals. It can be programmed to shut down and let other systems in the computer take over the bus lines. The chip select unit is also programmable. It generates the chip select bits to address the memory and peripherals. It can also be programmed to be in a READY or WAIT state. It is able to supply, among other things, A0 and A1 bits.

The 80186 DMA (direct memory controller) is able to directly address 1 megabyte of memory. The programmable DMA unit has two separate independent channels. These channels can transfer data between memory and I/O, memory to memory, and I/O to I/O. The data can be 8-bit bytes or 16-bit words. They can be transferred from even or odd addresses. Each channel has a 20-bit wide source or destination pointer that can be incremented or decremented by one or two after a data transfer.

Despite the fact that the 80186 was a greatly improved version of the 8086, the 186 never really became too popular. It was used in a few machines such as the Tandy 2000, but it never took off. One of the reasons for its non-use was the appearance of the 80286 and IBM. IBM made the 286 its processor of choice for its popular PC/AT series. As usual, many other manufacturers tooled up and introduced all sorts of AT clones and peripherals. The 286 took the architecture of the 186 a few important steps forward. Intel formally calls the 80186, the iAPX186 and the 80286, the iAPX286. Let us refer to them as the 186 and 286 for the rest of this discussion.

## FIRST LOOK AT THE 286

All of the members of the 8088-8086-186-286-386 family have a lot in common. The 8088 and 8086 are almost identical, except for a few design differences such as the 8088 having eight data pins and the 8086 with sixteen. The 186 is quite like the 8086 except for the additional support circuits on the chip. The 286 is like the 186 but takes micro-processing a few steps further. The 386 differences are covered in the next chapter.

The thread that binds them all together is their instruction set and registers that support the set. The 286 contains the same instruction set as all the rest of the family. The 286 has a super set of the 8088, 8086, and 186. Any program that can run on the 8088-8086 will also run directly on the 286.

In fact, when you first turn on a 286 computer, it comes up as an 8086. It defaults to an 8086. It runs all 8086 software immediately as if it is an 8086. It will continue to operate as an 8086 unless stopped and given special 286 instructions. There is only one major difference between the 286 in the 8086 mode and an actual 8086 machine. The 286 is much faster than the 8086. This speeds up processing to an astounding extent. Most of the time the increase in speed is a good feature. However, if you try running some game programs at the higher speed you won't be able to keep up with the activity.

| | | Clocks | | |
|---|---|---|---|---|
| Instruction | | 8088 | 8086 | 80286 |
| MOV | | 23 | 19 | 5 |
| MUL | | 144 | 140 | 24 |
| DIV | | 171 | 167 | 25 |
| ADD | | 31 | 23 | 5 |
| SUB | | 31 | 23 | 5 |

**Table 17-1. The 80286 has the Same Instruction Set as the 8088-8086 but Runs the Instructions with Less Clocks. This Makes the 286 Much Faster.**

While the 286 is designed to run with faster clock speeds, that isn't the main reason for the processing speedup. The design of the 286 has the processor executing instructions with less clock cycles. For example, in Table 17-1, a MOV instruction in an 8086 takes 19 clocks to be fully executed. The same MOV instruction in a 286 is completed in 5 clocks. A MUL (multiply) instruction in an 8086 takes 140 clocks. The MUL in the 286 only requires 24 clocks. All of the instructions right down the line need less clocks to execute in the 286 in contrast to the 8086. The 8088 requires even more clock cycles than the 8086, but the difference is not that great. The MOV in the 8088 needs 23 clocks. The MUL takes 144 clocks. Not too much difference between the 8086 and 8088. There is quite a difference when the 286 is run.

Besides the mode the 286 defaults to, called the Real Address Mode, it has a second mode called, the Protected Virtual Address Mode as seen in Fig. 17-3. The two modes are quite different. It's as if the 286 is two different processors on the same chip. In a way you could say the 286 is both an 8086 and a 286. The 286 has a complement of 150,000 transistors. The 8086 contains about 40,000. The 286 consists of the 40,000 8086 transistors plus another 110,000 that makes it two processors in one.

Note the two different modes deal expressly in addressing. They both execute code in much the same way except for addressing instructions. The addressing is where most of the differences lie. The Real Address Mode addresses one megabyte of physical memory with 20 address bits, A20-A0. The Protected Virtual Address Mode utilizes 24 address bits, A23-A0 (Fig. 17-4). It can address 16 megabytes of physical memory.

The instruction pointer register (Fig. 17-5) in the 286 is 32 bits wide, consisting of a 16-bit selector register and a 16-bit offset register. With some manipulation and some external support chips, the 32-bit register is able to address a billion bytes of address space for one task. This is, for all present practical purposes, an unlimited amount of addressing space. The programmer can use addresses to his heart's content without worrying about running out of space.

In the name, Protected Virtual Address Mode, the word Virtual conveys the following meaning. There are two kinds of address space. There is physical and virtual. Physical space describes addresses that are occupied by physical memory chips, for instance 4164s, the 64 K DRAM. Virtual space describes the addresses that the processor is able to access whether there are physical occupants or not. The 286 in Protected Virtual Address Mode supplies a billion bytes of virtual address space for one task.

If you tried to fill the billion byte space with 64 K DRAMs, it would take 131,072 of them. Obviously this is not practical. However, if you use memory such as hard disks, you could fill large sections of the billion byte space. The 286 in this mode is able to

## Operating Modes

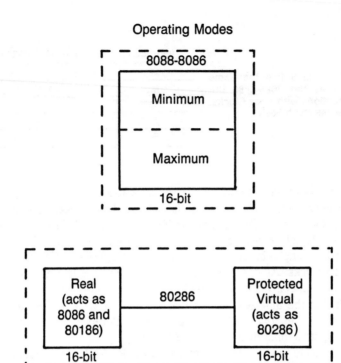

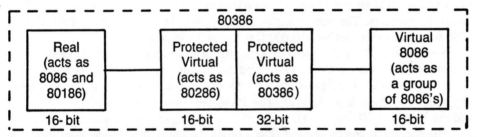

Fig. 17-3. The 8088-8086 processors can run in two modes, minimum and maximum. The 80286 also has two general modes. In Real mode it emulates an 8088-8086 or 80188-80186. In its Protected Virtual address mode it is in its natural state and operates as a 286. The 80386 is able to work in four modes. In Real mode it emulates the 8088-8086 or 80188-80186 also. Next it has a Protected Virtual mode that allows it to emulate a 286. Thirdly, it has its own native Protected Virtual mode where it acts as a 386. Finally it has a special Virtual 8086 mode. In this mode it can run a lot of 8086 programs at the same time.

manipulate addressing so that storage addresses on disks can become residents of the memory space. This type of data storage can then be addressed as if it is a form of RAM or ROM.

The word Protection in the name has to do with keeping the different features of the 286 from interfering with each other and crashing programs. There will be more detail on the Protection capability as multitasking and privilege levels are discussed next.

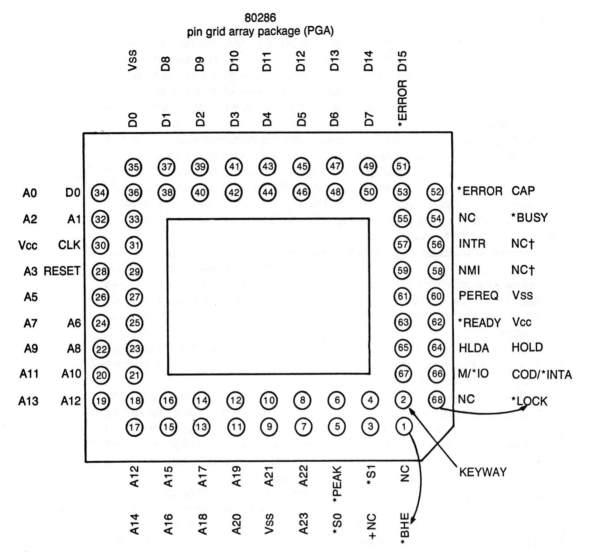

# 80286
## pin grid array package (PGA)

Fig. 17-4. The 286 is packaged in a 68-pin Pin Grid Array, PGA. Note there are 24 address pins, A23-A0. It can address 16 megabytes of physical memory.

+ Do not connect!

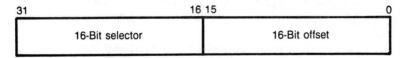

| 31 | 16 | 15 | 0 |
|---|---|---|---|
| 16-Bit selector | | 16-Bit offset | |

Fig. 17-5. The instruction pointer register in the 286 is 32-bits wide, 32-bits can address a billion bytes.

## Multitasking

While the 8086 mode typically is used by a single person with one machine, the 286 protected mode has capabilities to make it useful as a member of a network of computers. This capability allows the 286 machine to act as if it is a mini and not a microcomputer. In the protected mode, the 286 is able to run a number of programs at the same time without interfering with each other. Each program is called a "task" and the process is called multitasking.

Multitasking does not necessarily mean that a number of computers linked together has to be the case. A single user can also be able to enjoy the ability. For example, with multitasking, a businessman preparing a report can have the processor handle a number of tasks at the same time. Each task will act completely on its own and have it own register contents and virtual addressing space. The report might require three separate tasks. They could be editing text, have a spelling checker in operation, and loading the text into a spooler for temporary storage.

The three programs can be placed into the single billion byte addressing space. The application programs can be installed into RAM, onto disks, or even tape. The three applications are completely independent of each other. Each program believes it has its own billion byte space, even though they are all residing in the same gigabyte area. They have no contact between them. There is so much memory that they can remain completely apart.

Even though the application programs are unaware of each other, they all share the operating system that is running the show. The OS is also in the gigabyte memory space apart from the application programs.

As the user types his report the text editor is in charge and uses the general purpose registers to work with the editor program. When a word is misspelled, the spelling checker takes over, stores the contents of the registers, takes over the registers, and corrects the spelling error. At that time the spooler could take over and store the text that had been composed. These three tasks appear to go on simultaneously. The overall job proceeds and the three separate tasks keep performing.

Multitasking is defined in the following way. During multitasking operations, at any given instant in time, one task is running. That task is called the *current task*. At that instant, the current task has control of the general purpose 286 registers and is using the virtual memory space where its application programs are installed. The current task is also using the operating system programs.

Typically, the billion byte addressing space is arranged so that half the billion addresses are used for application programs, and the other half for operating system programs as in Fig. 17-6. Suppose there are three application programs and the operating system program in the memory space. The three application programs are in separate sections of their half-billion byte space. The operating system program is in the other half-billion space. The three applications are completely isolated from each other but they all share in using the operating system.

The operating system's half of the virtual address space is called the *Global Region*. The application program's half is called the *Local Region*. In the local area there can be many tasks. However, only one task can be active at one time. It is the current task.

Multitasking is the ability of the 286 to be able to operate a number of tasks one at a time. The 286 is also able to switch from task to task at breathtaking speed; so fast that

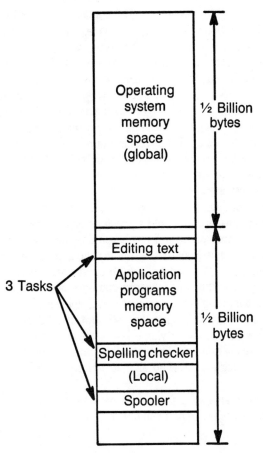

Fig. 17-6. Typically the billion byte virtual addressing space is divided in two. The lower addresses contain the application programs while the upper addresses hold the operating system programs.

the tasks appear to be running simultaneously. The switching is easy to perform. You can switch from one task to another with a special JMP or CALL instruction.

## PRIVILEGE LEVELS

The last section discussed multitasking used the Protected Virtual Address Mode of the 286. The billion byte addressing space the 286 is able to access has been described. It was shown how a number of tasks can be installed, completely independent of each other in the virtual address space. Besides being independent, each task is given another capability called Protection. The protection is afforded by means of Privilege Levels.

The protection given to each task is accomplished by arranging the code and data in memory at different privilege levels. The 286 is able to set up four privilege levels. What sort of privileges are given to the different levels?

At the lowest level, the 286 stops the program that is running from executing certain instructions that might cause troubles in the program run. At the lowest level the 286 conducts the users application programs. The application program might have in its repertoire some I/O instructions to peripheral devices. These instructions could possibly cause the program to crash, because the I/O activity is geared to operate at slower frequencies. These I/O instructions should be run at a different level, not at the lowest level. If the level specified for the I/O instructions is not the lowest one, the 286 will not permit the instructions to be executed in the lowest privilege level. The program run is thus protected from running these dangerous instructions by the privilege levels.

The 286 has four privilege levels. The lowest one, as mentioned, is the one that application programs are run at. The levels are numbered 0, 1, 2, and 3 as in Fig. 17-7. The least privileged or the lowest level is 3. 2 is more privileged, 1 even more, and 0 the most privileged. 3 is reserved for the user's application program running. 2, 1, and 0 usually handle the operating systems'.

When a programmer writes his program he usually divides the total program into modules. He then assigns each module a privilege level. The 286 will then watch over the program run. The more privileged levels running the operating system have practically no restrictions. The low level that is running the application program does not have full reign. The application program will be stopped from performing I/O instructions directly, from reading or writing to addresses that have been assigned a higher level, and from contacting the operating system except under special conditions.

These four levels of privilege give the 286 a lot of value that is appreciated by the programmer. As a technician the privilege levels are only of passing interest. The four levels need not be used in many applications. You can use one level. When only one level is used it must be the highest level so all instructions will be able to be executed and none restricted.

The privilege levels also keep a watchful eye on the tasks. If an attempt is made to switch tasks, but the switch is to be from one level to another, the 286 might not permit

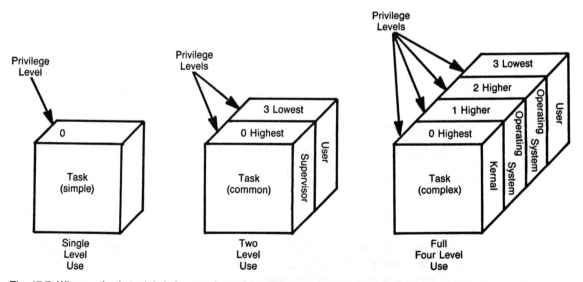

Fig. 17-7. When a simple task is being run, it can be set to operate at the 0 privilege level. If the task is not simple but common, it can be set to operate with two privilege levels of protection. Should a complex task be operating, all four protection levels can be brought into play.

it. Uncontrolled task switching could easily crash a program run. The 286 will allow a task switch to a level with the same privilege level or lower. If the switch is to a higher level the 286 will stop it.

To switch from one level to another, instructions similar to a task switch are used. These are variations of the same JMP and CALL instructions. These instructions can be executed directly as long as the destination address is allowed according to the rule of privilege levels.

When a level switch is not permitted since the destination is on a high level, caution is required. It probably means there is a fault in the program as written. However, there are ways to gain entry to higher privilege levels. The way to do it is through CALL Gates which are in the programmers province. If you want to be able to program the 286 in machine language there are a number of good books on the market or you can purchase Intel's programmers manual.

To summarize the last section, the 286 acts as two separate processors. It is a complete 8086 while in its Real Address Mode, but performs two and a half times faster than an actual 8086 at the same clock frequency. It is also a 286 in its Protected Virtual Address Mode. As a 286 it is able to perform multitasking with each task protected with four privilege levels. It is important for you as a technician to know about the special capabilities of this chip that is so advanced. Let's take a look at its registers and internal bus lines.

## THE PROGRAMMERS REGISTERS

It was mentioned in the last section that the billion byte memory space is divided in half. One half is used to store the code and data to run application programs. The other half is used by the operating system programs. The layout of the registers in the 286 follows suit. There are separate sets of registers. One set is assigned for use by the application programmer. The other set of registers is given exclusively to the operating system programmer. When the 286 is operating in Real Address Mode as an 8086, the operating system registers are ignored. However, when the 286 is running in Protected Mode, then all the registers are used by the OS programmer. The application programmer still does not use the OS registers even in Protected Mode.

There are fourteen registers that the applications programmer uses. They are the same ones found in the 8086. There are five more registers that OS programmers have need for (Fig. 17-8). While the application programmer uses his fourteen registers the OS programmer needs to use all nineteen of them.

The OS programmer with his five system registers sets up the machine for the applications to be run. The OS registers handle the multitasking and billion byte memory space that is available in Protected Mode. The first step the OS registers need is to be set up so the machine is put into Protected Mode. Remember, the 286 comes on either from a cold start or after a reset, in the Real Mode. It will stay in Real Mode and operate as a super fast 8086 unless the Protected Mode is activated.

The first step to get into Protected Mode is to initialize the Global Descriptor Table Register (GDTR) and the Interrupt Descriptor Table Register (IDTR), shown in Fig. 17-8. The next step is to initialize the Machine Status Word register (MSW). In the

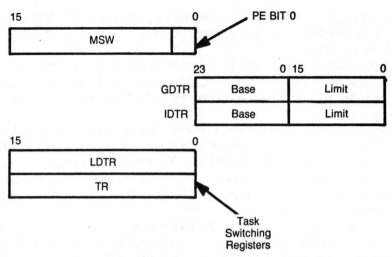

Fig. 17-8. Besides the fourteen application registers, the Operating System programmer needs five more registers for his work.

MSW is the Protection Enable bit (PE). The computer goes directly into Protected Mode when this bit is set.

With the computer in the Protected Mode the 286 begins running a task. If the task is all that is desired, the machine is off and running. If you want the 286 to run some other tasks too, then you operate the last two registers so you can effect task switching. You initialize the Task Register (TR) and the Local Descriptor Table Register (LDTR).

For most task executions, that's it. The actual details of the contents needed in these registers can be found in the 286 programming book. The 286 is arranged for Protected Mode operation. Once set, these registers need not, in most cases, be touched again. The fourteen application registers though, are not as easy to handle.

Note that the fourteen application registers have the same layout as the fourteen in an actual 8086. There are eight general purpose registers that do accumulator type duty. They are there mainly to store and manipulate the operands for the arithmetic and logic work. They are all 16-bit types. For the most part they are interchangeable. They are capable of handling either 8-bit or 16-bit pieces of data.

Five of the general purpose registers are able to store both address and data bits. As in Fig. 17-9, they are the BX, SI, DI, BP, and SP. When they perform addressing chores, the BX register usually will be given an address offset to hold that will point to a segment of data. A segment is a group of registers in the memory space that can hold either a collection of data or a collection of addresses. These segments are then called data segments or address segments. The two Index registers, source index, SI or destination index, DI, are also used to hold an offset that points to a particular data segment in memory.

The stack pointer register, SP, and the base pointer, BP are usually holding address offsets (displacements), that point to the top of a stack in memory.

Whenever these registers are not needed to hold an address offset, they can be used to hold data, both logic and arithmetic, that is to be processed by the 286. As a rule

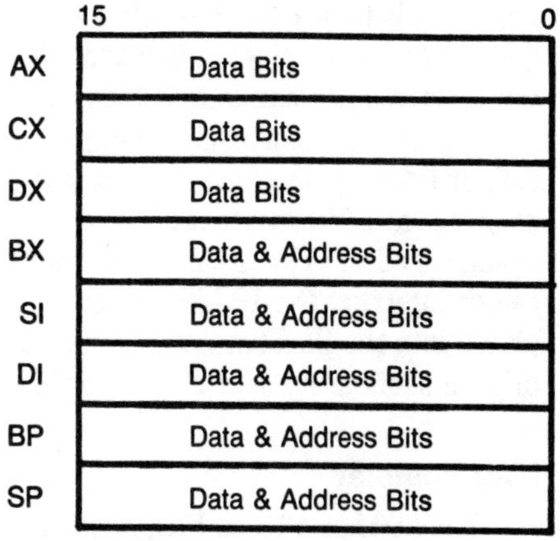

| | |
|---|---|
| AX | Data Bits |
| CX | Data Bits |
| DX | Data Bits |
| BX | Data & Address Bits |
| SI | Data & Address Bits |
| DI | Data & Address Bits |
| BP | Data & Address Bits |
| SP | Data & Address Bits |

Fig. 17-9. Typically three general purpose registers are used to hold data bits. The other five can contain both data and address bits.

though, the following usually applies. The BX, SP, and BP registers are assigned to do addressing duties, such as holding address offsets. The AX, DX, CX, and both index registers, SI and DI are used for logic and arithmetic data holding.

## Segment Registers

The general purpose registers are eight of the fourteen application registers. Next in line are four segment registers. As mentioned, a segment is a group of addresses in memory that contain either a batch of data or addresses. One segment in the 286 can be as large as 64 K bytes. The 16 bits in a segment register are able to address that many bytes.

There are four segment registers, code, CS, stack, SS, data, DS, and extra, ES, just like the ones in the 8086. Any address calculation that takes place in the 286 involves one of these segment registers. To put it another way, all of the code and data in memory is positioned relative to a segment address.

These segment pointer registers give the 286 a quality called relocatability. This is a valuable programming feature. What this means is, complete segments can be moved around in memory and get change of addresses easily. The new address is then easily applied by simply changing the segment register's base address. This is known as *position independence.*

This position independence of memory segments is available in both Real or Protected modes. The segmentation though is especially needed in Protected Mode. For multitasking with protection levels, segments must be used. Without segmenting the code and data in memory, there would be no distinct separation between the code and data and they would mix at certain times causing the program being run to crash. There would also be no distinction between physical memory and memory areas occupied by other storage means, such as disks. The virtual billion byte memory area would be a treacherous place for accessing activity.

## The Instruction Pointer

The Instruction Pointer acts somewhat like a program counter found in other processors. It will hold a 16-bit address offset that points to the instruction in a code segment that is to be executed. After the instruction is fetched and executed the IP is incremented to the next instruction address in sequence. The incrementation could be one or more bytes according to how many bytes there were in memory for the instruction.

The IP will keep on incrementing automatically unless an instruction such as a jump, call, or interrupt instruction is the one executed. Then the IP obeys the instruction and changes its address accordingly or takes the correct action. A jump simply causes a change of address but a call or interrupt causes further activity. During the execution of a call or interrupt the IP bits are pushed onto the stack. Then the change of address is placed into the IP. That way the stacked IP contents can be used to return the IP to its original sequencing once the call or interrupt is taken care of.

### Flag Register

The 286 has a 16-bit Flag register. These individual bits, each an independent register of its own, consist of six flags that affect logic and arithmetic activities, and five control flags, as shown in Fig. 17-10.

The Carry, Parity, Auxiliary Carry, Zero, Sign, and Overflow Flag are used to let the 286 know what happened as a result of the last logic or arithmetic operation. According to the results of the operation, a conditional branch decision is made.

The control flags are also affected by logic and arithmetic calculations. These controls consist of allowing single stepping of instructions for test purposes, permitting an interrupt to take place, giving the privilege level to execute I/O activities, determines whether a task is a nested type, and provides string instruction information on whether to increment or decrement through memory.

### ABOUT THE 80287 COPROCESSOR

Near the 286 in a computer, you will probably find a socket for an 80287 companion processor for the 286. the socket might or might not be filled. The 287 coprocessor is made to be a part of the 286 but installed into a different package. They are wired together and act as one unit. They are programmed as one even though they are two.

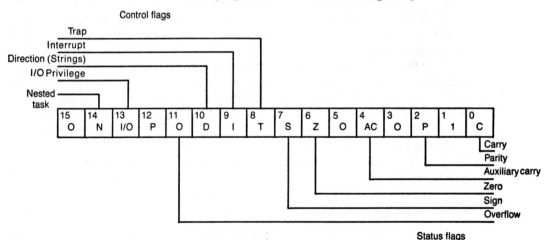

Fig. 17-10. The flag register of the 286 has six status flag bits and five control flag bits.

The 287 is a numeric processor. It is an upgrade of the 8087 that is used as a coprocessor with the 8086. There is also an 80387 that is used with the 80386 covered in the next chapter. These coprocessors are specifically designed to give the 8086, 286, and 386 additional accuracy when calculating large numbers.

There are eight general purpose registers in the 287 that act like the general purpose registers in the 286. The only thing is, the 287 registers are 80 bits wide. They can handle very large numeric values without having to round them off as the 286 must do by itself. These registers can perform register to register, memory to register, and register to memory arithmetic operations.

These registers only handle arithmetic. They do not perform any address calculations. All addressing is performed only in the 286. The 287 is restricted to holding operands for arithmetic. Its 80-bit register width simply provides more accuracy.

The eight 80-bit registers act as a form of special stack. The registers cannot be addressed individually. Only the top of the stack can be accessed. The numeric instructions contact the 287 registers in relation to the top register in the stack. There is a Flag Register in the 287. There is a bit called *Top of Stack*, TOS. The Flag Register in the 287 is controlled by the operating system, not by the application program. The TOS could indicate any one of the eight registers as the top of the stack. The TOS changes during the operations. As instructions are executed, those instructions that load or pop the stack cause the TOS to change the register designated as the top to move up or down according to the particular instruction.

A load instruction is a stack push. The load instruction decrements the TOS by one, and then pushes the value to be processed into the new TOS register. A store instruction is a stack pop. The store instruction pops the contents of the TOS register and then increments the TOS by one. Should you try to pop an empty stack, the 287 will tell the 286 that there is an error.

The 287 operates along with its host 286 in both Real and Protected Mode. There are two bits in the Machine Status Word register (MSW) in the 286 that deal with the 287. If you recall bit 0 of the MSW determined whether the machine should be in Real or Protected mode. When the PE bit is set, Protected Mode is enabled. Otherwise, the Real Mode is in charge. The next highest bit in that same MSW register is called Math Present (MP). The bit following that is Emulate Math (EM). These two bits arrange things for the 287 whether it is in its socket or not.

In Real Mode these bits are clear and are not included in the 287 activity. The 287 operates alone or in conjunction with the 286 as an 8086/8087 combination. In Protected Mode however, the operating system tests for the presence of the 287 in its socket. If the 287 is present then the Math Present bit is to be set. This enables the processors to operate as a 286/287 pair. This improves numeric performance.

If the 287 is not in its designated socket, the operating system notes the condition. In that event, the Emulate Math bit is set and the Math Present bit is left in a clear state. When the EM bit is set, the 286 knows it must act on its own without the help of the 287. The 286 then emulates the action of a 286/287 pair as best as it can. It uses software as a substitute for the 287 hardware. This is usually quite satisfactory. Incidentally, do not set both the MP and EM bits at the same time. This combination is used only in certain test procedures that went on during the manufacturing of the 286.

## THE PHYSICAL 80286

As mentioned, the 286 is a 68-pin chip. It is not packaged in a DIP. Figure 17-4 shows the pinout in a Pin Grid Array package, PGA. The address and data lines all have their very own pins, unlike the 8088-8086 packages that multiplex the various address and data lines with pin sharing.

The PGA packaging lays the pin structure out in a square. There is an outside row of pins and an inside row. This arrangement complicates pin testing. Care and patience is required to adequately test the pins one at a time. Fortunately, the PGA package is held in a 68-pin socket. If necessary, the chip can be tested by direct substitution with a known good 286. This is always the best test of the chip.

Figure 17-11 is the schematic drawing of a 286. This is drawn to show the signal flow of the 286. The pin locations in the schematic bear no physical resemblance to the PGA package layout. During testing, when you are using the schematic you must relate the schematic to the actual chip to find desired pins.

There are 24 address lines, A23-A0 at pins 7-28 and 32-34. The 16 data lines D15-D0 are found at pins 51-36.

Figure 17-12 is the block diagram of the 286 chip. Using both the schematic and the block diagram, you can see the 24 address lines emerging from the address latches and amplifiers. Also emerging with the address lines from the same circuits, out of pin 1 is *BHE, bus high enable, that is often hooked up with address line A0. Between A0 and *BHE they can select the high byte of a word, the low byte, the whole word or none of the word, in a memory location or from a peripheral. Another line from pin 67 that comes out of the same circuit is M/*IO, memory or I/O. When it is high, the 286 addresses memory. When it is low, the 286 addresses I/O devices.

The two-way data lines are connected to data amplifiers that operate on data either arriving or leaving. The data that is arriving can be instructions or operands. The instructions are channeled to the instruction decoder. The operands go to a data latch for processing. The data that is leaving for memory or I/O devices leaves through amplifiers and goes the other way over the bus lines.

### Controlling the Bus Lines

The bus lines are controlled with a number of inputs and outputs. They are *READY, an input at pin 63, and HOLD, another input at pin 64. The outputs are two status lines *S0, pin 5, *S1, pin 4, COD/INTA, pin 66, and HLDA at pin 65. These lines are able to run the important bus cycles. They operate in step with the CLK frequency that enters the 286 at pin 31. The bus cycles conduct all the reading, writing, and interrupting that takes place.

Intel has designed another smaller chip to help the 286 perform its cycle chores. It is the 82288 Bus Controller chip. It is a 20-pin DIP as shown in Fig. 17-13.

Three of the 286's bus control lines are connected directly to the 82288. They are the status lines, *S0 and *S1, and *M-*I/O. The bus controller chip in turn generates nine output control signals that the system bus will follow. First of all there are five read/write/interrupt outputs. They are *MRDC, a memory read, *MWTC, a memory write, *I/ORC, and I/O read, *I/OWC, and I/O write and *INTA, an interrupt acknowledge. Then there are four signals to control the address latching and the data two-way amplifi-

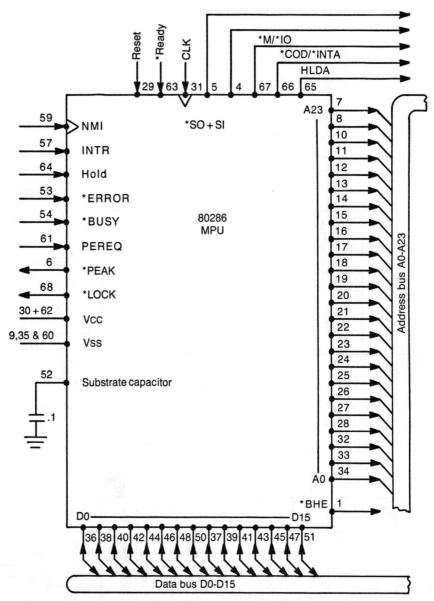

Fig. 17-11. The schematic drawing of the 286 shows the signals and flow direction of the inputs and outputs.

ers. These signals are ALE, address latch enable, *DEN, data enable, DT/*R, data transmit/receive. Figure 17-14 shows an arrangement of the 286 and it's bus controller in a typical system.

## The Arithmetic Logic Unit

The ALU circuits in the 286 are called the Execution Unit. The circuits are arranged around the ALU itself. They receive inputs from the instruction decoder. They receive

415

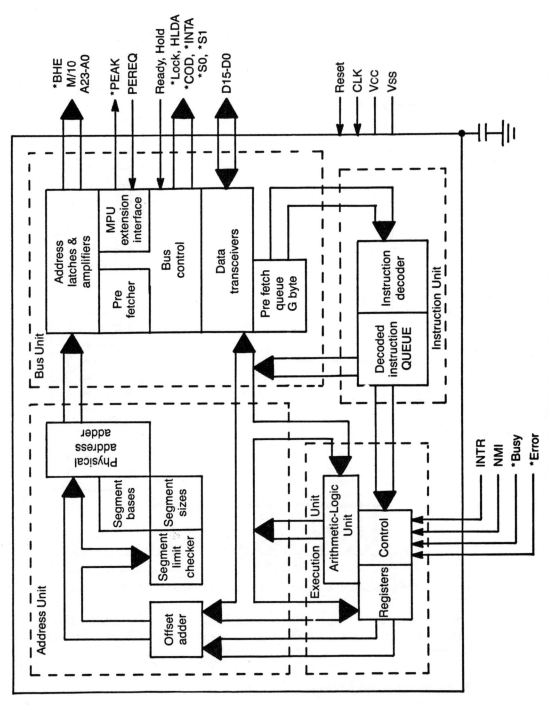

Fig. 17-12. The 286 has four Units. They are the Address, Bus, Execution, and Instruction. Between the schematic drawing and the block diagram, the general operation can be observed.

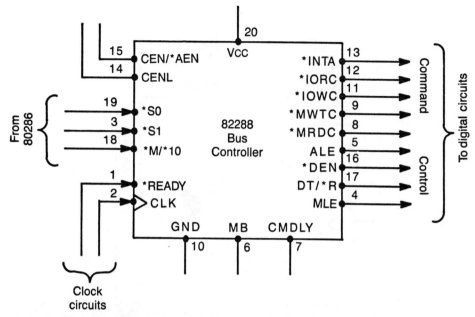

Fig. 17-13. There is a companion bus controller chip that is often used with the 286. It conditions a lot of the command and control lines.

inputs and also output to the two-way data latches. The control section of the Execution Unit receives input from the pins.

There is a *BUSY signal coming in at pin 54. An ERROR signal at pin 53. There is an available interrupt, INTR at pin 57, and a non-maskable interrupt at pin 59. In many Real Mode applications these pins are not useful and are disabled. For instance, pins 53 and 54 could be tied to +5 V, pin 59 to ground, and pin 57 just left disconnected. They do come in handy in Protected Mode.

The ALU is contained in a circuit enclave called the Execution Unit. In the unit there are a group of registers that operate with the ALU to do the arithmetic and logic processing that is the heart of the computing. The bus control circuits connect to the Execution Unit and feed data to the ALU. The bus control circuits are called the Bus Unit and is also a separate circuit enclave as the Execution Unit is.

There is a third enclave of circuits called the Instruction Unit. It receives instruction op codes from the Bus Unit. The Instruction Unit then decodes the instructions and sends the decoded instructions to the Execution Unit. The Execution Unit with its all-important ALU is the center of the computation activity.

Once the ALU finishes processing the data from the Bus Unit, it immediately sends the finished data back to the Bus Unit. The Bus Unit can then send the data back out onto the system bus.

The Execution Unit not only processes data but it deals in calculating addresses also. After it has done its part in the addressing calculations, the unit sends the address information to the fourth enclave type unit of the 286. The fourth unit is called the Address Unit.

417

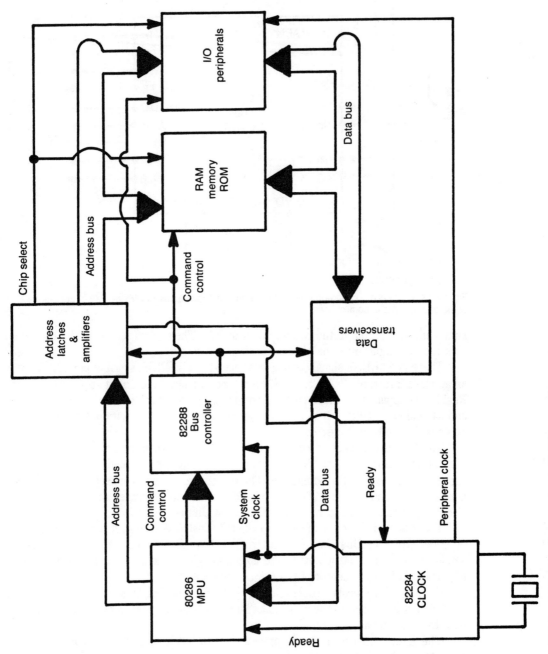

Fig. 17-14. This is a typical circuit arrangement of a 286 computer system.

## The Address Unit

The registers around the ALU connect to Address Unit registers called the Offset Adder. As its name suggests, the offset registers calculate the offset that will be used in the final addressing of the memory locations. The offset registers in turn connect to both the segment address base registers and the Physical Address Adder. Between these registers the effective address is calculated. The finished address is then coupled out of the Addressing Unit back to the Bus Unit and into the address latches. They are readied for their trip on the system bus and then output onto the bus.

This brings us to an important feature of the 286. It is called "pipelining." This is not a new technique. It has been used in mini and mainframe computers for many years. It is new in microcomputers. It is one of the reasons why the 286 is so powerful. It was not used in smaller processors such as the 8-bit types.

Note that there are four separate circuit enclaves on the 286 that are all wired together. Each enclave performs its particular duties. The separate steps of each program line are conducted in the units. The Bus Unit controls the cycles that drive the addresses and fetches data to and from memory. The Instruction Unit decodes the op codes. The Addressing Unit calculates the effective addresses. The Execution Unit processes all the data and helps in the address calculation.

Pipelining is the technique of having all four units conduct their jobs at the same time. In an 8-bit processor, each of the above steps also take place, but each step is conducted one at a time. In the larger 286 all four units conduct their operations, in their private enclaves, at the same time. The reason, of course, is to save time. Pipelining is one of the reasons why the 286, even in Real Mode when it is emulating an 8086, performs the 8086 jobs many times faster than an actual 8086.

## THE 286 BUS CYCLES

The 286, as a processor, generates five distinct types of bus cycles. They are Memory Read, Memory Write, I/O Read, I/O Write, and Interrupt Acknowledge. As discussed earlier, the 286 uses an 82288 bus controller chip. It injects the two status signals, *S0-*S1, and the M/*IO into the status decoder of the controller chip. The controller in turn can generate five command outputs. These five outputs represent the five types of bus cycles in the computer.

Figure 17-15 is the timing diagram of a read cycle in the 286. The top square wave depicts the beating of the clock. Note the designations for the previous cycle, the read cycle and the next cycle. Because of pipelining there is some overlap of the signals, since all four units of the 286 are operating at the same time.

The first step in the read cycle is putting the effective address out on the system bus. This happens as the previous cycle is near its end. At the same time the signals, M/*IO, and COD/*INTA are made valid. The 24 address bits, A23-A0 go out on the bus lines.

The *READY signal is turned on to signal the end of the previous cycle, then the status signals are activated. For a memory data read the signals *S0, *S1, M/*IO, COD/*INTA must be 1010, see Table 17-2. For a memory instruction read the signals must be 1011.

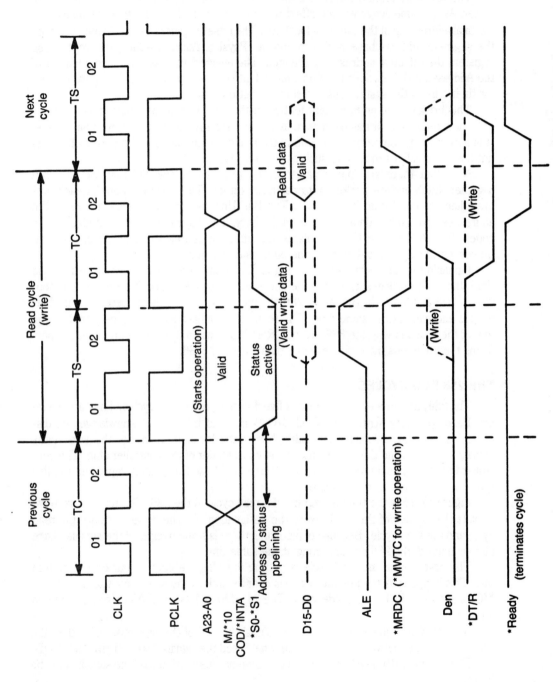

Fig. 17-15. Due to pipelining techniques, the Units in the chip are all running at the same time. Note the overlaps of signals in the previous cycle, the current read cycle and the next cycle.

| Bus Cycle | *S0 | *S1 | M/*10 | COD *INTA |
|---|---|---|---|---|
| Memory Data Read | 1 | 0 | 1 | 0 |
| Memory Instruction Read | 1 | 0 | 1 | 1 |
| Memory Data Write | 0 | 1 | 1 | 0 |
| I/O Read | 1 | 0 | 0 | 1 |
| I/O Write | 0 | 1 | 0 | 1 |
| Interrupt Acknowledge | 0 | 0 | 0 | 0 |

The bus controller decodes the signals and generates ALE and *MRDC, the address latch enable and the memory read signal. ALE goes active at the next clock edge after the bus controller has decoded the status signals. ALE turns on its latches and makes them hold the pipelined address for the rest of the cycle.

DEN, the data enable, and DTR, the data transmit/receive, set up the direction of signal flow from memory to processor. *MRDC then goes low and enables the read activity. The bits enter the processor at pins D15-D0 and the data is valid and accepted right at the end of the read cycle and the beginning of the next cycle. The *READY cycle then terminates the cycle.

The write cycle works in a similar manner but there are a few signal differences, the data travels in the other direction. The processor is writing to memory.

The addressing is the same. The status signals though are changed. For a memory data write, *SO-*S1, M/*IO, COD/*INTA must be 0110. The signals generated by the bus controller are the same ALE signal but a write signal, *MWTC instead of the read signal, *MRDC.

The DEN signal begins earlier and lasts well into the next cycle. *DT/R remains high throughout the write cycle. The *READY signal still terminates the cycle in the same way. With these signal changes, the data that is arriving is accepted in the data amplifier circuits.

This typical minimum bus cycle takes two processor clocks, PCLK, to execute. In an 8 MHz machine, each clock period is 125 nanoseconds. A bus cycle takes twice that time, 250 ns. As long as the computer is conducting business at this rate, there are no "wait states." A wait state is a clock period where a cycle is "stretched" past the 250 ns. Each wait state is 125 ns. Sometimes the 286 has to use wait states. The wait states are needed when the 286 is communicating with slower memory or I/O devices. The *READY signal that tells the system when the clock cycle is over, is used to stretch the bus cycles when it is necessary. The *READY signal can be withheld as long as necessary creating as many wait states as needed.

# 18
# 32-Bit Processors

When the 8-bit processors such as the 8085, Z80, 6800 and 6502 emerged in the late 70s and early 80s, they gave birth to a new species of inexpensive computers. These single board microcomputers had never existed before. They sold by the millions. Computer people, electronic technicians, experimenters, hobbyists, and just plain people snapped them up. They were fascinated and felt they were on to something unbelievable. They were, they had a helpmate for their brains.

There wasn't much software around in those days. It didn't matter too much. These computer pioneers were mainly interested in writing their own programs anyway. Today there is a hard core of millions of these people who spend untold hours on their Apple IIs, COMMODORE VIC 20, 64s, and 128s, CoCo 1s, 2s, and 3s, and others. I'm typing this manuscript on a ten year old CoCo 1 that I modified for my own purposes.

Then along came the 16-bit processors such as the 8088-8086 and the 68000, they gave birth to the IBM PC compatibles, the Macintosh, and the Amiga. While many of the 8-bit aficionados switched to the more advanced designs, the more important result was the advanced uses the new machines could undertake. They could be used for more serious jobs in education, business, and research. However, writing software for them was a prodigious task. Their success was astounding and immediate. They were a lot more expensive than the 8-bit types. The higher prices reduced sales to the average person. The machines made great inroads into the serious business-type applications. These 16-bit machines almost had the same capacity and power as the minicomputers that have been used in large business applications for years.

The next obvious step was the construction of 32-bit computers. The 80186 and 80286 were interim steps. The 80386 and the 68020 were true 32-bit processors. They can do the work a mini performs. They come close to matching the power of a mainframe. Their use in complex business situations is valuable beyond measure. The way the 80386 and 68020 is constructed and works is discussed in this chapter. Let's start with the Intel 386.

## THE COMPATIBILITY

When Intel designed the 8088-8086 it looked forward to the future. Intel appreciated the factor of compatibility. They realized that a lot of software and hardware would be designed around their processors. They built the 8088-8086 with an Instruction Set that could be expanded in future processors of the same family. The 8088-8086 was established as a standard. It was to be a sub-set of future super-sets.

The Instruction Set was cast into the chip. The set is a group of microinstructions built into a ROM-like structure on the 8086 chip. Portions of this microcode is run off according to an instruction that enters the 8086 instruction decoder from memory.

After the 8086, Intel came out with the 80186. The 186 contained a complete 8086 Instruction Set, a complete set of registers and other pertinent silicon cast circuits. In addition the 186 chip contained a lot of support circuitry. It was billed as a computer-on-a-chip. The additional support circuitry required the 186 Instruction Set to have ten more instructions than its predecessor the 8086, shown in Table 18-1.

After the 186 came the 286. The 286 was not to be a computer-on-a-chip. It's important advancement was the Protected Mode. However, it maintained compatibility by having the Real Mode. The Real Mode is nothing more than an 8086 processor installed on the chip. All of the Instruction Set from the 8086 and 80186 is in the 286 plus some more instructions to handle the different modes the 286 is able to run at. The 286 has a super-set of the 8086 Instruction Set. The additional instructions are in Table 18-2. All of the thousands of programs the 8086 is rich in can also be run on the 286. The 286 though runs the programs much faster and more efficiently.

The 386, with its 32-bit architecture, is even more so (Table 18-3). It covers all of the features of the 8086, the 286 and then adds on a lot of new goodies. It has three general modes. One of the three modes has two sub-modes. The first obvious mode is a Real Mode. This is the mode that completely emulates the 8086. In this mode the 386

**Table 18-1. The 80186 Has the Same Instruction Set as the 8086 Plus Ten More Instructions to Operate the Additional Circuits.**

| | Mnemonic | Operation |
|---|---|---|
| **DATA TRANSFER** | PUSH A<br>POP A | PUSH ON STACK (All registers)<br>POP OFF STACK (All Registers) |
| **STRING MANIPULATION** | INS<br>OUTS | Input Bytes or Word String<br>Output Bytes or Word string |
| | REPE/REPZ<br>REPNE/REPNZ | Repeat while Equal Zero<br>Repeat while Not Equal Not Zero |
| | ENTER<br>LEAVE<br>BOUND | Format Stack to Procedure Entry<br>Restore Stack for Procedure Exit<br>Detects Value Outside Prescribed Range |
| | NOP | No Operation |

**Table 18-2. The 80286 Also Has the Same 8086 Instruction
Set Plus These Additional Instructions for its Special Circuits.**

| | Mnemonic | Operation |
|---|---|---|
| **PROCESSOR CONTROL** { | LMSW | Load Machine Status Word |
| | SMSW | Store Machine Status Word |

**Table 18-3. The 80386 Follows the Same 8086 Compatibility
and Also Has These Additional Instructions for its Special Circuits.**

| | Mnemonic | Operation |
|---|---|---|
| **DATA TRANSFER** { | MOV/ZX | Move Byte or Word, DWord with Zero Extension |
| | MOV/SX | Move Byte or Word, DWord, Sign Extended |
| | CWD | Convert Word to DWord |
| | CWDE | Convert Word to DWord Extended |
| | CDQ | Convert DWord to QWord |
| | LFS | Load Pointer into F Segment Register |
| | LGS | Load Pointer into G Segment Register |
| | LSS | Load Pointer into S Segment Register |
| | PUSH FD | PUSH E Flags onto Stack |
| | POP FD | POP E Flags off Stack |
| **SHIFT/ ROTATE** { | SHLD | Double Shift Left |
| | SHRD | Double Shift Right |
| **BIT MANIPULATION** { | BT | Bit Test |
| | BTS | Bit Test and Set |
| | BTR | Bit Test and Reset |
| | BTC | Bit Test and Complement |
| | BSF | Bit Scan Forward |
| | BSR | Bit Scan Reverse |
| | IBTS | Insert Bit String |
| | XBTS | Exact Bit String |
| | SETCC | Set Byte Equal to Condition Code |
| **PROTECTION MODEL** { | SGDT | Store Global Descriptor Table |
| | SIDT | Store Interrupt Descriptor Table |
| | STR | Store Task Register |
| | SLDT | Store Local Descriptor Table |
| | LGDT | Load Global Descriptor Table |
| | LIDT | Load Interrupt Descriptor Table |
| | LTR | Load Task Register |
| | LLDT | Load Local Descriptor Table |
| | ARPL | Adjust Requested Privilege Level |
| | LAR | Load Access Rights |
| | LSL | Load Segment Limit |
| | VERR | Verify Segment for Reading |
| | VERW | Verify Segment for Writing |
| | LMSW | Load Machine Status Word |
| | SMSW | Store Machine Status Word |

acts as if it is a 8086. Like the 286, the 386 defaults to the Real Mode. As it comes on in the Real Mode it acts like a superfast 8086. It runs 8086 software at very fast speeds. It is so fast that some 8086 applications, such as graphics have to be slowed somewhat in order to make any sense of the displays.

The name Real Mode is so called because an 8086 is not able to directly address virtual memory. Virtual memory space, besides using RAM and ROM as addresses, is also able to use disks and other storage mediums. The 8086 can't perform the virtual memory tricks. It can only access its own physical memory.

Once the 386 is up and running, it can then be placed into the Protected Mode by software instructing it to do so. In Protected Mode, the 386 is able to operate in one of two sub-modes. The first sub-mode is a 16-bit form that emulates the 286. The 386, in effect contains a complete 286 processor, in addition to the 8086.

The 386 can also be instructed to operate in a 32-bit form. This is the true 386 operating type. This is the mode that all the 32-bit software that is written, will operate in.

Figure 17-3 illustrates the modes that ensure upward compatibility between the 8086, 80286, and 80386. The Real Mode has the 386 acting as an 8086. The 16-bit Protected Mode makes the 386 into a 286. The 32-bit section of the Protected Mode lets the 386 be itself, a full featured 386. Then there is one more Mode the 386 can get into.

This is a separate mode that is called Virtual 8086. This is an 8086 mode but it is different than the Real Mode. The Real Mode has the 386 acting the part of an ordinary 8086 except for the fact that it runs the 8086 application programs many times faster than an actual 8086 processor. In the Real Mode, as it emulates an 8086 the 386 is limited to running one program or task at a time. The Real Mode does not allow the 386 to perform multitasking. Because the Real Mode can run only one task at a time, it does not need any protection from interference with other tasks. About all the 386 is in Real Mode is a very fast 8086 with 1 MB of physical memory space.

In the Virtual 8086 Mode, the 386 sheds these restrictions. In the Virtual 8086 Mode the 386 is able to provide protection and is also able to run a number of 8086 application programs at the same time. Each 8086 task is assigned its own 1 MB memory space and runs as if it is the only task in operation. It is not aware of any other 8086 tasks that might be in operation at the same time. They all have their very own operating systems like DOS and perform under the overall protection of the master operating system provided to run the Virtual 8086 Mode. Besides running a number of 8086 programs in Virtual 8086 Mode, the 386 is able, at the same time, to run tasks in the 286 and 386 Protected Modes.

The three modes are distinguished from each other by their operating systems, the way the memory is addressed, and the amount of memory that each mode or sub-mode is able to use. The Real Mode only needs an operating system such as one of the DOS (disk operating system) types. The Protected Modes need more complex operating systems. The development of these systems is expensive and requires a lot of time to produce. The Protected 286 Mode is able to use OS/2, which is a single user multitasking operating system that will run 286 programs. OS/2 can only run the 286 mode of the 386. The 386 part of the mode requires more complex operating systems. At this writing there is very little software that can exploit the capabilities of the 386's native mode.

## The 386's Architecture

The 386 is a CMOS chip. It incorporates the low power needs of a CMOS and the high performance of an HMOS. There are about 250,000 transistors on the chip. The physical features of each transistor have been scaled down to a tiny measurement of 1.5 microns.

The chip comes in a 132-pin ceramic pin-grid-array, PGA. The 386 has three rows of pins as shown in Fig. 18-1. The illustration shows address pins A31-A2. A1 and A0 are connected internally at the 32-bit address register and emerge in combination with other signals.

A close look at the pinout shows a number of the same pins that were also on the 286 and 8086. Examples are reset, error, busy, ready, and so on. Another interesting pin

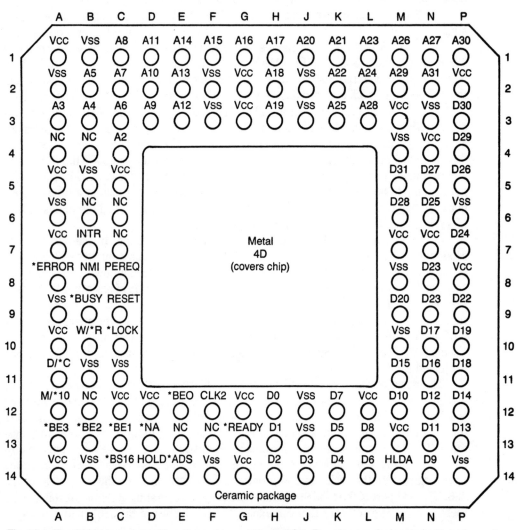

Fig. 18-1. The 80386 is packaged in a three pin row 132-pin PGA. The pins are designated with both numbers and letters to aid in identification.

arrangement is the large number of Vcc and Vss power connections. There are a lot of different circuit areas on the chip and it was not possible to service them all with power from a single VCC and VSS pair.

There are so may pins in the three rows that numbering them from 1 through 132 would be cumbersome. Intel arranged a row-column identification system. The top and bottom pin labels are arranged along a set of letters, A-P, leaving out I and O. The sides of the square are numbered 1-14. To identify a pin, you must read it out of the grid. For instance, the *READY pin is found in row 13 at column G. In other words *READY is found at the intersection of 13-G.

## CHIP REGISTERS

The 132 pins are connected to the chip in the center of the package under the metal lid. The pins are typically plugged into a socket. Running voltage or logic probe readings on the pins and trying to figure out troubles looks like and is a considerable job. Fortunately, special circuits and registers are built in the chip.

These are self-test circuits. They perform every time the computer is turned on. A number of tests are automatically performed. First of all about half of the 275,000 transistors are quickly tested for electrical faults. At the same time the test gets all the registers working. This powerup exercising determines whether the registers can do their jobs. At the end of the exercise program certain test results are placed into the general registers. You can check the results. If the predicted results are not correct the chip could be defective. The chip can then be replaced in its socket. There are some other test procedures to exercise certain memory areas to be sure they are operating properly.

The 386 architecture resembles the 286 but is more so, there is a full complement of 32-bit registers and the 386 internal bus lines are also 32-bits wide. There are eight 32-bit general registers. They can be used for one another to perform arithmetic and logic, be addressing registers, and do data register chores. The general registers can handle either 16-bit or 32 bit pieces of data. Four of the registers are also able to process 8-bit data. They appear in Fig. 18-2.

There is a 32-bit Flag register containing typical flags to signal results of the ALU and to effect control over processor work. There is also a 32-bit instruction pointer to help out during addressing. There are six 16-bit segment registers that work with the instruction pointer to produce effective addresses.

There are eight debug registers, two test registers, two system address registers, two system segment registers with two system descriptor registers, and four registers used for paging, a new ability. These last registers are used by the operating system programs and the application programs do not know they exist.

The operating system uses these registers for its own purposes. These include initializing the computer when it is turned on, performing multitasking, interrupt and exception jobs, setting breakpoints, running off the self-tests mentioned earlier, and other jobs.

The 386 works on a number of datatypes. The machine language programmer is very interested in what datatypes the 386 can work on. They are called $8-$, $16-$, and 32-bit integers and ordinals, packed and unpacked decimals, near and far pointers and

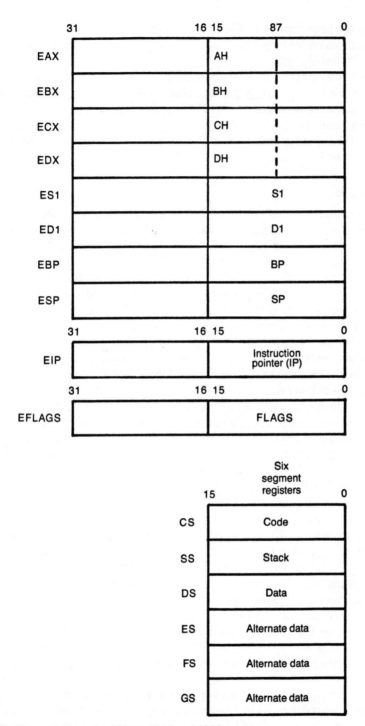

Fig. 18-2. The registers in the 386 are 32-bit and 16-bit types.

428

strings. The strings can be bits, bytes, words, and double words. For detailed explanations of these datatypes look them up in a programming manual.

These are the datatypes that the Instruction Set of the 386 are able to work on. The 386 Instruction Set is the largest of the three sets in the family. The 386 set includes the smaller 286 set and the even smaller 8086 set.

The 386 features pipelining as the 286 does, Fig. 18-3 shows the different units the 386 is arranged in. There is the Bus Unit, Instruction Prefetcher Unit, the Instructior Decoder, the Execution Unit, the Segment Unit and the new Paging Unit. All of these units are able to work, more or less, independent of each other and therefore are all able to do their jobs while the other units are busy doing there jobs. For instance, the Bus Unit can be moving data from place to place while at the same time the Prefetch Unit places the next four bytes of code into the prefetch queue. This is parallel operation rather than series operation where each unit must wait in line and take its turn operating. Pipelining speeds up the system.

These units that enable pipelining in the 386 are connected together with bus lines that are 32 bits wide. Besides allowing several instructions to be run at the same time, the various stages of the instruction sequence also overlap each other. While one instruction is being executed the next one can be decoded, and still another one can be read out of memory. However, the simultaneous execution of a number of instructions can only be performed when the program is being run one instruction after another from one memory address after another numerically. Should an instruction like an indirect jump come along, the pipelining feature has to be abandoned and the instructions that are not in numerical order must be run one at a time. Once the processor goes back to its sequential fetching of instructions the pipelining advantage can be used once again.

The eight general purpose registers are all 32-bit types. They can handle 32-bit pieces of data without having to divide up the four bytes. When 16-bit pieces are received by these registers, when the 286 or 8086 modes are used the registers can be accessed as if they are 16-bit types. The 16-bit pieces are installed in the lower end bits of the 32-bit registers. They appear to the 286 and 8086 modes as 16-bit registers. If 8-bit data is being processed, only the top four registers as shown in Fig. 18-2 are able to handle the 8 bits. They are processed in the lower bits of the 32-bit registers. Even though the 16-bit and 8-bit data pieces are installed into 32-bit registers, the registers adopt the size and act as if they are the size of the data widths. They even throw flags according to the size they adopt. For instance if there is a need for a Carry while handling 8 bits, the Carry flag will be activated.

## Mode Operations

When the 386 was designed, upward compatibility with the 286 and 8086 was one of the most important design goals. As mentioned earlier, the 386 is able to adopt three different modes with one of the modes having two sub-sections.

There are two separate modes for the 8086 emulation, the Real Mode and the Virtual 8086 Mode. They both run 8086 programs. They both use the common operating system known as DOS (disk operating system). The Real Mode acts as if the processor is an 8086. The processor uses 20 address lines and addresses 1 megabyte of physical memory. It cannot address disks or other such storage memory in a virtual memory

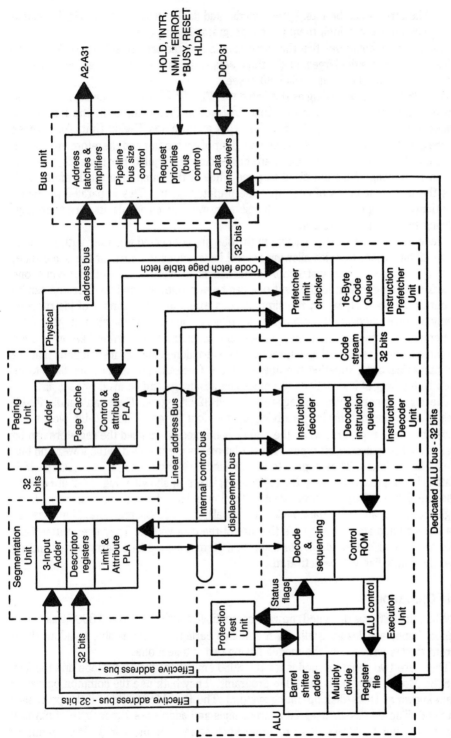

Fig. 18-3. There are six Units in the 386. They feature pipelining.

430

fashion. The Real Mode simply acts as if it is a very fast 8086, even faster than the way the 286 emulates the 8086. There are computers with a 386 processor that do not do anything but act as if it is a superfast 8086. The cther 386 features are never used, and in some machines there are not even any circuits that can access the full power of the 386.

The Virtual 8086 Mode is more versatile than the Real Mode. It is a protected mode, and requires an operating program other than ordinary DOS to get going. There are a number of special DOS programs that can activate the Virtual Mode. Once activated, the 8086 Virtual Mode is able to run, at the same time, a number of 8086 DOS based programs. This feature is valuable for many applications, especially when a number of computers are hooked together in a network. In Virtual 8086 Mode, each 8086 application task operates as if it were using its very own 8086 processor and its own 1 megabyte address space.

The 386 that is providing this 8086 multiple environment is working with a 4 gigabyte physical address space. Each 8086 task can be installed somewhere in the 4 gigabyte area. When it is time for that task to be addressed, the 386 maps the task to the first megabyte so the address numbers are correct. The 386 is able to do this trick with the Paging Unit that will be discussed later in this chapter.

When the 386 is in Virtual 8086 Mode, it is in a protected state. All the interrupts are vectored through special descriptor tables that control the interrupts outside of the 8086 application program. The 386 also traps privileged instructions and keeps control over the I/O ports.

Addressing in the virtual mode is quite like the Real Mode. 20-bit addresses are constructed in the same way as all the other 8086 addressing that goes on in an actual 8086 and 286. The address consists of two parts. There is the segment formed in the segment register and the offset. The segment register is shifted to the left by four bits and then the 16-bit offset is added to it.

The 386 also has its own Protected Virtual Modes for 16-bit 286 and 32-bit 386 operations. For these modes the technology ran ahead of the available software to run parts of these modes. The DOS operating system does not activate these modes. It is only useful in the 8086 modes.

There isn't too much trouble when the 386 emulates a 286. There is an operating system called OS/2. It is designed to be used by a single user desiring multitasking. It works on both the 286 and 386 processors to free up a Protected Virtual Addressing Mode. However, OS/2 only activates a protected 286 mode. In a 286 based machine this is fine. OS/2 allows the turn on of the 286 Protected Virtual Mode with its multitasking and privilege levels. When run in a 386 based machine, OS/2 only does the same thing. It activates the emulated 286 Protected Virtual Mode. It does not permit the operation of the 386 Virtual Mode. OS/2 in the 386 makes the processor act like a fast 286, not a 386.

In both the 286 and 386 it allows each processor to address 16 megabytes of physical memory and 1 gigabyte of virtual address space. This expanded memory is available because the 286 and 386 conduct segmentation in a different way than the 8086. The virtual address is installed into the Segment Unit. This unit converts it into an actual address number in memory that is in the 64 K segment in use at that time. This is the actual physical memory address.

The virtual address that was constructed and applied to the segment registers is the result of a 16-bit offset and a 16-bit selector. The 16-bit offset is used for the 286 Protected Mode. Should an address be calculated for the 386 Protected Mode, than a 32-bit offset is used as in Fig. 18-4.

The 16-bit selector is a pointer to a segment descriptor table. For the 386 mode, the value found in the table by the selector is added to the 32-bit offset. This produces a

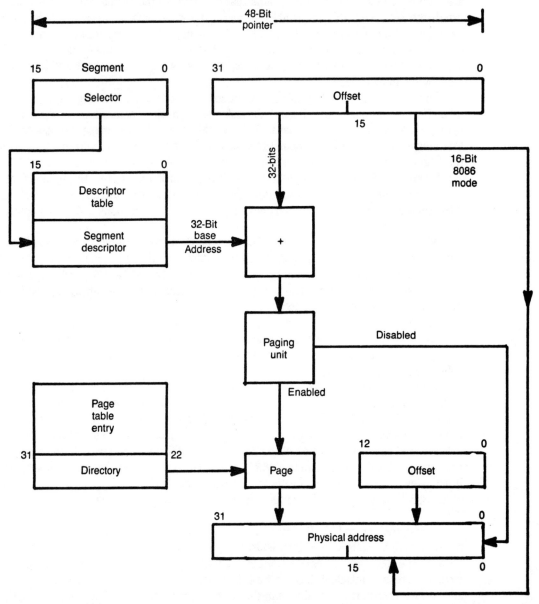

Fig. 18-4. The 386 generates 32-bit addresses that can locate data in 4 gigabytes of physical address space. It utilizes the actions of both segmenting and paging.

432

32-bit physical address. 32 bits are able to locate 4 gigabytes of address space. There is more detail on this procedure in the next section.

The value in the descriptor table is 16-bits wide and 14 of the bits are used to locate a physical address. This addition of bits results in an address that is 14 bits from the descriptor table and 32 bits from the offset. The resulting 46 bits can produce a virtual address space of 64 terabytes.

The 286 and 386 protected modes in the 386 are indeed powerful. They can operate at awesome clock speeds and address almost unlimited amounts of memory. The 286 is very well supported with versions of OS/2. The 386 though has its technology too far ahead of the software needed to exploit its capabilities. Software developers are scrambling to come to the marketplace with a good operating system that will free up the full features of the 32-bit 386 Protected Virtual Address Modes. At this writing there are some programs available but nothing yet that really does the job.

Virtual memory is a result of the action of the 286 and 386 that provides memory that far exceeds the actual physical memory. For instance, the 386 has a physical memory addressing ability based on using 32 bits. The 32 bits can contact 4 gigabytes or more than 4 billion 8-bit locations. The virtual memory uses 46 bits and can contact 64 terabytes or 64 trillion 8-bit locations. The 386 has registers that the addressing bits must pass through to result in a physical address. The address space is divided up into units of segments or pages. Both segmenting and paging is available in the 386. Only segmenting is available in the 286.

## Segments and Pages

The 386 has six segment registers. They are 16-bit registers. A segment in Real Mode can be any size from a single byte location up to a 64 K group of locations. The segment in memory is limited by the 16 bits it can use as an address. In Protected Mode, with all the additional descriptor register bits available, a segment in memory can still be as small as one byte but can be as large as 32 bits will allow, or 4 gigabytes.

In practice, memory is split up into segments. The various modules of a program are stored in segments. The segments can all be different sizes according to the size of the program module that is installed. In the protected mode each segment can be individually protected. Segments in the 386 can be as large as 4 gigabytes, which provides almost unlimited memory in a segment.

Figure 18-4 shows how segmentation produces an address in the vast virtual memory map. Note there is a 16-bit segment selector register. It chooses the segment to be accessed. Then there is a 32-bit offset that chooses the address in the chosen segment.

The 16-bit segment selector goes to a table that the operating system controls. The table yields an eight byte Descriptor from the table. The eight bytes contain the 32-bit base address and other pertinent addressing information about the segment to be located. The 32-bit base address is added to the offset to produce the actual address in virtual memory.

If there is no paging, this virtual address is also the physical address. When paging is used, this virtual address is passed into the Paging Unit. A page consists of small 4 K groups of memory. The technique keeps the memory organized like a book. The entire memory, if considered as a book, is composed of uniform 4 K byte pages.

The Paging Unit produces a 32-bit physical address. The highest ten bits come from a page directory table. This gives the page table address of the desired location. The next highest ten bits are added to the page table ten bits to produce the page number. The lowest 12 bits are then added to the page number to produce a 32-bit address that points to the physical address.

In the 386 segmentation and paging are individual systems. Segmentation can be used alone or with paging. Paging can also be used by itself or along with segmentation. The decision is made by the programmer.

The two systems are Memory Management options. Segmentation provides means to conduct data sharing, to use protection and perform multiple tasks. Paging deals with physical memory management. When both are used together, the segmentation system produces a 32-bit virtual address for the paging system. The Paging Unit converts the 32 bits into the actual physical address that goes out over the address bus.

## THE MOTOROLA 68020 32-BIT PROCESSOR

The 68020 is the 32-bit upgrade of the Motorola 68000 discussed earlier in the book. The 68000 contained address registers that had 32 bits. However, only 24 of the 32 bits were brought out to pins in its package. The 24 pins were able to address 16 megabytes of address space. In the 68020 the unused eight bits of the 68000 are placed into action. All of the bits are output from the 68020 package and as a result, the 68020 is able to address the full 4 gigabytes. The addressing capability is flat. All the complex addition of segments and offsets that the Intel family of processors uses to address memory is not needed in the Motorola group of processors. The 68000 and its upgrade the 68020 directly conduct addressing according to the bits in the addressing registers.

Figure 18-5 is a block diagram of the 68020 processor. It is a full 32-bit machine with separate 32-bit address and data buses. It is upward compatible with the 68000. It does have some more addressing modes that help it handle higher level languages that are used with it in addition to machine languages.

The 68020 is an HCMOS and has over 200,000 transistors cast on its chip. It operates with a 16 MHz frequency. The chip circuits are separated into a number of units. They are the Sequencer and Control Unit, the Execution Unit, the Bus Controller Unit, and the Instruction Prefetch and Decode Unit. The sequencer and control section is in the middle of the action. It connects to all the other units. It is the manager of the chip. It exerts control over the execution unit, the chip's registers, and internal bus lines.

The 32-bit external address bus is connected to the Execution Unit. The Execution Unit as the name implies performs all the calculations that the instructions and data require. The program counter is in the Execution Unit. In the program counter circuits all the instruction addresses are calculated. There is also a data section in the Execution Unit. The data section processes all the data in an ALU and its associated registers.

The bus controller handles the accessing of memory. It also contains an instruction cache. What is a cache?

It is a set aside portion of easily read memory. For example, the 80386 based computer can have a cache, a section of separate memory, installed between the main physical memory and the 386 internals. The cache is arranged so that it will store instructions or data that will be used constantly in a program run. That way, every time the MPU

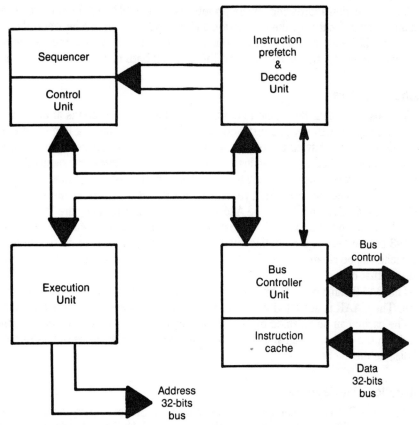

Fig. 18-5. The 68020 is divided into four sections. They generate 32-bit address and data signals.

needs some of this often used data, it checks the cache memory first before accessing main memory. If this needed data is in the cache, the MPU obtains it quickly and doesn't have to spend extra time accessing main memory. The cache usually consists of a small amount of memory.

The 68020 features an instruction cache on board in the Bus Controller Unit. The bus controller itself is the source of all the control lines that go out to and come in from the computer. These control lines were covered in the earlier 68000 discussion. They are just about the same lines except they are operating with a 32-bit 68020 instead of the 16-bit 68000. The instruction cache is connected to the 32-bit external data bus lines.

The Instruction Prefetch and Decode Unit works with the Execution Unit. It fetches and decodes instructions from memory. The prefetch section is a group of registers that fetch three instruction words at a time and then decode them. That way the MPU doesn't have to fetch instructions and decode them one at a time. As the instructions are needed by the MPU they are already in the MPU circuits and decoded. There is a lot of time saved as the fetching and decoding takes place at the same time as the previous instruction is being executed.

The instruction addressing for the prefetch is computed in a different circuit than the data addressing. That way, the instruction and data addressing can be worked out at the same time. If the instruction is installed in the instruction cache and the data is residing in the main memory, the instruction and the data can both be fetched at the same time.

## Cache Registers

The instruction cache is able to contain 256 bytes of instructions at one time. With these bytes filled with needed instructions, the MPU can obtain a large percentage of instructions without having to go outside of its package. This saves a great deal of time as the number of bus cycles for instruction fetches are drastically reduced. As mentioned, only instructions are stored in the cache. There is no data there.

The cache has two important registers, in Fig. 18-6. There is the Cache Control Register, the CACR, and the Cache Address Register, CAAR. They are 32-bit registers. The CACR only uses bits 0-3. The rest of the bits are always clear and set with lows. Bits 0-3 can be set. The operating system can cause the CACR to do one of four jobs. The cache can be cleared by setting bit 3, clear an entry, freeze the cache or enable the cache, in that order.

The CAAR can have a 32-bit address installed to locate a routine that will control the cache. The CAAR is activated when bit 3 of the CACR is set and clears the cache.

The cache can be disabled by an external signal. The pin *CDIS when enabled will shut down the cache. A signal into *CDIS will override any settings of bits in the cache and disable the cache.

## Instruction Overlapping

When the Bus Controller Unit and the Sequencer Unit are operating they could both be working on different instructions at the same time. In Fig. 18-7 such an activity is illustrated. At the top of the timing sketch are nine clocks. Beneath the clocks is a bus movement depicting a prefetch, a write, and the next instruction.

Beneath these entities is the activity of the bus controller and sequencer lined up with the timing of the clock. In this example it is shown how a Move instruction and a SUBtract instruction are operated on and overlap each other in the same time frame.

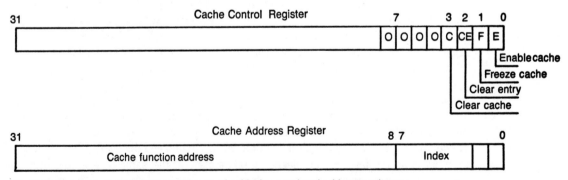

Fig. 18-6. The cache's important registers are the 32-bit control and address registers.

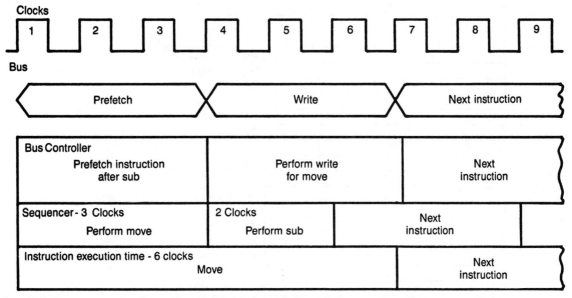

**Fig. 18-7.** The processor has instruction overlapping that speeds up the program execution.

The Move instruction takes six clocks to perform. The sequencer gets the Move executing in three clocks. The bus controller then takes over and performs the Move in the following three clocks. Meanwhile, after the third clock, the sequencer has finished with Move and is ready to do the next instruction that has been prefetched. This is the SUBtract instruction.

The SUBtract instruction does not need the services of the bus controller since the operation takes place in the MPU's Execution Unit and not out in memory. The sequencer thus can get the SUBtract instruction executed in two clocks. The overlap in execution time takes place in the 4th, 5th and 6th clocks. The two instructions were then executed at the same time. In fact, the 6th clock was used to get the next instruction started.

## THE PROGRAMMER'S BLOCK DIAGRAM (FIG. 18-8)

If you compare the 68020 programmer's registers with the 68000 registers you'll see a lot of similarity. They both have eight 32-bit general purpose data registers, seven address registers, stack pointers (the interrupt stack pointer is almost identical to the supervisor pointer in the 68000), program counter, and a 16-bit condition code register. Then there is the 32-bit vector base register, two 3-bit alternate function code registers, and a 16-bit status register. The all new registers are a master stack pointer and the two cache registers discussed earlier. These MPU registers make the 68020 code compatible with the 68000 family. The 68020 though has a few more addressing modes and some additional instructions. These new instructions are designed to have the 68020 work easier with higher level languages.

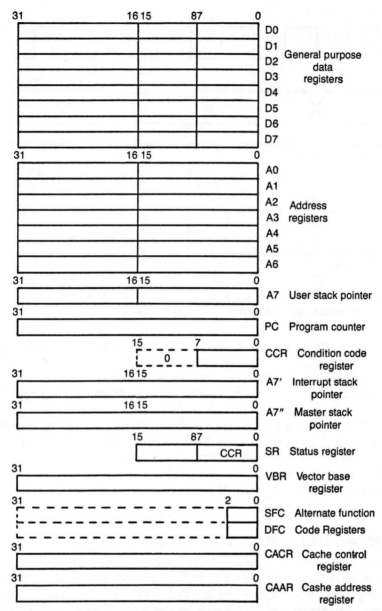

Fig. 18-8. The 68020 has eight general purpose data registers and seven address registers just like the 68000.

Chapter 14 discusses using the instruction set in a 68000. There are only two more addressing modes and a few more instructions in the 68020. If you are interested in programming the 68020 processor please refer to its programming manual.

## THE COMPUTER TECHNICIAN'S VIEWPOINT

At this juncture in the book, you have covered the material that a microcomputer technician should have a pretty good handle on. Micros are relatively new. They have evolved from the early 8-bit units that were of interest to the technically oriented to the 32-bit types that are quickly doing so many important jobs in the world today. Most of the important micros that are in use and how in general they work, have been touched upon in the last two parts of this book. The discussions for the most part have been "hands off." It is now time to get down to the nuts, bolts and chips. The third part of the book deals with "hands on."

# PART 3

# MAINTENANCE AND TROUBLESHOOTING

# 19

# Diagnosing
# Wear and Defects

The computer technician has the same excellent diagnostic tool the TV repairman enjoys. What is this grat aid? It is the video display. When trouble strikes the computer system, the problem is often clearly displayed on the screen. Typical general symptoms are shown in Fig. 19-1 through 19-5. They include garbage, no video with a display block, brightness but no video or display block, no brightness, not enough vertical sweep, no vertical sweep, not enough horizontal sweep, no horizontal sweep and dead computer.

Like the TV repairman, the computer technician takes time to examine and think about the symptoms. According to what particular symptom is encountered, a particular troubleshooting path of action is indicated (Fig. 19-6). For example, if the computer is dead (a common symptom), the power supply should be the first circuit to be tested. When the video is missing from the display block, the first test point is the video output of the video display generator chip. If there is a white horizontal line across an otherwise-dark screen, the vertical sweep circuits in the TV display circuit are the prime suspect. When the screen displays a block of garbage instead of logical lines, the inside digital world of the computer gets attention first. Each symptom points to the place where the trounle is happening. All you have to do is interpret the symptoms. Let's go through the common procedures needed to isolate the faulty circuit areas.

## TV-TYPE TROUBLES

Years ago, computer systems did not use the video display as an output device; today, a video display is a mandatory part of the computer. Recent studies show that better than 75 percent of microcomputer breakdowns are caused by video troubles.

The computer only needs part of an ordinary TV. It requires four general circuits to fire up the picture tube and show the logicl video it produces. The circuits are video out-

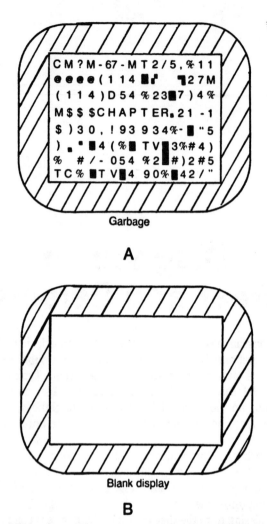

Garbage

**A**

Blank display

**B**

Fig. 19-1. A) This condition has the display full of meaningless characters, symbols, numbers, and blank spaces with and without illumination. It is caused by troubles in the digital circuits. B) No video in the display block. This is actually another form of garbage, and can be caused by the same digital components plus the video circuits.

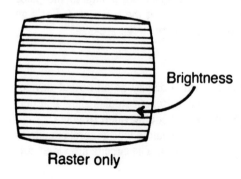

Brightness

Raster only

Fig. 19-2. Brightness but no display block. The raster is present but there is no display. The horizontal and vertical sync signals are gone and the display cannot be constructed.

444

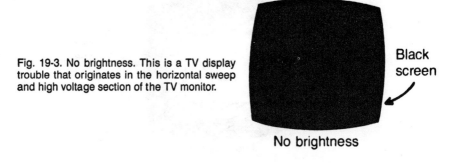

Fig. 19-3. No brightness. This is a TV display trouble that originates in the horizontal sweep and high voltage section of the TV monitor.

**Black screen**

**No brightness**

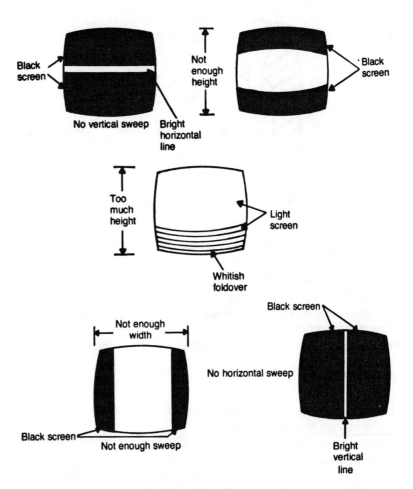

Black screen

Not enough height

Black screen

No vertical sweep    Bright horizontal line

Too much height

Light screen

Whitish foldover

Not enough width

No horizontal sweep

Black screen

Black screen    Not enough sweep

Bright vertical line

Fig. 19-4. Poor sweep. This includes not enough vertical sweep, no vertical sweep, too much vertical sweep, not enough horizontal sweep, and no horizontal sweep. All these troubles are caused by problems in the sweep circuits of the TV monitor.

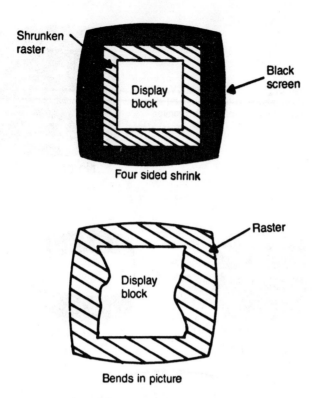

**Four sided shrink**

**Bends in picture**

Fig. 19-5. Four sided shrink, bends in the pictures, dead computer. These are all power supply troubles.

put, vertical sweep, horizontal sweep, and high voltage power supply. The other TV circuits (such as the tuner, i-f strip, etc.) are not found in the video monitor used by the computer. Of course, they are found in home TVs that computers can be attached to, but when a home TV breaks down, you have an ordinary TV service job on your hands, not a computer video monitor repair. We will not cover ordinary TV repairs here; we'll discuss only video monitor repairs.

When the display is the seat of the trouble, you'll see symptoms like this:

1. No brightness
2. Low brightness
3. Picture expands when brightness control is advanced
4. Not enough horizontal sweep
5. No horizontal sweep, only a bright white line from top to bottom of screen.
6. Not enough vertical sweep
7. No vertical sweep, only a bright white line from side to side of screen
8. No video or display block, but screen has light
9. Washed-out video
10. Smeared video

446

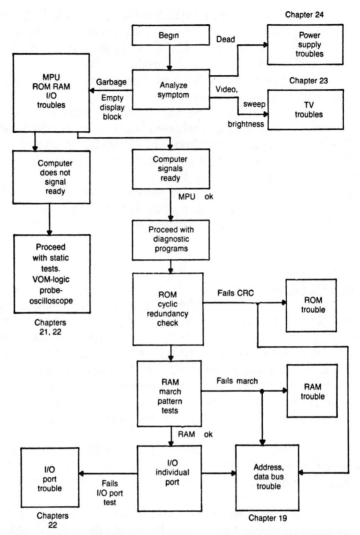

Fig. 19-6. The first step in any repair is to analyze the symptoms of trouble. Most of the time the display will point the way to the defective circuit area. If you follow this procedure, the rest of this book can be a general repair guide.

## POWER SUPPLY PROBLEMS

There are many variations of power uspplies in computers. The computers that connect to an independent monitor or TV have a supply of their own. The computers that have a built-in display share the supply between the display and all the other ciruits.

Power supplies that only have to energize a computer and not the video display only generate small voltages. Typically, such a supply only produces dc voltages like $\pm 12$ V and $\pm 5$ V. The voltages must be carefully regulated, but otherwise are easy to produce and maintain.

When these supplies fail the symptom you'll see is a completely dead computer. The off/on switch won't operate. Another symptom is due to one of the circuits that is specially fed −5 V, or one of the 12 volters. The +5 V line goes to practically every circuit in the machine so, when it dies the computer appears dead.

These low voltage power supply failures are usually easy to trace and repair. Chapter 24 goes into the repair techniques in detail.

When the power supply energizes the video display as well as the computer circuits, the supply is much larger. When this supply develops troubles, the display shows some symptoms besides the computer going dead. The symptoms are quite like ordinary TV troubles. The most obvious symptom is a completely dead computer. The TV display is black, and the computer is not doing anything.

Less apparent symptoms can be the four-sided shrink of the raster that happens if the voltage produced falls, and the raster bending with or without thick horizontal black stripes due to faulty filtering. All these symptoms and the techniques to locate them are discussed in Chapter 24.

## DIAGNOSTIC PROGRAMS

A computer has diagnostic capabilities far beyond other electronic gear. It can test itself! With the aid of the keyboard and other peripheral devices combined with test programs, most of the computer circuits cn be exercised. If the circuit works properly during the exercise, it is probably ok. When the circuit doesn't perform, the circuit might be the trouble. There is always the possibility, too, that a circuit isn't operating because another circuit is broken down, preventing the first from working properly.

When the power supply and display are exonerated, symptoms fall into one of two categories: a screenful of garbage, or a dead computer with a display that's lit. Both troubles can be caused by most of the digitan and/or video chips. The best place to start is with the ROM.

The ROM of the computer is the chip in control. It is the director of the computing operation. Before any of the digital circuits are tested, you must be sure the ROM is ok. Check the ROM by reading from it. If you can get the MPU to read from the ROM, you know it is operating.

When you first turn the computer on, the MPU automatically reads the start bytes of the ROM program. The computer signs in by printing its ready message on the TV screen. If this happens, the MPU is reading from ROM. Admittedly, the MPU is only reading a dozen or so start bytes, but the reading is going on. The ROM is probably ok.

When the ROM will sign in, you cn use the diagnostic programs for further testing. The rest of the ROM can be read from, RAM can be exercised, and all the other circuits can be checked out with the diagnostic software. We'll go through some of these tests shortly.

When the computer won't sign in, then the entire digital circuit area must be tested with the voltmeter, logic probe, oscilloscope, and other testing instruments, along with the aid of a schematic. These important techniques are discussed in Chapters 21 and 22.

## READING THE ROM

Most manufacturers supply diagnostic programs to exercise their particular circuits. Naturally, if the computer is down in a way that programs can't be run, these programs are worthless for the case. When the computer can run programs, diagnostics are invaluable. One of the programs tests every bit in the ROM. The ROM contains all the operating software the computer needs to work.

The ROM test that the TRS-80 Color Computer uses is typical of them all. The test is a program which reads each byte in the ROM, byte after byte. Each bit in each byte is run through a 16-bit shift register. The shift register XORs each incoming bit from ROM with its 6, 8, 11, and 15 bits. As each bit passes through, the value of the shift register changes.

The test number in the shift register is called a *CRC*. Since the register is 16 bits and four hex numbers code 16 bits, the test number is clled a *four-digit CRC*. CRC stands for Cyclic Redundancy Check, the name of the test. It is an error-checking test used by programmers to check the transmission of programs. We use it to read the ROM (and we thank the programmers for their contribution).

When the entire ROM has been tested bit by bit, the shift register is left with a hex value. This value, which is predetermined by the manufacturer, is printed on the screen. My machine prints the CRC hex number 9505 if the ROM has been read and is ok.

A ROM can become disabled if any shorts or opens occur in the burnt-in program bytes or control circuits. The test program is supposed to be able to pick out any defect in a ROM better than 99 percent of the time.

ROMs often contain checkout programs for other circuits such as the IBM post and other diagnostic programs (see appendix). For example, these ROMs will run a test program on all the RAM chips everytime the computer is turned on. This test is performed so the user does not get into the middle of a lengthy important program execution and then find it faulty because a RAM chip was dead. When the ROM runs an automatic start up RAM test, it shuts down the computer before it can get involved in a program. Let's examine this kind of RAM exercise.

## MARCHING THROUGH THE RAM

When the MPU reads all the way through a ROM, the MPU and the ROM are good. The RAM can be tested next. A static RAM chip becomes suspect when the computer is able to run some addresses of a program but not others. The addresses that won't respond properly could be on a defective chip. Since the data bus extends all eight lines to each individual chip, each byte is on one chip (Fig. 19-7).

This is different from dynamic RAM where the data bus extends only one line to each chip. Each memory byte is pread over the eight chips, one bit to a chip. Although a bad static RAM chip will not respond to the address on its chip, a dead dynamic RAM chip might not respond to any of the RAM addresses. One bit of ech byte is on every dynamic chip. All the dynamic chips are addressed at the same time with each addressing operation.

Even though static and dynamic RAMs have these basic bit and address differences, they both will respond to a software test. The test picks out a defective static RAM chip directly as it notes the defective address. The entire byte is at that address on one chip.

The test also picks out the exact defective address on the dynamic chip. However, since one address is spaced out over the eight chips in the RAM set, a further isolation technique might be needed to figure out which bit is inoperative in the suspect byte. The

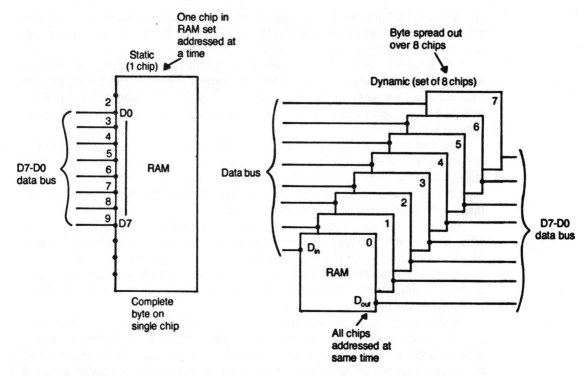

Fig. 19-7. During RAM testing, static and dynamic chips might need different tests due to the way the bytes are organized. Static has complete bytes on the same chip. Dynamic spreads the byte over the RAM array, one bit of a byte on each chip.

chips can be swapped around and the test byte is reexamined until the trouble is found, as it moves from bit position to bit position (Fig. 19-8).

## MARCH PATTERN

RAM can be checked out with a *march pattern*, which starts out by writing all 0s into every bit in memory (Fig. 19-9A). Next it begins reading each cell in return. If there is a 0 in the cell being read, the program writes a 1 to that successful cell (Fig. 19-9B). The program continues reading all the memory cells in the same way. Every cell with a 0 that is successfully read receives a 1 in return. After this march of 0s and 1s is completed, the next step in the test begins(Fig. 19-9C).

This march through the memory has produced some fine test results. We know, first of all, that the entire memory can store 0s. Second, the 0s can all be read successfully from the memory. Next, we were able to write 1s into all the bit locations. This demonstrates that the entire memory is able to transfer logic states between the MPU and the memory. If a bit is not able to have a logic state written and read, the program instantly stops at that bit and branches to another section of the program, which flashes a code of the defective bit's location onto the display.

The test so far has also proved or disproved the ability of the bits to hold their logic states as the next bit was exercised. That is, as a target bit was changed from a 0 to 1,

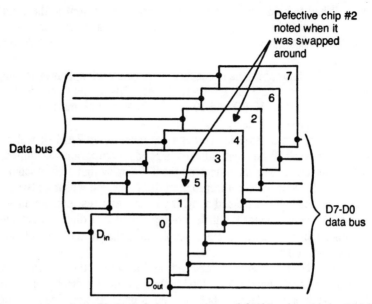

Fig. 19-8. In some computers with dynamic memory, once a defective address is located, it might be necessary to swap the chips around to note when the defect moved.

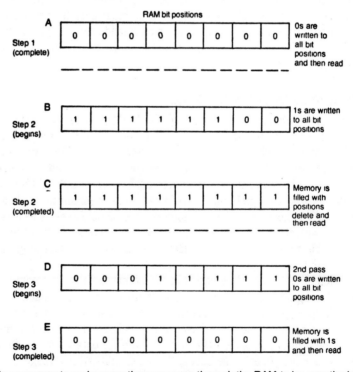

Fig. 19-9. It is necessary to make more than one pass through the RAM to be sure the bits on either side of a target bit remain intact as the electronic activity takes place.

the bit before it had to hold firm despite the electrical movement in the target bit. If it didn't, the program would signal failure. What about the bit after the target bit? It wasn't checked out for possible disturbance. If it failed and data changed, no failure sign would appear.

The bit after the target bit thus is checked next for stability. This is accomplished by reading every bit again to see if the 1 is there. When a 1 is present, a bit is deemed good and a 0 is written to it (Fig. 19-9D and 19-9E). If the complete march is able to be executed the memory passes the test.

As the march of bits takes place through the many K or RAM, it will on occasion encounter a defective bit. When that happens, a good test program will immediately stop the march. The program then announces on the TV display that a bit of failure has been discovered. If the RAM is statsic, the program then tells you whsat addsress has failed and also which bit position has passed away. If you and your test equipment were microscopic you would be able to test the little flip-flop circuit that died and actually pick out the short or open. Since you are not microscopic, take the word of the software that the bit position has gone down.

The indicated RAM chip is then replaced, and hopefully the computer is repaired. Often, however, the announced RAM chip number on the TV display of the program is wrong. The bit position is defective, but the chip is good; the trouble is in the bit input circuit in the address or data baus between the MPU and the RAM chip. We'll cover that eventuality next.

When the march program picks out a defect in dynamic RAM, some circuits are able to allow the program to pinpoint and display the actual chip that is defective. Other dynamic RAM circuits are built so the program cn provide the address of the defect but not the bit position. In those cases, the RAM chips must be swapped around to indicate which chip has the bad bit.

## ADDRESS AND DATA BUS TROUBLES

There are times when a CRC run through the ROM or a march program through the RAM indicates a defect, but the chips prove to be ok. When the indicated chip is replaced, the identical trouble still happens. This confusing result is often due to a short, or open circuit, in the address or data bus. The copper traces and their many connections, buffers, or latches can short to ground, to each other, or open. In 8-bit computers, there are 16 address lines and eight data lines. 16-bit computers can have up to 32 address lines and 16 data lines. 32-bit computers have 32 data lines as well as 32 address lines. In series with the lines can be all sorts of chip circuits. With software, a means should be available to isolate a defective line when it occurs. It is a program you could possibly compose.

When a defective address bus line is in the computer, the symptom could be that some parts of a grogram will run while other sections will not. If a defective data bus line happens, similar program problems will occur. The address line trouble causes the MPU to fail to reach an address when the defective line is needed to form the total address. The data bus line failure causes the MPU to fail to transfer data when the defective line is needed for the transfer. In extreme cases, the screen fills with garbage.

To find out which address bus line is gone, pick out sample addsresses and write to them. Then read the address to see if the data you wrote to the address arrived. You do not have to write to a ROM address, since it already contains data. When you find an address that won't respond, that address line is defective. To cover all those address lines in a 8-bit computer, the following addresses are written to. You'll notice that each address has 0s in all but one bit. The single bit containing a 1 is in the position of the line under test. The address formed cannot be contacted if the bus line is shorted or open.

### Test Address

| Binary | Hex | Bus Line |
|---|---|---|
| 0000000000000001 | 0001 | A0 |
| 0000000000000010 | 0002 | A1 |
| 0000000000000100 | 0004 | A2 |
| 0000000000001000 | 0008 | A3 |
| 0000000000010000 | 0010 | A4 |
| 0000000000100000 | 0020 | A5 |
| 0000000001000000 | 0040 | A6 |
| 0000000010000000 | 0080 | A7 |
| 0000000100000000 | 0100 | A8 |
| 0000001000000000 | 0200 | A9 |
| 0000010000000000 | 0400 | A10 |
| 0000100000000000 | 0800 | A11 |
| 0001000000000000 | 1000 | A12 |
| 0010000000000000 | 2000 | A13 |
| 0100000000000000 | 4000 | A14 |
| 1000000000000000 | 8000 | A15 |

With a small program along the same lines, the data bus cn be tested. The idea is to choose any known, good RAM address and write to it. Once the data is installed in the address, read it to see if it arrived intact. The data you transfer to the address is the following eight program bytes. Notice the arrangement of the 1s and 0s.

### Data Bytes

| Binary | Hex | Bus Line |
|---|---|---|
| 00000001 | 01 | D0 |
| 00000010 | 02 | D1 |
| 00000100 | 04 | D2 |
| 00001000 | 08 | D3 |

| Binary | Hex | Bus Line |
|--------|-----|----------|
| 00010000 | 10 | D4 |
| 00100000 | 20 | D5 |
| 01000000 | 40 | D6 |
| 10000000 | 80 | D7 |

Each binary 1 tests the data line that corresponds with its bit position. For example, if you poke hex 40 into a RAM location, when you peek into the location the 40 should be there. If it never arrived, data line D6 could have troubles. D6 corresponds with the binary 1 in bit 6 of the test data byte 01000000, which codes to hex 40.

The same test is just as valid on 16-or 32-bit computers as on 8-bit types. Just extend the number of address bits as needed. Also, the eight data bits are increased to 16, or 32.

## I/O DIAGNOSTICS

I/O trouble symptoms are easy to recognize. The affected peripheral stops working. For example, the keyboard can become inoperative. Pressing keys has no noticeable effect. Or the computer seems fine, but the printer doesn't murmur. In these cases, you must first determine whether the seat of the trouble is in the computer circuits or in the peripheral itself. The best test is to try another peripheral. If the new (known good) device also does not work, then the trouble is in the computer. Should the replacement peripheral operate, then the computer is ok and the old device needs looking at.

# 20
# Changing Chips Correctly

When a printed-circuit board is manufactured in today's factories, the board starts life at one end of the assembly line and comes alive at the other end with hardly a human finger touching it. The entire process is automated and the board is assembled by robots. A print board is nothing more than a laminated plastic board with copper foil bonded to both sides. A screen pattern is used to apply an etching solution and all of the copper except the designed wiring is then washed away. On boards that have DIPs installed there are holes punched through the board so the pins can be plugged into the holes and then the pins are soldered to the copper foil wiring (Fig. 20-1). On the boards that use surface mount devices, instead of holes, solder pads are used and the SMD legs are soldered to the pads as in Figs. 20-2 and 20-3. During maintenance and troubleshooting, you as a technician are liable to encounter both DIPs and SMDs as you work.

The factory robots are able to produce marvelous printed-circuit boards with pin-to-pin spacings smaller than 100 mils. The robotic devices solder these tiny pins with little trouble and when you look at the solder work you wonder how they are able to work so close and produce such a neat job. The awe you feel becomes even greater when one of these chips fail and you must desolder the package and resolder a new one in place. Unless you happen to be a print board artisan, your finished replacement job will not resemble the original factory robot installation in any respect.

However, don't worry, it really is not important that you reproduce the physical appearance of the original chip package on the board. What you must do though, is reproduce, in exact detail, the electronic workings of the dead chip so the computer will resume its designed performance without further ado.

## CHIP PACKAGING

As you look down on a print board, you'll see the chips laid out neatly. Surrounding all the chips are many support components such as resistors, capacitors, coils, switches,

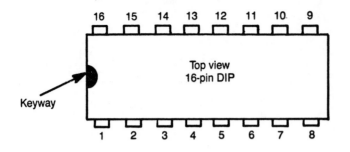

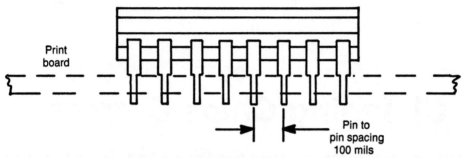

Fig. 20-1. A chip in a Dual-In-line package (DIP) has pins that are plugged through holes in a print board. Each pin is soldered to the copper foil connection on the bottom of the board.

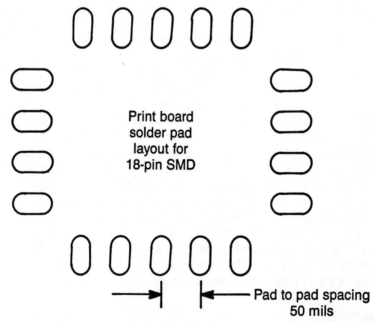

Fig. 20-2. A chip in a Surface-Mounted Device (SMD) has pins that have feet that stand on and are soldered to solder pads on one side of the board.

456

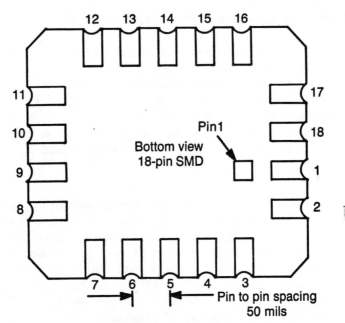

Fig. 20-3. This bottom view of an SMD shows the pins acting as feet. The pins are turned over inward on the SMD and match up with the solder pads on the board.

terminals, etc. Most of these components are relatively easy to desolder, replace, and resolder. That is because most of these support components possess very few pins. All you need are the replacement parts and the correct tools to do the job. The chips on the other hand, are not that easy unless they are socketed. The chips possess a lot of pins and the pins are very close together.

In years past, the chips for the most part were installed in DIPs. In recent years the same chips have been installed in newer type packages called SMDs. There are a number of SMD types. The DIPs important soldering characteristic is the fact that they are placed into and through board holes. Then the pins are soldered to the wiring on the bottom of the board. This method mounts the DIP on the topside of the board and connects the pins to the bottomside. In other words, the DIP uses both sides of the board. Using both sides of the board is considered wasteful.

In addition, the dual-in-line package has pins arranged on the two sides of the package. There are no pins emerging from the top and bottom of the package. This too is considered wasteful of space and a detriment to miniaturization. Those space wasting design features were among the reasons why new chip packages were conceived. Let's compare the different packages.

## The DIP

As mentioned, the DIPs are the little packages with the same number of in-line pins on either side of the narrow rectangular package. The pins are numbered counterclockwise starting at the left of the keyway, next to the keyway and working around to the last pin at the right of the same keyway. The keyway has been designated as a half moon grove, a paint dot, or both.

DIPs can be purchased in both plastic and ceramic forms. The pins are standardized and are spaced 100 mils apart. A mil equals 1/1000th of an inch. DIPs are hermetically sealed. The plastic DIP usually has tin-plated pins and can be worked with the usual electronics shop's 60/40 solder. The more expensive ceramic DIPs can be found with both tin-plated and gold-plated pins. When you find a defective DIP and prepare to desolder it and install a new replacement, you must consider these characteristics. There are more soldering technique details later on in this chapter.

## The SMD

The DIP, as described, uses both sides of the print board due to its plated through-hole mounting needs. There is no easy way to mount DIPs on both sides of the print board. That is where SMDs shine. The typical surface mount device does not have its pins pushed through holes. It's pins sit on solder pads. Solder pads can be placed on both sides of the board, SMDs can be mounted on the surface of both sides. This technique is especially handy for the print board cards that plug into the slots of today's computers. The cards stand up with their connections plugged into the slots. This keeps the two sides of the board out in the open air. Chips mounted on both sides of the board are feasible.

Besides being able to double up on chip population on one board because both board sides can be used, the SMD can be made smaller than the equivalent dual-in-line package.

The same chip that is inside a DIP can be installed into a smaller SMD package because all four sides of the SMD have pins. The DIP has no pins sticking out of its top and bottom. By utilizing the top and bottom for pin locations the SMD can be made 40% to 60% smaller in surface area than a DIP containing the same chip.

One common SMD type is called the CCP, for chip carrier package. The CCP, besides taking up less surface area on a print board, also has the shape of its pins changed. DIPs have straight pins that plug into holes. This is called plated through-hole technology. CCPs are designed with pins that look like feet. There are no holes on an SMD print board that uses CCPs. Instead of holes are the smaller solder pads mentioned before. The feet are designed to stand on the solder pads.

Once the feet are standing in the center of their designated pads, the area is heated, the solder melts, the feet sink into the solder and as the solder cools the feet attach themselves solidly to the pads. The connection is both physically and electrically strong. The CCPs are mounted directly on the surface of the board rather than through board holes. To top off the advantages, this surface mount process is considerably faster and cheaper to do than the plated through-hole technology.

The CCP solder pads have 50 mil centers. Two popular foot styles are the gull-wing shape and the J-lead shown in Figs. 20-4 and 20-5. The gull wing places a flat foot onto a solder pad while the J-lead bends over and places a knee onto the solder pad. When all the CCPs are placed on a board during manufacturing, the board can be heated and all the feet attach themselves at the same time onto the board.

458

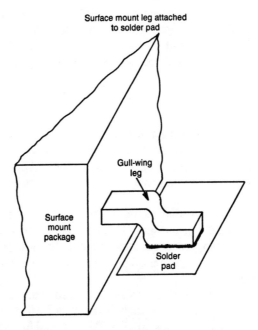

Fig. 20-4. There are a number of different style legs on SMDs. This is the so called "gull wing."

The New Surface Mount IC Package.

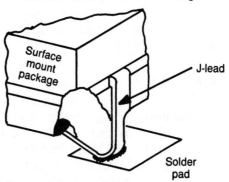

Fig. 20-5. An alternative leg shape on an SMD is the J-lead.

Because the board is not plated through, it need only be half as thick as one with DIPs. A typical DIP board has eight layers. The equivalent surface mount board only needs four layers. The savings can be illustrated by comparing an SMD one-megabyte board to an equivalent plated through-hole board. The SMD board will be 60% smaller in surface area, be half as thick, and cost 55% less than the DIP board.

However, when a chip on a surface mount board fails, you have a more difficult job troubleshooting and repairing it than a DIP board. The spaces between pins are very narrow and the solder pads are more trying to work with. The DIPs themselves are not that easy to test and replace, but the SMDs are even harder.

That doesn't mean you can't test and replace SMDs. You can. You must be careful and use the proper tools and techniques. With a bit of practice working with these small-sized components you'll be surprised how well you can manage. Later in this chapter we'll discuss the soldering tools and techniques required to replace both DIPs and SMDs.

## The COB

Another form of SMD you might encounter is called a COB, for chip-on-board. These chips are not replaceable under normal servicing conditions. The COB is a chip without the usual package. It is a chip that is wired and bonded directly to a print board along with the foil wiring between components. The silicon and its leads are part and parcel of the board itself.

Typically the COBs are sensitive memory integrated circuits. After the COB is wired and bonded to the board a plastic sealant is molded over the silicon and attached to the board. Once the attachment process is complete it is almost impossible to remove it from the board without destroying the chip. This is one of the reasons to use a COB. You can't access the COB physically.

The COB is used mostly to install and safeguard the software that could be in a specially designed ROM. The COB could possibly be used as RAM to save manufacturing money, but it is mostly a security technique. A ROM is packed full of permanent operating system and language interpreting system. These programs were written at considerable programming expense by manufacturers. These companies are not anxious to easily disclose the program lines by making the chips easily accessible. They install the ROMs as COBs, which provides a modicum of difficulty to anyone who wants to copy the ROM. If a COB should fail, it can't be replaced under ordinary means. The cost effective way to change a COB is to change the entire board it is bonded to.

## CHIP REPLACEMENT TECHNIQUES

Integrated circuit chips are much harder to troubleshoot and repair than the discrete components on the print board. The discrete components such as vacuum tubes, transistors, diodes, capacitors, resistors, etc., are relatively large and easily tested and replaced utilizing sockets, terminal tie points and plated through-holes. This is because discrete components have relatively few leads. A printed-circuit board with a defective discrete component, most of the time, is serviced routinely, the bad part is pinpointed and replaced. It would be very extravagant to replace a complete print board costing 500 dollars because a 50-cent capacitor shorted out.

These same type components are shrunk down into microscopic sizes and cast onto a silicon chip. They develop exactly the same type of electrical shorts, opens, and leaks. When these micro components go bad however, it is impossible to track down which germ sized component failed. You must therefore adopt the view that the chip is one black box component and your job then becomes deciding if the total chip is good or bad.

When you decide a chip is defective, the repair consists of replacing the entire chip. The techniques to locate the bad chip are somewhat different than pinpointing a bad discrete component, but not overly difficult. The next two chapters provide a lot of the available troubleshooting techniques to find bad chips.

The real difficulty arises after the faulty chip is located. It must be replaced. As discussed, the common ways that chips are packaged are in DIPs and SMDs. The packages are mounted on the print board in different ways. Each mounting method requires its very own replacement techniques. If the package is in a socket, most of the replacement effort is removed. To test a socketed chip, if you have a known good replacement, you gingerly pull the suspect out of its socket and install the new one. If the computer starts operating again the repair is over, the computer is fixed.

When you are checking a DIP with a low pin count and soldered through holes in the print board, the job is not too difficult. When this type DIP is a suspect, it can be tested pin-by-pin with the logic probe, VOM, or oscilloscope. The pin test results can then be compared with the voltages, logic states, or oscilloscope pictures on the computer schematic or test point charts. These are the prescribed test point results. According to the way the chip compares with the prescribed test results enables you to diagnose the chip as good or bad. When the chip is pronounced defective, it can then be replaced.

The technique is not difficult. You need a low-wattage iron and preferably some sort of solder sucker as shown in Fig. 20-6. The main trick is patience. If you examine the solder sucker iron, you'll see a tiny hole on the tip. The rubber bulb when squeezed will pump some air out of the hole. When the bulb is released, the air is sucked back through the bulb. If the tip of the iron is against molten solder, the solder will be sucked into the bulb. The suction does the job. This iron is used only for desoldering a chip. For resoldering I use an ordinary low-wattage iron.

When a DIP is desoldered, the iron is heated, the print board placed into a comfortable angle with a bright light shining on the bottom of the board focused on the chip to be

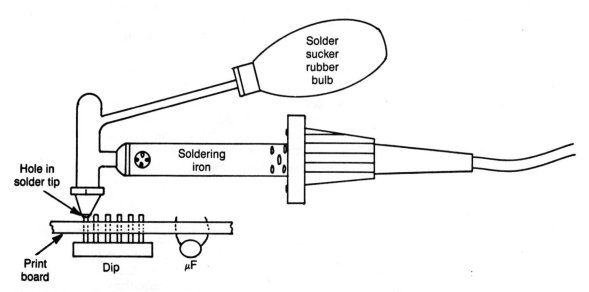

Fig. 20-6. It is difficult and tricky to safely desolder a DIP. The resoldering is easier in comparison. This type of solder sucker iron makes desoldering easier by vacuuming up some of the unwanted solder.

operated on. The bulb is then squeezed and the hole in the tip of the iron is placed over the first plated through-pin. You can see the solder melt. When the solder has turned liquid, you release the bulb. The solder at that pin is immediately sucked into the iron and into the bulb. Remove the iron and eject the solder by squeezing the bulb again.

If you are lucky you will have freed the pin. If the pin is still attached, repeat the process and keep repeating until the pin is free. Once the pin is free, go to the next pin and free it. Proceed from pin to pin until all the pins are free. Remove the defective chip. The new replacement chip can then be plugged into the open holes. Should one or more holes still have solder, either suck it clean or heat the solder and poke the excess out with a toothpick.

Making sure the new replacement chip is installed with the keyway correct (they will fit backwards but won't work), put the solder sucker aside and use a regular iron of 30 watts or less. Apply a tiny bit of solder to each pin. Be sure the solder does not drip and short across the tiny pins. This technique requires patience on your part. The desoldering can be tedious especially the repeated squeezing and releasing of the rubber bulb.

The job isn't too trying with the low count pin DIPs but as the count goes up, from 20 pins to 30, to 40, to 50 and so on, the tediousness of the job increases. However, that is the way the ordinary technician changing one chip does the job. In large service shops and manufacturing plants special desoldering equipment like large vacuum pumps with hollow tip irons are used. These vacuum desoldering systems cost hundreds of dollars. If you need such a system I've listed a few companies that deal in these items.

If you find that you will be replacing a lot of high pin count DIPs, these vacuum desoldering systems could become a must. Without one, the following happens again and again. As the pin count increases, the number of pins that defy immediate desoldering increases. These are the pins that take repeated heating and sucking efforts to free the pin. Even with the heat and sucking, these pins stubbornly refuse to pull free. You have to resort to some solder picking and more heat. The solder won't come off except speck by speck.

All the heat, even with the low-wattage iron, and all the solder sucking and pick stress can and does result in additional breaking of foil lines and otherwise harming or shorting of adjoining components as well as damaging the print board. The higher the pin count the more troubles will occur. Most of them are easily fixed, but who needs it? A deluxe desoldering system will save all this aggravation. Note it is only needed during desoldering. That is where the replacement problem exists. The resoldering is relatively easy.

## REPLACING SURFACE MOUNT DEVICES

When you open your machine and find it is full of SMDs, if you must replace one or more of them, you have a job on your hands. Since an SMD is soldered to only one side of the print board, you cannot get to the pins from the other side. Furthermore, there could be more SMDs on the other side of the board, making replacement complications multiplied manyfold. What can you do?

Let's start by examining the way a boardful of SMDs are installed in the first place. Typically a board is first constructed with all the solder pads installed. The pads are known to the technicians in the manufacturing plants as "footprints." There are footprints for every SMD and every pin on every chip. The pads are purposely made slightly larger than the foot on every pin. There is usually about 10-15 mils clearance around every pin. The pins are spaced 50 mils from center to center. The pins have feet such as the gull wing or J-lead, mentioned earlier.

Each footprint is given a layer of solder paste. The paste during manufacturing is usually installed in quantity through a stencil or screen. Often a print board needs to be recycled and have one or more chips replaced. In those cases the solder paste is applied to footprints one at a time with a hand syringe. When you replace solder paste during a chip replacement you can do the same job with a hand syringe.

Whatever, the paste is applied liberally onto the footprints with great care taken so the paste does not run off the pad. The paste serves a double purpose. First of all it aids the smooth flow of solder. Secondly, the paste on the footprint lets the pin foot sink into and stick to the pad. The paste holds the chip in place rather well and the chip won't slide off the pad and onto the bare board during soldering.

Once the paste has been properly applied, the surface mount device can be placed onto its footprints. In production the devices are installed by robotic pick-and-place machines at rapid speeds. If the board is being recycled and only one or a few chips are being changed, they are carefully placed by a technician by hand. The paste works well. When it is properly applied it will make up for chips that are installed slightly out of place. The paste will tend to make the chip self-align during the next step.

Once the paste and the SMDs are in place it is time to heat the solder pads so the solder will turn into a liquid and flow, connecting the wired up solder pads to the chip leg. When the solder cools and hardens, the chips are firmly installed. The solder should flow up the outside of the leg making a good solid connection.

The heating is conducted in an oven-type machine as seen in Fig. 20-7. The entire board is heated at the same time and all the solder on the board becomes molten and

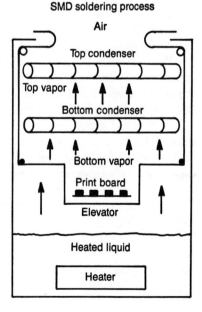

Fig. 20-7. SMDs can be soldered onto a print board all in one batch with the use of a special oven. The board full of chips is lowered into hot vapors in the oven on a timed elevator. After the solder flows the elevator rises and the board is removed.

flows simultaneously. In production this is fine as all the chips are connected at the same time. During recycling though, it is not necessary to heat the entire board since most of the chips are already well connected. In manufacturing plants they could have specially sized conduction soldering irons that will heat up all the pins on one chip at the same time. That way individual chips can be installed. These same special irons could also have a set of tongs to grasp the chip. This is handy for desoldering. That way they could heat all the pins at the same time and then lift the desoldered chip up and away with the tongs.

At any rate, getting back to the soldering of a full SMD board, in the oven is an elevator. In order to heat the board the elevator is able to descend into the heated oven environment at a carefully calculated rate of speed, pass through two layers of special vapors, and then arrive at the bottom of the elevator shaft. The temperature in the bottom vapor is about 215 degrees Centigrade. At the bottom a timer keeps the board still for between 10-30 seconds. The solder flows. The board is then raised back up to the top vapor layer where the molten solder becomes a solid once again. The legs are now securely connected to the footprints. The finished board is then removed from the oven area.

After the process the board is given a thorough cleaning to remove all of the solder flux that remains. The cleaning is performed with cleaning solvents that will take off all the residue and provide the components with good clearance between all connections. Now that you know how SMDs are installed in the factory, both a board at a time or individually, let's see what can be done to take them off and then reinstall them on your bench.

The solder sucker and other vacuum soldering machines aided in the removal of DIPs. They are not much help with the desoldering of SMDs. The tools needed for SMDs are lengths of solder braid, quantities of rosin, a fine-tipped low-wattage iron and a fine solder pick or small, sharp pocket-knife edges. Lastly, plenty of patience.

When the time arrives to desolder an SMD, position it in a bright light, flat on the bench top. Take a length of solder braid or solder wick and put generous amounts of rosin on the piece. Carefully place the solder braid across the pins on one of the four sides of the chip to be removed as in Fig. 20-8. Take the heated iron and place it against the braid. The braid will heat up and in turn the solder on the pins under the braid will become molten.

With the aid of the rosin, the braid starts soaking up the molten solder by capillary action. Rub the braid a bit on the pins to soak up as much of the solder as possible. When the braid becomes full of solder remove it from the pins. Snip off the section of the braid that is soaked with solder and continue with a new section of braid.

Work round and round the SMD carefully. You don't want to cause any heat problems or short excess solder across connections. Also, you do not want to ruin any solder pads or other print board wiring or components. Also, you don't want to kill the SMD in case it isn't defective after all. When you have soaked off as much solder as possible, you can stop using the solder braid.

Even with most of the solder removed, the SMD pins will still be sticking to the pads. However, they are now easily removed. With your fine-tipped iron and the solder pick heat each pin and pry it off the pad as the solder flows. Take your time and make sure each is free before starting on the next one. After awhile you'll have freed all the pins. The SMD can be lifted off. Before lifting though, make a note of the position of the keyway and pin locations.

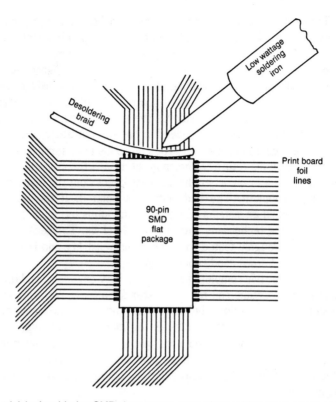

Fig. 20-8. The trick in desoldering SMDs is to sop up most of the solder with Desoldering braid or wick. The solder will be soaked up by capillary action.

To install the replacement SMD, the process is much easier. It is a good idea if you apply tiny dots of solder paste with a hand syringe onto the footprints as the factory technicians do. Then place the new chip into place pin for pin. Take your iron and solder one of the pins at or near a corner. Then do the other four corners. This tacks the chip down solidly. Finally with great care, solder all the pins into place. If you didn't accidentally cause any shorts, opens, or damage, the SMD replacement should be complete.

## BOARD SWAPPING

As described, testing print boards and then replacing defective micro-components in the field can be a very difficult if not impossible job except for the most expert, lavishly equipped technicians. As a result, most boards that fail in the field are usually "swapped" if a replacement board is readily available. For example, in a factory service department, the technicians are separated into two groups. Number one is the field servicemen. They are equipped with the latest in electronic service tools. In addition they are given a stock of known good print boards for the computers they will be servicing in the course of their day. Some of the boards are cards with a few chips while others can be motherboards with a hundred or more chips of all sizes and package types.

The second group of technicians are the benchmen. These fellows are the elite, they are the ones with the best troubleshooting and repair skills. Among them are some super elite. These are the ones who are print board artisans. They usually are the people who are able to quickly desolder and then resolder large pin count chips in DIP and SMD packages. About all they do all day is replace difficult chips.

When a computer system breaks down a field technician is dispatched. He arrives at a computer site and analyzes the trouble. He is usually able to isolate the seat of the trouble to a single print board. Once a print board is identified as containing the defect, without further ado, the technician removes the suspect board and replaces it with a known good board. If the trouble was indeed in the suspect board, the computer starts working again. The technician leaves and goes on to his next service call.

That evening, upon his return to the shop, he places the inoperative board into the factory servicing line. Later on, a bench technician checks out the board with the special factory servicing equipment. The bad chip is pinpointed. If the technician is good enough, he will go ahead an install a new chip. If the job is too much for him he passes the job on to one of the technicians with the artisan skills. The technician changes the chip, the board is thoroughly tested for quality and reliability and is then given to the parts department as a known good replacement.

As you can imagine, this complete procedure is very expensive and time consuming. However, computer downtime can mean disaster for a user. With this arrangement, a computer system that breaks down is back up and running in the least amount of time.

Board swapping, with a shop backup, is the main way bad chips are located and replaced. You can go this route if you must get a computer up and running at once. Whether time is of the essence or not, if you pinpoint a large pin count chip as the culprit and it is not in a socket, having the factory service operation do the chip replacement is probably the best way to go.

If you can determine which board has the bad chip during a bout of trouble, you can probably eliminate the need for a field technician. You could remove the board, take it to a factory service outlet and work something out with them. They might repair your board while you wait or perhaps service it overnight. They could give you an allowance for your defective board and make some sort of swap with you. I've worked out all sorts of arrangements as needed. Most computer dealers and the factory-type services they use are usually cooperative and want your system back on line as soon as possible. With a bit of tact and some electronic skill you can usually get them to help you without undue expense.

## STATIC ELECTRICITY CONSIDERATIONS

Electrostatic Discharge (ESD) is a main worry when chips are replaced. As Fig. 20-9 shows, there is a sensitive glassy insulator between the gate lead of an IGFET and the substrate. This insulator is the weak link in the FET. It will blow if it receives a shot of ESD. In chips, especially DRAMs, there are thousands upon thousands of these FETs equipped with these glassy insulators. You *must* take precautions to defend these chips from static electricity.

A few years ago the DRAM chips (like the 4 K types), only had a few thousand FETs on the substrate. The spacing between leads of these FETs were about five microns wide. Today, on about the same size chips there are more than a million FETs on the 1 megabit DRAMs. The lead spacing has been reduced to less than one micron. As a

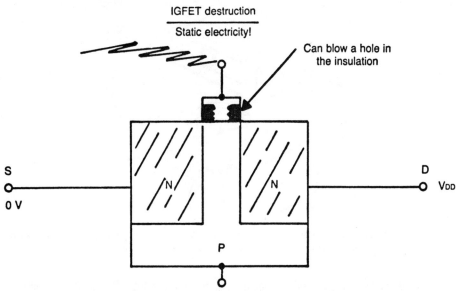

Fig. 20-9. On a chip there can be thousands upon thousands of these IGFETs. Each one has a microscopic piece of glassy insulation between the gate electrode and the channel. If one shorts through from static electricity, the entire chip could be ruined.

result the metallization between the FETs has also become vulnerable to electric shocks. It so happens that the smaller the sizes of features of the FETs on the chips, the more sensitive these chips are to ESD. Great care must be taken during chip replacement jobs. The handling techniques have been delineated by manufacturers. You must follow their instructions or you will cause yourself a lot of trouble.

Your body at all times, contains at least 100 or 200 V of static electricity potential. On a wet, humid day, there will be a minimum of about 100 V. On a dry day, the potential increases as you move around and brush your clothes against furniture, walls, the floor, and even the dry air itself, you can build up your personal static charge to a thousand volts or more. As you walk across a thick carpet, on a cold, dry day with low humidity and throw a spark at a doorknob, that shock could easily be measured in the thousands of volts. If a spark like this is passed through a chip during handling, odds of that chip surviving the ESD are not very good.

While a chip is residing on a print board, soldered securely in the circuit, it is fairly safe. Its pins are connected securely to the chassis ground and other secure circuits. It is energized as designed and there is very little chance of some ESD gaining access to the insulated gates of the FETs. The glassy gate insulators and the metallization between FETs though, are placed in peril when handled out-of-circuit. Especially on dry, low humidity days.

A professional technician is aware of the chip destruction static charges that could suddenly kill his new replacement chip that he might have waited weeks to receive. Before he unpackages the new chip, he first takes measures to lower the inherent static charge in his body, down to as close to zero volts as he can get. Zero volts is at earth ground. The technician connects himself to an earth ground such as a cold water pipe. Next he connects his work bench to earth ground. Then he reaches for his wrist strap.

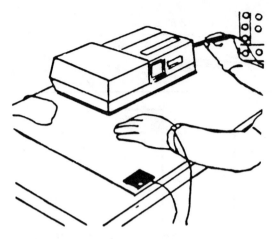

Fig. 20-10. When handling FET components static electricity can be rendered harmless with an anti-static kit like the one put out by RCA.

The wrist strap, illustrated in Fig. 20-10, comes in a kit. The RCA type is called their Antistatic Kit (Stock No. 162351); it consists of a static dissipative mat, a light-weight wrist strap, and coil cord. In addition there is a six-foot grounding cable that connects to earth ground. The wrist strap can be connected to either wrist although some technicians prefer to put the grounding bracelet on the hand they hold the probe or soldering iron with. They say that the closer the strap is to the hand that works on the chips, the less ESD will get through to the chips.

Because you will be grounded to earth while you are working, you must be careful not to touch any open electrical lines. That could be dangerous. To further insure that your grounding is safe, be sure that the outside of the wrist strap is insulated. In addition, there must be a resistor, such as a 1 megohm connected in series with the ground line at the wrist strap connection. That way, if you should cross a live electric line, the resistor will get zapped and not you.

There are a few more safety rules that will protect both you and the equipment you are working on.

- A device must never be inserted or removed from circuits unless the power to the circuits is off and the plug of the circuit is pulled out of electrical outlets.
- During the handling of chips, keep the chip in the conductive foam pad it came in. This keeps all the pins of the chips shorted together, which is the safest way for them to be, out-of-circuit.
- The chip must only be handled by the hand that is grounded with the bracelet grounding arrangement.
- All tools that contact the chip must be grounded at the time of contact. This includes chip pullers, chip inserters, pliers, screwdrivers, etc.

The soldering iron must have its tip grounded. The iron should have its plug pulled during the time the solder is heated or any time the iron touches the pins of the chip. This eliminates the possibility of the arc from the power company damaging the chip.

468

# 21

# Testing Chips and Bus Lines

When the computer fails and the display shows a screenful of garbage, the trouble is inside the digital circuits. The diagnostic software is useless. Diagnosis must be done with hardware test equipment that will show the condition of the test points on all the involved chips and connections.

The involved circuits are the MPU, ROM, RAM, and possibly I/O chips like the PIA. The garbage is being generated by an uncontrolled MPU. The MPU can go haywire if it or any of the circuits it communicates with has become defective. The first step in the garbage repair is to replace the indicated chips that are socketed. You start with a pencil and paper.

First, obtain or draw a chip location guide of the print board (Fig. 21-1). You will be paid back in time many times over. The chip location guide you acquire will familiarize you with the board and chips. It will save you from a lot of unnecessary hunting for components.

Next, the MPU, if it is socketed, should be carefully removed and a new replacement installed. If that doesn't cure the condition, a new ROM chip is next in line. If that still doesn't fix the trouble, RAMs and I/Os are then tested by direct replacement with known good chips. Be sure to exercise the necessary MOS chip-handling procedures so you do not shock good chips with static electricity during the replacements. Any chip electrocution will introduce a new trouble that could complicate the repair.

If the chip replacement is executed carefully, odds are good that the trouble will be gone. A good percentage of garbage repairs are due to defective circuits on one of the chips. Amazingly, though, the large MPU chip breaks down the least often of the group.

## THE BUS LINE TESTS

If chip replacement does not repair the garbage trouble, the next suspects are the address and data bus lines. In the factory, shorted and open bus lines are a matter of

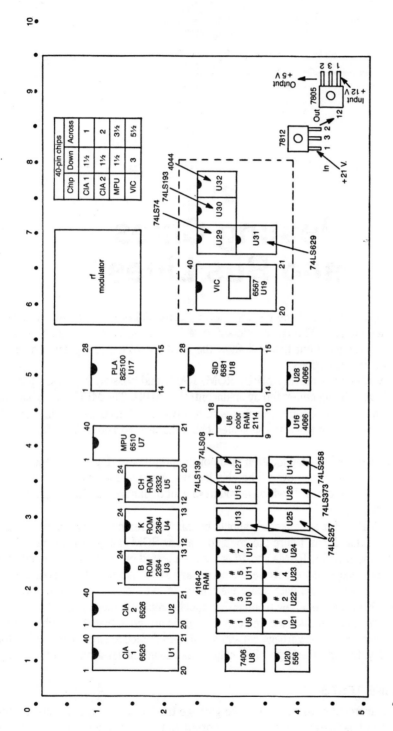

**Fig. 21-1. This is a chip location guide for the COMMODORE 64 that I drew. These type guides are usually the most used piece of service information.**

course. During production, a lot of fancy soldering goes on. Solder is applied by irons, by machines, in solder baths, and even sprayed. There is solder all over. As careful as the production line people might be, solder balls, slivers, and hairs get on the circuit boards. Even a tiny solder hair could cause the computer to go wild if it gets across the circuits and shorts out vitals.

In addition to solder, boards and components go through a lot of movement, heat, and stress. The connections are tiny, and require extraordinary handling and positioning. Mistakes are made, and open circuits can result.

Fortunately, the great majority of these troubles are caught on the production line by troubleshooters. Sometimes, though, a miniscule piece of solder gets through because it is on a spot that isn't causing trouble at the time. On occasion, a loose connection will test good in the factory but open while the computer is in transit or even during use. These complications must be tracked down and remedied in the field. They could (and often do) produce the garbage symptom.

The address and data bus lines run from chip to chip throughout the digital circuits. They can short or open anywhere in their run and cause troubles. They are the next items to be tested once the chips themselves have been deemed good and garbage is still on the screen.

The first test is visual. Look for solder pieces across lines. With a bright light, look for open connections or breaks in the copper traces. If you can't locate anything, grab the low-voltage continuity tester next.

First, test each address line and data line to the chassis ground. They should all read a high resistance to ground. Sometimes their resistance might not be too high, but they should at least all read about the same resistance to ground. If one or more is not the same as the others, this is a valid clue. That line could be where the trouble is. Check it out. This includes the pins of all the chips that the line is attached to.

Another test checks out the way any ground planes are installed beneath the print board. The ground plane acts as a shield, as well as being a handy place to attach to chassis ground. In lots of computers, the ground plane covers all the bottom wiring, connections, and components. The ground plane could be slightly askew or tightened in the wrong place. Also, a powered lead from a component, socket, or chip might be protruding too far out of the board and contacting ground. Sometimes a solder ball gets loose between the bottom of the print board and the ground plane, causing a short. If it is not prohibitive, remove the ground plane and trim any excess leads that can be seen. Reinstall the ground plane when you feel it is free of these problems.

## LOGIC STATE TESTING

If you have gone through the preceding quick checks and the computer is still displaying garbage, it is necessary to start probing test points with the computer energized. The place to begin is the MPU.

The 6809E is a typical 8-bit MPU (Fig. 21-2). It has 40 pins arranged in dual lines. Pin 1 starts at the left of the keyway, and the pins are numbered on that side to pin 20. Pin 21 begins at the same end of the chip as 20, on the other side. The pins are then numbered through to 40 which is opposite to pin 1. Note that the four ends of the chip rectangle are pins 1, 20, 21, and 40. As you relate the physical pins to the pins drawn on

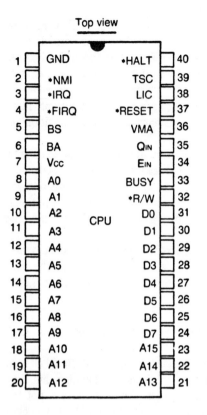

Top view

| Pin | Signal | | Signal | Pin |
|---|---|---|---|---|
| 1 | GND | | *HALT | 40 |
| 2 | *NMI | | TSC | 39 |
| 3 | *IRQ | | LIC | 38 |
| 4 | *FIRQ | | *RESET | 37 |
| 5 | BS | | VMA | 36 |
| 6 | BA | | Q$_{IN}$ | 35 |
| 7 | V$_{CC}$ | | E$_{IN}$ | 34 |
| 8 | A0 | | BUSY | 33 |
| 9 | A1 | | *R/W | 32 |
| 10 | A2 | CPU | D0 | 31 |
| 11 | A3 | | D1 | 30 |
| 12 | A4 | | D2 | 29 |
| 13 | A5 | | D3 | 28 |
| 14 | A6 | | D4 | 27 |
| 15 | A7 | | D5 | 26 |
| 16 | A8 | | D6 | 25 |
| 17 | A9 | | D7 | 24 |
| 18 | A10 | | A15 | 23 |
| 19 | A11 | | A14 | 22 |
| 20 | A12 | | A13 | 21 |

Fig. 21-2. If you look down on a 6809E MPU, the pins will be physically laid out on the print board in this arrangement.

the computer's schematic diagram (Fig. 21-3), you'll find they do not match up in any way. If you remember what the end numbers are on the actual chip it is easier to count the pins and make your tests.

The first two pins to test are VCC and ground (Fig. 21-4). VCC is supposed to be +5 V and ground is tied at 0 V. These two points are also high and low, or 1 and 0. It is best to use the logic probe for all the MPU testing, even VCC and ground. If the +5 V is missing, the probe will show any LED light. When the +5 V is present, the HIGH LED will shine. If the chip ground has disconnected, the probe will not light. When the ground is intact, the LOW LED goes on.

Once you've probed the supply voltage and it is ok, the next place to test is the address and data pins. There are 16 address pins and eight data pins. In this 6809E, the address lines light the HIGH LED when a 1 is on a line. For the line with a 0, nothing lights. You could see the start address in binary on the lines if the MPU has been able to read the ROM. Whether the ROM read has been started or not, a normal address line will light the PULSE LED on the probe. If the PULSE is not shown in any or all of the address lines, you have a valid clue. There is a problem in the clock or control inputs to the MPU, or the internal MPU circuits are defective.

The same reasoning can be applied to the eight data lines. There must be a pulsing output lighting the PULSE LED on the probe. The pulse is a form of MPU output. If it is not there, the trouble could be a defective clock or control line input. If the clock and

472

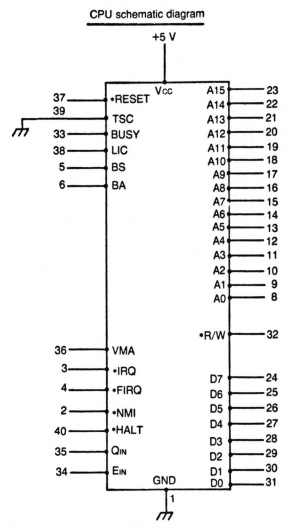

**Fig. 21-3.** If you look at the same 6809E drawn on the schematic the pins could be drawn in this fashion, bearing no resemblance to the physical layout.

control line inputs are ok, then the trouble is between the input and the output which is internal MPU circuits. A new MPU would be needed.

The companion line to the address and data buses is the R/*W pin 32. It is an output, and an important indicator. It is held high in the read position on the 6809E. The important indication is the PULSE LED that should light when the pin is probed. If it doesn't, the clock signal is not getting through the MPU correctly.

This particular 6809E uses the following inputs, which can all be tested quickly with the logic probe. First of all, there are two clock inputs called E and Q at pins 34 and 35. These inputs have frequencies of 0.89 MHz each and are spaced 90 degrees apart in their cycling. The logic probe shows a blinking pulse when they are present. All that is

| | Pin Number | VOM Reading | Logic Probe High (1) | Logic Probe Low (0) | Logic Probe Pulse |
|---|---|---|---|---|---|
| | Vcc 7 | +5 V | ✓ | | |
| | GND 1 | 0 V | | ✓ | |
| 16 Address Lines A0-A15 | 8 | | | | ✓ |
| | 9 | | | | ✓ |
| | 10 | | | | ✓ |
| | 11 | | | | ✓ |
| | 12 | | ✓ | | ✓ |
| | 13 | | | | ✓ |
| | 14 | | ✓ | | ✓ |
| | 15 | | ✓ | | ✓ |
| | 16 | | ✓ | | ✓ |
| | 17 | | ✓ | | ✓ |
| | 18 | 2.4 V - 4.0 V | ✓ | | ✓ |
| | 19 | | | | ✓ |
| | 20 | | | | ✓ |
| | 21 | | ✓ | | ✓ |
| | 22 | | | | ✓ |
| | 23 | | ✓ | | ✓ |
| 8 Data Lines D7-D0 | 24 | | | | ✓ |
| | 25 | | | | ✓ |
| | 26 | | | | ✓ |
| | 27 | | | | ✓ |
| | 28 | | | | ✓ |
| | 29 | | | | ✓ |
| | 30 | | | | ✓ |
| | 31 | | | | ✓ |
| | •Reset 37 | +5 V | ✓ | | |
| | •Irq 3 | +5 V | ✓ | | ✓ |
| | •Firq 4 | +5 V | ✓ | | |
| | •Nmi 2 | +5 V | ✓ | | |
| | •Halt 40 | +5 V | ✓ | | |
| Clock | QIN 35 | +2.4 V | | | Blinking |
| | EIN 34 | +2.4 V | | | Blinking |
| | •R/W 32 | +5 V | | | ✓ |

Fig. 21-4. The voltages and logic readings on this service chart should be present if the readings are correct. A deviation from this norm could be a clue.

necessary at this point in the procedure is a go/no go test. If the blinking LED occurs, they are considered ok for the present.

At pin 37 is *RESET. The asterisk indicates that the pin is held high. It goes into the reset procedure if a low is applied. The reset procedure causes the MPU to read the top two bytes of ROM. This configures all the computer chips. *RESET is held high by a connection to +5 V through a 100 K pullup resistor. The logic probe should read HIGH if the circuit is intact. If it reads LOW, or doesn't show anything, that is a valid indication of problems. The reset circuit needs further investigation.

Pin 39 is called TSC for three-state control. It is tied to ground. The probe should read a low. This keeps the MPU from going into a three-state condition. If the pin disconnects and starts floating, the MPU will stop operating.

Pin 40 is the halt input, *HALT. It is held high and if it goes low the address and data buses, as well as the R/*W output line start three-stating. The logic probe should read HIGH. If it does not, the +5 V halt pullup circuit could contain the defect. Pins 2, 3, and 4 are the MPU's three input interrupts. They all have asterisks: *NMI, *FIRQ, and *IRQ. They are normally held high during this type of testing. If you find one that is not high, that circuit is a lead to the trouble.

These tests will tell you if the MPU is running. When all the test points read normal, the MPU is operating. There is always the possibility that some exotic problem has developed that is not showing up, but it is not likely. Usually if these tests show the MPU is ok, there is little doubt about it. Also, when you do discover some bad test readings, they point at the circuit containing the defects. The pins that are held high are done so by little pullup circuits, which are easy to work through to find any bad parts.

While you are running the logic probe tests, take note as to the function of the pin under test. Is it an input that is receiving a signal from other digital circuits? For instance, *RESET and *IRQ are inputs. *RESET will receive a low when the reset button is pressed. *IRQ will receive a low when a peripheral device contacts the MPU.

Is the pin under test an output? All the address lines are outputs as well as the R/W line. The address lines are calling a memory location. The R/W line is telling the data bus which way to ship databytes.

The input/output observance is important. A good rule of thumb concerning how to interpret the logic probe test results of the pins is if an output line is showing wrong results, odds are good the chip under test is defective! The chip is not generating the correct output signal.

On the other hand, if a pin is an input and is reading incorrectly, chances are the chip under test is ok. The signal is coming from another source and it is not correct. The circuit feeding the signal to the pin is causing the trouble. Somewhere in that input circuit is the defect. Check out that circuit. If the *RESET pin is reading low all the time, test the *RESET circuit from the reset button to the input pin that yielded the clue.

## CHECKING THE BUS LINES

Once the MPU is checked and exonerated, the next circuits are the bus lines. They contain a lot of small chips and discrete components. There are buffers, latches, decoders, counters, multiplexers, and even capacitors and resistors.

## Data Bus Buffers

The data bus, whether 8-bit, 16-bit, or 32-bit, connects the MPU to all the locations in the memory map. The residents are registers in ROM, RAM, and the I/O chips. Most data buses need buffer circuits in series in the data lines (Fig. 21-5).

The main reason for the buffers is that the amount of current that leaves the MPU is miniscule. Each logic state, in the form of current, must travel a length of copper foil from the MPU to the addressed chip. In order to make the journey, the weak state must be amplified or it will never make it.

Another reason for the buffer is the physical makeup of the different MPUs, RAMs, and I/O chips. If the chips were wired directly the various types (TTL, NMOS, PMOS, etc.) would present many mismatches. Buffers can be designed to match them all up.

A third reason for buffers in the data bus is the fact that data must travel both to and from the MPU to the residents of the memory map. Three-state buffers installed in series in the memory map take care of these duties.

The buffers are YES gates. Two of them can be connected into one data line, wired head to toe. During a STORE operation, one buffer accepts an input from a data pin on the MPU. Its output goes to a bit in an addressed register. The amplifier circuit in the gate processes the state that enters. The same state leaves in an amplified, matched form and is stored in its addressed bit.

The second YES gate in the line, during a LOAD operation, accepts a logic state from a bit in an addressed location. It outputs the state into a data pin on the MPU. The same state leaves the buffer in an electrical condition the MPU can use.

While the data bus is moving bits for a STORE operation, the MPU-to-memory buffer is on and the other one is three-stated. During a LOAD operation, the memory-to-MPU buffer is on and the other one is three-stated into a high impedance condition.

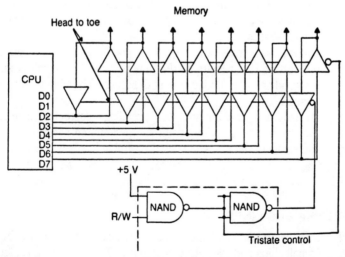

Fig. 21-5. The data bus in most computers will be equipped with three-state buffers wired head to toe in series with every data line in both directions.

476

The traffic direction can be controlled with the R/*W line, a NAND gate, and a NOT gate. The eight buffers that direct the bits to the memory are in series with each data bus line. Their three-state connections are all wired together.

The three-state control for the buffers comes from the output of the NAND gate. The NAND inputs are +5 V, a high, and the R/*W line. When the R/* line is in a write mode, it is low. With a high on one input and a low on the other, the NAND outputs a high. This high enables the buffers and they turn on, letting the MPU write to the memory.

Meanwhile, the buffers that are needed to direct traffic the other way are connected to the output of the NOT gate. The input of the NOT gate is the output of the NAND gate. During the write operation, the NAND gate is outputting a high. The NOT gate is connected to the buffers that take place in the read operation. The NOT gate, in this instance, outputs a low. This disables the read buffer participants. However, when the read operation goes on, the R/*W line goes high. The NAND gate then has two high inputs. The NAND outputs a low with these inputs. The low turns off the buffers that are used in the write operation and enters the NOT gate, where it is changed to a high output. The high now enables the buffers used in the read operation.

That is how the direction of the data bus signal flow is determined and executed. When the write buffers are enabled, the read buffers are disabled. As the read buffers are enabled, the write buffers are disabled. The R/*W line from the MPU is in control as it goes from high to low and back.

## Address Bus Buffers

The address bus can have buffers too, but for a different reason (Fig. 21-6). The address bits that leave the MPU travel in one direction only, from the MPU to the address that needs activation. The buffers are used to turn the bus on and off. There are times when the address bus is in the way and must be disabled. This occurs when the computer is transferring data between itself and some external devices. Most of the time, though, the address lines are on. The buffers are then enabled.

The address buffers are like the data buffers except for the fact that there is only one buffer set. The buffers, one for each address line, are in series with each line. They are connected with the input from the MPU and the output to the memory map.

The three-state line for all the buffers comes from the output of a NOT gate. The input to the gate can be a high, produced by attaching it to +5 V through a pullup resistor. This places a steady state low on the buffers. The low is the enabling signal for all the buffers.

The address lines thus stay on most of the time undisturbed. On the occasions the address lines must be three-stated, a low is applied to the NOT input, it outputs a high and the buffers are turned off.

## Bus Checkout

During checkout, the data and address buffer circuits are quickly tested with the aid of logic probe and the computer schematic. Some schematics are incomplete, so the use of the manufacturers spec sheet can also be helpful. The service notes are needed so you can physically locate the pins you want to take test readings on.

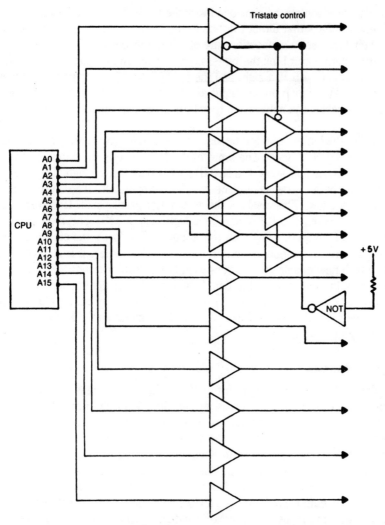

Fig. 21-6. The address bus only needs three-state buffers in one direction as addresses go to the memory map but not back.

The actual test examines the logic state on each pin that takes part in a bus line transfer. For example, in the data bus just discussed, a R/*W line should be held in the read position, a high, while the computer is waiting to be probed. The first touchdown point is the NAND input of the R/*W line. It should show a HIGH and a PULSE. If it does then the circuit is ok.

Next, the other NAND input should also read a HIGH but no pulse. The HIGH is the supply voltage through the resistor. The next test is at the output of the NAND gate. It should be a low according to the NAND truth table. If it is, the probe is moved to the input and output of the NOT gate. The input, which is tied to the NAND output, should be a LOW and the output a HIGH.

478

This read mode should place all the write buffers into a high impedance state and the read buffers on. The inputs and the outputs of the buffers can then be probed. The read buffers should show a logic state and pulse at the input and output. The write buffers should probe out with a logic state and pulse at the input but nothing on the output.

If you memorize the few truth tables required, you can proceed swiftly through the probing. In addition to the straight tests on the chip pins, you can employ simple test controls. For example, one of the inputs to the NAND gate is the +5 V. It can be shorted to ground as a test. There is no danger of damage, and the entire configuration will switch. This is the same effect as the R/*W line produces. You can use it as a test to see if all components are acting as they were designed to do.

## An Address Bus Variation

The buffering described in the last section used a lot of small chips to get the addressing done and the data transferred. For static RAM, this means of interaction between the MPU and memory locations is usually practical and is found in lots of machines. When dynamic RAM is needed, the number of transfer chips becomes unwieldly. Dynamic RAM also requires some refreshing circuits to keep the contents of read/write memory from leaking off. As a result, other special chips have been developed to take care of the buffering, latching, and refreshing.

One such chip is used with members of the 6800 MPU family. It is a 6883 40-pin type and called *SAM* for *Synchronous Address Multiplexer* (Fig. 21-7). During garbage troubles, SAM is one of the important suspects. It doesn't fail much, but it requires a lot of testing because it sits in the middle of the address line.

Looking down at the pinout, there are 16 address lines, A15-A0, spaced around the chip. These 16 lines connect directly to the 16 MPU address lines. The 16 bits the program counter puts out go straight to SAM (Fig. 21-8).Pin 15 of SAM receives the R/W input.

Pins 5 and 6 are the oscillator in and out connections. SAM takes care of generating the clock signal. The OSC in and out connections attach to the crystal circuit. Between this crystal discrete circuit and the SAM internal components, the clock E and Q signals are generated. Once produced, E and Q leave SAM at pins 13 and 14. They go to the MPU and the other destinations where they are needed.

Notice that SAM has no connections to the data bus. SAM is the controller for the dynamic RAM addressing, and the data bus is not involved in addressing. The inputs are the 16 address lines and the clock crystal circuit. SAM has two main jobs: doing all the addressing for the computer, and generating all the system timing.

SAM is controlled by an internal 16-bit register (Fig. 21-9). The register must contain data to control the various facets of SAM. Yet there is no data bus connection to SAM. In order to install the control bits into the register a different data transfer scheme is used. The bits are produced in each of the 16 bit holders by addressing each bit.

Each bit is built on the chip with two addresses. This gives the 16 bits in the register 32 addresses. Each bit has one even address and one odd address. When the even address is written to the circuit, it installs a 0 into the bit. If the odd address is written to, a 1 is installed in the bit. The register decides jobs to be done by SAM.

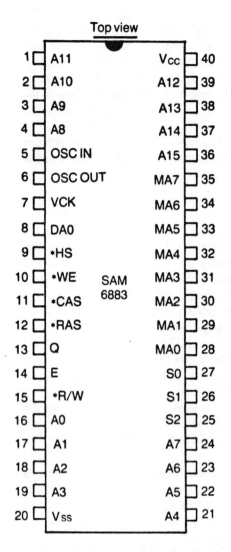

Top view

| Pin | Name | | Name | Pin |
|---|---|---|---|---|
| 1 | A11 | | Vcc | 40 |
| 2 | A10 | | A12 | 39 |
| 3 | A9 | | A13 | 38 |
| 4 | A8 | | A14 | 37 |
| 5 | OSC IN | | A15 | 36 |
| 6 | OSC OUT | | MA7 | 35 |
| 7 | VCK | | MA6 | 34 |
| 8 | DA0 | | MA5 | 33 |
| 9 | *HS | | MA4 | 32 |
| 10 | *WE | SAM | MA3 | 31 |
| 11 | *CAS | 6883 | MA2 | 30 |
| 12 | *RAS | | MA1 | 29 |
| 13 | Q | | MA0 | 28 |
| 14 | E | | S0 | 27 |
| 15 | *R/W | | S1 | 26 |
| 16 | A0 | | S2 | 25 |
| 17 | A1 | | A7 | 24 |
| 18 | A2 | | A6 | 23 |
| 19 | A3 | | A5 | 22 |
| 20 | Vss | | A4 | 21 |

Fig. 21-7. When dynamic memory is used with a chip like the 6800, a chip like this SAM is useful to multiplex the addresses and refresh the row addresses. Failure of the SAM circuits can cause garbage.

Two bits adjust SAM to various memory byte sizes. For instance, if both bits are cleared with 0s, the SAM is ready to operate with 4 K bytes. Two more bits determine the output frequencies of E and Q. Seven bits produce the video address. There are three bits to choose the mode the video display generator should operate in. One bit each decides the setting of the page switch and the map type. These bits can all be set or cleared by the software the programmer uses.

SAM outputs addresses and control signals, besides E and Q. Pins 25, 26, and 27 are high order bit outputs to select chips (Fig. 21-10). These three bits are sent to a decoder chip. The three bits can choose among eight outputs. This allows SAM to select from eight individual chips like RAMs, ROMs, and PIAs.

SAM outputs the address of the bit to be accessed in each dynamic RAM, through pins 28-35. These pins are MA7-MA0, multiplexed address bits. The low order bits of

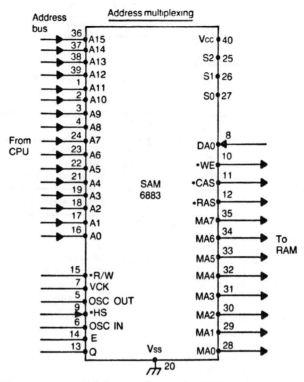

Address
bus

| Pin | Signal | | Signal | Pin |
|---|---|---|---|---|
| 36 | A15 | Vcc | | 40 |
| 37 | A14 | S2 | | 25 |
| 38 | A13 | S1 | | 26 |
| 39 | A12 | S0 | | 27 |
| 1 | A11 | | | |
| 2 | A10 | | | |
| 3 | A9 | | | |
| 4 | A8 | DA0 | | 8 |

From CPU

Fig. 21-8. The schematic drawing of the SAM chip shows lots of addressing involved pins but no data bus pins. It does not have anything to do with data. It is a helpmate for MPU addressing and clock signal generation.

the address is output first in time with the Row Address Strobe, RAS. This picks out the row in each chip that is being addressed. The high order bits of the address are then output over the same pins in time with the Column Address Strobe, CAS. This addresses the column in each chip desired. The desired bit is at the intersection of the row and column in each dynamic RAM chip. A copy of each bit is removed and sent to a latch chip.

The latch collects the eight bits and outputs them to their corresponding lines in the data bus. The data bus forwards the bits to the MPU.

### SAM Checkout

The best way to check out this SAM chip that takes over the address bus, is with a pin by pin checkout with a logic probe. A VOM is handy but is not as informative. The VOM will quickly read the +5 V supply and ground connections but the other pins are better tested with the logic probe (Fig. 21-11).

The logic probe is best because the SAM chip has pulses on every pin except 40 Vcc, 20 ground, 6 OSC in, and 5 OSC out. The supply voltages are steady state, but the OSC voltages are waveshapes. However, they are analog sine waves of the crystal frequencies and the logic probe deals in digital square wave types.

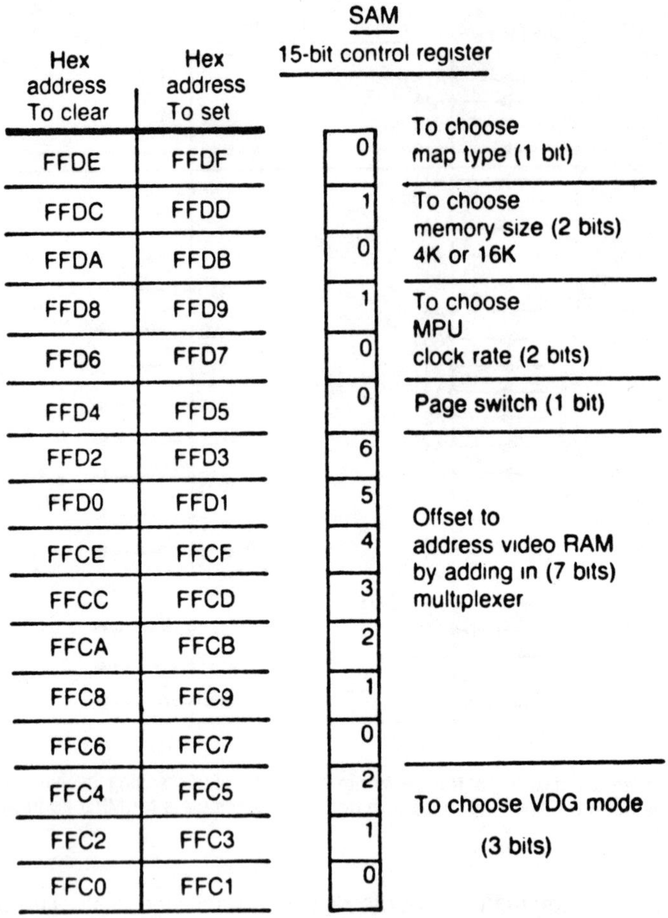

| Hex address To clear | Hex address To set | | |
|---|---|---|---|
| FFDE | FFDF | 0 | To choose map type (1 bit) |
| FFDC | FFDD | 1 | To choose memory size (2 bits) |
| FFDA | FFDB | 0 | 4K or 16K |
| FFD8 | FFD9 | 1 | To choose MPU |
| FFD6 | FFD7 | 0 | clock rate (2 bits) |
| FFD4 | FFD5 | 0 | Page switch (1 bit) |
| FFD2 | FFD3 | 6 | |
| FFD0 | FFD1 | 5 | |
| FFCE | FFCF | 4 | Offset to address video RAM |
| FFCC | FFCD | 3 | by adding in (7 bits) multiplexer |
| FFCA | FFCB | 2 | |
| FFC8 | FFC9 | 1 | |
| FFC6 | FFC7 | 0 | |
| FFC4 | FFC5 | 2 | To choose VDG mode |
| FFC2 | FFC3 | 1 | (3 bits) |
| FFC0 | FFC1 | 0 | |

Fig. 21-9. The 16-bit control register in SAM is set or cleared by addressing its 32 addresses. When an even location is addressed, the involved register bit is cleared. When an odd location is addressed, the bit is set.

All the rest of the pins should show a PULSE, since they are active. The address lines could have a HIGH in addition to the PULSE. A HIGH indicates an active 1 on the line. If only PULSE is present, the address bit can be considered a 0. Also if a LOW appears the bit is a 0.

The important test is the PULSE indication. It must be present or the computer is not operating. It should be on all the PULSE-designated pins. Even if a single required PULSE is missing, that is a sign of trouble. A good quick check is to touch down rapidly on each pin except the four mentioned above. Look for the PULSE indication at each pin. Odds are good that if the pulses are all present, the chip is probably good. If a pulse is missing, the clue will be obvious.

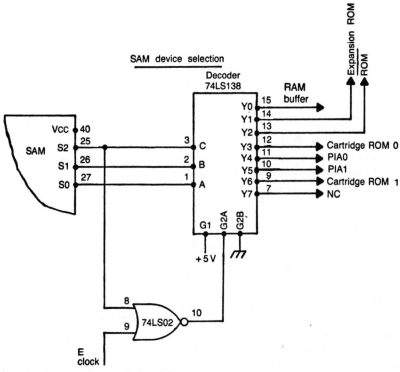

Fig. 21-10. SAM can select eight chips with the three address bits from S0, S1 and S2.

## SOPHISTICATED CHIP CHECKOUT

An expert technician maintains or repairs a computer with the fewest service moves and in the fastest time. For the most part, repair jobs are not the place for education or experimentation. During disassembly, only those areas in trouble are taken apart. There is no reason to disassemble the entire computer unless it is required for the repair. The defect is pinpointed as quickly as possible. When repairing a computer, the idea is to get the unit back in operation as quickly as possible. The great majority of repairs are straightforward, and do not need sophisticated techniques.

There comes a time, though, when engineering-level service moves are needed. Fortunately, these debugging measures are mostly needed in factories and not in the field. Computer hardware troubles are one of two kinds: trouble that has occurred to a computer that has been in operation and has worked fine until the breakdown, or trouble that is contained in a computer being developed or manufactured. The computer has never worked. It becomes the technician's job to get it operating for the first time.

The first type of problem is usually not overly difficult. The second kind of trouble can be a major project. This second type of trouble, where the computer has never operated, is the main opportunity to use sophisticated service measures; field service jobs do not often require them. We'll explore the factory techniques briefly.

In the factory, on the production line, some computer boards come off the line and do not work. Typical faults are address and data bus lines shorted to ground or together,

| Pin Number | | Sam Service Checkout Chart Logic Probe | | |
|---|---|---|---|---|
| | | High (1) | Low (0) | Pulse |
| Vcc | 40 | ✓ | | |
| GND | 20 | | ✓ | |
| A15 | 36 | ✓ | | ✓ |
| | 37 | | | ✓ |
| | 38 | ✓ | | ✓ |
| | 39 | | | ✓ |
| | 1 | | | ✓ |
| | 2 | ✓ | | ✓ |
| | 3 | ✓ | | ✓ |
| | 4 | ✓ | | ✓ |
| | 24 | ✓ | | ✓ |
| | 23 | ✓ | | ✓ |
| | 22 | | | ✓ |
| | 21 | ✓ | | ✓ |
| | 19 | | | ✓ |
| | 18 | | | ✓ |
| | 17 | | | ✓ |
| A0 | 16 | | | ✓ |
| OSC IN | 6 | | | |
| OSC OUT | 5 | | | |
| •R/W | 15 | ✓ | | ✓ |
| E | 14 | | | ✓ |
| Q | 13 | | | ✓ |
| S2 | 2 | | ✓ | ✓ |
| S1 | 26 | ✓ | | ✓ |
| S0 | 27 | | ✓ | ✓ |
| MA7 | 35 | | | ✓ |
| MA6 | 34 | | | ✓ |
| MA5 | 33 | | ✓ | ✓ |
| MA4 | 32 | | ✓ | ✓ |
| MA3 | 31 | | | ✓ |
| MA2 | 30 | | | ✓ |
| MA1 | 29 | | | ✓ |
| MA0 | 28 | | | ✓ |
| •CAS | 11 | | | ✓ |
| •RAS | 12 | | | ✓ |
| •WE | 10 | ✓ | | ✓ |
| •HS | 9 | ✓ | | ✓ |
| DA0 | 8 | ✓ | ✓ | ✓ |
| VCK | 7 | | | ✓ |

(16 Address Lines A0-A15 spans pins 36 through 16)

Fig. 21-11. SAM can be checked out in a pin-by-pin manner. If you have a logic probe service chart like this one, it will speed up the testing.

defective MOS chips that died during handling, broken TTL chips, open copper traces, and shorts between traces. Other possible defects are bad chip sockets, wrong components, chips installed backwards, and lead clippings trapped in places where they cause shorts or opens.

The type of trouble often comes in pairs, trios, and other multiples. They are much more difficult to diagnose than problems on computers that have been in use. When a computer in the field goes down, it usually has only a single trouble.

To expedite factory troubleshooting, engineers have defined a few different procedures. They are rarely needed in the field, but it is useful to have an idea of what they are.

## TEST JIG

Every production line troubleshooting bench has a test jig tailor-made for the computer being assembled.

For example, suppose a single board 8-bit computer is being mass-produced. At the end of the production line, the unit is energized and a specially-prepared program is run. If the program works, the board passes the test and is packaged. When the program won't run, the board is rejected and sent to the troubleshooter.

A new MPU is tried, but that's rarely the defective part. MPUs are amazingly reliable. Next step the servicer takes is removal of the MPU and the installation of the test jig (Fig. 21-12). The test jig could have an output plug that is a 40-pin DIP. The plug is inserted into the MPU socket on the print board.

The tester works on the principle that troubles in the computer are due to shorts, opens, and leaks in the hardware. These troubles are called *static*. Once the dielectric of

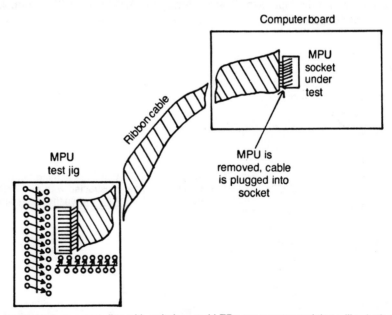

Fig. 21-12. In the factory test, jigs with switches and LEDs are constructed that will substitute for the MPU and allow the technician to conduct point by point static tests for shorts, opens, and leaks.

485

a capacitor springs a leak, the composition of a resistive element changes its net resistance, a piece of N and P semiconductor material changs its composition or cracks, two copper traces short together or a connection opens up, the trouble exists, and it does not go away by itself.

Compare this to a *dynamic* trouble, which could be a memory chip that stops operating only during certain conditions of humidity, voltage, current, or waveshapes. The trouble heals when the supply voltage is removed. The only way to make a test is to energize the unit and try to reproduce the trouble incurring environment. This is a difficult trouble to deal with; fortunately, it does not happen too often.

Static troubles are handled well with the static test jig, which is used only to pinpoint the circuit containing the static trouble. It substitutes for the MPU to test the surrounding circuits that the MPU operates with.

As far as ROM, RAM, and I/O chips go, the MPU only does two jobs. It reads from the memory map, and it writes data to the map. What the MPU does to the data is not a part of the memory map operation. The static tests have only to observe if the memory map and its environs are able to receive data from the MPU and send data to the MPU. With the test jig plugged into the MPU socket, these two functions can be checked out.

To do the check, the jig must be able to address the computer locations, send out a strobing or gating signal, and see if the data is transferred. The jig therefore must be able to produce a digital signal or be able to read a signal that is stored in memory.

There are three kinds of circuits needed in the jig. These circuits are each attached to individual pins. One circuit is able to read an incoming logic state (Fig. 21-13). A second circuit is able to output or write a logic state (Fig. 21-14). The third circuit is able to both read incoming signals and write output signals (Fig. 21-15).

Each MPU pin substitution circuit is an indicator. LEDs are installed in each input pin circuit to show if the input signals are entering the MPU socket. For example, input pins on a typical socket that read incoming signals are the interrupts and reset. If an

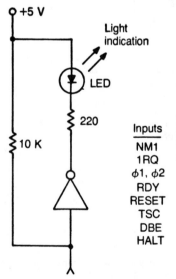

Inputs

NM1
1RQ
$\phi1$, $\phi2$
RDY
RESET
TSC
DBE
HALT

Fig. 21-13. An MPU test pin that does nothing but read inputs that enter the MPU can be constructed with an inverter, LED, and two resistors. The LED will light when the desired logic state enters the pin.

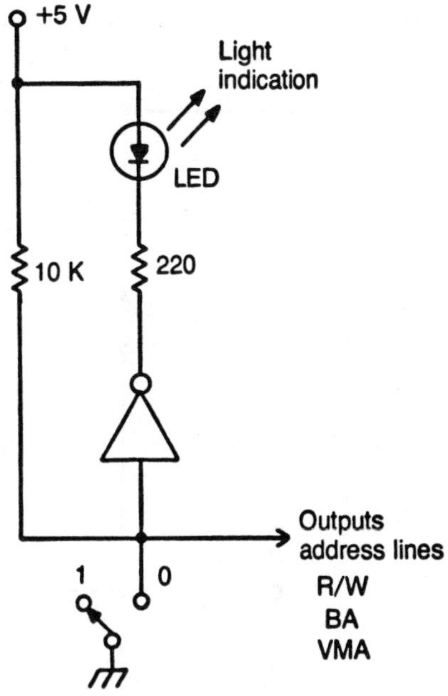

Fig. 21-14. An MPU test pin that does nothing but write outputs to the computer can be constructed with an inverter, LED, two resistors, and an off/on switch. The LED will light when the correct logic state is output.

*IRQ, *NMI, or *RESET pin receives a low, their monitoring LED lights, indicating the admission of the low.

The address lines are all outputs. They are built with switches in a circuit that can output either a high or low. The switch connects to +5 V to energize a logic state. To conduct a test, you can set the switches at any desired address. This dials up that location over the address bus.

The data lines are read/write types. For the input read, LEDs are installed in a separate input circuit. When a logic state enters a data pin, the LED lights.

In parallel with the input circuit, pin for pin, is an output circuit for the write function. The write circuit has individual switches for each data pin. You can set up a write output by setting the switches.

Once the MPU Substitution Machine is built for a particular computer board, it can take the MPUs place for electrical fault-finding purposes. You can take the computer board all the way through a complete data transfer operation, either reading from the board or writing to the board.

For example, suppose you want to see if the MPU is able to read from memory. Use the step by step procedure the MPU goes through as it executes a read. A good place to read from is the start address of the ROM on the board. For an MPU like the 6502, the read requires two steps. One is the setting of the address with the output switches. The address is in binary. The 1s are made by closing a switch. The 0s are produced by leaving a switch open. The second step is setting the R/*W line. The R/*W switch is set to a 1 for the read.

With the Substitution Machine plugged into the MPU socket, the address set, and the R/*W line is a 1, some or all of the eight data LEDs that do not light are 0s. The LEDs will provide a copy of the contents of the ROM start location you dialed up.

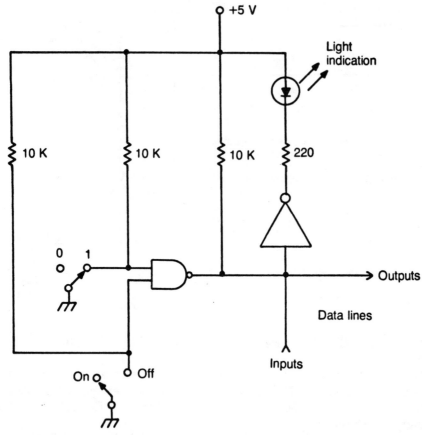

Fig. 21-15. An MPU test line that acts as a data pin can be built with the parts in the sketch. The circuit will indicate if a read or write is going on.

If the read operation is successful, then all the hardware involved in the test is considered ok. If the read try fails, the hardware becomes suspect. According to the way it fails, specific circuits or components are suspect.

If the result of the data read is not the data that you know is in the ROM, you could have contacted the wrong address. Check the address line bits. If only part of the data shows up on the LEDs, then a data line could be open.

To test static RAM and I/O chips, you can both read and write to the suspects and observe what happens. Dynamic RAM does not respond in simple static tests like these.

This type of testing device is usually built by a technician under the design instructions of an engineer at the startup of a production run. Production runs are not ordinarily the same, and the test machine often requires many design changes from run to run. It would be difficult to utilize one of these devices in a shop that does general servicing. While these MPU substitutors are invaluable on a long factory production run, they have restricted use in the field.

## ADVANCED TEST DEVICES

Before the wide proliferation of 16-bit and 32-bit microprocessors, the old tried and true methods of testing 8-bit integrated chip hardware was relatively easy using the methods just discussed. The newer, larger chips however, have placed hardships on the old pin-by-pin methods. For example, testing a 386 processor circuit, connected to 132 pins is a tough, time consuming job. As to be expected test equipment manufacturers have brought to market test instruments that take a lot of the effort out of these multi-pin difficulties.

These test instruments are expensive for the individual computer technician but relatively inexpensive for a large company that repairs more than a couple of hundred print boards a month. A typical test system can cost between $5,000 and $10,000. This sort of system consists of the following.

John Fluke Mfg. Co. in Everett, WA 98206, markets print board servicers they call their 9000 Series. One system is based around a model 9010A Troubleshooter mainframe, a second system is their model 9100A. These pieces resemble large desktop calculators or single board computers. They are designed expressly for testing and troubleshooting, as shown in Fig. 21-16.

A companion piece to the mainframes is an interface pod. The pod is a hand-held device with a wide ribbon cable coming out of one end, and an ordinary cable out of the

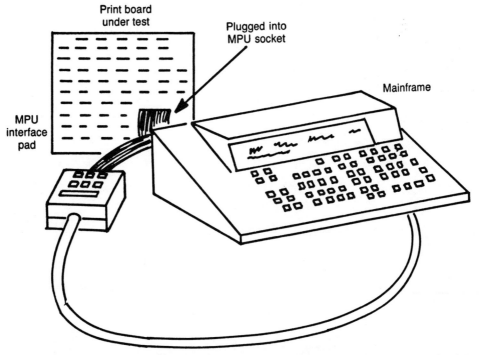

Fig. 21-16. This is an advanced MPU servicing system. The mainframe is a programmed device that can run all sorts of electronic tests on an ailing circuit board. The MPU Interface Pod is specially made to be specific to a particular MPU. For instance one pod can be made for the 8086. The 8086 is then replaced with a plug from the pod. The pod assumes the role of the 8086 on the defective board. The mainframe can then be used to test all the circuits connected to the 8086 socket.

other end. The pod is specific to the processor on the print board that is to be tested. There are pods for over 50 different processors including most of the ones discussed in this book. The pod is equipped with the ribbon cable connector that is designed to plug into the socket of the specific processor. The processor thus is removed and the pod connector plugged into the socket in the processors place. The other end of the pod connects to the mainframe.

The pod is a little computer in its own right. It has its own processor, RAM, ROM, and I/O circuits. It is dedicated to detect faults on print boards that contain the processor it is specific to. The pod can act as a computer and places the board being tested into the role of an I/O device. According to instructions the pod tests the board for faults.

Once connected and energized the pod starts running tests. The board under test does not need to be energized. These tests consist of checking the board bus lines, all of the RAM chips, the ROMs, the I/O circuits, and an AUTO test. The pod also runs various software exercises to determine the abilities of the board under test. For specific print boards and special test procedures you'll need to confer with the manufacturer's representative. These manufacturers are all constantly coming out with new advancements along the lines of these pieces of equipment.

# 22
# Testing I/O Circuits

When a computer fails to work with one or more of its peripheral devices the diagnosis of the trouble is simple. For example, if the computer won't respond to your keyboard strikes, then the trouble is indicated to be either in the keyboard itself or the keyboard input circuits. Should the printer stop churning out copy, the source of the trouble is either in the printer or its interface circuits. If the cassette or disk drive stops operation, the same troubleshooting reasoning is applied. Either the cassette or disk drive is defective or the computer's cassette or disk interface circuits have failed.

The first repair step, is to disconnect the peripheral that conked out and try a known good peripheral in its place. If the replacement device starts right up in fine fashion, then the trouble is pinpointed in the original peripheral. The old device is defective and needs repair or replacement. However, if the known good device won't work either, the odds are that the computer circuits that are interfaced to the device contain the trouble and require repair. In this chapter, we will examine some typical interface circuits and the techniques used to service them.

## VIDEO INTERFACE

The video circuits in a computer are there to generate a TV picture that can be injected into a video monitor. The picture display is a still that can be added to or moved about. The display can be produced in monochrome or color. Its all up to the capabilities of the video circuitry.

In small personal 8-bit computers, containing 30 to 40 chips, there is typically a single board mounted in the keyboard case. On the board, in addition to the digital circuits, there are video chips and other components to develop the TV display. Most of these computers produce a composite TV signal as in Fig. 22-1. This signal is then put into an RF modulator circuit that captures the composite TV and places the signal into a carrier

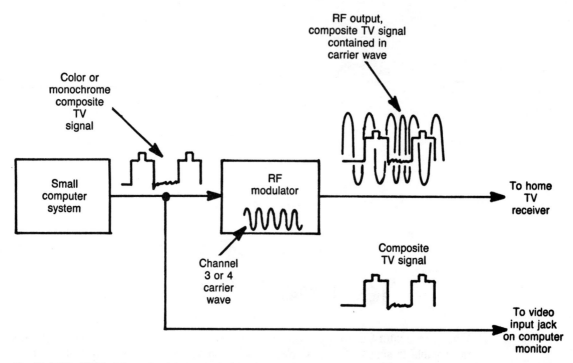

Fig. 22-1. The RF Modulator circuit is used when the home TV receiver acts as TV monitor. The RF Modulator installs the computer video output into a carrier wave the home TV can be tuned for. A computer monitor can accept the video output directly without a carrier wave.

wave. The carrier wave is tuned to channel 3 or 4. This RF output can then be attached to any home TV and the display will appear on the screen.

Some small computers, output the composite TV directly without the RF carrier wave. The composite signal can be monochrome or have color elements added to it. This signal can be plugged into a video input jack on some home TVs or into a computer TV monitor. This display system produces a better quality display than the RF carrier display.

Besides the composite TV signal, some computers are able to generate another type of color signal. This form of display is called RGBI and also just plain RGB. This output signal is different than the composite TV. The composite TV signal is quite like the one that commercial TV stations produce. The RGBI signal is entirely different, as shown in Fig. 22-2.

A color TV signal is made up of three signals to produce three different color lights, red, green, and blue. The lights are added together on your TV display screen. You see the result of the light addition. There will be more about this in the next chapter.

The composite TV signal the video circuits produce have the three colors contained in the single composite. The TV receiver takes the composite TV signal apart and separates the colors. The colors are then sent through amplifiers to the three color guns in the picture tube for display. The RGBI signal is treated differently. Rather than having the three colors separated in the TV receiver, the three colors are separated in the com-

492

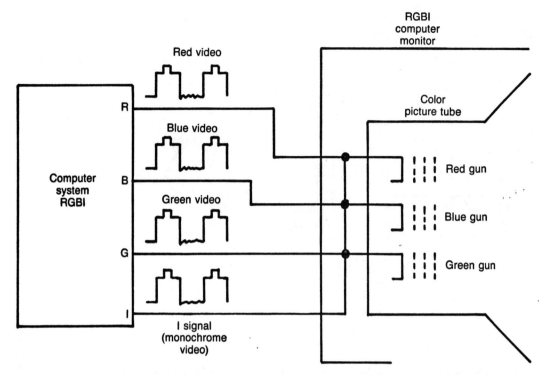

**Fig. 22-2.** The RGBI is composed of four signals, the three colors and a monochrome component. Each color plus the monochrome is fed to the color picture tube in the monitor.

puter video circuits. The computer then outputs each color separately through individual pins in the RGBI output plug. In the TV monitor the R, G, B, and I are all processed separately and applied individually to the three gun color CRT. Figure 22-2 shows the color distribution.

In the larger personal computers, the video circuits can be treated differently. Instead of being part and parcel of the print board, these computers have card slots as discussed in Chapter 16. In these cases the video circuits are not mounted on the motherboard. The video circuits are built on cards and are options. For example, the IBM PC can have a monochrome card in place or can plug in a color TV card.

Whatever the actual physical configuration is, the video circuits must generate a TV signal that will appear on the screen. The circuits must under normal circumstances produce three general displays. First of all they must produce the alphanumeric characters that are on the keyboard. Secondly, they must be able to display graphics. Thirdly, they should be able to combine the alphanumerics and graphics to show special effects.

### Typical Video Operation

When you strike a key, a row-column switch in the keyboard is shorted and generates a specific set of bits for that key. The bits pass through the interface chip, go to the processor and are promptly stored in RAM. A special section of RAM is set aside to hold keyboard generated bits. If the display is a 40 column, 25 row type, then 1000 video

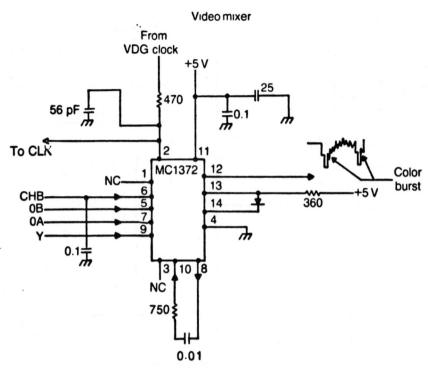

Fig. 22-3. Once the composite video signal is out of the VDG, it is injected into ordinary analog color video circuits like this video mixer chip. The analog scope, voltage, and resistance tests are used for troubleshooting.

RAM locations are reserved. They could be at decimal addresses 1024 through 2023. Each RAM location can hold one byte of code. Each RAM location is assigned to operate with one of the 1000 character blocks in the TV display. The RAM location controls what will appear in the character block.

Each of the 1000 character blocks can contain 64 dots of light that make up the shape of the character the block will display. Each dot of light can be turned on or off by the video display circuits. In the display circuits is a ROM that contains a table. In the table is the information to display the alphanumeric and graphics characters.

For example, in eight byte locations in the ROM are 64 permanent bits. Each bit is an off-on switch for one of the dots of light. If a bit is high, it can turn a dot on. When a low bit is used, it can turn a dot off. The video circuits, in action, take one of the keyboard generated codes from video RAM. The code is an address to a particular character in the character ROM. The video circuits access that character and apply the bits to the TV display block. The dots of light are turned off and on according to the pattern of bits in the eight bytes that were accessed.

In a typical video circuit, the 1000 bytes of video RAM could be scanned 60 times a second and copies of the RAM contents read. The video circuit then uses the video RAM codes to access the character ROM and obtain the bits needed for control of the character blocks. The bits are then applied to the TV display with the correct synchronization. The dots of light in the blocks are lit or darkened to produce the character. The video circuits are continually scanning video RAM and constantly updating the TV screen. You can walk away from a working computer and the video remains on the screen.

Whether the video circuits are contained on the motherboard or are mounted on a separate plug-in card, in general, the circuits display their character and graphic wares in about the same way. There is some changes in sync frequencies, some differences in specific output signals and other details, but they all produce displays.

When a video trouble occurs and the video circuits are on the main board, then they must be worked on directly as described next. If the video circuit is on a card that is a plug-in, you can test the circuits by replacing the suspect card with a known good card. If the trouble clears, you then know the card is bad. If the trouble remains, chances are the card is good and the trouble remains either in the card slot circuit or the TV display monitor.

In order to repair the card, you must obtain service notes, understand the theory behind the cards operation, and troubleshoot it. From a practical standpoint, the card can be swapped for a fee from a company that specializes in that specific type of repair.

### Testing A Typical Video Circuit

In Chapter 8 the Video Display Generator chip was discussed. It is one of those chips that converts keyboard digital codes into a composite video picture. It receives a number of digital inputs and puts out an analog composite color TV picture. When the picture disappears and the TV display circuits are deemed ok, then this VDG and its associated circuits become the prime suspect.

The VDG receives two multiple inputs. One is from an I/O chip like the PIA, and the other from video RAM. Besides these two inputs, there are a number of individual inputs and, of course, the +5 V supply voltage and ground return.

Video RAM is just ordinary RAM reserved for video duty. When the MPU addresses video RAM, it also sends a strobe signal to a video latch attached to the data bus. As the bits are written to the video RAM, they are simultaneously strobed into the video latch. The video latch in turn sends these video bits into the eight data pins of the VDG chip.

There are five control lines coming from the PIA to the VDG. These lines set up the display modes the VDG is able to produce. VDGs are usually able to produce three general modes: alphanumerics, semigraphics, and full graphics. These modes have variations. The VDG chip you saw in Fig. 8-15 had five input lines coming from the PIA. With five inputs, the VDG can receive code variations of 1s and 0s. Each binary arrangement can trigger a different display situation. The VDG is capable of adopting one out of 16 modes and is controlled by these five inputs from the PIA.

Three of these inputs connect to pins 30, 29, and 27, which are GM0, GM1, and GM2. Between these three pins eight separate modes can be dialed up. Pin 35, A/G, selects between semigraphics and full graphics.

The clock sends a color video signal to this VDG with a frequency of exactly 3.579545 MHz at pin 33. TV technicians will recognize this signal as the color oscillator. The signal is the most exact frequency in the computer. It is used by the color circuits to build the composite color video signal the display will show. Pin 22 is a line called DA0. It operates with the color oscillator signal to keep the color in sync. Pin 39, CSS, is a control line for the border around the display block. The two possible logic states can control two different color borders.

Once the data to be displayed and the mode controls are injected into the VDG, the chip can produce the desired composite video signal. Since the data and control signals are digital, and the output of the VDG is analog, the VDG is a video digital-to-analog device.

There are seven analog output pins that contain various parts of the total composite video signal. At pin 28 is the Y (luminance) signal, complete black and white TV signal. It contains sync pulses and blanking levels. This pin is the first place to check when a symptom of no video comes up. The ordinary service oscilloscope should show a very weak (about 1 volt peak to peak) signal, if it is present. When it is not there, further testing is needed (Table 8-2).

At pin 11 is a three level analog signal called *0A*. It is combined in the next stages with the Y signal and helps the Y to produce one of eight colors. *0B* is coming out of pin 13. It is a companion signal to 0A. It helps in the choosing of the color and also times the color burst signal properly. CHB is at pin 9. It is a dc reference signal to help during thermal tracking difficulties.

The signal at pins 37 and 38 are called *field sync* and *horizontal sync*. (Field sync is like vertical sync.) They are used to sync the VDG output video signal with the free-running sweep oscillators in the TV display circuits.

The VDG is an interface chip as well as an I/O chip. The input is digital and the output analog. This is different than the PIA. The PIA is an I/O chip, but it has digital inputs and digital outputs. The PIA outputs to D/A interface circuits.

The VDG then requires different types of testing at the input and the output. The inputs to the VDG are best tested with instruments like the logic probe. VDG outputs can be tested quickly with an ordinary service oscilloscope.

The best way to test the VDG in the field is with a service chart as shown in Table 8-2. The logic probe readings and the oscilloscope pictures you take should match up with the ones on the chart. Any discrepancy is a clue which could indicate the source of the trouble. For instance, if the inputs are good but an output or so is missing, the internal chip circuits could be defective. Another possibility is a defect in the external circuit attached to the indicated pin.

How can you get ahold of service charts like these? It is not easy. The best way is to make them yourself as you encounter various computers in the field. Once you have a service chart made, the next time you are working on the same make and model, you will be equipped with a valuable servicing tool. The first time you work on a particular computer is always the hardest. If you make service charts for yourself, the next time will be much easier.

The logic probe input tests and the oscilloscope output tests are very useful if the symptom is no video. However, if the trouble is a bit more subtle (there is some video, but it is faulty) then other tests are best.

Tricky troubles are best analyzed with test software. A test program can be obtained from the manufacturer or from other software companies. The program will be able to put the VDG through its paces. It can check each mode by changing the bits coming from the PIA. It can test colors and borders by further changing bits from the PIA. It can quickly exercise the entire VDG, if there is a picture of any sort shown on the screen.

If there is no video, but a weak Y signal is exiting the video generator circuit, then the video output circuit comes under scrutiny. At this stage of the testing, you are out of the digital circuit areas. The techniques required are all analog.

In this color video circuit we are testing, the video is applied to a typical color TV mixer chip (Fig. 22-3). The four output signals Y, 0A, 0B, and CHB enter at pins 9, 7, 5, and 6. The color clock signal of 3.58 MHz also enters the mixer at pin 2. The mixer puts all these signals together to produce a composite color TV signal complete with color burst. The signal is output at pin and reinput at pin 10 through a .01 $\mu$F capacitor. A 750 ohm resistor sets the luminance-to-chrominance ratio. The chip is able to do more than the computer requires. As a result, there are unused circuits and pins. Two such pins are 13 and 14, intended to be an RF oscillator in a home TV application. The oscillator circuit is extra baggage since the clock does all the timing chores. The extra circuit must be dampened so the unwanted oscillator doesn't start up and cause trouble. The diode and resistor at pins 13 and 14 take care of the dampening task. Incidentally, there are lots of unwanted circuits on chips throughout the computer. Be sure to be on the lookout for them, or you could lose time on false and misleading indications.

You can follow the composite video signal out of pin 12 of the mixer into a voltage divider in the base of Q1. Lastly, the signal can be picked up at the emitter of Q1. If you are in contact with the signal and you suddenly lose it, you could have found the circuit where a trouble exists. Should you trace the signal all the way to the input of the rf modulator or video monitor, then the computer video circuits are exonerated and the trouble is indicated to be in the display circuits. These are discussed in some detail in Chapter 21.

The signal finally exits the chip at pin 12. If you look at it on the oscilloscope it is exactly like the TV picture a station transmits. It is still too weak for the monitor to display. It must be amplified. A conventional transistorized TV video amplifier stage does the job. The amplifier is based around Q1 (Fig. 22-4).

Q1 is an npn current amplifier. The video enters at the base and has its current amplified. The output is taken from the emitter and is then sent to the TV display. If the computer is using a home TV for the display, then the emitter output is coupled into an rf modulator that mounts the video onto a TV carrier. The rf modulator can produce an oscillator carrier at the frequency for channel 3 or 4. The modulated TV signal can then be attached to the antenna terminals of any home TV for display.

When the computer uses a monitor, the video can be applied directly into the video circuit of the monitor, after the current amplification. Modulation can be dispensed with.

You can trace the video signal with an ordinary oscilloscope from the output of the VDG circuit right to the input of the rf modulator or monitor. The four signals that leave the VDG area are normally very weak. As they pass through the mixer they do not gain any strength but they are mixed together into the single output found on pin 12.

The mixer chip is the same one found in TV sets.

## DIGITAL-TO-DIGITAL INTERFACE

The VDG just discussed received digital data from the data bus inside the computer, and sent analog signals out to the TV circuits. The video circuit thus performs two con-

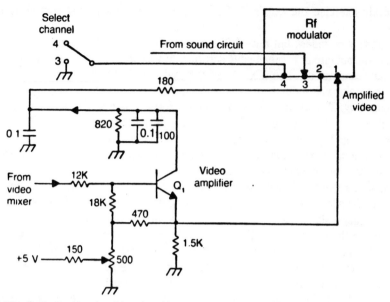

Fig. 22-4. The final stage for the video signal is a current amplifier based around a non-transistor.

version jobs. One, it gets the digital signal out of the digital world into the analog world. Two, it changes the digital to analog. Chips like UART and PIA, on the other hand, also receive digital data from the data bus, but then output digital signals to the external circuits. The outside analog circuits then must use additional D/A circuits to convert the digital data to the analog form they use. These I/O ports will not do that part of the job.

Servicing these digital-to-analog circuits is covered in the next section. For now, let's discuss the servicing of the digital-to-digital port. Earlier in the book we examined a PIA chip that is able to take data from the digital world and provide a port of entry for the data to enter the analog world. The PIA is also able to send data the other way, from the analog side to the internal data bus.

The service technique that will suffice during most PIA circuit failure was covered; the logic probe used with the computer energized. Each pin of the PIA is tested and its high, low and pulse state noted. If the state on a particular pin is not the prescribed state, that is a valid trouble clue. The circuit leading into that indicated pin is examined for defect. The reason for the incorrect pin reading is then discovered and remedied. Most of the time, the computer can then be placed back into service.

This technique did not require any outside devices besides the logic probe to uncover the clue; a VOM or continuity tester to locate the short, open, or leak; and perhaps a soldering iron to repair or replace a component. It was assumed that the MPU was known good and the only trouble was the single one in the I/O port area.

When these measures fail to produce a fix, then more sophisticated procedures are required. One of the best methods, after the easier techniques have been exhausted is with a test jig discussed in the last chapter. At this time, let's see how this is done. Let's test a computer with a 6800 MPU and some PIA chips as I/O.

The test jig is able to receive data bits from the data bus or various read, write, and read/write circuits. It is wired to correspond with the pin layout of the 6800. The 6800 chip is then removed and placed into a static-free protective container. The test plug is installed into the 6800's now-empty socket. The test jig is now the MPU the rest of the computer is attached to.

The test jig is able to receive data bits from the data bus or interrupt lines. It can also send out data bits via the data, address, or control lines. The device can reproduce all the addressing and data moving of the MPU. However, you and your movement of the switches are the clock. If you set a switch and then do other things, the bit you set does not change. It is static. This allows you to take careful, calculated logic state readings at every test point, taking as much time as you'd like to test and muse. The circuits will not be damaged by the lack of activity. This static situation is quite safe for the careful tester.

To get the most out of the test jig, you must be familiar with the steps the MPU takes to read from and write to the PIA. There is a definite designed step-by-step procedure the MPU goes through with every operation on the PIA. The MPU conducts a step with every beat of the clock. If the 6800 is running at 1 MHz, the 6800 performs a million steps a second. No matter what speed of the clock is, each step is individual, and is separate from each other. When you become the test clock, you will have to perform each step one at a time, then stop and take your test readings. Your clock speed might be one step every five minutes.

There aren't that many steps for a read or write operation. Let's itemize a series of steps that will imitate the MPU reading data from an I/O port.

The first step is to set up the address of the PIA to be selected and the register in the chip to be tested. A PIA register could be mapped at hex 4004 to start with. In binary this address reads A15-A0, 0100000000000100. You can address the PIA by setting the two switches at MPU pins 24 and 11. That places 1s on A14 and A2. The 0s are automatically in place while the switches are open.

At the PIA there are three chip selects, *CS2, CS1, CS0, and two register selects, RS1, and RS0. *CS2 is connected to A15, CS1 to A14, and CS0 to A2. RS1 is connected to A1, and RS0 to A0. To turn on the chip select with the asterisk requires a low or 0. To turn on the other select 1s are needed. The 1s in bits 14 and 2 selects the chip. Variations in the register selects picks out the desired register. The two 0s in register select bits 1 and 0 enables one of the registers.

The second step is to set the next switch, MPU pin 34 R/*W. When this is high, it tells all the components that a read operation is in progress.

In some circuits the PIA chip select is not permitted unless the MPU verifies that the address on the bus is valid. Pin 5 of the MPU socket is VMA, valid memory address. The third step is to set pin 5 of the test jig to a 1. The VMA 1 is ANDed with the 1 on A14 before application to pin 24 of the PIA. Once the ANDing results in a 1, the PIA can be considered addressed.

Now that the addressing is complete, you can test the address bus from beginning to end. The test points should show all the logical results of the switching you have just performed. The logic probe can be touched down at the chip pins and will show the state of each pin. It's as if you have frozen the states of the computer in time.

The test jigs will have different connections and different switch settings for each MPU and computer make and model. The step-by-step procedure will also vary, and different steps are needed according to whether the jig is testing I/O, RAM, ROM, or other circuits. The test jig becomes very useful if you have a lot of the same type of computer to check out.

## TYPICAL D/A INTERFACES

The computer is interested in receiving signals from and sending signals to our real world. In our world, computer-pertinent data is derived from items like voltages, positions of switches, and locations of shafts in horizontal and vertical planes.

The computer handles the values in the form of digital high and low voltages. We describe the various analog terms as *continuous analog voltages*, not simply one high and one low. The D/A circuits are charged with the responsibility of converting patterns of highs and lows into continuous voltages.

A typical D/A converter was shown in Fig. 15-4. The digital output is six bits. Six pins of one of the 8-bit ports is connected to the D/A converter circuit. The pins are PA7-PA2. The six pins are able to form 64 different patterns of highs and lows. The D/A converter has to be able to change each of the 64 different bit patterns into one individual voltage.

The D/A output circuit is a voltage divider and filter. There are six series resistors of various values that carries each of the six bits. The series resistors all terminate together between a 100 K load resistor and a 20 pF filter connected to ground. The 100 K resistor is connected to +5 V.

The series resistors are all held at the same voltage. When all six bits are outputting highs (111111), the voltage is at maximum, about +4.75 V. If all six bits are outputting lows (000000), the voltage is at minimum, about +0.25 V. Since there are 64 different bit patterns in the six bits, there are 64 different voltages the converter can output.

Between the six output pins of the I/O port and the six series resistors, there is a set of six buffers. The buffers impedance-match the six logic states to the output analog circuit which is the filtered voltage divider.

The circuit is easy to check out when it is a suspect. The logic probe will test the six pins of the I/O port. There should be a group of six highs and lows there. If one or more of the pins do not reveal a high or low, and the computer is operating, then a bit of trouble is indicated.

The same logic state that is found on the six pins should also be on the outputs of the six buffers. There again, a discrepancy is a clue of possible trouble. The output of the buffers is the end of the line for the logic probe. Its results are almost meaningless in the analog part of the circuit.

Once across the resistors, the VOM can take over. Voltage readings of the analog signal should be somewhere between +0.25 V and +4.75 V. The resistors and capacitor can also be tested safely with the ohmmeter in the VOM.

## TYPICAL A/D INTERFACES

The joystick input interface is a good example of an A/D circuit. The joystick is a device that controls digital signals with the position of the stick. The shaft is connected physically to a pair of potentiometers like ordinary volume controls. As your fingers move the shaft around, you are changing the setting of the two pots (Fig. 22-5). There is a +5

500

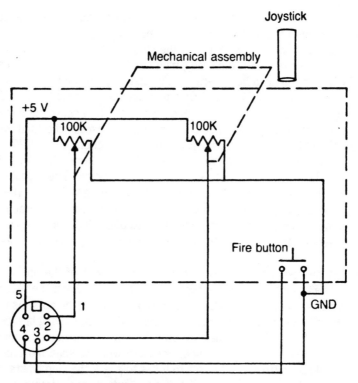

**Fig. 22-5.** The joystick is a device that develops varying voltages that describe the movement of a shaft. It is simply a pair of potentiometers that have their center wipers moved by the shaft.

V to ground across both pots. The center wipers therefore can output a voltage between 0 V and +5 V as you watch the TV display and cause objects to move on the screen. You are successfully converting the physical changing position of the shaft into an analog voltage.

At any one time, there are two varying voltages, one from each center wiper, sent to an analog multiplexer (as you saw in Fig. 15-5). If the computer is outfitted with two joysticks, the second one is hooked up to other pins on the multiplexer. The multiplexer is able to convert the joystick voltage inputs into a single analog voltage output. The output varies between 0 V and +5 V as you move the sticks. The single output is then sent to one of the inputs of a comparator chip.

Meanwhile, the computer, in response to software, is generating a stairstep voltage waveform. The stairstep signal is output from the D/A converter. It emanates as bits from the I/O chip such as a PIA. The bits pass through the buffers and produce an analog varying voltage from the resistor-capacitor voltage divide. The stairstep varies between 0 V and +5 V. It steps smoothly from level to level. The stairstep signal is sent to the other input of the comparator chip.

The comparator does not output any voltage as long as the two inputs are different. However, when both inputs are compared and found to be the same, the comparator outputs a logic state out of the output pin. The logic state is injected into a pin of an I/O port such as another PIA. The state is then sent to the data bus where it triggers off programmed activity that results in movement of an object on the display. The comparator is the key component in the analog to digital conversion.

The most common joystick trouble is the stick-potentiometer mechanism. When a new stick won't operate either; then the circuit needs testing. In order to test the circuit dynamically, a stairstep must be generated. The stairstep is produced in a diagnostic program. (If need be you could also use a game program that requires the use of the sticks.)

Once the stairstep waveshape is being output by the D/A converter into the comparator, you can test the comparator circuit with an ordinary oscilloscope and the VOM. The comparator circuit can be viewed as just another analog circuit (Fig. 22-6).

If you want to be certain that the stairstep is being generated, you can look at it on the PIA pins. The typical results are shown in the illustration. The stairstep will appear on the screen as a jaggedy line. You can then check the waveshape at the input of the comparator. The oscilloscope picture should be a bit more viewable, since the waveshape took a journey through the buffers at this point. If the stairstep is missing, the D/A circuit becomes the problem. As long as the stairstep is present and has even steps, the D/A circuit is ok.

The next test point for the oscilloscope is the output of the analog multiplexer. There should be a number of short straight haphazard lines. Each line represents a setting of the joysticks. They are dc values that are coming out of the pots. As you vary each pot, the lines will move as their dc value changes. If they are moving in accordance with the movement of the shaft, then they are probably working through the multiplexer ok. Should one or more of them be missing or not move with the shaft movement, then the multiplexer could be in trouble. The way to tell is to check the chip inputs. If the inputs are all dc voltages between 0 V and +5 V but the outputs are missing, then the multiplexer circuit is defective.

When the outputs are good, it is time for the comparator check. You have tested the comparator inputs and found them fine. Test the single comparator output. There should be a combination waveshape composed of the dc inputs and the stairstep as shown in the illustration. If the waveshape is missing, the comparator chip could be defective. Before you change it, though, be sure to double-check the +12 V to ground. It might be missing, indicating a power supply failure.

The trick to testing D/A and A/D circuits is a good understanding of the circuits. It is important to know where the digital circuits become analog and vice versa. The circuits are the doorway between the digital world and the analog world. You must use digital techniques on the computer side and analog techniques on the outer world side.

## RS-232 INTERFACE CIRCUITS

The RS-232 interface is an old system that was used to connect computers to teletype machines. The interface is a serial circuit that permits the computer to send signal to the device on one line and receive signal from a device on another line. The teletype has been replaced in today's computers with a keyboard and a line printer. The keyboard does not use the RS-232, but the line printer finds the serial input very convenient.

The line printer is a computer in its own right, and has an MPU and some memory. The interface is really between two computers. For instance, the computer itself could have its memory full of ASCII bytes that were installed by a typist with a word processor

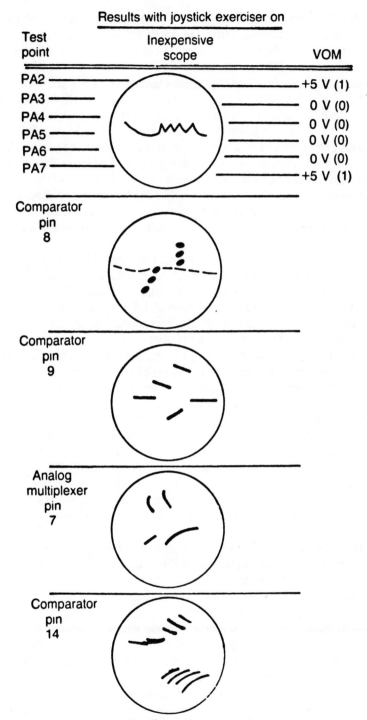

**Fig. 22-6.** The VOM and oscilloscope test results shown are the type that are found in the joystick circuit as the signal goes from analog in the potentiometer to digital at the PIA input pins.

program. When the typist is ready to print, the command is entered with the keyboard and the MPU starts sending outputting the ASCII bytes to the I/O chip. The I/O chip receives a byte from the data bus and converts the parallel byte to a line of serial bits. The bits are sent to the RS-232 interface.

The bits are nothing more than digital highs and lows of +5 V and 0 V. However, the highs and lows as +5 V and 0 V will not be accepted at the RS-232 interface in the printer. The RS-232 signal form is defined as the following. A high is any voltage larger than +3 V. A low is defined as any voltage less than −3 V. These definitions of highs and lows have been arranged as a standard by designers over the years. This way, the interface is universal, and can be used in many ways. The interface circuit therefore has the duty of changing the highs and lows to over +3 V and under −3 V.

A typical small computer can use a 4-pin RS-232 plug and interface successfully with many devices like printers and telephone modems. The plug is a DIN connector. The four pins are serial output, serial input, input status, and ground zero voltage, as you saw in Figs. 16-1 and 16-2.

The serial output pin 4 is fed signal from an op amp. The changing of +5 V to a voltage higher than +3 and 0 V to a voltage less than −3 is done in the op amp chip. The chip is powered with +12 V and −12 V at the supply inputs.

In the circuit shown, the op amp is biased at 1.4 V by the voltage divider between the +5 V supply connection and ground. This bias causes the op amp to switch between the +12 V and the −12 V as the serial input from the I/O chip changes from a high to a low. The op amp outputs to pin 4. The +12 V represented highs and the −12 V represented lows leave through pin 4 and proceeds to the device they are driving.

The serial input and input status pins are 2 and 1 respectively. Pin 3 is the chassis ground connection. Pins 2 and 1 are connected to identical RS-232 input circuits. Each input is based around a comparator circuit. Both are to receive signal from the external device and convert the signal to the +5 V and 0 V highs and lows the computer's I/O circuit is able to use.

The incoming bits from the external device are defined as RS-232 signals. The high is a voltage above +3 V and the low a voltage below −3 V. The serial input attached to pin 2 injects the device output which is a continuous flow of highs and low bits of intelligence. For example, a telephone modem can send a serial signal from another computer across town.

The status input at pin 1 receives a control signal. The signal could be from a printer that you are going to print some copy on. If the printer is ready to receive your ASCII code, it will send a continuous high. This means the printer is ready. If the printer is not ready, it will send a low. This control informs you that there is a problem and the printer is not ready to receive the ASCII for printing.

The serial input and the status input can use identical circuits. Even though the serial input is to receive a steady flow of serial bits and the status input only is given a single bit at a time, the circuits can be the same. The inputs are made into the anode of diodes. When the input signals are positive the diodes conduct. An impulse is sent to pins 4 and 6 of the twin comparators. As the signal swings negative the diodes shut off and no signal arrives at the comparator.

The two comparators have their pins 5 and 7 referenced at +2 V by a connection between the series resistors connected to +5 V and ground. With that arrangement, a

504

```
 5  POKE 65312,2 — SETS RS232OUT ON PIA
10  FOR X=0 TO 10:NEXT X — MARKS TIME
15  POKE 65312,0 — CLEARS RS232OUT ON
    PIA
20  FOR X=0 TO 10:NEXT X — MARKS SOME
    MORE TIME
25  GO TO 5 — CONTINUES SETTING AND
    CLEARING
```

Fig. 22-7. This little test program is a diagnostic to check out a 4-pin RS-232 interface.

**Table 22-1. Interface Service Chart.**

| OP AMP | TEST POINT | OSCILLOSCOPE | VOM |
|---|---|---|---|
| INPUT | 2 | SWITCHING | |
| OUTPUT | 6 | SWITCHING | +11 TO −11 |
| COMPARATORS | | | |
| INPUT | 4 | SWITCHING | 0 TO +10 |
| INPUT | 6 | SWITCHING | 0 TO +10 |
| OUTPUT | 1 | SWITCHING | |
| OUTPUT | 2 | SWITCHING | |

voltage of +2.6 V to pins 4 and 6 will switch on a comparator. The comparator outputs re connected directly to a pin of an I/O chip such as a PIA. The I/O chip latches the serial input out of the comparator and sends it out over the data bus for processing.

When the printer or modem isn't operative and the devices have been checked out and are good, the interface circuits are indicated as containing the trouble. A good way to test the circuits is by connecting the input to the output. A little test program can then be used to turn on the circuit. The oscilloscope and VOM are then used to test all the inputs and outputs. A discrepancy from the prescribed program results is an indication of trouble. The illustration shows a test program and a service chart that does the job on the TRS-80 Color Computer (Fig. 22-7 and Table 22-1).

Pins 1 and 2 of the RS-232 plug are shorted to pin 4. The program is then able to output a switching signal from the serial output circuit right back into the two input circuits. That way, the signal just goes on and on making it easy to take valid oscilloscope and VOM readings. The readings are then compared to the service chart. Once a test point is found that is not reporting the correct oscilloscope or VOM reading, the computer can be turned off and the suspect circuit leg checked out, component by component, with static resistance and replacement tests.

# 23
# Video Display
# Repair Techniques

The Video Display Generator (VDG) chip discussed at the end of the last chapter was one of the early composite color TV signal makers used in 8-bit computer.. It was the chip that generated color TV in the Tandy Color Computer 1. About the same time COMMODORE arrived on the scene with it's various Video Interface Chips (VIC). These chips were designed to operate using a home TV as the display monitor.

As a result, the chips were set to control the conventional TV raster (Fig. 23-1). A raster is the 525 brightness lines that are scanned onto a TV screen. The 525 lines are scanned like writing from left to right, only one on top of the other. The lines are drawn at a horizontal frequency of about 15,750 cycles per second. The lines are begun at the top of the screen and drawn down at a rate of about 60 times a second, the vertical frequency.

These frequencies are developed in the VDG or VIC so the computer output can be synchronized with the TV oscillators that originate the television's scanning frequencies. In the TV there is a vertical oscillator that runs at 60 Hz and a horizontal oscillator that perks along at 15,750 Hz. When the computer's vertical and horizontal sync signals are applied to the TV oscillators, the video from the computer and the TV raster are in sync. If the computer is producing 1,000 character blocks, these blocks will line up on the display as they are supposed to. Should the computer be putting out 2,000 character blocks, these blocks will also line up on the display with the same horizontal and vertical frequencies.

The 1,000 blocks are arranged 40 blocks across and 25 down. The 2,000 blocks are 80 blocks across and 25 down. There are twice as many blocks across and the same number down. As a result, the blocks across are each half as wide while the blocks down retain the same height. The 80 column letters are tall and skinny in comparison to the 40 column blocks. The 40 column lettering can be drawn with twice as many dots as the 80 column lettering.

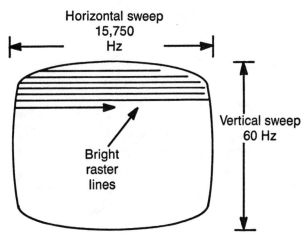

Fig. 23-1. A raster is the name for the group of horizontal brightness lines that are scanned across a TV screen.

## RESOLUTION

Like type, a letter on the TV display is composed of a number of points. In the TV display, these points are picture elements or they are called pixels. Each drawn line is composed of a number of pixels, Fig. 23-2. These pixels are switched on and off by the state of the bit in video RAM that controls that pixel. In a computer that syncs with the display at 15,750 Hz horizontal and 60 Hz vertical, there could be 320 pixels on one drawn line. The pixels in the line will be off and on in accordance with its controlling RAM bit.

In a vertical column, since it is not as long as a line, there could be 200 pixels. With this arrangement, it is said that the display has a resolution of 320 × 200. This gives the display block 64,000 pixels of resolution. Resolution is a direct result of the number of pixels. The more pixels there are the better is the resolution. Resolution is a direct result of the number of pixels. The more pixels there are the better is the resolution. The better the resolution the sharper and crisper the picture will be.

In order to increase resolution, one of the things that can be done is increase the horizontal sync signal that comes out of the video generator, Fig. 23-3. Instead of using 15.75 kHz, sync signals of 21.8 kHz, 31.5 kHz, 35 kHz and even higher can be output from the video generator. The vertical frequency remains around 60 Hz. The vertical frequency from display to display can vary a bit, from about 40 Hz to 75 Hz.

With the horizontal frequency increased and the vertical held about the same, the scanning produces a lot more horizontal lines for each cycle the vertical pulls the lines down from the top of the display. The increased number of lines in the picture fills in the spaces between lines. It becomes harder to discern the scanning lines, increasing the picture clarity. There are a lot more pixels in the picture too. Each additional line adds its pixel content to the total pixel number.

A second way to improve resolution, has to do with picture bandwidth. The bandwidth is the measurement of the speed a pixel is made to turn off or on, Fig. 23-4. The faster a pixel is made to turn off and on, the more pixels can be placed on a line. The

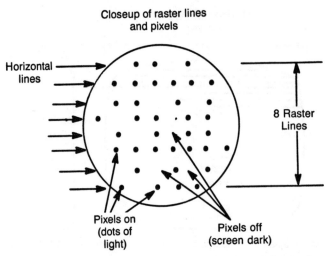

Fig. 23-2. Each line of the raster is intensity modulated by a number of picture element dots called pixels. The dots can be turned off and on by the computer.

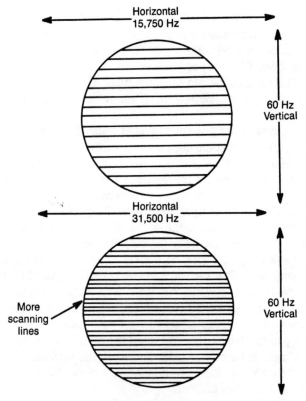

Fig. 23-3. One of the ways to improve resolution is by increasing the horizontal sweep frequency while keeping the vertical sweep frequency the same. The increased horizontal frequency increases the number of lines in the raster.

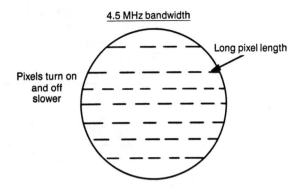

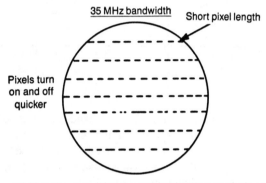

Fig. 23-4. The picture bandwidth is the speed that the monitor has to turn pixels on and off. The higher the speed or frequency, the shorter the pixel's length is and the better is the resolution.

more pixels there are the better is the resolution, which is what this effort is all about. Graphics become sharper and sharper as the resolution increases. In many applications such as computer-aided drafting (CAD), medical imaging, government defenses, and others resolution can be vitally important.

The ordinary TV set has a bandwidth of about 4.5 MHz. One set of horizontal lines is drawn at this rate. This means that 80 to 120 lines are drawn during the time one megahertz takes place. This is a relatively slow pace to turn pixels off and on. The resolution will be average. Not good enough for high resolution needs.

In higher resolution displays, the bandwidth is picked up to about 35 MHz or higher. At these higher frequencies the pixels are switched at a quicker pace. Exceptional high resolution pictures can be produced at these higher bandwidths.

Table 23-1 shows a list of some of the more popular display systems that are found in personal computers. These are the ones that are in the IBM created, CGA, EGA, and VGA, the Macintosh II system, and the NEC Multisync. There will be more about these systems later in this chapter.

The computer does its part to increase resolution by increasing the horizontal scanning frequency and increasing the bandwidth of its TV output. The increased horizontal

**Table 23-1. These are Some of the More Popular Display Systems that are Available.**

| Display Name | Typical Display Characteristics | | | | |
| --- | --- | --- | --- | --- | --- |
| | Resolution | Bandwidth | Input | Horiz. Sweep | Vert. Sweep |
| CGA Color Graphics Adapter | 320 × 200 4 of 16 colors | 35 MHz | Digital | 15.6 Hz | 60 Hz |
| EGA Enhanced Graphics Adapter | 640 × 350 16 of 64 Colors | 35 MHz | Digital | 21.8 Hz | 60 Hz |
| VGA Video Graphics Array | 320 × 200 256 of 256,000 Colors | 35 MHz | Analog | 31.5 KHz | 60 Hz |
| MacIntosh II | 16 Million Colors | | Analog | 35 KHz | 60 Hz |
| NEC Multisync | 1024 × 768 and Lower | 65 MHz | Analog Digital | Variable 15.75-35.5 KHz | 60 Hz |

frequency puts more lines on the screen. The increased bandwidth puts more pixels on a line. The larger the total number of pixels, the better is the resolution.

The idea is to fool the human eye. If the pixels are increased in number and each pixel made smaller, the eye can't see individual pixels. The eye sees one picture with fine detail. Just like a fine photo with many tiny points.

## DIGITAL AND ANALOG DISPLAY SYSTEMS

Early in the book, the differences between digital and analog signals were discussed. The TV signals that are generated in the computer, can also be digital or analog. If the signal is digital, there can be only a few different voltage levels. When the signal is analog in nature, there can be an infinite number of voltage levels.

The composite TV signal is analog. As the signal is output from the computer, the video section of the composite varies from voltage to voltage in a continuous manner. The varying voltage represents the brightness level of the signal. If the signal is a black and white one, then the voltage is varying from black to white with an infinite number of shades of gray in between.

Should the signal be color, then there are three signals. One signal for red, one for blue, and one for green. Each signal is like the black and white. The difference is the red signal varies from an intense red to a very pale red with shades of red in between. The companion blue and green signals perform in the same way.

In order to display a color picture, these three signals light up three colors of phosphor, each color individually. The three dots of phosphor are spaced closely on the screen in trios, as in Fig. 23-5. As these three colors are lit, the light generated adds

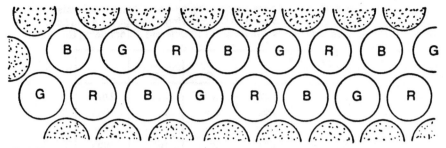

Fig. 23-5. The color phosphor dots can be laid out on the glass faceplate in triad patterns.

together. The dots are so close the human eye is only able to see the color addition observed as a single resultant color. Each dot trio on the TV screen is considered as one dot of light. A few of these dot triads can form a color pixel. There will be more about this later in this chapter.

The continuous analog color signals are able to each form an almost infinite number of voltage levels. This gives the analog output the ability to produce an almost infinite number of colors. Even though the possibility of an infinite number of colors can be produced, the actual number of analog colors are limited to the ability of the video display circuits in the computer. The latest IBM VGA circuits can output up to 265,000 colors. The Macintosh II can produce more than 16 million colors.

Digital signal outputs, in comparison to analog, are very limited in the number of colors they can put out. There are three color signals that must add together to produce a color resultant for digital outputs too. In addition, the overall brightness signal, called I for intensity, is also added when the resultant color light is produced.

Each of these signals, R, G, B, and I have their voltages fixed at their digital levels. The signals can be high or low (Table 23-2). Since there are four signals, each being able to go high or low, there are 16 possible total voltage levels that can be added together. Each total voltage level when applied to the TV screen produces a color. In the CGA video board, the digital output can produce a total of 16 colors.

To increase the total number of colors, some boards divide each color into two levels instead of just the one. In the EGA adapter, there are two sets of levels for each color, R1, R2, B1, B2, G1, G2, I1, and I2. This produces eight levels. With eight levels there are 64 possible combinations to add together giving a total of 64 possible colors.

## TV MONITORS

While the computer is the originator of the video and sync signals to produce the TV display, the signals need a monitor to do their stuff. The TV monitor, in comparison to a TV receiver, is rather simple. It doesn't have all the circuits needed to pull in and control a commercial transmitted or cable TV picture. It only has to display a computer pixel output. A monochrome monitor only needs a video amplifier and output, horizontal and vertical oscillators and outputs, a high voltage and low voltage power supply, and a monochrome picture tube, shown in Fig. 23-6. The phosphor on the screen is one color. It could be green, amber, blue, white or perhaps some other color.

A color monitor is typically quite the same except for the color needs. Instead of just one monochrome video amplifier and output, it needs four of them. There is one each for

**Table 23-2. Since There are Four Digital Color Signals Generated
on the CGA Board with Each Color Having a Voltage High and Low,
16 Different Voltage Levels Will Result in 16 Different Colors Being Generated.**

| COLOR – | R | G | B | I |
|---|---|---|---|---|
| 1 | Low | Low | Low | Low |
| 2 | Low | Low | Low | High |
| 3 | Low | Low | High | Low |
| 4 | Low | Low | High | High |
| 5 | Low | High | Low | Low |
| 6 | Low | High | Low | High |
| 7 | Low | High | High | Low |
| 8 | Low | High | High | High |
| 9 | High | Low | Low | Low |
| 10 | High | Low | Low | High |
| 11 | High | Low | High | Low |
| 12 | High | Low | High | High |
| 13 | High | High | Low | Low |
| 14 | High | High | Low | High |
| 15 | High | High | High | Low |
| 16 | High | High | High | High |

the red video, blue video, and green video. Then the color monitor requires a color picture tube and a few extra circuits to control the color.

## Monochrome Monitor

The signal to be seen is residing in bits in video RAM. The picture is a window into
the video RAM, Fig. 23-7. The video is output from the video generator to the monitor.
The signal is installed in the composite video. You can view the composite signal with an
ordinary TV repair oscilloscope at the output of the computer or at the input of the monitor. If the monitor is not showing the picture, as in Fig. 23-8, this is a good test point.
Should the oscilloscope show the composite video, then the monitor is in trouble. When
the signal is missing before it enters the monitor, then the computer has the trouble.

## Video Amplifier

Once the signal does enter the monitor, it is applied to a video amplifier. There can
be a number of amplifier stages that boosts the weak computer output of about 1 V peak
to peak to about 20 V p-p. In this circuit the signal first passes through one transistor
amplifier, then through an IC buffer that conditions the signal, through two more transistors until it is at the 20 V p-p level. The signal is then injected into the cathode of the
single gun monochrome picture tube. The composite video enters the CRT in serial
form. The signal is placed into action so that each line gets its pixel switching instructions
at precisely the right time.

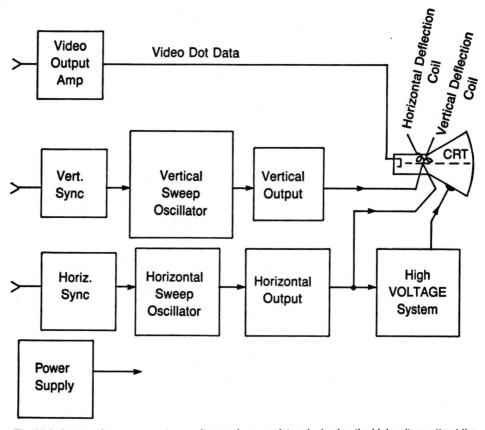

Fig. 23-6. A monochrome computer monitor produces a picture by having the high voltage attract the electron beam to land on and light up the single color phosphor, the video output modulating the beam with video dot data, the horizontal deflection coil scanning the beam from side to side and the vertical deflection coil scanning the beam up and down.

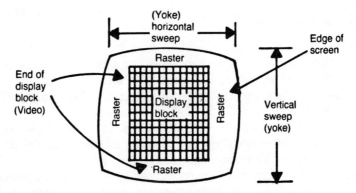

Fig. 23-7. The monitor display is a window showing the contents of video RAM.

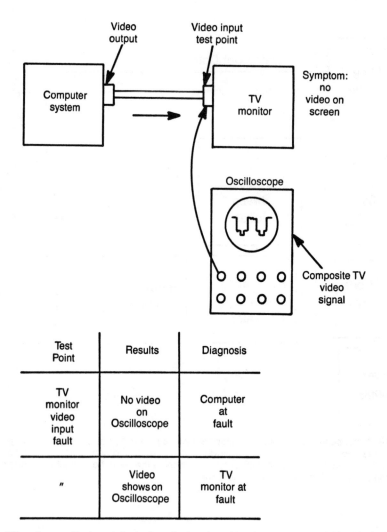

Fig. 23-8. When the monitor is not displaying, the monitor video input can be quickly checked with an ordinary TV service oscilloscope.

As an example, an 8-bit computer could produce a display that consists of 512 character blocks, 32 across and 16 down. In video RAM there are 512 bytes reserved. Byte 0 corresponds with the upper left-hand corner character block, and byte 511 is at the bottom right-hand corner, and all other blocks are in between.

Each byte in RAM contains a set of ASCII bits. The video display generator chip codes the ASCII bits into a video keyboard character that can be displayed in the correct block on the TV screen. The video is installed in the composite TV signal. The video is coupled to the monitor from the computer through a piece of 72 ohm coaxial cable. The connections of the cable are test points where you can view the composite signal on the oscilloscope.

514

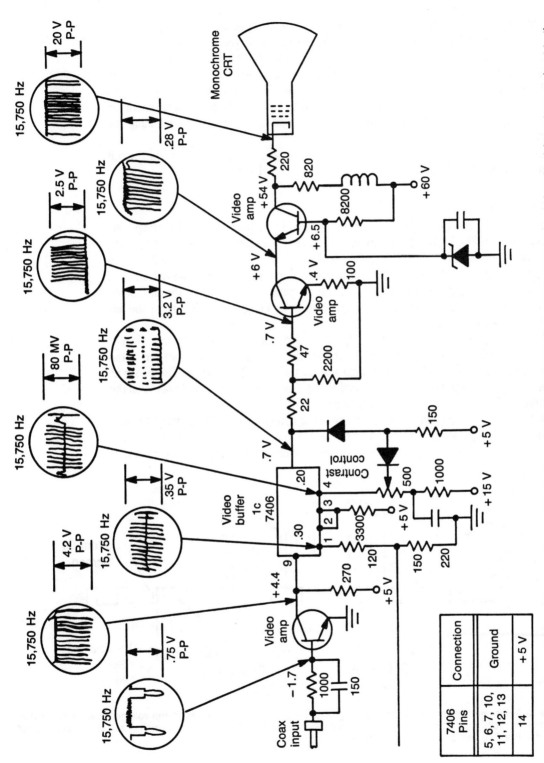

Fig. 23-9. This is a typical monochrome video amplifier in the monitor. The TV oscilloscope permits you to trace the signal from the coax input to the cathode of the CRT. The voltages and resistances can be tested with a volt-ohmmeter.

515

Once inside the monitor, the signal gets amplified from stage to stage until it has enough voltage to drive the cathode of the CRT. You can trace the signal with an oscilloscope from the coax input all the way to the CRT, as in Fig. 23-9. Starting at the coax input, a good video amp section will show ever increasing peak to peak voltage video signals as you touch down stage after stage. When the video circuits have troubles, you can detect where the trouble is occurring as you signal trace. Should the signal suddenly not appear at the next test point, you have just passed over the circuit containing the trouble.

Once you have pinpointed the troubled circuit, each component in the circuit becomes a suspect and can be tested with voltage and resistance checks.

## Sync Circuits

In addition to the video, the composite signal contains horizontal and vertical sync signals, shown in Fig. 23-10. These signals, in this example, are 15.75 kHz for horizontal and 60 Hz for vertical. These signals are placed into the composite signal so they trigger the scanning of the lines. The horizontal sync pulse is placed at the end of each line of light. It triggers the horizontal oscillator to pulse, which causes the line being drawn to halt at the right side of the screen, retrace, and begin the next line at the left side of the screen.

The vertical sync pulse is placed at the end of every complete raster scan. It triggers the vertical oscillator to pulse. This makes the vertical sweep stop at the bottom of the picture, retrace, and begin the next vertical scan at the top of the picture. The two sync pulses are vital to keep the display block and all the little character blocks in place on the TV screen. The display is then the window into video RAM.

In this example arrangement, each raster frame consists of 264 horizontal scan lines that are drawn one beneath the other. Out of the 264 available lines, only 192 are lit up to display the RAM window, 72 lines at the top and bottom are blacked out to form a bor-

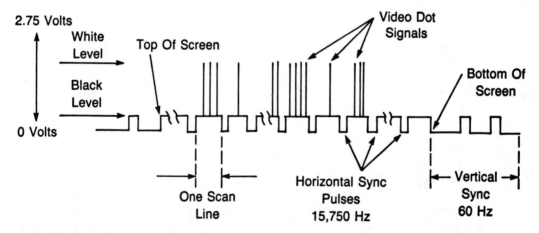

Fig. 23-10. The monochrome video signal can be graphed with time across the bottom and voltage in the vertical plane. This signal has voltages ranging from 0 to 2.75. One screenful of lines is shown. Note there are horizontal sync pulses after every scan line. The vertical sync pulses occur at the end of every screenful.

der. Also the beginning of each scan line and the end is blacked out to form the side borders of the display block.

Figure 23-10 shows a typical composite monochrome signal a computer can generate. The signal could vary from zero to 2.75 V peak to peak. Each level of voltage causes a change in the brightness of the picture as that level enters the cathode of the CRT. At zero volts, the picture is cut off and the pixels or light dots at that spot are black. At 2.75 V, the picture dots concerned are at their brightest, and if it is a black and white CRT they are at their whitest.

As the picture is scanned the pixels that are to be lit get the higher voltage, while the dots that are to remain black remain at the low zero volts. The illustration depicts the voltages for one raster scan. Each square wave duration is at the zero volt level. These durations are the scan lines. Perched on top of the scan lines are the pixel or dot switching signals. When a pixel is to be lit, there is a quick high spike shown as a line extending up to the white level. Should a pixel be off, there is no spike, the scan line voltage just remains at the black level. The horizontal sync pulses are between each scan line. The sync pulses extend down into the "blacker than black" voltage region, below zero volts. This keeps the raster blacked out during the horizontal retrace.

Once a raster is scanned, line by line, from the top of the screen to the bottom of the screen, then the vertical sync pulses are activated. They retrace the raster back up to the top of the screen. Note the vertical sync pulses are really durations of the square wave. They are also in the "blacker than black" region. This keeps the raster blacked out during the vertical retrace.

The computer video circuits are constantly at work scanning the video RAM, raster after raster. This keeps a steady stream of video entering the monitor. In this way the display stays put and is constantly updated as the display changes during computer activity.

You can see many troubles in the computer's logic circuits as the symptoms show up in the 192 lines of the display block. The commonest computer logic trouble is known as garbage. The symptom is evidenced by the display filling up the little blocks with meaningless characters, symbols, numbers, and random blackouts. The entire 512 blocks can fill with garbage, or only sections will show the nonsense. A variation of garbage is the appearance of a blank display area. Whichever version appears, the symptom indicates troubles in the digital logic areas of the computer. This includes all the sections that use binary and the video display generator.

If the display block itself should disappear and only the raster remains then the entire composite signal is not getting through. This trouble is likely to be located in the video amplifier section of the monitor. The signal is probably getting to the transistors, but not past them. The test is easy with the oscilloscope. Look for the signal at the circuit input and output. If the signal is at the input but not at the output, then the amplifier is defective.

Should the signal be present at the circuit output, trace it to the cathode of the CRT. A defective electron gun in the CRT could possibly kill the video. A new CRT would be needed in that case.

This loss of signal can be blamed on the computer circuits if the oscilloscope shows the signal is not at the input. Trace back through the input circuits.

Besides the video-fed cathode, the electron gun has these inputs; +15 V filaments, a control grid, screen grid, and focus grid. These elements comprise the electron gun of the CRT in Fig. 23-11. If the filaments open up, the CRT screen will go dark. Dead filaments are obvious to the troubleshooter.

When the other grids short together or open up, the picture will be black, have fixed brightness with or without video, lose focus, or display other CRT troubles. The best test of the electron gun in the CRT is to try a new CRT.

In order to produce a raster from the cathode ray, some external forces must grab ahold of the cathode ray as it passes through the neck of the CRT. These forces are elec-

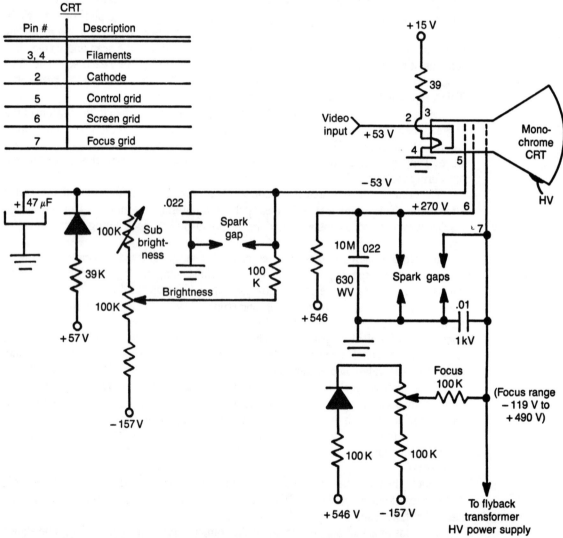

| CRT | |
|-----|-------------|
| Pin # | Description |
| 3, 4 | Filaments |
| 2 | Cathode |
| 5 | Control grid |
| 6 | Screen grid |
| 7 | Focus grid |

Fig. 23-11. This monochrome CRT has video inserted at the cathode. The rest of the electron gun elements need voltages too. The control grid has the brightness control circuit connected. The screen grid is given a +270 V attraction for electrons. The focus grid has the focus control circuit.

518

tromagnetic from a yoke around the neck and electrostatic high voltage around the bell of the CRT, shown in Fig. 23-12. Let's go through the circuits that sweep the cathode ray and produce the scan lines of the raster.

## VERTICAL OSCILLATOR

The vertical oscillator is the originator of a 60 Hz sweep frequency (Fig. 23-13). This frequency is used to draw the cathode ray down and up. As the lines are scanned, the vertical frequency causes them to start at the top of the screen and then be drawn one after and beneath the other. A single frame is made up of 264 lines. Each frame appears 60 times a second.

In this sample circuit, the vertical oscillator is based around a unijunction transistor. It is built to run free at 50 Hz, not 60 Hz. A sync pulse from the computer is going to force it to perform at 60 Hz. The 60 Hz pulse comes from the MPU circuit and is applied to the gate of the oscillator through a .01$\mu$F capacitor and a diode.

After the 60 Hz pulse is generated, it continues on to a voltage follower pnp. The follower feeds some signal back to the oscillator through a 20 K vertical linearity pot. This gives the circuit some control over the linearity of the 60 Hz sawtooth waveform.

When trouble strikes in the vertical oscillator, the vertical sweep will collapse into a bright horizontal line across the screen if the oscillator stops running. This could happen

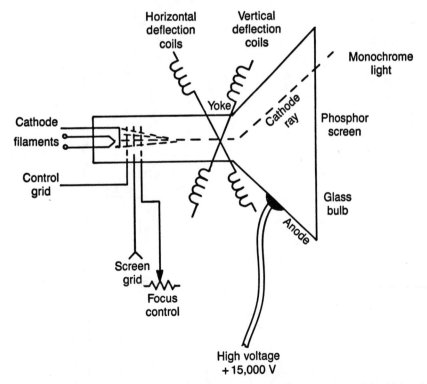

Fig. 23-12. The remaining elements to drive the CRT are the deflection coils and the high voltage anode.

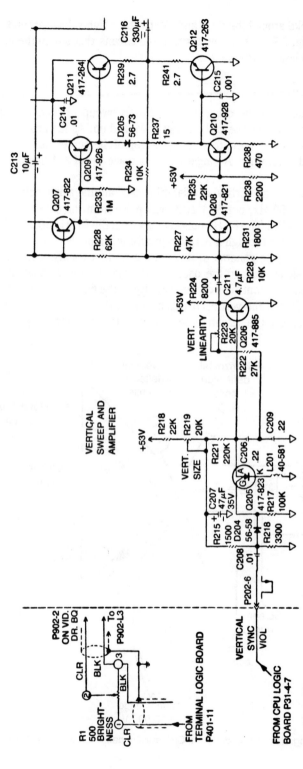

Fig. 23-13. The vertical sweep circuits originate in a unijunction transistor that runs free around 50 Hz. It needs vertical sync from the computer to operate at its prescribed 60 Hz.

if the sync pulse from the computer does not arrive, if one of the oscillator transistors dies, or if any of the related components quit.

If the picture happens to develop vertical jittering, the capacitors between the two transistors could have shorted or changed value. Should the vertical sweep be insufficient, the resistors around the vertical size pot or the pot resistive element itself could have failed.

## VERTICAL OUTPUT

The vertical output circuit is based around a half-dozen bipolar transistors. They do the job of amplifying the vertical sawtooth generated by the oscillator into a large enough signal that it will be able to be used by the yoke circuit. The circuit outputs its signal through a capacitor between a pair of output transistors' tied together emitters.

The vertical windings in the yoke take the sawtooth waveshape and deflects the cathode ray down and up the CRT face at a 60 Hz rate. When the vertical output circuit fails, the picture could have a bright white line exactly like the symptom the oscillator can cause.

The vertical output can also exhibit a decrease in vertical sweep like the oscillator might. However, the vertical output circuit can also produce too much vertical sweep during trouble times. When there is too much vertical sweep, the picture is likely to fold over on the bottom with a whitish haze appearing.

## HORIZONTAL OSCILLATOR

While the vertical sweep circuit is deflecting the cathode ray from the top of the screen and then back up, the horizontal sweep circuit is drawing the cathode ray from the left-hand side of the screen to the right and back (Fig. 23-14). The rate of the scan lines is 264 lines for every vertical deflection cycle.

The side-to-side scanning is magnetically performed by the horizontal windings of the deflection yoke. The horizontal oscillator is the originator of the sawtooth waveshape that does the job.

The waveshape has its beginnings in two timing chips that are like flip-flops. The two chips are able to oscillate at a frequency of about 15,750 Hz. They are triggered into oscillation by a horizontal sync pulse that comes from the MPU circuits. There are a group of discrete components that are in the oscillator circuit that help the chips generate the sawtooth horizontal deflection frequency.

A horizontal centering pot is in series with the +6 V supply line. Adjusting the pot varies the width of the output pulse. The actual frequency the timers pulse is at, is determined by the 3900 ohm resistor and the .0047$\mu$F capacitor in parallel with the centering pot. They cause the output pulse from pin 3 to have 20 microsecond intervals. With the pulse forced to have a specified width and specified time delay, the pulse is then transferred to the horizontal output circuit through a driver npn and a driver transformer.

When trouble strikes in the horizontal oscillator circuit, there are two common troubles in these chip-based circuits: the loss of horizontal sweep, and no horizontal centering ability.

The loss of horizontal sweep resembles the symptom of no vertical sweep. There will be a bright vertical line on the screen. A variation of this symptom is loss of bright-

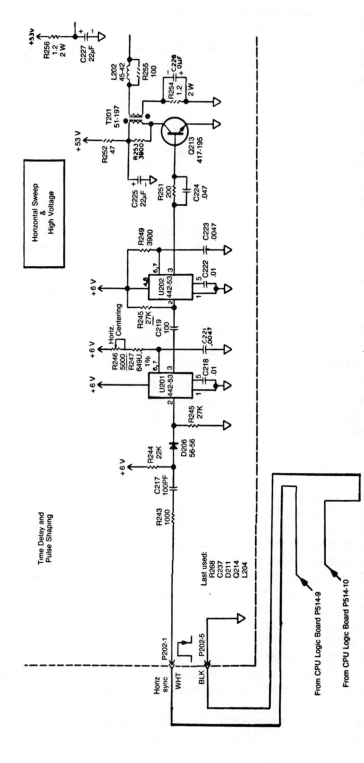

**Fig. 23-14.** The horizontal sweep originates in two IC timing chips. They are triggered into an oscillation of 15,750 Hz by sync pulses from the computer.

ness. The horizontal sweep is lost; however, the trouble often causes the CRT's high voltage to also die. This kills the brightness.

When you have horizontal sweep, the oscilloscope shows an output from the timing chips into the driver transistor. If you lose sweep, the oscilloscope will still reveal the horizontal sync pulse coming from the MPU circuits, but the oscillator will not be running and the oscilloscope will not display any waveshapes in the oscillator.

Any of the components from the sync input to the output of the driver transformer could possibly kill the oscillator. Especially vulnerable are the diode, chips, and transistor. The resistors and capacitors rarely die since the supply voltages are so tiny.

Poor centering is usually due to the timer chip, although the series components are suspects during a failure.

## HORIZONTAL OUTPUT

A large percentage of troubles in the monitor are due to failure of the horizontal output transistor (Fig. 23-15). When there is a loss of brightness, this power transistor is a prime suspect.

The well-shaped horizontal pulse generated in the oscillator is transferred into the horizontal output transistor through the driver transformer. The transistor is a switch that controls the flow of current through the horizontal output transformer known as the flyback. The flyback connects to the horizontal windings of the deflection yoke around the CRT neck. The windings in turn deflects the cathode ray across the screen. The deflection scheme is tricky and works like the following.

When the transistor is forced to turn on, current flows to the +53 V supply. The current takes a path from ground through a 1 μF capacitor, a 52 microhenry choke, a 19 microhenry width coil, the horizontal deflection coils, and the primary windings of the flyback. During this passage of current, the yoke current increases in a linear fashion and deflects the cathode ray to the right side of the screen. Note, that the ray is being drawn all the way to the edge of the screen, not the end of the display window that the video RAM uses to show its contents.

When the ray reaches the right side, the output transistor switches off. This sudden turn-off transfers the energy that was stored in the yokes to the .006μF capacitor that is bypassing the yoke windings. This energy takes the form of a halfwave voltage pulse with an amplitude of 550 V. As the yoke drops to zero, the cathode ray is drawn to screen center. The capacitor is then able to discharge current back into the yoke. The current now going the other way is able to draw the cathode ray the rest of the distance to the left side of the screen.

As the capacitor discharges to zero, it joins with the yoke and primary of the flyback to form a resonant circuit that tries to ring. As it tries to oscillate, the energy that had been transferred to the yoke now draws the ray back to screen center. The damper diode then acts by dampening the impending oscillation and charging the capacitor for the first half of the scanning. As the output transistor switches on and off, it is able to control the cathode ray and cause it to scan the screen horizontally.

The two coils in series with the yoke are the *width* and *horizontal linearity* coils. The width control adjusts the total current through the yoke. The amount of current can

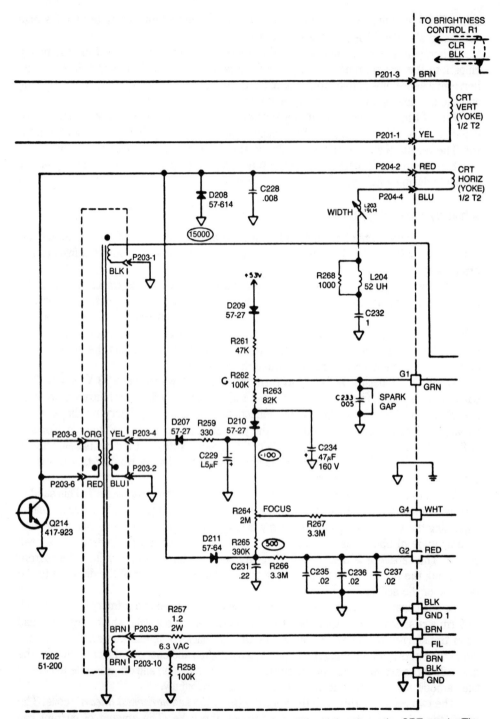

Fig. 23-15. The horizontal output circuit is also the source of the high voltage the CRT needs. The flyback transformer produces about 15 kV$_{ac}$.

spread or shrink the scan somewhat. The linearity coil is fixed and provides a certain amount of linearity correction to the scan lines.

The monitor is, in effect, a raster manufacturing plant. The raster in the monitor is almost identical to the raster developed in TV receivers. The vertical and horizontal sweep circuits, as they operate in unison, draw the scanning lines. The only contribution the computer makes are the triggering horizontal and vertical sync pulses that keep the raster in control by the MPU.

## HIGH VOLTAGE

In order for the cathode ray to arrive at the phosphor screen and the electrons to smack the phosphor hard enough to light it up, a dc high voltage of around 15,000 V must be on the bell. This attraction voltage is developed as a byproduct of the *flyback transformer*.

The flyback is so called because of the voltage pulse that is developed during the horizontal retrace. The retrace is the time between the end of one scan line and the beginning of the next scan line. That is the interval when the scan line has ended on the right side and is drawn back to the beginning on the left side. The brightness is blanked off during that time.

The primary of the flyback is coupled to three secondary windings. The top winding is where an ac version of the high voltage is developed. The flyback pulse developed in the collector of the transistor is stepped up to a 15 kV level. This ac HV is then rectified by an HV diode and applied to the bell of the CRT through the HV well in the side of the bell, seen in Fig. 23-16. The internal capacitance of the CRT bell is about 500 pF and acts as the filter for the HV. Once the 15 kV is installed in the bell as filtered dc, it can do its electron attraction job.

The bottom flyback winding has an output of 6.3 V at 450 milliamps. This is sufficient to light and heat the filaments in this CRT. The center winding is for a $-100V_{dc}$ supply. The winding produces the $-100$ V, and the diode and capacitor rectifies and filters the voltage until the output is $-100$ $V_{dc}$. Another flyback-related output is a tap into the output transistor collector line. This voltage is needed by the screen grid of the CRT as an acceleration voltage for the cathode ray.

The focus voltage for the CRT is taken from a tap between the $-100$ and the $+500$ voltages. The focus control and the series 390 K resistor are a variable voltage divider to obtain a correct focus voltage. Still another voltage divider from $+53$ V, of a diode, a 47 K resistor and a 100 K pot provide the control grid with an adjustable bias.

These assorted voltages provide the CRT with the following voltages and abilities. The 6.3 $V_{ac}$ heats the filaments. The cathode gets hot and emits a cathode ray. The ray passes through the control grid and has its intensity adjusted which adjusts CRT brightness levels. The electrons are then accelerated by the screen grid's $+500$ V. The focus grid then narrows the beam into a well focused condition. The ray then passes through the varying electromagnetic influence of the deflection yoke and is scanned across and back by the horizontal winding and down and up by the vertical windings. The 15 kV then attracts the electrons and makes them impinge on the phosphor screen to produce the raster.

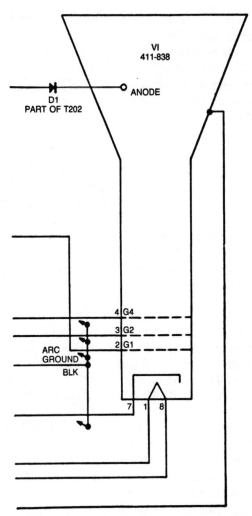

Fig. 23-16. The CRT has a diode at the anode to rectify the 15 kV$_{ac}$ to dc. The internal anode capacitance filters the high dc voltage. The electron gun receives filament voltage, video, screen grid voltage, and focus grid voltage.

When trouble strikes in the horizontal and HV circuits, the symptom is usually no brightness. Due to the complex interaction between all the circuits from the IC timers to the anode of the CRT, most of the components in these circuits could be suspects. Therefore, it would be a good idea to narrow the search area down before checking individual components. This can be done with a neon bulb, an HV probe, and a test horizontal output signal substitution. The neon bulb will light if the rf of the flyback is active.

The HV probe is used to check to see if the 15 kV$_{dc}$ is present on the CRT well. A signal substitute device is usually one of the standby pieces of test equipment in a TV repair shop. Once the circuit area is narrowed down a bit, the components in the suspect area can then be tested with normal analog measures.

526

## COLOR MONITORS

Most monochrome monitors are relatively simple devices. All that is needed to drive it is a monochrome composite signal replete with pixel switching information and sync signals. You can purchase a decent monochrome monitor for under $100.

A color monitor is a much more complex device. The main reason for the complications is the need for a color picture tube instead of a monochrome type. A monochrome CRT, invented about 80 years ago, consists of a single electron gun, contained in a bulb and pointed at a single color phosphor screen. The electron gun fires negatively charged electrons at the highly positively charged phosphor screen and lights the phosphor. A focus electrode in the gun narrows the beam into a round shape. A deflection yoke sweeps the beam over the screen like writing, starting at the upper left-hand corner.

On the other hand, a color tube must show a wide range of colors, not just varying shades of one color. In order to show color, three different color phosphors, red, green, and blue, must be laid out on the screen. The colored phosphors are put down in dots or stripes. The dot or stripe layout must be precise and placed closely together.

For instance, three dots are placed together in a triad as mentioned earlier. They must be so close together, that when they are lit, the colors add together and fool the eye into thinking the three dots are only one colored dot. In addition to that the triads must be placed together to fool the eye that all the triads are one expanse of phosphor. The closer the dots are placed the clearer the eye will see the total picture.

The distance between the dots is called dot pitch. The distance between the dot triads is called tridot pitch. The tridot pitch is usually considered a benchmark measurement of the color tube. Typical good quality tridot pitches range from a high of 0.32 millimeters to a low of 0.25 mm. The smaller the tridot pitch, the better is the resolution and fine detail in graphics displays show up satisfactorily.

While the monochrome CRT only requires a single electron gun to light up the single expanse of phosphor, a color CRT needs three guns, one for each color. There is a red gun, a green gun, and a blue gun, Fig. 23-17. These three guns produce three beams of electrons. Each beam is aimed at its corresponding phosphor on the screen. Each beam produces one of the three primary colors by lighting its own phosphor.

You might have heard of some color tubes that have a single gun. This is true but the gun is divided into three sections and each part fires a beam. There are still three beams to light up the phosphors even if they do originate in one cathode of a single gun.

There is one more item in a color tube. It is called, the shadow mask. The shadow mask is a thin metal plate perforated with one hole for each dot triad. When the three beams arrive at the mask, they must converge at the holes. That way, the three beams pass through the holes, diverge and hit the dot they are aimed at. The rest of the electrons are absorbed by the metal mask.

The reason for the shadow mask is to separate the three beams so they impinge only on their assigned phosphor dots. If the mask was not there, all of the electrons in all three beams would strike all three color phosphors on the screen. The mask shadows the electron beams from striking all the phosphors. Only the electrons that make it through the holes reach the phosphor.

Figure 23-18 shows a section of a shadow mask with round holes and the way the three beams reach their assigned phosphor dot targets. Figure 23-19 illustrates a

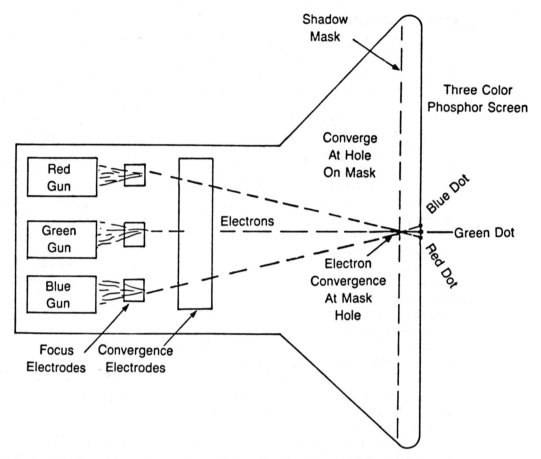

Fig. 23-17. A color picture tube consists of a glass envelope with a three-gun assembly at the rear end and a three color phosphor target at the face. A shadow mask in the electron gun has one hole for every color dot triad. The three electron beams converge at the mask and then separate to land on their assigned color dot.

shadow mask section with slotted apertures. This slotted arrangement is used when the three beams are to strike phosphor stripes rather than dots.

Like the monochrome CRT, the color picture tube has a deflection yoke around the neck of the bulb to grab ahold of the three beams electromagnetically and scan them over the screen in horizontal and vertical patterns. Unlike the monochrome CRT, the color CRT has more devices wrapped around the neck of the bulb. First of all there is a purity magnet.

Purity deals with making the three beams impinge only on their own phosphor and not on adjoining phosphors. When the beams are only striking their assigned phosphor, the purity of the colors is assured.

Next, there are two sets of convergence magnets, static and dynamic. These magnets are used to make sure the three beams converge at the holes in the shadow mask. The static magnets when adjusted affect the center of the TV screen where there is little

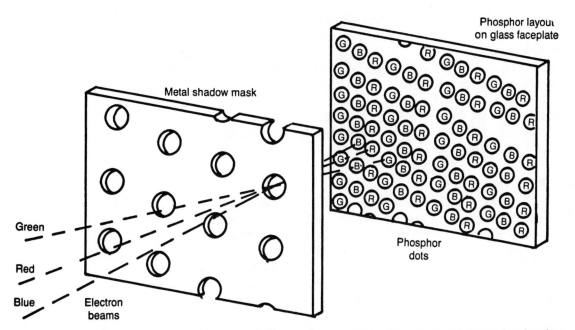

Fig. 23-18. The three color beams converge at one shadow mask hole and then diverge to land on three phosphor dots.

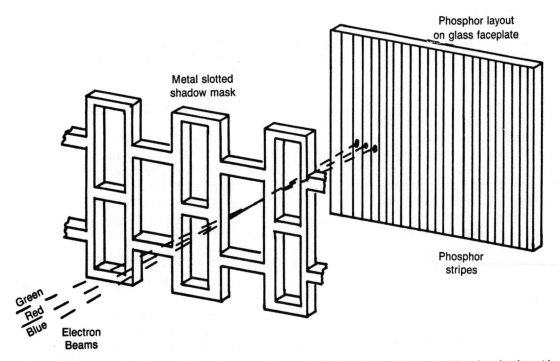

Fig. 23-19. Some color CRTs use a shadow mask with slots instead of holes. When slots are used the phosphor layout is composed of stripes instead of dots.

or no deflection taking place. The dynamic magnets are usually electromagnetic coils rather than permanent magnets like the purity and statics. The dynamic magnets affect all of the screen, top, bottom, and both sides. They can handle convergence problems no matter what the deflection angles might be. At the end of the chapter the way to make these adjustments are described.

The color CRT display is becoming vitally important as computers proliferate and new applications are discovered. There is a constant race going on between color monitor manufacturers to come up with better and better displays. As a technician you will encounter many color monitors.

## Typical Block Diagram

A color monitor can be considered as an abbreviated color TV. Quite often when I check out a monitor or TV, I use an ordinary oscilloscope and begin at the output and work backwards into the TV toward the input. I start at the cathodes of the color CRT. The color signals are injected into the CRT at the cathode.

As Fig. 23-20 shows, the three color signals are displayed on the oscilloscope as video signals. The oscilloscope shows them to be all alike since the oscilloscope is not equipped to display colors. The three color signals in this example are each present and have a peak to peak voltage of 60 V.

Moving back over the three output stages, which are based around discrete full sized transistors, the p-p voltage for each signal is still showing 60 V. Moving still further back, over the three driver stages, with more discrete transistors, the p-p voltage drops. At these touchdown points the p-p comes down to a lowly 2 V. The drivers gave the 2 V a boost up to 60 V.

The next touchdown point is over the amp stages. The oscilloscope pictures are not as clear cut. In the amp stages each of the color amps are combined with a black and white brightness signal called I for intensity. For instance, the red video checks out at 1.4 V p-p. The I signal has a p-p voltage of 0.6 V. The I is mixed with the R and the resultant is the 2 V p-p we read earlier. All three colors are mixed with the I in the same way. The I signal is coming from the computer too.

At this juncture we come to the four input stages for R, B, G, and I. The oscilloscope shows that the actual p-p voltage inputs are 2.5 V. They are fed to the inverter stages where they are inverted and amplified to 4 V. Incidentally, this example monitor uses conventional scanning frequencies of 15.75 kHz for horizontal and 60 Hz for vertical. These p-p oscilloscope readings we have been taking have been at the 15.75 kHz setting. If the monitor had been one with a higher horizontal frequency, the oscilloscope would be set at the higher frequency in order to be able to view the oscilloscope picture.

So far we have examined four of the monitors inputs, R, B, G, and I. The I was mixed with the R, B, and G, and the resultants connected to the three cathodes of the three CRT guns. There are two more inputs from the computer. They are the horizontal and vertical sync signals.

These two sync signals are sent to the inputs of the horizontal and vertical sweep circuits. These circuits do three jobs. One, they drive the deflection yoke. In the yoke are two separate coil sections. The yoke is wrapped around the neck of the CRT bulb. The three electron beams therefore stream right through the center of the yoke where

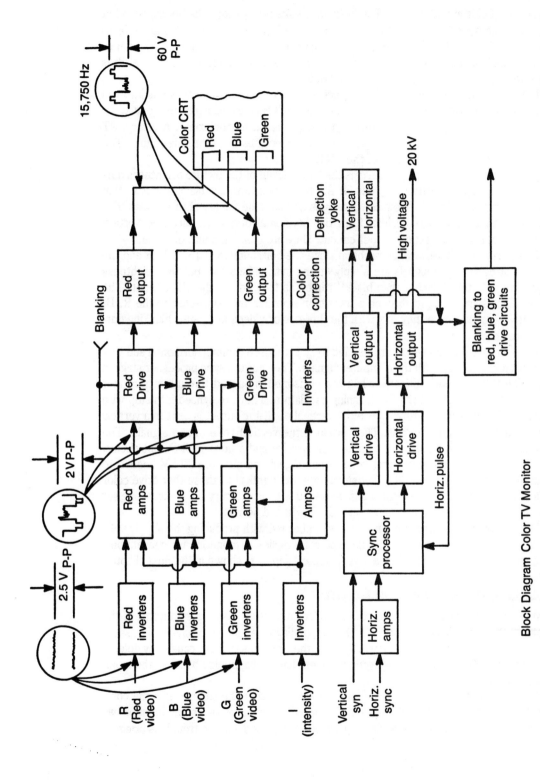

Block Diagram Color TV Monitor

Fig. 23-20. The color TV monitor has a complex video arrangement because it must process R, B, G and I. However, each color video circuit is tested in about the same way as the one monochrome video circuit.

the magnetic fields are developed. The horizontal yoke part sweeps the beams from left to right, retraces from right back to left, and then left to right again and again. Meanwhile the vertical yoke section sweeps the beams from the top of the picture to the bottom, retraces back to the top and then back to the bottom again and again. The result is a full screen sweep producing brightness full of logic.

The second job the sweep circuits do, actually only the horizontal sweep is involved in this one, is work with the horizontal output and the flyback transformer to produce the high voltage. A color CRT needs more high voltage than a monochrome. A color CRT could use at least 20,000 $V_{dc}$ in order to attract the electrons from the three guns. The HV is placed into a well in the side of the CRT.

The third job these circuits perform is the blanking out of the picture brightness during the horizontal and vertical retraces. If the brightness was not blanked out at that time, the retrace lines would show as white lines and hurt the fidelity of the display. The horizontal blanking signal is derived from the horizontal output circuit. The vertical blanking signal from the vertical output circuit. They are combined into one line.

This presents no interference problem since the horizontal is at 15.75 kHz and the vertical is at 60 Hz. The signals are simply strong sync pulses that put the brightness voltage level into the "blacker than black" region as they add to the video input. The blanking signals are then put through a transistor amplifier and connected to the R, B, and G driver inputs where they mix with the three color videos and cause blanking during retrace time.

The sync signals themselves are needed to sync the free running horizontal and vertical oscillators into step with the computer signals. They enter a sync processor stage in an IC. The vertical enters directly while the horizontal is passed through a transistor amplifier first. In the IC are the free running oscillators. They are synced into step with the video signal movement. From there the vertical oscillator output is sent to a vertical drive and a vertical output circuit. They produce the vertical yoke sweep signals. The horizontal oscillator output is sent to a horizontal drive and a horizontal output circuit. This circuit produces the horizontal yoke sweep signal and also the 20 kV needed to attract electrons in the color CRT. These circuits are identical to those that drive color CRTs in TV receivers. These circuits can be traced with an ordinary TV oscilloscope set to the frequency of the circuit under test, 15.75 kHz and 60 Hz.

The rest of the circuitry in the monitor is concerned with producing the supply voltages for the circuits just discussed. These power supplies in monitors are conventional and resemble supplies found in home TVs. A typical supply is shown in the next chapter.

## TROUBLESHOOTING A COLOR MONITOR

When computer troubles strike, the monitor quite often displays symptoms of the trouble. In the beginning of Chapter 19, the way to diagnose the symptoms is discussed. There are two types of troubles. First, there are the problems that are caused by defects in the computer. Second are the TV type troubles that are happening because the monitor has a fault.

The isolation test is simple. If you are not sure whether the trouble is in the computer or monitor, try a different, known good monitor. If the replacement monitor has the same symptoms, chances are the suspect monitor is good and the trouble is originating in the computer. When the replacement monitor works, then the suspect monitor indeed contains the fault.

In the color monitor, troubles break down into a few categories shown in Table 23-3. They are all color TV type troubles. In order to troubleshoot these conditions you need the arsenal of test equipment that a TV repairman must have to service color TVs. For example, if there is no vertical sweep, just a white horizontal line, you need a signal generator that outputs a 60 Hz signal. The signals is injected into the vertical sweep circuit at various test points in an effort to restore the sweep with the test signal. When you are able to restore the sweep with the test signal you are near the source of the trouble.

The same sort of signal injection technique is needed to test a horizontal circuit trouble. Loss of horizontal sweep or even loss of raster can be tested with a 15.75 kHz signal. If you find a spot where the signal produces the return of the raster or the sweep, you are near the fault.

Red, blue, and green picture losses or mixups can often be fixed with the aid of video-type injection signals. The signal is injected into various test points in the three color amplifier lines. The injected signal can alter or restore color losses. Then you must figure out what has failed, and why the injection signal is producing its results.

The troubleshooting table lists the common troubles that could befall the monitor, the test approach that should be taken to pinpoint the circuit, and the circuits that are indicated as prime suspects. For further troubleshooting and repair techniques consult some color TV repair books. When you are working on monitors, you are working on TVs.

## COLOR MONITOR ADJUSTMENTS

The color monitor only has a few inside adjustments available. You'll need the service notes for the specific monitor for some of the adjustments. For instance the dc B+ voltage that the power supply puts out, is adjustable. In the IBM PC you must connect a voltmeter to a test point and adjust a control for exactly +115 V output. To adjust the horizontal hold, you are instructed to connect a .1 microfarad capacitor from a test point to ground. The control is adjusted until the display floats around the picture. To produce a display an RGB color bar generator is advised. These type adjustments are specific to the monitor you are working on. The service notes spell out what should be done.

Less specific and more universal are the adjustments that are often required to produce a color display that is true. Around the neck of the color CRT bulb are a number of devices mentioned earlier. There is the deflection yoke, convergence magnets, and a purity magnet. There are also some potentiometer controls on the chassis that are associated with these devices. They are all adjustable in most monitors. They are the magnetic and resistive devices that control the path of the three electron beams that travel from the electron guns, through the shadow mask and land on the phosphor targets. Let's examine what they do. These adjustments can cure the following symptoms of trouble.

### Poor Monochrome Picture

In a color monitor, when the three colors are perfectly adjusted, a perfect black and white picture can be attained as the three colors add together. If you are not getting a

**Table 23-3. Typical Color Monitor Troubles.**

### Dead Set

| Approach | Suspects |
|---|---|
| Check Voltages with VOM | Low Voltage Supply<br>High Voltage Supply<br>(Chapter 24) |

### Shrunken Picture

| | |
|---|---|
| Check Voltages with VOM | Horiz. Output<br>Vertical Output<br>Low Voltage Supply<br>High Voltage Supply |

### Picture Out of Sync

| | |
|---|---|
| Check Horiz. &<br>Vertical Sync from<br>Computer with<br>Oscilloscope | Computer Sync<br>Output Circuits<br>Monitor Sync<br>Input Circuits |

### No Picture with Raster OK

| | |
|---|---|
| Check Video from<br>Computer. Test from<br>Monitor Input, to<br>Video Amplifiers<br>to CRT Cathode<br>with Oscilloscope | Video Amplifiers<br>CRT Electron Gun |

### Bright Red or Greenish-Blue Picture

| | |
|---|---|
| (Inject Video Signal)<br>Check R Video<br>Amplifiers with<br>VOM D Oscilloscope | R Video<br>Amplifiers |

### Bright Blue or Greenish-Red Picture

| | |
|---|---|
| (Inject Video Signal)<br>Check B Video<br>Amplifiers with<br>VOM and Oscilloscope | B Video<br>Amplifiers |

### Bright Green or Blueish-Red Picture

| | |
|---|---|
| (Inject Video Signal)<br>Check G Video<br>Amplifiers with<br>VOM and Oscilloscope | G Video<br>Amplifiers |

### Picture Too Dark or Too Bright

| | |
|---|---|
| Check I Video<br>Amplifiers with<br>VOM and Oscilloscope | I Video<br>Amplifiers |

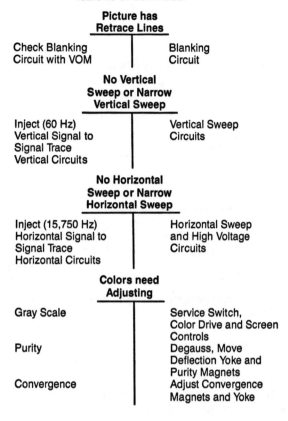

**Table 23-3. Continued.**

| Picture has Retrace Lines | |
|---|---|
| Check Blanking Circuit with VOM | Blanking Circuit |

| No Vertical Sweep or Narrow Vertical Sweep | |
|---|---|
| Inject (60 Hz) Vertical Signal to Signal Trace Vertical Circuits | Vertical Sweep Circuits |

| No Horizontal Sweep or Narrow Horizontal Sweep | |
|---|---|
| Inject (15,750 Hz) Horizontal Signal to Signal Trace Horizontal Circuits | Horizontal Sweep and High Voltage Circuits |

| Colors need Adjusting | |
|---|---|
| Gray Scale | Service Switch, Color Drive and Screen Controls |
| Purity | Degauss, Move Deflection Yoke and Purity Magnets |
| Convergence | Adjust Convergence Magnets and Yoke |

good black and white picture, the colors are not adding properly, as in Fig. 23-21. They need adjusting. This adjustment is often called, the color temperature adjustment, which is confusing the first time you see the term. I prefer to call it gray scale tracking. What is needed is the mixing of the three primary colors on the screen to fool the eye into thinking a black and white picture is there.

Lots of monitors follow color TV chassis design and provide what is called a Service Switch. When you flick the switch, the vertical sweep is killed leaving a horizontal line. The next step is to adjust the Red, Blue, and Green Drive controls. These controls make the lines bright or dim red, blue, and green. Adjust the three lines until they are superimposed on top of one another, and they produce a dim black and white picture. Reset the Service Switch and the full display will reappear. It should be a fairly good black and white display. If it is slightly off, readjust the Blue and Green Drive controls until the black and white picture is true.

## Poor Purity

One serious drawback with the three gun color CRT is that the three beams can be affected by the lines of force in the earth's magnetic field. It has been suggested that a

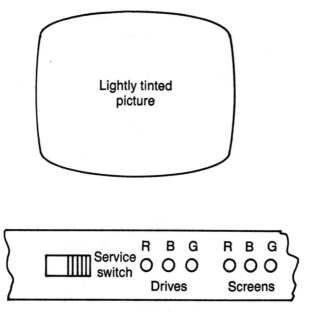

Fig. 23-21. When the color monitor cannot display a perfect black and white picture and is tinted, the colors are not adding together properly. These adjustments could eliminate the problem.

color CRT should operate in a north-south position so it is not cutting the earth's magnetic field.

Another problem in the same vein occurs when some of the metal in the monitor becomes magnetized. This too can affect the paths of the beams and produce distorted colors. The symptoms of the trouble that happens due to extraneous magnetic influences is color splotches in the display, Fig. 23-22, especially around the perimeter of the CRT face. The splotches can be any color and can be caused by spurious magnetization or misadjusted CRT neck devices.

The first step in curing poor picture purity is to demagnetize the magnetized spots. Technicians call it degaussing. Usually a color CRT will have a degaussing coil wound around the bulb near the faceplate. The degaussing coil is then automatically activated everytime the monitor is turned on. You can see the effect of the coil. The picture, especially around the perimeter will show moving color rainbows for a few seconds at turn on. This demagnetizes the area.

Sometimes the built-in coil is not strong enough to do the job. Then you must employ an external degaussing coil. It's easy; just energize and rotate the round coil from around the perimeter of the faceplate. You can do it with the set on or off, before, during, or after the repair. Just keep the coil away from the rear of the TV. You don't want to demagnetize the magnets in the monitor.

If after degaussing, some color splotches still remain, analyze their screen position. Are they around the rim of the tube or near screen center?

Screen center impurities can be removed by adjusting the purity magnets. Follow this procedure. Turn the Blue and Green Drive controls all the way down. This leaves a red picture. Adjust the Red Drive control so the red picture is vivid and the impurities

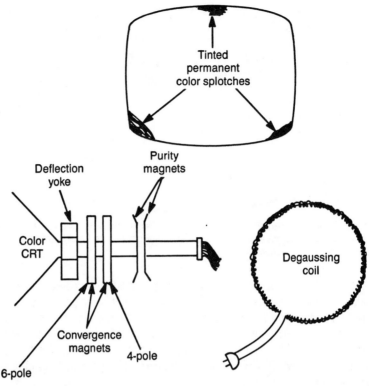

Fig. 23-22. When the three beams do not land on their assigned phosphor, color splotches will be seen. The purity problem can be remedied with use of a degaussing coil, adjusting the purity magnets and moving the yoke.

stand out. Adjust the purity tabs that move the purity magnets until the splotches are gone and a uniform red picture is displayed.

When the color splotches are around the perimeter of the screen, the cure is to loosen and move the deflection yoke back and forth until the red picture is uniform. There could be a lot of interaction between the purity magnets and the yoke movement. You will probably have to go back and forth between the purity tabs and the yoke positioning until you obtain your uniform red field. If you care to, you could even degauss again.

Once you have a uniform red field you can perform the gray scale tracking procedure to restore a true black and white picture.

## Color Bleeding

The gray scale tracking adds the proper amounts of red, blue, and green lights to produce black and white. The purity adjustments adjust the trajectory of the three beams so they only land on their assigned phosphor. A third trouble is bleeding colors. In the picture, sometimes you will observe an extraneous color bleeding out of the edges of objects on the screen (Fig. 23-23). The bleeding is most noticeable during a black and white display. Red, blue, or green outlines will appear around figures. It looks almost like

**Fig. 23-23.** When the characters in the display have unwanted color fringes, the three beams are not converging at their shadow mask apertures. Good convergence can be adjusted in with the convergence magnet and the deflection yoke.

a TV ghost trouble but it is different. It is being caused by incorrect trajectories of the three beams. The beams could be landing on the correct color phosphors, but the three beams are not converging at the holes in the shadow mask at the spots showing the bleeding. The cure is to make them converge and the bleeding will disappear.

To see where the bleeding is occurring you should connect a dot-bar generator to the monitor and display either a dot or bar pattern. The dots or bars clearly show the bleeding locations.

There are two sets of magnets around the bulb neck that adjust the trajectories of the three beams so they can be made to converge at the shadow mask holes once again (Fig. 23-22). One set of magnets adjusts bleeding at screen center. The other magnets adjust for bleeding around the perimeter of the CRT. The center adjusters are permanent magnets. The perimeter magnets could be permanent magnets, electromagnets, or the deflection yoke according to the specific monitor being tested.

In the IBM PC monitor we have been using as an example, the magnets are all permanent except for the deflection yoke. The following is the prescribed procedure to cure misconvergence. With an RGB dot-bar pattern entering the monitor, a dot pattern is used first. The dot pattern is handier to adjust center convergence.

There are two sets of permanent magnets on this monitor, a 4-pole and a 6-pole set. The deflection yoke is also needed for the perimeter convergence adjustments. With the dot pattern displayed, the 4-pole magnet is adjusted to converge the red and blue dots at the center of the screen. Then the 6-pole magnets are used to converge the green dots over on top of the red-blue dots. This produces white dots.

Next, a cross hatch pattern is displayed. The deflection yoke is loosened. The deflection yoke is then manipulated. The effect is, when the yoke is tilted up and down, the vertical lines at the top and bottom of the screen and the horizontal lines at the left and right of the screen can be converged.

When the yoke is tilted from side to side, the horizontal lines at the top and bottom and the vertical lines at the sides can be converged. The converged lines will be white with no bleeding. You must take your time and observe the lines carefully until you elimi-

538

nate the bleeding to the best of your ability. It will never be absolutely perfect but get as close to perfection as you can. It will usually be satisfactory.

## SPECIFIC COMPUTER MONITORS

When you are working on a computer monitor, you are in effect a TV technician. Unless the trouble is easily spotted and fixed, you will probably need the specific service notes for the unit. In the past few years as resolution and color needs have become vital, there are many kinds of monitors at all sorts of prices appearing on the market.

Since the advent of the IBM PC with its expansion slots, computers have not been limited to certain monitors. The IBM PC family and clones, as well as Apple's Macintosh and imitators do not as a rule, have the video display generators built onto the motherboard. The video generators have been installed onto cards and plug into the motherboard slots. As a result, users can easily change monitor types by purchasing the latest video output cards and plugging them in.

In the same computer you can switch from a monochrome monitor to a color monitor. You can then go from an inexpensive color monitor to a much better performer with better resolution. These advanced monitors have one drawback. When they need repairing they are found to be more complex than their predecessors.

Basically though, they are still only forms of color TVs. In order to be prepared, when you find you are getting into a complicated repair job, be sure to be equipped with TV service test instruments and the monitor's service notes.

# 24
# Power Supplies

Most computers are plugged into a wall socket and obtain the electrical energy that runs it, from the electric company. The electric company provides a typical 120-V, 60 Hz ac current. In other countries, their electric companies could provide different voltages and frequencies. For instance, some countries could provide 220 volts at 50 Hz.

Getting back to the U.S. Standard of 120-V, 60 Hz, although this form enters computer systems, the raw electricity cannot be used as-is by the computer. The components to be energized need special forms of electricity. In computers and monitors are digital chips, op amp chips, discrete transistors, and other components. The 120-V 60 Hz ac current must be conditioned or else it won't be able to energize the components.

Practically all the integrated chips need a supply of +5 or −5 V current. Op amps and discrete transistors often require +12 and −12 V current. In computer monitors, TV type supply voltages are required that can be +5 V, +12 V, +50 V, +115 V and more according to the circuits. Some CRT focus voltages are around +500 V. In addition the CRT needs a high voltage. Monochrome CRTs run with 10-15 kilovolts and color CRTs with 20 to 30,000 volts. All of these required dc voltages are derived from the original 120 V, 60 Hz, ac current.

If you liken electric energy from the utility company to water supplies, the voltage is analogous to water pressure. The frequencies could be compared to pulsating water that comes out of the spigot. Then there is electrical current, this is like the amount of water the utility charges you for. The electric company will sell you as much current as you need. As the amperes course into your house, the meter runs and charges you. They calibrate it in kilowatt hours but they are charging you for amps. A watt is simply the voltage times amps. The voltage is fixed at 120 but the number of amps you draw changes every month according to your needs.

On the power supply schematic, you'll find the input plug symbol is accompanied by the voltage and the amount of current the computer system draws. For instance, the

Apple II plug reads 120 V$_{ac}$, 290 mA. The mA means milliamps or mils. It is .290 amperes, not very much. The IBM PC reads 120 V$_{ac}$, 800 mA.

If you multiply 120 × .290, it equals, 34.8 watts. The Apple is rated at 34.8 watts. The IBM PC, 120 × .800 = 96 watts. This wattage is the amount of power the supplies in these machines can deliver. The power energizes all the components in the units. The supply must also power any print cards that might get plugged into the expansion slots. The Apple has eight expansion slots but none of the cards draw very much current. It can get by, most of the time, with a 34 watt supply. The IBM PC only has five slots but the cards that plug into those slots draw a lot more current. Some of the cards have complete video systems on them, others that are heavy duty could possess a modem, memory expansions, disk drives, and other useful accessories. Should a card be needed but draws too much current, it can't be used. For instance a disk drive card would overload the supply. An external drive must be employed with its own power supply.

The IBM XT, as a result was built with a supply that is able to draw 130 watts. The IBM AT enjoys 175 watts. They are able to utilize floppy and hard disk drive cards plugged into their expansion slots. The newer PS/2 machines from IBM have a 94 watt supply in the Model 50, 207 watts in the Model 60 and 225 watts available in the Model 80.

In a computer, the supply not only converts ac to prescribed dc levels, but the dc levels must be closely regulated. This means there cannot be any frequency ripples in the steady dc level.

## DC REGULATION

In old vacuum tube devices, dc regulation was usually not included in the power supplies. If some ripple did get into the dc output of the supply the results were tolerable. This is not the case in microcomputers or their monitors. The lack of regulation would put interference into the digital signals and either cause errors or decimate the signal altogether.

What exactly is dc regulation? This question brings up the story of the Giant Storage Battery. Just suppose, that instead of the electric company, your neighborhood used a giant storage battery. This giant battery is able to supply all the amperes or kilowatt hours that your neighborhood needed and still have plenty more current left over.

All the electronic equipment in your neighborhood would not need complex power supplies. The battery would put out a dc voltage that would hold at the desired volt level without varying a fraction of a volt either way. Usually when equipment is first turned on, there is a sudden burst of current that flows and the voltage supply suffers a small lowering of voltage until the current flow stabilizes. When the current supply is so plentiful as in this magical battery, turning on equipment would not affect the voltage. The voltage would be regulated perfectly and not vary.

If the battery was not a giant, but much smaller, when equipment is turned on, there would be a loss of voltage for a short period of time. This loss of voltage would be a voltage spike in the steady dc output of the battery. This spike would be applied to all the chips in any computers on the line. The spike could get into a byte of signal and change the value of the byte. The program being run would have errors or even crash. Voltage regulation is essential in these sensitive electronic machines.

Since there are no giant storage batteries putting out a perfectly regulated dc voltage to energize computer systems, regulation must be installed in the power supplies. An actual regulator is discussed later in this chapter.

Voltage regulators are defined as devices that supply dc voltages to a circuit's load. They automatically keep the dc voltage at or near a constant voltage. They perform this regulation no matter what the variations are in ac line voltage or the amount of current that the load draws.

In battery operated computers such as portables and laptops, batteries are used to power the units. The straight dc from the batteries are ideal and the voltage is regulated by the natural state of the battery. AC driven computer supplies though, have to first change the ac to unregulated dc and then duplicate the dc battery regulated output with the regulator devices. Let's examine a typical small computer's power supply that is able to eliminate these unwanted ac ripples and voltage spikes that are so potentially damaging.

## POWER SUPPLY INPUT

The input to most computers enters from the 120 V, 60 Hz house line through a polarized plug. The plug has two active lines that send the $120V_{ac}$ to a power transformer that is fused in the high input line. The ground connection on the polarized plug is connected to the chassis ground of the computer. As shown in Fig. 24-1 there is 0.01 $\mu$F HV capacitor to ground from the high input line (120 V). There is a second HV capacitor from the low input line (0 V) to ground. There is a third HV capacitor between the high and low input lines. These bypass capacitors eliminate incoming noise spikes that might be on the power lines.

In the transformer secondary there are two windings. Both are centertapped to the chassis ground. They are stepdown windings. The 120 $V_{ac}$ input is stepped down to about 18 $V_{ac}$ in the two windings. The computer can use the top winding for the +12 V, -12 V and -5 V needs. The bottom winding is then left to do the job of providing the 2 amps at +5 V the rest of the computer requires.

The power supply is one of the most common sources of trouble. It is subject to all the typical power supply troubles that technicians have become familiar with in all elec-

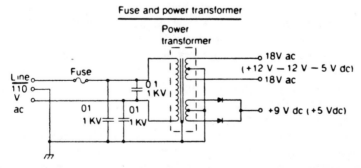

Fig. 24-1. This computer power supply input steps down the 110 $V_{ac}$ house current to a pair of 18 $V_{ac}$ lines and a +9 $V_{dc}$ line.

tronic gear. The fuse can blow, the rectifiers short or open, the transformer can open or start smoking from internal wiring shorts.

The typical symptom of power supply trouble is the dead computer. The first test, of course, is a fuse replacement. Sometimes that cures, but usually the replacement fuse will also blow and further tests must take place. Let's examine the circuits in detail.

## +5 VOLT LINE

The bottom winding of the transformer secondary is connected to the anodes of two rectifier diodes (Fig. 24-1). This provides a full wave rectification circuit. The high voltage peak of the 120 V sine wave input is rectified by one diode and the low voltage valley of the sine wave is rectified by the other diode. The cathodes of the diodes are tied together so the two rectified pulses are output together.

The twin diode output is a dc with ripple. After the rectification the dc has a voltage of +9 V. The dc has the ripple removed by being passed over the top of a 10,000 $\mu$F filter in Fig. 24-2. The smoothed out +9 V is then injected into the emitter of a discrete pnp transistor. The emitter is biased with a 68 ohm resistor from the base of the pnp.

The transistor is in charge of the amount of current the +5 V line will be permitted to have. The pnp is in turn controlled by the output of a 723C Adjustable Voltage Regula-

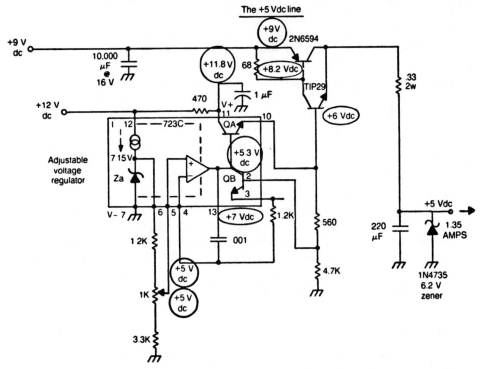

Fig. 24-2. The 723C regulator chip with some buffer and pass transistors is able to output a well regulated +5 V$_{dc}$ with heavy current abilities.

tor chip. This is a common voltage regulator that is found in a lot of computer power supplies. The regulator is vital to the correct processing of data in the digital circuits. Without it meaningless data bits would appear in programs and cause havoc.

The 723C is contained in a 14-pin DIP. The circuit consists of two zener diodes, two npn transistors, and a buffer amplifier. The 723C has the job of regulating the amount of current that flows through a series-pass power transistor. It constantly samples the current flow through the transistor and automatically adjusts the flow with its connection to the base. If some ripple tends to be generated, the adjustment cancels the ripple and allows only a steady dc to power the computer components.

The regulator voltage exits pin 10 of the 723. It is connected to the base of the npn, which in turn is driving the series-pass pnp. The output of the pnp then goes to the .33 ohm resistor. From there, the voltage passes over a 6.2 V zener diode and a 220 micro-farad filter. The voltage emerges from the circuit as the desired regulated +5 V. This circuit can supply 1.35 amps without any problems. The zener diode is normally off. It is only there in case a short develops between the +5 V line and the +12 V line. It will start conducting if the voltage rises above 6.2 V and will not permit any of the higher voltages into the +5 V rated circuits. The +12 V is applied to the chip at pin 12. It passes through a coil and arrives at the cathode of zener diode Za. The zener is rated at 7.15 V and this voltage is thus applied to pin 6. This is the voltage reference for the chip and it can be adjusted slightly by a 1 K pot in a voltage divider consisting of a 1.2 K and a 3.3 K besides the pot. The voltage divider ends at ground.

The 723C itself is powered by the +12 V line. The +12 V is applied to the chip at pin 12. It passes through a coil and arrives at the cathode of zener diode Za. The zener is rated at 7.15 V and this voltage is thus applied to pin 6. This is the voltage reference for the chip and it can be adjusted slightly by a 1 K pot in a voltage divider consisting of a 1.2 K and a 3.3 K besides the pot. The voltage divider ends at gorund.

The reference voltage is set at exactly +5 V and the wiper arm on the pot, with the +5 V connected to pin 5. Pins 4 and 5 are the inputs to a comparator on the chip called the *error amp*. Pin 13 is one output of the error amp. Pin 13 has a frequency compensating .001 μF capacitor connected.

Another output of the error amp controls the npn QA. QA is driving the regulator output that is emerging at pin 10. The third error amp output goes to QB, which is also exercising some control over QA. QB is controlled at its base through the current limit set by the 560 and 4.7 K resistors in the base of the npn attached to pin 10.

The net result of all these controls and compensations is to adjust the pnp series-pass transistor so that it will only output a regulated +5 V up to 1.35 amps. The error amp does all the sensitive work. It constantly checks its two inputs at its output. If the comparison senses a rising or falling voltage, it will adjust the output back to the +5 V.


## +12 VOLT LINE

The 400 milliamp current the +12 V line is required to supply can be regulated easily with a 7812 12 V regulator (Fig. 24-3). The 7812 is a three-pin component that resembles a power transistor. The three pins are the input, output and ground.

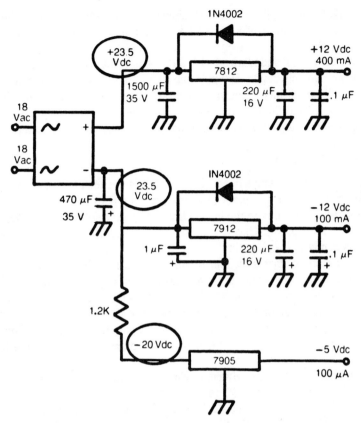

Fig. 24-3. The +12, −12, and −5 V$_{dc}$ outputs are obtained from the two 18 V$_{ac}$ lines.

The input receives a +23.5 V$_{dc}$ input from a set of bridge rectifiers that are connected to a secondary winding of the power transformer. The dc is filtered by a 1500 microfarad capacitor at 35 working volts. A diode is placed across the regulator for protection. The cathode of the diode attaches to the transformer side of the regulator. The output of the regulator is then further filtered by a pair of capacitors, a 220 μF and a .1 μF. Without further ado the +12 V leaves the supply and proceeds to its destinations.

## NEGATIVE VOLTAGES

The −12 V and −5 V lines are both drawn from the same bridge diodes the +12 V line receives its input. The diodes have one output for the +12 V supply and a second output for the negative voltages. Both −12 V and −5 V use the same filter, a 470 μF at 35 WV. The bridge-filter arrangement outputs −23.5 V$_{dc}$.

Two leads are taken from the −23.5 V$_{dc}$ leg. One line is for the −12 V supply and the second is to supply the −5 V needs. The −12 V lead is attached directly to a 7912 12 V regulator. The second lead goes to a 1.2 K current limiting resistor and then on to a 7905 5 V regulator. The 1.2 K resistor changes the −23.5 V$_{dc}$ to −20 V$_{dc}$.

The $-12$ V circuit is like the $+12$ V circuit with these few changes. The regulator is a 7912 in the $-12$ V line while the $+12$ V line has a 7812. The protective diode is the same one but the polarity is reversed to accommodate the minus voltage. The regulator's input filter is a $\mu$F and is wired with the $+$ end connected to the ground. Lastly the $-12$ V circuit can only supply 100 milliamps while the $+12$ V line provides 400 mils.

The $-5$ V circuit has a similar configuration, except the protective diode and the output 220 microfarad filtering are not needed. The $-5$ V line only has to deliver 100 microamps and the regulator can handle that without any additional components.

## TROUBLESHOOTING

When the computer stops dead, the first step is to check the power supply. When a particular function of the computer fails, the first step is to test the supply voltages that are supposed to be coming to the circuit from the power supply. Power supply troubles are fairly easy to diagnose. Once the power supply is indicated as the seat of a trouble, the VOM is handy to check it out.

The best place to start is the four regulator outputs. If all of the outputs are missing, then the trouble is probably in the power supply input circuit around the fuse area. The fuse, power transformer, diodes, and HV capacitors need testing.

If one of the regulator outputs is missing, then that line is indicated as containing trouble. For instance, if you discover the $-12$ $V_{dc}$ is gone, that circuit from the bridge diode output to the regulator output, contains a defect. Each part in the line must be tested.

The troubleshooting is not always as simple as that. First of all, the $+12$ V line supplies the voltage to drive the 723C regulator in the $+5$ V supply circuit. Second, zener diodes like the 6.2 V type in the $+5$ V output line will automatically short to ground if more than 6.2 V is applied to the line. This could be confusing and lead to false troubleshooting paths that go nowhere.

Therefore, if there is no voltage at the $+5$ V regulator output, the next stop is a test of the $+12$ V output. If the $+12$ V is also missing, then the $+12$ V line is really the primary source of the trouble. When the $+12$ V is present, then the $+5$ V line is the source of its own trouble. The next step in the $+5$ V line is to disconnect the 6.2 V zener, since it could be causing a false symptom. If the voltage returns with the zener disconnected, the diode is being overloaded. Find the overload before going any further. It could be a defective regulator. Disconnect the .33 ohm 2 watt resistor to avoid damaging other components, and test the regulator.

When there is no voltage in any of the lines and the fuse area checks out ok, then run resistance tests from the supply to ground. It is possible that a bypass component or the board itself has developed a short to ground.

When none of the above methods yield a repair, then a point by point test with the computer on is called for. The VOM will read the test nodes. The bridge diodes can be tested at their outputs. The $+23.5$ V and the $-23.5$ V are checked. If both are missing, the bridge could be bad. If one or the other of the voltages are gone, then the filter on the regulator has broken down. The $+5$ V line can be traced by following the voltage from the +5 V$_{dc}$ output. As soon as you arrive at a wrong voltage you are near the bad component.

## MONITOR POWER SUPPLY

Part of the monitor's power supply works in the same way the computer's supply operated. There is a polarized plug that goes into a wall socket. Near the plug on the schematic in Fig. 24-4 are the markings, 120 V$_{ac}$ and 340 mA. 120 × .340 = 40.8 watts. This is the amount of wattage the monitor needs to operate.

Next is a step down transformer that converts the 120 V$_{ac}$ to 22 V$_{ac}$. The transformer is capable of outputting 1.6 amps. The 22 V$_{ac}$ is then passed through a full-wave rectifier circuit. The 22-V$_{ac}$ is rectified to 25.9 V, 979 mA dc. From there the dc goes to a regulator network based around a series pass transistor and an IC. The regulator output, a steady as a rock dc current flow, goes to an intersection with three roads. The top road outputs about +15 V$_{dc}$, the middle road about +14 V$_{dc}$ and the bottom road, about +5 V$_{dc}$. All three outputs are dc regulated.

Note the oscilloscope wave shapes at the rectifier output, and the regulator output. The rectifier output is an unregulated pulsating dc. The regulator output is a smooth, steady dc. The regulator circuit is actually an electronic emulation of a filter capacitor system.

These three outputs are used to drive the video, vertical sweep and horizontal sweep circuits. In these circuits are some ICs and discrete transistors. The +5 and +15 V outputs do their job well for these circuits. However, in the monitor, there are some other heavy duty voltages needed. There is a video output transistor that requires +55 V. In addition, the picture tube has very large voltage needs.

The picture tube requires about 100 V difference in potential between the cathode and control grid in the electron gun. Next the CRT needs +270 V on the screen grid in the gun. Finally the gun circuits have to have a focus grid voltage that can vary, by adjusting the control, between −119 and +490 V$_{dc}$.

Besides these voltages, the picture tube has an anode hole in the side of the glass funnel. A dc voltage of about 15,000 V must be applied there. This is called the "high voltage." The anode hole is an important test point.

### High Voltage Supply

In this example monitor, which is somewhat like the IBM monochrome monitor, the high voltage power supply has four outputs. There is no need to go through a lot of dc regulation. The circuits that are driven with these four outputs can do very well without perfect regulation. They draw little or no current from the supply. From a practical viewpoint you could consider that they do not draw any current. Since they do not draw current they do not load down the supply and cause voltage spikes.

With no current being drawn, it is easy to develop very high voltages and the voltages are not deadly. If you should accidentally contact them you could be thrown across the room, but no deadly current will pass through you. At any rate, be careful working on the high voltage power supply.

Because there is no current to speak of that is drawn by the CRT circuits, it is easy to develop the high voltages. The HV supply is designed to be a by-product of the hori-

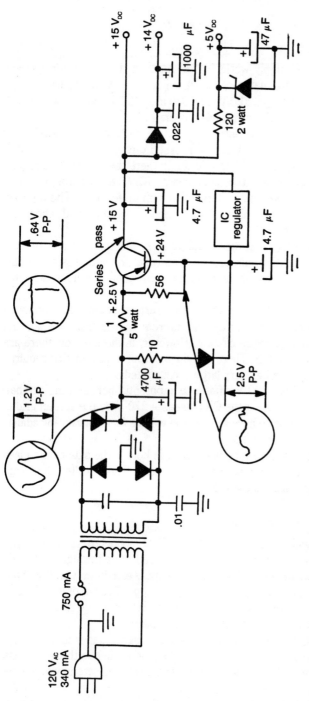

Fig. 24-4. The monochrome monitor low voltage supply produces +15, +14, and +5 V_dc.

zontal sweep circuit. The sweep circuit drives the deflection yoke that produces the scanning of the cathode ray across and up and down over the CRT face.

A special transformer called the "flyback" is also wired with the horizontal coils of the deflection yoke, in Fig. 24-5. The flyback has its primary windings connected with the yoke windings. The flyback has two step up secondary windings. The top secondary winding steps up the sweep voltage into the kilovolt ac range at one tap and into the hundreds of ac volts at another tap. These ac voltages are passed through rectifiers and become +15,000 V and +546 V. These two dc voltages are then available. The +15 kV is plugged into the CRT anode hole and the +546 is connected to the CRT focus circuit for application to the electron gun focus grid.

The bottom secondary winding of the flyback is split into three outputs. At one tap +57 V is obtained. At the other tap, a negative dc voltage of −167 is available. These voltages are applied to the other grids in the electron gun input circuits and to the video output transistor's collector circuit.

The flyback transformer gets its name because of the way it handles the primary input signal. The input signal is the horizontal sweep waveshape. The waveshape is a sawtooth operating at the horizontal sweep frequency. In this monitor, that is 15,750 Hz. The sawtooth, starts its movement at a low voltage and gradually increases its voltage as it draws the cathode beam across the screen. At the end of one line, the sawtooth has risen to its highest voltage. The sawtooth is then ready for its retrace. To accomplish the retrace, it drops from the highest voltage it has attained back to the low start voltage once again. The voltage drop from high to low takes place in only a fraction of the time the voltage took to rise and trace out a line.

This sudden voltage drop is called a flyback. This flyback pulse is coupled into the flyback primary winding. The suddenness of the pulse is coupled to the step up secondary windings. The top winding is able to step up the flyback pulse tremendously since no current is drawn. The flyback secondary pulse easily reaches 15,000 V for the instant the pulse is taking place. The pulse is then quickly rectified to a dc and filtered. The high voltage is thus produced. The rest of the flyback power supply voltages are developed in the same way. They are all high voltages that are fine working potentials as long as they do not draw any current to speak of.

## Troubleshooting the Monitor Power Supply

When the monitor power supply goes bad, the most common symptom is a dead monitor. It is a good idea to try another monitor and make sure the monitor is really at fault and not the computer or a video output card in a slot causing the trouble.

Once you are sure the monitor is at fault, you must then determine which part of the supply the trouble is occurring in. Is the problem in the low voltage or high voltage section of the supply? You can't tell right off unless there is some tell-tale visual or audible tipoff, like smoke, arcing or burning. Aside from that start in the low voltage supply.

The first obvious step is to test the ac line fuse. If it is blown, try a new one of the exact same size. That might be all that is wrong. Chances are you won't be so lucky, the fuse opened due to excessive current drain because of a short. The prime suspects then become the four rectifier diodes and the diode leading into the IC. Odds are good one or

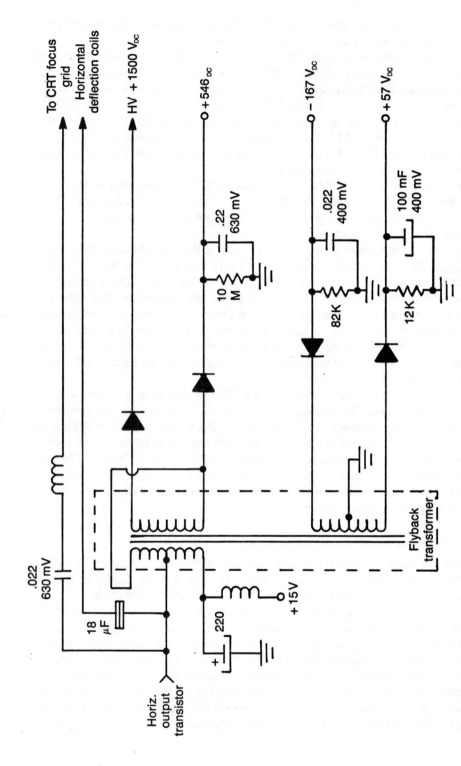

**Fig. 24-5.** The monochrome high voltage supply produces voltages that range from $-167\ V_{dc}$ to $+15{,}000\ V_{dc}$.

550

more of the rectifier diodes has shorted through. Replacing a bad rectifier diode should restore all.

Secondary suspects that could blow the ac fuse are the diode leading to the IC, the regulator transistor, the power transformer and it's nearby capacitors.

When the fuse is not blown, the approach is different. Energize the monitor and take oscilloscope readings at a low frequency at the output of the rectifiers and the output of the regulator. The rectifier output should reveal a pulsating voltage with a peak to peak of one or two volts. This is the unregulated dc and the ripple in the voltage is seen. The regulator oscilloscope picture should show a straight horizontal line with a peak to peak under a volt. This is the regulated dc.

If one or both are missing, the trouble is in that section of circuits. The components all become suspect and must be tested one at a time. Check the voltages shown on the schematic. A wrong voltage will indicate a nearby defect.

When the oscilloscope pictures are present, test the three source voltages. Two of them are about $+15$ V and the third about $+5$ V. Should one of them be missing or severely incorrect, it's line and the components in the line are suspect. Check them out until you uncover the problem.

Once the low voltage supply is exonerated, the high voltage supply comes under suspicion. The high voltage system is involved with the horizontal sweep circuits. Besides the components in the HV supply being possible culprits, any part of the horizontal circuit could also be under suspicion.

The first step is to see if the $+15,000$ V is being generated. This can be accomplished simply by placing a neon bulb tester near the flyback area. The flyback emanates an RF signal at 15,750 Hz. If the flyback is running, the neon will light up. If it does, then you must test the high voltage at the CRT funnel hole. This can only be done safely with a high voltage probe connected to a volt meter. Experienced technicians will draw an HV spark from the disconnected anode lead but this can be hazardous to both the circuits and the technician. The best way is with a high voltage probe.

If the neon lights but there is no high voltage at the CRT anode, then the components from the flyback to the CRT anode are suspect. The usual problem is a defective high voltage rectifier. If you can see the rectifier it can be replaced and cure the condition. Unfortunately, in this example monitor, the rectifier is internal to the flyback. When it dies, the replacement might be too much trouble and it's best to install a new flyback.

Should the HV be present at the CRT anode but the display won't show, the electron gun circuits could be defective. Test the CRT socket for the voltages. If they are incorrect, especially the focus voltage, the trouble could be the CRT or the circuits feeding the gun. Track each voltage from the source to the gun. As soon as you lose the voltage or it becomes grossly incorrect, you probably have just passed over the defect. Test the components in that line.

When there is no HV either at the anode hole or in the flyback, then the entire horizontal sweep circuit becomes the suspect. The first test is to read the voltage on the collector of the horizontal output transistor. It should have about $+15$ V, Fig. 24-6. If the voltage is missing, trace the voltage component by component back to the $+15$ V source in the low voltage supply. The voltage is coming to the output transistor through the flyback primary, over a 220 $\mu$F capacitor and through a coil. Any of them could be open or defective. A tap at the collector is made by an 18 $\mu$F capacitor to the horizontal deflection

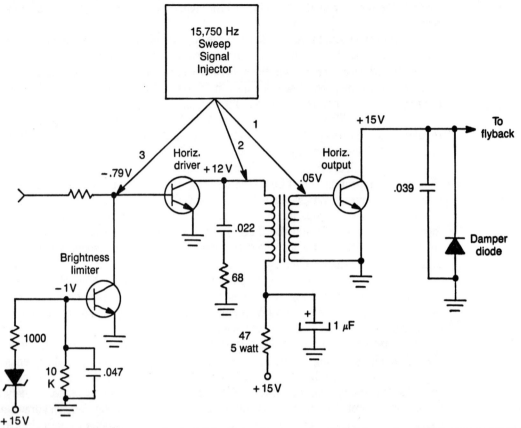

Fig. 24-6. Should the horizontal sweep circuits fail the high voltage supply will shut down. A good test procedure is to isolate the trouble with a horizontal sweep signal injector.

yoke coils. The capacitor or the deflection yoke are possible suspects too. Also, in the line are the damper diode with its anode connected to ground and a bypass .039 capacitor. The damper diode has a history of shorting and killing HV. Once all those circuits are tested and deemed ok, it is time to check the horizontal sweep itself. If the horizontal sweep has died, the HV supply will too. In order to work it needs the flyback pulse generated by the sweep.

In the service shop, there is usually a piece of test equipment that generates a 15,750 Hz sweep signal. This signal must now be injected at the base of the output transistor. If the HV and screen brightness returns upon injection, then all the circuits from the base of the output transistor to the picture are cleared. The trouble is indicated to be in the horizontal drive transistor circuits. If the HV does not return, you missed something. The trouble is still in the circuits you just tested.

However, when the HV does return move the injection point backwards to the collector of the horizontal driver transistor. If the brightness returns, then the driver transformer you just passed over is ok. When the brightness does not appear then the little transformer and the components connected to it are possible suspects and must be tested.

When the brightness did return, inject the signal into the base of the driver. If there is now no HV then the driver transistor and its adjoining components are indicated to be causing the trouble. The suspected components are tested one by one until the bad one is found. Usually there is only one defect at a time and replacing it will give you the fix.

# Appendix
# Buying Parts and Equipment

In order to be a successful computer technician, you must fill your head with the subjects covered in this book. This knowledge permits you to approach and begin operating on a computer that needs work. Once you dig in however, you then are required to reach for tools, test equipment, service manuals, and replacement parts. The amount of, and the quality of these items will then have a direct bearing on how well the computer job will go you are assigned to perform.

Out in computerworld, there are literally thousands of suppliers who are ready and waiting to sell you the things that will make your job go as smoothly as possible. If you look in the Yellow Pages you will probably find some good electronic supply houses near you. In case there are none in your area, don't fret. There are also a number of national mail order supply houses that are as near as your telephone. You can call or write to any of these companies and they will gladly send you a catalog.

## TOOLS

At the beginning of most jobs you must take the computer apart. As simple as this sounds, it must be done right and with the correct tools. There are all sorts of screws, nuts, clips, and solder connections holding different computer cases together. You have to have an assortment of screwdrivers, wrenches, soldering irons and other hand tools to properly take the machine out of its case. Using the wrong tool can prove difficult and cause complications.

Once the print board is in the open and a bad chip or other component is pinpointed, the item must be removed from the board and a new replacement installed. According to the component, the job could be as simple as changing a socketed chip or as trying as desoldering and resoldering a high-pin count surface mount device.

Once the job is complete, the computer must be put back into its case. While the computer came out easily enough you must be careful to put it back together without leaving any screws, clips or solder connections off.

There are companies that have studied this process carefully and have in their inventory all the handiest tools to do the disassembly, parts replacement, and reassembly jobs in the easiest and quickest manner. I've listed a few of them.

Jensen Tools Inc.
7815 S. 46th St.
Phoenix, AZ 85044-5399
(602) 968-6231

Fordham Radio
260 Motor Parkway
Hauppage, NY 11788
In NY state, 800-832-1446
Out of state, 800-645-9518

Jameco Electronics
1355 Shoreway Rd.
Belmont CA, 94002
(415) 592-8121

DIGI-KEY Corporation
701 Brooks Ave. South
P.O. Box 677
Thief River Falls, MN 56701-0677

JDR Microdevices
1256 South Bascom Ave.
San Jose, CA
800-538-5000

Endeco Desoldering and Soldering Equipment
Leads Metal Products, Inc.
5127 East 65th Street
Indianapolis, IN 46220
(317) 251-1231

## TEST EQUIPMENT

After you take a computer apart, it is to be tested. Your fingers, eyes, ears, sense of smell and sense of taste can take you only so far. In order to check out the voltages, logic states and other characteristics, you need extensions for your senses. The usual computer test pieces are the logic probe, VOM, oscilloscope and other devices mentioned throughout the book. There are hundreds of different companies that manufacturer test equipment. The manufacturer sells these units to your local supply houses or national supply houses like the ones just listed.

According to the type of computer you work on and the type of job you are assigned to do, your test equipment will vary. The following is a partial list of what is available to make your job easier.

Power Supplies
Digital Multimeters (DMM)
Logic Probes with and without test tones
Logic Pulsers
Logic Clips
Logic Comparators
Current Tracers
A wide variety of oscilloscopes, from simple TV types to lab models
Frequency Counters
Signal Tracer/Injectors
Programmable IC Tester
Digital Chip Tester
Breakout Boxes
DRAM Chip Tester
Power Line Monitor

Besides hardware devices like the above, there are also many types of software diagnostics. The software, of course, will only work if the computer is somewhat operable. Software is useless when a computer is dead.

When you can use software to diagnose trouble, you can save time. A lot of the computer manufacturers include some diagnostic software in the operating system that goes with the computer. For example, IBM has a program in it's operating system that tests the computer upon turn on. If there is a problem, a code number appears on the screen, indicating where in the computer the trouble is located.

You can purchase service diagnostics from your electronic supplier or call a company that writes service diagnostic software such as

SUPERSOFT, INC.
P.O. Box 611328
San Jose, CA 95161-1328
1-800-678-3600
408-745-0234

## SERVICE MANUALS

When you take a fast look at a print board, it appears complex and confusing. To take all the confusion out of the view, you need the service manual for that specific computer. In a good manual, ideally you should find the following pages of information.

The Schematic Diagrams
The IC Pinouts
The Voltages and Logic States for all chip pins
The oscilloscope pictures for selected test points
Disassembly Instructions
Adjustment and Alignment Instructions
Chip Location Guides
A Block Diagram
Theory of Operation
Troubleshooting Guide
Details on Self-Test programs, when present
Detailed Complete Parts List

This information is found in the Technical Reference Manual or Troubleshooting and Repair Book for the specific computer you are working on. There is in existence, for every important microcomputer made, these vital manuals and books.

To obtain these service books your first stop should be a dealer who sells the specific computer. Quite often he will have the books you want in stock. If he doesn't he will be able to clue you in to where the manuals are available. If the dealer can't help you contact the factory service department of the specific computer. They will often be cooperative and sell you the desired books.

Another possible source of service information are the electronic supply houses. They often sell service note packages for many of the popular microcomputers.

## REPLACEMENT PARTS

After you troubleshoot a computer and pin the condition to a specific part, unless the part can be repaired, it must be replaced. You might have some parts in stock, but often you must obtain a replacement part. When that happens, it could be easy or difficult. Whichever, obtaining the part requires some detective work. First of all you must identify the part.

With a bright light and a magnifier, examine the part for all the numbers that are stamped or engraved on it. List the numbers. You'll probably see some sort of logo. This should identify the manufacturer. If you handle a lot of parts you'll become familiar with the different logos. For instance a fancy M in a circle is used by Motorola.

Besides the logo, there is usually a code date. This is the date the part was made. For example you might see an 89-2. This means the part was coded in February (2), of 1989 (89).

In addition to that there is usually the manufacturers part number. For example, I have a 40-pin chip in front of me with the number MC6821P/M9N8442 printed on it. This is the Motorola part number. If I want a replacement, I would order with this number. An additional hint is, there is a 6821 embedded into the total part number. This identifies the part generically. It is a 6821 PIA chip, discussed earlier in the book.

Not all of the part numbers are that simple. Different manufacturers have different systems to label parts and they can be confusing. To avoid difficulties, have all the numbers listed on a piece of paper when you order. Supply houses are loaded with cross-reference books to identify practically any part as long as you have all the numbers.

As time goes by and you work on computer after computer, you will accumulate a library of service manuals and repair books. The confusion will gradually straighten out and become understanding.

# Index